T0331218

GROUP FORMATION IN ECONOMICS

Diverse activities are conducted within and by organized groups of individuals, including political, economic, and social activities. How groups form and are organized to conduct these activities are subjects of intense game-theoretic research. Some of the topics investigated are trade networks, coauthorship networks, buyer–seller networks with differentiated products, and networks of information sharing. Other topics are social norms on punctuality, the adoption of new technologies, clubs and the provision of club goods and public goods, collusive alliances among corporations, international alliances, and trading agreements. This volume introduces the reader to recent literature on game-theoretic treatments of organized groups, with networks, clubs, and coalitions.

Gabrielle Demange is Director of Studies at the Ecole des Hautes Etudes en Sciences Sociales, Paris. She has been coeditor of the journal *Economic Theory* since 1998 and associate editor of *Review of Economic Design* since 1998 and of *Mathematical Social Sciences* and *Finance* since 2000. Professor Demange was elected as a Fellow of the Econometric Society in 1992 and is a Fellow of the Centre for Economic Policy Research, London. She has conducted research in the areas of social choice theory and cooperative game theory. Professor Demange's works on two-sided matching games and multi-item auction with David Gale were among the first in a now-large field. Much of her recent research concerns risk sharing in financial markets and the design of social security systems. Apart from research articles in eminent journals, Professor Demange has written three textbooks on finance and game theory.

Myrna Wooders is Professor of Economics at Vanderbilt University and the University of Warwick. Professor Wooders is founding editor of the *Economics Bulletin*, editor of the *Journal of Public Economic Theory*, and president of the Association for Public Economic Theory. Her research has been primarily in the areas of public economic theory and game theory – especially in the interface between the two. Her work, alone and with others, on multijurisdictional economies is well known and widely cited. Professor Wooders has published in leading journals in economics and game theory, including *Econometrica,* the *Journal of Economic Theory*, and *Proceedings of the National Academy of Sciences*. She has also edited a volume. Her awards include the prestigious Connaught Fellowship in the Social Sciences, a Humboldt Research Award for Foreign Scientists (Germany), and a research award from the Director General of Universities of Catalunya. Professor Wooders is a Fellow of the Econometric Society, an elected member of the Game Theory Society Council, and a Research Fellow of the German-based CESifo Research Network.

Group Formation in Economics

Networks, Clubs, and Coalitions

Edited by

GABRIELLE DEMANGE
Ecole des Hautes Etudes en Sciences Sociales

MYRNA WOODERS
Vanderbilt University and University of Warwick

CAMBRIDGE
UNIVERSITY PRESS

32 Avenue of the Americas, New York NY 10013-2473, USA

Cambridge University Press is part of the University of Cambridge.

It furthers the University's mission by disseminating knowledge in the pursuit of education, learning and research at the highest international levels of excellence.

www.cambridge.org
Information on this title: www.cambridge.org/9780521842716

First published 2005
First paperback edition 2012

A catalogue record for this publication is available from the British Library

Library of Congress Cataloguing in Publication data
Group formation in economics : networks, clubs, and coalitions / edited by Gabrielle Demange, Myrna Wooders.
p. cm.
Includes bibliographical references and index.
ISBN 0-521-84271-9
1. Social networks – Economic aspects. 2. Social groups – Economic aspects.
3. Game theory. I. Demange, Gabrielle. II. Wooders, Myrna Holtz
HM741.G76 2005
302.4 – dc22 2004045929

ISBN 978-0-521-84271-6 Hardback
ISBN 978-1-107-40738-1 Paperback

The editors are indebted to the British Academy, the European Commission, and the University of Warwick for support for a 2001 Warwick Euro Workshop and a conference on Networks, where this volume was initiated. We also thank Domenico Moro for technical assistance in preparation of the volume.

Contents

Contributors

Francis Bloch   GREQAM, Centre de la Vieille Charité, 2 rue de la Charité, 13002 Marseille, France
e-mail: bloch@ehess.cnrs-mrs.fr
http://www.vcharite.univ-mrs.fr/PP/bloch/introduction.htm

Carlo Carraro   Dipartimento di Scienze Economiche, Università di Veneiza, San Giobbe 873,30121 Venezia, Italy
e-mail: ccarraro@univ.it
http://www.dse.univ.it/professori/Carraro/Carraro.html

John Conley   Department of Economics, Vanderbilt University, 414 Calhoun Hall, Nashville, TN 37235, USA
e-mail: j.p.conley@vanderbilt.edu
http://people.vanderbilt.edu/~j.p.conley/

Gabrielle Demange   EHESS, 48 Boulevard Jourdan, 75014 Paris, France
e-mail: demange@java.ens.fr
http://www.delta.ens.fr/demange/

Amrita Dhillon   University of Warwick, Department of Economics, Coventry, CV4 7AL, UK
e-mail: A.Dhillon@warwick.ac.uk
http://www2.warwick.ac.uk/fac/soc/economics/staff/faculty/dhillon/

Marcel Fafchamps   University of Oxford, Department of Economics, Manor Road, Oxford OX1 3UQ, UK
e-mail: Marcel.Fafchamps@economics.ox.ac.uk

Garance Genicot   Department of Economics, Georgetown University, 559 ICC, 37th & O Streets NW, Washington, DC 20057, USA
e-mail: gg58@georgetown.edu
http://www.georgetown.edu/faculty/gg58

Sanjeev Goyal   Department of Economics, University of Essex, Colchester CO4 3SQ, UK
e-mail: sgoyal@essex.ac.uk
http://privatewww.essex.ac.uk/~sgoyal/

Matthew O. Jackson   Division of the Humanities and Social Sciences, 228–77, California Institute of Technology, Pasadena, CA 91125, USA
e-mail: jacksonm@hss.caltech.edu

Fernando Jaramillo   Universidad de los Andes, Facultad de Economía, Carrera 1 N° 18A-70, Bloque C Columbia
e-mail: fjaramil@uniandes.edu.co

Samir Kamat   Potfolio Management Group, Wachovia Corporation, Atlanta, GA 30303, USA
e-mail: Samir.kamat2@wachovia.copr

Hubert Kempf   Université Paris-1 Panthéon-Sorbonne, EUREQua, Bureau 305, 106-112, Boulevard de l'Hôpital, 75013 Paris, France
e-mail: kempf@univ-paris1.fr
http://eurequa.univ-paris1.fr/membres/kempf/francais/cvcomp.htm

Alexander Kovalenkov   University of North Carolina at Chapel Hill, Department of Economics, 107 Gardner Hall, CB# 3305, Chapel Hill, NC 27599, USA
e-mail: akovalen@email.unc.edu
http://www.unc.edu/depts/econ/directory/kovalenkov.html

Michel Le Breton   IDEI, Université de Toulouse I, 21 allée de Brienne, 31000 Toulouse, France
e-mail: lebreton@cict.fr
http://www.idei.asso.fr/French/FCv/CvChercheurs/FrameLebreton.htm

Fabien Moizeau   GREMAQ, Université de Toulouse I, Manufacture des tabacs, 21 allée de Brienne, 31000 Toulouse, France
e-mail: moizeau@gremaq.univ-tlse1.fr

Anne van den Nouweland   Department of Economics, University of Oregon, Eugene, OR, USA, and Fellow, Department of Economics, The University of Melbourne, Australia
e-mail: annev@oregon.uoregon.edu
http://darkwing.uoregon.edu/~annev/

Frank H. Page, Jr.   University of Alabama, Department of Finance, Tuscaloosa, AL 35487, USA
e-mail: fpage@cba.ua.edu
http://www.cba.ua.edu/personnel/FrankPage.html

Debraj Ray   Department of Economics, New York University, New York, NY
10012, USA
e-mail: debraj.ray@nyu.edu
http://www.econ.nyu.edu/user/debraj/

Stefani Smith   Liberty Fund, Inc., 8335 Allison Pointe Trail, Suite 300, Indianapolis,
IN 46250, USA
e-mail: ssmith@libertyfund.org

Shlomo Weber   Department of Economics, Southern Methodist University, Dallas,
TX 75275, USA
e-mail: sweber@mail.smu.edu
http://faculty.smu.edu/sweber/

Mika Widgrén   Turku School of Economics, Department of Economics, Turku,
Finland
e-mail: Mika.Widgren@tukkk.fi

Myrna Wooders   Department of Economics, Vanderbilt University, Nashville, TN
37235-1819, USA, and Department of Economics, University of Warwick, Coventry
CV4 7AL, UK
e-mail: myrna.wooders@vanderbilt.edu
www.myrnawooders.com

Introduction

Gabrielle Demange and Myrna Wooders

Diverse activities are conducted within and by organized groups of individuals, including political, economic, and social activities. These activities have increasingly become subjects of intense game-theoretic research. A sample of the subjects treated are trade networks, coauthorship networks, buyer-seller networks with differentiated products, and networks of information sharing. Other subjects are social norms are punctuality, the adoption of new technologies, clubs and the provision of club goods and public goods, and collusive alliances, among corporations, international alliances, and trading agreements. This volume, which has three main parts, is an introduction to game-theoretic treatments of organized groups, with networks, clubs, and coalitions, including some illustrations and applications.

Part One is an introduction to recent studies on network formation with bilateral relationships as its principal focus. Although this promising approach is not yet fully developed and is still primarily theoretical, the literature is already vast. There is a wide literature in sociology and economics that makes the importance of social networks clear. One topic of this literature, for example, is the crucial role of personal contacts in obtaining information about job opportunities. Networks of relationships also underlie the trade and exchange of goods in noncentralized markets, and the provision of mutual insurance in developing countries. The aim of much recent research on networks in economics and game theory is to give strategic foundations to network formation.

Part Two discusses societies that may be partitioned into multiple groups. The situations treated range from ones with social activities, public goods, and competition under increasing returns to scale to formation of nations and secession. The literature on these topics, inspired by seminal works of Charles Tiebout, James Buchanan, and Frank Westhoff is, by itself, already large. This part focuses on collective activities, such as those carried out by firms, clubs, and jurisdictions.

Part Three studies strategic approaches to group formation and cooperation in political and economic contexts. The areas include the formation of parties, design of constitutions, alliances among firms, growth and environmental economics, and informal arrangements for risk sharing and trade. This part stresses the role of protocols (rules governing the coalition formation process), the extent of spillovers

1

between coalitions, and the possibilities of enforcing rules governing coalition formation.

At this point, let us make our vocabulary more precise, and clarify how we distinguish between groups, networks, clubs, and coalitions. The term *group* is the most neutral – it does not suggest that the group members engage in any collective or cooperative activity. Coalitions are groups of players whose members decide to cooperate, possibly by establishing binding agreements. The set of coalitions and the payoffs they can achieve constitute the primitives of a cooperative game, as first described by von Neumann and Morgenstern in a transferable utility setting. Networks are described by bilateral links between decision makers (nodes or players). Although links are decided bilaterally, a group of connected decision makers may act collectively as a coalition. The precise structure of the links connecting a coalition may influence the payoffs to its members. A club allows a group of players to engage in some collective activity, such as the provision of a public good subject to congestion. The club members may also engage in other activities (e.g., trade of private goods) with other individuals and other groups or clubs.

Although the parts differ widely in many aspects, a premise of all chapters is that whether groups are small or large, whether they are many or few, and whether they form or threaten to form coalitions, should depend on the context and should be determined endogenously. In line with the distinction just described, Part One focuses on predicting which networks may form, whereas Part Two and Part Three focus on the expected coalition structures (partitions of the players into coalitions) and their properties.

Turning to the predictions of group formation, these presumably depend on the modeling approach. One of the goals of the analysis is to gain a better understanding of this dependence and to identify when and how the "rules of the game" matter. Two approaches underpin much of the research presented. The first approach is based on an explicit game in strategic form, most often a two-stage game. Loosely speaking, the first stage determines the structure of collaboration based on individuals' strategy choices. In the second stage, given the collaboration structure, the distribution of benefits among individuals is determined. The second approach is more closely aligned with core theory, cooperative games and price- (or tax-) taking equilibrium. Core theory takes equilibrium as a situation in which no group of individuals could do better for themselves, using their own resources. From a club theoretic perspective, no group of participants can do better by forming a new club, given the choices of other individuals. These first and second approaches are, however, not entirely distinct (e.g., the core or equal cost sharing may be used in the second stage of a strategic game). Let us illustrate the differences with two examples.

In environmental problems, sovereign countries must decide whether to improve environmental quality – namely to provide an environmental global public good – on a voluntary basis. In practice, countries negotiate on an international agreement that defines emission targets for each signatory and often the way to achieve these targets as well. Applying the first approach, the negotiation protocol is modeled as a two-stage game. In the first stage nations decide on whether to join an agreement. Then, in the second stage, nations within the agreement abide by its rules but otherwise all behaviour is noncooperative.

In the second approach, for instance, individuals with diverse preferences may decide to share some public good and allocate the costs. Or countries may form clubs to invest jointly in a growth-enhancing technology. In equilibrium, no coalition of individuals would prefer to form a new group and allocate costs differently among themselves.

Clearly, the chapters differ in the situations and issues addressed and in the analytical tools used, but all advance our understanding of the impact of groups on social outcomes.

Part One: Network Formation, Communication, and Learning

The four chapters in this part acquaint the reader with recent developments in game-theoretic models of network formation. They survey the results that have been obtained so far, ranging from learning to stability and efficiency of networks; provide an overview of several directions in the literature; and present a diverse and informative collection of examples.

"A Survey of Network Formation Models: Stability and Efficiency" by Matthew Jackson introduces the reader to the diversity of situations described, in the recent literature, by networks. Indeed, networks can be many things. The main focus of the chapter is to relate network formation to allocation rules. For example, if any group of connected players must equally share the surplus generated by the group, then individuals have incentives to link to more productive players. The question is whether there are allocation rules that lead to equilibrium networks with desirable properties. The focus is on the compatibility of efficiency with individual incentives to form and sever links.

"Models of Network Formation in Cooperative Games" by Anne van den Nouweland, surveys the first works that address coalition formation through formation of bilateral links. In these works, payoffs to coalitions are derived from a cooperative game and are invariant to the precise structure of links between the coalition members. The chapter starts with the work of Aumann-Myerson, who model network formation through an extensive game in which once a link is established it cannot be broken. The chapter then discusses a one-shot static game, in which any individual can break a link with another individual and any two players, if they agree, can form a link. The pattern of equilibrium networks is studied as a function of the properties of the underlying game (e.g., convexity or whether a coalition can do at least as well for its membership as any partition of the coalition into smaller coalitions) and the solution concept employed.

In "Farsighted Stability in Network Formation," by Frank Page and Samir Kamat the main two issues are the rules governing network formation and what networks are likely to emerge and persist if individuals are farsighted. Farsighted individuals anticipate possible reactions to their link formation activities. The chapter treats directed networks in which a link may go from one node to another but not in the reverse direction. Moreover, links are allowed to vary in intensity. To illustrate some applications, citations are not generally bilateral and, while A may list B among his friends, B does not necessarily list A among his; moreover, the intensities of their affections may differ. Also loops are allowed, and links may be used in multiple ways. A rumor for example may go from A to B to C and then back to A. The framework presented accommodates all these situations. Remarkably, farsightedly stable networks exist; some examples demonstrate their properties.

In "Learning in Networks," Sanjeev Goyal discusses the relationships between learning and the structure of interaction among decision makers. In a wide range of situations, individuals make decisions without being fully informed about their consequences, and take advantage of their previous experiences and their observations of the experiences of others. The precise ways in which individuals interact can influence the generation and dissemination of information. The chapter addresses this issue, modeling the interaction structure as a network in which individuals learn from their neighbors. Two sorts of situations are considered. In the first, some network linking decision makers is given. The effects of the form of networks on learning are studied. In the second, the dissemination of information feeds back on the network structure, thus making link formation endogenous. A central application is the adoption of new technologies.

Part Two: On Equilibrium Formation of Groups: A Theoretical Assesment

Our focus turns to coalitions and clubs. The typical motivation for coalition formation and clubs is increasing returns to cooperation in some aspects and decreasing returns in others. Such situations abound both in politics and in economics. Classic examples are shared facilities such as swimming pools. The benefits of cost sharing imply increasing returns to larger club membership, but congestion, diversity in individual tastes, or both – some swimmers may like company whereas others may prefer doing laps in solitude – may hamper full exploitation of increasing returns to cost sharing and lead to the splitting of the society into smaller groups. Whether such splitting is optimal depends on the strength of the increasing returns, the mechanism by which the gains to cooperation are divided, and the compromises required by heterogeneous individuals in belonging to one group, club, or coalition. If congestion effects are sufficiently strong, then multiple groups may be required for the achievement of socially optimal outcomes. The chapters in this section treat firm formation, the financing of public projects, local public goods, and clubs.

There are two major premises: free mobility and free entry. Under free mobility, agents are free to join any group, provided they abide by the rules governing group formation. This is a natural economic assumption. For example, it is common to be able to "buy into" clubs by paying a membership fee or into communities by paying the price of a house. A theoretical motivation for free mobility comes from large coalitions in large economies, where it is natural to assume that individuals have nearly negligible influence on other members of a coalition. Free entry describes a situation in which coalitions can freely form. When there are trade-offs between the size of coalitions and diversity, free entry or some price system taking into account all possibilities is required to ensure that a sufficient variety of coalitional activities is on offer or can be provided. All chapters in this section concern both free entry and free mobility but from differing perspectives. A major issue is the distribution of costs and benefits from group formation, the tax or admission price systems, or profits and their effects on optimality and stability.

In "Group Formation: The Interaction of Increasing Returns and Preferences Diversity," Gabrielle Demange focuses on situations in which the diversity in individuals, either in their tastes or in their income, is the driving force behind the splitting of the society. An important application is the analysis of oligopoly in a differentiated goods economy. Despite increasing returns to scale, several firms may be active, each one attracting a different set of customers through a different policy. Free entry introduces the threat that a successful entrant will trigger a reallocation of the customers among the firms. In view of the theory of contestable markets, a main issue is whether free entry results in a stable and efficient oligopoly, or instead is "destructive," calling for regulation. After examining this issue, the chapter discusses the crucial features that shape group formation in more general models. Finally group formation is addressed in situations in which individuals may have a negative impact on a group they join. Free mobility places a major constraint on group formation. For example, jurisdictions face such constraints on their redistributive policies, which generate negative externalities on some individuals, typically the wealthy one.

In "Games and Economies with Near Exhaustion of Gains to Scale," Alexander Kovalenkov and Myrna Wooders concentrate on the marketlike properties of situations with many participants, in which almost all gains to collective activities are exhausted, including situations in which the whole group is optimal. The game-theoretic model encompasses clubs, local public goods, and other deviations from the standard exchange economy model. The authors argue that, if there are some small frictions preventing free and completely costless formation of coalitions, then an economy has stable and near optimal group structures – "almost free" entry equilibrium exists and equilibrium outcomes are optimal or nearly optimal. Free mobility of individuals between groups is expressed as price-taking equilibrium in which the commodities are the players themselves. With sufficiently many players, free mobility and free entry lead to the same set of outcomes. Numerous examples are presented to demonstrate the broad applicability of the results. There may be combinations of positive or negative externalities, and there may be many or few large or small groups.

In "Coalitions and Clubs: Tiebout Equilibrium in Large Economies," John Conley and Stefani Smith survey research studying how the worth of players to groups is determined. The crucial determinants of a player's worth are those characteristics of the player that directly influence others (his or her "crowding type"). If these characteristics are observable, such as gender, personality, occupation, and so on, then, remarkably, competitive admission prices to clubs that depend only on the crowding types of players yield optimal outcomes. The price-taking equilibrium concept allows free mobility of individuals between groups and also free entry of new clubs given prices. Two different models are treated: one in which the crowding types of agents are exogenous (such as gender or height) and another in which agents choose their crowding types, perhaps at some cost, such as the cost of an education. Although they may hold in special cases, if all individuals face the same educational cost function for instance, equilibria exhibiting population stratification in general are not possible.

In "Secession-Proof Cost Allocations and Stable Group Structures in Models of Horizontal Differentiation," Michel Le Breton and Shlomo Weber focus on the impact of cost-sharing schemes on public decisions and their stability. There may be institutional constraints, constraints on information, or ideals of fairness and equity that impede the use of a competitive cost sharing. Despite these considerations, in practice, a government has to select an explicit scheme to cover the costs of a project. This chapter seeks to deepen our understanding of the importance of the cost allocation scheme in determining whether "secession" can be avoided. The analysis is carried out in a horizontal differentiation model in which individuals have different rankings over elements of policy space (in opposition to vertical differentiation models in which individuals differ only in their incomes).

Part Three: Groups, Clubs, and Alliances in Political and Economic Environments

This part analyzes group formation and cooperation in various contexts mainly from a strategic perspective. The first two chapters in this part bear on political issues and coalition formation. The first chapter focuses on strategic issues and the second concerns assessment of coalitional power and the relationship to institutions.

In "Political Parties and Coalition Formation," Amrita Dhillon surveys a recent literature that analyzes coalition formation in politics. Coalitions are crucial at different stages in politics: at the preelectoral stage, a coalition of individuals or of candidates forms a party that campaigns for election whereas at the postelectoral stage, a coalition of candidates or of parties may try to form a government. Instead of treating a political party as a unitary actor, recent works take into account the diversity of preferences in political party formation. Accordingly, in that respect, the models here share many features of the chapters in the previous part: forming a party entails costs, in particular the costs of compromise. On the other hand, the expected benefits depend on the stage being modeled and on individual motivations, which are most often classified as office seeking, vote seeking, and policy seeking. Broadly speaking, forming a party would increase the possibilities of satisfying these motivations. Traditional questions about the size and number of parties are revisited: Are parties minimal winning coalitions? Do more parties form under majority than plurality rule (Duverger's hypothesis)? An important insight gained from the analysis is that some traditional results based on a unidimensional set of alternatives do not extend to more general setups.

In "Power in the Design of Constitutional Rules" Mika Widgrén addresses the crucial question of measuring decision power in real-life institutions. A debate on the European Union has recently been sparked between scholars who study cooperative approaches and power index models, on the one hand, and scholars who study noncooperative approaches and spatial voting models on the other. The verdict of the latter group is that power indices exclude important variables (such as institutions and strategies) and are influenced by computational formulas and hidden assumptions. The justification of the former group is that power indices deal with institutional design without the need for explicit decision procedures and specific preferences. However, institutional design often has to consider procedures and interinstitutional aspects. Widgren's chapter examines models from both sides of the debate. He argues that the two sides can be seen as extremes of a unified approach. Like spatial voting games, this approach is based on a posterior analysis but, when necessary information on players' preferences is not available, it can be used for a priori analysis, like the power indices of cooperative games. Using EU decision making as an example, the chapter demonstrates what elements of procedural voting the two so far very distinct approaches can accommodate. It also discusses how the unified approach is able to contribute to the analysis both theoretically and empirically.

The following two chapters treat environmental agreements and industrial organization. Both entail spillovers or, in other words, externalities across coalitions, which are excluded in most analyses of cooperative game theory. In the presence of spillovers, the payoff to a coalition depends on the coalitions formed by other players. This has several consequences. First, the basic representation of coalitional gains is a game in partition function form, meaning that the payoffs to a coalition depend on the entire coalition structure and not only on the membership of the coalition. Second, whenever a coalition forms, its members must anticipate how other players organize themselves into coalitions. This is a very important distinctive feature of the formation of groups in Chapters 11 and 12.

In "Group and Network Formation in Industrial Organization: A survey," Francis Bloch describes recent analyses that seek to understand the forms of cooperation that arise among firms or among traders. Three domains are investigated: (i) the formation of collusive agreements, (ii) the formation of cost-reducing alliances, and (iii) the formation of trade networks. The study of collusion focuses on endogenous cartel formation, both in oligopolistic markets and in auctions. Typically a free rider problem arises in a quantity-setting market: each firm prefers other firms to collude to restrict output but is itself better off outside of the cartel. In the analysis of strategic alliances, this feature is no longer true. Assuming that firms cooperate, in reducing production costs for instance, but compete on the market, the alliances (or networks of cooperative links) that emerge are characterized. Finally the formation of trade markets in which strategic traders can choose their trading partners is analyzed, both in strategic market games and in buyer-seller networks.

In "Institution Design for Managing Global Commons: Lessons from Coalition Theory," Carlo Carraro discusses the impact of institutional design on the emergence of cooperative international agreements to manage global commons. The chapter studies how different accession rules, minimum participation rules, and negotiation rules affect a country's decision to sign a treaty to protect a global common (i.e. to join a coalition that provides a global public good). The chapter also analyzes what the outcome of the negotiations would be if treaty design (for example, the minimum participation rule or the negotiation agenda) were endogenized and strategically chosen by the negotiating countries. In this latter case, players not only choose whether to join a coalition, but, in a preceding stage of the game also chose the rules of the coalition game.

In "Inequality and Growth Clubs," Fernando Jaramillo, Hubert Kempf, and Fabien Moizeau apply coalition theory to macroeconomics. Indeed various institutions shape and organize the functioning of an economy at the macroeconomic level. That the growth process across countries does not converge is now a well-established fact but contradicts the standard neoclassical model. The convergence debate and the attempts based on various types of segmentation (through education, for instance) to reconcile theory with empirics is first summarized. Although the link between the dynamics of inequality and growth rates has been emphasized, the difference in aggregate human capital across countries is left unexplained. The second part of the chapter builds up a model, based on coalition theory, to fill this gap. Countries voluntarily form clubs so as to share some resources that are necessary for growth. The formation of endogenous growth clubs therefore depends on the initial distribution of resources across countries. The model provides a microfoundation for the divergence in growth rates (the so-called twin peaks or multipeaks phenomena).

The final two chapters focus on the enforceability problem of cooperative agreements. The notion that binding cooperative agreements can be enforced has underpinned the cooperative approach to coalition formation. For instance, in Chapter 12, once a treaty has been signed, it is assumed that the signatories abide by the rules of the treaty. The following two chapters treat situations in which cooperative agreements are informal and must be self-enforcing.

In "Informal Insurance, Enforcement Constraints, and Group Formation," Garance Genicot and Debraj Ray discuss informal insurance arrangements in developing countries. Although there is considerable evidence of mutual insurance in village communities, the same studies reveal a large departure from perfect insurance. Apart from asymmetry of information and moral hazard, the lack of enforceability could impede widespread risk sharing. The starting point of the chapter is the following observation: if a large group – a village community for instance – could foresee the benefits of mutual risk sharing, smaller groups could do the same and deviate from insurance arrangements created by larger groups. The chapter formulates a recursive definition of group stability and applies it to the insurance problem. In contrast to the predictions of the standard insurance model, stable groups are always bounded in size, and an increase in environmental riskiness can lower the overall provision of insurance.

In "Spontaneous Market Emergence and Social Networks," Marcel Fafchamps investigates how market exchange is partly shaped by social networks and equilibrium dynamics. Markets at early stages of development are characterized by trade based on mutual trust and on the sharing of information among acquaintances. Also in credit, labor, and business markets, courts are seldom used to enforce commercial contracts. Other forms of punishment, such as stigmatization of defectors from an informal arrangement, may be employed. This chapter explains how different sorts of patterns of exchange can take place in a dynamic setting when no formal market institutions exist that exclude or punish cheaters. The role of social networks, which are predetermined by nonmarket forces (such as ethnic, religious, and family affiliation) in providing valuable information on partners, is emphasized.

PART ONE

Network Formation, Communication, and Learning

1

A Survey of Network Formation Models:
Stability and Efficiency

Matthew O. Jackson

1.1. Introduction

The set of economic situations in which network structures play an important role is wide and varied. For instance, personal contacts play critical roles in obtaining information about job opportunities.[1] Such networks of relationships also underlie the trade and exchange of goods in noncentralized markets,[2] the provision of mutual insurance in developing countries,[3] research and development and collusive alliances among corporations,[4] and international alliances and trading agreements[5] to mention just a few examples.

Given both the prevalence of situations in which networks of relationships play a role and their importance in determining the outcome of the interaction, it is essential to have theories about how such network structures matter and how they form. To get a feeling for what kinds of issues arise and why we might be interested, consider a brief example. We know from extensive research in both the sociology and labor economics literature that social connections are the leading source of information about jobs and that ultimately many (and in some professions most) jobs are obtained through personal contacts.[6] The reason we might care

[1] See, for example, Rees (1966), Granovetter (1973, 1974), Boorman (1975), Montgomery (1991), Topa (2001), Arrow and Borzekowski (2000), Calvo-Armengol (2000), Calvo-Armengol and Jackson (2001, 2004), Cahuc and Fontaine (2002), and Ioannides and Datcher Loury (2002).
[2] See, for example, Tesfatsion (1997, 1998); Corominas-Bosch (1999); Weisbuch, Kirman, and Herreiner (2000); Charness, Corominas-Bosch, and Frechette (2001); Kranton and Minehart (2001); and Wang and Watts (2002).
[3] See Fafchamps and Lund (2000) and De Weerdt (2002).
[4] See Bloch (2001), Belleflamme and Bloch (2002), Goyal and Moraga (2001), Goyal and Joshi (2000), and Billard and Bravard (2002).
[5] See Goyal and Joshi (1999), Casella and Rauch (2001), and Furusawa and Konishi (2002).
[6] The introduction in Montgomery (1991) provides a nice and quick overview of some of the studies on this. Some of the seminal references are Granovetter (1973, 1974), who found that over 50 percent of surveyed residents of a Massachusetts town had obtained their jobs through social contacts, and Rees (1966), who found, in a similar study, that over 60 percent had done so.

I thank Jernej Copic, Gabrielle Demange Sanjeev Goyal, Anne Van den Nouweland and Myrna Wooders for comments on earlier drafts. Financial support from the Lee Center for Advanced Networking is gratefully acknowledged.

about this is that the structure of the social network then turns out to be a key determinant of

(i) who gets which jobs, which has implications for social mobility;

(ii) how patterns of unemployment relate to ethnicity, education, geography, and other variables, and, for instance, why there might be persistent differences in employment between races;

(iii) whether or not jobs are being efficiently filled; and

(iv) the incentives that individuals have to educate themselves and to participate in the workforce.

Related to all of these issues are what the impact of these things is on how people "network" or what social ties they maintain, whether the resulting labor markets ultimately work efficiently, and how different policies (for instance, affirmative action, subsidization of education, etc.) will affect labor markets and how they might be best structured.[7] Although this is quite a list of an extensive issues to consider, it makes clear why understanding how networks operate is important.

At this point it is useful to crudely divide situations in which networks are important into two different categories to make clear what the scope of this survey will be. In one category, the network structure is a distribution or service network that is the choice of a single actor. For instance, the routing of planes by an airline[8] falls into this category as do many routing, transmission, and distribution network problems. In the other category of situations in which networks are critical, the network structure connects different individuals and the formation of the network depends on the decisions of many participants. This includes the preceding examples of labor markets, political alliances, and generally any social network. It is this second category of network problems, in which the networks connect several individuals, that I survey here.[9]

The recent and rapidly growing literature on network formation among individuals addresses various questions. I concentrate on the following three:

(i) How are such network relationships important in determining the outcome of economic interaction?

(ii) How can we predict which networks are likely to form when individuals have the discretion to choose their connections?

(iii) How efficient are the networks that form, and how does that depend on the way that the value of a network is allocated among the individuals?

In answering question (i), I will focus primarily on examples (see Section 1.3), and the principal emphasis will be on questions (ii) and (iii).

---

[7] See Calvo-Armengol and Jackson (2001, 2004) for a look at some of these issues.
[8] See, for instance, Starr and Stinchcombe (1992) and Hendricks, Piccione, and Tan (1995).
[9] There is some overlap as, for instance, in the case of the choices of Internet backbone providers that affects the structure of the Internet (e.g., see Badasyan and Chakrabarti 2003).

Beyond the literature surveyed here, there is a well-established and vast literature in sociology on social networks.[10] That literature makes clear the importance
of social networks in many contexts and provides a detailed look at many issues
associated with social networks, ranging from measuring power and centrality to
understanding the roles of different kinds of social ties. Although that literature
provides a wealth of knowledge on the workings of network interactions, largely
missing from it are strategic models of how networks are formed and in particular an understanding of the relationship between individual incentives and overall
societal welfare. The development of game-theoretic reasoning over past decades
and its influx into economic models has now come together with a realization that
network relationships play important roles in many economic interactions. This has
resulted in the birth of a literature that uses game-theoretic reasoning to develop such
models of self-organizing network relationships. This is a rapidly growing literature
on a wide-open landscape with numerous important questions to be addressed and
a huge variety of potential applications. As such, I cannot hope to cover all of this
burgeoning literature here. I have the more modest aim of providing a look at some
of the modeling approaches, a feeling for the tension between individual incentives
to form links and societal welfare, and a glimpse of some of the applications of the
developing theories.

1.2. Defining Network Games

Network relationships come in many shapes and sizes, and so there is no single
model that encompasses them all. Here I focus on one way of modeling networks
that will be fairly broad and flexible enough to capture a multitude of applications.
As we proceed, I will try to make clear what is being admitted and what is being
ruled out.

1.2.1. Players

$N = \{1, \ldots, n\}$ is a set of players or individuals connected in some network
relationship.

In this chapter, I will refer to the individuals as "players" with the idea that they
may be individual people, firms or other organizations, or even countries.

These players will be the nodes or vertices in a graph that will describe the network
relationships.

A common aspect to the papers in the literature surveyed here is that they model
situations in which each player has discretion in forming his or her links in the
network relationship. These may be people deciding on whom they wish to be friends
with, or contract with, or pass job information to; these may be firms deciding on
which partnerships to engage in; or these may be countries deciding on which trade
or defense alliances to enter into.

---

[10] An excellent and broad introductory text to the social networks literature is Wasserman and Faust
(1994).

1.2.2. Networks

The network relationship may take different forms as determined by the context. The simplest form is a nondirected graph, where two players are either connected or not. For instance, in a network in which links represent direct family relationships, the network is naturally a nondirected one. Two players are either related to each other or not, but it cannot be that one is related to the second without the second being related to the first. This is generally true of many social and economic relationships such as partnerships, friendships, alliances, and acquaintances. This type of network will be central to the following discussion. However, also discussed are other situations modeled as directed networks in which one player may be connected to a second without the second being connected to the first. For instance, a network that keeps track of which authors reference which other authors, or which Web sites have links to which others would naturally be a directed network.

The distinction between directed and nondirected networks is not a mere technicality. It is fundamental to the analysis because the applications and modeling are quite different. In particular, when links are necessarily reciprocal, then it will generally be the case that joint consent is needed to establish and maintain the link. For instance, in order to form a trading partnership, both partners need to agree. To maintain a friendship, we find that the same is generally true, as is maintaining a business relationship, alliance, and so on. In the case of directed networks, one individual may direct a link at another without the other's consent. These dissimilarities result in some basic differences in the modeling of network formation.

Most economic applications fall into the reciprocal link (and mutual consent) framework, and, as such, nondirected networks will be our central focus. Nevertheless, directed networks are also of interest, and I will return to discuss them briefly at the end of this chapter.

In many situations, links may also have some intensity associated with them. For instance, if links represent friendships, some may be stronger than others and this might have consequences, such as affecting the chance that information passes through a given link. Much of the literature on network formation to date has been restricted to the case in which links are either present or not and do not have intensities associated with them.[11] This makes representing networks somewhat easier, for we can just keep track of which links are present.

Although the focus on 0–1 links is restrictive, it is still of significant interest for at least two reasons. First, much of the insight obtained in this framework is fairly robust, and so this is a useful starting point. Second, the value and costs generated by links may differ across them, thus already allowing for substantial heterogeneity and admitting enough flexibility to ensure a diversity of interesting applications.

A network g is a list of which pairs of players are linked to each other. A network is then a list of unordered pairs of players $\{i, j\}$.

---

[11] For exceptions, see Calvo, Lasaga, and van den Nouweland (1999); Calvo-Armengol and Jackson (2001, 2004); Goyal and Moraga (2001); and Page, Wooders, and Kamat (2001).

For any pair of players i and j, $\{i, j\} \in g$ indicates that i and j are linked under the network g.

For simplicity, write ij to represent the link $\{i, j\}$, and so $ij \in g$ indicates that i and j are linked under the network g.

For instance, if $N = \{1, 2, 3\}$, then $g = \{12, 23\}$ is the network in which there is a link between players 1 and 2 and a link between players 2 and 3 but no link between players 1 and 3.

Let g^N be the set of all subsets of N of size 2, $G = \{g \subset g^N\}$ denotes the set of all possible networks or graphs on N.

The network g^N is referred to as the "complete" network.

Another prominent network structure is that of a "star," which is a network in which some player i exists such that every link in the network involves player i. In this case, i is referred to as the center of the star.[12]

A shorthand notation for the network obtained by adding link ij to an existing network g is $g + ij$, and for the network obtained by deleting link ij from an existing network g is $g - ij$.

Let

$$g|_S = \{ij : ij \in g \quad \text{and} \quad i \in S, j \in S\}.$$

Thus, $g|_S$ is the network found deleting all links except those that are between players in S.

For any network g, let $N(g)$ be the set of players who have at least one link in the network g. That is, $N(g) = \{i \mid \exists j \text{ s.t. } ij \in g\}$.

1.2.3. Paths and Components

A *path* in a network $g \in G$ between players i and j is a sequence of players $i_1, \ldots, i_K$ such that $i_k i_{k+1} \in g$ for each $k \in \{1, \ldots, K - 1\}$ with $i_1 = i$ and $i_K = j$.

Looking at the path relationships in a network naturally partitions a network into different connected subgraphs commonly referred to as components.

A *component* of a network g is a nonempty subnetwork $g' \subset g$ such that

- if $i \in N(g')$ and $j \in N(g')$, where $j \neq i$, then there exists a path in g' between i and j, and
- if $i \in N(g')$ and $ij \in g$, then $ij \in g'$.

Thus, the components of a network are the distinct, connected subgraphs of a network. In the following figure, there are two components with five agents each.

---

[12] This definition follows Jackson and Wolinsky (1996). Subsequently, this term has been used to refer to several variations on such a structure.

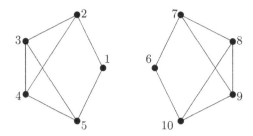

The set of components of g is denoted as $C(g)$. Note that $g = \cup_{g' \in C(g)} g'$.

Note that under this definition of a component, a completely isolated player who has no links is not considered a component. If one wants to have a definition of a component that includes isolated nodes as a special case, then the partition induced by the network can be considered.

Knowing the components of a network, we can partition the players into groups within which players are connected. Let $\Pi(g)$ denote the partition of N induced by the network g.[13]

1.2.4. Value Functions

The network structure is the key determinant of the level of productivity or utility to the society of the players involved. For instance, a buyer's expected utility from trade may depend on how many sellers that buyer is negotiating with, how many other buyers they are connected to, and so on (as in Corominas-Bosch 1999 and Kranton and Minehart 2001). Similarly, a network in which players have very few acquaintances with whom they share information will result in different employment patterns than one in which players have many such acquaintances (as in Calvo-Armengol and Jackson 2001, 2004).

Methods of keeping track of the overall value generated by a particular network, as well as how it is allocated across players, are through a value function and an allocation rule. These are the natural extensions of the notions of characteristic function and imputation rule from cooperative game theory. In cooperative game theory, these would depend just on the set of players involved, whereas here in the network setting they depend on the full network structure rather than simply a coalition. In fact, in the special case in which the value generated only depends on connected components rather than network structure, the value function and allocation rule reduce to a characteristic function (for a cooperative game in partition function form) and imputation rule.

A *value function* is a function $v : G \to \mathbb{R}$.

For simplicity, in what follows I maintain the normalization that $v(\emptyset) = 0$.

The set of all possible value functions is denoted v.

---

[13] That is, $S \in \Pi(g)$ if and only if either there exists $h \in C(g)$ such that $S = N(h)$ or there exists $i \notin N(g)$ such that $S = \{i\}$.

A value function allows the value of a network to depend in arbitrary ways on the structure of the networks. This allows for arbitrary externalities in the generation of value.

A prominent subclass of value functions is the set of component additive ones.

A value function v is *component additive* if $\sum_{h \in C(g)} v(h) = v(g)$.

Component additivity is a condition that rules out externalities across components but still allows them within components. It is quite natural in some contexts, such as social interactions, and not in others – for instance in an oligopoly setting in which links are alliances of some type and different firms compete with each other.

Another prominent subclass of value functions is the set of anonymous ones.

Given a permutation of players π (a bijection from N to N) and any $g \in G$, let $g^\pi = \{\pi(i)\pi(j) | ij \in g\}$. Thus, g^π is a network that shares the same architecture as g but with the players relabeled according to π.

A value function is *anonymous* if, for any permutation of the set of players π, $v(g^\pi) = v(g)$.

Anonymity says that the value of a network is derived from its structure and not the labels of the players who occupy various positions.

It is important to note that the various networks that connect the same players may lead to different values. This makes a value function a much richer object than a characteristic function used in cooperative game theory. For instance, a society $N = \{1, 2, 3\}$ may have a different value depending on whether it is connected via the network $g = \{12, 23\}$ or the network $g^N = \{12, 23, 13\}$.

The special case in which the value function depends only on the groups of players that are connected, but not how they are connected, corresponds to the communications networks (or cooperation structures) first considered by Myerson (1977) and surveyed in Chapter 2 of this volume. Specifically, Myerson started with a transferable utility cooperative game in characteristic function form and layered on top of that network structures that indicated which players could communicate. A coalition could only generate value if its members were connected via paths in the network. But, the particular structure of the network did not matter as long as the coalition's members were connected somehow.

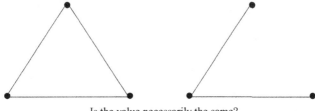

Is the value necessarily the same?

The approach surveyed here follows Jackson and Wolinsky (1996), who defined the value as a function that is allowed to depend on the specific network structure. A special case is one in which $v(g)$ only depends on the coalitions induced by the component structure of g, which corresponds to the communications games. In most applications, however, there may be some cost to links and thus some difference in total value across networks even if they connect the same sets of players, and so this more general and flexible formulation is more powerful and encompasses more applications.

It is also important to note that the value function can incorporate costs to links as well as benefits. This allows for costs and benefits to vary across networks in very general ways. Thus, a value function allows for externalities both within and across components of a network.

1.2.5. Network Games

A *network game* is a pair (N, v), where N is the set of players and v is a value function on networks among those players.

This notion of a network game might be thought of as the analog of a cooperative game (rather than a noncooperative game), for the allocation of values among players is not specified. The use of such games will involve both cooperative and noncooperative perspectives because they will be the basis for network formation. The augmenting of a network game by an allocation rule, which we turn to next, will be what allows us to model the formation of the network.

1.2.6. Allocation Rules

Beyond knowing how much total value is generated by a network, it is critical to keep track of how that value is allocated or distributed among the players in the society. This is captured by the concept of an allocation rule.

An *allocation rule* is a function $Y : G \times v \to \mathbb{R}^N$ such that $\sum_i Y_i(g, v) = v(g)$ for all v and g. Note that balance, $\sum_i Y_i(g, v) = v(g)$, is made part of this definition of allocation rule.

Generally, there will be some natural way in which the value is allocated in a given network situation. This might simply be the utility that the players directly receive, accounting for both the costs and benefits of maintaining their links (e.g., in a social network). This might also be the result of some bargaining about the terms of trade such as in a network of international trading relationships. Beyond the allocations that come naturally with the network, we might also be interested in designing the allocation rule; that is, reallocating value using taxes, subsidies, and other transfers. This might be motivated in several ways, including trying to affect the incentives of players to form networks, or more simply for fairness reasons. Regardless of the perspective taken, an allocation rule captures either an allocation that arises naturally or an allocation of value that is imposed.

It is important to note that an allocation rule depends on both g and v. This allows an allocation rule to take full account of a player i's role in the network. This includes not only what the network configuration is but also how the value generated depends on the overall network structure. For instance, consider a network $g = \{12, 23\}$ in a situation in which the value generated is 1 ($v(g) = 1$). Player 2's allocation might be very different as determined by the values of other networks. For instance, if

$v(\{12, 23, 13\}) = 0 = v(\{13\})$, then 2 is essential to the network and may receive a large allocation. If, on the other hand, $v(g') = 1$ for all networks, then 2's role is not particularly special. This information can be relevant, especially in bargaining situations, which is why the allocation rule is allowed to depend on it. I return to discuss this in more detail below.

Before moving on, I note two properties of allocation rules that will come up repeatedly in what follows.

1.2.7. Component Balance

An allocation rule Y is *component balanced* if $\sum_{i \in S} Y_i(g, v) = v(g|_S)$ for each component additive v, $g \in G$ and $S \in \Pi(g)$.

Component balance requires that the value of a given component of a network be allocated to the members of that component in cases in which the value of the component is independent of how other components are organized. This tends to arise naturally. It also is a condition that an intervening planner or government would like to respect to avoid secession by components of the network.

1.2.8. Anonymity of an Allocation Rule

Given a permutation $\pi : N \to N$, let v^π be defined by $v^\pi(g) = v(g^{\pi^{-1}})$ for each $g \in G$ (recalling the definition of g^π from Section 1.2.4.). This is just the value function obtained when agents' names are relabeled through π.

An allocation rule Y is *anonymous* if for any $v \in v$, $g \in G$ and permutation of the set of players π, $Y_{\pi(i)}(g^\pi, v^\pi) = Y_i(g, v)$.

Anonymity of an allocation rule requires that, if all that has changed are the labels of the players and the value generated by networks has changed in an exactly corresponding fashion, then the allocation only changes according to the relabeling.[14]

1.3. Some Examples

In order to fix some ideas and illustrate the preceding definitions, I now describe a few examples of network situations that have been analyzed in the literature.

Example 1.1. The Connections Model (Jackson and Wolinsky 1996). *In this model, links represent social relationships between players such as friendships. These relationships offer benefits in terms of favors, information, and so on and also involve some costs. Moreover, players benefit from indirect relationships. A "friend of a friend," also results in some benefits, although of a lesser value than a "friend," as do "friends of a friend of a friend," and so forth. The benefit deteriorates in the "distance" of the relationship. For instance, in the network $g = \{12, 23, 34\}$, player 1 gets a benefit of δ from the direct connection with player 2, an indirect*

---

[14] Note that the definition does not require that v be anonymous or that g be symmetric.

benefit of δ^2 from the indirect connection with player 3, and an indirect benefit of δ^3 from the indirect connection with player 4. For $\delta < 1$ this leads to a lower benefit from an indirect connection than a direct one. Players only pay costs, however, for maintaining their direct relationships. These payoffs and benefits may be relation specific and so are indexed by ij.

Formally, the payoff player i receives from network g is[15]

$$Y_i(g) = \sum_{j \neq i} \delta_{ij}^{d(i,j)} - \sum_{j:ij \in g} c_{ij},$$

where $d(i, j)$ is the number of links in the shortest path (the "geodesic") between i and j (setting $d(i, j) = \infty$ if there is no path between i and j). The value function in the connections model of a network g is simply $v(g) = \sum_i Y_i(g)$.

The case in which there are common δ and c such that $\delta_{ij} = \delta$ and $c_{ij} = c$ for all i and j is referred to as the "symmetric connections model."

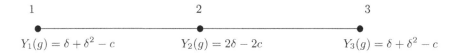

$$
\begin{array}{ccc}
1 & 2 & 3 \\
\bullet & \bullet & \bullet \\
Y_1(g) = \delta + \delta^2 - c & Y_2(g) = 2\delta - 2c & Y_3(g) = \delta + \delta^2 - c
\end{array}
$$

Example 1.2. The Spatial Connections Model (Johnson and Gilles 2000). *An interesting version of the connections model is studied by Johnson and Gilles (2000). This is a version with spatial costs, where there is a geography to locations and c_{ij} is related to distance. For instance, if players are spaced equally on a line and i's location is at the point i, then costs are proportional to $|i - j|$.*

This variation of the connections model introduces natural asymmetries among the players and yields interesting variations on the networks that form and the ones that are most efficient from society's perspective.

Example 1.3. Free-Trade Networks (Furusawa and Konishi 2002). *Furusawa and Konishi (2002) consider a model in which the players in the network are countries. A link between two countries is interpreted as a free-trade agreement, which means that the goods produced in either of the countries can be traded without any tariff to consumers in the other country. In the absence of a link, goods are traded with some tariff. A link between two countries has direct effects in the trade between those two countries because there will be a greater flow of goods (possibly in both directions) in the absence of any tariffs. There are also indirect effects from links. Countries not directly involved in a link still feel some effects, for the relative prices for goods imported from a country change while a free-trade agreement (link) between two other countries is put into place.*

Once demands of the consumers, the production possibilities, and the tariffs for imports from other countries (in the absence of links) are specified for each country, then the payoffs to each country can be calculated as a function of the network of

---

[15] I omit the notation v in $Y_i(g, v)$ in a slight abuse of notation. Here, the allocation or payoff Y is particular to the problem, and the value function is defined based on it.

free-trade agreements as well as the total value generated by all countries. Thus, we end up with a well-defined value function and allocation rule, making it possible to study the incentives for countries to form free-trade agreements.

Example 1.4. Market Sharing Agreements (Belleflamme and Bloch 2002). *In this model, the n players are firms that each have a home market for their goods. Firms are symmetric to start with, and so any asymmetries that arise will come from the network structure that is formed. In this model a link represents an agreement between two firms. In the absence of any agreement between firms i and j, firm i will sell goods on firm j's market and vice versa. If firms i and j form a link, then that is interpreted as a market-sharing agreement in which firm i refrains from selling on j's market and vice versa.*

The profits a firm makes from selling its goods on any market are given by a function that is the profit to a firm selling on market j as a function of n_j, which is the number of firms selling on market j. Once this profit function is specified, it is possible to calculate the payoff to each firm as a function of the network structure in place.

Example 1.5. Labor Markets (Calvo-Armengol and Jackson 2001, 2004). *In this model, each worker maintains social ties with other workers. Over time, workers randomly lose jobs and new job opportunities arise. As information about a new job comes to a given worker, he or she might do several things with it. First, if the worker is unemployed or the new job opportunity looks more attractive than that person's current job, he or she might take the job (or at least apply and obtain the job with some probability). Second, if the job is not right for the worker personally, he or she may pass that information on to one or more friends; that is, the information about the job may be passed on to some of those players to whom the worker is linked in the network. This passing of information leads to some probabilities that these workers' friends might obtain the job. The model can also allow for the possibility that these friends might further pass the information on, and so forth.*

The set of possibilities for how information might be passed through the network can be quite complicated. However, all that really matters in this model is what the probability is that each player ends up getting a (new) job as a function of what the current status of all the players in the network is. Once this is specified, a well-defined random (Markov) process results from which one can calculate the probability distribution of any worker's employment and wage status for any date given any information about the state of the network and employment statuses and wages on some previous date. The structure of the network and the initial starting state then provide predictions for the future expected discounted stream of any worker's wages.

With this network of information passing in place, and the predictions it yields for the stream of workers' wages, one can ask what the incentives of the workers are to maintain their position in the network rather than dropping out of it. One might also ask what their incentives are to maintain or sever links, and so on.

Example 1.6. The Coauthor Model (Jackson and Wolinsky 1996). *In the coauthor model, each player is a researcher who spends time working on research projects. If two researchers are connected, then they are working on a project together. Each player has a fixed amount of time to spend on research, and so the time that researcher i spends on a given project is inversely related to the number of projects, n_i, that he or she is involved in. The synergy between two researchers depends on how much time they spend together, and this is captured by a term $\frac{1}{n_i n_j}$. Here, the more projects a researcher is involved with, the lower the synergy that is obtained per project.*

Player i's payoff is represented by

$$Y_i(g) = \sum_{j:ij \in g} \left(\frac{1}{n_i} + \frac{1}{n_j} + \frac{1}{n_i n_j} \right)$$

for $n_i > 0$, and $Y_i(g) = 1$ if $n_i = 0$.

Thus, the value generated by any given research project is proportional to the sum of the time that i puts into the project, the time that j puts into it, and a synergy that is dependent on an interaction between the time that the two researchers put into the project.

The total value generated by all researchers is $v(g) = \sum_i Y_i(g)$.

Note that in the coauthor model there are no directly modeled costs to links. Costs come indirectly in terms of diluted synergy in interaction with coauthors.

Example 1.7. Organizations and Externalities (Currarini 2002). *Although the general model of a network game allows for arbitrary forms of externalities, it is useful to understand how the particular structure of externalities matters in determining which networks form. We can gain some insight from looking at various models. For instance, we see positive externalities to other players (not involved in a new link) when a player forms a new link in the connections model, and we see negative externalities to other players when a given player forms a new link in the coauthor model. Although these allow us to see some effects of different kinds of externalities, the models differ in too many dimensions to be able to disentangle exactly what the impact of different forms of externalities is.*

An approach to studying how different forms of externalities affect network formation is to specify a model that has a flexible enough structure to permit positive and negative externalities to be included as special cases, and yet at the same time we need the model to be specialized enough to permit pointed predictions. Currarini's (2002) model is motivated in this way.

In Currarini's model, the value of a network depends only on the partition of players induced by the components of the network. That is, any network partitions the players into different subsets, and two players are in the same subset if and only if there is some path in the network that includes them both. The simplifying assumption that he makes is that the value of a network g depends only on $\Pi(g)$, and so we can write $v(\Pi(g))$.[16]

---

[16] The v in Currarini's analysis, considered more carefully, is a richer object than the value function defined in this survey because Currarini's version specifies the value of each component as a function of the partition.

The reason that the network structure still plays an important role in Currarini's analysis is that, if some group of players change their links, the resulting network (and thus partition structure that results) depends on how they were connected to start with. For instance, if player 2 severs all links in the network {12, 23}, the resulting partition of players is different from what happens when player 2 severs all links in the network {12, 23, 13}.

Currarini's definition of positive and negative externalities is based on whether value increases or decreases as the partition of players becomes finer.

Example 1.8. Unequal Connections (Goyal and Joshi 2003). *Goyal and Joshi (2003) provide a different model of externalities but one that is similar to Currarini's in its spirit of having a specialized enough structure to allow for pointed predictions while having sufficient flexibility to allow for both positive and negative externalities.*

In the Goyal and Joshi model, the allocation to a given player as a function of the network can be written as

$$Y_i(g) = b_i(g) - n_i(g)c,$$

where c is a cost, n_i is the number of links that i has, and b_i is a benefit function. In particular the benefit function is assumed to take one of two forms. In the "playing the field" version,

$$b_i(g + ij) - b_i(g) = \phi\left(n_i(g), \sum_{k \neq i} n_k(g_{-i})\right),$$

where ϕ is common to all players and g_{-i} is the network with all links to i removed. Under this assumption, players care only about how many links they have and how many links all other players have in total. Essentially, players benefit (or suffer) from others' links in symmetric ways regardless of the particulars of the path structure. The other version of the model that they consider is the "local spillovers" version, where there is a function ψ such that

$$b_i(g + ij) - b_i(g) = \psi(n_i(g), n_j(g)).$$

Here the marginal value of a link depends only on how connected the two players are and not on the particulars of whom they are connected to or other aspects of the network.

Under these assumptions on marginal benefits from links, Goyal and Joshi can then look at positive and negative spillovers by considering how these functions change with the n_i's and n_j's. Under different possible scenarios, they can compute the networks that will be formed and see how these vary with the scenario.

Example 1.9. A Bilateral Bargaining Model (Corominas-Bosch 1999). *Corominas-Bosch (1999) considers a bargaining model in which buyers and sellers bargain over prices for trade. A link is necessary between a buyer and seller for a transaction to occur, but if a player has several links, then there are several possibilities as to whom he or she might transact with. Thus, the network structure essentially determines bargaining power of various buyers and sellers.*

More specifically, each seller has a single unit of an indivisible good to sell that has no value to the seller. Buyers have a valuation of 1 for a single unit of the good. If a buyer and seller exchange at a price p, then the buyer receives a payoff of $1 - p$ and the seller a payoff of p. A link in the network represents the opportunity for a buyer and seller to bargain and potentially exchange a good.[17]

Corominas-Bosch models bargaining via the following variation on a Rubinstein bargaining protocol. In the first period sellers simultaneously each call out a price. A buyer can only select from the prices that he or she has heard called out by the sellers with whom there are links. Buyers simultaneously respond by either choosing to accept some single price offer they have received or to reject all of them. If there are several sellers who have called out the same price, several buyers who have accepted the same price, or both, and there is any discretion under the given network connections as to which trades should occur, then there is a careful protocol for determining which trades occur (which is essentially designed to maximize the number of eventual transactions).

At the end of the period, trades are made and buyers and sellers who have traded are cleared from the market. In the next period the situation reverses and buyers call out prices. These are then either accepted or rejected by the sellers connected to them in the same way. In each period the role of proposer and responder switches, and this process repeats itself indefinitely until all remaining buyers and sellers are no longer linked to each other. Buyers and sellers are impatient and discount according to a common discount factor $0 < \delta < 1$. Thus, a transaction at price p in period t is worth $\delta^t p$ to a seller and $\delta^t(1 - p)$ to a buyer.

Given this specification and some specification of the costs of links, one can calculate the expected payoff to every buyer and seller (the allocation rule) as a function of the network structure.

Example 1.10. A Model of Buyer–Seller Networks (Kranton and Minehart 2001). *The Kranton and Minehart model of buyer–seller networks is similar to the Corominas-Bosch model described in the preceding example except that the valuations of the buyers for a good are random and the determination of prices is made through an auction rather than alternating-offers bargaining.*

The Kranton and Minehart model is described as follows. Again, each seller has an indivisible object for sale. Buyers have independently and identically distributed utilities for the object denoted u_i. Each buyer knows his or her own valuation (but only the distribution over other buyers' valuations), and, similarly, sellers know only the distribution of buyers' valuations.

Again, link patterns represent the potential transactions; however, the transactions and prices are determined by an auction rather than bargaining. In particular, prices rise simultaneously across all sellers. Buyers drop out when the price exceeds their valuation (as they would in an English or ascending oral auction). As buyers drop out, sets of sellers emerge for whom the remaining buyers still linked to those sellers

---

[17] Note that in the Corominas-Bosch framework links can only form between buyers and sellers. This fits into the setting we are considering here in which links can form between any players simply by having the value function and allocation rule ignore any links except those between buyers and sellers.

are no larger than the set of sellers. Those sellers transact with the buyers still linked to them. The exact matching of who trades with whom given the link pattern is done carefully to maximize the number of transactions. Those sellers and buyers are cleared from the market, and the prices continue to rise among remaining sellers. The process then repeats itself.

For each link pattern, every player has a well-defined expected payoff from the process just defined (from an ex ante perspective before buyers know their u_i's). The costs of maintaining links to buyers and sellers can be deducted from this expected payoff to obtain a prediction of net payoffs as a function of the network structure or, in other words, the allocation rule.

Example 1.11. Buyer–Seller Networks with Quality Differentiated Products (Wang and Watts 2002). *The Wang and Watts model of buyer–seller networks enriches the preceding bargaining models in the following ways. First, sellers have a choice of selling goods of either high or low quality (which is observable to the buyer). Also, in addition to having links between buyers and sellers, buyers and sellers may link with each other to form buyers associations and sellers associations. The advantage of forming such associations is that they influence the bargaining power and the eventual prices that emerge. The disadvantage is that sales may be rationed among members of an association. For instance, if a sellers association has an excess number of members relative to the number of buyers who have linked with it, then the determination of who gets to sell is made by randomization. This model brings together issues of how network structure affects bargaining power and how collective structures can influence such power.*

The examples presented above provide an idea of how rich and varied the potential applications of network models are. This is only a subset of the models in the literature. Let us now turn to look at the ways in which the formation of networks has been analyzed.

1.4. Modeling Network Formation

There are many possible approaches to modeling network formation.[18] An obvious one is simply to model it explicitly as a noncooperative game. Let us start with this approach as the literature did as well.[19]

1.4.1. An Extensive Form Game

Aumann and Myerson (1988) were the first to model network formation explicitly as a game and did so by describing an extensive form game for the formation of a

---

[18] The discussion here focuses on situations in which players decide to participate, or not to do so, in a link modeled in various ways. Brueckner (2003) examines an interesting alternative in which players put in effort and then links are determined randomly but with increasing probability in players' efforts.

[19] Another possibility is simply to specify some exogenous rule for adding and deleting links in a network environment and then to run simulations. That method of studying self-organizing networks is seen in some of the social networks literature. The idea of studying incentives and explicitly modeling the strategic aspects of network formation is to try to put more structure and understanding behind this process to see which networks form and why.

network in the context of cooperative games with communications structures.[20] In their game, players sequentially propose links which are then accepted or rejected. The extensive form possibly begins with an ordering over links. Let this ranking be $(i_1 j_1, \ldots, i_n j_n)$. The game is such that the pair of players $i_k j_k$ decide on whether or not to form that link knowing the decisions of all pairs coming before them and forecasting the play that will come after them. A decision to form a link is binding and cannot be undone. If a pair $i_k j_k$ decide not to form a link, but some other pair coming after them forms a link, then $i_k j_k$ are allowed to reconsider their decision. This feature allows player 1 to make a credible threat to 2 of the form "I will not form a link with 3 if you do not. But if you do form a link with 3, then I will also do so."

In terms of its usefulness as an approach to modeling network formation, this game has some nice features. However, the extensive form makes it difficult to analyze beyond very simple examples, and the ordering of links can have a nontrivial impact on which networks emerge. These hurdles have prompted some other approaches.

1.4.2. A Simultaneous Move Game

Myerson (1991) suggests a different game for modeling network formation. It is in a way the simplest one possible and as such is a natural one. It can be described as follows.[21] The strategy space of each player is the list of other players. So the strategy space of i is $S_i = 2^{N \setminus \{i\}}$. Players (simultaneously) announce which other players they wish to be connected to. If $s \in S_1 \times \cdots \times S_n$ is the set of strategies played, then link ij forms if and only if both $j \in s_i$ and $i \in s_j$.

This game has the advantage of being very simple and rather directly capturing the idea of forming links. Unfortunately, it generally has a large multiplicity of Nash equilibria. For instance, $s_i = \emptyset$, for all i is *always* a Nash equilibrium regardless of what the payoffs to various networks are. The idea is that no player suggests any links under the correct expectation that no players will reciprocate. This is especially unnatural in situations in which links result in some positive payoff. This means that, in order to make use of this game, one must really use some refinement of Nash equilibrium. Moreover, to really deal with the fact that it takes two players to form a link, something beyond refinements like undominated Nash equilibrium or trembling-hand perfection is necessary. One needs to employ concepts such as strong equilibrium or coalition-proof Nash equilibrium. Dutta and Mutuswami (1997) discuss such refinements in detail,[22] and the relationship of the equilibria to the concept of pairwise stability, which is the concept that I discuss next.

The fact that mutual consent is needed to form a link is generally a hurdle for trying to use any off-the-shelf, noncooperative, game-theoretic approach. In whatever game one specifies for link formation, requiring the consent of two players to form a link

---

[20] See Chapter 2 of this volume for a detailed discussion of this game.

[21] See Chapter 2 of this volume for a discussion of some results for this game.

[22] See also Dutta, van den Nouweland, and Tijs (1998); Harrison and Munoz (2002); and an earlier use of the game in Qin (1996). See also McBride (2002) for a variation of the game and a solution concept to allow for incomplete information of players regarding their payoffs and structure of the network.

means that either some type of coalitional equilibrium concept is necessary or the game needs to be an extensive form with a protocol for proposing and accepting links in some sequence. Another serious challenge to the off-the-shelf, noncooperative, game-theoretic approach is that the game is necessarily ad hoc, and fine details of the protocol (e.g., the ordering of who proposes links when, whether or not the game has a finite horizon or if players are impatient, etc.) generally matter.

1.4.3. Pairwise Stability

A different approach to modeling network formation is to dispense with the specifics of a noncooperative game and simply to model a notion of what a stable network is directly. This is the approach that was taken by Jackson and Wolinsky (1996) and is captured in the following definition.

A network g is *pairwise stable* with respect to allocation rule Y and value function v if

(i) for all $ij \in g$, $Y_i(g, v) \geq Y_i(g - ij, v)$ and $Y_j(g, v) \geq Y_j(g - ij, v)$, and

(ii) for all $ij \notin g$, if $Y_i(g + ij, v) > Y_i(g, v)$, then $Y_j(g + ij, v) < Y_j(g, v)$.

The first part of the definition of pairwise stability requires that no player wish to delete a link that he or she is involved in. Implicitly, any player has the discretion to unilaterally terminate relationships in which he or she is involved. The second part of the definition requires that if some link is not in the network and one of the involved players would benefit from adding it, then it must be that the other player would suffer from the addition of the link. Here it is implicit that the consent of both players is needed for adding a link.[23] This seems to be an aspect that is pervasive in applications, and it is thus important to incorporate this idea into a solution concept.

Although pairwise stability is natural and quite easy to work with, there are some limitations of the concept that deserve discussion.

First, it is a weak notion because it only considers deviations on a single link at a time. This is part of what makes it easy to apply. However, if other types of deviations are viable and attractive, then pairwise stability may be too weak a concept.[24] For instance, it could be that a player would not benefit from severing any single link but rather from severing several links simultaneously, and yet the network would still be pairwise stable. Second, pairwise stability considers only deviations by at most a pair of players at a time. Perhaps the players in some group could all be made better off by some more complicated reorganization of their links, which is not accounted for under pairwise stability. To the extent that larger groups can coordinate their actions in making changes in a network, a stronger solution concept may be needed.

---

[23] Jackson and Wolinsky (1996) also study another stability concept in which side payments are possible. That is, one player can pay another (or provide some sort of favors) so that new links form whenever the total benefit to the two players involved is positive. See that paper for details.

[24] One can augment pairwise stability by various extra considerations – for instance, allowing players to sever many links at once. For a look at different variations of this kind, see, for instance, Belleflamme and Bloch (2001) and Goyal and Joshi (1999).

In both of these regards, pairwise stability might be thought of as a necessary but not sufficient requirement for a network to be stable over time. Nevertheless, pairwise stability still turns out to be quite useful and in particular often provides narrow predictions about the set of stable networks.

1.4.4. Strong Stability

Alternatives to pairwise stability that allow for larger coalitions than just pairs of players to deviate were first considered by Dutta and Mutuswami (1997).[25] The following definition is in that spirit and is due to Jackson and van den Nouweland (2000).[26]

A network $g' \in G$ is *obtainable from* $g \in G$ *via deviations by* S if

(i) $ij \in g'$ and $ij \notin g$ implies $ij \subset S$, and

(ii) $ij \in g$ and $ij \notin g'$ implies $ij \cap S \neq \emptyset$.

This definition identifies changes in a network that can be made by a coalition S without the consent of any players outside of S. Part (i) requires that any new links that are added can only be between players in S. This requirement arises because the consent of both players is needed to add a link. Part (ii) requires that at least one player of any deleted link be in S. This is because either player in a link can unilaterally sever the relationship.

A network g is *strongly stable* with respect to allocation rule Y and value function v if for any $S \subset N$, g' that is obtainable from g via deviations by S, and $i \in S$ such that $Y_i(g', v) > Y_i(g, v)$, there exists $j \in S$ such that $Y_j(g', v) < Y_j(g, v)$.[27]

Strong stability provides a powerful refinement of pairwise stability. The concept of strong stability mainly makes sense in smaller network situations in which players have substantial information about the overall structure and potential payoffs and can coordinate their actions. Thus, for instance, strong stability might be more applicable to agreements between firms in an oligopoly than modeling friendships in a large society.

Strong stability also faces some high hurdles for its existence because it is a very demanding concept. In fact, one might argue that this is too demanding a concept, for what appears to be an improving deviation might not be taken if one started to forecast how the other players might react. This issue is addressed in the recently developed notions of "farsighted" network formation, which is discussed

---

[25] Core-based notions had been discussed in the exchange network literature mainly in terms of bargaining over value, as adapted from the cooperative game theory literature. See Bienenstock and Bonacich (1997) for an overview.

[26] Konishi and Ünver (2003) develop an interesting variation of strong stability for matching games.

[27] The difference between this definition of strong stability from Jackson and van den Nouweland (2000) and that of Dutta and Mutuswami (1997) is as follows. The preceding definition allows for a deviation to be valid if some members are strictly better off and others are weakly better off, whereas the definition in Dutta and Mutuswami (1997) considers a deviation valid only if all members of a coalition are strictly better off. Although the difference is fairly minor, this stronger notion implies pairwise stability whereas Dutta and Mutuswami's (1997) definition does not.

in Chapter 3 of this volume. Nevertheless, when strongly stable networks exist, they have very nice properties.

1.4.5. Forming a Network and Bargaining

The preceding methods of modeling network formation are such that the network formation process and the allocation of value among players in a network are separated. Currarini and Morelli (2000) provide an interesting approach in which the allocation of value among players takes place simultaneously with the link formation inasmuch as players may bargain over their shares of value as they negotiate whether or not to add a link.[28]

The game that Currarini and Morelli analyze can be described as follows. Players are ordered exogenously according to a function $\rho : N \to N$. Without loss of generality, assume that this is in the order of their labels, and so player 1 moves first, then player 2, and so forth. A player i announces the set of players with whom he or she is willing to be linked ($a_i \in 2^{N \setminus \{i\}}$) and a payoff demand $d_i \in \mathbb{R}$. The outcome of the game is then as follows. The actions $a = (a_1, \ldots, a_n)$ determine a network $g(a)$ by requiring that a link ij be in $g(a)$ if and only if $j \in a_i$ and $i \in a_j$. However, the network that is eventually formed is determined by checking which components of $g(a)$ are actually feasible in terms of the demands submitted. That is, if $h \in C(g(a))$, then h is actually formed if and only if $\sum_{i \in N(h)} d_i \leq v(h)$.[29] When $\sum_{i \in N(h)} d_i > v(h)$, the links in h are all deleted and the players in $N(h)$ are left without any links.

As I discuss below, the simultaneous bargaining over allocations and network formation can make an important difference in conclusions about the efficiency of the networks that are formed. This means that it is an idea that must be carefully accounted for. The main difficulty with this approach is the specification of the bargaining game, whose fine details (such as how the game ends) can be very important in determining what networks form and how value is distributed.

1.4.6. Dynamic Models

Beyond the one-time models of network formation, one can also take a dynamic perspective in which networks are formed over time. The first such approach was taken by Watts (1997) in the context of the symmetric connections model (Example 1.1). She modeled this as follows. First let me introduce some terminology that will be useful later and is helpful in discussing Watts's ideas.

A network g' is *adjacent* to a network g if $g' = g + ij$ or $g' = g - ij$ for some ij.

---

[28] See also Slikker and van den Nouweland (2001b), Mutuswami and Winter (2000), Navarro and Perea (2001), and Nieva (2002) for similar approaches, and see Chapter 2 of this volume for a detailed description. A new paper by Bloch and Jackson (2004) examines the networks that emerge from a variety of bargaining protocols.

[29] To understand these definitions, you will find that it is useful to think of v as component additive, and thus $\sum_{h \in C(g)} v(h) = v(g)$.

A network g' *defeats* another network g if either $g' = g - ij$ and $Y_i(g', v) > Y_i(g', v)$, or if $g' = g + ij$ with $Y_i(g', v) \geq Y_i(g', v)$, $Y_j(g', v) \geq Y_j(g', v)$, and at least one inequality holding strictly.

Note that, under this terminology, a network is pairwise stable if and only if it is not defeated by an (adjacent) network.

Watts's process can then be described as follows. The network begins as an empty network. At each time $t \in \{1, 2, \ldots\}$, a link is randomly identified. The current network is altered if and only if the addition or deletion of the link would defeat the current network. Thus, players add or delete links through myopic considerations of whether this would increase their payoffs.

Watts says that a network is a *stable state* if there is some time t after which no links would ever be added or deleted.

The set of stable states is clearly a subset of the pairwise stable networks.

The following notion from Jackson and Watts (2002a) captures this idea of sequences of networks, where each network defeats the previous one.

An *improving path*[30] is a sequence of networks $\{g_1, g_2, \ldots, g_K\}$ in which each network g_k is defeated by the subsequent (adjacent) network g_{k+1}. This is illustrated in Figure 1.1.

An improving path in this example is the sequence of networks $\{12, 23\}$, $\{12\}$, $\{12, 34\}$. Here $\{12, 23\}$ is defeated by $\{12\}$ because 2 benefits by severing the link 23, and this in turn is defeated by $\{12, 34\}$ because 3 and 4 both benefit by adding the link 34.

A network is pairwise stable if and only if it has no improving paths emanating from it. Note that a stable state is any pairwise stable network that can be reached by an improving path from the empty network.

A difficulty with the idea of a stable state is that in some situations one can get stuck at the empty network because any single link results in a lower value even though the larger networks may be valuable. If it were possible to start at any network, then any pairwise stable network could be reached by an improving path. But without specifying the process more fully, it is not clear what the right starting conditions are. Introducing some stochastics into the picture solves this problem quite naturally.

1.4.7. Stochastic Dynamic Models

There are two dynamic approaches that can overcome this difficulty of getting stuck at a network. One is to do away with the myopic nature of players' choices, as discussed in the next section. This makes sense in situations in which the networks are relatively small and players know each other and can make good predictions about future plays. The other approach is to introduce some randomness into the network formation process. For example, links may be added or deleted via some exogenous stimulus or simply by error or experiment on the part of the players.

---

[30] The term *path* here refers to a sequence of networks and should not be confused with a path inside a network.

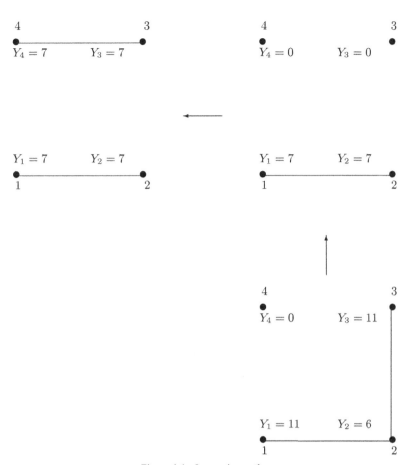

Figure 1.1: Improving paths.

This second approach of introducing random perturbations to the formation process was first studied by Jackson and Watts (2002a).[31] The setup is described as follows. Start at some network g. At each time $t \in \{1, 2, \ldots\}$, a link ij is randomly identified. Just as in the notion of an improving path, we check whether the players in question would like to add the link if it is not in the network or sever the link if it is in the network. What is new is that the intentions of the players are only carried out with probability $1 - \epsilon$, and with probability $\epsilon > 0$ the reverse happens. Given these random perturbations in the process, it will go on forever and has a chance of visiting any network. Some networks are more likely to be visited than others, for some can only be reached through a series of errors whereas others are more naturally reached through the intentions of the players. We can then

---

[31] This was further studied in the context of the play of noncooperative games by Jackson and Watts (2002b); Goyal and Vega-Redondo (2000); Droste, Gilles, and Johnson (2000); and Bramoullé et al. (2002). See also Skyrms and Pemantle (2000) for a reinforcement-based evolutionary analysis of games played on networks. See Chapter 4 of this volume for some discussion of those papers.

examine this process to see which networks have the highest probability of being reached.[32]

When pairwise-stable networks exist, then this analysis of stochastic stability will select a subset of them. When pairwise-stable networks do not exist, the limit of the process just described will involve cycles of networks that are randomly visited over time.

The advantages of these dynamic analyses is that they can select from among the pairwise-stable networks. In the case of stochastic stability, essentially the most robust or easy-to-reach networks are selected. The disadvantage with this approach is that the limit points of the dynamics can be difficult to identify in some applications.[33]

1.4.8. Farsighted Network Formation

Finally, as mentioned earlier, there is another aspect of network formation that deserves attention. The preceding definitions generally either have some myopic aspect to them or some artificial stopping point (a finite horizon to the game) that limits the ability of other players to react. For instance, the adding or severing of one link might lead to the subsequent addition or severing of another link. As determined by the context, this might be an important consideration. In large networks, players might have very little ability to forecast how the network could change in reaction to the addition or deletion of a link. In such situations the myopic solutions are quite reasonable. However, if players have very good information about how others might react to changes in the network, then these are things one wants to allow for either in the specification of the game or in the definition of the stability concept.[34] Recent work by Page, Wooders, and Kamat (2001); Watts (2002); Dutta, Ghosal, and Ray (2003); and Deroïan (2003) addresses this issue. This is surveyed in Chapter 3 of this volume, and so I will not discuss this idea here.

1.4.9. The Existence of Stable Networks

The existence of stable networks depends on which of the preceding approaches to modeling stability is taken.

In the case in which the sequential game of Aumann and Myerson (1988) or Currarini and Morelli (2000) is used, existence of a (subgame perfect) equilibrium can be established through results in the game-theoretic literature.[35]

---

[32] More formally, we end up with a finite-state, aperiodic, and irreducible Markov process. Techniques for characterizing the limiting distribution of such processes as $\epsilon \to 0$ are well developed. In particular, a theorem by Freidlin and Wentzell (1984), as adapted to the study of stochastic stability by Kandori, Mailath, and Rob (1993) and Young (1993), is the key tool. Jackson and Watts (2002a) provide details of the adaptation of this tool to the network setting.

[33] It does depend on the application. See Jackson and Watts (2002a) for more detail and some examples (such as the bipartite matching problems) where such techniques have sharp predictions.

[34] For an interesting set of experiments that compare myopic versus forward-looking behavior in network formation, see Pantz and Ziegelmeyer (2003). They find little evidence of forward-looking behavior – even in environments designed to elicit it. Although myopic behavior more closely matches the observed behavior in a variety of settings, there is still some behavior in the experiments that remains unexplained.

[35] The game of Aumann and Myerson is a finite-extensive form game of perfect information, and so existence follows easily from well-known theorems. Currarini and Morelli have a few more hoops to jump through because they have infinite action spaces.

When one looks at the simultaneous move game of Myerson (1991), the existence of a variety of equilibria types is easily established – again via standard theorems.

The main challenges arise in coming to grips with the issue of mutual consent needed to form a link. This occurs either in using a coalition-based solution concept to solve Myerson's game or when moving to notions such as pairwise stability, strong stability, and stable states. Let me turn to what is known about these issues.

Given the finite number of possible networks, it follows that if no pairwise-stable network exists, then there must be at least one cycle: an improving path $\{g_1, g_2, \ldots, g_K\}$, where $g_1 = g_K$. Indeed, there are situations in which no pairwise-stable network exists and following improving paths only leads to cycles (where every network is necessarily defeated by some other network).

This is demonstrated in the following example from Jackson and Watts (2002a).

Example 1.12. *Exchange Networks – Nonexistence of a Pairwise-Stable Network. The society consists of $n \geq 4$ players who get value from trading goods with each other. In general terms (see Jackson and Watts 2002a for details), the idea is that players have random endowments and may gain from trading with others. The greater the number of players who are linked, the greater the potential gains from trade but with a diminishing return to the number of players added. Moreover, there is an externality in that the link is costly to the players who are directly involved, but it may benefit other players through the improved flow of goods through the network. The nonexistence of a pairwise-stable network is due to these external effects. Players near the end of a "line" network of more than two wish to sever the link to the end players because that link is more costly to maintain than it is directly beneficial to the players involved. However, once the level of separate single links is reached, two of the players involved in different links would like to form a new link.*

This is illustrated in Figure 1.2.

A cycle in this example is $\{12, 34\}$ is defeated by $\{12, 23, 34\}$, which is defeated by $\{12, 23\}$, which is defeated by $\{12\}$, which is defeated by $\{12, 34\}$.

Jackson and Watts (2001) provide a result characterizing when it is that there are no cycles and pairwise-stable networks exist. (Note that if there are no pairwise-stable networks, then a cycle must exist.)

Observe that Y and v exhibit no indifference if, for any two adjacent networks, one defeats the other.

Proposition 1.1. *Fix v and Y. If there exists a function $w : G \to \mathbb{R}$ such that [g' defeats g] if and only if [$w(g') > w(g)$ and g' and g are adjacent], then there are no cycles. Conversely, if Y and v exhibit no indifference, then there are no cycles only if there exists a function $w : G \to \mathbb{R}$ such that [g' defeats g] if and only if [$w(g') > w(g)$ and g' and g are adjacent].*

The function w has an intuitive relationship to a potential function as defined in noncooperative games (see Monderer and Shapley 1996).

Although Proposition 1.1 seems difficult to use given that one must find some such w, it has some surprisingly simple applications. One application is to prove the existence of pairwise-stable networks under the Myerson value, which is a prominent allocation rule.

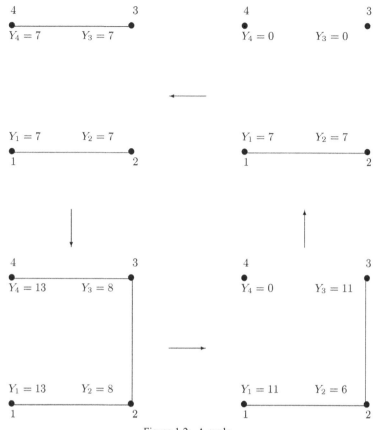

Figure 1.2: A cycle.

1.4.10. The Myerson Value

The Myerson value is an allocation rule defined by Myerson (1977) in the context of cooperative games with communication (also known as cooperation) structures and is a variation on the Shapley value. This rule was subsequently referred to as the Myerson value (see Aumann and Myerson 1988). The Myerson value also has a corresponding allocation rule in the context of network games as well, as shown by Jackson and Wolinsky (1996). That allocation rule is expressed as follows:

$$Y_i^{MV}(g, v) = \sum_{S \subset N \setminus \{i\}} (v(g|_{S \cup i}) - v(g|_S)) \left(\frac{\#S!(n - \#S - 1)!}{n!} \right).$$

The Myerson value follows Shapley value–style calculations and allocates value based on those calculations. That is, we can think of building up our network by adding players one by one and then seeing what value is generated through this process. Players are allocated their marginal contributions to generating overall value. There are many different orders in which this process could be performed, and the factor on the right-hand side accounts for averaging over all of the different orderings through which we could calculate the marginal contributions of players.

The following proposition is due to Jackson (2003a):

Proposition 1.2. *There exists a pairwise-stable network relative to* Y^{MV} *for every* v. *Moreover, all improving paths relative to* Y^{MV} *under any* v *emanating from any network lead to pairwise-stable networks. Thus, there are no cycles under the Myerson value allocation rule.*

This can be proven as a corollary to Proposition 1.1 by noting that

$$Y_i^{MV}(g, v) - Y_i^{MV}(g - ij, v) = w(g) - w(g - ij),$$

where

$$w(g) = \sum_{S \subset N} v(g|_S) \left(\frac{(\#S - 1)!(n - \#S)!}{n!} \right).$$

This proposition shows that existence of pairwise-stable networks is at least very well behaved for one prominent allocation rule. In fact, existence of pairwise-stable networks is also straightforward for two other natural rules: egalitarian and componentwise egalitarian allocation rules.

1.4.11. Egalitarian Rules

The following allocation rules were defined by Jackson and Wolinsky (1996).

The *egalitarian allocation rule* Y^e is defined by $Y_i^e(g, v) = \frac{v(g)}{n}$. Here, simply set $w(g) = \frac{v(g)}{n}$ and apply Proposition 1.1, or, alternatively, simply note that under the egalitarian rule any efficient network will be pairwise stable.

The *componentwise egalitarian allocation rule* Y^{ce} is defined as follows. For a component additive v and network, Y^{ce} is such that for any $h \in C(g)$ and each $i \in N(h)$

$$Y_i^{ce}(g, v) = \frac{v(h)}{\#N(h)}.$$

For a v that is not component additive, $Y^{ce}(g, v) = Y^e(g, v)$ for all g; thus, Y^{ce} splits the value $v(g)$ equally among all players if v is not component additive. The componentwise egalitarian rule is one in which the value of each component is split equally among the members of the component provided this can be done – that is, within the limits of component additivity.

Under the componentwise egalitarian rule, one can also always find a pairwise-stable network. However, for this rule Proposition 1.1 cannot be applied. Instead, one must follow other lines of proof. As noted by Jackson (2003a), an algorithm for finding a pairwise stable network is as follows:[36] find a component h that maximizes

---

[36] This is specified for component additive v's. For any other v, Y^e and Y^{ce} coincide.

the payoff $Y_i^{ce}(h, v)$ over i and h. Next, do the same on the remaining population $N \setminus N(h)$, and so on. The collection of resulting components forms the network.[37]

Now that we have seen some of the methods for modeling network formation, let us turn to one of the main foci of the literature: the relationship between stable and efficient networks.

1.5. The Relationship between Stability and Efficiency

Some of the very central questions about network formation concern the conditions under which the networks formed by the players turn out to be efficient from an overall societal perspective. In order to discuss these issues we need to define what we mean by efficiency.

An obvious notion of efficiency is simply the maximization of the overall total value among all possible networks. This notion was termed strong efficiency by Jackson and Wolinsky (1996), but I will refer to it as efficiency.

1.5.1. Efficiency

A network g is *efficient* relative to v if $v(g) \geq v(g')$ for all $g' \in G$.

It is clear that there will always be at least one efficient network given that there are only a finite set of networks.

Once we begin to define things relative to a fixed allocation rule, then there is another natural notion of efficiency: the standard notion of Pareto efficiency.

1.5.2. Pareto Efficiency

A network g is *Pareto efficient* relative to v and Y if no $g' \in G$ exists such that $Y_i(g', v) \geq Y_i(g, v)$ for all i with strict inequality for some i.

To understand the relationship between the two definitions, note that g is efficient relative to v if it is Pareto efficient relative to v and Y *for all Y*.

Thus, efficiency is the more natural notion in situations in which there is some freedom to reallocate value through transfers, whereas Pareto efficiency might be more reasonable in contexts in which the allocation rule is fixed (and we are not able or willing to make further transfers or to make interpersonal comparisons of utility).

Beyond these notions of efficiency, one may want to consider others. For instance, some reallocation of value may be possible, but only under the constraint that the allocations be balanced on each component. Such constraints lead to the following definition of constrained efficiency introduced by Jackson (2003a).

A network g is *constrained efficient* relative to v if and only if it is Pareto efficient relative to v and Y for every component-balanced and anonymous Y.

---

[37] This follows the same argument as existence of core-stable coalition structures under the weak-top coalition property in Banerjee, Konishi, and Sönmez (2001). Note, however, that the networks identified by this algorithm are not necessarily strongly stable under the definition used here.

With definitions of efficiency in hand, we can examine the central question of the relationship between stability and efficiency of networks.

I begin with a simple model – that of symmetric connections. Although this is a highly stylized model, it provides a preview of some of the tension between stability and efficiency and gives an idea of why such a conflict might arise.

The following propositions are from Jackson and Wolinsky (1996):

Proposition 1.3. *The unique efficient network structure in the symmetric connections model (Example 1.1) is*

(i) *the complete graph* g^N *if* $c < \delta - \delta^2$,

(ii) *a star encompassing everyone if* $\delta - \delta^2 < c < \delta + \frac{(N-2)}{2}\delta^2$, *and*

(iii) *no links if* $\delta + \frac{(N-2)}{2}\delta^2 < c$.

The efficient networks take simple and intuitive forms. If link costs are high, then it does not make sense to form any links (iii). If link costs are low enough ($c < \delta - \delta^2$), then it makes sense to form all links because the cost of adding a link is less then the gain from shortening any path of length at least two into a path of length one. The more interesting case arises for intermediate costs of links. Here the only efficient network structure is a star. To see why, note that a star has the minimal number of links needed to connect any set of players. Moreover, it is the (unique) network structure that minimizes the average path length given the minimal number of links.

Given that the star is the only efficient network for intermediate costs of links, we might expect to see some conflict between stability of a network and efficiency. In a star network in the connections model, the center player bears a great deal of cost and provides much of the externalities for other players but is not compensated for those externalities. Thus, there will be whole ranges of link costs in which the efficient networks are not pairwise stable. The description of pairwise-stable networks in the symmetric connections model from Jackson and Wolinsky (1996) is as follows:

Proposition 1.4. *In the symmetric connections model,*

(i) *A pairwise stable network has at most one (nonempty) component.*

(ii) *For* $c < \delta - \delta^2$, *the unique pairwise-stable network is the complete graph* g^N.

(iii) *For* $\delta - \delta^2 < c < \delta$, *a star encompassing all players is pairwise stable but not necessarily the unique pairwise stable graph.*

(iv) *For* $\delta < c$, *any pairwise-stable network that is nonempty is such that each player has at least two links and thus is inefficient.*[38]

As we expected, for high and low costs to links, efficient networks coincide with the pairwise-stable networks, and the problematic case is for intermediate costs to links.

---

[38] If $\delta + \frac{(N-2)}{2}\delta^2 > c$, then all pairwise-stable networks are inefficient because then the empty graph is also inefficient.

For instance, consider a situation in which $n = 4$ and $\delta < c < \delta + \frac{\delta^2}{2}$. Here a star network is the unique efficient structure. However, the only pairwise-stable network is the empty network. To see this, note that, because $c > \delta$, a player gets a positive payoff from a link only if it also offers an indirect connection. Thus, clearly the star will not be pairwise stable because the center bears more cost for each link than it gets in benefits. Moreover, this implies that if a network is nonempty and stable, then each player must have at least two links because, if i has only one link and it is to j, then j would benefit from severing that link. We can also see in this cost range that a player maintains at most two links because the payoff to a player with three links (given $n = 4$) is less than 0 given that $c > \delta$. So, a pairwise-stable network would have to be a ring (e.g., $\{12, 23, 34, 14\}$). However, such a network is not pairwise stable because the payoff to any player is increased by severing a link. For instance, 1's payoff in the ring is $2\delta + \delta^2 - 2c$, whereas severing the link 14 leads to $\delta + \delta^2 + \delta^3 - c$, which is higher because $c > \delta$.

Although the empty network is the unique pairwise-stable network, it is not even Pareto efficient. The empty network is Pareto dominated by a line (e.g., $g = \{12, 23, 34\}$). To see this, note that, under the line the payoff to the end players (1 and 4) is $\delta + \delta^2 + \delta^3 - c$, which is greater than 0, and to the middle two players (2 and 3) the payoff is $2\delta + \delta^2 - 2c$, which is also greater than 0 because $c < \delta + \frac{\delta^2}{2}$.

Thus, there exist cost ranges under the symmetric connections model for which all pairwise-stable networks are *Pareto* inefficient and other cost ranges for which all pairwise-stable networks are efficient. There are also some cost ranges for which some pairwise-stable networks are efficient and some other pairwise-stable networks are not even Pareto efficient.

Even when there are some pairwise-stable efficient networks in the symmetric connections model, they might not be reached. For instance, Watts (2001) shows that, as n increases, the probability that the resulting stable state is a star goes to 0. Thus, as the population increases, the particular ordering needed to form a star (the efficient network) becomes less and less likely relative to orderings leading to some other stable states. Watts's (2001) result is stated as follows:

Proposition 1.5. *Consider the symmetric connections model in the case in which $\delta - \delta^2 < c < \delta$. As the number of players grows, the probability that a stable state (under the process in which each link has an equal probability of being identified) is reached with the efficient network structure of a star goes to 0.*

The preceding propositions show us that there may be cases in which the networks that are pairwise stable (or stable states) are neither efficient nor even Pareto efficient.

At this point a series of important questions arises.

We begin to see from the connections model that some reallocation of value may be natural and may help reconcile efficiency and stability. For instance, the center of the star could negotiate with the other players to receive some payments or favors for maintaining his or her links with the other players.[39] If we start to account for such reallocations, can we reconcile efficiency and stability?

Because there are many ways to address these issues, let us list some of the questions that come to mind.

(1) If we can control the allocation rule, can we always design an allocation rule such that at least one efficient network is pairwise stable?

(2) Can we always design an allocation rule such that at least one efficient network is pairwise stable if we impose some minimal conditions on the allocation rule such as anonymity and component balance?

(3) If the answer to (2) is no, what if we weaken the demands on efficiency, or on anonymity, or on component balance?

(4) If the answer to (2) is no, is there some nice class of situations in which we can design an anonymous and component-balanced allocation rule such that at least one efficient network is pairwise stable?

(5) For a given allocation rule of interest, what are the classes of value functions for which efficient and stable networks coincide?

(6) What can we say about these questions for alternative stability notions?

(7) Will efficient networks be formed if bargaining over the allocation and the network formation is tied together?[40]

The answer to question (1) (whether we can design an allocation rule that reconciles efficiency and stability) is yes, and it is easy to see why. Consider the egalitarian allocation rule Y^e. This completely aligns player incentives and overall efficiency because players' payoffs are directly proportional to overall network value. Thus, under the egalitarian allocation rule every efficient network is pairwise stable and in fact strongly stable.

Although this is partly reassuring, it turns out that this answer is really dependent on such a full reallocation of value. A fully egalitarian rule has nice incentive properties, but it is an extreme rule and in particular requires that value be allocated across different components. That is, the egalitarian rule fails to satisfy component balance. In the long run this might be problematic because some components will be receiving less than their value and might benefit from seceding.

This takes us to question (2) (whether or not we can find an allocation rule for which efficiency and stability are reconciled while satisfying some simple conditions such as component balance and anonymity). The following proposition shows that there is no component-balanced and anonymous allocation rule for which it is always the case that some efficient network is pairwise stable. Thus, the answer to (2) is no. This proposition is due to Jackson and Wolinsky (1996).[41]

---

[39] In fact, intuition from the sociology literature would suggest that a player in such a central position should receive a high payoff (e.g., see Burt 1992).

[40] See Bloch and Jackson (2004) for an answer to this question.

[41] Jackson (2003a) shows that the proposition can be strengthened to require only equal treatment of equals rather than anonymity and that it also holds if efficiency of the network is replaced by constrained efficiency. Arguably, if one is requiring component balance of the allocation rule, then the efficiency notion should be similarly defined, and thus constrained efficiency is the appropriate notion. See Jackson (2003a) for details.

Proposition 1.6. *There does not exist any component-balanced and anonymous allocation rule such that for every v there exists an efficient network that is pairwise stable.*

The proof of Proposition 1.6 shows that there is a particular v such that for every component-balanced and anonymous allocation rule none of the constrained efficient networks are pairwise stable.

To see the proof, simply consider the following example with $n = 3$ players. Here v is such that any one-link network has a value of 1, any two-link network has a value of 13/12, and the complete network has a value of 1. This is as pictured in the following figure.

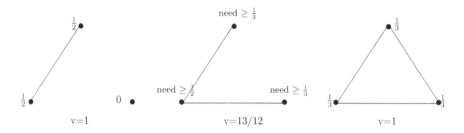

So, in this example the efficient network structure is a two-link one. Now let us consider what allocations are necessary. By anonymity and component balance, the allocations in one- and three-link networks are completely determined. Each player connected in a one-link network gets an allocation of $\frac{1}{2}$. Each player in the complete network gets an allocation of $\frac{1}{3}$. Let us consider what the possibilities are for a two-link network with the idea that we would like to make the two-link network pairwise stable. For a two-link network to be pairwise stable, the middle player (who has two links) must get an allocation of at least $\frac{1}{2}$ or else he or she would benefit from severing one of the links. Also, for a two-link network to be pairwise stable, the other two players must each get an allocation of at least $\frac{1}{3}$, or else they would benefit from adding a link between them. Unfortunately, $\frac{1}{2} + \frac{1}{3} + \frac{1}{3} > \frac{13}{12}$, and so this is not feasible. Thus, there is no possible allocation rule satisfying anonymity and component balance such that the efficient network is pairwise stable here.

The answer to question (3) is that the conditions of anonymity and component balance do play important roles in the incompatibility of stability and efficiency. If we drop either of the conditions, then we can reconcile efficiency and stability. That is, Proposition 1.6 is tight.

Let us examine each aspect of the proposition. If we drop component balance, then, as mentioned before, the egalitarian allocation rule will always have all efficient networks being (strongly) stable.

If we drop anonymity (or equal treatment of equals), then a careful and clever construction of Y by Dutta and Mutuswami (1997) ensures that some efficient network is strongly stable for a class of v. This is stated in the following proposition:

Let $v^* = \{v \in v \mid g \neq \emptyset \Rightarrow v(g) > 0\}$. This is a class of value functions in which any network generates a positive value.

The following proposition is due to Dutta and Mutuswami (1997).

Proposition 1.7. *There exists a component-balanced Y such that for any $v \in v^*$ some efficient network is pairwise stable. Moreover, although Y is not anonymous, it is still anonymous on some networks that are both efficient and pairwise stable.*[42]

This proposition shows that if one can design an allocation rule and only wishes to satisfy anonymity on stable networks, then efficiency and stability are compatible.

Next, let us consider the question of requiring the allocation rule to be component balanced and anonymous but weakening efficiency to require only Pareto efficiency. If we do this, then the componentwise egalitarian rule ensures that for any value function at least one pairwise-stable network is Pareto efficient, as stated in the following proposition:

Let $g(v, S) = \text{argmax}_{g \in g^S} \frac{v(g)}{\#N(g)}$ denote the network with the highest per capita value out of those that can be formed by players in $S \subset N$.

Given a component additive v, find a network g^v through the following algorithm. Pick some $h_1 \in g(v, N)$ with a maximal number of links. Next, pick some $h_2 \in g(v, N \setminus N(h_1))$ with a maximal number of links. Iteratively, at stage k pick a new component $h_k \in g(v, N \setminus N(\cup_{i \leq k-1} h_i))$ with a maximal number of links. Once there are only empty networks left, stop. The union of the components picked in this way defines a network g^v.

The following proposition is a variation on one due to Banerjee (1999)[43]:

Proposition 1.8. *Under a component additive v, a g^v defined by the preceding algorithm is a pairwise-stable and Pareto-efficient network under the component wise egalitarian rule.*

Although this proposition is of some interest given that we are allowing reallocation of value, it is not clear that Pareto efficiency is the right notion of efficiency. In particular, constrained efficiency seems to be more appropriate, and under that condition the proposition no longer is true, as we have seen already in Proposition 1.6 (and its footnote).

Consequently, reconciling the tension between stability and efficiency will require giving something up in terms of our desired conditions of anonymity, component balance, and efficiency; thus, to some extent this tension is a characteristic of network games.

---

[42] Dutta and Mutuswami work with a variation of strong stability. As mentioned before, their version of strong stability is not quite a strengthening of pairwise stability, for it only considers one network as defeating another if there is a deviation by a coalition that makes all of its members strictly better off; pairwise stability allows one of the two players adding a link to be indifferent. However, one can check that the construction of Dutta and Mutuswami extends to pairwise stability as well.

[43] Banerjee (1999) actually works with a weighted version of the component wise egalitarian rule, which is a straightforward generalization of this result. Also, he works with a notion of strong stability but one that only accounts for deviations that make all players strictly better off. Note that g^v will not always be strongly stable under the definition here. Finally, the algorithm here is somewhat different from his inasmuch as I require the maximal number of links in the definition of each h_k, which is critical to guaranteeing pairwise stability. Banerjee does not have to worry about this because his definition of stability only considers deviations for which all deviating players are strictly better off.

This leads us to another one of our questions (4): Is there some nice class of situations in which we can design an anonymous and component-balanced allocation rule such that at least one efficient network is pairwise stable? That is, the tension arises for some value functions but not all. What do we know about the structure of value functions for which there is (or is not) a tension?

The following proposition provides a partial answer to (4) by identifying a very particular feature of the tension between efficiency and stability. It shows that in situations in which efficient networks are such that each player has at least two links, there is no tension. So, problems arise only in situations in which efficient networks involve players who may be thought of as "loose ends."

A network g has *no loose ends* if for any $i \in N(g)$, $\#\{j | ij \in g\} \geq 2$.

The following proposition is due to Jackson (2003a):

Proposition 1.9. *There exists an anonymous and component-balanced allocation rule such that if v is anonymous and has an efficient network with no loose ends, then there is at least one efficient network (with no loose ends) that is pairwise stable.*

The proof of Proposition 1.9 is constructive, showing that a variation on the componentwise egalitarian allocation rule works. This tells us that the tension between efficiency and stability has some natural limits and must involve situations in which efficient networks are such that some players have just one link.

The analysis in the last few propositions took a "design" perspective because the question of whether there existed any allocation rule that would reconcile efficiency and stability was asked. More generally, however, the allocation rule might be determined naturally by the environment. To the extent that we cannot intervene (or prefer not to unless needed), it is important to know when there will be a tension between efficiency and stability for a given allocation rule.

The difficulty in addressing this issue is that the space of allocation rules is quite large, and so providing a characterization of when there are tensions and when there are none is an overwhelming task. What we might do is instead simply look at some natural allocation rules and natural settings. Many of the examples from Section 1.3 are ones for which this is the approach that has been taken. There a setting, value function, and allocation rule are given by the model, and then one analyzes which networks are stable and can address the issue of whether they are efficient. This is a valuable exercise and provides some insights. The results, however, are particular to the models in question. Given the limits on the length of this survey, I will not go over those results here.[44]

To get a somewhat broader view, we can look at question (5): For given allocation rules, what are the classes of value functions for which efficient and stable networks coincide?

---

[44] The reader is referred to the papers themselves. The reader can also find some comparison across some of the bargaining models in Jackson (2003a).

A natural starting point for this question is to work with the most obvious of component-balanced and anonymous allocation rules, the componentwise egalitarian rule. A strong reason for doing this is that we know the egalitarian rule has excellent incentive properties, and so the componentwise version would seem to be a good one to work with under the constraint of component balance. The following proposition provides a characterization of when the componentwise egalitarian rule works well.

A link ij is *critical* to the graph g if $g - ij$ has more components than g or if i is only linked to j under g.

A critical link is one such that if it is severed, the component that it was a part of will become two components (or one of the nodes will become disconnected). Let h denote a component that contains a critical link, and let h_1 and h_2 denote the components obtained from h by severing that link (where it may be that $h_1 = \emptyset$ or $h_2 = \emptyset$).

The pair (g, v) satisfies *critical link monotonicity* if, for any critical link in g and its associated components h, h_1, and h_2, we have that $v(h) \geq v(h_1) + v(h_2)$ implies that $v(h)/\#N(h) \geq \max[v(h_1)/\#N(h_1), v(h_2)/\#N(h_2)]$.

The following proposition is due to Jackson and Wolinsky (1996):

Proposition 1.10. *If g is efficient relative to a component additive v, then g is pairwise stable for Y^{ce} relative to v if and only if (g, v) satisfies critical-link monotonicity.*

Question (6) asks about the relationship between efficiency and stability for stability notions other than pairwise stability. Short of the consideration of bargaining together with network formation (question [7]), the only analysis has been in terms of strong stability.[45] Note that strong stability goes a long way toward guaranteeing at least Pareto efficiency simply by definition, and so it will not be too surprising that the issue will largely boil down to existence of strongly stable networks. It also turns out that an interesting implication of strong stability is that if we have a strongly stable efficient network, then the allocation we are working with must be the componentwise egalitarian rule – at least on the given network. This makes the componentwise egalitarian rule a natural one to focus on. These ideas are formalized as follows.

An allocation rule Y is *component decomposable* if $Y_i(g, v) = Y_i(g|_S, v)$ for each component additive $v, g \in G, S \in \Pi(g)$, and $i \in S$.

Component decomposability requires that, in situations in which v is component additive, the way in which value is allocated within a component does not depend on the structure of other components. Thus, in situations in which there are no externalities across components, the allocation within a component is independent of the rest of the network. For instance, the players within a component need not pay attention to, and might not even be aware of, the organization of other components.

---

[45] There is analysis of other formation models in the context of directed networks. One can find some discussion of this in Chapter 4 of this volume.

The following proposition is due to Jackson and van den Nouweland (2000):

Proposition 1.11. *Consider any anonymous and component-additive value function* $v \in v$. *If Y is an anonymous, component-decomposable, and component-balanced allocation rule and $g \in G$ with $\Pi(g) \neq \{N\}$ is a network that is strongly stable with respect to Y and v, then $Y(g, v) = Y^{ce}(g, v)$ and $Y_i(g, v) = \frac{v(g)}{n}$ for each $i \in N$.*

Although Proposition 1.11 only ties down the allocation rule on strongly stable networks, it still strongly suggests the componentwise egalitarian rule as a focal one. So let us examine when efficient networks are strongly stable under that allocation rule.

A value function v is *top convex* if some efficient network also maximizes the *per capita* value among players.[46] That is, the value function v is *top convex* if there exists an efficient g such that $\frac{v(g)}{n} \geq \frac{v(g')}{\#N(g')}$ for all g'.

Top convexity implies that all components of an efficient network must lead to the same per capita value. If some component led to a lower per capita value than the average, then another component would have to lead to a higher per capita value than the average, which would contradict top convexity.

Jackson and van den Nouweland (2000) prove the following proposition:

Proposition 1.12. *Consider any anonymous and component additive value function v. The set of efficient networks coincides with the set of strongly stable networks under the componentwise egalitarian rule if and only if v is top convex. Moreover, the set of strongly stable networks is nonempty under the componentwise egalitarian rule if and only if v is top convex.*

To get some feeling for the top-convexity condition, note that in the symmetric connections model v is top convex for all values of $\delta \in [0, 1]$ and $c \geq 0$, and thus all networks that are strongly stable with respect to Y^{ce} and v are efficient with respect to v. This means that top convexity is a condition that is satisfied in some natural situations. However, it is still a demanding condition that has strong implications.

1.5.3. Simultaneous Network Formation and Allocation of Value

Finally, let us turn to question (7) regarding what happens when the allocation of value and the formation of the network occur as part of the same bargaining process.

Currarini and Morelli (2000) show that, for a wide class of value functions, all subgame-perfect equilibria of their formation game are efficient. Because this applies for a fairly broad class of value functions, it shows that under some assumptions the tension between stability and efficiency may be overcome if bargaining over value is tied to link formation. Let us examine their result in more detail.

---

[46] A related condition is called "domination by the grand coalition" as defined in the context of a cooperative game by Chatterjee et al. (1993).

A value function v satisfies *size monotonicity* if $v(g) > v(g - ij)$ for every g and critical link $ij \in g$.

Although this is a demanding condition, it is one that is often satisfied in situations in which large networks are efficient. The demanding aspect of the condition is that it must hold for all g. It is not clear to what extent that aspect of the condition is vital to the following result.

The following proposition is due to Currarini and Morelli (2000):

Proposition 1.13. *If v satisfies size monotonicity, then every (subgame perfect) equilibrium of the Currarini and Morelli bargaining and network formation game leads to an efficient network.*

Mutuswami and Winter (2002) also discuss a similar network formation game and show that such positive results hold for even more general value functions under a slightly different formulation. In their analysis, players receive increasing benefits in the size of the network and incur increasing costs. The game is such that, instead of making demands on how much value they desire, players indicate how much they will contribute toward the cost of links. Moreover, Mutuswami and Winter show that a variation on the game results in payoffs that mirror the Shapley value calculations of a related cooperative game.

One aspect of these results deserves discussion. The finite ending point of the game provides for strong bargaining power for early players in the sequence. They essentially demand what can maximally be extracted given what the other players will end up getting from the subsequent game. The maximum value comes from the efficient network because the game really boils down to a bargaining one. It is not so clear what would happen if the bargaining protocol went on in some way either with discounting or with players being able to revise demands and actions. Proposition 1.13 is still very important in pointing out the potential role of simultaneous link formation and bargaining over value, but whether this will turn out to be robust to variations in the protocol is not yet clear.

1.6. The Myerson Value and Alternative Allocation Rules

In addition to the literature that has concentrated on questions of whether efficient networks are formed, there is also a literature that has looked in detail at the axiomatic foundations of some allocation rules. To some extent, the axiomatic treatment of allocation rules is the "cooperative" counterpart to the "noncooperative" analysis of network stability. The axiomatic literature largely grew out of the cooperative game theory literature and mostly followed cooperative games with communications or cooperation structures. However, almost all of the studies there have fairly easy extensions to the more general network game setting.

Much of the literature on cooperative games with communications structures is discussed in Chapter 2 of this volume, and so I only briefly discuss a small part of that axiomatic literature here. In particular I discuss a part that is closely related to the idea that networks are not fixed but something subject to the discretion of the players involved, which is the part that is most closely linked to ideas of network formation.

To discuss these issues, let us first observe a characterization of the Myerson value allocation rule, which is the most prominent allocation rule.

1.6.1. Equal Bargaining Power and the Myerson Value

An allocation rule satisfies equal bargaining power if for any component additive v and $g \in G$

$$Y_i(g) - Y_i(g - ij) = Y_j(g) - Y_j(g - ij).$$

Note that equal bargaining power does *not* require that players split the marginal value of a link. It just requires that they equally benefit or suffer from its addition. It is possible (and generally the case) that $Y_i(g) - Y_i(g - ij) + Y_j(g) - Y_j(g - ij) \neq v(g) - v(g - ij)$.

The following proposition from Jackson and Wolinsky (1996) is a fairly direct extension of Myerson's (1977) result from the setting of cooperative games with communications structures to the network game setting.

Proposition 1.14. *Y satisfies component balance and equal bargaining power if and only if $Y(g, v) = Y^{MV}(g, v)$ for all $g \in G$ and any component-additive v.*

Dutta and Mutuswami (1997) extend the characterization to allow for weighted bargaining power and show that one obtains a version of a weighted Shapley (Myerson) value.

Although the Myerson value is an interesting allocation rule, the perspective it takes is problematic from a network formation perspective.[47] The basic problem with it is that the value of other possible networks is not properly accounted for in its calculations. This is especially bothersome in situations in which the network is something that can be changed or is being formed. The basic idea is as follows. If the network is something that can be changed or is such that alternative possible network structures are taken into account when bargaining over how to allocate value, then values of alternative networks, *and not just subnetworks*, should be important in determining the allocation. If the network is completely fixed and cannot be changed, then it is not clear why the value of subnetworks (and only subnetworks) should enter allocation calculations.

These criticisms can be made more precise by looking at some very simple examples.

Example 1.13. A Criticism of the Myerson Value. *Consider a value function v, where $v(\{12\}) = v(\{23\}) = 1$, $v(\{12, 23\}) = 1$, and $v(g) = 0$ for all other networks. In this case only the network $\{12, 23\}$ and its nonempty subnetworks generate value.*

---

[47] See Jackson (2003b) for a detailed discussion.

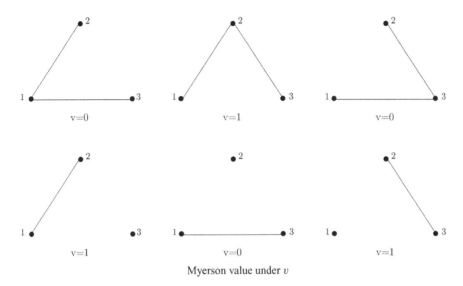

Myerson value under v

Consider another value function v' defined by $v'(g) = 1$ for all $g \neq \emptyset$. That is, under v' the value of every nonempty network is 1.

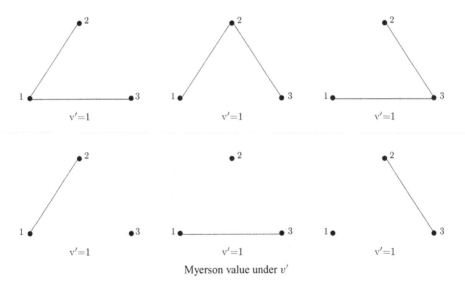

Myerson value under v'

Note that

$$Y^{MV}(\{12, 23\}, v) = Y^{MV}(\{12, 23\}, v') = \left(\frac{1}{6}, \frac{2}{3}, \frac{1}{6}\right).$$

The Myerson value allocation rule provides the same allocation on the network $\{12, 23\}$ regardless of whether the value function is v or v'. In particular, player 2 gets a bigger allocation in the network $\{12, 23\}$ than the other players. This reflects player 2's status in two links in the network and comes about through the Shapley *value – style calculations underlying the Myerson value, where we can think of building up the network* {12, 23} *by adding players one at a time.*

Although player 2's position is special in the network {12, 23}, *player 2's status is not at all special if the value function is v'. That is, any player could have equally well served that central position. In fact, any nonempty network would provide the same value as the network* {12, 23}. *To the extent that the network is something that can be altered, there is no reason that player 2 should enjoy special treatment under v', and one might argue that all players should receive equal payments.*

To see some of the issues in more detail, one can look at the conditions that characterize the Myerson value.

Example 1.14. A Criticism of the Equal Bargaining Power. *Next, let $v(\{12\}) = v(\{23\}) = 1$ and $v(g) = 0$ for all other networks. Here any single-link network that involves player 2 will generate a value of 1, whereas all other networks generate a value of 0.*

Any allocation rule, including the Myerson value, that satisfies equal bargaining power (and allocates 0 to the players on the empty network) will have $Y_1(\{12\}, v) = Y_2(\{12\}, v)$. Other networks have $v = 0$

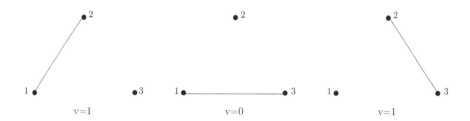

Here, there is a real asymmetry among the players, and player 2 is a more critical player than the others. It is not at all clear why we should require that the allocation to players 1 and 2 be the same in the network {12}, *for player 2 has a viable outside option whereas player 1 does not.*[48]

There are other criticisms that can be made, including pointing out problems with component balance. In response to these criticisms, Jackson (2003b) proposes the following allocation rule. First, an auxiliary definition is needed.

Given a value function v, its *monotonic cover* $\widehat{v}$ is defined by

$$\widehat{v}(g) = \max_{g' \subset g} v(g').$$

The monotonic cover of a value function looks at the highest value that can be achieved by building a network out of a given set of links. The monotonic cover captures the perspective that the network is flexible and thus can be reorganized to produce the highest possible value.

---

[48] For instance, if one brings in core-based considerations, then in fact the full value should be given to player 2 in this example.

Using this perspective leads to a natural adaptation of the Shapley value to network games, which results in the following allocation rule, which Jackson called the Player-Based Flexible Network Allocation rule.[49]

$$Y_i^{\text{PBFN}}(g, v) = \frac{v(g)}{\widehat{v}(g^N)} \sum_{S \subset N \setminus \{i\}} (\widehat{v}(g^{S \cup i}) - \widehat{v}(g^S)) \left(\frac{\#S!(n - \#S - 1)!}{n!} \right).$$

This allocation rule looks at the value that any group of players S could generate by forming the best possible network. Then, through Shapley-style calculations, the rule looks at the marginal value generated by adding a player to different groups; then the allocation is in proportion to these marginal contributions.

On a superficial level this rule bears some similarities to the Myerson value because we see Shapley value–style calculations. However, it is a quite different allocation rule. In fact, it violates both equal bargaining power and component balance and is characterized by conditions that are violated by the Myerson value. For instance, looking back at Example 1.13, we find that Y^{PBFN} provides allocations that differ on v and v'. In fact, it agrees with the Myerson value under v and, in contrast, is fully egalitarian under v'. In Example 1.14 it provides higher allocations to player 2 than the others, again which is in contrast to the Myerson value.

More generally, once the perspective that alternative network structures should matter in determining an allocation is taken, a variety of cooperative, game-theoretic solutions concepts, including, for example, the Nucleolus, can be called upon in addition to the Shapley value. The simple idea is that the monotonic cover $\widehat{v}$ can be used to define a cooperative game $w(S) = \widehat{v}(g^S)$, which can then be used as a basis for allocating value.[50]

1.7. Concluding Discussion

1.7.1. Directed Networks

This chapter has focused on nondirected networks. More specifically, the important aspect here is the treatment of situations in which a link between two players requires the consent of both parties. Although this nondirected or mutual consent case covers many (if not most) situations of interest, the case in which links are directed and may be formed unilaterally also includes some important settings. For instance, a Web site can provide a link or pointer to another Web site without the second Web site's permission. Likewise, if we consider a network of researchers and examine who cites whom, this is another network that is both directed and for which links can

---

[49] Jackson (2003b) also proposes other allocation rules. One is a slight variation on this and is "link based." For more on the idea of allocating value based on links rather than players, see Meessen (1988) and Borm, Owen, and Tijs (1992). The idea is instead to apply the value to links rather than players and then to assign the value to players based on the links that they control. Other variations involve using solution concepts such as the Nucleolus.

[50] See Jackson (2003b) for details.

be formed unilaterally in that one researcher can generally cite another researcher without the second researcher's permission.

Although the analysis of directed networks is different from that of nondirected networks, the overall themes end up being similar. The main differences are in modeling network formation, which is simpler owing to the unilateral action and of course in the applications covered. In particular, a tension between stability and efficiency is still present (see Dutta and Jackson 2000), and, again, there are situations in which efficient networks self-organize quite naturally. For instance, Bala and Goyal (2000b) consider a directed version of the connections model and find that, in situations in which the decay is not too high (δ is close to 1), efficient networks are the unique strict Nash equilibrium networks in a directed variation of Myerson's (1991) network formation game (see also Haller and Sarangi 2001). This is discussed in more detail in Chapter 4 of this volume, and so I will not say more here.

1.7.2. Closing Remarks

The literature surveyed in this chapter helps us to understand network formation. Because networks are pervasive in social and economic interactions, this literature was really inevitable. As we have seen, there are interesting and somewhat unexpected relationships between which networks are efficient from society's perspective and which networks form as the result of player incentives. We have also learned that explicit modeling of networks is tractable and that a valuable theory can be developed.

Although the literature has made some progress, there is still good news for researchers – namely, there are many important and interesting open questions in this area that are manageable and just waiting for attention. Some of these questions involve theoretical modeling such as developing greater understanding of the relationship between stable and efficient networks and how this depends on the setting, further exploring of the simultaneous bargaining over the allocation of value and the formation of networks, and more generally understanding how side payments may affect network formation. But these questions also go well beyond the theoretical to include the empirical and experimental analysis of models of economic networks. I have not really touched upon these here, partly because those areas are so wide open. Some analysts are pioneering into these areas, as we see on the experimental side in Corbae and Duffy (2000); Charness et al. (2001); Callander and Plott (2001); Pantz and Ziegelmeyer (2003); and Falk and Kosfeld (2003) (see Kosfeld 2003 for a recent survey).[51] Work on the empirical side has a longer tradition that dates back to early studies on contact networks in labor economics (e.g., Rees 1966) but is

---

[51] I should be careful to say that the experimental research on exchange networks from the sociological side is quite extensive (e.g., see Bienenstock and Bonacich (1993)) as is the empirical analysis of various network structures (e.g., see Wasserman and Faust (1994) and the references therein). So, here I am referring more to the questions of network formation and the testing of formal models of formation as well as analyses of the efficiency of observed networks.

enjoying new interest as in recent work by Topa (2000), Conley and Topa (2001), Fafchamps and Lund (2000), and Aizer and Currie (2002).

There are also some substantial challenges for the future literature on networks that are coming out of economics and game theory. One challenge is that of bridging to the sociology ("social networks") literature.[52] That literature is well established, very large, and full of interesting questions, insights, data sets, and knowledge of network structure and what influences it. The main challenge comes in the differences in terminology, the points of view, and the techniques of analysis. As the literatures continue to grow, the cross fertilization that is just beginning now should become more and more natural.

BIBLIOGRAPHY

[1] Aizer, A. and J. Currie (2002), "Networks, Neighborhoods, and the Utilization of Publicly-Funded Prenatal Care in California," mimeo., UCLA.

[2] Arrow, K. J. and R. Borzekowski (2000), "Limited Network Connections and the Distribution of Wages," mimeo., Stanford University.

[3] Aumann, R. and R. Myerson (1988), "Endogenous Formation of Links between Players and Coalitions: An Application of the Shapley Value," In: Roth, A. (ed.) *The Shapley Value*, Cambridge University Press, 175–191.

[4] Badasyan, N. and S. Chakrabarti (2003), "Private Peering among Internet Backbone Providers," mimeo., Virginia Tech.

[5] Bala, V. and S. Goyal (2000a), "A Strategic Analysis of Network Reliability," *Review of Economic Design* 5, 205–228.

[6] Bala, V. and S. Goyal (2000b), "A Non-cooperative Model of Network Formation," *Econometrica* 68, 1181–1230.

[7] Banerjee, S. (1999), "Efficiency and Stability in Economic Networks," mimeo., Boston University.

[8] Banerjee, S., H. Konishi, and T. Sönmez (2001), "Core in a Simple Coalition Formation Game," *Social Choice and Welfare* 18, 135–154.

[9] Belleflamme, P. and F. Bloch (2002), "Market Sharing Agreements and Stable Collusive Networks," mimeo., University of London and GREQAM.

[10] Bienenstock, E. and P. Bonacich (1993), "Game Theory Models for Social Exchange Networks: Experimental Results," *Sociological Perspectives* 36, 117–136.

[11] Bienenstock, E. and P. Bonacich (1997), "Network Exchange as a Cooperative Game," *Rationality and Society* 9, 37–65.

[12] Billard, P. and C. Bravard (2002), "Non-Cooperative Networks in Oligopolies," mimeo., University of Jean Monnet-Saint Etienne.

[13] Bloch, F. (2001), "Coalitions and Networks in Industrial Organization," mimeo., GREQAM.

[14] Bloch, F. and M. O. Jackson (2004), "The Formation of Networks with Transfers Among Players," California Institute of Technology, Social Science Working Paper 1194.

[15] Boorman, S. (1975), "A Combinatorial Optimization Model for Transmission of Job Information through Contact Networks," *Bell Journal of Economics* 6, 216–249.

---

[52] To a more limited extent, the same can be said for bridging to the agent-based computation models, where many network situations have been analyzed. There is more natural overlap there, because the underlying view of players' incentives and the terminology are closer to begin with.

[16] Borm, P., G. Owen, and S. Tijs (1992), "On the Position Value for Communication Situations," *SIAM Journal on Discrete Mathematics* 5, 305–320.

[17] Bramoullé, Y. (2000), "Congestion and Social Networks: an Evolutionary Analysis," mimeo., University of Maryland.

[18] Bramoullé, Y. (2001a), "Complementarity and Social Networks," mimeo., THEMA, Université de Paris X-Nanterre.

[19] Bramoullé, Y. (2001b), "Interdependent Utilities, Preference Indeterminacy and Social Networks," mimeo., THEMA, Université de Paris X-Nanterre.

[20] Bramoullé, Y. and R. Kranton (2003), "A Network Model of Public Goods: Experimentation and Social Learning," mimeo., University of Toulouse and University of Maryland.

[21] Bramoullé, Y., D. Lopez-Pintado, S. Goyal, and F. Vega-Redondo (2002), "Network Formation and Anti-coordination games," mimeo., Universidad de Alicante.

[22] Brueckner, J. K. (2003), "Friendship Networks," mimeo., University of Illinois.

[23] Burt, R. (1992), *Structural Holes: The Social Structure of Competition*, Cambridge, MA: Harvard University Press.

[24] Cahuc, P. and F. Fontaine (2002), "On the Efficiency of Job Search with Social Networks," mimeo., University of Paris 1-EUREQua.

[25] Callander, S. and C. Plott (2001), "Networks: An Experimental Study," California Institute of Technology Social Science Working Paper #1156. mimeo., Caltech.

[26] Calvo, E., J. Lasaga, and A. van den Nouweland (1999), "Values of Games with Probabilistic Graphs," *Mathematical Social Sciences* 37, 79–95.

[27] Calvo-Armengol, A. (1999), "Stable and Efficient Bargaining Networks," UAB mimeo.

[28] Calvo-Armengol, A. (2000), "Job Contact Networks," UAB mimeo.

[29] Calvo-Armengol, A. (2001), "Bargaining Power in Communication Networks," *Mathematical Social Sciences* 41, 69–88.

[30] Calvo-Armengol, A. and M. O. Jackson (2001a), "Social Networks in Determining Employment: Patterns, Dynamics, and Inequality," *American Economic Review*, 94, 3, June.

[31] Calvo-Armengol, A. and M.O. Jackson (2001b), "Networks in Labor Markets: Wage and Employment Dynamics and Inequality," mimeo., Caltech and Universitat Autònoma de Barcelona, http://www.hss.caltech.edu/~ jacksonm/dyngen.pdf.

[32] Carayol, N. and P. Roux (2003), "'Collective Innovation' in a Model of Network Formation with Preferential Meeting," mimeo., Université Louis Pasteur and Université de Toulouse I.

[33] Casella, A. and J. Rauch (2001), "Anonymous Market and Group Ties in International Trade," mimeo., Columbia University and University of California at San Diego.

[34] Charness, G. M. Corominas-Bosch, and G.R. Frechette (2001), "Bargaining on Networks: An Experiment," mimeo., University of California Santa Barbara.

[35] Chatterjee, K., B. Dutta, D. Ray, and S. Sengupta (1993), "A Noncooperative Theory of Coalitional Bargaining," *Review of Economic Studies* 60, 463–477.

[36] Chwe, M. S.-Y. (1994), "Farsighted Coalitional Stability," *Journal of Economic Theory* 63, 299–325.

[37] Conley, T. G., and G. Topa (2001), "Socio-Economic Distance and Spatial Patterns in Unemployment," mimeo., New York University.

[38] Corbae, D. and J. Duffy (2000), "Experiments with Network Economies," mimeo., University of Pittsburgh.

[39] Corominas-Bosch, M. (1999), "On Two-Sided Network Markets," Ph.D. dissertation: Universitat Pompeu Fabra.

[40] Currarini, S. (2002), "Stable Organizations with Externalities," mimeo., Universitá di Venezia.

[41] Currarini, S. and M. Morelli (2000), "Network Formation with Sequential Demands," *Review of Economic Design* 5, 229–250.

[42] Demange, G. (2002), "On Group Stability in Hierarchies and Networks" mimeo., DELTA.

[43] Deroïan, F. (2003), "Farsighted Strategies in the Formation of a Communication Network," *Economics Letters* 80, 343–349.

[44] Droste, E., R. P. Gilles and C. Johnson (2000), "Evolution of Conventions in Endogenous Social Networks," mimeo., Virginia Tech.

[45] Dutta, B., S. Ghosal, and D. Ray (2003), "Farsighted Network Formation," mimeo., University of Warwick and New York University.

[46] Dutta, B. and M. O. Jackson (2000), "The Stability and Efficiency of Directed Communication Networks," *Review of Economic Design* 5, 251–272.

[47] Dutta, B. and M. O. Jackson (2003a), "On the Formation of Networks and Groups," in *Networks and Groups: Models of Strategic Formation*, B. Dutta and M. O. Jackson (eds.), Heidelberg: Springer-Verlag.

[48] Dutta, B. and M. O. Jackson (2003b), editors: *Networks and Groups: Models of Strategic Formation*, Heidelberg: Springer-Verlag.

[49] Dutta, B. and S. Mutuswami (1997), "Stable Networks," *Journal of Economic Theory* 76, 322–344.

[50] Dutta, B., A. van den Nouweland, and S. Tijs (1998), "Link Formation in Cooperative Situations," *International Journal of Game Theory* 27, 245–256.

[51] De Weerdt, J. (2002), "Risk-Sharing and Endogenous Network Formation," mimeo., K. U. Leuven.

[52] Ellison, G. (1993), "Learning, Local Interaction, and Coordination," *Econometrica* 61, 1047–1071.

[53] Ellison, G. and D. Fudenberg (1995), "Word-of-Mouth Communication and Social Learning," *The Quarterly Journal of Economics* 110, 93–126.

[54] Fafchamps, M. and S. Lund (2000), "Risk-Sharing Networks in Rural Philippines," mimeo., Stanford University.

[55] Falk, A. and M. Kosfeld (2003), "It's All about Connections: Evidence on Network Formation," mimeo., University of Zurich.

[56] Feri, F. (2003), "Network Formation with Decay," Università Ca Foscari, Venice.

[57] Freidlin, M. and A. Wentzell (1984), *Random Perturbations of Dynamical Systems*, New York: Springer-Verlag, pp. 161–211.

[58] Furusawa, T. and H. Konishi (2002), "Free Trade Networks," mimeo., Yokohama National University and Boston College.

[59] Galeotti, A. and S. Goyal (2002), "Network Formation with Heterogeneous Players," mimeo., Erasmus University Rotterdam and University of London.

[60] Galeotti, A. and M. A. Meléndez-Jiménez (2003), "Strategic Multidimensionality and Social Interaction," mimeo., Erasmus University Rotterdam and University of Alicante.

[61] Gilles, R. P. and S. Sarangi (2003a), "The Role of Trust in Costly Network Formation," mimeo., Virginia Tech and Louisiana State University.

[62] Gilles, R. P. and S. Sarangi (2003b), "Rationalizing Trust in Network Formation," mimeo., Virginia Tech and Louisiana State University.

[63] Glaeser, E., B. Sacerdote, and J. Scheinkman (1996), "Crime and Social Interactions," *Quarterly Journal of Economics* 111, 507–548.

[64] Goyal, S. (1993), "Sustainable Communication Networks," Discussion Paper TI 93-250, Tinbergen Institute, Amsterdam–Rotterdam.

[65] Goyal, S. and S. Joshi (1999), "Bilateralism and Free Trade," mimeo., Tinbergen Econometric Institute Report 176.

[66] Goyal, S. and S. Joshi (2000), "Networks of Collaboration in Oligopoly," forthcoming: *Games and Economic Behavior*.

[67] Goyal, S. and S. Joshi (2003), "Unequal Connections," mimeo., University of London and George Washington University.

[68] Goyal, S., A. Konovalov, and J. -L. Moraga (2003), "Hybrid R and d," mimeo., Essex University.

[69] Goyal, S. and J. -L. Moraga (2001), "R and D Networks," *Rand Journal of Economics* 32, 686–707.

[70] Goyal, S. and F. Vega-Redondo (2000), "Learning, Network Formation and Coordination," mimeo., Erasmus University.

[71] Granovetter, M. (1973), "The Strength of Weak Ties," *American Journal of Sociology* 78, 1360–1380.

[72] Granovetter, M. [1974](1995), *Getting a Job: A Study of Contacts and Careers*, 2nd edition, University of Chicago Press.

[73] Haller, H. and S. Sarangi (2001), "Nash Networks with Heterogeneous Agents," mimeo., Virginia Tech and Louisiana State University.

[74] Harrison, R. and R. Munoz (2002), "Stability and Equilibrium Selection in a Link Formation Game," mimeo., Georgetown University and the University of Maryland.

[75] Hendricks, K., M. Piccione, and G. Tan (1995), "The Economics of Hubs: The Case of Monopoly," *Review of Economic Studies* 62, 83–100.

[76] Holland, P. W. and S. Leinhardt (1977), "A Dynamic Model for Social Networks," *Journal of Mathematical Sociology* 5, 5–20.

[77] Ioannides, Y. M. and L. Datcher Loury (2002), "Job Information Networks, Neighborhood Effects and Inequality," mimeo., Tufts University.

[78] Jackson, M. O. (2003a), "The Stability and Efficiency of Economic and Social Networks," in *Advances in Economic Design*, S. Koray and M. Sertel (eds.), Heidelberg: Springer-Verlag, and reprinted in *Networks and Groups: Models of Strategic Formation*, B. Dutta and M. O. Jackson (eds.), Heidelberg: Springer-Verlag.

[79] Jackson, M. O. (2003b). "Allocation Rules for Network Games," forthcoming in *Games and Economic Behavior*.

[80] Jackson, M. O. and A. van den Nouweland (2000), "Strongly Stable Networks," forthcoming: *Games and Economic Behavior*, http://www.hss.caltech.edu/~jacksonm/coopnet.pdf.

[81] Jackson, M. O. and A. Watts (2001), "The Existence of Pairwise Stable Networks," *Seoul Journal of Economics* 14, 3, 299–321.

[82] Jackson, M. O. and A. Watts (2002a), "The Evolution of Social and Economic Networks," *Journal of Economic Theory* 106, 2, 265–295.

[83] Jackson, M. O. and A. Watts, (2002b) "On the Formation of Interaction Networks in Social Coordination Games," *Games and Economic Behavior*, 41, 2, 265–291.

[84] Jackson, M. O. and A. Wolinsky (1996), "A Strategic Model of Social and Economic Networks," *Journal of Economic Theory* 71, 44–74.

[85] Johnson, C. and R. P. Gilles (2000), "Spatial Social Networks," *Review of Economic Design* 5, 273–300.

[86] Kandori, M., G. Mailath, and R. Rob (1993), "Learning, Mutation, and Long Run Equilibria in Games," *Econometrica* 61, 29–56.

[87] Katz, M. and C. Shapiro (1994), "Systems Competition and Networks Effects," *Journal of Economic Perspectives* 8, 93–115.

[88] Kirman, A. (1997), "The Economy as an Evolving Network," *Journal of Evolutionary Economics* 7, 339–353.

[89] Kirman, A., C. Oddou, and S. Weber (1986), "Stochastic Communication and Coalition Formation," *Econometrica* 54, 129–138.

[90] Konishi, H. and M. Utku Ünver (2003), "Credible Group-Stability in General Multi-Partner Matching Problems," mimeo., Boston College and Koc University.

[91] Kosfeld, M. (2003), "Network Experiments," mimeo., University of Zurich.

[92] Kranton, R. and D. Minehart (1996), "Link Patterns in Buyer–Seller Networks: Incentives and Allocations in Graphs," mimeo., University of Maryland and Boston University.

[93] Kranton, R. and D. Minehart (2000), "Competition for Goods in Buyer–Seller Networks," *Review of Economic Design* 5, 301–332.

[94] Kranton, R. and D. Minehart (2001), "A Theory of Buyer–Seller Networks," *American Economic Review* 91, 485–508.

[95] Lahari, S. (2003), "Stable Allocation Rules for Generalized Matching Problems," mimeo.

[96] Liebowitz, S. and S. Margolis (1994), "Network Externality: An Uncommon Tragedy," *Journal of Economic Perspectives* 8, 133–150.

[97] Lippert, S. and G. Spagnolo (2003), "Networks of Relations," mimeo., University of Mannheim.

[98] Mairesse, J. and L. Turner (2001), "Measurement and Explanation of the Intensity of Co-publication in Scientific Research: An Analysis at the Laboratory Level," EUREQua Working Paper 2001.53.

[99] Marsali, M., F. Vega-Redondo, and F. Slanina (2003), "The Rise and Fall of a Networked Society," mimeo., Pompeu Fabra.

[100] McBride, M. (2002), "Position-Specific Information in Social Networks," mimeo., University of California at Irvine.

[101] Meessen, R. (1988), "Communication Games," Master's thesis, Department of Mathematics, University of Nijmegen.

[102] Monderer, D. and L. Shapley (1996), "Potential Games," *Games and Economic Behavior* 14, 124–143.

[103] Monsuur, H. (2002), "Centrality and Network Dynamics," mimeo., Royal Netherlands Naval Academy.

[104] Montgomery, J. (1991), "Social Networks and Labor Market Outcomes," *The American Economic Review* 81, 1408–1418.

[105] Montgomery, J. (1992), "Job Search and Network Composition: Implications of the Strength-of-Weak-Ties Hypothesis," *American Sociological Review* 57, 586–596.

[106] Montgomery, J. (1994), "Weak Ties, Employment, and Inequality: An Equilibrium Analysis," *American Journal of Sociology* 99, 1212–1236.

[107] Moreno-Ternero, J. D. (2000), "Notes about a Strategic Model of Social and Economic Networks," Universidad de Alicante.

[108] Mutuswami, S. and E. Winter (2002), "Subscription Mechanisms for Network Formation," *Journal of Economic Theory* 106, 242–264.

[109] Myerson, R. (1977), "Graphs and Cooperation in Games," *Mathematics of Operations Research* 2, 225–229.

[110] Myerson, R. (1991), *Game Theory: Analysis of Conflict*, Cambridge, MA: Harvard University Press.

[111] Navarro, N. (2002), "Fair Allocation in Evolving Networks," mimeo., Universidad Carlos III de Madrid.

[112] Navarro, N. and A. Perea (2001), "Bargaining in Networks and the Myerson Value," mimeo., Universidad Carlos III de Madrid.

[113] Nieva, R. (2002), "An Extension of the Aumann–Myerson Solution for Reasonable Empty-Core Games," mimeo., Rochester Institute of Technology.

[114] Page, F., M. Wooders, and S. Kamat (2001), "Networks and Farsighted Stability," Working paper, University of Warwick, n. 621, *Journal of Economic Theory* (to appear).

[115] Pantz, K. and A. Ziegelmeyer (2003), "An Experimental Study of Network Formation," mimeo., Max Planck Institute.

[116] Polanski, A. (2003), "Bilateral Bargaining in Networks," mimeo., Universidad de Alicante.

[117] Qin, C.-Z. (1996), "Endogenous Formation of Cooperation Structures," *Journal of Economic Theory* 69, 218–226.

[118] Rees, A. (1966), "Information Networks in Labor Markets," *American Economic Review* 56, 559–566.

[119] Roth, A. and M. Sotomayor (1989), *Two-Sided Matching*, Econometric Society Monographs No. 18: Cambridge University Press.

[120] Santamaria-Garcia, J. (2003), "Gathering Information through Social Contacts: An Empirical Analysis of Labor Market Outcomes," mimeo., European University Institute.

[121] Sarangi, S., R. Kannan, and L. Ray (2003), "The Structure of Information Networks," mimeo., Louisiana State University.

[122] Skyrms, B. and R. Pemantle (2000), "A Dynamic Model of Social Network Formation," *Proceedings of the National Academy of Sciences* 97, 9340–9346.

[123] Slikker, M. (2000), *Decision Making and Cooperation Structures*, CentER Dissertation Series: Tilburg.

[124] Slikker, M., R P Gilles, H. Norde, and S. Tijs (2001), "Directed Networks," Allocation Properties and Hierarchy Formation, mimeo: Virginia Tech.

[125] Slikker, M. and A. van den Nouweland (2000), "Network Formation Models with Costs for Establishing Links," *Review of Economic Design* 5, 333–362.

[126] Slikker, M. and A. van den Nouweland (2001a), *Social and Economic Networks in Cooperative Game Theory*, Amsterdam: Kluwer Academic Publishers.

[127] Slikker, M. and A. van den Nouweland (2001b), "A One-Stage Model of Link Formation and Payoff Division," *Games and Economic Behavior* 34, 153–175.

[128] Starr, R. M. and M. B. Stinchcombe (1992), "Efficient Transportation Routing and Natural Monopoly in the Airline Industry: An Economic Analysis of Hub-Spoke and Related Systems," UCSD dp 92-25.

[129] Starr, R. M. and M. B. Stinchcombe (1999), "Exchange in a Network of Trading Posts," in *Markets, Information and Uncertainty*, G. Chichilnisky (ed.), Cambridge, UK: Cambridge University Press.

[130] Stole, L. and J. Zweibel (1996), "Intra-Firm Bargaining under Non-Binding Constraints," *Review of Economic Studies* 63, 375–410.

[131] Tassier, T. (2002), "A Markov Model of Referral-Based Hiring and Workplace Segregation," mimeo., University of Iowa.

[132] Tassier, T. and F. Menczer (2002), "Social Network Structure, Equality and Segregation in a Labor Market with Referral Hiring," mimeo., University of Iowa.

[133] Tesfatsion, L. (1997), "A Trade Network Game with Endogenous Partner Selection," in *Computational Approaches to Economic Problems*, H. Amman et al. (eds.), New York: Kluwer Academic Publishers, 249–269.

[134] Tesfatsion, L. (1998), "Gale–Shapley Matching in an Evolutionary Trade Network Game," Iowa State University Economic Report No. 43.

[135] Topa, G. (2001), "Social Interactions, Local Spillovers and Unemployment," *Review of Economic Studies* 68, 261–296.

[136] Vega-Redondo, F. (2002), "Building Up Social Capital in a Changing World," mimeo., Universidad de Alicante.

[137] Wang, P. and A. Watts (2002), "Formation of Buyer–Seller Trade Networks in a Quality-Differentiated Product Market," mimeo., Pennsylvania State University and Southern Illinois University.

[138] Wang, P. and Q. Wen (1998), "Network Bargaining," mimeo., Pennsylvania State University.

[139] Wasserman, S. and K. Faust (1994), *Social Network Analysis: Methods and Applications*, Cambridge, UK: Cambridge University Press.

[140] Watts, A. (2001), "A Dynamic Model of Network Formation," *Games and Economic Behavior* 34, 331–341.

[141] Watts, A. (2002), "A Note on Non-Myopic Network Formation," *Economics Letters* 74, 277–281.

[142] Watts, D. J. (1999), *Small Worlds: The Dynamics of Networks between Order and Randomness*, Princeton, NJ: Princeton University Press.

[143] Weisbuch, G., A. Kirman, and D. Herreiner (2000), "Market Organization," *Economica* 110, 411–436.

[144] Yoon, K. "Resale of Information and Stability of Networks," mimeo., Korea University.

[145] Young, H. P. (1993), "The Evolution of Conventions," *Econometrica* 61, 57–84.

[146] Young, H. P. (1998), *Individual Strategy and Social Structure*, Princeton, NJ: Princeton University Press.

Models of Network Formation in Cooperative Games[*]

Anne van den Nouweland

2.1. Introduction

Network structures play an important role in many economic situations. The types of networks considered in this chapter connect many individuals who each must establish and maintain their own links. I refer to such networks as communications networks; they describe the bilateral channels through which individuals can communicate and thereby coordinate their actions. The worth that coalitions of individuals can obtain by coordinating their actions is modeled by a coalitional game, which specifies for each coalition S of individuals a worth $v(S)$. Suppose, for example, that there are three individuals: one seller who has one indivisible unit of a good for sale and two potential buyers. Suppose the value of the good is 0 to the seller (s), 1 to the first buyer (b_1), and 2 to the second buyer (b_2). This situation can be modeled as a coalitional game with player set $\{s, b_1, b_2\}$ and $v(\{s\}) = v(\{b_1\}) = v(\{b_2\}) = v(\{b_1, b_2\}) = 0$, $v(\{s, b_1\}) = 1$, and $v(\{s, b_2\}) = v(\{s, b_1, b_2\}) = 2$. If only the two buyers are linked (the only link formed is $b_1 b_2$), then the seller cannot communicate with any of the buyers and thus no worth can be generated. If the seller is linked to the first buyer and the first buyer, in turn, is linked to the second buyer (the two links $s b_1$ and $b_1 b_2$ have been formed), then all three can communicate and coordinate their actions (the seller and the second buyer do so through the first buyer) and a worth of 2 can be generated by selling the good to the second buyer.

Note that in the approach based on coalitional games as explained above, the worth that players in a network can obtain primarily depends on which players are connected with one another (directly or indirectly) and not on how exactly these players are connected. Hence, issues such as the deterioration of information as it travels along longer paths are not taken into account. When we want to take these types of issues into account, we end up in the realm of value functions on networks, which are covered in Chapter 1 of this volume. Also, the approach based on coalitional games precludes externalities between different groups of interconnected players; the worth

[*] Most of what I cover in this chapter is also covered in Slikker and van den Nouweland (2001a). I am greatful to Macro Slikker, Matthew Jackson, and Myrna Wooders for helpful comments on an earlier version of this chapter.

generated by a group of interconnected players does not depend on whether players not in the group are connected to each other.

I illustrated in the opening paragraph how the worth that the players can obtain depends on the network. The discussion there concentrated on the worth that can be obtained by the players as a group if they cooperate. The issue of how this worth will then be divided among the players was not addressed. In general, this division will depend on the positions that the players take in the network. For example, if in the situation described above the two links sb_1 and b_1b_2 have been formed and the worth 2 is generated by selling the good to the second buyer, then the first buyer might get some share of the profits of the sale because his or her cooperation is needed for the seller and the second buyer to make a deal given that they cannot communicate directly (link sb_2 has not been formed). If, on the other hand, link sb_2 has been formed, then the worth 2 can still be generated by selling the good to the second buyer. But now since the seller and this second buyer do not need the assistance of the first buyer to complete the transaction, it seems reasonable that the seller and the second buyer will share the worth 2 between themselves. The specific way in which the worth generated by the players in a network is shared among them is specified by an allocation rule. In most of the models described in this chapter, it is assumed that such an allocation rule is exogenously given and the players decide which links to form given this allocation rule.[1]

A network is a collection of bilateral links between players who must establish and maintain their own links. To form a link is a strategic decision for a player because his links have an influence on the position that he will take in the network and thereby on the payoff that he or she expects to obtain, as specified by the allocation rule. Because the formation of links is a strategic decision, it is appropriate to model network formation as a noncooperative game. Perhaps the simplest way to model network formation is by means of a strategic-form game in which players simultaneously announce which links they want to form and in which a link between two players is formed if and only if both these players want to form it.[2] In this model, every network can emerge in a Nash equilibrium when the underlying coalitional game and the allocation rule are such that every player wants to have as many links as possible. This is because it takes the consent of two players to form a link, and thus a single player cannot form any new links through unilateral deviation. This motivates the study of refinements of Nash equilibrium for network-formation models.

In this chapter, I discuss the various (noncooperative) models of network formation in coalitional games that have been studied in the literature. The questions answered for these models concern which networks can be formed according to Nash equilibria or refinements thereof and what the payoffs are to the players in such networks. The models illustrate how differences in the circumstances under which the players form links and differences in ways in which jointly generated profits are distributed among them influence the networks they form.

---

[1] The exception is the model in Section 2.7, in which players bargain over link formation and payoff division simultaneously.

[2] This model is described in Section 2.4.

2.2. Definitions

All the models in this chapter start from a coalitional game (N, v), in which $N = \{1, 2, ..., n\}$ is the set of players and $v : 2^N \to I\!R$ is a characteristic function that assigns to each coalition $S \subseteq N$ of players a worth $v(S)$. It is always assumed that $v(\emptyset) = 0$. The interpretation of the worth $v(S)$ of a coalition S is that this is the payoff the members of S can obtain for themselves if they coordinate their actions and it is independent of the actions taken by the players who are not included in the coalition. However, in order to coordinate their actions, players have to be able to communicate.

Communication takes place through bilateral channels, which I refer to as (communications) links. The link between players i and j is denoted by ij and the set of all possible communications links between the players in N is denoted by $g^N = \{ij \mid i, j \in N, i \neq j\}$. In the models surveyed, it takes the consent of both players to form the link between them, and an existing link ij can be used costlessly by both players i and j. A network is a pair (N, g), where N is the set of players and $g \subseteq g^N$ is a set of links. When this does not lead to confusion, a network (N, g) is identified with its set of links and is simply denoted g. The network with all possible links, g^N, is referred to as the complete network. In a network g, two players can communicate (and, hence, coordinate their actions) if and only if there exists a path of communication between them. A path in g between players i and j is a sequence of players $i = i_1, i_2, ..., i_t = j$ with $t \geq 2$ such that $i_k i_{k+1} \in g$ for each $k \in \{1, 2, ..., t - 1\}$. If there exists such a path with $t = 2$, then $ij \in g$ and players i and j can communicate directly. Players can communicate indirectly through other players if a longer path exists between them. Players who are not connected by a path are in different components of the network, whereas players who are connected by a path are in the same component. The component containing player i is denoted by $C_i(g) = \{j \in N \mid j = i$ or j and i are connected by a path in $g\}$, and the set of all components of network (N, g) is denoted by $\pi(N, g) = \{C_i(g) \mid i \in N\}$. Network (N, g) is connected if it contains only one component, that is, if $C_i(g) = N$ for each $i \in N$ so that all players can communicate with each other.

A coalitional game and a network constitute a communications situation. Formally, a communications situation is a triple (N, v, g) consisting of a player set N, a characteristic function v, and a set of links g. I am interested in the formation of links given a coalitional game (N, v), and I denote the set of all communications situations with player set N and characteristic function v by CS_v^N.

For a communications situation (N, v, g), the network-restricted game (N, v^g) incorporates both the possible gains from cooperation for coalitions of players as modeled by the coalitional game (N, v) and the restrictions on communications reflected by communications network g. The players in a coalition $T \subseteq N$ have available the links in $g(T) = \{ij \in g \mid i \in T$ and $j \in T\}$ and this induces a partition $\pi(T, g)$ of this coalition into the components of the network $(T, g(T))$. The players in T can only coordinate their actions within these components. This motivates the definition of the characteristic function v^g as $v^g(T) = \sum_{C \in \pi(T,g)} v(C)$ for each $T \subseteq N$. Note that this definition implicitly assumes that there are no externalities between different components of a network; the worth of the players in a network is simply the sum of the worths of its components. Jackson and Wolinsky (1996) refer to this property as component additivity of the value function that assigns a value to every network. This property of the network-restricted game derived from a coalitional game is in accordance with the interpretation of the coalitional game as assigning to each coalition of players the worth that they can obtain *independently of the other players*. In addition, the definition of the characteristic function v^g is such that the worth of a coalition of players who form a component of a network does not depend on exactly which links exist between these players but only on whether these players are connected at all. This reflects the interpretation of the links as (costless) communications channels that allow players to cooperate.

Using the network-restricted game (N, v^g), Myerson (1977) defined an allocation rule for communications situations. An allocation rule on a class CS of communications situations is a function γ that assigns to each communications situation $(N, v, g) \in CS$ a payoff vector $\gamma(N, v, g) \in \mathbb{R}^N$. If allocation rule γ is used, then a player $i \in N$ expects to get a payoff $\gamma_i(N, v, g)$ from being in communications situation (N, v, g). The Myerson value μ is the Shapley value Φ (cf. Shapley 1953) of the network-restricted game

$$\mu_i(N, v, g) = \Phi_i(N, v^g) = \sum_{T \subset N: i \notin T} \frac{|T|!(|N| - 1 - |T|)!}{|N|!} (v^g(T \cup i) - v^g(T)) .^3$$

The Myerson value is by far the most widely used allocation rule for communications situations in the literature. One of the reasons for this popularity is undoubtedly its firm axiomatic grounding. Myerson (1977) showed that for any coalitional game (N, v) the Myerson value is the unique allocation rule on CS_v^N that satisfies the properties of component efficiency and fairness. Component efficiency of an allocation rule means that the players in a component distribute the value of this component, which they can obtain for themselves irrespective of the actions taken by the players not in the component, among themselves. The fairness property signifies that two players should gain or lose equally from forming the link between them. An allocation rule is fair if the payoffs of two players i and j increase or decrease by the same amount whenever the link connecting them is severed.[4]

Several other allocation rules for communications situations appear in the literature. The main one is the position value (cf. Borm, Owen, and Tijs 1992), which focuses on the importance of the communications links rather than the role of the players. Finding an axiomatic characterization of this allocation rule for a fixed coalitional game and variable networks has proven rather elusive over the years, but Slikker (2003) recently succeeded in finding one. He uses two axioms in his characterization of the position value: component efficiency and balanced total threats, a property that is reminiscent of the balanced contributions axiom that Myerson (1980) used to axiomatize the Myerson value and that can replace fairness in a

---

[3] Here, $|T|$ denotes the number of elements in a set T. Also, following popular tradition, I omit the set brackets {and} when I don't think such an omission will cause the reader any confusion.

[4] Jackson (see Chapter 1 of this volume) refers to this property as equal bargaining power.

characterization of the Myerson value. The axiomatization of the position value may well lead to new applications of this allocation rule in the future.

I will cover both extensive-form games of network formation and strategic-form ones. The network-formation game in extensive form is most easily described casually, and I will do exactly that in Section 2.3. A game in strategic form is a tuple $(N; (S_i)_{i \in N}; (f_i)_{i \in N})$ consisting of a player set N, a strategy set S_i for each player $i \in N$, and a payoff function $f_i : \prod_{i \in N} S_i \to I\!R$ for each player $i \in N$. In such a game, every player $i \in N$ chooses one of his or her strategies $s_i \in S_i$ and then each player i gets a payoff $f_i(s)$, where $s = (s_i)_{i \in N}$ denotes the strategy profile chosen. A strategy profile is a Nash equilibrium (cf. Nash 1950) if no player can increase his or her payoff by unilaterally deviating to a different strategy. In formulaic form, $s \in \prod_{i \in N} S_i$ is a Nash equilibrium if for each player $i \in N$ and each strategy $t_i \in S_i$ it holds that $f_i(s_i) \geq f_i(t_i, s_{-i})$, where $s_{-i} = (s_j)_{j \in N \setminus i}$ denotes the (fixed) strategies of the players other than i and (t_i, s_{-i}) denotes the strategy profile in which player i plays his or her strategy t_i and every player $j \in N \setminus i$ plays his or her strategy s_j.

I will use several refinements of Nash equilibria. A strategy s_i of a player i is undominated if there is no other strategy that gives this player at least as high a payoff and sometimes a higher payoff for all possible strategy choices of the other players. Hence, $s_i \in S_i$ is undominated if there is no other strategy $t_i \in S_i$ such that $f_i(s_i, s_{-i}) \leq f_i(t_i, s_{-i})$ for all $s_{-i} \in \prod_{j \in N \setminus i} S_j$ with the inequality being strict for at least one s_{-i}. An undominated Nash equilibrium is a Nash equilibrium in which each player plays an undominated strategy.

A strong Nash equilibrium (cf. Aumann 1959 and Bernheim, Peleg, and Whinston 1987) is a strategy profile that is stable against deviations not only by single players but by any coalition of players. Hence, $s \in \prod_{i \in N} S_i$ is a strong Nash equilibrium if for each coalition $T \subseteq N$ it holds that there is no strategy tuple $t_T = (t_i)_{i \in T} \in \prod_{i \in T} S_i$ such that $f_i(t_T, s_{N \setminus T}) \geq f_i(s)$ for all $i \in T$ and $f_i(t_T, s_{N \setminus T}) > f_i(s)$ for at least one $i \in T$. This definition of strong equilibrium is actually slightly different from that put forward in Aumann (1959) and Bernheim et al. (1987) in that it allows a coalition to deviate to a strategy profile that strictly increases the payoffs of some of its members without decreasing those of the other members, whereas the original definition allows only deviations that strictly increase the payoffs of all members of a deviating coalition. Both interpretations of strong Nash equilibrium are prominent in the literature, and in most games the two definitions lead to the same sets of strong Nash equilibria; however, the one that I use here is slightly more appealing in the context of network-formation games (see, e.g., Jackson and van den Nouweland 2001).

Coalition-proof Nash equilibria (cf. Bernheim et al. 1987) are similar to strong Nash equilibria in that they require a strategy profile to be stable against deviations by all coalitions of players. However, in a coalition-proof Nash equilibrium, the deviations are restricted to be stable themselves against further deviations by subcoalitions. To provide the formal definition of coalition-proof Nash equilibrium, which is inductive, I need some additional notation. Let $\Gamma = (N; (S_i)_{i \in N}; (f_i)_{i \in N})$ be a game in strategic form, $T \subset N$ a coalition, and $s^*_{N \setminus T} \in \prod_{i \in N \setminus T} S_i$. The strategic-form game $\Gamma(s^*_{N \setminus T}) = (T; (S_i)_{i \in T}; (f^*_i)_{i \in T})$ induced on the players of T by the strategies

$s^*_{N\setminus T}$ has payoff functions $f^*_i : \prod_{i\in T} S_i \to I\!R$ given by $f^*_i(s_T) = f_i(s_T, s^*_{N\setminus T})$ for all $s_T \in \prod_{i\in T} S_i$, for each $i \in T$. In a 1-player game $(\{i\}; S_i; f_i)$, a strategy $s^*_i \in S_i$ is a coalition-proof Nash equilibrium if s^*_i maximizes f_i over S_i. Let $\Gamma = (N; (S_i)_{i\in N}; (f_i)_{i\in N})$ be a game with $|N| > 1$ players and suppose that coalition-proof Nash equilibria have been defined for games with fewer than $|N|$ players. A strategy profile $s^* \in \prod_{i\in N} S_i$ is considered self enforcing if for all $T \subset N$, it holds that s^*_T is a coalition-proof Nash equilibrium of the game $\Gamma(s^*_{N\setminus T})$. A strategy profile s^* is a coalition-proof Nash equilibrium of Γ if s^* is self-enforcing and there is no other self-enforcing strategy profile $s \in S_N$ such that $f_i(s) > f_i(s^*)$ for all $i \in N$.

The last refinement of Nash equilibria that I use is defined only for strategic-form games that are potential games. A game $(N; (S_i)_{i\in N}; (f_i)_{i\in N})$ is a potential game (cf. Monderer and Shapley 1996) if there exists a potential function $P : \prod_{i\in N} S_i \to I\!R$ such that for every strategy profile $s \in \prod_{i\in N} S_i$, every $i \in N$, and every $t_i \in S_i$ it holds that $f_i(s_i, s_{-i}) - f_i(t_i, s_{-i}) = P(s_i, s_{-i}) - P(t_i, s_{-i})$. The function P provides information on changes in payoff when any player unilaterally changes his or her strategy choice. For a potential game, the potential maximizer selects the strategy profiles that maximize a potential function P. Monderer and Shapley (1996) prove that the potential maximizer is a well-defined refinement of Nash equilibria. Ui (2001) shows that Nash equilibria maximizing a potential function are generically robust, and Garratt and Qin (2003) provide justification for using the potential maximizer in network-formation games.

2.3. Network-Formation Game in Extensive Form

Network-formation games in extensive form were introduced by Aumann and Myerson (1988). The network-formation process in these games is sequential. Pairs of players get opportunities to form links according to some exogenous rule of order on the links. Links are formed one at a time, and players observe which pairs of players form links or decline to form links as the game progresses. Moreover, links cannot be broken once they have been formed. After each pair of players has had an opportunity to form a link in the order determined by the exogenous rule of order, every pair of players that has declined to form a link is given another opportunity to do so in an order determined by the same rule of order. This process is repeated as long as new links are formed in each round, but it stops when, after the latest link has been formed, all pairs of players who have not formed a link have had one final opportunity to change their minds and form it but have declined. The payoffs to the players are those found by applying the Myerson value μ to the network formed in combination with an underlying coalitional game. The network-formation game in extensive form as just described with underlying coalitional game (N, v), exogenous allocation rule μ (the Myerson value), and exogenous rule of order σ on all possible links between the players in N is denoted by $\Delta^{nf}(N, v, \mu, \sigma)$.

For the extensive-form games of network formation $\Delta^{nf}(N, v, \mu, \sigma)$, to the best of my knowledge no general results have been obtained. Results for these games are limited to a series of examples that illustrate which networks are supported by subgame-perfect Nash equilibria of the network-formation games for various underlying coalitional games. A subgame-perfect Nash equilibrium is a profile of strategies, one for each player, satisfying the requirement that, at each point in the game, every player's strategy yields the highest possible payoff in the remainder of the game given the strategies of the other players.[5]

The following example is taken from Aumann and Myerson (1988) and shows that, for a superadditive coalitional game, the extensive-form network-formation process may not lead to the formation of a complete network or even a connected network. A coalitional game (N, v) is superadditive if any two disjoint coalitions of players T and R (so $T \cap R = \emptyset$) can only benefit from joining forces, that is, $v(T \cup R) \geq v(T) + v(R)$.

Example 2.1. *Consider player set $N = \{1, 2, 3\}$ and assume that the economic possibilities of the players are captured in the superadditive coalitional game (N, v), where $v(T) = 0$ if $|T| \leq 1$, $v(T) = 60$ if $|T| = 2$, and $v(N) = 72$. For this underlying game, the payoffs to the players as determined by the Myerson value for the various possible networks are as follows. In the empty network, every player receives zero, that is,*

$$\mu_i(N, v, \emptyset) = 0 \quad \text{for each} \quad i \in N.$$

In a network with one link, the two linked players equally divide the value of a two-player coalition and the isolated player gets zero, that is,

$$\mu_k(N, v, \{ij\}) = \begin{cases} 0 & \text{if} \quad k \notin \{i, j\}; \\ 30 & \text{if} \quad k \in \{i, j\}. \end{cases}$$

In a network with two links, the payoffs are

$$\mu_r(N, v, \{ij, jk\}) = \begin{cases} 44 & \text{if} \quad r = j; \\ 14 & \text{if} \quad r \in \{i, k\}. \end{cases}$$

Finally, in the complete network each player receives the same payoff and

$$\mu_i(N, v, g^N) = 24 \quad \text{for each} \quad i \in N.$$

To find which networks are supported by subgame-perfect Nash equilibria of the game $\Delta^{nf}(N, v, \mu, \sigma)$, first note that each player receives a positive payoff if he or she forms any links at all, whereas all players receive zero if no links are formed. It follows that at least one link will be formed in a subgame-perfect Nash equilibrium. So, suppose that exactly one link has been formed – for instance, link ij. If no additional links are formed, players i and j will each receive a payoff of 30. Note that if one of them, for instance i, forms a link with the remaining player k, he or she would realize an increase in payoff to 44. However, in the network $(N, \{ij, ik\})$, players j and k receive only 14, and they can increase their payoffs to 24 by forming link jk. Hence, none of the players i and j will form a link with player k because this will cause the other player to do so as well and both their payoffs would be

---

5   Subgame-perfect Nash equilibria always exist for these games because they are finite and have perfect information.

only 24 rather than the 30 they each get in the network $(N, \{ij\})$. This shows that in a subgame-perfect Nash equilibrium exactly one link will be formed. The order σ on the links is not important in the sense that, for any order σ and for any one of the three links, there is a subgame-perfect Nash equilibrium that results in the formation of this particular link, as is discussed in detail in Slikker (2000).[6]

Since for superadditive coalitional games, the extensive-form network-formation process might not lead to the formation of a complete network, some research has focused on strengthening the requirement of superadditivity to convexity. A coalitional game (N, v) is convex if a player's contribution to a coalition increases (weakly) with the size of the coalition he or she joins – that is, for any player i and any two coalitions $T, R \subseteq N \setminus i$ with $T \subseteq R$, it holds that $v(T \cup i) - v(T) \leq v(R \cup i) - v(R)$. Convexity of a coalitional game seems to provide strong incentives for players to cooperate in the largest possible coalition. It is a long-standing open conjecture that for convex coalitional games, subgame-perfect Nash equilibria of the extensive-form game of network formation support the complete network. This conjecture was addressed in van den Nouweland (1993) and later in Slikker and Norde (2000). Van den Nouweland (1993) shows that the conjecture holds true if a second conjecture holds. This second conjecture is that, for any convex game and any network that is not the complete network, there exist two players who have not formed a link and whose Myerson values in the network are weakly smaller than their respective Myerson values in the complete network. However, this second conjecture was disproved by an example due to R. Holzman (private communication), which can be found as Example 6.3 in Slikker and van den Nouweland (2001a).

Slikker and Norde (2000) study the extensive-form network-formation games $\Delta^{nf}(N, v, \mu, \sigma)$ for underlying games that are convex and symmetric. A coalitional game (N, v) is symmetric if the worth of every coalition of players depends only on how many members it has, that is, $v(T) = v(R)$ for all coalitions $T, R \subseteq N$ with $|T| = |R|$. The additional requirement of symmetry makes it easier to analyze a game because it reduces its complexity considerably. Slikker and Norde (2000) are able to show that for convex, symmetric coalitional games with at least two and at most five players the complete network is supported by a subgame-perfect Nash equilibrium of the extensive-form games of network formation $\Delta^{nf}(N, v, \mu, \sigma)$ for any order σ. Moreover, they are able to show that for strictly convex[7] symmetric games (N, v) with at least two and at most five players, it holds that any network (N, g) supported by a subgame-perfect Nash equilibrium is payoff equivalent to the complete network, that is, $\mu(N, v, g) = \mu(N, v, g^N)$. This result cannot be extended to games with more than five players. Slikker and Norde (2000) study a six-player, strictly convex symmetric game (N, v) and show that for this game there exist networks that are not payoff equivalent to the complete network but are supported

---

[6] For some games, the order σ might influence which networks are supported by subgame-perfect Nash equilibria. Slikker and van den Nouweland (2001a) demonstrate this in their Example 6.2.

[7] A game (N, v) is strictly convex if the convexity inequalities all hold with strict inequality, that is, for any player i and any two coalitions $T, R \subseteq N \setminus i$ with $T \subset R$, it holds that $v(T \cup i) - v(T) < v(R \cup i) - v(R)$.

by subgame-perfect Nash equilibria of network-formation games $\Delta^{nf}(N, v, \mu, \sigma)$. However, it is still an open question whether for (strictly) convex (symmetric) games with more than five players the complete network is supported by a subgame-perfect Nash equilibrium of the extensive-form network-formation games.

Other coalitional games for which the extensive-form network-formation game has been studied are weighted majority games. A weighted majority game is a game that results from a situation in which each player $i \in N$ has a number of votes w_i and in which a coalition of players needs a total of q votes (the quota) to obtain the surplus, which is normalized to equal 1. The tuple $(N, q, (w_i)_{i \in N})$ is a weighted majority situation. To avoid the existence of two disjoint coalitions of players that can obtain the surplus, it is assumed that $\frac{1}{2} \sum_{i \in N} w_i < q$. The characteristic function v of the weighted majority game (N, v) associated with weighted majority situation $(N, q, (w_i)_{i \in N})$ is defined by

$$v(T) = \begin{cases} 1 & \text{if } \sum_{i \in T} w_i \geq q; \\ 0 & \text{otherwise} \end{cases}$$

for all $T \subseteq N$.

The following example considers a weighted majority game with one powerful player and several small ones – a so-called apex game. This example is due to Aumann and Myerson (1988).

Example 2.2. *Consider the weighted majority situation $(N, q, (w_i)_{i \in N})$ with player set $N = \{1, 2, 3, 4, 5\}$, quota $q = 4$, and numbers of votes $w_1 = 3$ and $w_2 = w_3 = w_4 = w_5 = 1$. Player 1 has more votes than each of the other players but still needs at least one of the players with few votes to obtain the surplus. Also, the players with few votes can obtain the surplus without player 1 if all four of them cooperate. The characteristic function of the associated weighted majority game (N, v) is*

$$v(T) = \begin{cases} 1 & \text{if } T = \{2, 3, 4, 5\} \text{ or if } 1 \in T \text{ and } |T| \geq 2; \\ 0 & \text{otherwise.} \end{cases}$$

Note that players 2 through 5 are symmetric in this game. Consequently, it suffices to discuss only the payoffs for some possible networks, and those for other networks can be found using this symmetry. If only a link between player 1 and player 2 is formed, then these two players depend on each other to obtain the surplus. This is expressed in the Myerson value, which gives each of them $\frac{1}{2}$. Of course, all isolated players receive 0. Player 1 can increase his or her payoff by linking with more players with few votes, for this will decrease player 1's dependence on these other players. In a network in which the three links between players 1, 2, and 3 are formed, player 1 gets $\frac{2}{3}$, whereas players 2 and 3 get $\frac{1}{6}$ each. In a network in which the six links between players 1, 2, 3, and 4 are formed, player 1 gets $\frac{3}{4}$ whereas players 2, 3, and 4 get $\frac{1}{12}$ each. When all the players are included, player 1's payoff decreases again because now he or she is no longer essential in obtaining the surplus. In the complete network, player 1 gets $\frac{3}{5}$ and the other players get only $\frac{1}{10}$ each. Players 2, 3, 4, and 5 get more if they do not include player 1; in the network in which the six links between players 2, 3, 4, and 5 are formed, these *players get $\frac{1}{4}$ each. However, any one of these players has the highest payoff in a network in which he or she alone is linked with player 1. But players 2, 3, 4, and 5 prefer to form the six links among themselves, excluding player 1, to linking up with player 1 and at least one other player (with few votes).*

It can be shown that only networks in which all links are formed within components are supported by subgame-perfect Nash equilibria, and so I restrict attention to those. I identify the formation of all links between the players in a coalition T with the formation of coalition T.

I use backward induction to find the coalitions whose formation is supported by subgame-perfect Nash equilibria. Suppose coalition $\{1, 2, 3, 4\}$ has been formed. Then players 2 and 5 can increase their payoffs (from $\frac{1}{12}$ and 0, respectively, to $\frac{1}{10}$) by forming a link, which eventually will result in the formation of coalition N. Hence, once a coalition with player 1 and three players with few votes has been formed, the remaining links will also be formed. Now, suppose that coalition $\{1, 2, 3\}$ has been formed. It was just shown that if any one of players 1, 2, or 3 forms an additional link with players 4 or 5, this will eventually result in the formation of coalition N. This would decrease the payoff of player 1 from $\frac{2}{3}$ to $\frac{3}{5}$ and that of players 2 and 3 from $\frac{1}{6}$ to $\frac{1}{10}$. Hence, no additional links will be formed once a coalition with player 1 and two players with few votes has been formed. This implies that once coalition $\{1, 2\}$ has been formed, player 1 can permanently improve his or her payoff from $\frac{1}{2}$ to $\frac{2}{3}$ by forming a link with player 3. Because this will also improve player 3's payoff, a coalition with player 1 and one player with few votes cannot be sustained in a subgame-perfect Nash equilibrium.

Alternatively, suppose players 2, 3, 4, and 5 have formed a coalition. If one of them forms a link with player 1, eventually the complete network will be formed, decreasing his or her payoff from $\frac{1}{4}$ to $\frac{1}{10}$. Hence, no additional links will be formed once coalition $\{2, 3, 4, 5\}$ has been formed.

The preceding analysis shows that only two types of networks can possibly be supported in subgame-perfect Nash equilibria: coalitions like $\{1, 2, 3\}$ with player 1 and two players with few votes, and coalition $\{2, 3, 4, 5\}$. Note that players 2 through 5 each have a higher payoff in coalition $\{2, 3, 4, 5\}$ than in either one of the coalitions that includes player 1 and two players with few votes. This implies that players 2 through 5 will refuse to form links with player 1 and form all links with each other. Hence, coalition $\{2, 3, 4, 5\}$ will be formed in a subgame-perfect Nash equilibrium.

Aumann and Myerson (1988) mention that, in apex games with a large player who has more than one and less than q votes and several small players with one vote each, in general the complete network on a minimal winning coalition of small players will be formed in subgame-perfect Nash equilibria.

To the best of my knowledge, no general results for other types of weighted majority games have been reported in the literature. Aumann and Myerson (1988) do, however, report on two weighted majority situations with two large players each in which both the coalitions with the large players and the coalitions with one large player and all small ones are supported by subgame-perfect Nash equilibria.

The following example is due to Feinberg (1998). In response to a question posed in Aumann and Myerson (1988), this example provides a weighted majority game and a network that is not internally complete with the property that no additional links will be formed in a subgame-perfect Nash equilibrium.

Example 2.3. *Consider the eight-player weighted majority situation in which the eight players have 5, 1, 2, 2, 2, 2, 4, and 1 votes, respectively, and the quota is 12 votes. The characteristic function of the associated weighted majority game (N, v) assigns a worth of 1 to every coalition $T \subseteq N = \{1, 2, 3, 4, 5, 6, 7, 8\}$ if and only if $\sum_{i \in T} w_i \geq 12$ and a worth of 0 otherwise. Feinberg (1998) shows that in the network-formation games $\Delta^{nf}(N, v, \mu, \sigma)$ it holds that once the network (N, g) with*

$$g = g^N \setminus \{37, 47, 57, 67, 18, 48, 58, 68\}$$

has been formed, no further links will be formed by the players. In this network, the payoffs according to the Myerson value are

$$\mu(N, v, g) = \left(\frac{123}{420}, \frac{27}{420}, \frac{42}{420}, \frac{38}{420}, \frac{38}{420}, \frac{38}{420}, \frac{91}{420}, \frac{23}{420} \right).$$

The payoffs according to the Myerson value in the complete network are

$$\mu(N, v, g^N) = \left(\frac{122}{420}, \frac{22}{420}, \frac{41}{420}, \frac{41}{420}, \frac{41}{420}, \frac{41}{420}, \frac{90}{420}, \frac{22}{420} \right).$$

This shows that the complete network is preferred to network (N, g) by players 4, 5, and 6, whereas all other players prefer network (N, g) to the complete network. However, in network (N, g), players 4, 5, and 6 have already formed all links except those with players 7 and 8. Hence, players 7 and 8 can prevent players 4, 5, and 6 from forming additional links. This shows that once network (N, g) is formed, no additional links will be formed. It is still unknown whether there exists a subgame-perfect Nash equilibrium of $\Delta^{nf}(N, v, \mu, \sigma)$ that results in the formation of network (N, g) if the formation process is started from the empty network.

2.4. Network-Formation Game in Strategic Form

The simplest game of network formation in coalitional games is the strategic-form game that was mentioned briefly in Myerson (1991, 448) and studied more extensively in Dutta, van den Nouweland, and Tijs (1998). In this game, the players each independently indicate the set of other players with whom they would like to form bilateral relations. A link is then formed between two players if both of them indicate they would like to form a relation with each other. The payoffs to the players are those found by applying an exogenous allocation rule to the network that is formed in combination with the underlying coalitional game.

To describe the network-formation game in strategic form formally, let (N, v) be a coalitional game and let γ be an allocation rule for communications situations. The strategy set of player $i \in N$ is $S_i = \{T \mid T \subseteq N \setminus i\}$, where a particular strategy $s_i \in S_i$ represents the set of players with whom player i would like to form links.

If the players play a strategy tuple $s = (s_i)_{i \in N} \in \prod_{i \in N} S_i$, then a link is formed between two players i and j if and only if $j \in s_i$ and $i \in s_j$. Denote the set of all links that are formed according to this rule by $g(s)$. The network-formation game in strategic form $\Gamma^{nf}(N, v, \gamma)$ is described by the tuple $(N; (S_i)_{i \in N}; (f_i^\gamma)_{i \in N})$, where $f_i^\gamma(s) = \gamma_i(N, v, g(s))$ for each $s \in S$.

A game $\Gamma^{nf}(N, v, \gamma)$ will in general have many Nash equilibria. The reason for this is that, if a player i indicates that he or she does not want to form a link with another player j, then it does not matter for the network formed (or the payoffs) whether player j wants to form a link with player i because this link will not be formed in either case. This reasoning underlies Theorem 2.1. To state this theorem formally, I need the three logically independent properties of allocation rules for communications situations that were used in Dutta, van den Nouweland and Tijs (1998). The class of allocation rules for communications situations satisfying these three properties is reasonably large, and it contains, for example, the Myerson value on the class of communications situations with a superadditive underlying game.

Component Efficiency An allocation rule γ on a class CS of communications situations satisfies component efficiency if for every communications situation $(N, v, g) \in CS$ and every component $C \in \pi(N, g)$ it holds that $\sum_{i \in C} \gamma_i(N, v, g) = v(C)$.

Component efficiency of an allocation rule means that the players in a component distribute the value of this component among themselves.

Weak Link Symmetry An allocation rule γ on a class CS of communications situations satisfies weak link symmetry if for every communications situation $(N, v, g) \in CS$ and every link ij it holds that if $\gamma_i(N, v, g \cup ij) > \gamma_i(N, v, g)$, then $\gamma_j(N, v, g \cup ij) > \gamma_j(N, v, g)$.[8]

Weak link symmetry is a form of fairness in which the formation of a new link between two players cannot strictly benefit just one of them.

Improvement Property An allocation rule γ on a class CS of communications situations satisfies the improvement property if for every communications situation $(N, v, g) \in CS$ and every link ij it holds that if there exists a $k \in N\backslash\{i, j\}$ such that $\gamma_k(N, v, g \cup ij) > \gamma_k(N, v, g)$, then $\gamma_i(N, v, g \cup ij) > \gamma_i(N, v, g)$ or $\gamma_j(N, v, g \cup ij) > \gamma_j(N, v, g)$.

This property stipulates that the formation of a new link cannot benefit some player who is not involved in the link without also benefiting at least one of the two players forming it.

Dutta et al. (1998) have shown that any allocation rule satisfying the three preceding properties necessarily satisfies a fourth property, link monotonicity, if the underlying coalitional game is superadditive. This property states that forming an additional link can never harm a player if the allocation rule is link monotonic.

---

[8] I omit details on domains on which a rule γ is defined because the domains that are considered are always closed with respect to the operations that appear in the properties.

Link Monotonicity An allocation rule γ on a class CS of communications situations satisfies link monotonicity if for every communications situation $(N, v, g) \in CS$ and every link ij it holds that $\gamma_i(N, v, g \cup ij) \geq \gamma_i(N, v, g)$.

Even though link monotonicity plays an important and prominent role in many of the results that are obtained for network-formation games $\Gamma^{nf}(N, v, \gamma)$, Slikker and van den Nouweland (2001a) demonstrate in examples that replacing weak link symmetry by link monotonicity, even in a context in which component efficiency and the improvement property hold, will not guarantee the validity of the statements in Theorems 2.2 and 2.3. Hence, link monotonicity should be viewed as an intermediate result only, albeit one that is interesting enough to warrant highlighting it as a separate property.

If an allocation rule satisfies link monotonicity, then a player never has an incentive to change strategy to prevent the formation of one or more of his or her links.[9] This implies that any network g can be supported by a Nash equilibrium of the network-formation game, namely the strategy profile in which each agent i chooses strategy $s_i = \{j \in N \mid ij \in g\}$ indicating the will to form exactly the links in g in which he or she is involved. In this strategy profile, no single player can induce the formation of an additional link because that would require a change in strategy by two players. A single player could prevent the formation of one or more of his or her links but has no incentive to do so under link monotonicity. This shows the validity of the following theorem.

Theorem 2.1. *(Dutta et al. 1998) Let (N, v) be a superadditive coalitional game and let γ be an allocation rule on CS_v^N that satisfies component efficiency, weak link symmetry, and the improvement property. Then any network g can be supported by a Nash equilibrium of the network-formation game $\Gamma^{nf}(N, v, \gamma)$.*

A driving force behind this theorem is that it takes two players to form a link, whereas the Nash equilibrium concept allows only single-player deviations. Hence, if two players each do not indicate that they want to form a link with each other, then none of them can unilaterally cause the link to be formed even if its formation would benefit the players. There are two ways around this. One is to consider undominated Nash equilibria, and the other is to look at equilibrium refinements that allow for deviations by multiple players.

In an undominated Nash equilibrium, if the formation of a link with another player is beneficial, a player should indicate a desire to form this link even if the other player does not do so and the link will not be formed. The reason is that if the first player is not certain whether the other player will want to form the link, then he or she does not want to block the possibility of the link being formed. For a superadditive coalitional game, the restriction to undominated strategies narrows down the set of equilibria considerably. Although there may be multiple undominated Nash equilibria, they all result in the formation of a network in which the payoffs are equal to those in the complete network, $\gamma(N, v, g^N)$. The complete network g^N itself is also supported

---

[9]   Note that this shows that link monotonicity implies that the strategy $s_i = N \setminus i$ is a weakly dominant strategy for each player $i \in N$.

by an undominated Nash equilibrium, the strategy profile $\bar{s}$ defined by $\bar{s}_i = N \backslash i$ for each $i \in N$.

Theorem 2.2. *(Dutta et al. 1998) Let (N, v) be a superadditive coalitional game and let γ be an allocation rule on CS_v^N that satisfies component efficiency, weak link symmetry, and the improvement property. Then $\bar{s}$ is an undominated Nash equilibrium of the network-formation game $\Gamma^{nf}(N, v, \gamma)$. Moreover, if s is an undominated Nash equilibrium of $\Gamma^{nf}(N, v, \gamma)$, then $\gamma(N, v, g(s)) = \gamma(N, v, g^N)$.*

The most obvious equilibrium refinement that allows for deviations by multiple players is strong Nash equilibrium. However, strong Nash equilibria might not exist in the game $\Gamma^{nf}(N, v, \gamma)$, not even under fairly strong requirements on the underlying coalitional game.[10] This motivates the consideration of coalition-proof Nash equilibria, which also allow for deviations by multiple players, but these deviations are restricted to be immune to further allowed deviations themselves. It turns out that for a superadditive coalitional game (N, v), there are no existence problems for coalition-proof Nash equilibria in the network-formation game $\Gamma^{nf}(N, v, \gamma)$ because the complete network g^N is always supported by a coalition-proof Nash equilibrium. Moreover, even though there might be multiple networks supported by coalition-proof Nash equilibria, the payoffs are the same in all of these networks. This shows that, even though undominated Nash equilibria and coalition-proof Nash equilibria may lead to very different payoffs to the players for strategic-form games in general, for the strategic-form games of network formation, coalition-proof Nash equilibria lead to outcomes similar to those of undominated Nash equilibria.

Theorem 2.3. *(Dutta et al. 1998) Let (N, v) be a superadditive coalitional game and let γ be an allocation rule on CS_v^N that satisfies component efficiency, weak link symmetry, and the improvement property. Then the strategy profile $\bar{s}$ is a coalition-proof Nash equilibrium of the network-formation game $\Gamma^{nf}(N, v, \gamma)$. Moreover, if s is a coalition-proof Nash equilibrium of $\Gamma^{nf}(N, v, \gamma)$, then $\gamma(N, v, g(s)) = \gamma(N, v, g^N)$.*

A different approach is taken by Qin (1996). He has shown that for any coalitional game (N, v) and any external allocation rule γ that is component efficient, the strategic-form network-formation game $\Gamma^{nf}(N, v, \gamma)$ is a potential game if and only if $\gamma = \mu$, that is, if the exogenous allocation rule used is the Myerson value. The essence of the proof that μ is the only component-efficient allocation rule for which $\Gamma^{nf}(N, v, \gamma)$ is a potential game consists of using a potential of $\Gamma^{nf}(N, v, \gamma)$ to show that γ must satisfy fairness. In his proof of the other implication that $\Gamma^{nf}(N, v, \mu)$ is a potential game, Qin (1996) uses a kind of cyclicity property for potential games

---

[10] Slikker and van den Nouweland (2001a) show that convexity of the underlying game does not guarantee existence of strong Nash equilibria (their Example 7.4) and that balancedness is not necessary for existence (their Example 7.5).

that has been shown by Monderer and Shapley (1996) to characterize games that admit a potential. Slikker and van den Nouweland (2001a) provide a proof of this implication that uses a representation theorem by Ui (2000), who shows that there is a relation between the existence of potential functions for games in strategic form and Shapley values of coalitional games.

Because the network-formation games $\Gamma^{nf}(N, v, \mu)$ are potential games, the potential-maximizing strategy profiles provide an equilibrium refinement for them. The following theorem shows that the application of this refinement leads to results similar to those obtained for other refinements.

Theorem 2.4. *(Qin 1996) Let (N, v) be a superadditive coalitional game and let P be a potential function for the network-formation game $\Gamma^{nf}(N, v, \mu)$. Then P assumes its maximum value at $\bar{s}$. Also, if s is a strategy profile in which P is maximal, then $\mu(N, v, g(s)) = \mu(N, v, g^N)$.*

The three preceding theorems show that undominated Nash equilibrium, coalition-proof Nash equilibrium, and potential-maximizing strategies (when appropriate) all support the formation of the complete network or a network that is payoff equivalent to the complete network when the underlying coalitional game is superadditive. Hence, all three equilibrium concepts provide the same unique prediction on the ultimate payoffs of the players – namely those associated with the complete network.[11] However, these theorems do not necessarily imply that these three types of equilibria support the same networks. They leave open the possibility that a noncomplete network that is payoff equivalent to the complete network is supported by one equilibrium concept but not by the other two. Little is known about exactly which networks are supported by the various equilibrium concepts. Exceptions are Garratt and Qin (2003) and Garratt et al. (2002), who shed some light on which networks are supported by potential-maximizing strategy profiles of network-formation games $\Gamma^{nf}(N, v, \mu)$ – specifically for three-player coalitional games.

Slikker et al. (2000) analyze hypergraph-formation games in strategic form. The hypergraph-formation games they study are straightforward extensions of the strategic-form network-formation games $\Gamma^{nf}(N, v, \mu)$ to situations in which players can form multilateral relationships rather than just bilateral ones. They derive results similar to Theorems 2.1, 2.2, and 2.3 in this more general setting. In addition, they prove that hypergraph-formation games are weighted potential games (cf. Monderer and Shapley 1996) if and only if a weighted Myerson value is used as an exogenous allocation rule. Using this, they are able to derive a result similar to that of Theorem 2.4 for weighted potentials.

---

[11] I point out that pairwise stability (see Chapter 1 of this volume) does not provide the same unique predictions. Although it is true that the complete network is pairwise stable if the underlying coalitional game is superadditive, there may be networks that are not payoff equivalent to the complete network that are pairwise stable. The reason for this is that the pairwise stability concept only considers the addition of one link at a time, and this can make a smaller network pairwise stable if the addition of more than one link is necessary to increase the payoffs to the players.

2.5. Comparison of the Network-Formation Models in Extensive and Strategic Forms

The differences between the games of network formation in extensive form and the games of network formation in strategic form are illustrated by considering the three-person game (N, v) with player set $N = \{1, 2, 3\}$ in which the worth of every one-player coalition equals 0, that of every two-player coalition equals 60, and that of the three-player grand coalition equals 72. This is the same game as in Example 2.1. That example illustrated that the prediction of the network-formation game in extensive form is that a network with one link will be formed. The reason that no additional links are formed is the following. Suppose that link ij has been formed. Then it seems beneficial for player i to form a link with the third player k to increase the payoff of player i from 30 to 44 and that of player k from 0 to 14. However, this would cause a drop in player j's payoff from 30 to 14, and now players j and k would have an incentive to form the third link and increase each of their payoffs from 14 to 24. Note that the payoff of player i falls to 24 as a result of this. Hence, player i will not form the link with player k because of player j's threat to retaliate by forming a link with player k as well. Note that executing this threat is in player j's best interest. Also, if all three links are formed, both players i and j are worse off than when only link ij is formed. Hence, the network $(N, \{ij\})$ is sustained by a pair of mutual threats of the kind "If you form a link with k, then so will I." Note, however, that such mutual threats can only be effective if the negotiation process is public and player j can observe whether player i forms a link with player k. These threats lose bite if bilateral negotiations are conducted secretly or when negotiations over different links are carried out simultaneously rather than sequentially and links cannot be broken once they have been formed. In such situations, if player k starts negotiations with players i and j separately after link ij has been formed, players i and j are basically playing the following game:

	l	nl
l	24,24	44,14
nl	14,44	30,30

Here, l and nl denote the strategies of forming a link with k and not forming a link with k, respectively. In this game, it is a dominant strategy for both players i and j to form a link with k. Note that this game describes a prisoners' dilemma situation. It shows that in the network-formation game in strategic form both players i and j will form a link with player k, and the complete network will be formed simply because players i and j cannot sign a binding agreement to abstain from forming a link with k.

2.6. Network Formation with Costs for Establishing Links

The network-formation games in extensive form and strategic form that were the subject of the previous two sections do not allow for the inclusion of costs for forming links. In these models, the worth of a connected coalition of players is the same whether they are connected by a minimum number of links, by all possible links, or something in between. Slikker and van den Nouweland (2000) investigate the effects of introducing costs for forming links into the two aforementioned games of link formation. To isolate the effect that such costs have on the networks formed in equilibrium, we take these costs to be as simple as possible – namely, constant across links. A cost-extended communication situation is a tuple (N, v, g, c) in which N is a set of players, (N, v) a coalitional game, (N, g) a communications network, and $c \geq 0$ the cost for establishing a communications link.

When links are costly, the worth that a coalition of players can obtain no longer just depends on whether they are connected but also on how many links they have formed. Because costs are associated with forming additional links, players have incentives to form only as many links as necessary to connect them to others. However, forming an additional link will put a player in a more central position in a network and might increase his or her payoff. Therefore, a player needs to balance the cost of an additional link against its benefits carefully. The inclusion of costs necessitates extending the notion of an allocation rule. Slikker and van den Nouweland (2000) extend the Myerson value and use this allocation rule in the link-formation games. To obtain the worth of a coalition of players, we need to subtract the costs of the links formed by these players from the benefits they can obtain in the presence of these links. Hence, the worth of a coalition $T \subseteq N$ of players in a cost-extended communication situation (N, v, g, c) is

$$v^{g,c}(T) = \sum_{C \in \pi(T,g)} v(C) - c \, |g(T)|.$$

The cost-extended Myerson value $v(N, v, g, c)$ is the Shapley value of the associated cost-extended network-restricted game $(N, v^{g,c})$, that is,

$$v(N, v, g, c) = \Phi(N, v^{g,c}).$$

Note that $v(N, v, g, c) = \mu(N, v, g)$ whenever $c = 0$, and thus the cost-extended Myerson value is indeed an extension of the Myerson value. The cost-extended Myerson value can be interpreted in two methodologically very different ways. One is as a solution to the bargaining problem in which the players bargain over the benefits and the costs of forming links simultaneously. This interpretation arises because the cost-extended Myerson value is based on the game $(N, v^{g,c})$, which includes both the benefits and the costs of forming links. Another interpretation is that players first form links, pay the costs for forming them, and then, when a network has been formed and the costs are sunk, bargain over the division of the benefits. This interpretation stems from the fact that the cost-extended network-restricted game $(N, v^{g,c})$ can be written in terms of the network-restricted game (N, v^g) as $v^{g,c} = v^g - c \sum_{ij \in g} u_{i,j}$,[12] which implies that

$$v_i(N, v, g, c) = \mu_i(N, v, g) - \frac{1}{2} \sum_{ij \in g} c$$

---

[12] $u_{i,j}$ denotes the characteristic function of the unanimity game on coalition $\{i, j\}$ and is defined by $u_{i,j}(T) = 1$ if $\{i, j\} \subseteq T$ and $u_{i,j}(T) = 0$ otherwise, for all $T \subseteq N$.

for each player i. This shows that benefits are allocated according to the Myerson value, whereas the cost of each link is simply split between the players who form it.

Focusing on the networks rather than the players, we can define a reward function $r^{v,c}$ that assigns to each network g the net worth that the players can obtain in this network:

$$r^{v,c}(g) = \sum_{C \in \pi(N,g)} v(C) - c\,|g|.$$

Such a reward function is a special case of a value function as discussed in Chapter 1 of this volume. Slikker and van den Nouweland (2001a) prove that the cost-extended Myerson value is a special case of the Myerson value defined for such value functions in Jackson and Wolinsky (1996).

The trade-off between the costs and benefits of an additional link can be illustrated by considering a three-player, symmetric coalitional game in which the worth of every one-player coalition equals $v_1 = 0$, that of every two-player coalition equals $v_2 \geq 0$, and that of the grand coalition consisting of all three players equals $v_3 \geq 0$. Then, in a network with two links, a player who is involved in only one link has a cost-extended Myerson value $v_i(N, v, \{ij, jk\}, c) = \frac{1}{3}v_3 - \frac{1}{6}v_2 - \frac{1}{2}c$. If this player were to form a link with the other player who is involved in only one link, then the complete network would result and each player's cost-extended Myerson value would become $v_i(N, v, \{ij, ik, jk\}, c) = \frac{1}{3}v_3 - c$. Hence, player i would prefer to form this third link if and only if $c < \frac{1}{3}v_2$, in which case the extra benefit of being more central in the network ($\frac{1}{6}v_2$) outweighs the extra cost of the link ($\frac{1}{2}c$).

Using the cost-extended Myerson value, we can study the effect of costs for forming links in both the extensive-form network-formation games $\Delta^{nf}(N, v, c, \nu, \sigma)$ and the strategic-form network-formation games $\Gamma^{nf}(N, v, c, \nu)$. Slikker and van den Nouweland (2000, 2001a, 2002) provide overviews that identify which networks are supported by various equilibrium refinements of these games as the costs for forming links change. They do so for all three-player games in which the underlying coalitional games are symmetric and nonnegative. Nonnegativity basically means that cooperation is beneficial in the sense that the worth of any multiplayer coalition is at least that of the sum of the individual worths of its members. I will not reproduce these overviews here. Overviews for subgame-perfect Nash equilibria of the extensive-form games of network formation and those for undominated Nash equilibria and coalition-proof Nash equilibria of the strategic-form games of network formation were first published in Slikker and van den Nouweland (2000), and those for Nash equilibria were published in Slikker and van den Nouweland (2001a). Slikker and van den Nouweland (2002) extend earlier results to cost-extended communications situations and show that for any coalitional game (N, v), any nonnegative cost c, and any component-efficient external allocation rule γ, the strategic-form network-formation game $\Gamma^{nf}(N, v, c, \gamma)$ is a potential game if and only if $\gamma = \nu$, that is, if the exogenous allocation rule used is the cost-extended Myerson value. Hence, for the potential games $\Gamma^{nf}(N, v, c, \nu)$, potential-maximizing strategy profiles can be used as an equilibrium refinement, and Slikker and van den Nouweland

(2002) provide overviews of networks supported by potential-maximizing strategy profiles.

I discuss the most striking results.[13]

It turns out that for three-player symmetric games (N, v) the pattern of equilibrium networks as a function of changing costs for forming links depends on whether the underlying game is superadditive, convex, or both. This holds for both the extensive-form games of network formation and the strategic-form games of network formation as well as for all of the equilibrium concepts studied. It is well known that a convex game is superadditive, whereas the reverse implication is not true in general. Hence, with respect to the network-formation games with costs for forming links, three types of underlying games need to be considered. They are nonsuperadditive games, superadditive games that are not convex, and convex games.

In strategic-form network-formation games, undominated Nash equilibrium, coalition-proof Nash equilibrium, and potential-maximizing strategy profiles provide the most useful predictions. Surprisingly, it turns out that for these games the predictions of coalition-proof Nash equilibrium refine those of undominated Nash equilibrium at the network level.[14] Also, the patterns of networks supported by potential-maximizing strategies are almost exactly the same as those for the coalition-proof Nash equilibrium.[15] Therefore, I concentrate on networks supported by coalition-proof Nash equilibria. These are as follows. For all underlying coalitional games, the complete network is supported for very low costs of link formation,[16] and the empty network (in which there are no links and, hence, every player is isolated) is supported for very high costs. It is for intermediate cost levels that the predictions depend on the structure of the underlying coalitional game.[17] If that game is nonsuperadditive, then for intermediate cost levels the formation of exactly one link is supported. If the underlying game is convex, networks with two links are supported for intermediate cost levels. Finally, if the coalitional game is superadditive but not convex, networks with two links are supported for lower costs, whereas for higher costs the formation of only one link is supported.

In extensive-form network-formation games, subgame-perfect Nash equilibrium is the most appropriate solution concept. The networks supported by subgame-perfect Nash equilibria are as follows. If the underlying coalitional game is non-superadditive, then for low costs only networks with one link are supported, whereas for high costs only the empty network results. Networks with more than one link are not supported for any level of the costs if the game is not superadditive. For convex coalitional games, the complete network is supported for very low costs,

---

[13] I remind the reader that the results discussed cover three-player coalitional games that are symmetric, zero-normalized, and nonnegative.

[14] Note that coalition-proof Nash equilibrium is not a refinement of undominated Nash equilibrium on the strategy level, not even for the class of strategic-form network-formation games.

[15] The only difference appears for nonsuperadditive games, where the level of the cost at which the transition from the complete network to networks with one link occurs is higher for the potential-maximizing strategy profiles than for coalition-proof Nash equilibria.

[16] If the game is nonsuperadditive, then the cutoff for "very low" costs might be negative, in which case the complete network is not supported for any nonnegative cost c.

[17] The levels of costs that are considered intermediate vary with the structure of the coalitional game.

networks with two links are supported for intermediate costs, and the empty network is supported for very high costs. The most interesting case turns out to be that of nonconvex superadditive coalitional games. For such games, the number of links whose formation is supported by coalition-proof Nash equilibria varies with the costs of forming links in a nonmonotonic way. For very low costs, networks with three links are supported.[18] For somewhat higher costs, networks with one link are supported. Then, if the costs increase from there, networks with two links are supported (thus an increase in the costs results in the formation of *more* links). If the costs keep increasing, the number of links formed in equilibrium decreases again. First, networks with one link are supported, whereas for very high costs the empty network (with 0 links) is supported.

The following example illustrates that an increase in the cost for establishing a communications link can result in more communication between the players in subgame-perfect Nash equilibria of the extensive-form game of network formation.

Example 2.4. *Let (N, v) be the three-player symmetric game (N, v) in which the worth of every one-player coalition equals 0, that of every two-player coalition equals 60, and that of the three-player grand coalition equals 72. Note that this game is superadditive but not convex. It is the same game that was studied in Example 2.1, where it was shown that if the cost for forming links is 0, only networks with one link are supported by subgame-perfect Nash equilibria. For low costs of forming links (to be precise, for $c < 20$), the discussion in Example 2.1 is still valid as is its conclusion that exactly one link will be formed.*

But the analysis changes if the costs are larger. I demonstrate this for $c = 22$. With these costs, the cost-extended Myerson values are as follows. An isolated player (one who does not form any links) gets 0. In a network with one link, the two players who have formed this link each get 19 (which is one-half of the revenue of 60 minus the cost of the link). In a network with two links, the central player (who has formed two links) gets 22, whereas the other two players each get 3. In the complete network, each player gets 2 (which is one-third of the revenue of 72 minus the cost of the three links).

The higher costs change the incentives of the players. In a network with two links, the two players who have not formed a link with each other have no incentive to do so because that would reduce their payoffs from 3 to 2. Then, in a network with one link, a player who is involved in this link has an incentive also to form a link with the isolated player. Doing this will increase his or her payoff (from 19 to 22) and, unlike for lower levels of the costs, there is no threat of the third link's being formed later on. Clearly, at least one link will be formed, so that some players will receive a strictly positive payoff. It follows that networks with two links are supported by subgame-perfect Nash equilibria if the costs are equal to 22. Note that this means that the increase of the cost, from 19 to 22 for instance, results in the formation of two links rather than one.

---

[18] For some games in this class the cutoff for "very low" costs might be negative, in which case the complete network is not supported for any nonnegative cost c.

The equilibrium concept for network-formation games in strategic form that is most similar in spirit to subgame perfection is undominated Nash equilibrium. However, there is a multiplicity of networks resulting from undominated Nash equilibria in the strategic-form network-formation games and coalition-proof Nash equilibrium provides a further refinement of these predictions. Therefore, a comparison of the cost-network patterns for subgame-perfect Nash equilibria in the network-formation games in extensive form with those for coalition-proof Nash equilibria in the network-formation games in strategic form is appropriate. The predictions according to subgame-perfect Nash equilibrium in the games in extensive form and those according to coalition-proof Nash equilibrium in the games in strategic form are remarkably similar. For convex games, the predictions in the extensive-form games and those in the strategic-form games are the same for all levels of the costs of link formation. For nonsuperadditive games, the predictions in both network-formation games are almost the same. The only difference is that the level of the costs that marks the transition from the complete network to a network with one link is possibly positive in the strategic-form game, whereas it is always negative (and therefore does not show up in the overview) in the extensive-form games.[19] The predictions of both types of network-formation games are most dissimilar if the underlying coalitional game is superadditive but not convex. In the extensive-form game a network with one link is supported if the costs are fairly low, but not very low, whereas in the strategic-form game for the same level of costs the complete network is supported. For all other levels of the cost, the predictions of both games are the same. The difference between the predictions of both network-formation games is a result of the validity of mutual threats in the network-formation game in extensive form, as discussed in Section 2.5, which is applicable to all games that are superadditive but not convex. These mutual threats also drive the remarkable result that higher costs may result in the formation of more links in the extensive-form network-formation game. Mutual threats will only be credible for lower costs because for higher costs a player who executes such a threat will permanently decrease his or her payoff.

For games with more than three players, it is no longer true that the pattern of networks formed in equilibrium depends only on whether a game is superadditive, convex, or both. Slikker and van den Nouweland (2000) illustrate this with two examples of symmetric four-player games that are superadditive but not convex and for which the patterns of equilibrium networks as a function of the cost of forming links are different. However, the most interesting result obtained for symmetric three-player games (namely that in the network-formation games in extensive form it is possible that the number of links formed in subgame-perfect Nash equilibria increases as the cost for establishing links increases) is still valid for games with more than three players. Slikker and van den Nouweland (2000) illustrate this in an example of a four-player game and also for n-player games with n odds. In contrast, Slikker and van den Nouweland (2002) extend the result that in strategic-form

---

[19] This level of the cost is higher and always positive if potential-maximizing strategies are used in the strategic-form games of network formation.

network-formation games the number of links formed in potential-maximizing strategy profiles decreases as the costs for forming links increase. They prove this for coalitional games with an arbitrary number of players that are not necessarily symmetric.

2.7. Simultaneous Bargaining over Network Formation and Payoff Division

In the three previous sections, an exogenous allocation rule was used to determine the payoffs to the players in various networks. This can be interpreted as network formation and bargaining occurring in two sequential stages; the first stage is the network-formation stage, and in the second stage the players bargain over payoffs given the network formed in the first stage. The second stage is collapsed into an exogenous allocation rule that provides the predicted outcome of the process of bargaining over payoffs. In contrast, Slikker and van den Nouweland (2001b)[20] study a model of network formation in which players bargain over the formation of links and the division of the payoffs simultaneously. In such a model, the use of an exogenous allocation rule is no longer justified. The link and claim game provides an integrated approach to network formation and payoff division. As in the games of network formation in extensive and strategic forms of Sections 2.3 and 2.4, the link and claim game is built around a coalitional game (N, v) describing the possibilities of cooperating coalitions of players. To keep notations as simple as possible, we assume the game is zero-normalized, that is, $v(i) = 0$ for each player $i \in N$. The link and claim game $\Gamma^{lc}(N, v)$ is a strategic-form game $(N; (S_i)_{i \in N}; (f_i)_{i \in N})$ with strategies and payoff functions as described immediately below. The strategy set of player i is

$$S_i = \{c^i \in A^N \mid c_i^i = P\},$$

where $A := \mathbb{R}_+ \cup \{P\}$, $\mathbb{R}_+ = [0, \infty)$, and P stands for Pass. A strategy for player i specifies a $c_j^i \in \mathbb{R}_+ \cup \{P\}$ for any player $j \in N$. The interpretation of $c_j^i = P$ is that player i is not willing to form a link with player j, and $c_j^i \in \mathbb{R}_+$ means that player i is willing to form a link with player j provided that he or she gets the amount c_j^i claimed for forming it. Because player i cannot form a link with himself, it is assumed that $c_i^i = P$ for all $c^i \in S_i$. Suppose the players play strategy profile $c = (c^i)_{i \in N} \in \prod_{i \in N} S_i$. The resulting payoffs to the players depend on the network that is formed. According to strategy profile c, the set $l(c)$ of links that the players are willing to form is

$$l(c) = \{ij \mid c_i^j, c_j^i \in \mathbb{R}_+\}$$

because the consent of both players is needed to form the link between them. However, the claims of the players for forming these links might add up to more than is available. Hence, it needs to be determined which of the links in $l(c)$ carry feasible

---

[20] Most results in this section are taken from Slikker and van den Nouweland (2001b). However, they also appear in Chapter 9 in Slikker and van den Nouweland (2001a), where they are presented more extensively and where the proofs are clearer in my opinion.

claims. Network $(N, l(c))$ partitions the player set into components. For every such component, the links in $l(c)$ between its members can only be formed if the total of the claims for these links does not exceed the worth of the coalition. Hence, the set $g(c)$ of links that are formed equals

$$g(c) = \{ij \in l(c) \mid \sum_{km \in l(c): k, m \in C_i(l(c))} (c_m^k + c_k^m) \leq v(C_i(l(c)))\},$$

where $C_i(l(c))$ denotes the component of network $(N, l(c))$ that contains player i. This construction of $g(c)$ implies that if the players in a component of $(N, l(c))$ collectively claim too much, they all end up being isolated.[21] The payoffs to the players can be found by adding their claims for the links that are actually formed:

$$f_i(c) = \sum_{j: ij \in g(c)} c_j^i. \text{[22]}$$

Note that this gives an isolated player his or her stand-alone payoff of zero.

The link and claim game $\Gamma^{lc}(N, v)$ is illustrated in the following example.

Example 2.5. *Let (N, v) be the three-person coalitional game with $N = \{1, 2, 3\}$ and characteristic function v with $v(T) = 0$ if $|T| = 1$, $v(T) = 30$ if $|T| = 2$, and $v(T) = 72$ if $T = N$. Consider the strategy profile*

$$c = (c^1, c^2, c^3) = ((P, 10, 10), (10, P, 10), (P, 10, P))$$

in the link and claim game $\Gamma^{lc}(N, v)$. The link between players 1 and 3 is not in $l(c)$ because, although player 1 would like to form this link ($c_3^1 = 10 \in \mathbb{R}_+$), player 3 does not ($c_1^3 = P$). Link 12 is in $l(c)$ because both players 1 and 2 want to form it. Proceeding in this way, we find that $l(c) = \{12, 23\}$. The network $(N, l(c))$ has one component, $\pi(N, l(c)) = \{\{1, 2, 3\}\}$. The total of the payoffs claimed for forming the links in $l(c)$ equals $c_2^1 + c_1^2 + c_3^2 + c_2^3 = 40 \leq 72 = v(N)$. Because these claims are feasible for coalition N, all links in $l(c)$ are formed and $g(c) = \{12, 23\}$. The corresponding payoffs to the players are $f_1(c) = c_2^1 = 10$, $f_2(c) = c_1^2 + c_3^2 = 20$, and $f_3(c) = c_2^3 = 10$.

The profile $\hat{c} = ((P, 20, 20), (20, P, P), (P, 20, P))$ is an example of a strategy profile in which the players claim too much for all the links in $l(\hat{c})$ to be formed. It holds that $l(\hat{c}) = \{12\}$ and $\hat{c}_2^1 + \hat{c}_1^2 = 40 > 30 = v(1, 2)$. Hence, $g(\hat{c}) = \emptyset$ and $f_i(\hat{c}) = 0$ for every $i \in N$.

For link and claim games the question is not only which networks are supported by (refinements of) Nash equilibria but also which payoff vectors are supported. For any coalitional game (N, v) it holds that a strategy profile in $\Gamma^{lc}(N, v)$ is not a Nash equilibrium if it results in the formation of a network containing a cycle and if at least one player claims a positive amount on one of the links in the cycle. A cycle is a path $i_1, i_2, ..., i_{t+1}$ in which $i_1, i_2, ..., i_t$ are all different players and $i_{t+1} = i_1$.

---

[21] See Slikker and van den Nouweland (2001a) for a discussion of alternative approaches.

[22] Note that this definition leaves open the possibility that the players claim less than what is available. This, however, will never happen in a Nash equilibrium and so it does not really matter whether the remainder is burned (as is the case for the expression that I provide here) or, for example, divided evenly among the players.

Theorem 2.5. *(Slikker and van den Nouweland 2001b) Let (N, v) be a zero-normalized coalitional game. For every Nash equilibrium c in the link and claim game $\Gamma^{lc}(N, v)$ it holds that all claims on links in cycles in $g(c)$ are equal to zero.*

I illustrate this theorem in the following example.

Example 2.6. *Consider the three-player game (N, v) in Example 2.5. The complete network is the only possible one for the three players that contains a cycle. This network can only be formed if the players play a strategy profile c with $c_j^i \in I\!R_+$ for each $i, j \in N$, $i \neq j$, and $c_2^1 + c_3^1 + c_1^2 + c_3^2 + c_1^3 + c_2^3 \leq 72$. If c is a Nash equilibrium of $\Gamma^{lc}(N, v)$, then no player can gain from unilaterally deviating to a strategy in which he simply raises one of his claims. Hence, $c_2^1 + c_3^1 + c_1^2 + c_3^2 + c_1^3 + c_2^3 = 72$ has to hold. Without loss of generality, assume that $c_2^1 > 0$, and thus player 1 gets a positive amount for forming link 12. Player 2 can increase his payoff by refusing to form link 12 and claiming the amount c_2^1 for himself by playing strategy $\hat{c}^2 = (P, P, c_1^2 + c_3^2 + c_2^1)$. Then network $(N, \{13, 23\})$ will be formed and the players can still obtain $v(N) = 72$. Hence, $f_2(c_1, \hat{c}_2, c_3) = c_1^2 + c_3^2 + c_2^1 > c_1^2 + c_3^2 = f_2(c)$. This demonstrates that player 2 has a profitable deviation from c, and therefore c is not a Nash equilibrium.*

Theorem 2.5 implies that for a zero-normalized coalitional game (N, v) with at least three players and a positive value for the grand coalition $(v(N) > 0)$, Nash equilibria do not support the formation of the complete network. Therefore, attention is shifted to connected networks. As is argued in Example 2.6, if a connected network is formed in a Nash equilibrium, then the payoffs must be efficient for the underlying coalitional game, that is, sum up to $v(N)$. Slikker and van den Nouweland (2001b) prove that, in general, a plethora of efficient payoff vectors are supported by Nash equilibria of the link and claim game $\Gamma^{lc}(N, v)$.[23] One of their main results is that all payoffs in the core are supported by Nash equilibria. The core of a coalitional game (N, v) consists of all efficient payoff vectors such that the members of each coalition $T \subseteq N$ collectively get at least the worth $v(T)$ that they can obtain independently of the players not included in the coalition; $\text{core}(N, v) = \{x \in I\!R^N \mid \sum_{i \in T} x_i \geq v(T)$ for all $T \subseteq N$ and $\sum_{i \in N} x_i = v(N)\}$.

Theorem 2.6. *(Slikker and van den Nouweland 2001b) For any zero-normalized coalitional game (N, v) it holds that for every payoff vector $x \in core(N, v)$ there exists a Nash equilibrium c of the link and claim game $\Gamma^{lc}(N, v)$ such that $f(c) = x$.*

Because Nash equilibrium itself supports very many payoff vectors, focus is shifted to strong Nash equilibria in an attempt to generate clearer predictions. An example shows that strong Nash equilibria of the link and claim game may support payoff vectors that are not efficient for the underlying coalitional game.

Example 2.7. *Let (N, v) be the four-person coalitional game with player set $N = \{1, 2, 3, 4\}$ and characteristic function v with $v(T) = 0$ if $|T| = 1$, $v(T) = 2$ if $|T| = 2$ or $|T| = 3$, and $v(T) = 3$ if $T = N$. The strategy profile c with*

---

[23] A Nash equilibrium c supports payoff vector x if $f(c) = x$.

$c^1 = (P, 1, P, P)$, $c^2 = (1, P, P, P)$, $c^3 = (P, P, P, 1)$, and $c^4 = (P, P, 1, P)$ is a strong Nash equilibrium of $\Gamma^{lc}(N, v)$. It results in the formation of the network $(N, \{12, 34\})$ and payoff vector $f(c) = (1, 1, 1, 1)$. This payoff vector is not efficient for the game (N, v) because the sum of the payoffs equals 4 whereas the worth of the grand coalition equals only 3.

The result in the previous example occurs because a partition of the player set into coalitions exists such that the sum of the worths of these coalitions is larger than the worth of the grand coalition. Slikker and van den Nouweland (2001b) show that if the game (N, v) is such that a partition with this property does not exist, then every strong Nash equilibrium of the link and claim game $\Gamma^{lc}(N, v)$ results in a payoff vector that is not only efficient but also in the core of the coalitional game (N, v). This, of course, implies that for such a coalitional game the set of strong Nash equilibria of $\Gamma^{lc}(N, v)$ is empty if the core of (N, v) is empty. The following example illustrates that not all payoff vectors in the core are necessarily supported by strong Nash equilibria.

Example 2.8. *Consider the coalitional game (N, v) with player set $N = \{1, 2, 3\}$ and $v(T) = 0$ if $|T| = 1$, $v(1, 2) = 120$, $v(1, 3) = 60$, $v(2, 3) = 80$, and $v(N) = 180$. Payoff vector $(60, 60, 60)$ is in the core of this game. I will show that there is no strong Nash equilibrium that results in payoff vector $(60, 60, 60)$ by demonstrating that every Nash equilibrium that supports this payoff vector cannot be strong. Suppose that c is a Nash equilibrium of $\Gamma^{lc}(N, v)$ such that $f(c) = (60, 60, 60)$. It follows from Theorem 2.5 that $(N, g(c))$ must have two links.*

Suppose that $g(c) = \{12, 23\}$. Together with $f(c) = (60, 60, 60)$, this implies that $c^2 = (c_1^2, P, 60 - c_1^2)$ for some $0 \le c_1^2 \le 60$, $c^1 = (P, 60, c_3^1)$, and $c^3 = (c_1^3, 60, P)$, where either $c_3^1 = P$ or $c_1^3 = P$ (or both). Because $f_2(c) = 60$, either $c_1^2 > 0$ or $c_3^2 = 60 - c_1^2 > 0$ (or both). Without loss of generality, assume that $c_3^2 > 0$. Strategy profile c is not a strong Nash equilibrium because players 1 and 3 can increase their payoffs by deviating to strategies $(\hat{c}^1, \hat{c}^3)$ defined by $\hat{c}^1 = (P, 60, \frac{c_3^2}{2})$ and $\hat{c}^3 = (60 + \frac{c_3^2}{2}, P, P)$. The strategy profile $(\hat{c}^1, c^2, \hat{c}^3)$ results in the formation of links 12 and 13 and payoff vector $(60 + \frac{c_3^2}{2}, c_1^2, 60 + \frac{c_3^2}{2})$, which means that players 1 and 3 both improved their payoffs through the deviation.

It can be demonstrated in a similar manner that c is not a strong Nash equilibrium if $g(c) = \{12, 13\}$ or $g(c) = \{13, 23\}$. This shows that there is no strong Nash equilibrium of $\Gamma^{lc}(N, v)$ that supports payoff vector $(60, 60, 60)$.

The reasoning above exploits the feature of the payoff vector $(60, 60, 60)$ that all its elements are positive, and thus any strategy profile c that supports this payoff vector leads to a middleman who gets a positive payoff. This idea can be extended and leads to the conclusion that none of the payoff vectors in which all coordinates are positive can be supported by a strong Nash equilibrium. For a payoff vector in the core such as $(70, 110, 0)$, in which one of the players has a payoff of zero, reasoning similar to that used previously cannot be applied. Indeed, the payoff vector $(70, 110, 0)$ is supported by the strong Nash equilibrium c in which $c^1 = (P, P, 70)$, $c^2 = (P, P, 110)$, and $c^3 = (0, 0, P)$.

The results in Example 2.8 hold in general. The following theorem identifies the payoff vectors that are supported by strong Nash equilibria of the link and claim game. The first part identifies a class of games for which the set of payoff vectors supported by strong Nash equilibria coincides with the core of the underlying coalitional game, and the second part describes a class of games for which the payoff vectors supported by strong Nash equilibria are all the payoff vectors in the core in which at least one of the players receives a zero payoff.

Theorem 2.7. *(Slikker and van den Nouweland 2001b) Let (N, v) be a zero-normalized coalitional game with the property that $v(N) \geq \sum_{k=1}^{t} v(B_k)$ for all partitions $\{B_1, \ldots, B_t\}$ of N, and let $\Gamma^{lc}(N, v)$ be the corresponding link and claim game.*

(i) If there exists a partition $\{B_1, \ldots, B_t\}$ of N such that $|B_k| = 2$ for all $k \in \{1, \ldots, t\}$ and $v(N) = \sum_{k=1}^{t} v(B_k)$, then

$$\{f(c) \mid c \text{ is a strong Nash equilibrium of } \Gamma^{lc}(N, v)\} = core(N, v).$$

(ii) If $v(N) > \sum_{k=1}^{t} v(B_k)$ for all partitions $\{B_1, \ldots, B_t\}$ of N in which $|B_k| = 2$ for each $k \in \{1, \ldots, t\}$[24], then

$$\{f(c) \mid c \text{ is a strong Nash equilibrium of } \Gamma^{lc}(N, v)\} =$$

$$\{x \in core(N, v) \mid \text{there exists a player } i \in N \text{ such that } x_i = 0\}.$$

Theorem 2.7 shows that, although strong Nash equilibria of the link and claim games often exist, the strong Nash equilibrium concept seems quite restrictive because it results in at least one of the players receiving a payoff of zero for a large class of coalitional games. One of the players receiving a zero payoff might even be the central player in a star. The reason that the payoff of a player in such a central position is kept low in a strong Nash equilibrium is that other players can avoid having to communicate through him or her by forming new links between themselves. However, such deviations are not necessarily stable against further deviations. This motivates the consideration of coalition-proof Nash equilibria. The following example demonstrates how the requirement that deviations be self-enforcing prevents the players from making certain deviations, and thus some strategies that are not stable against arbitrary deviations become sustainable.

Example 2.9. *Consider the coalitional game (N, v) in Example 2.8 and payoff vector $x = (60, 60, 60)$, which is in the core of (N, v) but not supported by a strong Nash equilibrium of the associated link and claim game $\Gamma^{lc}(N, v)$. Consider strategy profile c defined by $c^1 = (P, 60, P)$, $c^2 = (0, P, 60)$, and $c^3 = (P, 60, P)$, for which $g(c) = \{12, 23\}$ and $f(c) = x$. It is shown in the remainder of this example that c is a coalition-proof Nash equilibrium of $\Gamma^{lc}(N, v)$, which demonstrates that x is supported by a coalition-proof Nash equilibrium.*

It is easily seen that c is a Nash equilibrium because no player can unilaterally deviate to a strategy that gives him or her a higher payoff. Further, there are no

---

[24] Note that this condition is trivially satisfied for a game (N, v) with an odd number of players.

*deviations by coalition N that increase the payoffs of all players as $x_1 + x_2 + x_3 =$
$180 = v(N)$. Hence, to prove that c is a coalition-proof Nash equilibrium, it suffices
to show that there are no profitable deviations by two-player coalitions that are
stable against further deviations by members of the deviating coalition.*

*Start by considering a deviation by coalition $\{1, 2\}$. When c is played, players 1
and 2 together receive 120, which is the worth of coalition $\{1, 2\}$. Hence, to improve
their payoffs, players 1 and 2 need to deviate to a strategy profile that results in
the formation of at least one link with player 3. Because player 3 is still playing
strategy $(P, 60, P)$, this will have to be link 23, and player 3 will still receive 60 after
the deviation by coalition $\{1, 2\}$. But then players 1 and 2 together cannot obtain
more than $v(N) - 60 = 120 = x_1 + x_2$ after the deviation, and thus they cannot
both improve their payoffs. Similar arguments show that there are no profitable
deviations by coalition $\{2, 3\}$.*

*It remains to consider deviations by coalition $\{1, 3\}$. Because $x_1 + x_3 = 120 >$
$v(1, 3)$, any profitable deviation by players 1 and 3 has to result in the formation of
a connected network. To improve their payoffs, players 1 and 3 have to break a link
with player 2 on which player 2 has a positive claim. Hence, link 23 will be broken.
This is represented by the strategies*

$$\hat{c}^1 = (P, \hat{c}^1_2, \hat{c}^1_3) \qquad with \quad \hat{c}^1_2 + \hat{c}^1_3 = 60 + 60\alpha, 0 < \alpha < 1,$$
$$\hat{c}^3 = (60 + 60\beta, P, P) \quad with \quad 0 < \beta \leq 1 - \alpha.$$

*However, player 1 can deviate from strategy profile $(\hat{c}^1, c^2, \hat{c}^3)$ by playing $\tilde{c}^1 =$
$(P, 120, P)$, which induces the formation of network $(N, \{12\})$ and improves his or
her payoff from $60 + 60\alpha$ to $120 = v(1, 2) - c_1^2$. Because $\tilde{c}^1$ is a coalition-proof
Nash equilibrium in the reduced game that emerges when the strategies of players 2
and 3 are fixed to c^2 and $\hat{c}^3$, respectively, it follows that deviation $(\hat{c}^1, \hat{c}^3)$ is not
self-enforcing. We conclude that c is coalition-proof Nash equilibrium of $\Gamma^{lc}(N, v)$.*

Slikker and van den Nouweland (2001a) provide a description of all coalition-
proof Nash equilibria of the link and claim game $\Gamma^{lc}(N, v)$ and corresponding
payoffs for coalitional games (N, v) with three players. A remarkable result is that
for some coalitional games with a nonempty core, some efficient payoff vectors that
are not in the core of the game are nevertheless supported by coalition-proof Nash
equilibria. For the game (N, v) of Examples 2.8 and 2.9, the efficient payoff vector
$(100, 10, 70)$ is supported by the coalition-proof Nash equilibrium $c = (c^1, c^2, c^3)$
defined by $c^1 = (P, P, 100)$, $c^2 = (P, P, 10)$, and $c^3 = (70, 0, P)$,[25] but it is not
in the core of (N, v) (players 1 and 2 get less than $v(1, 2)$). The results in Slikker
and van den Nouweland (2001a) also imply that there exist coalition-proof Nash
equilibria of the link and claim game $\Gamma^{lc}(N, v)$ that result in efficient payoff vectors
even if the core of the game (N, v) is empty as long as $v(T) \leq v(N)$ for at least one
two-player coalition T.

Slikker (2000) shows that all the results obtained in Slikker and van den
Nouweland (2001a) on coalition-proof Nash equilibria still hold for something

---

[25] See Lemma 9.2 in Slikker and van den Nouweland (2001a).

he calls adjusted coalition-proof Nash equilibria. Adjusted coalition-proof Nash equilibrium is similar to coalition-proof Nash equilibrium, but it limits the size of deviating coalitions to be less than or equal to 2. This is an especially appealing limitation in a setting of network formation, where each link is formed by two players and a single player can break links.

2.8. Related Literature

In this chapter I have discussed the literature on the formation of networks in coalitional games. A coalitional game describes the possible gains from cooperation for all coalitions of players. The question of which coalitions will be formed by the players in a coalitional game is still largely unresolved. Models of network formation in coalitional games approach this question by adding structure to the game and thereby making it possible to consider bilateral cooperation that facilitates cooperation by larger coalitions of players. A network is a collection of bilateral relations between the players, and as such networks can be viewed as a generalization of coalition structures in the sense that a coalition of players can be identified with a network in which all the members of the coalition have formed bilateral links with each other. Hence, a coalition structure is a collection of complete networks. This is formalized in Slikker and van den Nouweland (2001a), who show that the value for games with coalition structures introduced in Aumann and Drèze (1974) coincides with the value for games with networks introduced in Myerson (1977) for the networks that model the coalition structures as just described. Networks are more general than coalition structures because they allow for nontransitivity of bilateral relations. This opens up the possibility of modeling communication between players who have no direct relation but who do have indirect relations via other players who act as intermediates. Just as in the case of coalition structures, players who have no direct or indirect relations cannot effectively communicate and hence cannot cooperate. For players who can communicate, the worth that they can obtain by cooperating is modeled by a coalitional game. In this approach, the value of a network primarily depends on which players it connects with one another (directly or indirectly) and not on how exactly it connects these players (the only exception being a model in which links are costly, see Section 2.6). Hence, issues such as the deterioration of information as it travels along longer paths are not taken into account. When we want to take these types of issues into account, we end up with models in which the worth of players in networks is given by a value function rather than derived from a coalitional game. The literature on networks with value functions is covered in Chapter 1 of this volume. Also, the approach based on coalitional games precludes externalities between different groups of interconnected players. Currarini (2002) looks at the formation of networks in situations in which such externalities can exist.[26]

---

[26] All of these papers look at static models of network formation. For a survey of the research on learning in networks I refer the reader to Chapter 4 of this volume.

There is a lively literature on the tensions between stability of networks and their efficiency in the sense of overall payoff maximization. Chapter 1 of this volume includes a discussion of this literature. Mostly, the models that I discuss illustrate this tension, which was shown in Jackson and Wolinsky (1996) to be quite pervasive even in settings of more general value functions than those based on coalitional games.

In this chapter, I concentrated on the basic models of network formation in which players form bilateral relations that are deterministic and symmetric and in which the possibilities of coalitions of players are given by a coalitional game with transferable utility. I believe that most of the issues that arise when studying network formation in coalitional games do so for this basic model. I refer the reader to Myerson (1980); van den Nouweland, Borm, and Tijs (1992); and Slikker et al. (2000) for extensions to situations in which players can form multilateral relations; to Calvo, Lasaga, and van den Nouweland (1999) for extensions to situations in which bilateral relations are not deterministic; to Slikker and van den Nouweland (2001a) and Casas-Méndez and Prada-Sánchez (2003) for situations in which utilities are not transferable; and to Slikker and Gilles et al. (2000) for situations in which players form relations that are not symmetric. For a much more elaborate treatment of the subject of network formation in coalitional games than I could provide in this survey, I refer the reader to Slikker and van den Nouweland (2001a), where the reader will also find most of the proofs I have omitted in this chapter.

BIBLIOGRAPHY

[1] Aumann, R. (1959), "Acceptable Points in General Cooperative *n*-Person Games," in A. Tucker and R. Luce (eds.), *Contributions to the Theory of Games IV*, Princeton University Press, pp. 287–324.

[2] Aumann, R. and J. Drèze (1974), "Cooperative Games with Coalition Structures," *International Journal of Game Theory* 3, 217–237.

[3] Aumann, R. and R. Myerson (1988), "Endogenous Formation of Links between Players and Coalitions: An Application of the Shapley Value," in A. Roth (ed.), *The Shapley Value*, Cambridge University Press, pp. 175–191.

[4] Bernheim, D., B. Peleg, and M. Whinston (1987), "Coalition-Proof Nash Equilibria I: Concepts," *Journal of Economic Theory* 42, 1–12.

[5] Borm, P., G. Owen, and S. Tijs (1992), "On the Position Value for Communication Situations," *SIAM Journal on Discrete Mathematics* 5, 305–320.

[6] Calvo, E., J. Lasaga, and A. van den Nouweland (1999), "Values of Games with Probabilistic Graphs," *Mathematical Social Sciences* 37, 79–95.

[7] Casas-Méndez, B. and J. Prada-Sánchez (2003), "On the Properties of Solutions for NTU Communication Situations," *Mathematical Methods of Operations Research* 58, 417–439.

[8] Currarini, S. (2002), "Stable Organizations with Externalities," Working Paper downloaded from http://www.grandcoalition.com/people/currarini.html.

[9] Dutta, B. and M. O. Jackson (2003), "On the Formation of Networks and Groups," in B. Dutta and M. O. Jackson (eds.), *Networks and Groups; Models of Strategic Formation*, Springer-Verlag, pp. 1–16.

[10] Dutta, B., A. van den Nouweland, and S. Tijs (1998), "Link Formation in Cooperative Situations," *International Journal of Game Theory* 27, 245–256.

[11] Feinberg, Y. (1998), "An Incomplete Cooperation Structure for a Voting Game Can Be Strategically Stable," *Games and Economic Behavior* 24, 2–9.

[12] Garratt, R., J. Parco, C. Qin, and A. Rapoport (2002), "Potential Maximization and Coalition Government Formation," Working Paper downloaded from http://www.econ.ucsb.edu/~garratt/faculty/garratt.htm.

[13] Garratt, R. and C. Qin (2003), "On Cooperation Structures Resulting from Simultaneous Proposals," *Economics Bulletin* 3, 1–9

[14] Jackson, M. O. and A. van den Nouweland (2001), "Strongly Stable Networks," Working Paper 2001-3, Department of Economics, University of Oregon. To appear in *Games and Economic Behavior*.

[15] Jackson, M. O. and A. Wolinsky (1996), "A Strategic Model of Social and Economic Networks," *Journal of Economic Theory* 71, 44–74.

[16] Monderer, D. and L. Shapley (1996), "Potential Games," *Games and Economic Behavior* 14, 124–143.

[17] Myerson, R. (1977), "Graphs and Cooperation in Games," *Mathematics of Operations Research* 2, 225–229.

[18] Myerson, R. (1980), "Conference Structures and Fair Allocation Rules," *International Journal of Game Theory* 9, 169–182.

[19] Myerson, R. (1991), *Game Theory: Analysis of Conflict*, Cambridge, MA: Harvard University Press.

[20] Nash, J. (1950), "Equilibrium Points in *n*-Person Games," *Proceedings of the National Academy of Sciences* 36, 48–49.

[21] Qin, C. (1996), "Endogenous Formation of Cooperation Structures," *Journal of Economic Theory* 69, 218–226.

[22] Shapley, L. (1953), "A Value for *n*-Person Games," in A. Tucker and H. Kuhn (eds.), *Contributions to the Theory of Games II*, Princeton University Press, pp. 307–317.

[23] Slikker, M. (2000), *Decision Making and Cooperation Restrictions,* Ph.D. Thesis, Tilburg University, Tilburg, The Netherlands.

[24] Slikker, M. (2003), "A Characterization of the Position Value," BETA Working Paper WP-96, Technische Universiteit Eindhoven, The Netherlands.

[25] Slikker, M., B. Dutta, A. van den Nouweland, and S. Tijs (2000), "Potential Maximizers and Network Formation," *Mathematical Social Sciences* 39, 55–70.

[26] Slikker, M., R. Gilles, H. Norde, and S. Tijs (2000), "Directed Communication Networks," CentER Discussion Paper 2000-84, Tilburg University, Tilburg, The Netherlands.

[27] Slikker, M. and H. Norde (2000), "Incomplete Stable Structures in Symmetric Convex Games," CentER Discussion Paper 2000-97, Tilburg University, Tilburg, The Netherlands. To appear in *Games and Economic Behavior*.

[28] Slikker, M. and A. van den Nouweland (2000), "Network Formation Models with Costs for Establishing Links," *Review of Economic Design* 5, 333–362.

[29] Slikker, M. and A. van den Nouweland (2001a), *Social and Economic Networks in Cooperative Game Theory*, Boston: Kluwer Academic Publishers.

[30] Slikker, M. and A. van den Nouweland (2001b), "A One-Stage Model of Link Formation and Payoff Division," *Games and Economic Behavior* 34, 153–175.

[31] Slikker, M. and A. van den Nouweland (2002), "Network Formation, Costs, and Potential Games," in P. Borm and H. Peters (eds.), *Chapters in Game Theory* (in honor of Stef Tijs), Boston: Kluwer Academic Publishers, pp. 223–246.

[32] Ui, T. (2000), "A Shapley Value Representation of Potential Games," *Games and Economic Behavior* 31, 121–135.

[33] Ui, T. (2001), "Robust Equilibria of Potential Games," *Econometrica* 69, 1373–1380.

[34] van den Nouweland, A. (1993), *Games and Graphs in Economic Situations*, Ph.D. Thesis, Tilburg University, Tilburg, The Netherlands.

[35] van den Nouweland, A., P. Borm, and S. Tijs (1992), "Allocation Rules for Hypergraph Communication Situations," *International Journal of Game Theory* 20, 255–268.

[36] van Huyck, J., R. Battalio, and R. Beil (1990), "Tactic Coordination Games, Strategic Uncertainty, and Coordination Failure," *American Economic Review* 35, 347–359.

Farsighted Stability in Network Formation

Frank H. Page, Jr., and Samir Kamat

3.1. Introduction

3.1.1. Overview

In this chapter, the objective is again to address network formation. In contrast to the first two chapters in this volume, here we assume that individuals are farsighted; that is, we assume that individuals are concerned with the eventual consequences of their immediate actions in forming connections and interacting with other individuals. To focus our discussion, we address the following question: Given the rules governing network formation (i.e., the rules governing what interactions are possible), and given the preferences of the individuals, what networks are likely to emerge and persist if individuals are farsighted? One possible approach to this question – an approach introduced by Page, Wooders, and Kamat (2001) and the approach taken in this chapter – is to think of each possible network representation of individual interactions as a node in a larger network in which the arcs represent coalitional preferences over networks and possible coalitional moves from one network to another. We call such a network of networks (or network formation network) a supernetwork. Given the structure of the supernetwork, we define a farsighted dominance relation on the networks composing the nodes of the supernetwork, and we consider three types of stable sets with respect to this supernetwork-determined farsighted dominance relation: farsightedly stable sets, farsightedly quasi-stable sets, and farsightedly consistent sets. Each of these three types of stable sets contains networks that can reasonably be thought of as likely to emerge and persist if individuals are farsighted. In this chapter, we present existence and nonemptiness results for all three of these notions of farsighted stability. In particular, we present results on the existence of farsightedly stable sets, the existence of farsightedly quasi-stable sets (these sets are automatically nonempty if they exist), and the existence and nonemptiness of farsightedly consistent sets. By considering the graph of the farsighted dominance relation over networks, we are able to reformulate classical

We thank Matt Jackson and Myrna Wooders for helpful comments.

results due to Berge (2001) and Richardson (1953) to obtain the existence of far-sightedly stable sets for certain types of supernetworks. Unlike farsightedly stable sets, farsightedly quasi-stable sets exist for all supernetworks – a consequence of a supernetwork variation on a classical result due to Chvatal and Lovasz (1972) for directed graphs. Using our supernetwork variation on this classical result, we then prove the nonemptiness of the farsightedly consistent set of networks for any supernetwork, thus extending to supernetworks Chwe's nonemptiness result for abstract games (see Chwe 1994, Corollary to Proposition 2). Finally, within the context of strategic information-sharing, we present two examples of information-sharing supernetworks. For each example, we compute the farsightedly consistent set of information-sharing networks, and we compare the farsightedly consistent set with the set of Nash information-sharing networks. In our first example, the Nash and farsightedly consistent sets are equal. We obtain our second example by slightly modifying the network payoffs in the first example. In the resulting supernetwork, the Nash and farsightedly consistent sets have changed and are nonintersecting.

Most of the literature on social and economic networks (e.g., Jackson and Wolinsky 1996; Dutta and Mutuswami 1997) focuses on linking networks. Here, we extend the definition of directed networks and focus on extended directed networks. Like all networks, the directed networks we consider are composed of nodes and arcs.[1] What differentiates a directed network (extended or not) from a linking network is that in a directed network each arc possesses an orientation or direction: arc j connecting nodes i and i' must either go from node i to node i' or must go from node i' to node i.[2] In an undirected (or linking) network, arc j would have no orientation and would simply indicate a connection or link between nodes i and i'. Under our extended definition, nodes are allowed to be connected by multiple arcs. For example, nodes i and i' might be connected by arcs j and j' with arc j running from node i to i' and arc j' running in the opposite direction (i.e., from node i' to node i).[3] Thus, if node i represents a seller and node i' a buyer, then arc j might represent a contract offer by the seller to the buyer, whereas arc j' might represent the acceptance or rejection of that contract offer. Also, under our extended definition, loops are allowed and arcs are allowed to be used multiple times in a given network.[4] For example, arc j might be used to connect nodes i and i' as well as nodes i' and i''. However, we do not allow arc j to go *from* node i *to* node i' multiple times. By allowing arcs to possess direction and be used multiple times and loops and nodes to be connected by multiple arcs, our extended definition makes possible the application of networks to a richer set of economic environments. Although here we focus on directed networks, the same approach, with minor modifications, can be used to analyze farsighted stability in the formation of undirected networks.

---

[1]   In most economic applications, nodes represent economic agents, and arcs represent connections or interactions between agents.

[2]   We denote arc j going from node i to node i' via the ordered pair $(j, (i, i'))$, where (i, i') is also an ordered pair. Alternatively, if arc j goes from node i' to node i, we write $(j, (i', i))$.

[3]   Under our extended definition, arc j' might also run in the same direction as arc j.

[4]   A loop is an arc going *from* a given node *to* that same node. For example, given arc j and node i, the ordered pair $(j, (i, i))$ is a loop.

Given a particular directed network, an agent or a coalition of agents can form a new network by simply adding, subtracting, or replacing arcs from the existing network in accordance with the rules of network formation represented via the supernetwork.[5] For example, if the nodes in a network represent agents, then the rule for adding an arc j from node i to node i' might require that both agents i and i' agree to add arc j, whereas the rule for subtracting arc j from node i to node i' might require that only agent i or agent i' agree to dissolve arc j.

3.1.2. Some History

In a given supernetwork, network G' (a node in the supernetwork) farsightedly dominates network G (another node in the supernetwork) if a finite path through the supernetwork going from G to G' exists such that each consecutive move along the path (from one network to another) can be brought about by some coalition and for each such coalition the network G' eventually reached by the path is preferred to the intermediate network altered by that coalition. Thus, farsighted dominance allows for coalitional defections from a given network that are not necessarily immediately preferred but eventually lead to a network that is preferred. Our supernetwork-based definition of farsighted dominance is closely related to the definition of farsighted dominance given by Chwe (1994) (see Li 1992, 1993 for an alternative definition of farsighted dominance). Farsighted dominance has two progenitors: the notion of effective preferences due to Guilbaud (1949) and the notion of indirect dominance due to Harsanyi (1974).

The notion of a farsightedly stable set of networks has deep roots in game theory. In particular, a farsightedly stable set is simply a von Neumann–Morgenstern stable set (or solution) with respect to the farsighted dominance relation determined by the supernetwork (see von Neumann and Morgenstern 1944). In graph theory, a stable set with respect to a binary relation $\prec$ is referred to as a kernel of the directed graph determined by $\prec$. Thus, in graph-theoretic terminology, a farsightedly stable set of networks is simply a kernel of the directed graph determined by the farsighted dominance relation (see Berge 2001). In any given supernetwork, a farsightedly stable set of networks is both externally and internally stable with respect to farsighted dominance. Therefore, any network not contained in the farsightedly stable set is farsightedly dominated by some network contained in the farsightedly stable set (external stability), and given any two networks contained in the farsightedly stable set, neither farsightedly dominates the other (internal stability).

The notion of a farsightedly quasi-stable set of networks has its origins in graph theory, and in particular, in the work of Chvatal and Lovasz (1972) (also see Galeana-Sanchez and Li 1998). In graph-theoretic terminology, a farsightedly quasi-stable set is a semikernel or quasi-kernel of the directed graph determined by the farsighted dominance relation. Although farsightedly quasi-stable sets are internally stable with respect to farsighted dominance, they are not necessarily externally

---

[5] Put differently, agents can change one network to another by adding, subtracting, or replacing ordered pairs, $(j, (i, i'))$ in accordance with certain rules.

stable – but they are externally quasi-stable. In particular, any network not contained in the farsightedly quasi-stable set is either (i) farsightedly dominated by some network contained in the farsightedly quasi-stable set, or (ii) is farsightedly dominated by some network that is, in turn, farsightedly dominated by some network contained in the farsightedly quasi-stable set.

The notion of a farsightedly consistent set of networks is a supernetwork rendition of Chwe's game-theoretic notion of a farsightedly consistent set (Chwe 1994). Given preferences (and hence coalitional preferences) and the rules governing network formation as represented by the supernetwork, a network (i.e., a particular node in the supernetwork) is said to be farsightedly consistent if no individual or coalition of individuals is willing to alter the network (via the addition, subtraction, or replacement of arcs representing interactions) for fear that such an alteration might induce further network alterations by other individuals or coalitions that would eventually lead to a network in which the initially deviating individual or coalition would not be better off – and would possibly be worse off. Farsightedly consistent sets are externally stable with respect to farsighted dominance but are not necessarily internally stable.

3.1.3. Other Approaches and Related Literature

Although the literature on stability in networks is well established and growing (e.g., see Dutta and Mutuswami 1997; Jackson 2003; Jackson and van den Nouweland 2001), the literature on farsighted stability in network formation is in its infancy. As far as we know, the work by Page, Wooders and Kamat (2001) is the first to address formally the issue of farsighted stability in network formation. Since Page et al. (2001), other papers have appeared focusing on nonmyopic behavior in network formation. Most notable are those by Watts (2002), Deroian (2003), and Dutta, Ghosal, and Ray (2003). These papers differ from our work in at least two respects:

1. All three papers analyze the nonmyopic formation of linking networks (rather than directed networks) and assume that network formation takes place one link at a time in accordance with a given set of rules usually requiring link addition to be bilateral while allowing link subtraction to be unilateral (thus, in all of these papers a particular set of network formation rules is assumed).
2. All three papers utilize a notion of farsightedness and farsighted dominance that differs from the notion we use. For example, Dutta et al. (2003) use a dynamic programming framework to capture farsightedness. Their work is closely related to the work of Konishi and Ray (2003) on dynamic coalition formation.

Our approach, although not explicitly dynamic, can be considered a dynamic network formation thought experiment carried out at a particular point in time in which the future network consequences of individual or coalitional defections from the status quo network are fully taken into account.[6] Unlike Watts (2002), Deroian (2003), and

---

[6] Other important works on dynamic network formation that do not explicitly address the issue of farsightedness are, for example, Watts (2001) and Jackson and Watts (2002).

Dutta et al. (2003), in our network formation model we use a supernetwork extension of Chwe's (1994) notion of farsighted dominance, and in our thought experiment a move from network G to network G' might occur if network G' farsightedly dominates network G.

Other approaches to farsightedness in network formation are suggested by the work of Xue (1998, 2000), Luo (2001), Mariotti and Xue (2002), Bhattacharya and Ziad (2003), and Mauleon and Vannetelbosch (2003) on farsightedness in games and coalition formation. With the exception of Mauleon and Vannetelbosch (2003), all of these papers take as their starting point Greenberg (1990). See also Chapter 1 in this volume for further discussion of models with farsighted players. Here, we will follow the approach introduced in Page et al. (2001).

3.2. Directed Networks

We begin by giving a formal definition of the class of directed networks to be considered. Let N be a finite set of nodes with a typical element denoted by i, and let A be a finite set of arcs with a typical element denoted by j. Arcs represent potential connections between nodes, as dictated by the application, nodes can represent economic agents or economic objects such as markets or firms.[7]

Definition 3.1. *(Directed Networks). Given node set N and arc set A, a directed network G is a subset of $A \times (N \times N)$. We will denote by $\mathbb{N}(N, A)$ the collection of all directed networks given N and A.*

A directed network $G \in \mathbb{N}(N, A)$ specifies how the nodes in N are connected via the arcs in A. Note that order matters in a directed network. In particular, if $(j, (i, i')) \in G$, this means that arc j *goes from* node i *to* node i'. Also, note that under our definition of a directed network, loops are allowed – that is, we allow an arc to go from a given node back to that given node. Finally, note that under our definition an arc can be used multiple times in a given network and multiple arcs can go from one node to another. However, our definition does not allow an arc j to go from a node i to a node i' multiple times.

The following notation is useful in describing networks. Given directed network $G \subseteq A \times (N \times N)$, let

$$
\begin{cases}
G(j) := \left\{ (i, i') \in N \times N : (j, (i, i')) \in G \right\}, \\
G(i) := \left\{ j \in A : (j, (i, i')) \in G \text{ or } (j, (i', i)) \in G \right\} \\
G(i, i') := \left\{ j \in A : (j, (i, i')) \in G \right\}, \\
G(j, i) := \left\{ i' \in N : (j, (i, i')) \in G \right\}.
\end{cases}
\tag{3.1}
$$

---

[7] Of course, in a supernetwork, nodes represent networks.

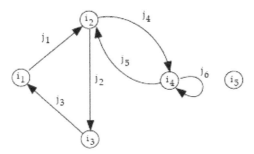

Figure 3.1: Network G.

Thus,

$G(j)$ is the *set of node pairs* connected by arc j in network G,
$G(i)$ is the *set of arcs* going from node i or coming to node i in network G,
$G(i, i')$ is the *set of arcs* going from node i to node i' in network G,
and
$G(j, i)$ is the *set of nodes* that can be reached by arc j from node i in network G.

Note that if for some arc $j \in A$, $G(j)$ is empty, then arc j is not used in network G. Moreover, if for some node $i \in N$, $G(i)$ is empty, then node i is not used in network G and node i is said to be isolated relative to network G.

If in our definition of a directed network we had required that $G(j)$ be single valued and nonempty for all arcs $j \in A$, then our definition would have been the same as that given by Rockafellar (1984).

Suppose that the node set N is given by $N = \{i_1, i_2, \dots, i_5\}$, whereas the arc set A is given by $A = \{j_1, j_2, \dots, j_5, j_6, j_7\}$. Consider the network G depicted in Figure 3.1. In network G, $G(j_6) = \{(i_4, i_4)\}$. Thus, $(j_6, (i_4, i_4)) \in G$ is a loop. Also, in network G, arc j_7 is not used. Thus, $G(j_7) = \emptyset$.[8] Finally, note that $G(i_4) = \{j_4, j_5, j_6\}$, whereas $G(i_5) = \emptyset$. Thus, node i_5 is *isolated* relative to G.[9]

Consider the new network, $G' \in \mathbb{N}(N, A)$ depicted in Figure 3.2.

In network G', $G'(j_1) = \{(i_1, i_2), (i_3, i_1)\}$. Thus, $(j_1, (i_1, i_2)) \in G'$ and $(j_1, (i_3, i_1)) \in G'$. Note that in network G', node i_5 is no longer isolated. In particular, $G'(i_5) = \{j_6, j_7\}$. Also, note that nodes i_2 and i_4 are connected by two different arcs pointed in opposite directions. Under our definition of a directed network it would be possible to alter network G' by replacing arc j_5 from i_4 to i_2 with arc j_4 *from* i_4 *to* i_2. However, it would *not* be possible under our definition to replace arc j_5 from i_4 to i_2 with arc j_4 from i_2 to i_4 because our definition does not allow j_4 to go *from* i_2

---

[8] The fact that arc j_7 is not used in network G can also be denoted by writing

$$j_7 \notin proj_A G,$$

where $proj_A G$ denotes the projection onto A of the subset

$$G \subseteq A \times (N \times N)$$

representing the network.

[9] If the loop $(j_7, (i_5, i_5))$ were part of network G in Figure 3.1, then node i_5 would no longer be considered isolated under our definition. Moreover, we would have $G(i_5) = \{j_7\}$.

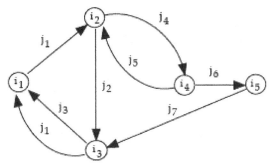

Figure 3.2: Network G'.

to i_4 multiple times. Finally, note that nodes i_1 and i_3 are also connected by two different arcs, but arcs pointed in the same direction. In particular, $G(i_3, i_1) = \{j_1, j_3\}$.

3.2.1. Remark

Under our extended definition of a directed network, a directed graph or digraph can be viewed as a special case of a directed network. A directed graph consists of a pair, (N, E), where N is a finite set of nodes or vertices and E is a finite set of ordered pairs of nodes. Given node set N, arc set A, and directed network $G \in \mathbb{N}(N, A)$, for each arc $j \in A$, $(N, G(j))$ is a directed graph where, as in expression (3.1) above, $G(j)$ is the set of ordered pairs of nodes connected by arc j given by

$$G(j) := \{(i, i') \in N \times N : (j, (i, i')) \in G\}.$$

Thus, a directed network is the graph of a graph-valued mapping, $j \to_\bullet G(j)$.

3.3. Supernetworks

3.3.1. Definition

Let D denote a nonempty set of agents (or economic decision-making units) with a typical element denoted by d, and let $\Gamma(D)$ denote the collection of all *nonempty* subsets (or coalitions) of D with a typical element denoted by S.

Given collection of directed networks $\mathbb{G} \subseteq \mathbb{N}(N, A)$, we assume that each agent's preferences over networks in $\mathbb{G}$ are specified via a network payoff function

$$v_d(\cdot) : \mathbb{G} \to \mathbb{R}.$$

For each agent $d \in D$ and each directed network $G \in \mathbb{G}$, $v_d(G)$ is the payoff to agent d in network G. Agent d then prefers network G' to network G if and only if

$$v_d(G') > v_d(G).$$

Moreover, coalition $S' \in \Gamma(D)$ prefers network G' to network G if and only if

$$v_d(G') > v_d(G) \quad \text{for all } d \in S'.$$

Note that the payoff function of an agent depends on the entire network. Thus, an agent may be affected by directed links between other agents even when this agent has no direct or indirect connection with those agents. Intuitively, "widespread" network externalities are allowed.

By viewing each network G in a given collection of directed networks $\mathbb{G} \subseteq \mathbb{N}(N, A)$ as a node in a larger network, we can give a precise network representation of the rules governing network formation as well as agents' preferences. To begin, let

$\mathbb{M} := \{m_S : S \in \Gamma(D)\}$ denote the set of move arcs (or m-arcs for short),
$\mathbb{P} := \{p_S : S \in \Gamma(D)\}$ denote the set of preference arcs (or p-arcs for short),
and
$\mathbb{A} := \mathbb{M} \cup \mathbb{P}$.

Given networks G and G' in $\mathbb{G}$, we denote by

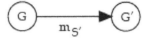

(i.e., by an m-arc belonging to coalition S' going from node G to node G') that coalition $S' \in \Gamma(D)$ can change network G to network G' by adding, subtracting, or replacing arcs in network G. Moreover, we denote by

$$\left(G\right)\dashrightarrow\left(G'\right)$$
$$p_{S'}$$

(i.e., by a p-arc belonging to coalition S' going from node G to node G') that each agent in coalition $S' \in \Gamma(D)$ prefers network G' to network G.

Definition 3.2. *(Supernetworks). Given directed networks* $\mathbb{G} \subseteq \mathbb{N}(N, A)$, *agent payoff functions* $\{v_d(\cdot) : d \in D\}$, *and arc set* $\mathbb{A} := \mathbb{M} \cup \mathbb{P}$, *a supernetwork* **G** *is a subset of* $\mathbb{A} \times (\mathbb{G} \times \mathbb{G})$ *such that for all networks* G *and* G' *in* $\mathbb{G}$ *and for every coalition* $S' \in \Gamma(D)$,

$(m_{S'}, (G, G')) \in$ **G** *if and only if coalition* S' *can change network* G *to network* G',
$G' \neq G$, *by adding, subtracting, or replacing arcs in network* G,
and
$(p_{S'}, (G, G')) \in$ **G** *if and only if* $v_d(G') > v_d(G)$ *for all* $d \in S'$.

Thus, a supernetwork **G** specifies how the networks in $\mathbb{G}$ are connected via coalitional moves and coalitional preferences and thus provides a *network representation* of agent preferences and the rules governing network formation.

Remarks

(1) Under our definition of a supernetwork, m-arc loops and p-arc loops are ruled out. Thus, for any network G and coalition S',

$$(m_{S'}, (G, G)) \notin \mathbf{G} \quad \text{and} \quad (p_{S'}, (G, G)) \notin \mathbf{G}.$$

Although m-arc loops are ruled out by definition, the absence of p-arc loops in supernetworks arises because each agent's preferences over networks are irreflexive.

(2) The definition of agent preferences via the network payoff functions,

$$\{v_d(\cdot) : d \in D\},$$

also rules out the following types of p-arc connections:

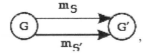

Thus, for all coalitions $S' \in \Gamma(D)$ and networks G and G' contained in $\mathbb{G}$,

$$\text{if } (p_{S'}, (G, G')) \in \mathbf{G}, \text{ then} (p_{S'}, (G', G)) \notin \mathbf{G}.$$

(3) For all coalitions $S' \in \Gamma(D)$ and networks G and G' contained in $\mathbb{G}$, if

$$(p_{S'}, (G, G')) \in \mathbf{G}, \text{ then}$$

$$(p_S, (G, G')) \in \mathbf{G} \text{ for all subcoalitions } S \text{ of } S'.$$

(4) Under our definition of a supernetwork, multiple m-arcs, as well as multiple p-arcs, connecting networks G and G' in supernetwork $\mathbf{G}$ are allowed. Thus, in supernetwork $\mathbf{G}$ the following types of m-arc and p-arc connections are possible:

For coalitions S and S', with $S \neq S'$,

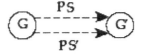

and

However, multiple m-arcs or multiple p-arcs from network $G \in \mathbf{G}$ to network $G' \in \mathbf{G}$ belonging to the *same* coalition are not allowed – and moreover, are unnecessary. Allowing multiple arcs can be very useful in many applications. For example, multiple m-arcs (not belonging to the same coalition) connecting networks G and G' in a given supernetwork $\mathbf{G}$ denote that in supernetwork $\mathbf{G}$ there is more than one way to get from network G to network G'.

(5) In many economic applications, the set of nodes, N used in defining the networks in the collection $\mathbb{G}$ and the set of economic agents D are one and the same (i.e., in many applications $N = D$).

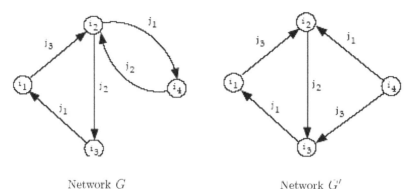

Network G Network G'

Figure 3.3: The networks in collection $\mathbb{G}$.

3.3.2. Examples: Supernetworks and the Rules of Network Formation

In this section we present two examples illustrating the connections between preferences and the rules governing network formation and the resulting supernetwork. We take as our collection of directed networks

$$\mathbb{G} := \{G, G'\},$$

where G and G' are as depicted in Figure 3.3.

Each node in the set

$$N = \{i_1, i_2, i_3, i_4\}$$

represents an agent (i.e., $N - D$), whereas each arc in the set

$$A = \{j_1, j_2, j_3\}$$

represents a particular type of interaction between two agents. Thus, $(j, (i, i')) \in A \times (N \times N)$ denotes a type j interaction between agents i and i', and agent i' is the initiating agent and agent i' is the receiving agent.

Network G is given by

$$G = \{(j_1, (i_3, i_1)), (j_1, (i_2, i_4)), (j_2, (i_2, i_3)), (j_2, (i_4, i_2)), (j_3, (i_1, i_2))\},$$

and network G' is given by

$$G' = \{(j_1, (i_3, i_1)), (j_1, (i_4, i_2)), (j_2, (i_2, i_3)), (j_3, (i_1, i_2)), (j_3, (i_4, i_3))\}.$$

In moving from network G to network G',

$$(j_1, (i_2, i_4)) \text{ is subtracted and } (j_1, (i_4, i_2)) \text{ is added,}$$
$$\text{and}$$
$$(j_2, (i_4, i_2)) \text{ is subtracted and } (j_3, (i_4, i_3)) \text{ is added.}$$

In moving from network G' to network G,

$$(j_1, (i_4, i_2)) \text{ is subtracted and } (j_1, (i_2, i_4)) \text{ is added,}$$
$$\text{and}$$
$$(j_3, (i_4, i_3)) \text{ is subtracted and } (j_2, (i_4, i_2)) \text{ is added.}$$

Suppose that agent preferences are as follows:

$$v_1(G) = v_1(G'),$$
$$v_2(G) > v_2(G'),$$
$$v_3(G) < v_3(G'),$$
$$v_4(G) > v_4(G').$$

Moreover, suppose that the rules governing network formation (i.e., the rules governing the addition and subtraction of arcs) are as follows:

Rules 1 (Bilateral and Unilateral Rules)

(1) In order to establish an interaction of type j_1 or type j_2 between two agents (i.e., to add an arc of type j_k, $k = 1, 2$), both agents must agree.

(2) In order to terminate an interaction of type j_1 or type j_2 between two agents (i.e., to subtract an arc of type j_k, $k = 1, 2$), the initiating agent must agree.

(3) In order to establish an interaction of type j_3 between two agents (i.e., to add an arc of type j_3), the initiating agent must agree.

(4) In order to terminate an interaction of type j_3 between two agents (i.e., to subtract an arc of type j_3), the receiving agent must agree.

Moving from network G to network G': According to Rules 1, to subtract $(j_1, (i_2, i_4))$ from network G, agent i_2 must agree, and to add $(j_1, (i_4, i_2))$ to network G, agents i_2 and i_4 must agree. Moreover, to subtract $(j_2, (i_4, i_2))$, agent i_4 must agree, and to add $(j_3, (i_4, i_3))$, agent i_4 must agree. Thus, the move from network G to network G' can be represented via a move arc belonging to coalition

$$S' = \{i_2\} \cup \{i_2, i_4\} \cup \{i_4\} \cup \{i_4\} = \{i_2, i_4\}.$$

Moving from network G' to network G: According to Rules 1, to subtract $(j_1, (i_4, i_2))$, agent i_4 must agree, and to add $(j_1, (i_2, i_4))$, agents i_2 and i_4 must agree. Moreover, to subtract $(j_3, (i_4, i_3))$, agent i_3 must agree, and to add $(j_2, (i_4, i_2))$, agents i_4 and i_2 must agree. Thus, the move from network G' to network G can be represented via a move arc belonging to coalition

$$S = \{i_4\} \cup \{i_2, i_4\} \cup \{i_3\} \cup \{i_4, i_2\} = \{i_2, i_3, i_4\}.$$

Figure 3.4 depicts the supernetwork corresponding to agent preferences and network formation Rules 1.

Note that in Figure 3.4 we have only pictured the p-arc from G' to G belonging to the largest coalition preferring G' to G. We will adopt this convention throughout in drawing p-arcs.

Rules 1 can be described as a mix of bilateral and unilateral rules. For example, adding $(j_1, (i_4, i_2))$ requires that both agents i_4 and i_2 agree. Thus, the addition of a j_1

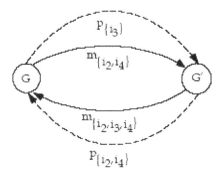

Figure 3.4: Supernetwork 1.

arc requires bilateral cooperation and agreement. However, subtracting $(j_1, (i_4, i_2))$ requires only that the initiating agent i_4 agree. Thus, the subtraction of a j_1 arc is a unilateral action. It is important to note that move arc $m_{\{i_2,i_3,i_4\}}$ from G' to G does not require that all three agents i_2, i_3, and i_4 act cooperatively; rather, arc $m_{\{i_2,i_3,i_4\}}$ simply requires that all three agents act simultaneously whether cooperatively or not. A similar comment applies to arc $m_{\{i_2,i_4\}}$. Thus, under Rules 1 the move from network G' to network G via arc $m_{\{i_2,i_3,i_4\}}$ involves some bilateral cooperation as well as some unilateral actions. This mix of bilateral and unilateral rules, allowable in our supernetwork framework, differs substantially from the rules of network formation assumed in the literature on noncooperative network formation (e.g., Bala and Goyal 2000). In this literature, the rules are unilateral. In particular, in models of noncooperative network formation, the addition or subtraction of arcs requires only that the initiating agent agree.

Keeping network preferences the same, suppose now we assume that the rules of network formation are unilateral and given as follows:

Rules 2 (Unilateral Rules – The Initiating Agent). In order to establish or terminate an interaction $j \in A$ of any type (i.e., to add or subtract an arc of any type), only the initiating agent must agree.

Figure 3.5 depicts the supernetwork corresponding to agent preferences and network formation Rules 2.

Because there is an $m_{\{i_2,i_4\}}$-arc from network G to network G' *and* an $m_{\{i_2,i_4\}}$-arc from network G' to network G, the $m_{\{i_2,i_4\}}$-arc connecting networks G and G' in

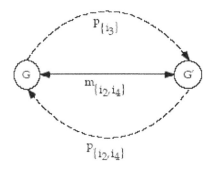

Figure 3.5: Supernetwork 2.

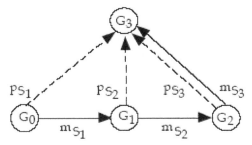

Figure 3.6: G_3 farsightedly dominates G_0.

Figure 3.5 has arrowheads at both ends. Under Rules 2, arc $m_{\{i_2,i_4\}}$ from G to G' and arc $m_{\{i_2,i_4\}}$ from G' to G indicate that agents i_2 and i_4 each act unilaterally but simultaneously.

3.4. Notions of Farsighted Stability in Network Formation

3.4.1. Farsighted Dominance

Given supernetwork $\mathbf{G} \subset \mathbb{A} \times (\mathbb{G} \times \mathbb{G})$, we say that network $G' \in \mathbb{G}$ farsightedly dominates network $G \in \mathbb{G}$ if there is a finite sequence of networks

$$G_0, G_1, \ldots, G_h$$

with $G = G_0$, $G' = G_h$, and $G_k \in \mathbb{G}$ for $k = 0, 1, \ldots, h$, and a corresponding sequence of coalitions

$$S_1, S_2, \ldots, S_h$$

such that for $k = 1, 2, \ldots, h$

$$(m_{S_k}, (G_{k-1}, G_k)) \in \mathbf{G},$$
$$\text{and}$$
$$(p_{S_k}, (G_{k-1}, G_h)) \in \mathbf{G}.$$

We denote by $G \lhd\lhd G'$ that network $G' \in \mathbb{G}$ farsightedly dominates network $G \in \mathbb{G}$.

Figure 3.6 provides a network representation of the farsighted dominance relation in terms of m-arcs and p-arcs. In Figure 3.6, network G_3 farsightedly dominates network G_0. Note that what matters to the initially deviating coalition S_1, as well as coalitions S_2 and S_3, is the ultimate network outcome G_3. Thus, the initially deviating coalition S_1 will not be deterred even if

$$(p_{S_1}, (G_0, G_1)) \notin \mathbf{G}$$

as long as the ultimate network outcome G_3 is preferred to G_0, that is, as long as G_3 is such that

$$(p_{S_1}, (G_0, G_3)) \in \mathbf{G}.$$

3.4.2. Farsighted Quasi-Stability and Farsighted Stability

Given supernetwork $\mathbf{G} \subset \mathbb{A} \times (\mathbb{G} \times \mathbb{G})$, we say that a sequence of networks $\{G_k\}_k$ in $\mathbb{G}$ is a *farsighted domination path*, written $\lhd\lhd$-path, *through supernetwork* $\mathbf{G}$ if for any two consecutive networks G_{k-1} and G_k, G_k farsightedly dominates G_{k-1}, that is, if

$$G_{k-1} \lhd\lhd G_k.$$

We can think of the farsighted dominance relation $G_{k-1} \lhd\lhd G_k$ between networks G_k and G_{k-1} as defining a $\lhd\lhd$-arc *from* network G_{k-1} *to* network G_k. Given $\lhd\lhd$-path $\{G_h\}_h$ through $\mathbf{G}$, the *length* of this path is defined to be the number of $\lhd\lhd$-arcs in the path. We say that network $G_1 \in \mathbb{G}$ is $\lhd\lhd$-*reachable* from network $G_0 \in \mathbb{G}$ in $\mathbf{G}$ if there exists a finite $\lhd\lhd$-path in $\mathbf{G}$ from G_0 to G_1 (i.e., a $\lhd\lhd$-path in $\mathbf{G}$ from G_0 to G_1 of finite length). If network $G_0 \in \mathbb{G}$ is $\lhd\lhd$-reachable from network G_0 in $\mathbf{G}$, then we say that supernetwork $\mathbf{G}$ contains a $\lhd\lhd$-*circuit*. Thus, a $\lhd\lhd$-circuit in $\mathbf{G}$ starting at network $G_0 \in \mathbb{G}$ is a finite $\lhd\lhd$-path from G_0 to G_0. A $\lhd\lhd$-circuit of length 1 is called a $\lhd\lhd$-loop. Note that because preferences are irreflexive, $\lhd\lhd$-loops are in fact ruled out. However, because the farsighted dominance relation $\lhd\lhd$ is *not transitive*, it is possible to have $\lhd\lhd$ circuits of length greater than 1.

We define the $\lhd\lhd$-*distance* from G_0 to G_1 to be the length of the shortest $\lhd\lhd$-path from G_0 to G_1 if G_1 is $\lhd\lhd$-*reachable* from G_0 in $\mathbf{G}$, and $+\infty$ if G_1 is not reachable from G_0 in $\mathbf{G}$. We denote the distance *from* G_0 to G_1 in $\mathbf{G}$ by $d_{\mathbf{G}}^{\lhd\lhd}(G_0, G_1)$. Thus,

$$d_{\mathbf{G}}^{\lhd\lhd}(G_0, G_1) := \begin{cases} \text{length of shortest } \lhd\lhd\text{-path from } G_0 \text{ to } G_1 \text{ in } \mathbf{G}, \\ \text{if } G_1 \text{ is reachable from } G_0, \\ +\infty, \text{ if } G_1 \text{ is not reachable from } G_0 \text{ in } \mathbf{G}. \end{cases}$$

Definition 3.3. *(Farsightedly Quasi-Stable Sets and Farsightedly Stable Sets). Let $\mathbb{G} \subseteq \mathbb{N}(N, A)$ be a collection of directed networks and let $\mathbf{G} \subset \mathbb{A} \times (\mathbb{G} \times \mathbb{G})$ be a supernetwork.*

(1) A subset $\mathbb{Q}$ of directed networks in $\mathbb{G}$ is said to be farsightedly quasi-stable given supernetwork $\mathbf{G}$ if

(a) (internal stability) $d_{\mathbf{G}}^{\lhd\lhd}(G_0, G_1) \geq 2$, whenever G_0 and G_1 are in $\mathbb{Q}$, with $G_0 \neq G_1$, and
(b) (external quasi-stability) given any $G_0 \notin \mathbb{Q}$, there exists $G_1 \in \mathbb{Q}$ with $d_{\mathbf{G}}^{\lhd\lhd}(G_0, G_1) \leq 2$.

(2) A subset $\mathbb{S}$ of directed networks in $\mathbb{G}$ is said to be

(a) (internal stability) $d_{\mathbf{G}}^{\lhd\lhd}(G_0, G_1) \geq 2$, whenever G_0 and G_1 are in $\mathbb{S}$, with $G_0 \neq G_1$, and
(b) (external stability) given any $G_0 \notin \mathbb{S}$, there exists $G_1 \in \mathbb{S}$ with $d_{\mathbf{G}}^{\lhd\lhd}(G_0, G_1) \leq 1$.

If we let

$$P_{\triangleright\triangleright}(G_0) := \{G \in \mathbb{G} : G \triangleright\triangleright G_0\},$$

an alternative way to write part (2) of the definition above is as follows:

(2)′ A subset $\mathbb{S}$ of directed networks in $\mathbb{G}$ is said to be farsightedly stable given supernetwork **G** if

(a) (internal stability) $G \in \mathbb{S}$ implies that $P_{\triangleright\triangleright}(G) \cap \mathbb{S} = \emptyset$, and

(b) (external stability) $G \notin \mathbb{S}$ implies that $P_{\triangleright\triangleright}(G) \cap \mathbb{S} \neq \emptyset$.

If $\mathbb{S}$ is farsightedly stable (or farsightedly quasi-stable), then it is automatically nonempty. Note that a farsightedly stable set $\mathbb{S}$ is simply a von Neuman–Morgenstern stable set with respect to the farsighted dominance relation $\triangleright\triangleright$ defined on $\mathbb{G}$. Also, note that if $\mathbb{S}$ is farsightedly stable, then it is automatically farsightedly quasi-stable.

We now state and prove a remarkably simple result on the existence of farsightedly quasi-stable sets. This result is a supernetwork variation on a general result due to Chvatal and Lovasz (1974) on the existence of quasi-stable sets in directed graphs.

Theorem 3.1. *(Existence of Farsightedly Quasi-Stable Sets). Given any collection of directed networks $\mathbb{G} \subseteq \mathbb{N}(N, A)$ and any supernetwork $\mathbf{G} \subset \mathbb{A} \times (\mathbb{G} \times \mathbb{G})$, there exists a farsightedly quasi-stable set $\mathbb{Q}$ in $\mathbb{G}$ given supernetwork $\mathbf{G}$.*

Proof. We proceed by induction on the number of networks in $\mathbb{G}$. First, suppose $\mathbb{G}$ contains a single network. Then the result holds trivially.

Next, suppose $\mathbb{G}$ contains n networks and let $\mathbf{G} \subset \mathbb{A} \times (\mathbb{G} \times \mathbb{G})$ be a supernetwork. For $G_0 \in \mathbb{G}$, define

$$P_{\triangleright\triangleright}^{-1}(G_0) := \{G \in \mathbb{G} : G_0 \in P_{\triangleright\triangleright}(G)\} = \{G \in \mathbb{G} : G_0 \triangleright\triangleright G\}.$$

Also, for any subset $\mathbb{H}$ of networks in $\mathbb{G}$, let $\mathbf{G}\backslash\mathbb{H}$ denote the supernetwork derived from supernetwork **G** by deleting the nodes in $\mathbb{H}$ and deleting all m-arc and p-arc connections between the nodes in $\mathbb{G}\backslash\mathbb{H}$ and the nodes in $\mathbb{H}$ in supernetwork **G**. Now consider the collection of networks

$$\mathbb{G}\backslash\{G_0\} \cup P_{\triangleright\triangleright}^{-1}(G_0) \text{ for } G_0 \in \mathbb{G} \text{ and supernetwork } \mathbf{G}\backslash\{G_0\} \cup P_{\triangleright\triangleright}^{-1}(G_0).$$

Note that if $\mathbb{G} = \{G_0\} \cup P_{\triangleright\triangleright}^{-1}(G_0)$, then $\{G_0\}$ is a stable set for $\mathbb{G}$ in supernetwork **G** and the proof is complete. Assume that

$$\mathbb{G}\backslash\{G_0\} \cup P_{\triangleright\triangleright}^{-1}(G_0) \neq \emptyset.$$

By the induction hypothesis, a farsightedly quasi-stable set $\mathbb{Q}'$ exists for collection $\mathbb{G}\backslash\{G_0\} \cup P_{\triangleright\triangleright}^{-1}(G_0)$ in supernetwork $\mathbf{G}\backslash\{G_0\} \cup P_{\triangleright\triangleright}^{-1}(G_0)$.

Note that if G_0 is an isolated node, then $\mathbb{Q}' \cup \{G_0\}$ is a farsightedly quasi-stable set for $\mathbb{G}$ in supernetwork **G** and the proof is complete. Moreover, if $\mathbb{Q}' \cup \{G_0\}$ is internally stable, then $\mathbb{Q}' \cup \{G_0\}$ is a farsightedly quasi-stable set for $\mathbb{G}$ in supernetwork **G**.

Suppose that G_0 is not an isolated node in supernetwork **G** and that $\mathbb{Q}' \cup \{G_0\}$ is not internally stable. Because $\mathbb{Q}' \cup \{G_0\}$ is not internally stable, a node $G_1 \in \mathbb{Q}'$

exists connected to G_0 by a $\lhd\lhd$-arc. Given that $G_1 \notin P_{\rhd\rhd}^{-1}(G_0)$, it must be true that $G_1 \rhd\rhd G_0$. Thus, $\mathbb{Q}'$ is a farsightedly quasi-stable set in $\mathbb{G}$ given supernetwork **G**. ∎

In fact, it follows from the theorem due to Chvatal and Lovasz (1972) that any finite set $\mathbb{Z}$ equipped with a binary relation $\prec$ has a $\prec$-quasi-stable set. Moreover, if the relation $\prec$ is transitive, then any $\prec$-quasi-stable set is $\prec$-stable.

Next we state two results on the existence of farsightedly stable sets.

Theorem 3.2. *(Existence of Farsightedly Stable Sets). Let* $\mathbb{G} \subseteq \mathbb{N}(N, A)$ *be any collection of directed networks and let* **G** $\subset \mathbb{A} \times (\mathbb{G} \times \mathbb{G})$ *be any supernetwork.*

(1) If **G** *contains no* $\lhd\lhd$-*circuits, then there exists a unique farsightedly stable set* $\mathbb{S}$ *in* $\mathbb{G}$ *given supernetwork* **G**.
(2) If **G** *contains no* $\lhd\lhd$-*circuits of odd length, then there exists a farsightedly stable set* $\mathbb{S}$ *in* $\mathbb{G}$ *given supernetwork* **G**.

Part (1) of Theorem 3.2 is an immediate consequence of a 1958 result due to Berge (see Theorem 4, p. 48, in Berge 2001). Part (2) of Theorem 3.2 is a supernetwork version of the classical result due to Richardson (1953). A $\lhd\lhd$-circuit in supernetwork **G** from network G_0 to network G_0 is said to be of odd length if $d_{\mathbf{G}}^{\lhd\lhd}(G_0, G_0)$ is an odd number.

3.4.3. Farsighted Consistency

Definition 3.4. *(Farsightedly Consistent Sets). Let* $\mathbb{G} \subseteq \mathbb{N}(N, A)$ *be a collection of directed networks and let* **G** $\subset \mathbb{A} \times (\mathbb{G} \times \mathbb{G})$ *be a supernetwork.*
A subset $\mathbb{F}$ *of directed networks in* $\mathbb{G}$ *is said to be farsightedly consistent if,*

$$\text{for all } G_0 \in \mathbb{F},$$
$$(m_{S_1}, (G_0, G_1)) \in \mathbf{G} \text{ for some } G_1 \in \mathbb{G} \text{ and some coalition } S_1 \text{ implies that}$$
$$\text{there exists } G_2 \in \mathbb{F}$$
$$\text{with } G_2 = G_1 \text{ or } G_2 \rhd\rhd G_1 \text{ such that}$$
$$(p_{S_1}, (G_0, G_2)) \notin \mathbf{G}.$$

In words, a subset of directed networks $\mathbb{F}$ is said to be farsightedly consistent if, given any network $G_0 \in \mathbb{F}$ and any m_{S_1}-deviation to network $G_1 \in \mathbb{G}$ by coalition S_1 (via adding, subtracting, or replacing arcs in accordance with **G**), there exists further deviations leading to some network $G_2 \in \mathbb{F}$ where the initially deviating coalition S_1 is not better off – and possibly worse off. A network $G \in \mathbb{G}$ is said to be farsightedly consistent if $G \in \mathbb{F}$, where $\mathbb{F}$ is a farsightedly consistent set corresponding to supernetwork **G**.

There can be many farsightedly consistent sets. We denote by $\mathbb{F}^*$ the largest farsightedly consistent set. Thus, if $\mathbb{F}$ is a farsightedly consistent set, then $\mathbb{F} \subseteq \mathbb{F}^*$.

Unlike farsightedly quasi-stable sets and farsightedly stable sets where existence implies nonemptiness, in considering farsightedly consistent sets two critical questions arise: (i) Given supernetwork **G**, does there exist a largest farsightedly consistent set of networks in **G**, and (ii) is it nonempty?

3.4.3.1. Existence

Our first result resolves the existence issue. The method of proving existence is a straightforward, supernetwork rendition of Chwe's (1994) method and is similar to the method introduced by Roth (1975, 1977).

Theorem 3.3. *(Existence of* $\mathbb{F}^*$*, Chwe 1994, Proposition 1). Let* $\mathbb{G} \subseteq \mathbb{N}(N, A)$ *be a collection of directed networks. Given any supernetwork* $\mathbf{G} \subset \mathbb{A} \times (\mathbb{G} \times \mathbb{G})$*, there exists a unique, largest farsightedly consistent set* $\mathbb{F}^*$ *in* $\mathbf{G}$*.*

Proof. Let $2^{\mathbb{G}}$ denote the collection of *all* subsets of $\mathbb{G}$ (including the empty set), and define the mapping

$$\Lambda_{\mathbf{G}}(\cdot) : 2^{\mathbb{G}} \to 2^{\mathbb{G}}$$

as follows:

for subcollection of networks $\mathbb{H} \in 2^{\mathbb{G}}$ and network $G_0 \in \mathbb{G}$,
G_0 is contained in $\Lambda_{\mathbf{G}}(\mathbb{H})$
if and only if
$\forall\, G_1 \in \mathbb{G}$ such that $(m_S, (G_0, G_1)) \in \mathbf{G}$ for some coalition $S \in \Gamma(D)$
$\exists$ a network $G_2 \in \mathbb{H}$ such that
(i) $G_2 = G_1$ or $G_2 \rhd\rhd G_1$, and
(ii) $(p_S, (G_0, G_2)) \notin \mathbf{G}$, that is, $v_d(G_2) \leq v_d(G_0)$ for some $d \in S$.

First, note that a set $\mathbb{F}$ is a farsightedly consistent set if and only if $\mathbb{F}$ is a fixed point of the mapping $\Lambda_{\mathbf{G}}(\cdot)$. Second, note that $\Lambda_{\mathbf{G}}(\cdot)$ is monotone increasing; that is, for any subcollections $\mathbb{H}$ and $\mathbb{E}$ of $\mathbb{G}$,

$$\mathbb{H} \subseteq \mathbb{E} \text{ implies that } \Lambda_{\mathbf{G}}(\mathbb{H}) \subseteq \Lambda_{\mathbf{G}}(\mathbb{E}).$$

To see that $\Lambda_{\mathbf{G}}(\cdot)$ has a unique, largest fixed point, consider the following. Let

$$\Sigma = \left\{ \mathbb{H} \in 2^{\mathbb{G}} : \mathbb{H} \subseteq \Lambda_{\mathbf{G}}(\mathbb{H}) \right\}.$$

Note that Σ is nonempty because the empty subcollection $\emptyset \in 2^{\mathbb{G}}$ is contained in Σ; that is, $\emptyset \subseteq \Lambda_{\mathbf{G}}(\emptyset)$. Let $\mathbb{F}^* = \bigcup_{\mathbb{H} \in \Sigma} \mathbb{H}$. By the monotonicity of $\Lambda_{\mathbf{G}}(\cdot)$ and the definition of Σ,

$$\mathbb{H} \subseteq \Lambda_{\mathbf{G}}(\mathbb{H}) \subseteq \Lambda_{\mathbf{G}}(\mathbb{F}^*) \quad \text{for all } \mathbb{H} \in \Sigma.$$

Hence,

$$\mathbb{F}^* = \bigcup_{\mathbb{H} \in \Sigma} \mathbb{H} \subseteq \bigcup_{\mathbb{H} \in \Sigma} \Lambda_{\mathbf{G}}(\mathbb{H}) \subseteq \Lambda_{\mathbf{G}}(\mathbb{F}^*).$$

Thus,

$$\mathbb{F}^* \subseteq \Lambda_{\mathbf{G}}(\mathbb{F}^*).$$

Moreover, by the monotonicity of $\Lambda_{\mathbf{G}}(\cdot)$,

$$\Lambda_{\mathbf{G}}(\mathbb{F}^*) \subseteq \Lambda_{\mathbf{G}}\left(\Lambda_{\mathbf{G}}(\mathbb{F}^*)\right).$$

Thus, we have, $\Lambda_G(\mathbb{F}^*) \in \Sigma$ and $\Lambda_G(\mathbb{F}^*) \subseteq \mathbb{F}^*$, and we can conclude that

$$\mathbb{F}^* = \Lambda_G(\mathbb{F}^*).$$

The set $\mathbb{F}^*$ is the largest farsightedly consistent set because, if $\mathbb{F}'$ is any other fixed point (i.e., if $\mathbb{F}' = \Lambda_G(\mathbb{F}')$), then $\mathbb{F}' \in \Sigma$ and hence $\mathbb{F}' \subseteq \mathbb{F}^*$. ∎

3.4.3.2. Nonemptiness

It follows from the proof of Theorem 3.3 that, in order to demonstrate that the largest farsightedly consistent set is nonempty, it suffices to show that

$$\mathbb{H} \subseteq \Lambda_G(\mathbb{H}) \text{ for some nonempty subset of networks } \mathbb{H} \in 2^{\mathbb{G}}.$$

In this section, our objective will be to find just such a subcollection of networks.[10] Our approach to nonemptiness is similar to that taken by Chwe (1994) and Gillies (1959). In particular, we begin by defining a new *transitive*, farsighted dominance relation on the collection of networks $\mathbb{G}$ consistent with the supernetwork. We then consider the stable sets with respect to this new relation. Given transitivity, the existence of stable sets with respect to this new relation is guaranteed by our Theorem 3.1 on the existence of quasi-stable sets.

The Relation $\rhd_{\mathbb{H}}$ and $\rhd_{\mathbb{H}}$-Stability. For any nonempty subset of networks $\mathbb{H}$, we define the relation $\rhd_{\mathbb{H}}$ on $\mathbb{G}$ as follows: for G^1 and G^0 in $\mathbb{G}$,

$$G_1 \rhd_{\mathbb{H}} G_0 \text{ if and only if } \begin{cases} \text{(a) } G_1 \in \mathbb{H} \cap P_{\rhd\rhd}(G_0), \text{ and} \\ \text{(b) } \mathbb{H} \cap P_{\rhd\rhd}(G_1) \subseteq P_{\rhd\rhd}(G_0). \end{cases}$$

Recall that

$$P_{\rhd\rhd}(G_0) := \{G \in \mathbb{G} : G \rhd\rhd G_0\}.$$

Lemma 3.1. *($\rhd_{\mathbb{H}}$-transitivity). If $G_2 \rhd_{\mathbb{H}} G_1$ and $G_1 \rhd_{\mathbb{H}} G_0$, then $G_2 \rhd_{\mathbb{H}} G_0$.*

Proof. First, we have $G_2 \in \mathbb{H} \cap P_{\rhd\rhd}(G_1)$. Because $G_1 \rhd_{\mathbb{H}} G_0$, we have $\mathbb{H} \cap P_{\rhd\rhd}(G_1) \subseteq P_{\rhd\rhd}(G_0)$. Thus, $G_2 \in \mathbb{H} \cap P_{\rhd\rhd}(G_0)$.
We must show that

$$\mathbb{H} \cap P_{\rhd\rhd}(G_2) \subseteq P_{\rhd\rhd}(G_0).$$

Because $G_2 \rhd_{\mathbb{H}} G_1$, we have

$$\mathbb{H} \cap P_{\rhd\rhd}(G_2) \subseteq P_{\rhd\rhd}(G_1).$$

Because $G_1 \rhd_{\mathbb{H}} G_0$, we have

$$\mathbb{H} \cap P_{\rhd\rhd}(G_1) \subseteq P_{\rhd\rhd}(G_0).$$

Thus, $\mathbb{H} \cap P_{\rhd\rhd}(G_2) \subseteq \mathbb{H} \cap P_{\rhd\rhd}(G_1) \subseteq P_{\rhd\rhd}(G_0)$, and we have $G_2 \rhd_{\mathbb{H}} G_0$. ∎

---

[10] If we extend Proposition 3 in Chwe (1994) to supernetworks, it can be shown that if $\mathbb{S}$ is a farsightedly stable set in collection $\mathbb{G}$ given supernetwork $\mathbf{G}$, then $\mathbb{S} \subseteq \Lambda_G(\mathbb{S})$. Thus, if supernetwork $\mathbf{G}$ possesses a farsightedly stable set $\mathbb{S}$, then the largest farsightedly consistent set $\mathbb{F}^*$ is nonempty and $\mathbb{S} \subseteq \mathbb{F}^*$.

The following result is an immediate consequence of $\rhd_{\mathbb{H}}$-transitivity and Theorem 3.1.

Theorem 3.4. *(Existence of $\rhd_{\mathbb{H}}$-Stable Sets). Let $\mathbb{G} \subseteq \mathbb{N}(N, A)$ be a collection of directed networks and let $\mathbf{G} \subset \mathbb{A} \times (\mathbb{G} \times \mathbb{G})$ be a supernetwork. Given any subcollection of networks $\mathbb{H} \subseteq \mathbb{G}$, there exists a subset of networks $\mathbb{E}$ in $\mathbb{G}$ such that $\mathbb{E}$ is $\rhd_{\mathbb{H}}$-stable in $\mathbf{G}$; that is, there exists a subset of networks $\mathbb{E}$ in $\mathbb{G}$ such that in supernetwork $\mathbf{G}$*

(a) $\mathbb{E}$ is internally $\rhd_{\mathbb{H}}$-stable; that is, $G \in \mathbb{E}$ implies that $P_{\rhd_{\mathbb{H}}}(G) \cap \mathbb{E} = \emptyset$, and

(b) $\mathbb{E}$ is externally $\rhd_{\mathbb{H}}$-stable; that is, $G \notin \mathbb{E}$ implies that $P_{\rhd_{\mathbb{H}}}(G) \cap \mathbb{E} \neq \emptyset$.

The set $P_{\rhd_{\mathbb{H}}}(G)$ is given by

$$P_{\rhd_{\mathbb{H}}}(G) := \{G' \in \mathbb{G} : G' \rhd_{\mathbb{H}} G\}.$$

We say that a nonempty subset of networks $\mathbb{E}$ is $\rhd_{\mathbb{H}}$-consistent if $\mathbb{E}$ is $\rhd_{\mathbb{H}}$-stable and $\mathbb{E} = \mathbb{H}$.

Theorem 3.5. *(Existence of $\rhd_{\mathbb{H}}$-Consistent Sets). Let $\mathbb{G} \subseteq \mathbb{N}(N, A)$ be a collection of directed networks. Given any supernetwork $\mathbf{G} \subset \mathbb{A} \times (\mathbb{G} \times \mathbb{G})$, there exists a subset of networks $\mathbb{H}^*$ in $\mathbb{G}$ such that $\mathbb{H}^*$ is $\rhd_{\mathbb{H}^*}$-consistent in $\mathbf{G}$; that is, there exists a subset of networks $\mathbb{H}^*$ in $\mathbb{G}$ such that in supernetwork $\mathbf{G}$*

(a) $G \in \mathbb{H}^*$ implies that $P_{\rhd_{\mathbb{H}^*}}(G) \cap \mathbb{H}^* = \emptyset$, and

(b) $G \notin \mathbb{H}^*$ implies that $P_{\rhd_{\mathbb{H}^*}}(G) \cap \mathbb{H}^* \neq \emptyset$.

Proof. Let $\mathbb{H}^0 = \mathbb{G}$ and define a sequence of sets $\{\mathbb{H}^n\}_{n=1}^{\infty}$ recursively as follows: let $\mathbb{H}^n$ be a $\rhd_{\mathbb{H}^{n-1}}$-stable set in $\mathbf{G}$. By induction, we will show that $\mathbb{H}^n \subseteq \mathbb{H}^{n-1}$ for all n. Clearly, $\mathbb{H}^1 \subseteq \mathbb{H}^0$. By the induction hypothesis, $\mathbb{H}^{n-1} \subseteq \mathbb{H}^{n-2}$. We must now show that this implies that $\mathbb{H}^n \subseteq \mathbb{H}^{n-1}$.

Suppose that $G_0 \in \mathbb{H}^n$ but $G_0 \notin \mathbb{H}^{n-1}$. Because $\mathbb{H}^{n-1}$ is a $\rhd_{\mathbb{H}^{n-2}}$-stable set, $G_0 \notin \mathbb{H}^{n-1}$ implies that $P_{\rhd_{\mathbb{H}^{n-2}}}(G_0) \cap \mathbb{H}^{n-1} \neq \emptyset$. Let

$$G_1 \in P_{\rhd_{\mathbb{H}^{n-2}}}(G_0) \cap \mathbb{H}^{n-1}.$$

Thus, because $G_1 \in P_{\rhd_{\mathbb{H}^{n-2}}}(G_0)$, we have

$$G_1 \in \mathbb{H}^{n-2} \cap P_{\rhd\rhd}(G_0),$$
$$\text{and}$$
$$\mathbb{H}^{n-2} \cap P_{\rhd\rhd}(G_1) \subseteq P_{\rhd\rhd}(G_0).$$

In fact, $G_1 \in \mathbb{H}^{n-1} \cap P_{\rhd\rhd}(G_0)$ and by the induction hypothesis

$$\mathbb{H}^{n-1} \cap P_{\rhd\rhd}(G_1) \subseteq \mathbb{H}^{n-2} \cap P_{\rhd\rhd}(G_1) \subseteq P_{\rhd\rhd}(G_0).$$

Thus,

$$G_1 \in P_{\rhd_{\mathbb{H}^{n-1}}}(G_0).$$

If $G_1 \in \mathbb{H}^n$, then $G_1 \in P_{\rhd_{\mathbb{H}^{n-1}}}(G_0) \cap \mathbb{H}^n$, which is a contradiction because $G_0 \in \mathbb{H}^n$.

If $G_1 \notin \mathbb{H}^n$, then there exists

$$G_2 \in P_{\rhd_{\mathbb{H}^{n-1}}}(G_1) \cap \mathbb{H}^n.$$

Thus, we have

$$G_2 \in \mathbb{H}^n,$$
$$\text{and}$$
$$G_2 \rhd_{\mathbb{H}^{n-1}} G_1 \rhd_{\mathbb{H}^{n-1}} G_0.$$

By transitivity $G_2 \rhd_{\mathbb{H}^{n-1}} G_0$, and so

$$G_2 \in P_{\rhd_{\mathbb{H}^{n-1}}}(G_0) \cap \mathbb{H}^n,$$

which is a contradiction because $G_0 \in \mathbb{H}^n$.

Because $\mathbb{G}$ is finite, there exists an n such that

$$\mathbb{H}^n = \mathbb{H}^{n+1} = \cdots = \mathbb{H}^*.$$

The subset of networks $\mathbb{H}^*$ is $\rhd_{\mathbb{H}^*}$-consistent in $\mathbf{G}$. ∎

Now we have our main result on the nonemptiness of the largest farsightedly consistent set. This result extends to supernetworks (Chwe 1994, Proposition 2 and its corollary).

Theorem 3.6. *(Nonemptiness of the Largest Farsightedly Consistent Set). Let $\mathbb{G} \subseteq \mathbb{N}(N, A)$ be a collection of directed networks. Given any supernetwork $\mathbf{G} \subset \mathbb{A} \times (\mathbb{G} \times \mathbb{G})$, there exists a nonempty subset of networks $\mathbb{F}^*$ in $\mathbb{G}$ such that $\mathbb{F}^*$ is the largest farsightedly consistent set given supernetwork $\mathbf{G}$. Moreover, $\mathbb{F}^*$ is externally $\rhd\rhd$-stable in supernetwork $\mathbf{G}$; that is,*

$$G \notin \mathbb{F}^* \text{ implies that } P_{\rhd\rhd}(G) \cap \mathbb{F}^* \neq \emptyset.$$

Proof. Let $\mathbb{H}^*$ be a $\rhd_{\mathbb{H}^*}$-consistent set in $\mathbf{G}$. It suffices to show that

$$\mathbb{H}^* \subseteq \Lambda_{\mathbf{G}}(\mathbb{H}^*).$$

Suppose that $G_0 \in \mathbb{H}^*$ but $G_0 \notin \Lambda_{\mathbf{G}}(\mathbb{H}^*)$. Then there exists a network $G_1 \in \mathbb{G}$ with

$$(m_{S_1}, (G_0 G_1)) \in \mathbf{G}$$

for some coalition S_1 such that for all networks $G_2 \in \mathbb{H}^*$ with $G_2 = G_1$ or $G_2 \rhd\rhd G_1$

$$(p_{S_1}, (G_0 G_2)) \in \mathbf{G}.$$

Thus, if $G_1 \in \mathbb{H}^*$, then

(a) $G_1 \in \mathbb{H}^* \cap P_{\rhd\rhd}(G_0)$, and
(b) $\mathbb{H}^* \cap P_{\rhd\rhd}(G_1) \subseteq P_{\rhd\rhd}(G_0)$;

and if $G_1 \notin \mathbb{H}^*$, then

$$\mathbb{H}^* \cap P_{\rhd\rhd}(G_1) \subseteq P_{\rhd\rhd}(G_0).$$

Hence, if $G_1 \in \mathbb{H}^*$,

$$G_1 \rhd_{\mathbb{H}^*} G_0,$$

which contradicts the facts that $G_0 \in \mathbb{H}^*$ and $\mathbb{H}^*$ is $\rhd_{\mathbb{H}^*}$-consistent in $\mathbf{G}$.

If $G_1 \notin \mathbb{H}^*$, then there exists $G_2 \in \mathbb{H}^*$ such that $G_2 \rhd_{\mathbb{H}^*} G_1$. Thus,

(a) $G_2 \in \mathbb{H}^* \cap P_{\rhd\rhd}(G_1)$, and
(b) $\mathbb{H}^* \cap P_{\rhd\rhd}(G_2) \subseteq P_{\rhd\rhd}(G_1)$.

Because $G_0 \notin \Lambda_\mathbf{G}(\mathbb{H}^*)$,

$$\mathbb{H}^* \cap P_{\rhd\rhd}(G_1) \subseteq P_{\rhd\rhd}(G_0),$$

and so we have

$$G_2 \in \mathbb{H}^* \cap P_{\rhd\rhd}(G_0).$$

Because $G_2 \rhd_{\mathbb{H}^*} G_1$,

$$\mathbb{H}^* \cap P_{\rhd\rhd}(G_2) \subseteq P_{\rhd\rhd}(G_1),$$

and so we have

$$\mathbb{H}^* \cap P_{\rhd\rhd}(G_2) \subseteq P_{\rhd\rhd}(G_0).$$

Hence,

$$G_2 \rhd_{\mathbb{H}^*} G_0,$$

which contradicts the facts that $G_0 \in \mathbb{H}^*$ and $\mathbb{H}^*$ is $\rhd_{\mathbb{H}^*}$-consistent in $\mathbf{G}$. ∎

3.5. Computational Examples: Strategic Information Sharing

In this section, we compute the farsightedly consistent sets for two supernetwork examples of strategic information sharing. All of our computations are carried out using a Mathematica® package developed by Kamat and Page (2001).

3.5.1. Information Sharing Networks

Consider a situation in which three agents i_1, i_2, and i_3 have private information. Figure 3.7 depicts three possible information-sharing networks. The basic idea is as follows: in network G_{10}, the j_1 arc running from agent i_1 to agent i_3 indicates that agent i_1 observes the private information of agent i_3. The loops in network G_{10} at each node, for example $(j_3, (i_3, i_3))$, indicate that each agent observes his or her own private information. Note that in network G_{10}, agent i_3 observes only his or her own private information. In network G_{64} there is full information sharing: each agent observes the private information of the other agents directly and indirectly. For example, in G_{64} agent i_1 observes $i_3's$ private information indirectly via his or her indirect link to agent i_3 given by

$$i_1 \xrightarrow{j_1} i_2 \xrightarrow{j_2} i_3.$$

Because in network G_{64} agent i_1 already observes $i_3's$ private information directly, $i_1's$ indirect observation of i_3 can be thought of as confirming the information gained via his or her direct observation of i_3.

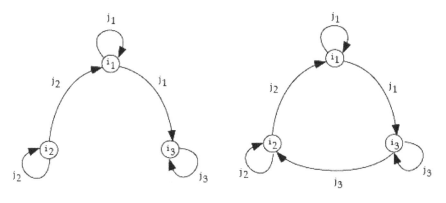

Information-Sharing Network G_{10} Information-Sharing Network G_{42}

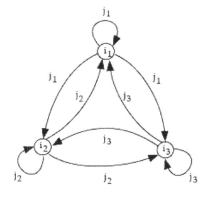

Information-Sharing Network G_{64}

Figure 3.7: Three possible information-sharing networks.

In this example, the set of nodes $N = \{i_1, i_2, i_3\}$ and the set of agents D are one and the same, and the subscript on each arc denotes the agent to whom the arc belongs and thus identifies the node from which the arc must emanate. Also, in this example, arc addition and subtraction are unilateral and can be simultaneous. The m-arc connections between networks G_{10} and G_{42} and between networks G_{42} and G_{64} are depicted below.

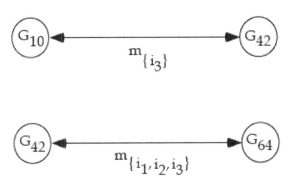

With reference to the first figure above, note that the move from network G_{10} to network G_{42} brought about by agent i_3 can be reversed by agent i_3 (hence, the $m_{\{i_3\}}$-arc connecting networks G_{10} and G_{42} has arrowheads at both ends). This is because arc addition and subtraction are unilateral on the part of the initiating agent. The same can be said about the move from network G_{42} to network G_{64} brought about by coalition $\{i_1, i_2, i_3\}$.

Table 3.1, consisting of four panels, lists all possible information-sharing networks. Denote the collection of all possible information-sharing networks by $\mathbb{G}_I$.

Table 3.1: *All possible information-sharing networks,* $\mathbb{G}_I$

	$(j_3, (i_3, i_3))$			
	$(j_2, (i_2, i_2))$	$\begin{pmatrix} (j_2, (i_2, i_2)), \\ (j_2, (i_2, i_1)) \end{pmatrix}$	$\begin{pmatrix} (j_2, (i_2, i_2)), \\ (j_2, (i_2, i_3)) \end{pmatrix}$	$\begin{pmatrix} (j_2, (i_2, i_2)), \\ (j_2, (i_2, i_1)), \\ (j_1, (i_2, i_3)) \end{pmatrix}$
$(j_1, (i_1, i_1))$	G_1	G_2	G_3	G_4
$\begin{pmatrix} (j_1, (i_1, i_1)), \\ (j_1, (i_1, i_2)) \end{pmatrix}$	G_5	G_6	G_7	G_8
$\begin{pmatrix} (j_1, (i_1, i_1)), \\ (j_1, (i_1, i_3)) \end{pmatrix}$	G_9	G_{10}	G_{11}	G_{12}
$\begin{pmatrix} (j_1, (i_1, i_1)), \\ (j_1, (i_1, i_2)), \\ (j_1, (i_1, i_3)) \end{pmatrix}$	G_{13}	G_{14}	G_{15}	G_{16}

	$\begin{pmatrix} (j_3, (i_3, i_3)), \\ (j_3, (i_3, i_1)) \end{pmatrix}$			
	$(j_2, (i_2, i_2))$	$\begin{pmatrix} (j_2, (i_2, i_2)), \\ (j_2, (i_2, i_1)) \end{pmatrix}$	$\begin{pmatrix} (j_2, (i_2, i_2)), \\ (j_2, (i_2, i_3)) \end{pmatrix}$	$\begin{pmatrix} (j_2, (i_2, i_2)), \\ (j_2, (i_2, i_1)), \\ (j_1, (i_2, i_3)) \end{pmatrix}$
$(j_1, (i_1, i_1))$	G_{17}	G_{18}	G_{19}	G_{20}
$\begin{pmatrix} (j_1, (i_1, i_1)), \\ (j_1, (i_1, i_2)) \end{pmatrix}$	G_{21}	G_{22}	G_{23}	G_{24}
$\begin{pmatrix} (j_1, (i_1, i_1)), \\ (j_1, (i_1, i_3)) \end{pmatrix}$	G_{25}	G_{26}	G_{27}	G_{28}
$\begin{pmatrix} (j_1, (i_1, i_1)), \\ (j_1, (i_1, i_2)), \\ (j_1, (i_1, i_3)) \end{pmatrix}$	G_{29}	G_{30}	G_{31}	G_{32}

(continued)

Table 3.1 *(continued)*

$$\begin{pmatrix} (j_3, (i_3, i_3)), \\ (j_3, (i_3, i_2)) \end{pmatrix}$$

	$(j_2, (i_2, i_2))$	$\begin{pmatrix} (j_2, (i_2, i_2)), \\ (j_2, (i_2, i_1)) \end{pmatrix}$	$\begin{pmatrix} (j_2, (i_2, i_2)), \\ (j_2, (i_2, i_3)) \end{pmatrix}$	$\begin{pmatrix} (j_2, (i_2, i_2)), \\ (j_2, (i_2, i_1)), \\ (j_1, (i_2, i_3)) \end{pmatrix}$
$(j_1, (i_1, i_1))$	G_{33}	G_{34}	G_{35}	G_{36}
$\begin{pmatrix} (j_1, (i_1, i_1)), \\ (j_1, (i_1, i_2)) \end{pmatrix}$	G_{37}	G_{38}	G_{39}	G_{40}
$\begin{pmatrix} (j_1, (i_1, i_1)), \\ (j_1, (i_1, i_3)) \end{pmatrix}$	G_{41}	G_{42}	G_{43}	G_{44}
$\begin{pmatrix} (j_1, (i_1, i_1)), \\ (j_1, (i_1, i_2)), \\ (j_1, (i_1, i_3)) \end{pmatrix}$	G_{45}	G_{46}	G_{47}	G_{48}

$$\begin{pmatrix} (j_3, (i_3, i_3)), \\ (j_3, (i_3, i_1)), \\ (j_3, (i_3, i_2)) \end{pmatrix}$$

	$(j_2, (i_2, i_2))$	$\begin{pmatrix} (j_2, (i_2, i_2)), \\ (j_2, (i_2, i_1)) \end{pmatrix}$	$\begin{pmatrix} (j_2, (i_2, i_2)), \\ (j_2, (i_2, i_3)) \end{pmatrix}$	$\begin{pmatrix} (j_2, (i_2, i_2)), \\ (j_2, (i_2, i_1)), \\ (j_1, (i_2, i_3)) \end{pmatrix}$
$(j_1, (i_1, i_1))$	G_{49}	G_{50}	G_{51}	G_{52}
$\begin{pmatrix} (j_1, (i_1, i_1)), \\ (j_1, (i_1, i_2)) \end{pmatrix}$	G_{53}	G_{54}	G_{55}	G_{56}
$\begin{pmatrix} (j_1, (i_1, i_1)), \\ (j_1, (i_1, i_3)) \end{pmatrix}$	G_{57}	G_{58}	G_{59}	G_{60}
$\begin{pmatrix} (j_1, (i_1, i_1)), \\ (j_1, (i_1, i_2)), \\ (j_1, (i_1, i_3)) \end{pmatrix}$	G_{61}	G_{62}	G_{63}	G_{64}

Table 3.2: *Costs and benefits in supernetworks* $\mathbf{G}_1$ *and* $\mathbf{G}_2$

variables	$\mathbf{G}_1$	$\mathbf{G}_2$
b_1 = value to 1 of his own private information	1	1
r_{12} = benefit to 1 of directly observing the private information of 2	3	3
r_{13} = benefit to 1 of directly observing the private information of 3	2	2
c_{12} = cost to 1 of directly observing the private information of 2	2	2
c_{13} = cost to 1 of directly observing the private information of 3	2	2
e_{12} = benefit to 1 of indirectly observing the private information of 2	.25	.25
e_{13} = benefit to 1 of indirectly observing the private information of 3	.5	.5

Costs and Benefits to Agent 1

variables	$\mathbf{G}_1$	$\mathbf{G}_2$
b_2 = value to 2 of his own private information	1	1
r_{21} = benefit to 2 of directly observing the private information of 1	1	1
r_{23} = benefit to 2 of directly observing the private information of 3	3	3
c_{21} = cost to 2 of directly observing the private information of 1	2	2
c_{23} = cost to 2 of directly observing the private information of 3	2	2
e_{21} = benefit to 2 of indirectly observing the private information of 1	.25	.25
e_{23} = benefit to 2 of indirectly observing the private information of 3	.5	.5

Costs and Benefits to Agent 2

variables	$\mathbf{G}_1$	$\mathbf{G}_2$
b_3 = value to 3 of his own private information	1	1
r_{31} = benefit to 3 of directly observing the private information of 1	1	1
r_{32} = benefit to 3 of directly observing the private information of 2	1	1
c_{31} = cost to 3 of directly observing the private information of 1	2	2
c_{32} = cost to 3 of directly observing the private information of 2	2	2
e_{31} = benefit to 3 of indirectly observing the private information of 1	.5	1.5
e_{32} = benefit to 3 of indirectly observing the private information of 2	.5	1.5

Costs and Benefits to Agent 3

3.5.2. Network Payoffs and Preferences

We construct two possible supernetworks, $\mathbf{G}_1$ and $\mathbf{G}_2$, over the collection $\mathbb{G}_I$ by varying the costs and benefits to each agent of observing, either directly or indirectly, the private information of other agents. Table 3.2, consisting of three panels, summarizes the possibilities.

For example, in constructing supernetwork $\mathbf{G}_1$, we assume that the benefit to agent i_3 of directly observing the private information of agent i_1 is 1 (see the entry in the second row, the $\mathbf{G}_1$ column, in panel 3). Using the numbers in Table 3.2, we can compute the network payoffs, $\{v_d(\cdot) : d \in \{i_1, i_2, i_3\}\}$ for each of the sixty-four information-sharing networks in the collection $\mathbb{G}_I$ under the cost–benefit assumptions corresponding to each of our two supernetworks $\mathbf{G}_1$ and $\mathbf{G}_2$.

Table 3.3 lists all possible network payoffs given the cost–benefit assumptions corresponding to supernetwork $\mathbf{G}_1$.

Table 3.3: *All possible network payoffs in supernetwork* $\mathbf{G}_I$

	$(j_3, (i_3, i_3))$			
	$(j_2, (i_2, i_2))$	$\begin{pmatrix}(j_2, (i_2, i_2)),\\(j_2, (i_2, i_1))\end{pmatrix}$	$\begin{pmatrix}(j_2, (i_2, i_2)),\\(j_2, (i_2, i_3))\end{pmatrix}$	$\begin{pmatrix}(j_2, (i_2, i_2)),\\(j_2, (i_2, i_1)),\\(j_1, (i_2, i_3))\end{pmatrix}$
$(j_1, (i_1, i_1))$	$(1, 1, 1)_1$	$(1, 0, 1)_2$	$(1, 2, 1)_3$	$(1, 1, 1)_4$
$\begin{pmatrix}(j_1, (i_1, i_1)),\\(j_1, (i_1, i_2))\end{pmatrix}$	$(2, 1, 1)_5$	$(2, 0, 1)_6$	$(2.5, 2, 1)_7$	$(2.5, 1, 1)_8$
$\begin{pmatrix}(j_1, (i_1, i_1)),\\(j_1, (i_1, i_3))\end{pmatrix}$	$(1, 1, 1)_9$	$(1, .5, 1)_{10}$	$(1, 2, 1)_{11}$	$(1, 1, 1)_{12}$
$\begin{pmatrix}(j_1, (i_1, i_1)),\\(j_1, (i_1, i_2)),\\(j_1, (i_1, i_3))\end{pmatrix}$	$(2, 1, 1)_{13}$	$(2, .5, 1)_{14}$	$(2.5, 2, 1)_{15}$	$(2.5, 1.5, 1)_{16}$

	$\begin{pmatrix}(j_3, (i_3, i_3)),\\(j_3, (i_3, i_1))\end{pmatrix}$			
	$(j_2, (i_2, i_2))$	$\begin{pmatrix}(j_2, (i_2, i_2)),\\(j_2, (i_2, i_1))\end{pmatrix}$	$\begin{pmatrix}(j_2, (i_2, i_2)),\\(j_2, (i_2, i_3))\end{pmatrix}$	$\begin{pmatrix}(j_2, (i_2, i_2)),\\(j_2, (i_2, i_1)),\\(j_1, (i_2, i_3))\end{pmatrix}$
$(j_1, (i_1, i_1))$	$(1, 1, 0)_{17}$	$(1, 0, 0)_{18}$	$(1, 2.25, 0)_{19}$	$(1, 1.25, 0)_{20}$
$\begin{pmatrix}(j_1, (i_1, i_1)),\\(j_1, (i_1, i_2))\end{pmatrix}$	$(2, 1, .5)_{21}$	$(2, 0, .5)_{22}$	$(2.5, 2.25, .5)_{23}$	$(2.5, 1.25, .5)_{24}$
$\begin{pmatrix}(j_1, (i_1, i_1)),\\(j_1, (i_1, i_3))\end{pmatrix}$	$(1, 1, 0)_{25}$	$(1, .5, 0)_{26}$	$(1, 2.25, 0)_{27}$	$(1, 1.75, 0)_{28}$
$\begin{pmatrix}(j_1, (i_1, i_1)),\\(j_1, (i_1, i_2)),\\(j_1, (i_1, i_3))\end{pmatrix}$	$(2, 1, .5)_{29}$	$(2, .5, .5)_{30}$	$(2.5, 2.25, .5)_{31}$	$(2.5, 1.75, .5)_{32}$

$$\begin{pmatrix} (j_3,(i_3,i_3)), \\ (j_3,(i_3,i_2)) \end{pmatrix}$$

	$(j_2,(i_2,i_2))$	$\begin{pmatrix}(j_2,(i_2,i_2)),\\(j_2,(i_2,i_1))\end{pmatrix}$	$\begin{pmatrix}(j_2,(i_2,i_2)),\\(j_2,(i_2,i_3))\end{pmatrix}$	$\begin{pmatrix}(j_2,(i_2,i_2)),\\(j_2,(i_2,i_1)),\\(j_1,(i_2,i_3))\end{pmatrix}$
$(j_1,(i_1,i_1))$	$(1,1,0)_{33}$	$(1,0,.5)_{34}$	$(1,2,.5)_{35}$	$(1,1,.5)_{36}$
$\begin{pmatrix}(j_1,(i_1,i_1)),\\(j_1,(i_1,i_2))\end{pmatrix}$	$(2,1,0)_{37}$	$(2,0,.5)_{38}$	$(2.5,2,0)_{39}$	$(2.5,2,0)_{40}$
$\begin{pmatrix}(j_1,(i_1,i_1)),\\(j_1,(i_1,i_3))\end{pmatrix}$	$(1.25,1,0)_{41}$	$(1.25,.5,.5)_{42}$	$(1.25,2,0)_{43}$	$(1.25,1.5,.5)_{44}$
$\begin{pmatrix}(j_1,(i_1,i_1)),\\(j_1,(i_1,i_2)),\\(j_1,(i_1,i_3))\end{pmatrix}$	$(2.25,1,0)_{45}$	$(2.25,.5,.5)_{46}$	$(2.75,2,0)_{47}$	$(2.75,1.5,.5)_{48}$

$$\begin{pmatrix} (j_3,(i_3,i_3)), \\ (j_3,(i_3,i_1)), \\ (j_3,(i_3,i_2)) \end{pmatrix}$$

	$(j_2,(i_2,i_2))$	$\begin{pmatrix}(j_2,(i_2,i_2)),\\(j_2,(i_2,i_1))\end{pmatrix}$	$\begin{pmatrix}(j_2,(i_2,i_2)),\\(j_2,(i_2,i_3))\end{pmatrix}$	$\begin{pmatrix}(j_2,(i_2,i_2)),\\(j_2,(i_2,i_1)),\\(j_1,(i_2,i_3))\end{pmatrix}$
$(j_1,(i_1,i_1))$	$(1,1,-1)_{49}$	$(1,0,-.5)_{50}$	$(1,2.25,-1)_{51}$	$(1,1.25,-.5)_{52}$
$\begin{pmatrix}(j_1,(i_1,i_1)),\\(j_1,(i_1,i_2))\end{pmatrix}$	$(2,1,-.5)_{53}$	$(2,0,0)_{54}$	$(2.5,2.25,-.5)_{55}$	$(2.5,1.25,0)_{56}$
$\begin{pmatrix}(j_1,(i_1,i_1)),\\(j_1,(i_1,i_3))\end{pmatrix}$	$(1.25,1,-1)_{57}$	$(1.25,.5,-.5)_{58}$	$(1.25,2.25,-1)_{59}$	$(1.25,1.75,-.5)_{60}$
$\begin{pmatrix}(j_1,(i_1,i_1)),\\(j_1,(i_1,i_2)),\\(j_1,(i_1,i_3))\end{pmatrix}$	$(2.25,1,-1)_{61}$	$(2.25,.5,0)_{62}$	$(2.75,2.25,-.5)_{63}$	$(2.75,1.75,0)_{64}$

For example, consider network G_{10}. Under the cost–benefit assumptions corresponding to supernetwork $\mathbf{G}_1$, we have

$$v_{i_1}(G_{10}) = b_1 + (r_{13} - c_{13}) = 1 + (2 - 2) = 1,$$
$$v_{i_2}(G_{10}) = b_2 + (r_{21} - c_{21}) + e_{23} = 1 + (1 - 2) + .5 = .5,$$
$$v_{i_3}(G_{10}) = b_3 = 1,$$
and therefore
$$\left(v_{i_1}(G_{10}), v_{i_2}(G_{10}), v_{i_3}(G_{10})\right) = (1, .5, 1).$$

Table 3.4 lists all possible network payoffs given the cost–benefit assumptions corresponding to supernetwork $\mathbf{G}_2$.

Table 3.4: *All possible network payoffs in supernetwork $\mathbf{G}_1$*

	$(j_3, (i_3, i_3))$			
	$(j_2, (i_2, i_2))$	$\begin{pmatrix} (j_2, (i_2, i_2)), \\ (j_2, (i_2, i_1)) \end{pmatrix}$	$\begin{pmatrix} (j_2, (i_2, i_2)), \\ (j_2, (i_2, i_3)) \end{pmatrix}$	$\begin{pmatrix} (j_2, (i_2, i_2)), \\ (j_2, (i_2, i_1)), \\ (j_1, (i_2, i_3)) \end{pmatrix}$
$(j_1, (i_1, i_1))$	$(1, 1, 1)_1$	$(1, 0, 1)_2$	$(1, 2, 1)_3$	$(1, 1, 1)_4$
$\begin{pmatrix} (j_1, (i_1, i_1)), \\ (j_1, (i_1, i_2)) \end{pmatrix}$	$(2, 1, 1)_5$	$(2, 0, 1)_6$	$(2.5, 2, 1)_7$	$(2.5, 1, 1)_8$
$\begin{pmatrix} (j_1, (i_1, i_1)), \\ (j_1, (i_1, i_3)) \end{pmatrix}$	$(1, 1, 1)_9$	$(1, .5, 1)_{10}$	$(1, 2, 1)_{11}$	$(1, 1, 1)_{12}$
$\begin{pmatrix} (j_1, (i_1, i_1)), \\ (j_1, (i_1, i_2)), \\ (j_1, (i_1, i_3)) \end{pmatrix}$	$(2, 1, 1)_{13}$	$(2, .5, 1)_{14}$	$(2.5, 2, 1)_{15}$	$(2.5, 1.5, 1)_{16}$

	$\begin{pmatrix} (j_3, (i_3, i_3)), \\ (j_3, (i_3, i_2)) \end{pmatrix}$			
	$(j_2, (i_2, i_2))$	$\begin{pmatrix} (j_2, (i_2, i_2)), \\ (j_2, (i_2, i_1)) \end{pmatrix}$	$\begin{pmatrix} (j_2, (i_2, i_2)), \\ (j_2, (i_2, i_3)) \end{pmatrix}$	$\begin{pmatrix} (j_2, (i_2, i_2)), \\ (j_2, (i_2, i_1)), \\ (j_1, (i_2, i_3)) \end{pmatrix}$
$(j_1, (i_1, i_1))$	$(1, 1, 0)_{17}$	$(1, 0, 0)_{18}$	$(1, 2.25, 0)_{19}$	$(1, 1.25, 0)_{20}$
$\begin{pmatrix} (j_1, (i_1, i_1)), \\ (j_1, (i_1, i_2)) \end{pmatrix}$	$(2, 1, 1.5)_{21}$	$(2, 0, 1.5)_{22}$	$(2.5, 2.25, 1.5)_{23}$	$(2.5, 1.25, 1.5)_{24}$
$\begin{pmatrix} (j_1, (i_1, i_1)), \\ (j_1, (i_1, i_3)) \end{pmatrix}$	$(1, 1, 0)_{25}$	$(1, .5, 0)_{26}$	$(1, 2.25, 0)_{27}$	$(1, 1.75, 0)_{28}$
$\begin{pmatrix} (j_1, (i_1, i_1)), \\ (j_1, (i_1, i_2)), \\ (j_1, (i_1, i_3)) \end{pmatrix}$	$(2, 1, 1.5)_{29}$	$(2, .5, 1.5)_{30}$	$(2.5, 2.25, 1.5)_{31}$	$(2.5, 1.75, 1.5)_{32}$

$$\begin{pmatrix} (j_3, (i_3, i_3)), \\ (j_3, (i_3, i_2)) \end{pmatrix}$$

	$(j_2, (i_2, i_2))$	$\begin{pmatrix} (j_2, (i_2, i_2)), \\ (j_2, (i_2, i_1)) \end{pmatrix}$	$\begin{pmatrix} (j_2, (i_2, i_2)), \\ (j_2, (i_2, i_3)) \end{pmatrix}$	$\begin{pmatrix} (j_2, (i_2, i_2)), \\ (j_2, (i_2, i_1)), \\ (j_1, (i_2, i_3)) \end{pmatrix}$
$(j_1, (i_1, i_1))$	$(1, 1, 0)_{33}$	$(1, 0, 1.5)_{34}$	$(1, 2, 1.5)_{35}$	$(1, 1, .5)_{36}$
$\begin{pmatrix} (j_1, (i_1, i_1)), \\ (j_1, (i_1, i_2)) \end{pmatrix}$	$(2, 1, 0)_{37}$	$(2, 0, 1.5)_{38}$	$(2.5, 2, 0)_{39}$	$(2.5, 1, 1.5)_{40}$
$\begin{pmatrix} (j_1, (i_1, i_1)), \\ (j_1, (i_1, i_3)) \end{pmatrix}$	$(1.25, 1, 0)_{41}$	$(1.25, .5, 1.5)_{42}$	$(1.25, 2, 0)_{43}$	$(1.25, 1.5, 1.5)_{44}$
$\begin{pmatrix} (j_1, (i_1, i_1)), \\ (j_1, (i_1, i_2)), \\ (j_1, (i_1, i_3)) \end{pmatrix}$	$(2.25, 1, 0)_{45}$	$(2.25, .5, 1.5)_{46}$	$(2.75, 2, 0)_{47}$	$(2.75, 1.5, 1.5)_{48}$

$$\begin{pmatrix} (j_3, (i_3, i_3)), \\ (j_3, (i_3, i_1)), \\ (j_3, (i_3, i_2)) \end{pmatrix}$$

	$(j_2, (i_2, i_2))$	$\begin{pmatrix} (j_2, (i_2, i_2)), \\ (j_2, (i_2, i_1)) \end{pmatrix}$	$\begin{pmatrix} (j_2, (i_2, i_2)), \\ (j_2, (i_2, i_3)) \end{pmatrix}$	$\begin{pmatrix} (j_2, (i_2, i_2)), \\ (j_2, (i_2, i_1)), \\ (j_1, (i_2, i_3)) \end{pmatrix}$
$(j_1, (i_1, i_1))$	$(1, 1, -1)_{49}$	$(1, 0, .5)_{50}$	$(1, 2.25, -1)_{51}$	$(1, 1.25, .5)_{52}$
$\begin{pmatrix} (j_1, (i_1, i_1)), \\ (j_1, (i_1, i_2)) \end{pmatrix}$	$(2, 1, .5)_{53}$	$(2, 0, 2)_{54}$	$(2.5, 2.25, .5)_{55}$	$(2.5, 1.25, 2)_{56}$
$\begin{pmatrix} (j_1, (i_1, i_1)), \\ (j_1, (i_1, i_3)) \end{pmatrix}$	$(1.25, 1, -1)_{57}$	$(1.25, .5, .5)_{58}$	$(1.25, 2.25, -1)_{59}$	$(1.25, 1.75, .5)_{60}$
$\begin{pmatrix} (j_1, (i_1, i_1)), \\ (j_1, (i_1, i_2)), \\ (j_1, (i_1, i_3)) \end{pmatrix}$	$(2.25, 1, .5)_{61}$	$(2.25, .5, 2)_{62}$	$(2.75, 2.25, .5)_{63}$	$(2.75, 1.75, 2)_{64}$

Table 3.5: *Farsightedly consistent sets and Nash sets*
corresponding to supernetworks $\mathbf{G}_1$ *and* $\mathbf{G}_2$

	$\mathbf{G}_1$	$\mathbf{G}_2$
Farsightedly consistent set $\mathbb{F}^*$	$\{G_7, G_{15}\}$	$\{G_{23}, G_{31}\}$
Nash networks	$\{G_7, G_{15}\}$	$\{G_{21}, G_{29}\}$

3.5.3. Computational Results

In Table 3.5 we list the farsightedly consistent sets corresponding to supernetworks $\mathbf{G}_1$ and $\mathbf{G}_2$. We also list the Nash networks for each of our supernetworks.

Figure 3.8 depicts the farsightedly consistent networks as well as the Nash networks in supernetwork $\mathbf{G}_1$.

Note that in the Nash and farsightedly consistent networks G_7 and G_{15}, agent i_3 observes only his or her own private information. The reason for this can be seen in the $\mathbf{G}_1$ column in the third panel of Table 3.2: there is a net loss to agent i_3 in directly observing the private information of the other agents, and this net loss is not compensated by agent $i_3's$ indirectly observing the private information of the other agents. In particular,

$$(r_{31} - c_{31}) + (r_{32} - c_{32}) = (-1) + (-1) = -2,$$
$$\text{whereas}$$
$$e_{31} + e_{32} = (.5) + (.5) = 1.$$

In supernetwork $\mathbf{G}_2$ we have changed the benefits to agent i_3 of indirectly observing the private information of the other agents. In particular, note that in the $\mathbf{G}_2$

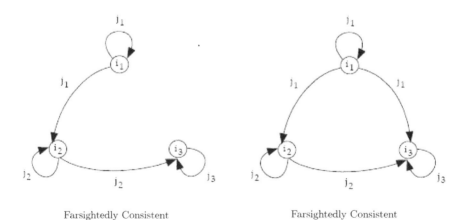

Farsightedly Consistent   Farsightedly Consistent

and Nash Network G_7 and Nash Network G_{15}

Figure 3.8: The farsightedly consistent networks and Nash networks in supernetwork $\mathbf{G}_1$.

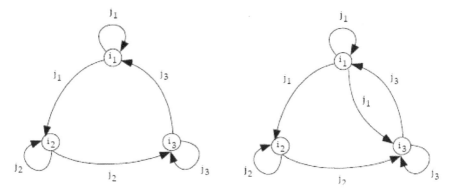

Farsightedly Consistent Network G_{23} Farsightedly Consistent Network G_{31}

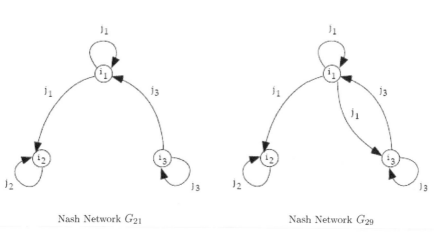

Nash Network G_{21} Nash Network G_{29}

Figure 3.9: The farsightedly stable networks and Nash networks in supernetwork $\mathbf{G}_2$.

column of the third panel of Table 3.2 we now have

$$e_{31} = 1.5 \quad \text{and} \quad e_{32} = 1.5.$$

Also note that in Table 3.2 this is the *only* modification we have made in the specification of benefits and costs in order to change supernetwork $\mathbf{G}_1$ to supernetwork $\mathbf{G}_2$. But even this small change greatly alters the farsightedly consistent set and the Nash set. In supernetwork $\mathbf{G}_2$, the farsightedly consistent set is $\{G_{23}, G_{31}\}$, whereas the Nash set is $\{G_{21}, G_{29}\}$. Thus, now the farsightedly consistent set and the Nash set are nonintersecting. Figure 3.9 depicts the farsightedly consistent networks and the Nash networks in supernetwork $\mathbf{G}_2$.

In supernetwork $\mathbf{G}_2$, the benefits to agent i_3 of indirectly observing the private information of the other agents have been increased. As a result, in the farsightedly consistent networks, as well as the Nash networks in supernetwork $\mathbf{G}_2$, agent i_3

directly observes the private information of agent i_1 at a loss in order to gain the benefit of indirectly observing the private information of agent i_2.

BIBLIOGRAPHY

[1] Bala, V. and S. Goyal (2000), "A Noncooperative Model of Network Formation," *Econometrica* 68, 1181–1229.

[2] Berge, C. (2001), *The Theory of Graphs*, Mineola, NY: Dover. (reprint of the translated French edition published by Dunod, Paris, 1958).

[3] Bhattacharya, A. and A. Ziad (2003), "On Conservative Stable Standards of Behavior in Situations with Perfect Foresight," CORE Discussion Paper 2003/49.

[4] Chvatal, V. and L. Lovasz (1972), "Every Directed Graph Has a Semi-Kernel," in *Hypergraph Seminar*, Lecture Notes in Mathematics 411, Berlin: Springer-Verlag.

[5] Chwe, M. (1994), "Farsighted Coalitional Stability," *Journal of Economic Theory* 63, 299–325.

[6] Deroian, F. (2003), "Farsighted Strategies in the Formation of a Communication Network," *Economic Letters* 80, 343–349.

[7] Dutta, B., S. Ghosal, and D. Ray (2003), "Farsighted Network Formation," typescript, New York University.

[8] Dutta, B. and S. Mutuswami (1997), "Stable Networks," *Journal of Economic Theory* 76, 322–344.

[9] Galeana-Sanchez, H. and Xueliang Li (1998), "Semikernels and (k, l)-Kernels in Digraphs," *SIAM Journal of Discrete Mathematics* 11, 340–346.

[10] Gillies, D. B. (1959), "Solutions to General Non-Zero Games," in A. W. Tucker and R. D. Luce (eds.), *Contributions to the Theory of Games*, 4. Vols. Princeton University Press.

[11] Greenberg, J. (1990), *The Theory of Social Situations: An Alternative Game-Theoretic Approach.* Cambridge, UK: Cambridge University Press.

[12] Guilbaud, G. T. (1949), "La Theorie des Jeux," *Economie Appliquee* 2, 18.

[13] Harsanyi, J. C. (1974), "An Equilibrium-Point Interpretation of Stable Sets and a Proposed Alternative Definition," *Management Science* 20, 1472–1495.

[14] Jackson, M. O. (2003), "The Stability and Efficiency of Economic and Social Networks," in M. Sertel and S. Koray (eds.), *Advances in Economic Design.* Berlin: Springer-Verlag.

[15] Jackson, M. O. and A. van den Nouweland (2001), "Strongly Stable Networks," typescript, California Institute of Technology.

[16] Jackson, M. O. and A. Watts (2002), "The Evolution of Social and Economic Networks," *Journal of Economic Theory* 106, 265–295.

[17] Jackson, M. O. and A. Wolinsky (1996), "A Strategic Model of Social and Economic Networks," *Journal of Economic Theory* 71, 44–74.

[18] Kamat, S. and F. H. Page, Jr. (2001), "Computing Farsighted Stable Sets," typescript, University of Alabama.

[19] Konishi, H. and D. Ray (2003), "Coalition Formation as a Dynamic Process," typescript, New York University, *Journal of Economic Theory* 110, 1–41.

[20] Li, S. (1992), "Far-sighted Strong Equilibrium and Oligopoly," *Economic Letters* 40, 39–44.

[21] Li, S. (1993), "Stability of Voting Games," *Social Choice and Welfare*, 10, 51–56.

[22] Luo, X. (2001), "General Systems and φ-Stable Sets – A Formal Analysis of Socio-economic Environments," *Journal of Mathematical Economics* 36, 95–109.

[23] Mariotti, M. and L. Xue (2002), "Farsightedness in Coalition Formation," typescript, University of Aarhus.

[24] Mauleon, A. and V. Vannetelbosch (2003), "Farsightedness and Cautiousness in Coalition Formation," Nota Di Lavoro 52.2003, Fondazione Eni Enrico Mattei.

[25] Page, Jr., F. H., M. H. Wooders, and S. Kamat (2001), "Networks and Farsighted Stability," Warwick Economic Research Papers, No. 621, University of Warwick to appear in *Journal of Economic Theory*.

[26] Richardson, M. (1953), "Solutions of Irreflexive Relations," *Annals of Mathematics* 58, 573–580.

[27] Rockafellar, R. T. (1984), *Network Flows and Monotropic Optimization*, New York: John Wiley & Sons Inc.

[28] Roth, A. E. (1975), "A Lattice Fixed-Point Theorem with Constraints," *Annals of Mathematics* 81, 136–138.

[29] Roth, A. E. (1977), "A Fixed-Point Approach to Stability in Cooperative Games," S. Karamardian (ed.), *Fixed Points: Algorithms and Applications*. New York: Academic Press.

[30] von Neumann, J. and O. Morgenstern (1944) *Theory of Games and Economic Behavior*, Princeton University Press.

[31] Watts, A. (2001), "A Dynamic Model of Network Formation," *Games and Economic Behavior* 34, 331–341.

[32] Watts, A. (2002), "Non-myopic Formation of Circle Networks," *Economic Letters* 74, 277–282.

[33] Xue, L. (1998), "Coalitional Stability under Perfect Foresight," *Economic Theory* 11, 603–627.

[34] Xue, L. (2000), "Negotiation-Proof Nash Equilibrium," *International Journal of Game Theory* 29, 339–357.

4

Learning in Networks

Sanjeev Goyal

4.1. Introduction

In a wide range of economic situations, individuals make decisions without being fully informed about the rewards from different options. In many of these instances the decision problems are recurrent, and it is natural that individuals use their past experience and the experience of others in making current decisions. The experience of others is important for two reasons:

(1) It may yield information on different actions per se (as in the case of the choice of new consumer products, agricultural practices, or medicines prescribed).

(2) In many settings the rewards from an action depend on the choices made by others, and so there is a direct value to knowing about other's actions (as in the case of which credit card to use, which language to learn, or whether to buy a fax machine).

This suggests that the precise way in which individuals interact can influence the generation and dissemination of useful information and that this could shape individual choices and social outcomes. In recent years, these considerations have motivated a substantial body of work on learning in economics, which takes explicit account of the structure of interaction among individual entities. The present chapter provides a survey of this research.

I will consider the following simple framework: there is a set of individuals located on nodes of a network, and the arcs of the network reflect relations between these individuals. At regular intervals, individuals choose an action from a set of alternatives. They are uncertain about the rewards from different actions. They use their own past experience and gather information from their neighbors (individuals who are linked to them) as the basis for choosing an action that maximizes individual payoffs. I start by studying the influence of network structure on individual and social learning. In this part the network is taken as given. In the second part

I would like to thank Yann Bramoulle, William Brock, Leigh Tesfatsion, Antonella Ianni, Werner Raub, Larry Samuelson, Gerhard Sorger, Brian Skyrms, and Fernando Vega-Redondo for useful comments on an earlier version of the chapter.

of the chapter I explore learning in a setting in which the network itself is evolving owing to individual choices on link formation. Here, the focus will be on the way that individual incentives shape the evolution of structure as well as economic performance.[1]

This framework allows for a rich set of interpretations, and I provide some examples to illustrate this:

- Adoption of consumer products: Consumers make decisions on brand choice without complete knowledge of the alternatives. They try out different brands and also gather information from market surveys and their friends and acquaintances to make more informed choices.
- Medical innovation: Doctors have to decide on new treatments for ailments without complete knowledge of their efficacy and side effects; they read professional journals and exchange information with other doctors to determine whether to prescribe a new treatment.
- Agricultural practices: Farmers decide on whether to adopt new seeds and farming packages without full knowledge of their suitability for the specific soil and weather conditions they face. They use the experience of neighboring farms and extension services in making decisions.

In these examples, individuals use their links with others primarily to gather useful information on product characteristics or suitability. In the next set of examples, there is strategic interaction between individuals, and the rewards from an action depend on the actions of others.

- Adoption of new information technology: Individuals decide on whether to adopt fax machines or a new computer operating system without full knowledge of its usefulness. This usefulness is related to the choices of others with whom they would like to communicate.
- Language choice: Individuals choose which language to learn at school as a second language. Here the rewards depend on the choices of others with whom they expect to interact in the future.
- Credit card choice: Individual consumers choose a credit without full knowledge of the card's benefits because they do not know how often the card can be used. The benefit in turn depends on the credit cards adopted by shops that they frequent. The shopkeepers face a similar decision problem.
- Social norms on punctuality: Individuals decide whether to be on time for their appointments or to arrive somewhat late. The returns from being on time and the costs associated with being late depend on the choices of others whom they are going to meet.

---

[1] In this chapter I will be mostly concerned with learning in models in which agents are either fully rational or the departures from full rationality are relatively minor. Moreover, the focus is entirely on analytical results. I will therefore not be discussing the large literature on agent-based modeling and computational economics that studies similar issues. For surveys of this work, see Judd and Tesfatsion (2004 forthcoming) and Kirman and Zimmermann (2001). For surveys on static models of network formation, see the first three chapters of this volume.

The work discussed in this survey should be seen as part of a larger research program in economics that examines the role of informal institutions and nonmarket interaction in shaping economic activity; for general introductions to this area, see Goyal (1999), Kirman (1997), and Young (1998). I now briefly mention some closely related strands of research. There is a large and growing body of empirical work that studies the influence of the network – interaction structure on economic outcomes.[2] This work documents the different ways in which individual behavior is sensitive to the patterns of interaction and also illustrates how changes in the patterns of interaction lead to changes in individual behavior and social outcomes. There is also a significant body of experimental research on the effects of networks and nonmarket interaction on individual behavior and social learning.[3]

The study of learning has been one of the most active fields of research in economics in the last two decades. Different aspects of this research have been surveyed in articles and books; see, for example, Blume and Easley (1995), Fudenberg and Levine (1999), Kandori (1997), Marimon (1997), and Samuelson (1997). The distinctive feature of this chapter is its focus on the role of interaction structures in learning.

I would next like to mention the early work of Coleman (1966) and Schelling (1975) and the large body of work in economic sociology that studies the effects of social structure on economic performance. For an introduction to some of the themes in this body of work, see Burt (1994), Granovetter (1974, 1985), Raub and Weesie (1990), and Smelser and Swedberg (1994). There is also an extensive literature on network formation in mathematical sociology; for recent work in this area see Banks and Carley (1996), Doreian and Stokman (2001), and Snijders (2001). I would like briefly to relate the work in economics and sociology. Traditionally, the relationship between economics research and sociology research has been seen as follows: In the economics strand, most of the research has a relatively simple formulation of the objective function – maximization of a payoff function – but a relatively rich formulation of the strategic possibilities inherent in the network formation process. On the other hand, the work in sociology endows individuals with a rich and varied set of motivations but pays relatively less attention to the strategic aspects of the network formation process. A second difference is the emphasis on the relationship between individual incentives and social efficiency in economics, which is something that seems to be less studied by sociologists. In recent years, as the rational choice school has become more prominent in sociology, the research methodology in the two subjects has become more similar.

---

[2] See, for example, Hagerstrand (1969), Griliches (1957), and Ryan and Gross (1943) on diffusion of new agricultural practices; Coleman (1966) and Taylor (1979) on diffusion and patterns of medical practices; Young (1998) on the spread of traffic norms; Elias (1978) on the history of social customs and manner; Munshi (2003) on migration and social networks; Watkins (1991) on the spread of norms in marriage and fertility; Burke and Young (2001) on norms in contracting; and Glaeser, Sacredote and Scheinkman (1996) on local interaction and criminal activity. For a discussion on the technical issues arising in the measurement of local effects, see Glaeser and Scheinkman (2002), Brock and Durlauf (2001), and Manski (2000).

[3] Kosfeld (2004) provides a survey of the experimental work.

Finally, I mention the rapidly growing literature in physics on the subject of networks. This work highlights statistical regularities of actual networks such as the World Wide Web, the Internet, the network of coauthors (in different disciplines), and the network of actors. The empirical work shows that these networks display small-world features (the average distance between nodes in the network is relatively short), clustering (high overlap between the connections of connected nodes), and a scale-free distribution of links. The research has also developed simple dynamic models of expanding networks that generate these statistical properties. For comprehensive surveys of this work in physics, see Albert and Barabasi (2002) and Dorogovtsev and Mendes (2003). The distinctive element of the research in economics is the emphasis on individual incentives and strategic interaction.

I believe that the issues addressed here are of general interest, and so I have tried to make this survey accessible to readers with different backgrounds. The main results are presented precisely, and the intuition behind them is developed in some detail. On occasion, to keep the exposition smooth, I have taken the liberty of omitting some technical assumptions (or qualifications). To make up for this, I have provided complete references for all the results reported, and the enthusiastic reader is encouraged to refer to the originals for the mathematical proofs.

The rest of the chapter is organized as follows. In Section 4.2, I introduce networks and present the basic terminology to be used throughout the survey. I start with a presentation of results on learning within a given network. Section 4.3 considers learning about optimal actions in nonstrategic environments, whereas Section 4.4 considers learning about optimal actions in strategic environments. I then discuss learning in evolving networks. Section 4.5 discusses learning about optimal link decisions, and Section 4.6 examines learning about optimal links as well as actions in strategic games. Section 4.7 concludes.

4.2. Networks

Let $N = \{1, 2, \ldots, n\}$ be a finite set of individuals or decision makers, each of whom is located (and identified with) a distinct node of a network. An arc or a link between two individuals i and j is denoted by $g_{i,j}$, where $g_{i,j} \in \{0, 1\}$. Here, $g_{i,j} = 1$ reflects the presence of a link, whereas $g_{i,j} = 0$ denotes the absence of a line from i to j. In Figure 4.1, for example, there are three players: 1, 2 and 3, and $g_{1,3} = g_{3,1} = g_{1,2} = 1$. We denote a network by g and the set of all networks by $\mathcal{G}$. There is a one-to-one correspondence between the set of directed networks on n vertices and the set $\mathcal{G}$. We say there is a *path* from j to i in g either if $g_{i,j} = 1$ or there exist distinct players $j_1, \ldots, j_m$ different from i and j such that $g_{i,j_1} = g_{j_1,j_2} = \cdots = g_{j_m,j} = 1$. For example, in Figure 4.2 there is a path from player 2 to player 3. The notation "$j \xrightarrow{g} i$" indicates that a path exists from j to i in g. A network g is said to be connected if there is a path between any pair of players i and j in g. The (geodesic) distance from player j to player i in g is the number of links in the shortest path from j to i and is denoted $d_{i,j}(g)$. We set $d_{i,j}(g) = \infty$ if there is no path from j to i in g.

Figure 4.1: A directed network.

I now define neighborhoods of players in a network. Let $N^d(i; g) = \{k \in N | g_{i,k} = 1\}$ be the set of individuals with whom i has a direct link in network g. We refer to $N^d(i; g)$ as the set of direct neighbors of i in network g. Let $N(i; g) = \{k \in N | k \xrightarrow{g} i\}$ be the set of individuals whom i can directly or indirectly access in network g. Let $\eta_i^d : \mathcal{G} \to \{0, \ldots, n-1\}$ be defined as $\eta_i^d(g) \equiv |N^d(i; g)|$. Here, $\eta_i^d(g)$ is the number of individuals with whom i is directly linked in network g. The term $\eta_i(g)$ is defined correspondingly. Thus, in Figure 4.1, $N(1; g) = \{1, 2, 3\}$, $N(2; g) = \{2\}$, $N(3; g) = \{1, 2, 3\}$, whereas $N^d(1; g) = \{2, 3\}$, $N^d(2; g) = \phi$, and $N^d(3; g) = \{1\}$.

A component of g is a subset $C \subset N$ and the set of all links between the members of C in g with the property that for every distinct pair of players i and j in C I have $j \xrightarrow{g} i$ (equivalently, $j \in N(i; g)$), and there is no strict superset C' of C in g for which this is true. A network g is said to be *minimal* if the deletion of any link increases the number of components in g. We can also say that a network g is *connected* if it has a unique component. If the unique component is minimal, g is described as being *minimally connected*. A network that is not connected is referred to as being *disconnected*. A network is said to be *empty* if $N(i; g) = \{i\}$, and it is called *complete* if $N^d(i; g) = N\backslash\{i\}$ for all $i \in N$. We denote the empty and the complete network by g^e and g^c, respectively. A *star* network has a central player i such that $g_{i,j} = g_{j,i} = 1$ for all $j \in N\backslash\{i\}$ and there are no other links. A *wheel* network is one in which the players are arranged as $\{i_1, \ldots, i_n\}$ with $g_{i_2,i_1} = \cdots = g_{i_n,i_{n-1}} = g_{i_1,i_n} = 1$ and there are no other links. The wheel network is denoted g^w. Figure 4.2 presents these networks for a society with four people.

Two networks $g \in \mathcal{G}$ and $g' \in \mathcal{G}$ are equivalent if g' can be obtained by a relabeling of the players in g. For example, if g is the network in Figure 4.1 and g' is the network in which players 1 and 2 are interchanged, then g and g' are equivalent. The equivalence relation partitions $\mathcal{G}$ into classes: each class is referred to as an

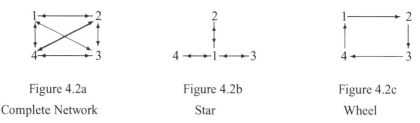

Figure 4.2a	Figure 4.2b	Figure 4.2c
Complete Network	Star	Wheel

Figure 4.2: Some well-known network.

architecture. For example, there are n possible "star" networks, all of which come under the equivalence class of the star architecture. Likewise, the wheel architecture is the equivalence class of $(n - 1)!$ networks consisting of all permutations of n individuals in a circle.

We say that a network graph is *regular* if all individuals have the same number of neighbors, $N^d(i; g) = k$, for some $k \in \{0, 1, 2 \ldots, n - 1\}$. In this case the number of neighbors is referred to as the *degree* of the network.

The preceding description is for directed networks – that is, networks in which there is an explicit direction to the arc between two nodes. In particular, in directed networks the presence of a link $g_{i,j} = 1$ says nothing about the status of the link $g_{j,i}$. By contrast, in undirected networks, a link has no orientation or direction and $g_{i,j} = g_{j,i}$. In some parts of the survey, I will discuss undirected networks; the concepts and terminology for these networks can be developed analogously.

4.3. Nonstrategic Interaction

This section addresses learning about optimal actions in a setting in which the rewards from an action do not depend on the actions chosen by other individuals.

I consider the following general framework. There are many decision makers, each of whom faces a similar decision problem: to choose an action at regular intervals without knowing the true payoffs from the different actions. The action chosen generates a random reward and also provides information concerning the true payoffs. An individual uses this information as well as the experience of a subset of the society – that person's *neighbors* – to update his or her prior beliefs. Given the updated beliefs, an individual chooses an action that maximizes one-period expected utility. I study the dynamic process of individuals' beliefs, actions, and utilities. Our interest is in the influence of the structure of neighborhoods on the actions that individuals choose and the transmission of information. I first present the analysis of learning in fixed networks and then discuss random networks.

4.3.1. Learning from Neighbors

The nature of neighborhood influence on individual choice has been studied in early papers by Allen (1982) and Ellison and Fudenberg (1993). In this section I first present the papers by Bala and Goyal (1998, 2001), as these papers fit in more naturally within the general framework of the survey – which involves a finite number of individuals located in a deterministic network structure, finite actions, and myopic best-response decision rules. I will discuss the papers by Allen and Ellison and Fudenberg later in this section.

Decision Problem. Time is assumed to be discrete and is indexed by $t = 1, 2, \ldots$. There are $n \geq 3$ individuals; an individual i chooses an action from a finite set of alternatives denoted by S_i. In this section, I assume that $S_i = S_j = A$ for every pair of individuals i and j. The payoffs from an action depend on the state of the world

θ, which belongs to a finite set Θ. If θ is the true state and an individual chooses action $a \in A$, then he or she observes an outcome $y \in Y$ with conditional density $\phi(y, a; \theta)$ and obtains a reward $r(a, y)$. To simplify matters, I will assume that Y is the real line and that the reward function $r(a, .)$ is bounded.

Individuals do not know the true state of the world; their private information is summarized in a prior belief over the set of states. For individual i this prior is denoted by $\mu_{i,1}$. The set of prior beliefs is denoted by $\mathcal{P}(\Theta)$. I assume that priors of all individuals are interior, that is, $\mu_{i,1}(\theta) > 0, \forall\, \theta$, and $\forall\, i \in N$. Given belief μ, an individual's one-period expected utility from action a is given by

$$u(a, \mu) = \sum_{\theta \in \Theta} \mu(\theta) \int_Y r(a, y)\phi(y, a; \theta)dy. \qquad (4.3.1)$$

I assume that individuals have similar preferences reflected in a common reward function $r(., .)$. I will consider the role of heterogeneity later. Let $G : \mathcal{P}(\Theta) \to X$ be the one-period optimality correspondence:

$$G(\mu) = \{a \in A | u(a, \mu) \geq u(a', \mu), \forall a' \in A\} \qquad (4.3.2)$$

Let δ_θ represent point mass belief on the state θ; then $G(\delta_\theta)$ denotes the set of optimal actions if the true state is θ. I now provide an example (of a two-arm bandit problem), which is a special case of the framework outlined above in this section.

Example 4.1. *Suppose $A = \{a_0, a_1\}$ and $\Theta = \{\theta_o, \theta_1\}$. In state θ_1, action a_1 yields Bernoulli-distributed payoffs with parameter $\pi \in (1/2, 1)$, that is, it yields 1 with probability π and 0 with probability $1 - \pi$. In state θ_o, action a_1 yields a payoff of 1 with probability $1 - \pi$ and 0 with probability π. Furthermore, in both states, action a_o yields payoffs that are Bernoulli distributed with probability $1/2$. Hence, action a_1 is optimal in state θ_1, whereas action a_o is optimal in state θ_o. The belief of an individual is a number $\mu \in (0, 1)$, which represents the probability that the true state is θ_1. The one-period optimality correspondence is given by*

$$G(\mu) = \begin{cases} a_1 & \text{if } \mu \geq 1/2 \\ a_o & \text{if } \mu \leq 1/2. \end{cases}$$

Dynamics. For each $i \in N$, let $\psi : \mathcal{P} \to A$ be a selection from the one-period optimality correspondence G. In period 1, each individual chooses $\psi(\mu_{i,1})$ and observes the outcome; individual i also observes the actions and outcomes of each of his or her neighbors, $j \in N^d(i)$. I assume that individuals use this information to update their prior $\mu_{i,1}$ and then make a decision in period 2, and so on. In particular, I assume that an individual does not take into account that the actions of his or her neighbors may provide information about what these neighbors have observed about their neighbors. There are two reasons for this assumption. The first reason is descriptive realism: I feel that agents either do not have the computational capacity to work through these inferences or do not find the computations involved worthwhile. The second reason is tractability of the model. This assumption as well as the assumption of myopic optimization helps me to simplify the model and allows me to focus on the role of interaction structure directly.

I need some additional notation to describe the dynamic process. For a fixed θ, let $(\Omega, \mathcal{F}, P^\theta)$ define the probability triple, where Ω contains all the sample realizations of all the individuals over time and P^θ is the probability measure induced over the sample paths by $\theta \in \Theta$. For a subset $B \subset \Theta$ and H, a measurable subset of Ω, let $P_i(B \times H)$ be given by

$$P_i(B \times H) = \sum_{\theta \in B} \mu_{i,1}(\theta) P^\theta(H) \tag{4.3.3}$$

for each individual $i \in N$. A typical sample path is of the form $\omega = (\theta, \omega')$, where θ is the state of nature and $w' = ((y_{i,1}^a)_{a \in A, i \in N}, (y_{i,2}^a)_{a \in A, i \in N}, \ldots, (y_{i,t}^a)_{a \in A, i \in N} \cdots)$, where $y_{i,t}^a \in Y_{i,t}^a = Y$. Let $C_{i,t} = \Psi(\mu_{i,t})$ denote the action of individual i in period t, $Z_{i,t}$ the outcome of this action, and $U_{i,t}(\omega) = u(C_{i,t}, \mu_{i,t})$ the expected utility of i with respect to his or her own action at time t. Given this notation I can now write down the posterior beliefs of individual i in period $t + 1$ as follows:

$$\mu_{i,t+1}(\theta) = \frac{\prod_{j \in N^d(i;g) \cup \{i\}} \phi(Z_{j,t}; C_{j,t}, \theta) \mu_{i,t}(\theta)}{\sum_{\theta' \in \Theta} \prod_{j \in N^d(i;g) \cup \{i\}} \phi(Z_{j,t}; C_{j,t}, \theta) \mu_{i,t}(\theta)}. \tag{4.3.4}$$

Our interest is in studying the influence of network structure on the evolution of individual actions, beliefs, and utilities, $(a_{i,t}, \mu_{i,t}, U_{i,t})_{i \in N}$.

The following result, due to Bala and Goyal (1998), shows that the beliefs and utilities of individuals converge in the long run.

Theorem 4.3.1. *The beliefs and utilities of every individual converge:* $\lim_{t \to \infty} \mu_{i,t}(\omega) = \mu_{i,\infty}(\omega)$ *and* $\lim_{t \to \infty} U_{i,t}(\omega) = U_{i,\infty}(\omega)$, *for every* $i \in N$, *with probability 1.*

The first part of the statement follows as a corollary of the Martingale Convergence theorem (see e.g., Billingsley 1985). Let $A_i(\omega)$ be the set of actions chosen infinitely often by individual i along sample path ω. It is intuitive that each of these actions must be optimal with respect to limit beliefs and must yield the same utility in each of the states that are in the support of the limit belief $\mu_{i,\infty}(\omega)$. The result on limiting utilities follows from this observation.

I now examine whether all information is communicated efficiently in a connected society. There are different ways of addressing this issue. One way would be to ask if different persons get the same payoffs in the long run. This would suggest that they each possess a similar amount of "useful" information. The following result, due to Bala and Goyal (1998), is in this spirit.

Theorem 4.3.2. *Every individual in a connected society gets the same long-run utility:* $U_{i,\infty} = U_{j,\infty}$ *for every* $i, j \in N$ *with probability 1.*

We note that this result obtains in a setting in which all individuals have the same reward function. The idea behind the preceding result is as follows: if i observes the actions and outcomes of j, then he or she must be able to do as well as j in the long run. Next note that this must be true by transitivity for any person k who observes j indirectly. The final step is to note that, in a connected society, there is an information path from any player i to any player j. This result shows that in a connected society information transmission is good enough to ensure that every person gets the same utility in the long run. The preceding results lead me to the question, Do beliefs converge to the truth, and are individuals choosing the optimal action and earning the maximal possible utility in the long run?

We assume that θ_1 is the true state of the world. The long-run actions of a player i are said to be optimal if $A^i(\omega) \subset G(\delta_{\theta_1})$. Social learning is said to be complete if for all $i \in N$, $A^i(\omega) \subset G(\delta_{\theta_1})$ on a set of sample paths, which has probability 1 (with respect to the true state θ_1). The analysis of long-run learning rests on the informativeness of actions. An action is said to be fully informative if it can help an individual distinguish between all the states: if for all $\theta, \theta' \in \Theta$, with $\theta \neq \theta'$,

$$\int_Y |\phi(y; a, \theta) - \phi(y; a, \theta')| dy > 0. \qquad (4.3.5)$$

By contrast, an action a is uninformative if $\phi(., a; \theta)$ is independent of θ. In Example 4.1, action a_o is uninformative whereas action a_1 is fully informative.

It is natural that prior beliefs have to be restricted if individuals are to learn the optimal action. For instance, in Example 4.1 if everyone has priors such that the uninformative action is optimal, then no additional information is emerging in the society and nothing is going to change over time. Optimism by itself is, however, not sufficient. To see this, consider a society with a finite number of individuals, and suppose that we are in the setting of Example 4.1 and that everyone has optimistic priors, $\mu_{i,1} > 1/2$, for all $i \in N$. Thus, in period 1, everyone will choose action a_1. There is a well-defined number of realizations of 0, T for instance, after which an individual will switch to the uninformative action a_o. Because individual trials are independent, the probability of such a sequence of bad realizations is positive. Given that the number of individuals is finite, there is also a positive probability that everyone gets such a poor sequence of realizations in the first T trials. Thus, there is a positive probability that everyone will choose the uninformative action a_0 after a finite time T.[4] The foregoing argument also shows that the probability of incomplete learning is strictly positive in any finite society. Although this finding is useful, it leaves open two related questions:

(1) What is the relative attractiveness of different networks for social learning in finite societies?

(2) What happens to the probability of learning in different networks as the number of players gets large and in the limit goes to infinity? I am not aware of any general results on the first question; Bala and Goyal (1998) develop some results on question (2), and I report then now.

Consider therefore a large society in which everyone is optimistic, that is, $\mu_{i,1}(\theta_1) > 1/2$. I explore the role of information networks in this setting. Suppose that the

---

[4] This line of reasoning has been developed and elaborated upon in the Bayesian learning literature; see, for example, Rothschild (1974), Easley and Kiefer (1988), McLennan (1984).

decision problem is as in Example 4.1, and for concreteness suppose that beliefs satisfy the following condition:

$$\inf_{i \in N} \mu_{i,1} > \frac{1}{2}; \quad \sup_{i \in N} \mu_{i,1} < \frac{1}{1 + x^2}, \quad (4.3.6)$$

where $x = (1 - \pi)/\pi \in (0, 1)$. From the optimality correspondence formula, it follows that every person chooses a_1 in period 1. Suppose that individuals are arranged along the integer points of the real line and that the direct neighborhood of players is as follows: $N^d(i; g) = \{i - 1, i + 1\} \cup \{1, 2, 3, 4, 5\}$. I will refer to the commonly observed group of individuals $\{1, 2, 3, 4, 5\}$ as the "royal family." This structure corresponds to situations in which individuals have access to local as well as some common or public source of information. For example, such a structure arises naturally in the context of agriculture, for individual farmers observe their neighboring farmers but all the farmers observe a few large farms and agricultural laboratories. Similarly, in academic research, individual researchers keep track of developments in their own field of specialization and also try and keep abreast of the work of pioneers and intellectual leaders in their subject more broadly defined.

Suppose that the true state is θ_1 and a_1 is the optimal action. I now argue that there is a strictly positive probability of incomplete learning in this society. The argument is quite simple: suppose that every person in the royal family is unlucky in the first period and gets an outcome of 0. Consider any individual i and note that this person can get at most three positive signals from his or her immediate neighborhood. Thus, any person in this society will have a minimum residual of two negative signals on the true state. Given the assumptions on the priors, this negative information is sufficient to push the posteriors below the critical cutoff level of $1/2$, and this will induce a collective switch to action a_o in period 2. From then on, no further information is generated and society gets locked into the uninformative and suboptimal action. Notice that this argument does not use the size of the society, and thus I have obtained an upper bound that is less than 1 on the probability of learning for all n. This example illustrates how a few common signals can block out and overwhelm a vast amount of locally available information. This example also suggests a possible mechanism for getting out of the problem: looking at networks in which local information is given due weight.

I now present a simple network, g, in which local information is given enough scope and ultimately prevails. Consider a society in which for every i, $N^d(i; g) = \{i - 1, i + 1\}$. It is possible to show that in this society complete learning obtains. The argument is as follows. First, I fix an individual i and apply the strong law of large numbers to claim that there is a set of sample paths with positive probability on which the experience on the optimal action a_1 always remains positive on the average. This means that if we start with optimistic priors, individual i will persist with action a_1 forever on this set of sample paths if he or she were isolated. I then similarly construct a set of sample paths for each of the neighbors of player i on which players $i - 1$ and $i + 1$, respectively, receive positive information on average. Exploiting independence of trials across players, I infer that the probability the three players $i - 1$, i, and $i + 1$ will receive positive information on average is strictly positive $- q > 0$, for instance, hence, the probability that individual i will choose the suboptimal action a_o is bounded above by $1 - q$. I finally note that along this set of sample paths the experience of other individuals outside the neighborhood cannot alter the choices of individual i. Similarly, I can construct a set of sample paths for individual $i + 3$, whose information neighborhood is $\{i + 2, i + 3, i + 4\}$. Since the actions of individuals have independent and identical distributions, I can deduce that the probability of this sample of paths is $q > 0$ as well. Note next that, because individuals i and $i + 3$ do not share any neighbors, the two events, that neither i nor $i + 3$ tries the optimal action in the long run, are independent, and the probability of this joint event is therefore bounded above by $(1 - q)^2$. In a society in which $\bar{N}^d(i; g) - \{i - 1, i + 1\}$, and given that $q > 0$, it now follows that learning can be made arbitrarily close to 1 by suitably raising the number of individuals.

This example illustrates in a simple way how the architecture of the information network affects the possibilities of social learning. In particular, it shows that the probability of learning can be increased by decreasing the number of information links and thereby restricting flow of information in society. More generally, it helps us identify a structural feature of information networks that facilitate learning, *local independence*. I will say that two individuals i and j are locally independent if $N^d(i; g) \cap N^d(j; g) = \emptyset$. In a society with a royal family, the positive information generated on the optimal actions in different parts of the society is overturned by the negative information generated by the royal family. By contrast, in a society with local ties only, negative information does arise over time, but it cannot simultaneously overrule the positive information generated in different parts of the society. This allows the positive local information to gain a foothold and eventually spread across the whole society. This insight is fairly general and is summarized in the following result due to Bala and Goyal (1998). A player i has optimistic prior beliefs if $g_i(\mu_{i,1}) \subset G(\delta_{\theta_1})$.

Theorem 4.3.3. *Suppose a society is connected. In such a society the probability of learning can be made arbitrarily close to 1 by suitably increasing the number of locally independent optimistic players.*

Conformism vs. Diversity. I now briefly discuss the question, Do all individuals choose the same action in a connected society? I will say that a long-run action profile exhibits conformism if all individuals choose the same action, and it exhibits diversity if there is a positive fraction of individuals that chooses different actions. Theorem 4.3.2 says that in a connected society all individuals will obtain the same utility in the long run. If there is a unique optimal action for every state, this implies that all individuals will choose the same action as well. In case there are multiple optimal actions for the same state, however, the result does not say anything about conformism and diversity. This motivates a study of the relative likelihood of conformism and diversity as a function of the network structure. Bala and Goyal (2001) study a class of societies in which there are completely linked groups and the society's level of integration is given by the number of cross-group links. They find that diversity obtains if there are relatively few cross-group links, whereas conformism is guaranteed if the groups are fully interconnected and the society forms a complete network.

Heterogeneous preferences: This result on conformism, and indeed all the results reported so far, are obtained in a setting in which all individuals have the same reward functions. In a society with heterogeneous preferences, the analogue of this result would be as follows: in a connected society, all individuals with the same preferences obtain the same utility. Bala and Goyal (2001) show by example that this conjecture is false. In this example, preference differences can create information blockages that impede the transmission of useful information and thereby sustain different utility levels for individuals with similar preferences. This leads then to a proposal of a stronger notion of connectedness: *groupwise connectedness*. A society is said to be groupwise connected if, for every pair of individuals i and j of the same preference type, either j is a neighbor of i or there exists a path from j to i with all members of the path being individuals having the same preference as i and j. Theorem 4.3.2 obtains for members with the same preferences in societies that satisfy this stronger connectedness requirement.

I now discuss the papers by Allen (1982) and Ellison and Fudenberg (1993). Allen studies technology adoption by a set of individuals located on nodes of a graph who are subject to local influences. This is clearly very close in spirit to the motivation behind the framework developed in Bala and Goyal (1998). Allen shows that, if every action is chosen with a positive probability, then there exists a unique global (joint) distribution on actions given any local influence structure. These results tell us something about the consistency requirements imposed by local influences, but they leave open the issue of the dynamics of how local influences work their way through to the global level, which is the focus of this chapter.

Ellison and Fudenberg (1993) consider a setting with a unit measure of individuals, each of whom makes a choice between two actions. The relative profitability of these technologies is unknown. In each period, a fraction of the population gets an opportunity to revise their choices. These individuals observe the average payoffs of the two actions in the previous period and pick the action that yields the higher payoff. The authors examine the share of the population adopting different actions over time.

Let f and h be the two technologies and suppose the payoffs are given as follows: $u_t^h - u_t^f = \beta + \epsilon_t$. The value of β is unknown, and the ϵ is a random variable with mean 0 and a cumulative distribution H. The distribution of ϵ is such that Probability$[u_t^h - u_t^f \geq 0] = p > 0$. Thus, it may happen that action h gets higher payoffs in a period even though the action f is better, that is, $\beta < 0$.

Let x^t denote the fraction of individuals choosing action h in period t. The first result they obtain says that the time average of x^t converges to its expectation with respect to the unique invariant measure, ν. Moreover, this average corresponds in a simple way to the distribution of the noise in the payoffs function of the two actions: $E_\nu(x) = p$.

It is easy to see that a decision based solely on comparing previous-period payoffs does not really allow the superior quality of an action to express itself, and as a result the process fluctuates with the noise and does not actually settle down on any one action in the long run. To allow for the history of past experiences to have greater influence, Ellison and Fudenberg (1993) next consider a decision rule that gives some weight to the relative popularity of the different actions. In particular, they use the following decision rule: an individual prefers action h if the observed payoff difference $u_t^h - u_t^f \geq m(1 - 2x^t)$, where m refers to the weight on the relative popularity of the actions. It is clear that, given some m, a larger x^t makes it more likely that the inequality will be satisfied and action h will be chosen. For all $x^t \neq 1/2$, a larger m signifies greater weight on the popularity of different actions. Suppose that the distribution of shocks ϵ_t is uniform on $[-\sigma, \sigma]$. Given this assumption, I can state the following result, due to Ellison and Fudenberg (1993), on the behavior of x^t for different values of m:

Theorem 4.3.4. *If $m = \sigma$, then x^t converges to 1 if h is optimal ($\beta > 0$), and it converges to 0 if f is optimal ($\beta < 0$). For $m < \sigma$, the process need not converge, whereas for $m > \sigma$ it always converges but the limit is sensitive to the initial state x_0.*

This result suggests that there is an optimal weight for popularity in the decision rule: $m < \sigma$ represents underweighting, whereas $m > \sigma$ reflects overweighting of the popularity.

Ellison and Fudenberg also consider a spatial model of learning, where payoffs are sensitive to location. Suppose that the measure of individuals is arranged along a line and each individual is surrounded by a window of observation. Moreover suppose that the payoffs are given as follows: $u_t^h(\theta) = \theta + \beta\theta + \epsilon_{ht}$ for technology h at location θ, and $u_t^f(\theta) = \beta\theta + \epsilon_{ft}$ for technology f. With this formulation, it follows that there is a cutoff for the optimal technology at $\theta = 0$, with h being the optimal choice for $\theta > 0$, whereas f is the optimal choice for $\theta < 0$. In each period, individuals observe the average payoffs of the two technologies in their window of observation. For individual θ, the window is an interval given by $[\theta - w, \theta + w]$. They choose the action that yields a higher average payoff in this window. Suppose there is a boundary point x_0 at the start. Ellison and Fudenberg study the evolution of this boundary. From our point of view, their main result pertains to the effect of the size of the window of observation on the long-run properties of the system. They find that, under some regularity conditions on the distribution of the error terms, the steady-state welfare is decreasing in the size of the interval. Thus, smaller intervals are better from a long-term welfare point of view. However, if w is small, then the cutoff point moves slowly over time if the initial state is far from the optimum and this creates a trade-off: increasing w leads to a short-term welfare gain but a long-term welfare loss.

4.3.2. Related Themes

So far I have discussed learning in a setting in which every player has a fixed set of neighbors, and the implicit assumption is that they constitute a small subset of the whole population. An alternative way to think of information transmission is as follows: in every decision period, an individual gets to observe a sample of other people chosen at random from the population. This individual uses the information obtained from the sample – which could relate to the relative popularity of different actions, or actions and outcomes of different trials – in making his or her choices. This approach has been explored by Ellison and Fudenberg (1995) among others. In this approach, the attention has been on the size of the sample, the type of information extracted from the sample, and the nature of the decision rule that maps this information into the choice of individuals (boundedly rational or Bayesian).

It is useful to examine briefly the effects of random sampling in the decision-problem framework developed in Bala and Goyal (1998). Suppose the number of players is finite. Then I can employ standard mathematical arguments to show that random sampling implies that every person observes every other person infinitely often (with probability 1). The society will therefore be "fully connected" in a stochastic sense, and I expect that the analogues of Theorems 4.3.1 and 4.3.2 will obtain. The argument on incomplete learning in finite societies can also be extended straightforwardly. Thus, I will need large, that is, infinite, societies to obtain complete learning within the random network setting. To get an impression of the issues that arise in settings with large populations, I now discuss a model developed by Ellison and Fudenberg (1995).

Consider a unit measure of individuals, each of whom makes a choice between two actions. The relative profitability of these technologies is unknown. In each period a fraction of the population gets an opportunity to revise its choices. These individuals observe a random sample of other persons, compare the average payoffs of the two actions in this sample (they also use their own experience in arriving at this average), and pick the action that yields the higher payoff. I examine the share of the population adopting different actions over time.

The two actions are denoted by f and h. Suppose that the payoffs to individual i choosing action f are given by $\bar{f}_t + \epsilon_{ift}$ and the payoffs from action h are given by $\bar{h}_t + \epsilon_{iht}$. The second term reflects the idiosyncratic shocks, whereas the first term refers to the aggregate level of payoffs in that period. The idiosyncratic shocks are assumed to be i.i.d across players and time. They have mean 0 and standard deviation σ. It is assumed that $\beta_t = \bar{h}_t - \bar{f}_t$ and that β_t has a binomial distribution with Probability$(\beta_t = \beta) = p > 0$, whereas Probability$(\beta_t = -\beta) = 1 - p$.

In each period t, a fraction α of the individuals gets an opportunity to revise its decisions. Each person faced with this choice gets to observe the actions and payoffs of K randomly chosen other individuals. He or she supplements this information from personal experience, arrives at an estimate of the average payoffs from the two actions, and chooses the action with the higher average payoff. In case individual i was choosing action f and does not observe any trials with action h, he or she is obliged to persist with action f irrespective of the information on action f. Let x^t denote the fraction of individuals choosing action h in period t. The authors study the behavior of x^t for different values of the sample size K.

The main results of the paper concern the relative likelihood of social conformism and diversity. The first result, due to Ellison and Fudenberg (1995), is for the case in which both actions have the same payoffs.

Theorem 4.3.5. *Suppose that $p = 1/2$ and the actions are on average equally good. Then x^t converges to an endpoint with everyone choosing the same action if the sample size is small. If the sample size is large, then x^t exhibits diversity in the long run.*

The intuition behind this result is as follows: If sample sizes are large, then individual idiosyncratic noise gets washed out for individuals who are revising their choices, and the process is governed by the aggregate shocks captured in the variable β. Since β is binomial, the process x^t oscillates and a positive fraction of the population chooses each of the two actions in the long run. On the other hand, if the sample is small, then aggregate shocks are mediated by individual shocks and percolate slowly through the system. In such a setting, there is a tendency for popular actions to be reinforced, and the system always converges to an endpoint.

The second result, due to Ellison and Fudenberg (1995), covers the case in which the two actions have different payoffs.

Theorem 4.3.6. *Suppose that $p > 1/2$ and action h is, on average, superior. Then x^t converges to an endpoint with everyone choosing the same action if the sample size is small. This action can be either f or h, and so inefficient conformism can occur. If sample size is moderate, then x^t converges to the efficient action h, whereas if sample size is large, then x^t exhibits diversity in the long run.*

The relationship between sample size and long-run learning is due to the combination of aggregate and idiosyncratic noise. To see this, I briefly consider the two limit cases: the first with no aggregate uncertainty ($p = 1$), and the second with no idiosyncratic noise. The first case permits a clean comparison with the learning in the fixed networks framework presented earlier. In that decision environment, there is a true (stochastic) quality level for each action and individual trials yield independent draws; hence, it has no aggregate uncertainty but does have idiosyncratic noise. We note that, in the preceding result, the critical sample sizes depend on the value of p, and for the limit case with $p = 1$, it can be shown that efficient conformism obtains for all sample sizes. The intuition for this builds on the arguments presented for Theorem 4.3.5. In case $p = 1$, there is no aggregate uncertainty, and as samples get large, the influence of idiosyncratic noise is less and thus the superior technology dominates. Consider next the case in which there are aggregate shocks but no idiosyncratic noise. In this situation, sample size is only relevant insofar as it affects the probability of individuals' accessing at least one draw of each action.

I would like to conclude by mentioning the literature on herding and informational cascades (Banerjee 1992; Bikhchandani, Hirshleifer and Welch 1992). In this literature there is a single sequence of privately informed individuals who take one action each. Before making his or her choice, an individual gets to observe the actions of all the people who have moved earlier. The person moving in a period thus uses the actions of his or her predecessors as signals for private information and uses these signals to supplement his or her own private information. This is quite different from the framework developed in this section in which individuals can access the entire experience – the actions as well as rewards – of a subset of individuals, their

2 1	α	β
α	a, a	d, e
β	e, d	b, b

Figure 4.3: Coordination game.

neighbors. Thus, there is learning from actions and payoffs; moreover, different individuals have access to different aspects of the social information on the basis of their location in the society. For a study of social learning from actions in the context of social networks, see Gale and Kariv (2003).

4.4. Strategic Interaction

In this section I will study learning of optimal actions in a setting in which the rewards from different actions depend on the actions chosen by other individuals. Given our interest in the influence of network structure on individual choice, this leads me to a study of strategic interaction among individuals located in networks. I will consider both games of coordination and games of conflict. As before, our interest is in the question, What is the influence of the structure of interaction on individual choice and the behavior of the system as a whole?

4.4.1. Coordination Games

Suppose there are two players 1 and 2 and they are engaged in the 2×2 game shown in Figure 4.3. I will assume that payoffs satisfy the following restrictions:

$$a > d; \quad b > d; \quad d > e; \quad a + d > b + e. \tag{4.4.1}$$

These restrictions imply that there are two pure strategy equilibria of the game, (α, α) and (β, β), and that coordinating on either of them is better than not coordinating at all. The assumption that $a + e > b + d$ implies that α is the *risk-dominant* strategy. It is worth noting that α can be risk dominant even if it is not efficient (that is even if $b > a$). Given the restrictions on the payoffs, these equilibria are strict in the sense that the best response in the equilibrium yields a strictly higher payoff than the other option. It is well known that strict equilibria are robust to standard refinements of Nash equilibrium; thus, players engaged in such a game face a coordination problem.

I will consider a group of players engaged in playing this coordination game. The structure of interaction will be modeled in terms of an *undirected* network whose nodes are the players, and an arc between two players signifies that the two players play the game with each other. I start with a discussion of the static problem and then take up the issue of learning.

Suppose there are n players located on vertices of an undirected network with each player being located on a distinct node. To distinguish between a directed and an undirected link, I use the notation $\bar{g}_{i,j} \in \{0, 1\}$ to denote a undirected link between players i and j. As before, $\bar{g}_{i,j} = 1$ denotes the existence of a link, and $\bar{g}_{i,j} = 0$ denotes the absence of a link between players i and j. Let $\bar{g}$ denote an undirected network, and let $\bar{G}$ denote the set of all undirected networks with n nodes. Recall that $N^d(i; \bar{g}) = \{j \in N | \bar{g}_{i,j} = 1\}$ refers to the set of players with whom i is linked in network $\bar{g}$. I will use s_i to signify a strategy of player i and $S_i = \{\alpha, \beta\}$ to denote the strategy set. I will use $S = \Pi_{i \in N} S_i$ to signify the set of all strategy profiles in the game and s to refer to a typical member of this set. In this two-person game, let $\pi(x, y)$ denote the payoffs to player i when this player chooses action x and his or her opponent chooses action y. The payoffs to a player i from a strategy s_i, given that the other players are choosing s_{-i}, is

$$\prod_i (s_i, s_{-i}) = \sum_{j \in N^d(i; \bar{g})} \pi(s_i, s_j) \tag{4.4.2}$$

This formulation reflects the idea that a player i interacts with each of the players in the set $N_i^d(\bar{g})$. A strategy profile $s^* = \{s_1^*, s_2^*, \ldots, s_n^*\}$ is a Nash equilibrium if $\Pi_i(s_i^*, s_{-i}^*) \geq \Pi_i(s_i, s_{-i}^*)$, for all $s_i \in S_i$, for all players $i \in N$. The equilibrium is strict if the inequalities are strict for every player.

4.4.1.1. Multiple Equilibria

I start by describing the nature of Nash equilibria under different network structures. The first point I note is that the strategy profile $s_i = x$ for all $i \in N$, where $x \in \{\alpha, \beta\}$ is a Nash equilibrium given any network structure. This is straightforward to check, given the restrictions on the payoffs. Thus, the issue is, Are there any other equilibria, and how is the answer to this question related to the network structure? The second point to note, then, is that if the network is complete (i.e., every pair of players has a link), then the aforementioned outcomes with social conformism are the only equilibria possible. However, if networks are incomplete, then a variety of other strategy profiles can arise in a Nash equilibrium. To see this, I consider some specific network structures. Consider a society of N players divided into two groups, N_1 and N_2, with $N_1 \cup N_2 = N$. Suppose that $\bar{g}_{i,j} = 1$ if and only if $i, j \in N_k$ for $k = 1, 2$. In other words, a link exists between every pair of players in a group and there are no links across players of the two groups. In this simple network it is an equilibrium for players in group 1 to choose action α, whereas members of group 2 choose β. (The converse pattern with members of group 1 choosing action β and members of group 2 choosing α is clearly also an equilibrium. These are the only two possible equilibria in this network.) This example exploits the separation of the two groups of players and leads us to ask, Can diversity arise in a connected network? By way of illustration, suppose that the two groups N_1 and N_2 are relatively large and there is one link between two players in different groups. A society with this network is connected, but it is easy to see that different actions can still be sustained in equilibrium in the two groups. These observations are summarized as follows:

Theorem 4.4.1. *For any action, an outcome in which everyone chooses this action is a Nash equilibrium. If the network is complete, then these are the only Nash equilibria. If the network is incomplete, then mixed equilibria may exist as well.*

This result yields two insights: (1) there is a multiplicity of equilibria in general, and (2) the possibility and nature of mixed equilibria depend on the network architecture.

These observations lead me to a closer examination of the plausibility of different equilibria and how this is in turn related to the structure of interaction. I will study plausibility in terms of dynamic stability. I start with a simple decision rule for individuals and examine the behavior of the dynamic process generated by this rule.

4.4.1.2. Dynamic Stability and Equilibrium Selection

Suppose that time is discrete and given by $t = 1, 2, 3, \ldots$. In each period, with probability $p \in (0, 1)$, a player gets an opportunity to revise his or her strategy. Faced with this opportunity, player i chooses an action that will maximize payoff under the assumption that the strategy profile of his or her neighbors remains the same as in the previous period. If more than one action is optimal, then the player persists with the current action. Denote the strategy of a player i in period t by s_i^t. If player i is not active in period t, then it follows that $s_i^t = s_i^{t-1}$. This simple best-response strategy revision rule generates a transition probability function $P_{ss'}(\bar{g}) : S \times S \to [0, 1]$, which governs the evolution of the state of the system $s^t(\bar{g})$. Recall that a strategy profile (or state) is said to be absorbing if the dynamic process cannot escape from the state once it reaches it. Equipped with this notation and terminology, I can now present a general convergence and characterization result.

Theorem 4.4.2. *Fix some network of interaction $g \in G$. If we start from any strategy profile, the dynamic process $s^t(g)$ converges to an absorbing strategy profile in finite time, with probability 1. There is an equivalence between the set of absorbing strategy profiles and the set of Nash equilibria of the static social game.*[5]

The equivalence between absorbing states and Nash equilibria of the social game of coordination is easy to see. The arguments underlying the convergence result are as follows: start at some state s_o. Consider the set of players who are not playing a best response. If this set is empty, then we are at a Nash equilibrium profile and this is an absorbing state of the process. Suppose, therefore, that there are some players who are currently choosing action α but would prefer to choose β. Allow them this

---

[5] One may wonder if there is any relationship between the Nash equilibria of the social game and the original 2 × 2 game I started with. This issue has been studied by Mailath, Samuelson, and Shaked (1997), who show that the Nash equilibria of the static social game is equivalent to the set of correlated equilibria of the 2 × 2 game. Ianni (2001) studies convergence to correlated equilibria under myopic best-response dynamics.

choice and let s_1 be the new state of the system (this transition occurs with positive probability given the process defined). Now examine the players doing α in state s_1 who would like to switch actions. If there are such players, then have them switch to β and define the new state as s_2. Clearly, this process of having α players switch will end in finite time (because the number of players in the society is finite). Let the state with this property be $\hat{s}$. Either there will be no players left choosing α or there will be some players choosing α in $\hat{s}$. In the former case we are clearly at a Nash equilibrium. Let us take up the second possibility then. Check if there are any players choosing β who would like to switch actions. If there are none, then we are at an absorbing state. If there are some β players who would like to switch, then follow the process just outlined to reach a state in which there is no player who wishes to switch from β to α. Let this state be denoted by $\bar{s}$. Next observe that no player who was choosing α (and did not want to switch actions) in $\hat{s}$ would be interested in switching to β. This is true because the game is a coordination game, and the set of players choosing α has (weakly) increased in the transition from $\hat{s}$ to $\bar{s}$. Hence, we have arrived (with positive probability) at a state in which no player has any incentive to switch actions. This is an absorbing state of the dynamics; because the initial state was arbitrary, and the transition just described occurs with positive probability, the theory of Markov chains tells us that the transition to an absorbing state will occur in finite time with probability 1.

An early result on convergence of dynamics to a Nash equilibrium in regular networks (where every player has the same number of neighbors) is presented in Anderlini and Ianni (1996). In their model, a player is randomly matched to play with one other player in his or her direct neighborhood. Moreover, every player gets a chance to move in every period. Finally, a player who plans to switch actions can make an error with some probability. They refer to this as noise on the margin. With this decision rule, the dynamic process of choices converges to a Nash equilibrium for a class of regular networks. The result I present here holds for all networks and does not rely on mistakes for convergence. Instead, I rely on inertia and the coordination nature of the game.

The preceding result shows that the learning process with regard to actions converges in due time. The result also says that every Nash equilibrium (for the given network of interaction) is an absorbing state of the process. Thus, one cannot hope to select across the variety of equilibria identified earlier with this dynamic process. This motivates a study of stability with respect to small but repeated perturbations. This is formally done using the idea of stochastic stability.

I suppose that, occasionally, players make mistakes, experiment, or simply disregard payoff considerations in choosing their strategies.[6] Specifically, I assume that, conditional on receiving a revision opportunity, a player chooses his or her strategy at random with some small "mutation" probability $\epsilon > 0$. Given a network g, and for any $\epsilon > 0$, the mutation process defines a Markov chain that is aperiodic and irreducible and therefore has a unique invariant probability distribution; let us denote

---

[6] In the context of economics, the notion of stochastic stability was introduced by Kandori, Mailath, and Rob (1993) and Young (1993).

this distribution by $v_\epsilon(\bar{g})$. I analyze the support of $v_\epsilon(\bar{g})$ as the probability of mistakes becomes very small, that is, as ϵ converges to zero. Define $\lim_{\epsilon \to 0} v_\epsilon(\bar{g}) = \hat{v}_{\bar{g}}$. I will say that a state s is stochastically stable if $\hat{v}_{\bar{g}}(s) > 0$. This notion of stability identifies states that are relatively more stable with respect to occasional errors or experiments by individuals.

The ideas underlying stochastic stability can be informally described as follows. Suppose that s and s' are the two absorbing states of the best-response dynamics. Given that s is an absorbing state, a movement from s to s' requires an error on the part of one or more of the players. Similarly, the transition from s' to s requires errors on the part of some subset of players. The state s is stochastically stable if it requires relatively more errors to exit from s than from the other state s'. If it takes the same number of mutations to exit the two states, then the two states are both stochastically stable.

I will be using the notion of stochastic stability extensively in what follows. It is therefore important to point out some limitations of this approach as a way to select for equilibrium. One limitation is the lack of an explicit model which explains the individual errors and experimentation. A second limitation of this approach is that, in most applications, the number of mutations needed is of the order of the number of players, and thus in large societies, as the probability of errors becomes small, the process moves very slowly and the rate of convergence can be very slow. For an overall account of the concepts, techniques, and applications of stochastic stability, see Young (1998).[7]

I start with two examples: interaction with every player in a complete network and interaction with immediate neighbors among players located around a circle. These examples show that the risk-dominant action α is stochastically stable. I first take up the complete network. Suppose that player 1 is deciding on whether to choose action α or β. It is easy to verify that the minimum number of players choosing α needed to induce player 1 to choose α is given by $k = (n-1)(b-d)/[(a-e)+(b-d)]$. Similarly, the minimum number of players choosing action β needed to induce player 1 to choose action β is given by $l = (n-1)(a-e)/[(a-e)+(b-d)]$. Given our assumption that $a+d > b+e$, it follows that $k < \frac{n-1}{2} < l$. It now follows that if we are in a state in which everyone is choosing α, then it takes l mutations to transit to a state in which everyone is choosing action β; likewise, if we are in a state in which everyone is choosing β, then it takes k mutations to transit to a state in which everyone is choosing action α. From now follows that, in the complete network, everyone choosing the risk-dominant action α is the unique stochastically stable outcome.

I now turn to interaction with immediate neighbors among players located around a circle. This example is taken from Ellison (1993). Suppose that at the start everyone is choosing action β. Now suppose that two adjacent players i and $i+1$ choose action α by way of experimentation. It is now easy to verify that, in the next period, the immediate neighbors of i and $i+1$, players $i-1$ and $i+2$, will find it optimal

---

[7] For an exposition of the original mathematical results, refer to Freidlin and Wentzell (1984).

to switch to action α (this is due to the assumption that α is risk dominant and $a + d > b + e$). Moreover, in the period after that the immediate neighbors of $i - 1$ and $i + 2$ will have a similar incentive, and so there is a contagion process under way that leads to everyone's choosing action α in finite time. On the other hand, if we were to start in a state with everyone choosing α, then it would be difficult to generate a similar contagion process. To see why, note that a player bases his or her decision on the actions of immediate neighbors, and so long as at least one of the neighbors is choosing α the optimal action is to do likewise. Hence, so long as there are two players choosing action α, the action will revive and take over the whole population. This simple argument suggests that it is relatively easy to perturb the state in which everyone is doing β whereas it is significantly more difficult to perturb the state in which everyone is choosing α. These observations, taken along with the earlier remarks on stochastic stability, show that choosing the risk-dominant action is the unique, stochastically stable action when players are arranged on a circle and interact with their immediate neighbors.

The simplicity of the preceding arguments may lead one to conjecture that the risk-dominant outcome obtains in all networks. I now present an example, which is taken from Jackson and Watts 2002b, to show that this conjecture is false. Suppose that players are arranged in a star network. Recall that this is a network in which one player has links with all the other $n - 1$ players, whereas the other players have no links between them. It is easily verified that, in a star network, a perturbation that switches the action of the central player is necessary as well as sufficient to obtain a switch of all the other players. Hence, the number of perturbations needed to go from an all-α state to an all-β state is equal to the number of perturbations needed for the reverse transition. Thus, both states are equally vulnerable and are stochastically stable as well.

The arguments above illustrate how the network structure can shape the nature of the long-run outcome. These examples lead us to the question, Are there circumstances under which the stochastically stable states are independent of the network structure? One response to this question is provided by a result in Young (1998). This result proceeds by making the mutations in individual strategy sensitive to payoff losses. To present this result, I need to develop some additional notation. I will say that in every period t, an individual i is drawn at random and chooses an action (say) α according to a probability distribution $p_i^\gamma(\alpha|s^t)$, where $\gamma > 0$ and s^t is the strategy profile at time t. The probability distribution is obtained via the following formula:

$$p_i^\gamma(\alpha|s^t) = \frac{e^{\gamma \cdot \Pi_i(\alpha, s_{-i}^t)}}{e^{\gamma \cdot \Pi_i(\alpha, s_{-i}^t)} + e^{\gamma \cdot \Pi_i(\beta, s_{-i}^t)}} . \tag{4.4.3}$$

This is referred to as the log-linear response rule. This rule was first studied in Blume (1993) in the context of games played on lattices.[8] Note that for large values of γ the probability distribution will place most of the probability mass on the best-response action. Define $\Delta_i(s) = \Pi_i(\beta, s_{-i}) - \Pi_i(\alpha, s_{-i})$, and say that $\rho = e^{-\gamma}$. Then, for

---

[8] For a general treatment of the theory of statistical mechanics, refer to Liggett (1985).

large γ, I can express the probability of action α as follows:

$$p_i^{\gamma}(\alpha|s^t) = \frac{e^{-\gamma \cdot \Delta_i(s^t)}}{1 + e^{-\gamma \cdot \Delta_i(s^t)}} \cong e^{-\gamma \Delta_i(s^t)} = \rho^{\Delta_i(s^t)}. \tag{4.4.4}$$

This expression says that the probability of not choosing the best response exponentially declines in the payoff loss from the deviation. Equipped with these additional concepts, I am ready to state the following general result, due to Young (1998).

Theorem 4.4.3. *Let $\bar{g}$ be an arbitrary connected network. Suppose that in each period an individual is picked at random to revise choices. In revising choices, this individual uses the log-linear response rule. Then the stochastically stable outcome is one in which every player chooses the risk-dominant action.*

To get some intuition for the result, let us briefly discuss the effects of the log-linear decision rule on the dynamic process in the star network. In that example, the simplest way to get a transition is via a switch in the action of the central player. In the standard model, with payoff-insensitive mutations, the probability of the central player's making a switch from α to β is the same as it is the other way around. Under the log-linear response rule, matters are different. If the number of players is large then there is a significant difference in the payoff losses involved, and the probabilities of switching from α to β are significantly smaller as compared with the probability of switching from β to α. This difference is crucial for obtaining Theorem 4.4.3.

In the models above, the dynamics are Markovian, and if there is a unique invariant distribution, then standard mathematical results suggest that the rate of convergence is exponential. In other words, there is some number $\rho < 1$ such that the probability distribution of actions at time t, σ^t, approaches the invariant distribution σ^* at a rate approximately given by ρ^t. Although this result is helpful, it is easy to see that this property allows a fairly wide range of convergence rates as determined by the value of ρ. The convergence rate is important because it clarifies the relative importance of the initial conditions and the evolutionary, dynamic forces, respectively. If ρ is close to 1, then the process is essentially determined by the initial configuration σ_0 for a long period, whereas if ρ is close to 0, initial conditions play a less important role and dynamics shape individual choices quickly. The work of Ellison (1993) focused attention on the role of interaction structure in shaping the rate of convergence. He argued that if interaction were random or in a complete network, then transition between strict Nash equilibria based on mutations would take a very long time in large populations because the number of mutations needed is of the order of the population. By contrast, if interaction takes place between immediate neighbors who are arranged on a circle, then it is easy to see that a few mutations (followed by best responses) would be sufficient to initiate a transition to the risk-dominant action. Thus, local interaction leads to dramatically faster rates of convergence to the risk-dominant action. In a recent paper, Young (2003) shows that the role of local interaction in speeding up rate of convergence to risk-dominant outcome is quite general: in any society in which people are organized in clusters with considerable overlap between neighborhoods, the rate of convergence is quite rapid and essentially independent of population size.

4.4.1.3. Related Themes

In the last ten years, research on the subject of coordination games has been very active, and a significant part of this work deals with interaction models. To conclude this section, I briefly mention some of the other issues that have been explored. I first take up the issue of alternative decision rules (this issue is also related to the issue of how mutations and experiments shape the set of stochastically stable outcomes, which was discussed earlier in this section). In this connection, I would like to discuss two issues that have been examined in the literature. The first is imitation-based decision rules, and the second is state-dependent mutations. In the discussion so far, I have assumed that in revising strategies each player chooses a myopic best response to the current strategy profile. An alternative decision rule would require that an individual compare the realized payoffs from different actions in the previous period and choose the action yielding the highest payoffs. I will refer to this as the imitate-the-best-action rule. Robson and Vega-Redondo (1996) show how this rule, taken together with alternative matching rules, causes the efficient action (which is not necessarily risk-dominant) to be always stochastically stable. The second issue concerns the modeling of the mutations. Bergin and Lipman (1996) have argued that any outcome could be supported as stochastically stable under a suitable mutation structure. This "anything is possible" result should not come entirely as a surprise given our earlier observations on stochastically stable states when players are located on a star. This result has provoked several responses, and I mention two of them here. The first response interprets mutations as errors and says that these errors can be controlled at some cost. Their argument has been developed in van Damme and Weibull (2002). Their paper shows that incorporating this cost structure leads us back to the risk-dominant equilibrium. This line of research has been further extended to cover local interaction on general weighted graphs by Baron et al. (2002). A second response is to argue that risk-dominance obtains for all possible mutation rules if some additional conditions are satisfied. In this vein, a recent paper by Lee, Szeidl, and Valentinyi (2003) argues that if interaction is on a two-dimensional lattice, then the dynamics select for the risk-dominant action for any state-dependent mutation structure provided the number of players is sufficiently large.

A second concern has been the role of random initial configurations. Lee and Valentinyi (2000) study the spread of actions on a two-dimensional lattice. They suppose that, at the start, every player chooses each of the two actions with positive probability whereas subsequent decisions are based on a myopic best-response rule. They find that if there are sufficiently large numbers of players, then all of them choose the risk-dominant action. This result should be seen in the context of Theorem 4.4.1. The result of Lee and Valentinyi suggests that such diversity is unlikely to obtain in a probabilistic sense.

The third concern has been the issue of openness of different interaction structures to change. Suppose that there is one-shot introduction of players choosing a new practice into a population following a different action. What are the prospects of the new action's catching on in the population and how is this likelihood related to the interaction structure? This question has been addressed in Goyal (1996) and Morris (2000). Using a general framework of analysis, Morris shows that diffusion is easier in networks in which there is substantial overlap in neighborhoods. In particular, he is able to parameterize the receptiveness of a network to new actions in terms of a contagion threshold and finds that local interaction on a circle is maximally receptive.

The fourth issue that has been discussed is the role of interaction structure in shaping behavior in games in which players wish to coordinate on action combinations $\{\alpha, \beta\}$ or $\{\beta, \alpha\}$. In other words, there are two (pure strategy) Nash equilibria, but they both involve players choosing different actions. Bramoulle (2002) refers to these as congestion games and finds that network structure affects the static equilibria quite differently as compared with the coordination games I have discussed in this section. For example, in the coordination games studied in this section, we observed that the outcomes in which everyone chooses the same action are Nash equilibria irrespective of the network of interaction. This is clearly not true when we are dealing with congestion games. More generally, the welfare properties of the networks are quite different as well because, in congestion games, complete bipartite graphs are particularly attractive.

4.4.2. Games of Conflict

I now examine the role of interaction structure in shaping individual behavior in the context of games of conflict. There are many different ways in which conflict in games can be modeled. I study a particularly simple model because it allows me to draw out the role of interaction structure in a straightforward manner and also points to some interesting open issues in this area.

Suppose that there are many players, each of whom has a choice between two actions A and E. I will think of A as referring to an altruistic or cooperative action and E as referring to an egoistic or "defect" action. Let $s_i \in S_i = \{A, E\}$ denote the strategy of player i and let $s = \{s_1, s_2, s_3 \ldots s_n\}$ refer to the strategy profile of the players. I use $n(A, s_{-i})$ to refer to the number of players who choose action A in the strategy profile s_{-i} (of all the players other than player i). Consider first the case in which a player interacts with all the other players, that is, the complete network. In this case, the payoffs to player i from action A, given the strategy profile s_{-i} of other players, are as follows:

$$\prod_i (A, s_{-i}) = n(A, s_{-i}) - c, \tag{4.4.5}$$

where $c > 0$ is the cost associated with action A (or the costs of altruism). Similarly, the payoffs to player i from action E are given by

$$\prod_i (E, s_{-i}) = n(A, s_{-i}). \tag{4.4.6}$$

Because $c > 0$, it follows that action E is strongly dominated by action A. So, if players are payoff optimizers (given the strategies of others), they will never choose A.

Thus, it is necessary to have at least some players using alternative decision rules if there is to be any chance of action A's being adopted.

4.4.2.1. Local Interaction, Imitation, and Altruism

I follow Eshel, Samuelson, and Shaked (1998) and assume that all players use a variant of the imitate-the-best-action rule: each player compares the average payoffs from the two actions and chooses the action that attains the higher payoff. If all players choose the same action in the current strategy profile, then a player follows this action.

I first note that if players are in the complete network, then, in a configuration in which both actions are present, the average payoffs from choosing action E are higher. Thus, if players follow the imitate-the-best-action (on average) rule, the outcome in which everyone chooses action E will obtain (unless we start with everyone choosing action A, which is an uninteresting case). This negative result on the prospects of action A leads us to consider the role of interaction structure.

By way of illustration, suppose therefore that players are located around a circle and that their payoffs depend on the choices of their immediate neighbors only.[9] Let $\{i-1, i, i+1\}$ be the neighborhood of player i and suppose that the payoffs to player i are given by $n(A, s_{i-1}, s_{i+1}) - c$ if player 1 chooses A and by $n(A, s_{i-1}, s_{i+1})$ if he or she chooses action E. Here we have specialized the term $n(a, s_{i-1}, s_{i+1})$ to refer to the number of players who choose action a among the neighbors of player i. I will now also make the model dynamic and suppose that time is discrete and that in each period every player gets a chance to revise his or her strategy. Let the strategy profile at time t be denoted by s^t. The decision rules (along with an initial profile, s^1) define a Markovian dynamic process in which the states of the process are the strategy profiles s. The probability of transition from s to s' is either 0 or 1. I am interested in exploring the long-run behavior of the dynamic process. Recall that a state (or a set of states) is said to be absorbing if the process cannot escape from the state once it reaches it. I also note that every absorbing state (or set of states) has associated with it a corresponding stationary distribution of the Markov process.

I begin the analysis of this model by clarifying the role of local interaction. To rule out uninteresting cases, I suppose that $c < 1/2$.[10] Suppose that there is a string of three players choosing action A and they are surrounded on both sides by a population of players choosing E. Given the decision rule, any change in actions can only occur at the boundaries. What are the payoffs observed by the player's choosing action A on the boundary? Well, this person observes one player choosing E with a payoff of 1 while he or she observes one player choosing action A with payoff $2 - c$. Moreover, this same player observes his or her own payoff of $1 - c$

---

[9] For a related model of cooperative behavior with local interaction in games with conflict, see Tieman, Houba, and van der Laan (2000). In their model, players are located on a network and play a generalized (many-action) version of the prisoner's dilemma. They find that with local interaction and a tit-for-tat type decision rule, superior payoff actions that are dominated can survive in the population in the long run.

[10] The restriction that $c < 1/2$ is made to ensure that it is attractive for players to switch from E to A under some configurations.

as well. Given that $c < 1/2$, it follows that he or she prefers action A. On the other hand, the player on the boundary choosing action E observes one player choosing action E with payoff 0, one player choosing action A with payoff $1 - c$, and himself or herself with a payoff 1. Given that $c < 1/2$, this player prefers to switch to action A. This suggests that the region of altruists will expand. Note, however, that if everyone except one player is choosing action A, then the player choosing E will get a payoff of 2, and because this is the maximum possible payoff, this will induce his or her neighbors to switch to action E. However, as they expand, this group of egoists will find their payoffs fall (because the interior of the interval can no longer free ride on the altruists). These considerations suggest that a long string of players choosing action A can be sustained, whereas a long string of players choosing E will be difficult to sustain. These arguments are summarized in the following result due to Eshel et al. (1998).

Theorem 4.4.4. *Absorbing sets are of two types: (1) they contain a singleton state in which all players choose either action A or action E, and (2), they contain states in which there are strings of A players of length 3 or more separated by strings of E players of length 2 or less (on average). In the latter case, at least 60% of the players choose action A (on average).*

It is worth commenting on the relative proportions of A players in mixed configurations. First note that a string of E players cannot be of size 3 or larger (in an absorbing state). If it is, the boundary E players will each have two players choosing A on one side and a player choosing E who is surrounded by E players. It is easy to show that these boundary players will switch to A. Likewise, there have to be at least three players in each string of A players; otherwise, the boundary players will switch to E. These considerations yield the proportions mentioned in the result in Theorem 4.4.4.[11]

Given the preceding arguments, it is easily seen that a string of five players choosing A cannot shrink over time. If players' strategies are randomly chosen initially, it follows that the probability of such a string of A players can be made arbitrarily close to 1 by suitably increasing the number of players. This idea is summarized in the following result due to Eshel et al. (1998).

Theorem 4.4.5. *Suppose that players' initial strategy choices are determined by independent, identically distributed variables for which the probability of each strategy is positive. Then the probability of convergence to an absorbing set containing states with at least 60% of A players goes to one as n gets large.*

This result suggests that the set of states from which the system moves to a majority altruistic society is relatively large. Eshel et al. (1998) also study stochastic stability of different absorbing sets. They show that the states identified in Theorem 4.4.5 are also the stochastically stable ones. In other words, we should expect a society to

---

[11] The term within brackets "on average" refers to the possibility of a cycle between two states, one in which there is a string of three players choosing E and the other in which there is a one-player string choosing E. In this case, there are on average two players choosing E.

spend most of the time in a state in which a large share of the players are choosing the altruistic action.

4.4.2.2. Related Themes

The findings reported in the previous section should be seen as part of an extensive literature on spatial evolution of social norms. This literature spans the fields of biology, computer science, philosophy, and political science in addition to economics. First, I note that the idea of local emergence of cooperative norms and their gradual spread in a social space has been discussed by different authors (see, e.g., Ullman-Margalit 1977 and Axelrod 1997). The model and the arguments developed in the previous section, should be seen as providing a formal account of this line of reasoning.

Second, I would like to explore the scope of the preceding argument in explaining altruism in richer interaction structures. In the model above, the persistence and spread of altruism appears to be related to the presence of A players who are protected from E players and therefore secure sufficiently high payoffs so that other A players on the boundary persist with action A as well. In larger dimensional interaction (e.g., k-dimensional lattices) or asymmetric interaction (as in a star) this protective wall may be harder to generate, and this may make altruism more vulnerable. For example, in the case of a star, mixed configurations are not sustainable, and it seems very easy to make the transition from a purely altruistic society to a purely egoist society (via the switch by the central player alone). The reverse transition requires switches by at least three players. Thus, if interaction is in a star, then we should expect to see a society of egoists only in the long run. These arguments suggest that the robustness of altruistic behavior needs to be explored further. Existing work on this subject seems to be mostly based on simulations (Nowak and May 1992). This work suggests that, in the absence of mutations, altruism can survive in a variety of interaction settings. There is also an extensive literature in evolutionary biology on the emergence and persistence of altruistic traits in different species. In this work the spread of altruistic traits is attributed to greater reproductive success. This success leads to the larger set of altruists spilling into neighboring areas, and this in turn leads to a growth of the trait over time (see, e.g., Wynne-Edwards 1986; Eshel and Cavalli-Sforza 1982).

Third, I would like to discuss the scope of cooperation in repeated games when they are played on networks. Although the literature on repeated games is very large, it seems that there is relatively little on repeated games with local interaction. In a recent paper, Haag and Lagunoff (2000) examine a setting in which players play the repeated prisoners' dilemma games with their immediate neighbors. Haag and Lagunoff examine the network architectures that support high cooperation when discount factors vary across players. Their main result shows that, under some restrictions on strategies allowed to players, a desirable interaction structure has the following properties: there is a clique of patient players (who are fully linked among themselves), each of whom is linked to a limited set of impatient players. In equilibrium, the clique of patient players will play cooperatively, whereas the impatient players at the periphery will defect. However, given their high patience level, and in a desire to sustain cooperation with their patient partners, the core group of players will tolerate this defection by peripheral players.

4.5. Evolving Networks

So far I have been discussing the nature of learning in the context of a given network. Our discussion suggests that in both strategic and nonstrategic contexts, the architecture of the network has an important impact on individual learning and social outcomes. This leads us to ask, Which networks are plausible? In many contexts of interest, the links that individuals have place them at a relative advantage or disadvantage. It is therefore natural to examine the incentives of individuals to form links and the implications of such link formation for social and economic interaction. This is the principal motivation for the recent research on the theory of network formation.

The process of learning in a setting in which the network itself is evolving is complicated. It seems desirable to proceed in steps. In this section I will focus on the pure network formation problem: individuals learn about the optimality of links with different individuals and revise their choices in response. This leads to an evolving network. In my discussion, I will focus on the model of connections that has been extensively studied in the literature.

4.5.1. The Connections Model

This model is based on the notion that social networks are formed by individual decisions that trade off the costs of forming and maintaining links against the potential rewards from doing so. A link with another individual allows access, in part and in due course, to the benefits available to the latter via his or her own links. Thus, links generate externalities and define the economic background for the network formation process. As before, let $N = \{1, \ldots, n\}$, with $n \geq 3$, be the set of players and let i and j be typical members of this set. A strategy of player $i \in N$ is a (row) vector $g_i = (g_{i,1}, \ldots, g_{i,i-1}, g_{i,i+1}, \ldots, g_{i,n})$, where $g_{i,j} \in \{0, 1\}$ for each $j \in N\setminus\{i\}$. I say player i has a *link* with j if $g_{i,j} = 1$. In this framework, links are *one-sided* in the sense that they can be formed on individual initiative, and (as will become clear shortly) this individual pays for the costs of forming links as well. This approach to link formation was developed in Bala and Goyal (2000a).[12] A natural interpretation of links is that they are information channels. A link between player i and j can allow for either one-way (asymmetric) or two-way (symmetric) flow of information. With one-way communication, the link $g_{i,j} = 1$ enables player i to access j's information but not vice versa. For example, i could access j's Web site or read a paper written by j. With two-way communication, a link $g_{i,j}$ enables i and

---

[12] The static model of one-sided links was introduced in Goyal (1993), and the dynamics were introduced in Bala (1997), notes on network formation (personal communication). The work of Bala and Goyal (2000a) subsumes these earlier individual attempts.

 The term *connections model* is due to Jackson and Wolinsky (1996), who developed a closely related model in which a link requires the consent of both players involved. This model is presented later in this section.

j to share information. An example of this is a telephone call between two players. A second interpretation is that a link reflects a social relation, which involves the giving of gifts and reciprocal favors. The set of (pure) strategies of player i is denoted by $\mathcal{G}_i$. Since player i has the option of forming or not forming a link with each of the remaining $n - 1$ players, the number of strategies of player i is clearly $|\mathcal{G}_i| = 2^{n-1}$. The set $\mathcal{G} = \mathcal{G}_1 \times \cdots \times \mathcal{G}_n$ is the space of pure strategies of all the players.

The link $g_{i,j} = 1$ is represented by an *edge* starting at j with the arrowhead pointing at i. Figure 4.1 provides an example with $n = 3$ players. Here player 1 has formed links with players 2 and 3, player 3 has a link with player 1, and player 2 does not link up with any other player. Note that there is a one-to-one correspondence between the set of all directed networks with n vertices and the set $\mathcal{G}$.

With a slight abuse of our earlier notation, I can say that $N^d(i; g) = \{k \in N \mid g_{i,k} = 1\}$ is the set of players with whom i *maintains* a link. The notation "$j \xrightarrow{g} i$" indicates that there exists a path from j to i in g. Furthermore, I define $N(i; g) = \{k \in N \mid k \xrightarrow{g} i\} \cup \{i\}$. This is the set of all players whom i accesses either through a direct link or a sequence of links. Recall that $\eta_i^d(g) \equiv |N^d(i; g)|$ and $\eta_i(g) \equiv |N(i; g)|$ for $g \in \mathcal{G}$.

I wish to model a situation in which it is advantageous to access a larger number of people and links are costly to maintain. I will first discuss the case of one-way flow of benefits. Denote the set of nonnegative integers by Z_+. Let $\phi : \mathcal{Z}_+^2 \to \mathcal{R}$ be such that $\phi(x, y)$ is strictly increasing in x and strictly decreasing in y. Define each player's payoff function $\Pi_i : \mathcal{G} \to R$ as

$$\prod_i(g) = \phi(\eta_i(g), \eta_i^d(g)). \qquad (4.5.1)$$

Given the properties I have assumed for the function ϕ, $\eta_i(g)$ can be interpreted as providing the "benefit" that player i receives from his or her links, and $\eta_i^d(g)$ measures the "cost" associated with maintaining them. I note that this formulation assumes that the players are ex ante identical; for a study of the impact of heterogeneity on network formation, see Galeotti and Goyal (2002).

A special case of (4.5.1) occurs when payoffs are linear. To define this, I specify two parameters $V > 0$ and $c > 0$, where V is regarded as the *value* of each player's information (to himself or herself and to others), whereas c is this player's *cost* of link formation. Without loss of generality, V can be normalized to 1. I now define $\phi(x, y) = x - yc$, that is,

$$\prod_i(g) = \eta_i(g) - \eta_i^d(g)c. \qquad (4.5.2)$$

In other words, player i's payoffs are the number of players he or she observes less the total cost of link formation. I identify three parameter ranges of importance. If $c \in (0, 1)$, then player i will be willing to form a link with player j for the sake of j's value alone. When $c \in (1, n - 1)$, player i will require j to observe some additional players to induce him or her to form a link with j. Finally, if $c > n - 1$, then the cost of link formation exceeds the total benefit of information available from the rest of society. Here, it is a dominant strategy for i not to form a link with any player.

Given a network $g \in \mathcal{G}$, let g_{-i} denote the network obtained when all of player i's links are removed. The network g can be written as $g = g_i \oplus g_{-i}$, where the $\oplus$ indicates that g is formed as the union of the links in g_i and g_{-i}. Recall that a strategy profile g^* is a Nash equilibrium if $\Pi_i(g_i^* \oplus g_{-i}^*) \geq \Pi_i(g_i \oplus g_{-i}^*)$ for all $g_i \in \mathcal{G}_i$ and for all $i \in N$. A *strict* Nash equilibrium is a Nash equilibrium in which each player gets strictly higher payoffs with his or her current strategy than would be the case with any other strategy.

I first study the static network formation problem. Recall that a wheel is a network in which each player forms exactly one link represented by an arrow pointing to the player. The following result, due to Bala and Goyal (2000a), provides a complete characterization of equilibrium networks in the preceding model.

Theorem 4.5.1. *Let the payoffs be given by equation (4.5.1). Then a strict Nash network is either the wheel or the empty network.*

In particular, in the context of the linear model, the wheel is the unique equilibrium network if $c < 1$, the wheel and the empty network are the only equilibria for $1 < c < n - 1$, and the empty network is the unique network for $c > n - 1$. I now provide a sketch of the main arguments underlying Theorem 4.5.1. The first step in the proof is to show that a Nash network is either connected or empty. Consider a nonempty Nash network and suppose that player i is the player who observes the largest number of players in this network. Suppose i does not observe everyone. Then there is some player j who is not observed by i and who does not observe i (for otherwise j would observe more players than i). Inasmuch as i gets value from his or her links and payoffs are symmetric, j must also have some links. Let j deviate from his or her Nash strategy by forming a link with i alone. By doing so j will observe strictly more players than i does, for he or she has the additional benefit of observing i. Since j was observing no more players than i in his or her original strategy, j's payoffs are increased by the deviation of forming a link with i alone. This contradiction implies that i must observe every player in the society. It then follows that every other player will have an incentive either to link with i or to observe him or her through a sequence of links so that the network is connected. If the network is not minimally connected, then some player could delete a link and still observe all players, which would contradict Nash. The second step exploits the refinement of strictness and is based on the following observation: if two players i and j have a link with the same player k, then one of them, i for instance, will be indifferent between forming a link with k or instead forming a link with j. We know that Nash networks are either connected or empty. This means that in the one-way flow model a (nonempty) strict Nash network has exactly n links. The wheel is the unique such network, and the result follows.

Theorem 4.5.1 shows that individual incentives restrict the range of possible network architectures quite dramatically. This characterization of equilibrium networks, however, raises the issue, How do individuals choose links if they start with some different network, and is there some pressure moving them to the equilibrium networks identified above? In other words, will individuals learn to coordinate their links and arrive at a wheel network?

Bala and Goyal (2000a) introduced the study of learning dynamics in the formation of networks, and I will follow their approach here. They used a variant of the myopic best-response dynamic to study the preceding question. Two features of the process are important: (1) There is some probability that an individual exhibits *inertia*, that is, chooses the same strategy as in the previous period. This ensures that players do not perpetually miscoordinate. (2) If more than one strategy is optimal for some individual, then he or she *randomizes* across the optimal strategies. This requirement implies, in particular, that a nonstrict Nash network can never be a steady state of the dynamics. The rules on individual behavior define a Markov chain on the state space of all networks; moreover, the set of absorbing states of the Markov chain coincides with the set of strict Nash networks of the one-shot game. The following result, due to Bala and Goyal (2000a), shows that the learning process converges to the equilibrium networks just identified.

Theorem 4.5.2. *Let the payoff functions be given by equation (4.5.1) and let g be some initial network. Then the dynamic process converges to the wheel or the empty network in finite time with probability one.*

In the context of the linear model, the process converges to the wheel for $0 < c < 1$, the wheel or the empty network for $1 < c < n - 1$, and the empty network for $c > n - 1$. The proof of Theorem 4.5.2 exploits the idea that well-connected individuals generate positive externalities. Fix a network g and suppose that there is a player i who accesses all people in g directly or indirectly. Consider a player j farthest away from i in the network g – in other words $j \in \text{argmax}_{k \in N} d_{i,k}(g)$. This also means that player j is not critical for player i in the network g, that is, player i is able to access everyone even if player j deletes all of his or her links. (It is easy to see that such a player j will always exist.) Allow player j to move; he or she can form a single link with player i and access all the different individuals accessed by player i. Thus, if forming links is at all profitable for player j, then one best-response strategy is to form a single link with player i. This strategy in turn makes player j well connected. We now consider some person k who is not critical for j and apply the same idea. Repeated application of this argument leads to a network in which everyone accesses everyone else via a single link, that is, a wheel network.

I now consider the case in which the flow of benefits is two way. In this case, benefits flow between two players so long as one of the two has formed the link with the other. To capture this two-way flow, I define $\hat{g}_{i,j} = \max\{g_{i,j}, g_{j,i}\}$. The link $g_{i,j} = 1$ is represented by an *edge* between i and j; a filled circle lying on the edge near player i indicates that it is this player who has initiated the link. Figure 4.4 depicts the example of Figure 4.1 for the two-way model. As before, player 1 has formed links with players 2 and 3, player 3 has formed a link with agent 1, and agent 2 does not link up with any other agent.[13] Given the strategy profile g, it is now straightforward to define a network $\hat{g}$ using the operation above. Every strategy profile g has a unique representation in the manner shown in Figure 4.4.

---

[13] Since players choose strategies independently of each other, two players may simultaneously initiate a two-way link, as seen in Figure 4.4.

Figure 4.4: Two-way flow network.

I can extend the notion of path as follows: there is a *tw-path* (for two-way) in g between i and j if either $\hat{g}_{i,j} = 1$ or there exist agents $j_1, \ldots, j_m$ distinct from each other and i and j such that $\hat{g}_{i,j_1} = \cdots = \hat{g}_{j_m,j} = 1$. I write $i \xrightarrow{\hat{g}} j$ to indicate a tw-path between i and j in g. Let $N^d(i; g)$ and $\eta_i^d(g)$ be defined as in the case of directed networks. The set $N(i; \hat{g}) = \{k \mid i \xrightarrow{\hat{g}} k\} \cup \{i\}$ consists of agents that i observes in $\hat{g}$ under two-way communication, and $\eta_i(\hat{g}) \equiv |N(i; \hat{g})|$ is its cardinality. In the two-way flow model, the payoff to player i with a strategy g_i, faced with a profile g_{-i}, is given by

$$\hat{\prod}_i(g) = \phi\big(\eta_i(\hat{g}), \eta_i^d(g)\big), \tag{4.5.3}$$

where $\phi(.,.)$ is as in the one-way flow model. The case of linear payoffs is $\phi(x, y) = x - yc$ as before. I obtain the following, which is analogous to equation (4.5.2):

$$\hat{\prod}_i(g) = \eta_i(\hat{g}) - \eta_i^d(g)c. \tag{4.5.4}$$

The parameter ranges $c \in (0, 1)$, $c \in (1, n - 1)$, and $c > n - 1$ have the same interpretation as above. A center-sponsored star is a network in which the center forms and hence pays for all the links. The following result, due to Bala and Goyal (2000a), provides a complete characterization of the architecture of strict Nash networks in the two-way flow case.

Theorem 4.5.3. *Let the payoffs be given by equation (4.5.3). A strict Nash network is either a center-sponsored star or the empty network.*

In particular, in the linear model given by equation (4.5.4), the center-sponsored star is the unique (strict) equilibrium network for $0 < c < 1$, whereas the empty network is the unique equilibrium for $c > 1$. I now sketch the main arguments underlying the proof. The first step in the proof is to show that a Nash network is either empty or connected. The second step exploits the following observation: if player n has a link with j, then no other player can have a link with j. The idea behind this is that if two agents i and j have a link with the same agent k, then one of them, for instance i, will be indifferent between forming a link with k or instead forming a link with j. As a Nash network is connected, this implies that n must be the center of a star. A further implication of the foregoing observation is that every link in this star must be formed or "sponsored" by the center. The dynamics of the two-way flow model are well behaved. The following result, due to Bala and Goyal (2000a), provides a characterization.

Theorem 4.5.4. *Let the payoff functions be given by equation (4.5.3) and let g be some initial network. If $\phi(x + 1, y + 1) > (<)\phi(x, y)$ for all $y \in \{0, 1, \ldots, n - 2\}$*

and $x \in \{y + 1, y + 2, \ldots, n - 1\}$, *then the dynamic process converges to the center-sponsored star (empty network) in finite time with probability 1.*

The preceding model of connections supposes that links can be formed by single individuals. In many economic applications – such as two firms collaborating on a project or two countries signing a bilateral trade agreement – it is natural to suppose that the formation of a link requires the acquiescence of both the players who are directly involved. This leads us to a model of two-sided link formation. Jackson and Wolinsky (1996) develop a general model of two-sided link formation as well as a solution concept for such games: *pairwise stability.*[14] A network *g* is said to be pairwise stable (pw-stable for short) if no individual has an incentive to delete any link that exists in the network and no pair of players has an incentive to form a link that does not exist in the network. I now present a variant of this model of connections to illustrate the role of different link formation assumptions. I will then turn to the issue of learning and dynamics in two-sided networks.

A link is denoted by $\bar{g}_{i,j} \in \{0, 1\}$, where it is assumed that $\bar{g}_{i,j} = \bar{g}_{j,i}$. A network $\bar{g} = (\{\bar{g}_{i,j}\})_{i,j \in N}$; the space of all networks $\bar{\mathcal{G}}$ is equivalent to the set of all undirected networks on *n* vertices. The notions of path, component, distance, and connectedness extend to this set of networks naturally. I suppose that the value of every player is 1, and I also assume that there is decay (given by $\delta \in [0, 1)$) of value in indirect links, which is related to the distance between players. Let $d_{i,j}(\bar{g})$ refer to the (geodesic) distance between two players *i* and *j* in network $\bar{g}$ and let $\eta_i^d(\bar{g})$ refer to the number of players with whom player *i* forms a link in network *g*. The payoffs to player *i* in a network $\bar{g}$ are

$$\prod_i(\bar{g}) = 1 + \sum_{j \in N(i;\bar{g})} \delta^{d_{i,j}(\bar{g})} - \eta_i^d(\bar{g})c. \tag{4.5.5}$$

The following result, due to Jackson and Wolinsky (1996), offers a partial characterization of pairwise stable networks.

Theorem 4.5.5. *Suppose payoffs are given by equation (4.5.5). A pw-stable network has at most one non-singleton component. For $c < \delta - \delta^2$, the unique pw-stable network is the complete network g^c. For $\delta - \delta^2 < c < \delta$, a star is a pw-stable network (it is not the unique stable one). For $\delta < c$, the empty network is pw-stable and any pw-stable network that is nonempty is such that each player has least two links.*

For details of this result, I refer the reader to Chapter 1 of this volume. As in the one-sided link model, I now explore the dynamics of network formation in the two-sided link formation case. I suppose that in each period one pair of players is randomly picked and has a choice of forming (or not forming) a link. If a link is already present, then the players can decide whether to sever it. If no link exists, they can decide to form a link, and at the same time each of the players can also delete any subset of the links that they currently maintain (so long as both players agree to this). I also assume that they make decisions on the basis of myopic payoff maximization.

---

[14] For a more complete discussion of two-sided link formation, I refer the reader to Chapter 1 of this volume.

The following result, due to Watts (2001), presents a partial characterization of the behavior of the preceding dynamic process.

Theorem 4.5.6. *If $0 < c < \delta - \delta^2$, then every link will form and the process converges to the complete network in finite time with probability 1. If $\delta - \delta^2 < c < \delta$, then there is a positive probability that the star network will emerge. However, this probability is decreasing in the number of players and goes to 0 as the number of players gets large. If $c > \delta$, then no link will be formed and the network remains empty with probability 1.*

The arguments underlying the first and third statements follow directly from the assumption on parameters and the myopic decison rule. The argument for the formation of the star is as follows: fix a player 1 and get each of the other players, starting from 2, 3, and so on until n, to have an opportunity to form links with player 1. It follows from the facts that $c < \delta$, the initial network is empty, and that players are myopic that every pair of players with an opportunity to form a link will do so. The star emerges at the end of period $n - 1$ and, given the rules about matching, this pairing sequence occurs with positive probability. The result on the decreasing probability of a star with respect to number of players exploits the following observation: for the star to form, every player $j \neq 1$ must meet player 1 before he or she meets any other player. This is true because if, for instance, players 1 and 2 meet in period 1 and players 3 and 4 meet in period 2, then at the end of period 2 there will be two linked pairs. Now, suppose player 1 meets player 3 in period 3. Clearly, they will form a link under the assumption that $c < \delta$ and players are myopic. To get a star with player 1 at the center, we must have players 1 and 4 meet and form a link. However, if they meet, player 1 will not agree to form a link with player 4 because the net payoff $(\delta - c) - \delta^2 < 0$. The proof follows by noting that the probability that every player meets player 1 before meeting any other player goes to 0 as n gets large.

4.5.2. Related Themes

I now briefly discuss one other issue: the rate of convergence of the dynamics. This is an important issue because the state space of the dynamic process is large. There are $2^{n(n-1)}$ networks with n agents; thus, for instance, in a game with eight players, there are $2^{56} = 7 \times 10^{16}$ possible directed networks, which suggests that a slow rate of convergence is a real possibility. The dynamics are Markovian, and so convergence to the limiting distribution is exponential. As noted in Section 4.4.1, however, this allows for a wide range of convergence speeds. The rate of convergence is studied using simulations in Bala and Goyal (2000a). They find that both in the one-way flow model as well as the two-way flow model, the dynamics converge rapidly to the limit network. For instance, in a game with eight players, the average time to convergence is less than 250 periods in the one-way flow model, whereas the average time to convergence is 28 periods in the two-way model. (These numbers are for a high probability of strategy revision in every period; the rates of convergence remain fast as this probability is varied.)

Several other issues, such as the relation between individual incentives and social efficiency, heterogeneity in valuations, costs of forming links, imperfect reliability of links, link formation by far-sighted players, and imperfect information on network structure, have been studied in the literature on network formation. I refer the reader to Chapters 1 and 2 of this volume for a discussion of these issues.

4.6. Optimal Links and Actions in Games

I now turn to an exploration of models in which individuals choose links (and thereby shape the network) and also choose actions in strategic games they play with those with whom they have formed connections. There are a variety of economic examples that fit naturally in this framework. Firms collaborate on research with each other and subsequently compete in the product market, whereas individuals invest in relationships and then choose actions in the social interaction (the action could be whether to smoke, to indulge in criminal activity, or pertain to the choice of learning different softwares or languages). In this section, I will focus on coordination games.[15]

4.6.1. Coordination Games

I present a simple model in which players their partners and an action in the coordination games they play with their different partners. This framework allows us to endogenize the nature of interaction and study the effect of partner choice on the way players coordinate their actions in the coordination game.

The issue of endogenous structures of interaction on coordination has been explored in Bhaskar and Vega-Redondo (2004); Ely (2002); Mailath, Samuelson, and Shaked (1997); and Oechssler (1997). They use a framework in which players are located on islands. Moving from one island to another implies severing all ties with the former island and instead playing the game with all the players on the new island. Thus, neighborhoods are made endogenous via the choice of islands. In my exposition, I will follow some of the more recent papers on this subject because they fit in more naturally with the framework I am using in this survey. I will briefly discuss the relationship between the different approaches later in this section.

As before, I will suppose that $N = \{1, 2, \ldots, n\}$ is the set of players, where $n \geq 3$. Each player has a strategy $s_i = \{g_i, a_i\} \in \mathcal{G}_i$, where g_i refers to the links he or she forms whereas $a_i \in A_i$ refers to the choice of action in the accompanying coordination game. Any profile of link decisions $g = (g_1, g_2 \ldots g_n)$ defines a directed network. Given a network g, I say that a pair of players i and j are directly linked if at least one of them has established a link with the other one, that is, if $\max\{g_{ij}, g_{ji}\} = 1$. To describe the pattern of players' links, I will take recourse to

---

[15] There is relatively little research and few general results on evolving networks in games of conflict. For some recent work, I refer the reader to Annen (2003) and Vega-Redondo (2002). A related earlier paper that uses a different framework of analysis is Hirshleifer and Rasmusen (1989).

our earlier notation and define $\hat{g}_{ij} = \max\{g_{ij}, g_{ji}\}$ for every pair i and j in N. I refer to g_{ij} as an active link for player i and a passive link for player j. I will say that a network g is essential if $g_{ij}g_{ji} = 0$ for every pair of players i and j. Also, let $G^c(M) \equiv \{g : \forall i, j \in M, \ \hat{g}_{ij} = 1, \ g_{ij}g_{ji} = 0\}$ stand for the set of complete and essential networks on the set of players M. I will say that $s = (g, a) \in S^h$ for some $h \in \{\alpha, \beta\}$ if $g \in G^c(N)$ and $a_i = h$ for all $i \in N$. More generally, I will write $s = (g, a) \in S^{\alpha\beta}$ if there exists a partition of the population into two subgroups, N^α and N^β (one of them possibly empty) and corresponding components of g, g^α, and g^β such that (i) $g^a \in G^c(N^\alpha)$, $g^\beta \in G^c(N^\beta)$ and (ii) $\forall i \in N^\alpha, \ a_i = \alpha; \ \forall i \in N^\beta,$ $a_i = \beta$.

Individuals located in a social network play a 2×2 symmetric game with a common action set. The set of partners of player i depends on his or her location in the network. In particular, I assume that player i plays a game with all other players in the set $N^d(i; \hat{g})$. The bilateral game is the same as the coordination game discussed in Section 4.3. Recall that there is a common set of actions $A = \{\alpha, \beta\}$. I will assume that the restrictions stated in equation 4.4.1 hold. Recall that these restrictions imply that there are two pure strategy equilibria of the game – (α, α) and (β, β) – and that coordinating on either of them is better than not coordinating at all. I also assume that $b \geq a$ in what follows.

Every player who establishes a link with some other player incurs a cost $c > 0$. Given the strategies of other players, $s_{-i} = (s_1, \ldots s_{i-1}, s_{i+1}, \ldots s_n)$, the payoffs to a player i from playing some strategy $s_i = (g_i, a_i)$ are given by

$$\Pi_i(s_i, s_{-i}) = \sum_{j \in N^d(i; \hat{g})} \pi(a_i, a_j) - \eta^d(i; g) \cdot c. \tag{4.6.1}$$

I make two remarks about this formulation.

(1) Individual payoffs are aggregated across the games played by each player. This seems appropriate in the present setting because the number of games an individual plays is endogenous. I want to account explicitly for the influence of the size of the neighborhood and thus choose the aggregate payoff formulation.
(2) The description of strategies and the payoff formulation reflect the assumption that every player i is obliged to choose the same action in the (possibly) several bilateral games in which he or she is engaged.

This assumption is natural in the present context: if players were allowed to choose a different action for every two-person game they are involved in, this would make their behavior in any particular game insensitive to the network structure.

I start with the following result, due to Goyal and Vega-Redondo (2004), which provides a complete characterization of equilibrium outcomes.

Theorem 4.6.1. *Suppose payoffs satisfy equation (4.4.1) and $b > a$. (a) If $c < d$, then the set of equilibrium profiles $S^* = S^\alpha \cup S^\beta$; (b) if $d < c < a$, then $S^\alpha \cup S^\beta \subset S^* \subset S^{\alpha\beta}$, the first inclusion being strict for large enough n; (c) if $a < c < b$, then $S^* = S^\beta \cup \{(g^e, (\alpha, \alpha, \ldots, \alpha))\}$, (d) if $c > b$, then $S^* = \{g^e\} \times A^n$.*

I provide a sketch of the main arguments underlying this result. The first step derives restrictions on equilibrium network architectures implied by individual incentives. If costs of link formation are low ($c < e$), for instance, then a player has an incentive to link up with other players irrespective of the actions the other players are choosing. On the other hand, when costs are quite high (specifically, $a < c < b$), then everyone who is linked must be choosing the efficient action. This, however, implies that it is attractive to form a link with every other player and thus to obtain the complete network again. In contrast, if costs are at an intermediate level ($d < c < a$), a richer set of configurations is possible. On the one hand, because $c > d(> e)$, the link formation is only worthwhile if other players are choosing the same action. On the other hand, because $c < u(< b)$, coordinating at either of the two equilibria (in the underlying coordination game) is better than not playing the game at all. This allows for networks with two disconnected components in equilibria. In view of these considerations, parts (a) and (c) follow quite directly. I now elaborate on the coexistence equilibria identified in part (b). In these equilibria, there are two unconnected groups with each group adopting a common action (different in each group). The strategic stability of this configuration rests on the appeal of "passive" links. A link such as $g_{ij} = 1$ is paid for by player i, but both players i and j derive payoffs from it. In a mixed equilibrium configuration, the links in each group must be, roughly, evenly distributed. This means that all players enjoy some benefits from passive links. In contrast, if a player were to switch actions and then to derive the full benefits of this switch, he or she would have to form (active) links with everyone in the new group. This lowers the incentives to switch, which is a consideration that becomes decisive if the number of passive links is large enough (hence the requirement of large n).

The preceding result says that individual incentives restrict the range of network architectures quite sharply in this setting, and this has a bearing on the extent of heterogeneity that is permissible. However, there is a residual multiplicity: in parts (a) and (c), this multiplicity permits alternative states in which either of the two actions is homogeneously chosen by the whole population, whereas in part (b), the multiplicity allows for a wide range of possible states for which neither action homogeneity nor full connectedness necessarily prevails. Are these outcomes all equally stable? This question leads me to examine the stochastic stability of different equilibria.

4.6.1.1. Coevolution of Structure and Behavior

Time is discrete $t = 1, 2, 3, \ldots$. At each t, the state of the system is given by the strategy profile $s(t) \equiv [(g_i(t), a_i(t))]_{i=1}^{n}$ specifying the action played, and links established, by each player $i \in N$. I will suppose that the decision rules are the same as in the one-sided link formation model described in Section 4.5. In every period, there is a positive independent probability that any given individual gets a chance to revise his or her strategy. If the player receives this opportunity, I assume that he or she chooses a best response to what other players chose in the preceding period. If there are several strategies that fulfill this requirement, then any one of them is taken to be selected with equal probability, for instance. This strategy revision process defines a simple Markov chain on $S \equiv S_1 \times \cdots \times S_n$. I then define the perturbed dynamics as in Section 4.4 with a small "mutation" probability $\epsilon > 0$. For any $\epsilon > 0$, the process defines a Markov chain that is aperiodic and irreducible and therefore has a unique invariant probability distribution. Let us denote this distribution by η_ϵ. I analyze the form of η_ϵ as the probability of mistakes becomes very small – that is, formally, as ϵ converges to zero. Define $\lim_{\epsilon \to 0} \eta_\epsilon = \hat{\eta}$. When a state $s = (s_1, s_2, \ldots, s_n)$ has $\hat{\eta}(s) > 0$, that is, it is in the support of $\hat{\eta}$, I say that it is *stochastically stable*.

The following result, due to Goyal and Vega-Redondo (2004), provides a complete characterization of stochastically stable social networks and actions in the coordination game.

Theorem 4.6.2. *Suppose equation (4.4.1) and $b > a$. There exists some $\bar{c} \in (e, a)$ such that if $c < \bar{c}$, then $\hat{S} = S^\alpha$ whereas if $\bar{c} < c < b$, then $\hat{S} = S^\beta$. Finally, if $c > b$, then $\hat{S} = \{g^e\} \times A^n$.*

This result illustrates that the *dynamics* of link formation play a crucial role in the model. I observe that the only architecture that is stochastically stable (within the interesting parameter range) is the complete one, although players' behavior in the coordination game is *different* depending on the costs of forming links. However, if the network were to remain fixed throughout, standard arguments indicate that the risk-dominant action must prevail in the long run (cf. Kandori, Mailath, and Rob 1993). Thus, it is the link formation *process* that, by allowing for the coevolution of the links and actions, shapes individual behavior in the coordination game.

I now briefly provide some intuition on the sharp relationship found between the *costs* of forming links and the corresponding behavior displayed by players in the coordination game. On the one hand, when the cost of forming links is small, players wish to be linked with everyone irrespective of the actions they choose. Hence, from an individual perspective, the relative attractiveness of different actions is quite *insensitive* to what is the network structure faced by any given player at the time his or her choices are revised. In essence, a player must make fresh choices as if he or she were in a complete network. In this case, therefore, the risk-dominant (and possibly) inefficient convention prevails because, under complete connectivity, this convention is harder to destabilize (through mutations) than the efficient but risk-dominated one. By contrast, if costs of forming links are high, individual players choose to form links only with those who are known (or perceived) to be playing the same action. This lowers the strategic uncertainty in the interaction and thus facilitates the emergence of the efficient action.

I comment on two features of the model: the one-sided link formation and the simultaneous choice of links and actions in the coordination game. It is possible to show that the main result on stochastically stable networks and the relation between costs of link formation and coordination remains essentially unchanged if link formation is two-sided and costs are borne by both players. However, a model with two-sided links and sequential choice of links and actions yields quite different outcomes. This formulation has been explored by Jackson and Watts (2002b). They consider a two-sided link formation model in which pairs of players are given an opportunity to form links. They make a decision on forming links under the assumption that their actions (in the corresponding coordination game) will remain the same as in the previous period. Once the network is in place, a player is selected at random to choose an action in the coordination game. This player chooses an action that maximizes current payoff given the current network and the actions of players in the previous period. The choices of players can be perturbed or randomly altered with small probability, and I look for stochastically stable outcomes. The following result, due to Jackson and Watts (2002b), provides a complete characterization of stochastically stable outcomes in this setting.[16]

Theorem 4.6.3. *Suppose that equation (4.4.1) holds and $a < b$. Suppose that link formation is two-sided and choice of links and actions in the coordination game is sequential. (a) If $0 < c < e$, then a complete network with everyone choosing α is the unique, stochastically stable outcome; (b) if $e < c < a$, then a complete network with everyone choosing either α or β can be the stochastically stable outcome; and (c) if $a < c < b$, then a complete network with everyone choosing β or the empty network with everyone choosing α are the stochastically stable outcomes.*

The ideas behind parts (a) and (c) are close to the ones mentioned in the case of one-sided links. The impact of the sequentiality of links and actions is reflected clearly in part (b), and I discuss this result now. Suppose we are a complete network with everyone choosing action α. Now let there be two trembles that lead to two players switching actions to β. Then players choosing action α would like to delete their links with these two players, and a component of two players choosing β arises. This component can grow with single mutations to β until it takes over the population. Jackson and Watts show that the process of transition from an all-β state to an all-α state is symmetric, and so the complete network with everyone choosing action α or β is both stochastically stable outcomes. In this process, notice that players who have "trembled" from (say) α to β cannot switch actions and simultaneously offer to form links with the other players. If this simultaneous change were possible, then the players will want to switch actions and form links with the other $n - 2$ players, and these other players will accept these links (under the parameter conditions given), and the process will revert to an all-α state. Thus, the assumption of sequentiality of link formation and action choice is central to the preceding result.

In a closely related paper, Droste, Gilles, and Johnson (1999) explore a model of networks and coordination in which there is an ex ante spatial structure with all players located around a circle and the costs of link formation are higher for players who are other away. In this case, long-run outcomes have richer spatial interaction structures, but the risk-dominant action prevails in the interesting parameter ranges.

I now discuss the connections between the preceding results and the earlier work of Ely (2002), Mailath et al. (1997); Oechssler (1997); and Bhaskar and Vega-Redondo (2004). The basic insight flowing from the earlier work is that, if individuals can easily separate or insulate themselves from those who are playing an inefficient

---

[16] For an application of stochastic stability ideas to link formation models more generally, see Jackson and Watts (2002a).

action (e.g., the risk-dominant action), then efficient "enclaves" will readily be formed and eventually attract the "migration" of others who will eventually adopt the efficient action. One may be tempted to identify *easy* mobility with *low* costs of forming links. However, the considerations involved in the two approaches turn out to be very different. This is evident from the differences in the results: recall that in the network formation approach, the risk-dominant outcome prevails if the costs of forming links are small. There are two main reasons for this contrast. First, in the network formation approach, players do not *indirectly* choose their pattern of interaction with others by moving across a *prespecified* network of locations (as in the case of player mobility). Rather, they *directly* construct their interaction network (with no exogenous restrictions) by choosing those agents with whom they want to play the game. Second, the cost of link formation is paid per link formed and thus becomes truly effective only if it is high enough. Thus, it is precisely the restricted "mobility" induced by high costs that helps insulate (and thus protect) the individuals who are choosing the efficient action. If the costs of link formation are low, then the extensive interaction this facilitates may have the unfortunate consequence of rendering risk-dominance considerations decisive.

4.6.1.2. Related Themes

I now briefly discuss some other issues that have been studied in the literature. In the framework discussed, individuals choose links and actions to maximize current payoffs. An alternative formulation consisting of reinforcement in link formation along with the imitation of the highest payoff action has been studied in a recent paper by Skyrms and Pemantle (2000). They study the stag game (in which the payoffs to a player from the risk-dominant action are independent of the choice of the partner). The dynamics of links are driven by reinforcement: a link becomes likely in the future if the current experience is positive. They find that if the speed of adjustment of actions is relatively slow as compared with the speed at which reinforcement works on links, then all players converge to the efficient (but risk-dominated) action. On the other hand, the likelihood of choosing the efficient action declines quite sharply as the speed of switching actions increases. These are interesting findings and seem to be in line with the earlier work on mobility discussed in this section earlier, where efficiency in coordination games becomes more likely as mobility – in the sense of switching partners – becomes easier.

I conclude this section by briefly discussing some work on learning of optimal links and actions in games of congestion. Recall these are two-player, two-action games in which there are two pure strategy equilibria $\{\alpha, \beta\}$ and $\{\beta, \alpha\}$. Bramoulle et al. (2002) study these games. They show that the density of the network varies inversely with respect to the costs of forming links: for low costs the equilibrium network is complete, for moderate costs the equilibrium network is a bipartite graph; whereas for high costs the equilibrium network is empty. Moreover, the relative proportions of the individuals choosing the different actions depend crucially on the cost of forming links. For low costs, only the complete and essential graph with a unique proportion of individuals performing each action arises in equilibrium. However, for moderate costs there is a wide variety of proportions that can arise in equilibrium. These proportions have very different welfare properties, and typically equilibrium networks are not efficient. Finally, Bramoulle et al. find that in contrast to the preceding coordination game analysis, all equilibria of the game are stochastically stable.

4.7. Concluding Remarks

Traditionally, economists have studied social and economic phenomena using models with centralized and anonymous interaction among individual entities. Moreover, prices have been the main coordinating device for the interaction among individuals. In recent years, we have developed a richer repertoire of models that allow for decentralized (and local) interaction among individuals, and coordination is attained via a variety of nonprice mechanisms. The research on learning in networks surveyed in this chapter should be seen as part of this general research program. In this section I summarize what we have learned so far and also propose some open questions.

I started the chapter with results on learning for a given network of interaction. Existing results show clearly that, both in strategic and nonstrategic settings, the network structure influences the actions individuals take and this in turn has serious implications for the level of welfare they can hope to attain in the short run as well as in the long run. In the context of nonstrategic learning, we know that individuals with similar ranking of actions who are located in a connected society will eventually all earn the same payoff. However, the level of this payoff – whether it is the maximum attainable – will depend on the architecture of the network of communication. Existing work has explored the possibilities of complete learning in societies with an infinite number of players. The main finding here is that a desirable communications network should allow for "local independence" – people having distinct sources of information that facilitate experimentation and gathering of new information – and at the same time the network should have channels of communication across these localities to spread successful actions. The optimality of this network, especially with regard to finite societies, remains an open question.

In the context of coordination games played on networks, the main finding is that in random matching models or in complete networks, equilibrium outcomes correspond to the pure strategy of the underlying game. Moreover, the stochastically stable outcome is typically the risk-dominant equilibrium. However, with local interaction, a variety of outcomes are possible, and this is also true when we restrict attention to stochastically stable outcomes. The stochastic stability results have been obtained for myopic best-response decision rules and equiprobable deviations. These results can be greatly strengthened and refined if we suppose that deviations from best response follow a log linear function (which makes deviations from optimal actions sensitive to payoff differences). In particular, it can be shown that dynamics always select the risk-dominant equilibrium and that convergence to this outcome is rapid and essentially independent of the size of the population for a wide class of local interaction networks. The class of interaction networks identified here also emphasizes close-knit local communities, which is similar in spirit to the local independence idea developed in the nonstrategic learning setting. The differences in results between best-response dynamics and log-linear decision–based dynamics lead me to wonder if there are close relations between interaction structure and decision rules. For instance, is imitation easier and more effective in local interaction settings? My discussion of games of conflict played on networks focused on prisoners' dilemma games and also highlighted this connection between decision rules and interaction structure. The main result obtained here is that a combination of imitation-based decision making and local interaction ensures high levels of cooperation in society. This result has been obtained for interaction on a circle only, and an interesting open question here is the robustness of altruism and the possibility of cooperation in more general networks of interaction.

I then moved to a discussion of learning in a setting in which the network of structure itself is evolving as a result of individual decisions on links with others. This is a relatively new strand of the research, and several fascinating questions remain open. My presentation focused on the connections model of networks. There are two general findings here: the first is that strategic link formation implies sharp predictions on equilibrium network architectures, and the second is that the dynamics of link formation based on individual learning have strong self-organizing properties. The process converges, the limit networks can be explicitly characterized (and have simple and classical architectures such as stars and wheels) and the rate of convergence to the limit networks is fast. The model of connections is a natural one for networks with nonrival goods because it captures one type of positive externality of linking activity. But there are a variety of other externalities – positive and negative as well as a mixture of the two – that arise in networks. A systematic analysis of these spillovers and their bearing on network architectures is an open problem.

In the final part of the chapter, I studied games in which the strategies involve links as well as other actions. The study of these models is still at an early stage. An exploration of link formation and learning optimal actions in a nonstrategic setting (as explored in Section 4.3) seems to be a very promising area for further work. In the context of coordination games, the main finding of existing work is that the costs of forming links decisively shape individual behavior and determine long-run equilibrium. This finding should be seen as a first step in the exploration of a wide range of issues relating to evolving social structures and economic performance. For instance, one may wonder if it is desirable to allow persons to form links freely or if some restrictions on link activity may be socially desirable. The existing models are very stylized, and richer models can be useful to study phenomenon such as ghettos and the formation of exclusive clubs.

BIBLIOGRAPHY

[1] Albert, Reka and Albert-Laslo Barabasi (2002), "Statistical Mechanics of Complex Networks," *Review of Modern Physics* 74, 47–100.

[2] Allen, Beth (1982), "Some Stochastic Processes of Interdependent Demand and Technological Diffusion of an Innovation Exhibiting Externalities among Adopters," *International Economic Review* 23, 595–607.

[3] Anderlini, Luca and Antonella Ianni (1996), "Path Dependence and Learning from Neighbors," *Games and Economic Behavior* 13, 141–177.

[4] Annen, Kurt (2003), "Social Capital, Inclusive Networks, and Economic Performance," *Journal of Economic Behavior and Organization* 50, 449–463.

[5] Axelrod, Robert (1997), *The Complexity of Cooperation: Agent-Based Models of Competition and Collaboration*. Princeton University Press.

[6] Bala, Venkatesh and Sanjeev Goyal (1998), "Learning from Neighbours," *Review of Economic Studies* 65, 595–621.

[7] Bala, Venkatesh and Sanjeev Goyal (2000a), "A Non-Cooperative Model of Network Formation," *Econometrica* 68, 5, 1181–1231.

[8] Bala, Venkatesh and Sanjeev Goyal (2000b), "A Strategic Analysis of Network Reliability," *Review of Economic Design* 5, 3, 205–229.

[9] Bala, Venkatesh and Sanjeev Goyal (2001), "Conformism and Diversity under Social Learning," *Economic Theory* 17, 101–120.

[10] Banerjee, Abhijit (1992), "A Simple Model of Herd Behavior," *Quarterly Journal of Economics* 107, 797–817.

[11] Banks, David and Kathleen Carley (1996), "Models of Social Network Evolution," *Journal of Mathematical Sociology* 21, 173–196.

[12] Baron, Robert, Jean Durieu, Hans Haller, and Philippe Solal (2002), "A Note on Control Costs and Potential Functions for Strategic Games," *Journal of Evolutionary Economics* 12, 563–575.

[13] Bergin, James and Bart Lipman (1996), "Evolution of State Dependent Mutations," *Econometrica* 64, 943–956.

[14] Bhaskar, Venkataraman and Fernando Vega-Redondo (2004), "Migration and the Evolution of Conventions," *Journal of Economic Behavior and Organization*, in press.

[15] Bikhchandani, Sushil, David Hirshleifer, and Ivo Welch (1992), "A Theory of Fads, Fashion, Custom, and Cultural Change as Informational Cascades," *Journal of Political Economy* 100, 992–1023.

[16] Billingsley, Patrick (1985), *Probability and Measure*. New York: Wiley.

[17] Blume, Larry (1993), "The Statistical Mechanics of Strategic Interaction," *Games and Economic Behavior* 4, 387–424.

[18] Blume, Larry and David Easley (1995), What Has the Rational Learning Literature Taught Us?," in A. Kirman and M. Salmon (eds.), *Learning and Rationality in Economics*, Oxford University Press.

[19] Boorman, Steven (1975), "A Combinatorial Optimization Model for Transmission of Job Information through Contact Networks," *Bell Journal of Economics* 6, 1, 216–249.

[20] Bramoulle, Yann (2002), Complementarity and Social Networks, *CSED Working Paper No. 24*, Brookings Institution.

[21] Bramoulle, Yann, Dunia Lopez, Sanjeev Goyal, and Fernando Vega-Redondo (2002), Network Formation in Anti-coordination Games, *IVIE Working Paper, WP-AD 2002–25*, University of Alicante.

[22] Brock, William and Steven Durlauf (2001), "Interactions-Based Models," in Heckman and Leamer (eds.), *Handbook of Econometrics: Volume V*. Amsterdam: North Holland.

[23] Burke, Mary and Peyton Young (2001), "Competition and Custom in Economic Contracts: A Case Study of Illinois Agriculture," *American Economic Review* 91, 559–573.

[24] Burt, Ronald (1994), *Structural Holes: The Social Structure of Competition*, Harvard University Press.

[25] Coleman, James (1966), *Medical Innovation: A Diffusion Study*, Second Edition. Indianapolis: Bobbs-Merrill.

[26] Doreian, Patrick and Frans Stokman (2001), "Evolution of Social Networks," Special Volume: *Journal of Mathematical Sociology* 25.

[27] Dorogovtsev, S.N. and J. F. Mendes (2003), Evolution of Networks: From Biological Nets to the Internet and www. Oxford_Oxford University Press.

[28] Droste, Edward, Robert Gilles, and Kathleen Johnson (1999), "Endogenous Interaction and the Evolution of Conventions," in *Adaptive Behavior in Economic and Social Environments*, Ph.D Thesis. Center, University of Tilburg.

[29] Dutta, Bhaskar and Matthew Jackson (2001), (eds.) *Models of the Strategic Formation of Networks and Groups.* Springer-Verlag.

[30] Easley, David and Nicholas Kiefer (1988), "Controlling a Stochastic Process with Unknown Parameters," *Econometrica* 56, 1045–1064.

[31] Elias, Norbert (1978), *The History of Manners*, Part 1 of *The Civilizing Process.* Pantheon Books.

[32] Ellison, Glenn (1993), "Learning, Local Interaction, and Coordination," *Econometrica* 61, 1047–1071.

[33] Ellison, Glenn and Drew Fudenberg (1993), "Rules of Thumb for Social Learning," *Journal of Political Economy* 101, 612–644.

[34] Ellison, Glenn and Drew Fudenberg (1995), "Word-of-Mouth Communication and Social Learning," *Quarterly Journal of Economics* 109, 93–125.

[35] Ely, Jeff (2002), "Local Conventions," *Berkeley Electronic Press Journals, Advances in Theoretical Economics* 2, 1, 1.

[36] Eshel, Ilan and L. L. Cavalli-Sforza, (1982), "Assortment of Encounters and Evolution of Cooperativeness," *Proceedings of the National Academy of Sciences* 79, 4, 1331–1335.

[37] Eshel, Ilan, Larry Samuelson, and Avner Shaked (1998), "Altruists, Egoists, and Hooligans in a Local Interaction Model," *American Economic Review* 88, 157–179.

[38] Freidlin, M. I. and A. D. Wentzell (1984), *Random Perturbations of Dynamical Systems.* Translation of Freïdlin and Venttsel' (1979) by J. Szücs. New York: Springer-Verlag.

[39] Fudenberg, Drew and David Levine (1999), *The Theory of Learning in Games.* Cambridge, MA: MIT Press.

[40] Gale, Douglas and Shachar Kariv (2003), Bayesian Learning in Social Networks, *Games and Economic Behavior*, forthcoming.

[41] Galeotti, Andrea and Sanjeev Goyal (2002), "Network Formation with Heterogeneous Players, Tinbergen Institute Discussion Paper, TI 2002–69.

[42] Glaeser, Edward, Bruce Sacredote, and Jose Scheinkman (1996), "Crime and Social Interactions," *Quarterly Journal of Economics* 111, 507–548.

[43] Glaeser, Edward and Jose Scheinkman (2002), "Non-Market Interactions," in *Advances in Economics and Econometrics: Theory and Applications, Eight World Congress*, M. Dewatripont, L. P. Hansen and P. Turnovsky (eds). Cambridge University Press.

[44] Goyal, Sanjeev (1993), "Sustainable Communication Networks," Tinbergen Institute Discussion Paper, TI 93–250.

[45] Goyal, Sanjeev (1996), "Interaction Structure and Social Change," *Journal of Institutional and Theoretical Economics* 152, 3, 472–495.

[46] Goyal, Sanjeev (1999), *Networks, Learning and Equilibrium,* Inaugural Lecture, Erasmus University. Delft: Eburon Press.

[47] Goyal, Sanjeev and Fernando Vega-Redondo (2004), "Network Formation and Social Coordination," Games and Economic Behavior, Forthcoming, IVIE Working Paper-AD 2001–19. University of Alicante.

[48] Granovetter, Mark (1974), *Getting a Job: A Study of Contacts and Careers*, Harvard University Press.

[49] Granovetter, Mark (1985), "Economic Action and Social Structure: The Problem of Embeddedness," *American Journal of Sociology* 3, 481–510.

[50] Griliches, Zvi (1957), "Hybrid Corn: An Exploration in the Economics of Technological Change," *Econometrica* 25, 501–522.

[51] Haag, Mathew and Roger Lagunoff (2000), "Social Norms, Local Interaction, and Neighborhood Planning," *David Levine's Working Paper Archive 2049*. Department of Economics, UCLA.

[52] Hirshleifer, David, and Eric Rasmusen (1989), "Cooperation in a Repeated Prisoner's Dilemma with Ostracism," *Journal of Economic Behaviour and Organization* 12, 1, 87–106.

[53] Ianni, Antonella (2001), "Correlated Equilibria in Population Games," *Mathematical Social Sciences* 42, 3, 271–294.

[54] Jackson, Matthew and Allison Watts (2002a), "The Evolution of Social and Economic Networks," *Journal of Economic Theory* 106, 2, 265–295.

[55] Jackson, Matthew and Allison Watts (2002b), "On the Formation of Interaction Networks in Social Coordination Games," *Games and Economic Behavior* 41, 2, 265–291.

[56] Jackson, Matthew and Asher Wolinsky (1996), "A Strategic Model of Economic and Social Networks," *Journal of Economic Theory* 71, 1, 44–74.

[57] Judd, Kenneth and Leigh Tesfatsion (2004), *Handbook of Computation Economics II: Agent-Based Computational Economics.* Amsterdam: North Holland.

[58] Kandori, Michihiro (1997), "Evolutionary Game Theory in Economics," in *Advances in Economics and Econometrics: Theory and Applications*, Kreps and Wallis (eds). Cambridge University Press.

[59] Kandori, Michihiro, George Mailath, and Rafael Rob (1993), "Learning, Mutation and Long-Run Equilibria in Games," *Econometrica* 61, 29–56.

[60] Kirman, Alan (1997), "The Economy as an Evolving Network," *Journal of Evolutionary Economics* 7, 339–353.

[61] Kirman, Alan and Jean-Benoit Zimmermann (2001), *Economics with Heterogeneous Interacting Agents*, Series: Lecture Notes in Economics and Mathematical Systems. Springer-Verlag.

[62] Kosfeld, Michael (2004), "Economic Networks in the Laboratory: A Survey Review of Network Economics," 3, 20–41.

[63] Lee, In-ho, Adam Szeidl, and Akos Valentinyi (2003), "Contagion and State Dependent Mutations," *Berkeley Electronic Press Journals, Advances in Economics* 3, 1, 2.

[64] Lee, In-ho and Akos Valentinyi (2000), "Noisy Contagion without Mutation," *Review of Economic Studies*, 67, 1, 17–47.

[65] Liggett, Thomas (1985), *Interacting Particle Systems*. New York: Springer-Verlag.

[66] Mailath, George, Larry Samuelson, and Avner Shaked (1997), "Correlated Equilibria and Local Interaction," *Economic Theory* 9, 551–568.

[67] Manski, Charles (2000), "Economic Analysis of Social Interactions," *Journal of Economic Perspectives* 14, 3, 115–136.

[68] Marimon, Ramon (1997), "Learning from Learning in Economics," in *Advances in Economics and Econometrics: Theory and Applications,* D. Kreps and K. Wallis (eds.). Cambridge University Press.

[69] McLennan, Andrew (1984), "Price Dispersion and Incomplete Learning in the Long Run," *Journal of Economic Dynamics and Control* 7, 331–347.

[70] Morris, Stephen (2000), "Contagion," *Review of Economic Studies* 67, 1, 57–79.

[71] Munshi, Kaivan (2003), "Networks in the Modern Economy: Mexican Migrants in the U. S. Labor Market," *Quarterly Journal of Economics* 118, 2, 549–597.

[72] Nowak, Martin and Robert May (1992), "Evolutionary Games and Spatial Chaos," *Nature* 359, 826–829.

[73] Oechssler, Joerg (1997), "Decentralization and the Coordination Problem," *Journal of Economic Behavior and Organization* 32, 119–135.

[74] Raub, Werner and Jeoren Weesie (1990), "Reputation and Efficiency in Social Interactions," *American Journal of Sociology* 96, 626–655.

[75] Robson, Arthur and Fernando Vega-Redondo (1996), "Efficient Equilibrium Selection in Evolutionary Games with Random Matching," *Journal of Economic Theory* 70, 65–92.

[76] Rothschild, Michael (1974), "A Two-Arm Bandit Theory of Market Pricing," *Journal of Economic Theory* 9, 185–202.

[77] Ryan, Bryce and Neal Gross (1943), "The Diffusion of Hybrid Seed Corn in Two Iowa Communities," *Rural Sociology* 8, 15–24.

[78] Samuelson, Larry (1997), *Evolutionary Games and Equilibrium Selection.* Cambridge, MA: MIT Press.

[79] Schelling, Thomas (1975), *Micromotives and Macrobehavior.* New York: Norton.

[80] Skyrms, Brian and Robert Pemantle (2000), "A Dynamic Model of Social Network Formation, *Proceedings of the National Academy of Sciences* 97, 16, 9340–9346.

[81] Smelser, Neil and Richard Swedberg (1994), *The Handbook of Economic Sociology*, Princeton University Press.

[82] Snijders, Tom (2001), "The Statistical Evaluation of Social Network Dynamics," *Sociological Methodology* 31, 361–395.

[83] Taylor, Robert (1979), *Medicine Out of the Control: The Anatomy of a Malignant Technology.* Sun Books.

[84] Tieman, Alexander, Harold Houba, and Gerard van der Laan (2000), "On the Level of Cooperative Behavior in a Local Interaction Model," *Journal of Economics* 71, 1–30.

[85] Ullman-Margalit, Edna (1977), *The Emergence of Norms.* Oxford, UK: Clarendon Press.

[86] van Damme, Eric and Jurgen Weibull (2002), "Evolution and Refinement with Endogenous Mistake Probabilities," *Journal of Economic Theory*, 106, 296–315.

[87] Vega-Redondo, Fernando (2002), "Building Social Capital in a Changing World," IVIE Working Paper AD 2002–26. University of Alicante.

[88] Watkins, Susan (1991), *Provinces into Nations: Demographic Integration in Western Europe, 1870–1960.* Princeton University Press.

[89] Wynne-Edwards, Vero (1986), *Evolution through Group Selection.* Oxford, UK: Blackwell Publishers.

[90] Young, Peyton (1998), *Individual Strategy and Social Structure.* Princeton University Press.

[91] Young, Peyton (2003), "Diffusion of Innovations in Social Networks," in *Economy as a Complex Evolving System, Volume III*, L. Blume and S. Durlauf (eds.). Oxford University Press.

PART TWO

On Equilibrium Formation of Groups:
A Theoretical Assessment

Group Formation: The Interaction of Increasing Returns and Preferences Diversity

Gabrielle Demange

5.1. Introduction

In a large range of political and economic situations a group of individuals sharing common interests can pursue them more efficiently through a coordinated action. Returns to coordinated action explain why decisions are conducted within organized groups. Most often also, individuals differ in some aspects. The diversity in individual tastes hampers a full exploitation of coordination and encourages the splitting of society into smaller self-sufficient groups. The main purpose of this chapter is to analyze group formation under these two opposite forces: increasing returns to size and to coordination on the one hand and heterogeneity of preferences on the other. In particular, we try to understand which kind of competition among groups allows for an efficient and stable organization. Competition among firms under increasing returns to scale and competition among large communities are two prominent domains of application.

Most often there is a tension between the exploitation of the potential gains to collective action and the introduction of some form of competition among groups. To illustrate this tension, consider an industry in which the exploitation of increasing returns to scale calls for a small number of active firms, each one serving a large set of customers. As a result, competition between active firms is softened. The proponents of contestable markets argue that the perfect freedom of entry and exit in the industry introduces a very strong competitive force, which promotes efficiency (Baumol, Panzer, and Willig 1982). This force however is so strong that it may result in instability, which is a situation sometimes referred to as "destructive" competition.

A similar difficulty arises more generally when the formation of groups is subject to two "natural" competitive pressures generated by free mobility and free entry.[1] Under *free mobility*, each individual can choose any existing group without restriction. Under *free entry*, any new group can form and coordinate action without cost. The difficulty is that, on the one hand, free-mobility equilibria exist but are typically

I thank Francis Bloch and Myrna Wooders for helpful remarks.

[1] See, for example, the analysis of competition among jurisdictions by Bewley (1981).

numerous and inefficient, and on the other hand a free-mobility and free-entry equilibrium is efficient but may fail to exist.

At this point, it is useful to qualify this claim and to divide the situations of group formation crudely into two categories. In the first category, almost all gains to cooperation are realized through small coalitions. Then, the competitive pressure exercised by individuals (free mobility) is powerful enough to ensure near optimality,[2] as made precise in Chapters 6 and 7 of this volume. This chapter, instead, analyzes the second category of situations in which, owing to increasing returns, efficiency and competition across groups are unlikely to foster the formation of small coalitions. One of our main objectives is to identify clear conditions under which free mobility and free entry are compatible in that setup.[3]

The chapter first investigates competition among firms that select the characteristics of their products. Consumers may differ in their tastes or income and the technology exhibits increasing returns to scale. The main issue is whether free entry is bound to be destructive, which, if true, would call for some regulation. Although there are increasing returns to scale, differences in individuals may allow for several active firms, each one attracting a different group of customers through an appropriate product design and price policy. Thus, the idea of contestable markets must be extended to an oligopoly. If entry is free, any opportunity to make a positive profit with an alternative offer targeted toward a group of customers triggers entry. Under some conditions, free-entry competition is not destructive but instead results in a *sustainable* oligopoly configuration in which a stable and optimal variety of products are offered (Demange and Henriet 1991). One condition bears on preferences and requires a specific form of heterogeneity called *intermediate preferences*. The other crucial condition is to allow the number of active firms and their offers to be endogenous and affected by the relative strength between the increasing returns to scale and the individual tastes of heterogeneity.

To what extent is competition across groups in other settings similar to competition among firms? Consider, for example, jurisdictions. Choosing public goods levels and their financing is subject to objections from part of the population. Also, these decisions are affected by the ability of individuals to move to another jurisdiction or to another country. Accordingly, free entry and free mobility are competitive forces at work. Also, public goods generate returns to scale. If jurisdictions are viewed as controlled by land owners or developers who behave as firm managers, competition among jurisdictions is similar in many aspects to competition among firms under increasing returns to scale. Jurisdictions, however, are run by elected people, and the tax tools that can be used may be limited. How do these features affect competition across jurisdictions? Similarly, issues such as stratification, fiscal competition, and breakup of nations can be discussed within a model of competition among regions or countries.[4] If one is willing to highlight

---

[2] The intuition was given by Tiebout (1956) in what he called the *severe* model: "Let the number of communities be infinite and let each announce a different pattern of expenditures on public goods. [...] The consumer-voters will move to that community which *exactly* satisfies their preferences. (p. 421)"

[3] See also Chapter 8 of this volume for a complementary analysis.

[4] Following Westhoff (1977), the literature on these issues is large. See Guesnerie and Oddou (1981), Greenberg and Weber (1986), and more recently Alesina and Spolaore (1997) to name a few.

such issues, the robustness of the results to the specific modeling assumptions should matter.

Cooperative game theory provides useful tools for conducting such a robustness analysis. Indeed, free entry, which encompasses the possibility for a new group to form if it is in the interest of its members, is basically a no-blocking condition. In the situations we are interested in, the splitting of the society into smaller self-sufficient groups may be an efficient outcome: the underlying game is not necessarily superadditive contrary to the standard setup.[5] It turns out that, under a condition of no spillovers across coalitions, standard results on the core are very useful. These results shed some light on conditions that are somewhat necessary for a stable and efficient partition of the society into self-sufficient groups to result from free entry and free mobility.

Albeit useful, the core approach is not appropriate in all situations. In particular, the interaction between free mobility and free entry is properly addressed by the core only if returns to coalitions are increasing. Returns to coalitions fail to increase in situations in which an individual who wants to join a group imposes a negative externality on some members of that group. This failure can be due to various factors. For instance, constitutional constraints, such as the use of majority rule within coalitions, may prevent all members from benefiting from a newcomer even if a Pareto improvement would be feasible. Most importantly, adverse selection generates negative externalities. In such a context, if a group is unable to screen newcomers, the ability of individuals to move places a major constraint on the decisions within groups.[6] Jurisdictions that perform redistribution among citizens typically face such constraints, as shown for example by Epple and Romer (1991). Therefore, addressing competition among groups under negative externalities is an important, although difficult, topic. This chapter concludes by discussing this issue in a simple public goods economy.

The chapter is organized as follows. Section 5.2 focuses on competition in a simple economy under increasing returns to scale and heterogeneous consumers. The concept of sustainable oligopoly is discussed and analyzed. Section 5.3 studies, in a more general and abstract setup, competition among groups in the absence of spillovers. Whereas Section 5.3 develops some insights of Section 5.2, it can be read first. Finally, Section 5.4 analyzes public decisions in a simple public goods economy through the previous approach and addresses the interaction between free mobility and free entry under negative externalities.

5.2. Competition under Increasing Returns

Most often, whereas economic activities are performed under some form of increasing returns to scale, exploiting these returns imposes constraints on consumers. For instance, a unique large shopping center instead of several smaller ones may save on

---

[5] Superadditivity may fail even under "technological" increasing returns to scale. This failure is due to the very fact that individuals differ and that, most often, personalized prices or personalized taxes cannot be charged.

[6] In competitive insurance markets, the constraints stemming from adverse selection have been well known since the work of Rothschild and Stiglitz (1976).

cost but requires a longer travel time for some customers. Also exploiting increasing returns to scale in the production of a good – a cultural good for instance – entails standardization and uniformity. The greater the variance across individuals' tastes, the more likely it is that some individuals will be dissatisfied. As a result, a group of similar customers who are close in their location, their tastes, or their income may be better off by being offered a service closer to their aspirations even if the lower scale of production entails a larger price.

The purpose of this section is to explore how competition works in a simple economy that combines these two features: *increasing returns to scale*, which promotes standardization, and the *individuals' preferences diversity*, which promotes differentiation.[7] We first describe the economy and give some examples.

5.2.1. An Economy with Differentiated Goods

We consider an economy with two goods: money and a differentiated consumption good. The consumption good may have different characteristics, such as location, quality, and color. The good can be private or public, divisible or indivisible, or be associated with a package of products such as access to various services through a network.

Offers. An *offer* specifies the parameters of the transaction proposed by a producer. For a divisible good, for example, an offer is represented by a vector (q_1, q_2, p, t), where q_1 is the quality of the product, q_2 is its location, p is its unit price, and t is a fixed fee. If the good is public, it is simply (q_1, q_2, t), where q_1 and q_2 are interpreted as above and t may be either a tax fee (poll tax) or a proportional scheme based on observed income. The set of a priori possible offers is a subset A of a finite-dimensional space, which may be discrete in the case of indivisible goods.

Consumers. The set of consumers, denoted by N, is finite. Each individual is interested in one offer at most. Thus, preferences are defined on the set A: $u_i(a)$ denotes the utility level that consumer i achieves by choosing offer a. For instance, if the good is divisible, this level represents the indirect utility obtained by choosing the optimal quantity. Consumers also have an outside option of suppress for instance buying no good and paying nothing. This option is represented by a fictitious offer in A denoted by a_0.

Production. The number of firms is not given a priori. The same technology is available to each potential firm. The profit of providing an offer a to a set S of consumers is denoted by $\pi(a, S)$. By convention, the profit associated with the fictitious offer is null whatever set $S : \pi(a_0, S) = 0$. As said in the introduction, we are interested in situations in which production is performed under some form of increasing returns to scale.

There are increasing returns to scale if $\pi(a, S) \geq 0$ implies $\pi(a, S') \geq 0$ for any S' containing S.

---

[7] This section mainly builds on Demange and Henriet (1991).

This condition states a weak form of increasing returns to scale: any offer that makes no loss when chosen by a set of customers makes no loss either if chosen by more customers. For instance, let offer $a = (q, t)$ represent the access to a service with quality q at a fixed fee t. Returns to scale are increasing if, given quality q, the cost of production is composed of a fixed cost $f(q)$ plus a variable cost $sc(q)$ proportional to the number of customers s. A null marginal cost, $c(q) = 0$, represents the case of a pure public good.

Because each firm has access to the same technology, established firms do not enjoy cost or reputation advantages. Accordingly, our approach takes a "long-run" perspective in which all costs, including research and development, determine the profit function.

Examples. Product differentiation, either vertical or horizontal, price discrimination, and congestion effects can be analyzed in the preceding framework.

Example 5.1. *Differentiation models have been used extensively to study imperfect competition.*

In horizontal differentiation models à la Hotelling (1929), individuals differ in their "location." Each individual is characterized by his or her location parameter θ. The parameter can represent a true location or, more generally, be interpreted as a characteristic specifying, for example, preferences over colors, or over movies (see the survey of Gabszewicz and Thisse 1986). Most often, the parameter is assumed to belong to a line, or to a circle. An offer $a = (q, p)$ specifies the location of the product and its unit price. Each individual buys zero or one unit of a product, a car for instance, and derives a utility that depends on the "distance" between his or her location and that of the product as given, for example, by

$$u(q, p, \theta) - v - p - f(|q - \theta|),$$

where f is a convex transportation cost. Competition encourages firms to differentiate according to their location, thereby attracting groups of consumers that are located in nonoverlapping zones.

Vertical differentiation models are similar except that products differ in quality instead of location. All individuals agree on the ranking of quality but differ in their valuation for it because, for example, they differ in their income level θ (Shaked and Sutton 1983). An offer $a = (q, p)$ specifies the quality of the product and its unit price. Examples of utility functions are $u(q, p, \theta) = q(\theta - p)$ or

$$u(q, p, \theta) = v(q, \theta) - p$$

under a Spence–Mirrlees condition $\frac{\partial^2 v}{\partial \theta \partial q} > 0$, which says that the marginal utility for quality increases with the characteristic θ. Here competition should lead firms to differentiate according to the quality of the product they offer, thereby attracting groups of individuals with different income levels or different valuations.

Example 5.2. Price Discrimination. *Consider an homogeneous good, without scope for differentiation either through quality or location. Firms may nevertheless discriminate between customers by proposing two-part tariffs. Thus, an offer is* *written as $a = (t, p)$, where t is the access cost and p is the unit price. Given a utility function $v(x, \theta) + m$, where m is the numeraire and x is the amount of the good consumed (number of visits, telephone calls, and so on), an individual facing tariff (p, t) chooses the optimal quantity and compares different offers according to the indirect utility*

$$u(p, t, \theta) = \max_x \{v(x, \theta) - px - t\}.$$

Example 5.3. Communications Network. *The characteristics of a product represent all the services to which an individual may have access. They can be represented by the set of connections between two points: $q = (q_{i,j})$ in which $q_{i,j}$ is equal to 1 if i is joined to j through the network and 0 otherwise. Whenever the cost to serve a set of customers through a given network consists of the sum of a fixed cost of building the network, $f(q)$, and a cost proportional to the number of users, increasing returns to scale are met.*[8]

Example 5.4. Congestion. *Let an offer represent the access to a service, the quality of which is endogenous, affected by the number of customers who have access to the service. A minimal capacity denoted by $K(q, s)$ is needed to provide the quality q to a number of users s. There are congestion effects if the capacity that ensures a given quality increases as the set of consumers expands: $K(q, s)$ increases with s. Profit is given by*

$$\pi(q, t, S) = st - C(K(q, s)),$$

where s is the number of individuals in S and $C(k)$ is the cost of building capacity k. Increasing returns to scale hold if the per user cost does not increase with the number of users, that is, if $C(K(q, s))/s$ does not increase with s. Thus, congestion effects and increasing returns to scale are compatible: both are present if the cost to provide a given quality to several users increases with the number of users (congestion) but less than proportionately to that number (increasing returns). This form of congestion is not too severe and is weaker than in club theory as explained in 5.2.5.

These examples provide an idea of the trade-off faced by firms. On one hand, owing to the differences in individuals' tastes, firms have incentives to differentiate by offering products with different characteristics so as to avoid sharp competition. On the other hand, exploiting increasing returns calls for products that attract as many consumers as possible. We now turn to the analysis of this trade-off in a competitive framework.

---

[8] Increasing returns to scale differ from the property of *economies of scope*. Economies of scope prevail if the cost of connecting two nodes decreases as the existing network expands. Therefore the property specifies how the fixed cost f varies with the network q (see Sharkey 1982 for an analysis of competition in that setup). More generally, economies of scope can be defined as follows in our model. Consider two firms, each one proposing an offer, for instance a and a', to two disjoint sets of customers S and S'. There are economies of scope if the sum of their cost is larger than the cost borne by a unique firm that jointly proposes these two offers to the same sets of customers. We preclude this form of economies of scope. Note, however, that economies of scope are possible within the different components of a multidimensional offer a.

5.2.2. Sustainable Oligopoly Configuration

Competition is analyzed here through the equilibrium concept of *sustainable oligopoly*. Other approaches and a related framework are discussed at the end of this section.

Before defining sustainability, we need to describe how an oligopoly may organize itself. An *oligopoly configuration* specifies for each active firm its proposed offer and its (nonempty) set of customers, which is hereafter denoted by (a_ℓ, S_ℓ) for firm ℓ. It is important to allow the number of firms or offers to vary: this number, denoted by L, must be affected by the strength of the increasing returns to scale relative to the scope of preferences' heterogeneity. Also, recall that customers have the option of buying nothing (option denoted by the fictitious offer a_0). Let S_0 denote the set, possibly empty, of customers who choose that option. It is convenient to include (a_0, S_0) in a configuration even if S_0 is empty. Because each individual is interested in one offer at most, the various groups of customers form a partition of the whole set N.

Definition 5.1. *An oligopoly configuration is given by a set of pairs* $(a_\ell, S_\ell)_{\ell=0,\ldots,L}$ *in which* S_ℓ *is the set of customers of offer* a_ℓ, S_ℓ *is nonempty for* $\ell > 0$, *and* $(S_\ell)_{\ell=0,\ldots,L}$ *is a partition of the set of consumers* N. *The configuration is feasible if* $\pi(a_\ell, S_\ell) \geq 0$ *for each* $\ell = 1, \ldots, L$.

In the sequel, given a partition of N, $\ell(i)$ denotes the set to which i belongs.

Our purpose is to explore how free competition between all firms, active and potential, affects an oligopoly configuration. Sustainability basically describes an equilibrium in a competitive environment in which each consumer can choose whatever offer is proposed, and each firm, active or not, has the opportunity to propose a new offer.

Definition 5.2. *A configuration* $(a_\ell, S_\ell)_{\ell=0,\ldots,L}$ *is sustainable if*
(free choice or free mobility) each consumer chooses among the offers he or she prefers:

for each i, $u_i(a_{\ell(i)}) \geq u_i(a_k)$ for each $k = 0, \ldots, L$
(firms make no loss) $\pi(a_\ell, S_\ell) \geq 0$ *for each* $\ell = 1, \ldots, L$
(free entry) there are no offer b *and subset of customers* T *that satisfy*
$\pi(b, T) \geq 0$ *and* $u_i(b) > u_i(a_{\ell(i)})$ *for each* $i \in T$.

Free choice or free mobility states the standard behavior of consumers who are "product and price" takers. This behavior can be justified in an infinite population, as we will see in Section 5.2.3.3. The no-loss condition is clear. Free entry says that no firm, active or not, has the opportunity to propose a new offer that would attract some consumers and make a profit. This condition needs more comment.

It should first be noted that free entry is a strong competitive force. To see this, consider the situation in which an offer (q, p) specifies the quality of a product q and the unit price p. Assume that the price p can be changed by any small amount. Free entry implies competition in prices à la Bertrand, which drives profit down to zero. The argument is standard and is based on an undercutting strategy: if firm

ℓ makes positive profit, an entrant can propose a product with an identical quality q_ℓ but at a slightly lower unit price than p_ℓ. All customers in S_ℓ are better off while the entrant makes a positive profit in contradiction to free entry. By a similar argument, each firm maximizes profit; otherwise, entry would be profitable. More generally, profits are driven to zero under free entry whenever at least one characteristic in the offer – price, quality, or location – can be adjusted in a continuous way. Thus, free entry is indeed a very competitive force. We now discuss two factors that might raise difficulties for this force to be effective.

First, the free-entry condition makes sense if any firm, established or potential, faces the same profit function. It may be argued that fixed costs in production generate an asymmetry. Even worse, the fact that established firms have already incurred the fixed costs creates an advantage in their favor vis-à-vis potential entrants: fixed costs will constitute barriers to entry. As argued by Baumol et al. (1982), established firms do not enjoy any advantage if fixed costs are recoverable, which means that firms recover without a loss the fixed costs they may have incurred during their activity when they leave the market. Then any possibility of making profit triggers entry, possibly for a short time, because exit is free as well (the so-called hit-and-run strategy), which justifies the free-entry condition.[9]

Second, the threat of entry that underlies the free entry condition is credible only if firms have enough information on customers. A firm, incumbent or entrant, must know there is an offer preferred by a group of customers to their current choice and that selling that offer to that group will be profitable. This informational requirement is rather weak under increasing returns to scale. To see this, note that whenever entry is profitable with an offer attracting a given set of customers it is also profitable by attracting even more customers. Therefore, an entrant does not need to screen among the consumers and can agree to serve any consumer who asks to be served. Accordingly, to decide whether entry is profitable, a firm only needs to know the distribution of characteristics or tastes within the population.

5.2.3. Existence of a Sustainable Oligopoly Configuration

As we have just seen, sustainability imposes demanding requirements. A first task is to examine whether a sustainable configuration exists under reasonable conditions. Simple examples first illustrate the problem.

5.2.3.1. Some Simple Cases

Increasing returns and preferences' heterogeneity generate two opposite forces. In the first two examples below, one of the two forces does not operate. In such situations, a sustainable configuration exists, which moreover displays a very simple

---

[9] If fixed costs are (partially) sunk (i.e., cannot be entirely recovered), then indeed an asymmetry between active firms and potential entrants arises: an incumbent, who has already paid the sunk costs and knows that an entrant has not may have a credible incentive to react to entry. For a discussion on these issues, see Gabszewicz and Thisse (2002).

structure. In the third example, the two opposite forces operate, leading to a tradeoff that raises existence problems.

Increasing Returns to Scale and Homogeneous Population. Intuitively, if individuals are all alike and there are increasing returns to scale, there is no rationale behind a variety of different offers. This is indeed true.

Consider configurations of the form (a, N) in which a unique offer is bought by the whole set of consumers. Choose an "efficient" offer a^*, which maximizes each (identical) consumer's utility $u(a)$ under the no-loss condition $\pi(a, N) \geq 0$ (most often a^* is unique). The configuration (a^*, N) is sustainable because any other offer that is strictly preferred by a group of customers will surely result in a loss. Furthermore, all sustainable configurations are obtained that way under mild additional assumptions.[10] As an illustration, consider Example 5.4 in which a public service is subject to some mild form of congestion. Sustainability requires all customers to access the same service, the quality of which maximizes each individual's utility under average cost pricing, that is, quality q that maximizes $u(q, C(K(q, n))/n)$.

Decreasing Returns to Scale. Returns to scale are (weakly) decreasing if any offer that makes no loss when chosen by a set of customers makes no loss either if chosen by *fewer* customers. Consider the "autarky" configuration in which each consumer produces his or her preferred good for personal consumption under the no-loss condition (so there are as many offers as consumers). If there are decreasing returns to scale, autarky is clearly sustainable.[11]

As these two extreme cases make clear, it is the exploitation of increasing returns to scale by firms facing different types of individuals that generates a nontrivial variety of distinct offers, each one attracting a group of possibly different types of customers.

Destructive Competition. We define an economy characterized by three parameters: the individuals' valuation for a public good such as a swimming pool, the cost of producing one unit of the public good, and a transportation cost. The example illustrates the two following points:

(1) The number of offers at a sustainable configuration (if any) depends on the economy parameters.
(2) A sustainable configuration fails to exist for a nonnegligible set of parameter values.

---

[10] Consider a sustainable configuration. If a unique offer a is proposed, it satisfies $\pi(a, N) \geq 0$; a must be efficient because otherwise an efficient offer would attract all consumers and be profitable. If distinct offers are proposed, free mobility requires each individual to be indifferent between all the proposed offers. Let offer a be bought by S, a strict subset N. If increasing returns to scale are strict, $0 \leq \pi(a, S) < \pi(a, N)$. Thus, if offers can be adjusted slightly – for example if the price component is in small enough units – a new offer can be designed to make each consumer strictly better off and generate profits.

[11] Assuming the number and the characteristics of offers to be endogenous is crucial to obtaining the sustainability of autarky. Under constraints on the number of firms, for instance, autarky might not be feasible.

Three towns – X, Y, and Z – each populated with the same number of citizens s, are equidistant along a circle at a distance d from each other. An offer specifies the location of a swimming pool and the access price to use it, which is common to all individuals. Citizens are all alike except for their location. Their valuation for the swimming pool is v, and the per unit transportation cost is c. Thus, the utility of an individual who pays p for the access to a swimming pool at a distance l is

$$v - p - cl. \tag{5.1}$$

The once-for-all cost of building a swimming pool is F. So $f = F/s$ denotes the per citizen cost if a swimming pool is used by the citizens of only one town.

We claim that no sustainable configuration exists if

$$v < f, (f + cd)/2 < v \quad \text{and} \quad v < f/3 + cd. \tag{5.2}$$

Consider a sustainable configuration.

First, if $v < f$, there is at most one swimming pool. To show this, note that a swimming pool is necessarily used by more than one-third of the population (otherwise the access price would be larger than f and no citizen would use the swimming pool). This excludes three swimming pools. This also implies that, in the case of two swimming pools, the citizens of one town, say X, use both. By free mobility, the X-inhabitants are indifferent between the two places. Lowering the access price to one swimming pool slightly without changing its location would attract all the X-inhabitants, thereby strictly increasing profits: sustainability requires a unique swimming pool.

Second, if $(f + cd)/2 < v$, there is surely one swimming pool; otherwise, a swimming pool located equidistant between two towns at an access price slightly larger than $f/2$ would make all the citizens of the two towns better off and generate profits: entry would be profitable.

Third, if $v < f/3 + cd$, citizens at a distance larger than d from a swimming pool prefer not to use it even if they pay $f/3$, the smallest possible access price. Thus, under equation (5.2), we are left with only one possibility: a configuration with a unique swimming pool located between two towns X and Y for instance, possibly closer to X, and that is used by X and Y only. The configuration is not sustainable: entry between Z and Y, a little closer to Y than Z, at an access price slightly larger than $f/2$ attracts all citizens of Y and Z and makes profit.

This last example shows that a sustainable configuration may not exist even under standard preferences. It should be clear that, if the towns were located along a line instead of a circle, symmetry would be broken and a sustainable configuration would exist. It turns out that existence in such a case follows from a more general existence result (Theorem 5.1 below). Before stating this result, we need to define the intermediate preferences property introduced in social sciences by Kemeny and Snell (1962) (see also Grandmont 1978).

5.2.3.2. Intermediate Preferences

The property bears on a family of preferences – all defined on the same set. Here we restrict attention to preferences that are parameterized by a one-dimensional characteristic. It turns out that this restriction is satisfied in the standard models of product differentiation and price discrimination described in Section 5.2.1.

Consider orders of preferences on A. An order is said to be *between* two other orders if it ranks alternative a before b whenever the two others both rank a before b. Consider now a family of preferences parameterized by a one-dimensional parameter. Given three parameters, one parameter is between the other two. The property of intermediate preferences holds if the associated preferences follow the same comparison.[12] Formally,

Definition 5.3. *The family $\{u(.,\theta), \theta \in [\underline{\theta}, \overline{\theta}]\}$ of utility functions on A indexed by the one-dimensional parameter θ defines intermediate preferences if, for any a and b in A, the sets $\{\theta, u(a, \theta) > u(b, \theta)\}$ and $\{\theta, u(a, \theta) \geq u(b, \theta)\}$ are intervals.*

So the property specifies that the preferences in the family are related among each other while preserving some heterogeneity in tastes. Whereas the characteristic is a scalar, alternatives may be multidimensional. Consider some examples of Section 5.2.1.

In a vertical differentiation model in which $u(q, p, \theta) = v(q, \theta) - p$, the Spence–Mirrlees condition ($\frac{\partial^2 v}{\partial \theta \partial q}$ of constant sign) ensures that preferences are intermediate.[13] In a horizontal differentiation model, consider firms that not only choose their location q_2 but also the quality of their product q_1. Utility functions

$$u(q_1, q_2, p, \theta) = v(q_1) - p - f(|q_2 - \theta|)$$

define intermediate preferences under the standard assumption of an increasing and convex transportation cost f. Finally, consider the price discrimination example in which consumers choose the optimal quantity according to a proposed two-part tariff. Indirect utility is given by

$$u(p, t, \theta) = \max_{x}\{v(x, \theta) - px - t\}.$$

A family of intermediate preferences is obtained whenever the utility for the good, $v(x, \theta)$, satisfies the Spence–Mirrlees condition (from the first example, it suffices to check that indirect utility u inherits the Spence–Mirrlees property).

---

[12] The definition extends to any set of parameters endowed with a "between" relation such as a convex set. Intermediate preferences hold if, given three parameters, where one parameter is between the other two, the associated preferences follow the same comparison. Contrary to a one-dimensional parameter, three parameters may not be comparable, in which case the corresponding preferences are not necessarily comparable either.

[13] Given $a = (q, p)$ and $a' = (q', p')$, let $I = \{\theta/v(q, \theta) - v(q', \theta) > p - p'\}$. We have to prove that I is an interval. If $q = q'$, I is either empty or the whole interval $[\underline{\theta}, \overline{\theta}]$. If $q \neq q'$, the function $\theta \to v(q, \theta) - v(q', \theta)$ is strictly monotone thanks to the Spence–Mirrlees condition; hence, I is an interval. The proof is similar if the inequality defining I is weak.

5.2.3.3. Existence Result

We are now ready to state the following existence result.

Theorem 5.1. *Under increasing returns to scale and one-dimensional intermediate preferences, a sustainable configuration exists. Individuals cluster according to their types: if two individuals choose the same offer, all individuals with preferences between them also choose the same offer.*

Consider a vertical differentiation model in which offers are of the form (q, p) and individuals' preferences given by $u(q, p, \theta) = \theta(q - p)$. The clustering property implies that all individuals with income θ within some range choose the same offer. By free mobility, the quality of the product chosen by individuals is increasing in their income. More generally, the clustering property means that each offer is bought by all individuals whose characteristic belongs to a given interval of characteristics hereafter called an "interval" of individuals.

The proof is constructive (see Demange and Henriet 1991 for details). One first builds a configuration that satisfies two adequate properties:[14]

(a) S_ℓ, the set of consumers who buy a given offer a_ℓ, is an interval.

(b) No firm can enter profitably by attracting an interval of customers, that is, free entry holds for "intervals" of customers.

Thanks to intermediate preferences, a single-peaked preferences property is satisfied at the configuration: the utility of an individual decreases over the offers chosen by individuals with either increasing characteristics or decreasing ones. In the case of increasing returns to scale, this property implies that the free-entry condition holds for any group of customers.

Discussion. Intermediate preferences can be defined for parameters that are not necessarily one-dimensional (see footnote 12). A natural question is whether Theorem 5.1 extends to these settings. We consider two cases.

First, let characteristic θ belong to a multidimensional convex set. Preferences are intermediate if, for any alternatives a and b, the sets $\{\theta, u(a, \theta) > u(b, \theta)\}$ and $\{\theta, u(a, \theta) \geq u(b, \theta)\}$ are convex. Unfortunately, Theorem 5.1 does not extend to that setting; that is, a sustainable configuration does not necessarily exist if intermediate preferences and increasing returns hold but the characteristic is multidimensional (see Demange and Henriet 1991 for an example).

---

[14] Order individuals by their characteristics. Starting with individual n, define "guarantee levels" inductively as follows: $\gamma(n)$ is the maximum utility level that individual n can get, $\gamma(i)$ is the maximum utility level that i can get over offers that are feasible if bought by an interval of consumers $[i, i + r]$ with r nonnegative, and that give to each j in that interval his or her guarantee level $\gamma(j)$ at least. There is a configuration that ensures each individual's guarantee level is obtained as a minimum: (1) By construction there is a coalition, for instance, $[1, i_1]$, that can ensure each of its members the level $\gamma(i)$; (2) if $i_1 < n$, there is a coalition $[i_1 + 1, i_2]$ that can ensure each of its members the level $\gamma(i)$, and so on. This configuration satisfies the two required properties (in case of ties, some care is needed).

Second, let the characteristic belong to a graph.[15] Preferences are intermediate if for any alternatives a and b the sets $\{\theta, u(a, \theta) > u(\theta, b)\}$ and $\{\theta, u(a, \theta) \geq u(\theta, b)\}$ are connected. The existence of a sustainable configuration is ensured if the graph is a tree (see Section 5.4) but not if the graph contains a cycle, as shown by the example in Section 5.2.3.1.

Finally, Theorem 5.1 holds if, instead of the intermediate preferences assumption, preferences are assumed to be single peaked on a one-dimensional set of alternatives (Greenberg and Weber 1993). Although these preferences' assumptions[16] differ, they both entail a one-dimensional requirement – either on the set of alternatives (for single-peaked preferences) or on the set of characteristics (for intermediate preferences). Section 5.4 investigates the natural question of whether this unidimensionality requirement can be dropped.

Justifying Competitive Customers. According to the free-choice or free-mobility condition, individuals are "price and product takers." Such a competitive behavior is justified if each individual has a negligible impact on the product and the price that is chosen by a firm. This occurs if there are many consumers per offer. The question is whether a sustainable oligopoly exists with this property. The natural setup to investigate this question is a continuum of consumers. Assume that an offer is not profitable if a *small* proportion of the population buys it. More precisely, if one normalizes the size of the whole population to 1, there is a size $s > 0$ such that whatever offer is made results in a loss if only a group of size smaller s chooses it. Under this additional assumption, Theorem 4.1 can be extended: a sustainable configuration exists (see Demange and Henriet 1991). Furthermore, because each offer must be profitable, each one is bought by an "infinite" number of consumers (at least a proportion s of the whole population), thereby justifying competitive behavior.

Given that a sustainable configuration exists under reasonable conditions, efficiency properties can now be investigated.

5.2.4. On the Optimality of a Sustainable Configuration

To assess the optimality of a sustainable configuration, one can check whether all individuals are better off at another feasible configuration. We will not be limited to that comparison. Feasibility, as defined before, requires each offer not to sustain a loss, which is meaningful in a competitive environment in which each offer is proposed by a different firm. In a context of increasing returns, however, a natural question is whether a monopoly, by proposing several offers and implementing cross subsidies between them, would achieve a Pareto improvement. If this were the case,

---

[15] Recall that a graph or a network g on N is a set of unordered pairs, or links, of distinct elements of N. A *path* of g is a sequence $i_1 \cdots, i_m$, where (i_k, i_{k+1}) are links for $k = 1, \ldots, m - 1$ and are all distinct. A graph is a *tree* if any two distinct elements are linked by a unique path. A subset S of N is *g-connected* if the path between two elements of S is contained in S (see also the chapters in the first part of this volume).

[16] Two preferences with the same peak do not necessarily coincide: they can differ on the ordering of a pair formed with one alternative to the right and one to the left of the peak. In many examples, however, single-peaked preferences are parameterized by their peaks and satisfy intermediate preferences.

an argument in favor of restricting entry and of regulating a monopoly could be made. This leads us to extend the set of feasible configurations by allowing cross subsidies between offers and to investigate the efficiency of a sustainable configuration within this larger set.

Definition 5.4. *A configuration $(a_\ell, S_\ell)_{\ell=0,\dots,L}$ is feasible, possibly with cross subsidies, if*

$$\sum_{\ell=1,\dots,L} \pi(a_\ell, S_\ell) \geq 0. \tag{5.3}$$

Equation (5.3) states the feasibility condition in terms of the consumption good, the numeraire. Cross subsidies between offers are allowed because the no-loss condition is not required for each offer.

Theorem 5.2. *A sustainable configuration is Pareto optimal among all configurations that are feasible possibly with cross subsidies:*

if $(a_\ell, S_\ell)_{\ell=0,\dots,L}$ is sustainable and $(a'_\ell, S'_\ell)_{\ell=0,\dots,L'}$ is feasible, possibly with cross subsidies, it is not true that for each i $u_i(a_{\ell(i)}) < u_i(a'_{\ell'(i)})$.

The argument is very simple and general. Let us assume by contradiction that a feasible configuration Pareto dominates a sustainable one. By the feasibility condition (5.3), the profit of at least one offer, for instance (a'_ℓ, S'_ℓ), is nonnegative. Because every member of S'_ℓ is better off than under the sustainable configuration, this contradicts free entry.

This result of course implies that a sustainable configuration is optimal among the configurations for which each offer makes no loss. This confirms that free entry, if not destructive, plays a very positive role.

5.2.5. Related Framework

Competition under Increasing Returns or Differentiation. Two distinct strands in the literature are related to our analysis: the theory of contestable markets, which focuses on increasing returns, and the literature on differentiation, which focuses on the endogenous choice of variants or location.

Baumol et al. (1982) consider a "natural monopoly" situation, meaning that a given output vector is produced at a lower cost by one organization than by several. They argue that, if the market is contestable, which means that entry is free, a unique firm cannot exploit its monopoly position. The industry is efficiently organized with a unique active firm without bearing the usual distortions associated with a monopoly. A major difficulty is that an equilibrium under free entry may not exist. The setup considered by Baumol et al. (1982) differs from ours in several aspects. Economies of scope in joint production incite firms to propose offers composed of several products, the characteristics of the products are exogenous, and the consumers' behavior is described by a demand function. Hence, the choice of the characteristics that best suit the customers' taste is left aside, and only the price policy is flexible. In contrast, our modeling of the consumption side allows us to treat firms symmetrically, to know how the demand is split up between several firms, and to determine the number and the characteristics of the products in an endogenous way.

The literature on differentiation uses a different model than ours to analyze the choice of products competition. Following Hotelling, a two-stage game is considered in which firms first choose the characteristics of their product (the location on the beach) and then compete in prices. The competition phase may be one shot or repeated as determined by whether the product specifications are somewhat irreversible or not. As usual, the existence of an equilibrium, the structure of the economy – the number of competitors, products, or both – and the efficiency properties may be quite sensitive to the game. For an elaboration of these issues, see the survey of Gabszewicz and Thisse (1986).

In conclusion, our approach can be viewed as an attempt to integrate the concern of contestable markets into a differentiation model.

Club Theory. Club theory basically examines the same question as we do. I outline here only what I see as the main differences. In the initial club model proposed by Buchanan (1965), individuals are identical.[17] The reason why groups form on the one hand and are limited in size on the other is that there is some form of positive externality among individuals but only up to a certain limit in the size of the group: there is a finite "efficient" size for a group. A service subject to congestion is a typical example. Under most equilibrium concepts the population should split into groups – all with the efficient size. This is clearly impossible when the overall population size is not a multiple of the efficient size. Consequently, even in this very simple framework with identical agents, an equilibrium may not exist because of an "integer" problem. In contrast, such a failure does not exist in our setup. As seen in Section 5.2.3.1, with identical individuals, a sustainable configuration exists in which all customers choose the same offer: the "efficient" size is always equal to the population size.

Thus, the issues we are interested in clearly differ from those of club theory. We are concerned with the difficulties of exploiting increasing returns stemming from the differences in individuals' tastes. Whereas club theory has been extended in various directions so as to handle heterogeneous population and multiple goods, most developments assume that only "small" groups are effective. In contrast, this chapter considers that large organizations are worth forming even with an infinite population (as in Section 5.2.3).

Jurisdictions and Tiebout Equilibrium. In the local public goods model proposed by Tiebout (1956), communities set up local taxes and offer various facilities such as schools, protection, and sport centers. Citizens differ in their preferences over local public goods as dictated by the number and age of their children, their income level, and their leisure activities. Thus, both increasing returns to size and

---

[17] See Chapters 6 and 7 of this volume and the references therein for subsequent developments.

preferences heterogeneity are present. Some political issues, such as the location of a government or fiscal decisions (vertical differentiation) under competition between governments, can be analyzed by adapting the horizontal and vertical differentiation models introduced in Section 5.2.1. Let us just change our vocabulary as follows:

- A consumer is called a *citizen*. There is free mobility if each citizen picks the community that best satisfies his or her preferences.
- A group of consumers is a *jurisdiction or local community*.
- An offer specifies the public good characteristics and how it is financed – possibly through income taxes.
- *City managers* choose offers[18] (the location of the good, the level of taxes), and finally the profit is the city *budget*.

Free mobility simply says that citizens can choose whatever community they wish. Free entry means that no group of citizens could be better off by seceding and choosing another tax policy and public good levels. In this interpretation, a sustainable configuration is called a Tiebout equilibrium. Greenberg and Weber (1986) show that a Tiebout equilibrium exists if jurisdictions are endogenous in an economy in which citizens differ in income only and the public good is financed by either a proportional or constant tax scheme. More generally, provided that the assumptions of Theorem 5.1 are satisfied, a Tiebout equilibrium exists. If citizens differ in income only, the clustering property implies stratification.

In this interpretation, city managers behave as firm managers. This assumption is somewhat dubious. After all, city managers are elected. What is their objective? The answer to this question is not easy. As is well known, if decisions are to be taken in a democratic way to reflect individuals' preferences, no objective or decision rule imposes itself. Nevertheless, most often, the way decisions are taken within a group is constrained: decisions must be taken through a specified mechanism.[19] Of particular relevance is the majority rule. To discuss competition across jurisdictions, or more generally across groups, it is convenient to introduce a more general model.

5.3. On Competition across Groups

Our aim in this section is to highlight the role of some crucial features that shape the formation of groups. To that purpose, we introduce a more general and abstract setting than in the previous section. Three key ingredients must be specified:

- How decisions are taken by the members of a group,
- What the possible moves are for the individuals,
- What the possibilities are for new groups to emerge.

---

[18] It should be clear that this sketched model is a very simplified representation of jurisdictions. In particular, it does not address the interaction between city managers and landowners, who could also propose facilities to increase the value of land.

[19] In public good contexts, fixed decision schemes have been considered by many authors starting with Rose-Ackerman (1979) and Greenberg and Shitovitz (1988). See also Haeringer (2000) and Chapter 8 of this volume, which considers the impact of cost allocation rules on secession in the context of a public project.

We will conduct the analysis within the framework of cooperative games. This framework introduces the preceding specifications in a simple but quite general setup. Given a set of individuals, N, sometimes called the *society*, a nonempty subset of N is called a *coalition*. The primitives are the set of actions that each coalition can take when its members collaborate and the associated utility levels or payoffs. In what follows, only games without spillovers will be considered. Although restrictive, the set of situations that can be analyzed through games without spillovers is very rich, starting with competition within jurisdictions. Furthermore, the lessons that can be drawn on the formation of groups are, in our view, important.

5.3.1. Games without Spillovers

A game is said to be *without spillovers* if the actions that are feasible for a coalition, if it forms, as well as the payoffs to its members, are not affected by the organization of outside agents. In other words, there are no externalities across coalitions as far as feasibility and payoffs are concerned. As will be made clear later on, even in the absence of spillovers, the full organization of the society is relevant to assess its stability. If, for instance, individuals can move or new groups can form, their opportunities to do so depend on all standing groups.[20]

Without spillovers, the set of feasible actions in alternatives, or decisions for a coalition can be described by a single set independently of the organization of outsiders. Let $A(S)$ denote the set of feasible actions for coalition S. The welfare of an individual depends on the decision taken by the coalition to which he or she belongs: If S chooses a, the member i of S obtains utility level $u_i(a)$. Therefore, each vector of utility levels $(u_i(a))_{i \in S}$ when a runs in $A(S)$ can be achieved by the coalition of its members. The set of attainable utility levels is assumed to be bounded and closed for each coalition S. This is ensured, for example, if each feasible set $A(S)$ is compact and utility function u_i is continuous for each i.

The description of the feasible sets depends on the problem at hand. Indeed, the feasible set of a group integrates not only the technological constraints that the group faces if it forms, but also the various "institutional" constraints that may restrict the way decisions are made. For instance, within a community, most often the voting rule is imposed, or the tax tools must be of a specific form, or the information on citizens is poor, thereby excluding some types of redistribution. Feasible sets are affected accordingly. In the extreme case where coalitions pick their decision according to a fixed rule, feasible sets boil down to singletons. As a result, the payoff to a player is entirely determined by the coalition to which he belongs: the utility level of individual i who is a member of S can be written simply as $u_i(S)$. Aumann and Dreze (1974) introduced these games, and called them *hedonic* games.[21]

---

[20] Whereas spillovers (or externalities) across groups, negative or positive, are likely to have an important impact, their analysis is still restricted to specific situations. See, for example, Yi (1997) for a noncooperative approach to the formation of coalitions, chapter 11 of this volume for applications to industrial organization, and Currarini (2003) for an analysis of hierarchical structures.

[21] Hedonic games arise in various noneconomic contexts, in sport games for example, if each player is concerned only with the composition of the team he joins (precluding cash transfers).

Examples

It should be noted first that this setting encompasses the economy of Section 5.2. Some macroeconomic and political issues can also be analyzed through cooperative games without spillovers.

Example 5.5. *The economy of Section 5.2 is represented by a game without spillovers in which a coalition is a group of customers who set up a firm or a cooperative. A feasible action for S is an offer that makes no loss when each individual in S buys it:* $A(S) = \{a, \pi(a, S) \geq 0\}$.

Example 5.6. *The analysis of Chapter 13 of this volume fits our setup. The chapter provides an explanation for the persistent difference in growth rates across countries by the formation of coalitions of countries. Once a coalition is formed, each country within the coalition decides on its own contribution to a growth-enhancing public good. This gives use to a hedonic game. We refer the reader to Chapter 13 of this volume for a precise description and analysis.*

Example 5.7. *The formation of nations, as analyzed by Alesina and Spolaore (1997), gives rise to a cooperative game without spillovers. Consider a horizontal differentiation model à la Hotelling in which individuals are all alike except for their location. Assuming that individuals are located over an interval, a "country/coalition" is characterized by its borders populated with the individuals living within the interval.[22] A country needs a government, which costs a fixed amount c. Within a country, citizens vote on the location of the government using majority rule, and the government cost is financed through an equal tax. Finally assume utility given by the income y minus the tax minus the "preference" distance between the individual's location and that of the government. Under these assumptions, a majority winner exists within a country: the government is located at the median location of the citizens. Therefore a hedonic game is obtained.*

For instance, let us compute the payoffs assuming that individuals are uniformly distributed over $[0, 1]$. *If country* $[\theta_1, \theta_2]$ *forms, the cost per citizen is* $c/(\theta_2 - \theta_1)$, *and the government is located at the middle* $(\theta_1 + \theta_2)/2$. *This yields the utility level*

$$y - \frac{c}{(\theta_2 - \theta_1)} - \left| \theta - \frac{\theta_1 + \theta_2}{2} \right|$$

to a citizen located at θ *in the country.*

Payoffs. Given feasibility sets and utility functions, one can associate the set of payoffs to each coalition S.[23] Here, we adopt the so-called Shapley convention, which defines all sets of payoffs as a subset of $\Re^N$ (instead of $\Re^S$ for S) as follows:

$$V(S) = \{x \in \Re^N / \text{ there is } a \in A(S) \text{ such that } \forall i \in S, x_i \leq u_i(a)\}. \tag{5.4}$$

---

[22] If a country is formed with several disconnected intervals, each interval needs to have its own government. This allows one to consider intervals only.

[23] In the case of transferable utilities, the set of feasible payoffs can be represented more simply by a single number, the "value" to the coalition.

This convention is especially convenient to describe the payoffs that can be achieved by two disjoint coalitions acting separately. Let S and T be two disjoint coalitions. S can achieve any payoff in $V(S)$ to its members and T can do so in $V(T)$. Therefore, thanks to the absence of spillovers, *any payoff in $V(S) \cap V(T)$ can be achieved by the two disjoint coalitions S and T acting separately.*

5.3.2. Incentives to Form Coalitions

The incentives to form coalitions primarily depend on whether the members of a coalition derive some benefit by accepting new members and whether coalitions gain by splitting into smaller groups. We make these notions precise.

5.3.2.1. Increasing Returns to Coalitions

We start with notions of increasing returns.

Definition 5.5. *Feasible sets are increasing if, for any two coalitions S and T where S is contained in T, $A(S)$ is contained in $A(T)$: $A(S) \subset A(T)$.*

Returns to coalitions are increasing if, for any two coalitions S and T where S is contained in T, for any a in $A(S)$ there is b in $A(T)$ such that

$$u_i(b) \geq u_i(a), \forall i \in S.$$

Feasible sets are increasing if any feasible action for a coalition remains feasible when new members join that coalition. In the differentiated goods economy of Section 5.2, feasible sets are increasing whenever there are increasing returns to scale. Returns to coalitions are increasing if the sets of payoffs are increasing with coalitions: a coalition can, possibly by changing the current decision, accommodate any newcomer without hurting any of its current members. Clearly, increasing feasible sets imply increasing returns to coalitions.

It is important to note that, in situations in which a fixed decision rule is used, the rule has an impact on whether returns to coalitions are increasing. Indeed, increasing returns encompass two conditions. The first is that a coalition can derive gains by accepting newcomers, which is a "technological" increasing returns condition. The second is that the distribution of these gains among the coalition members as induced by the fixed rule makes each one better off. As an example, consider communities that decide on the level and financing of some pure public service so that there are technological increasing returns. If the public good is financed through a poll tax that is chosen according to majority rule, the second condition is not necessarily met. To see this, assume that individuals differ only with respect to their income level. Under standard assumptions, majority rule selects the decision preferred by the voter with median income within the jurisdiction under consideration. If an outsider joins a jurisdiction, the median voter of the enlarged jurisdiction typically differs from the former one. As a result, for some citizens the gains from having more citizens financing the public good can be offset by the losses due to a change in the median voter. Therefore, even if Pareto improvements over the current decision exist, the majority mechanism may not pick one of them.

As we will see in Section 5.3.5, whether increasing returns hold or not has important consequences for the interaction between free mobility and free entry.

5.3.2.2. Superadditivity, Coalition Structures, and Efficiency

The benefits for disjoint groups to join crucially determine group formation. A game in which each coalition is always at least as efficient as any of its partition is called *superadditive*. Recall that $V(S) \cap V(T)$ are the payoffs that can be achieved by two disjoint coalitions S and T acting separately. Therefore, superadditivity may be expressed as

$$V(S) \cap V(T) \subset V(S \cup T) \quad \text{whenever } S \text{ and } T \text{ are disjoint.}$$

As for increasing returns, the decision process used within coalitions may affect superadditivity (see the analysis of a public goods economy in Section 5.4.1).

Under superadditivity, efficiency can always be reached by the whole group N. Instead, in situations in which the members of a group can all be made better off by being partitioned into smaller self-sufficient groups, there is no reason to exclude this possibility. A coalition structure precisely takes into account the splitting possibilities.

Definition 5.6. *A coalition structure of N is a family $(a_\ell, S_\ell)_{\ell=1,\dots,L}$, where $(S_\ell)_{\ell=1,\dots,L}$ is a partition of N and a_ℓ is feasible for $S_\ell, \ell = 1, \dots, L$.*

In the economy of Section 5.2, a coalition is a group of customers who buy the same offer, and a coalition structure amounts to a feasible configuration.

At a structure $(a_\ell, S_\ell)_{\ell=1,\dots,L}$, i's utility level is equal to $u_i(a_{\ell(i)})$, where, as before, $\ell(i)$ denotes the coalition to which i belongs. So a coalition structure that is Pareto optimal among all coalition structures is called efficient, defined by

Definition 5.7. *A coalition structure $(a_\ell, S_\ell)_{\ell=1,\dots,L}$ is efficient if no other coalition structure makes everybody better off, for no coalition structure $(a'_\ell, S'_\ell)_{\ell=1,\dots,L'}$ $u(a_{\ell'(i)}) > u(a_{\ell(i)})$ for each i.*

Efficiency implies efficiency within coalitions, which is a notion termed *intragroup efficiency*. Formally, a structure $(a_\ell, S_\ell)_{\ell=1,\dots,L}$ is said to be *intragroup efficient* if a_ℓ is Pareto optimal for S_ℓ among the alternatives of $A(S_\ell)$. For example, a structure (a, N) composed with a Pareto-efficient decision for the whole society is intragroup efficient. Also, in a hedonic game, any structure is intragroup efficient because a coalition has a single possible decision. As made clear by these examples, which coalitions form also matters for a structure to be efficient. Thus, efficiency is stronger than intragroup efficiency; which coalitions form also matters for a structure to be efficient.

Superadditive Cover. For games that are not superadditive, allowing coalition structures enlarges the set of feasible payoffs. The *superadditive cover* $\hat{V}$ of the initial game V precisely assigns to each group the set of payoffs that it can reach through all its coalition structures. To define $\hat{V}(T)$, note that if T splits into the partition $(T_\ell)_{\ell=1,\dots,L}$, it can reach any payoff in $\cap_{\ell=1,\dots,L} V(T_\ell)$. Thus, $\hat{V}(T)$ is obtained as the union of these payoffs over all partitions of T:

$$\hat{V}(T) = \cup_{\{(T_l)l=1,...,L \text{ partition of } T\}} \cap_{l=1,...,L} V(T_l). \tag{5.5}$$

Clearly, $\hat{V}$ is superadditive. Also, if V is superadditive, $\hat{V}$ coincides with V.

On the Number of Groups at an Efficient Coalition Structure. Quite naturally, the number of coalitions necessary to reach efficiency depends on the underlying game. Some insight can be gained from the analysis of Guesnerie and Oddou (1987). They focus on situations in which efficiency is reached by a unique coalition, the whole society. By definition, N is always as efficient as several disjoint coalitions if, for any coalition structure $(a_\ell, S_\ell)_{\ell=1,...,L}$ of N, there is an action b feasible for N that makes everybody as well off, namely such that

for any i in N, $u_i(b) \geq u_i(a_{\ell(i)})$.

This property, which is weaker than superadditivity,[24] is called the *universal efficiency* of N. Interestingly, Guesnerie and Oddou provide a necessary condition for universal efficiency that is easy to interpret. To introduce this condition, let us consider the simple situation in which N is partitioned into two sets such as S and T. Let us pick two agents, as "dictators," respectively, in S and T, meaning that each one chooses his or her preferred action, respectively, in $A(S)$ and $A(T)$. If N is universally efficient, then surely the two dictators can find a mutually advantageous decision under the condition that the whole society forms and applies this decision. Note that this must hold whatever the partition under consideration and whatever the couple of agents that are designated as dictators. This yields the condition of binary superadditivity:

A game is binary superadditive if for any partition of N into two coalitions S and T, any i in S, j in T, a in $A(S)$, and b in $A(T)$ there exists c in $A(N)$ such that

$$u_i(c) \geq u_i(a), \quad u_j(c) \geq u_j(b).$$

Binary superadditivity is necessary for the whole society to be universally efficient. It should be clear that the more homogeneous the population and the larger the returns to size, the more likely it is that the game will be binary superadditive. It turns out that if the set of alternatives is one-dimensional, binary superadditivity is also sufficient for N to be universally efficient. This is not true if the set of alternatives is multidimensional. Then, a stronger condition called multilateral merging agreements guarantees the universal efficiency of N. Agreement has to be found for partitions into more than two groups. Furthermore, the maximal number of groups in these partitions increases with the dimension of the alternative space. Thus, quite naturally, the larger the dimension, the more numerous the partitions to consider, and the stronger the condition of multilateral merging agreements (we refer the interested reader to Guesnerie and Oddou 1987 for a precise definition).

Whereas this analysis treats the universal efficiency of the whole society, it can be carried out on coalitions. In particular, if the whole society is not universally

---

[24] Note that superadditivity requires *each* coalition to be universally efficient.

efficient, finding the coalitions that are universally efficient can give an insight into the maximal number of coalitions that form at an efficient structure.

The main issue we are concerned with is whether some form of competition helps, or forces, the group N to reach an efficient structure. We start by examining the pressure exercised by individuals who are free to move and join any existing coalition. This gives rise to the free-mobility conditions. We proceed with the pressure exercised by coalitions, which gives rise to the free entry conditions. The relationships between free mobility and free entry are investigated afterwards.

5.3.3. Free Mobility Coalition Structures

Given a coalition structure, consider an individual who contemplates leaving the coalition to which he or she belongs. Under free mobility, this person has the opportunity to stay single or to join an existing coalition and decides according to the expected benefits of each alternative. The expected payoff from staying single is simply the maximum utility level over the individual's feasibility set, the *individual rationality level*. The expected payoff from joining a coalition is more ambiguous because it is affected by the impact that the individual expects to have on the action taken by the coalition.

In most situations we are interested in, coalitions are large and engaged in a collective activity such as the levels of public goods and their financing through taxes. Then, an individual joining a coalition naturally expects to have no impact:[25] this person takes the action of the coalition as "given" without attempting to change this action or considering the externality he or she may impose on the group members. This assumption coincides in the differentiated goods economy with consumers who are "price and product takers," as already considered. We start with this situation. For stating the definition it is convenient to introduce a fictitious action a_0, where $u_i(a_0)$ is set equal to i's individual rationality level.

Definition 5.8. *A coalition structure* $(a_\ell, S_\ell)_{\ell=1,\dots,L}$ *satisfies free mobility if*

$$\text{for each } i, \ u_i(a_{\ell(i)}) \geq u_i(a_k) \quad \text{any } k = 0, 1, \dots, L.$$

Structures that satisfy free mobility typically exist, and in fact are numerous. Furthermore most of them are inefficient, and even intragroup inefficient. To see this, consider a structure (a, N) where only the whole group N forms. Free mobility is satisfied if action a gives to each individual at least his/her rational utility level: for each i, $u_i(a) \geq u_i(a_0)$. In most problems of interest, there are many such actions. Moreover, most of them are Pareto dominated by another feasible action for N, in which case the structure is not only inefficient but also intragroup inefficient.

We now consider the case where an individual has an impact on the decision taken by the coalition he contemplates joining. If the individual is aware of this impact, free mobility should be defined in the line of a Nash equilibrium. We restrict here to hedonic games. In these games the payoff accruing to a player who joins

---

[25] To make sense, an action must be "anonymous," which means that the action taken by a coalition can be applied without ambiguity to an outsider. This is the case in all the examples we have seen so far.

a coalition is uniquely defined, hence can be anticipated without ambiguity.[26] A coalition structure, which simply amounts to a partition $(S_\ell)_{\ell=1,...,L}$ of the society N, is *Nash stable* if setting $S_0 = \emptyset$

$$\text{for each } i, u_i(S_{\ell(i)}) \geq u_i(S_k \cup i) \quad \text{for any } k = 0, 1, \ldots L.$$

For the same reasons as for free mobility, Nash stability does not imply efficiency or even intragroup efficiency.

The intuition for why single individual moves are far from ensuring efficiency is quite clear: efficiently exploiting returns to collective action requires some coordination. This inefficiency result, however, may not be so problematic, for because of these returns, coordinated moves, and not only moves by single individuals, are likely to be at work. We examine now coordinated moves and whether they restore efficiency.

5.3.4. Free Entry Coalition Structures

Coordinated actions within a group are presumably the driving forces that explain competition across groups. These forces can be modeled through the standard blocking conditions properly extended to coalition structures.

Definition 5.9. *A coalition structure* $(a_\ell, S_\ell)_{\ell=1,...,L}$:

– is blocked by coalition S if there is an action b feasible for S that makes every member of S better off :

$$\text{for some } b \text{ in } A(S) \ u_i(b) > u_i(a_{\ell(i)}) \text{ each } i \text{ in } S,$$

– satisfies free entry (or is stable under free entry) if it is blocked by no coalition, or equivalently, if the payoff vector $(u_i(a_{\ell(i)}))_{i \in N}$ *belongs to the core of the superadditive cover* $\hat{V}$ *defined by equation (5.5).*

Under free entry, any group can form, and does form, if it is in the members' interests. It is important to note that, even in the absence of spillovers, the full organization of the society is relevant to assess its stability: the opportunity of a move for the members of a given coalition is determined by the organization of outside agents. Stability under free entry corresponds to the standard stability notion of the core applied to the situation in which the society can partition itself. We draw three consequences from this simple remark. Although straightforward, the first consequence is nevertheless important. Because a core outcome is always Pareto efficient, *a coalition structure that satisfies free entry is efficient among all feasible coalition structures.* As a result, *several* coalitions form only if the

---

[26] In games that are not hedonic, because no decesion mechanism is fixed within a coalition for instance, the reaction to the arrival of a new member may not be uniquely defined. Hence individuals' incentives to move are affected by their conjectures about these reactions. This difficulty does not arise in a hedonic game.

splitting of the society into smaller groups is triggered by efficiency forces, that is, in nonsuperadditive games.[27]

In settings in which a divisible good can be transferred across coalitions, balanced transfers do not lead to a Pareto improvement either, as argued in Theorem 5.2. *A coalition structure that satisfies free entry is Pareto efficient among coalition structures with cross subsidies.*

Efficiency results from free entry but not from alternative coalition threats. To see this, consider the model of nation formation, as described in Example 5.3 of Section 5.2. The location of a government within a nation is chosen according to majority rule. This gives rise to a hedonic game. In this game, a new "nation" forms and blocks if, given the majority winner within this new nation, each member is made better off than under the current structure. A stable structure can be shown to exist. It is efficient in the hedonic game, that is, among all structures in which majority rule within a country is used.

Alesina and Spolaore (1997) consider a different notion of stability, or equivalently, of secession. They assume that a new "nation" forms if the modification is approved by a majority in each of the existing countries affected by the change of the borders. It is important to understand that majority rule here is used at two distinct levels: at a first level within a country for choosing the location of the government, and at a second level for modifying and destabilizing the borders of the countries. Therefore, in contrast to blocking, *unanimity* within a destabilizing coalition is not required, which makes secession easier. As a result, inefficiency results, that is, too many nations form.[28]

It should be noted that the rules that usually apply to form a new jurisdiction (the second level) differ from the rules that apply to take decisions within each jurisdiction (the first level); indeed they are much more stringent than simple majority. Even though unanimity may not be required to form a new jurisdiction, the blocking condition is likely to be closer to normal practice.

Existence. The *second* consequence that can be drawn from the core analysis is rather negative. As has been well known since Shapley (1967), the core of a superadditive game may be empty. Thus, without further restrictions, free-entry coalition structures may not exist. The previous section has shown that, under some restrictions on preferences, the intermediate preferences property, existence of a free entry structure is obtained. Restrictions on free entry may also help to ensure existence. How serious are these restrictions? Section 5.3.6 below examines this question.

Fee Entry Structure without Increasing Returns. Finally, the *third* consequence looks a priori more technical but is very important in many applications. Increasing

---

[27] Exploiting this result, Demange and Guesnerie (1997) provide a setup in which the whole society may collaborate without being blocked.

[28] Again, inefficiencies are here assessed in the game that takes the majority rule within a country (the first level) as a constraint.

returns to coalitions are not at all necessary for a free-entry coalition structure to exist. To see this, note that a free-entry coalition structure exists when the core of the superadditive cover $\hat{V}$ is nonempty, which is independent of whether the sets of payoffs $V(S)$ increase with S. Why do we stress this point? It turns out that, without increasing returns, a coalition structure that is stable under free entry may not satisfy free mobility. If some individuals do not belong to the group they prefer, is a free-entry coalition structure stable in some reasonable sense? We investigate this question now.

5.3.5. Free Mobility, Free Entry, and Increasing Returns

It is first important to understand that free entry does not a priori imply free mobility. The reason is that, under free mobility, an individual contemplates joining a standing coalition without evaluating the welfare of the insiders. Therefore, an individual i may want to join a coalition S_ℓ even if the members of S_ℓ do not benefit from the newcomer. This means that, even if the enlarged coalition formed with the insiders and the newcomer $S_\ell \cup i$ does not block, i may want to join S_ℓ: free entry does not imply free mobility.

If feasible sets are increasing, however, free mobility most often follows from free entry. The argument is as follows. Consider an individual who is strictly better off by joining an existing group under the current action taken by that group. By keeping the action unchanged, the insiders are equally well off. Therefore, the enlarged coalition formed with the insiders and the newcomer blocks in a "weak" sense. Under a smoothness assumption, the action can be slightly modified so that every member is strictly better off, thus contradicting free entry. This gives the following property.

Assume that feasible sets are increasing. Under smooth payoffs, a coalition structure that satisfies free entry and satisfies free mobility as well.

What can be said about the stability of a free-entry coalition structure if feasible sets are not increasing? In a situation in which a group can prevent newcomers from joining it, it will use this possibility whenever it is in the members' interest. Consider, for example, that an individual can join a group only if each member of that group agrees. Free mobility then amounts to free mobility under agreement. We describe this condition, in the simple setup of a hedonic game.[29]

A coalition structure $(S_\ell)_{\ell=1,\ldots,L}$ satisfies *free mobility under agreement* if, for each i, each S one of the existing community S_ℓ, $\ell = 1, \ldots, L$ or $S = \emptyset$ it is not true that

$$u_i(S \cup i) > u_i(S_{\ell(i)}) \quad \text{and} \quad u_j(S \cup i) \geq u_j(S) \quad \text{for any } j \text{ in } S.$$

---

[29] For various definitions and discussions of free mobility in hedonic games, see Bogomolnaia and Jackson (2002). Immigration rules under which a jurisdiction accepts immigrants can be seen as a form of restriction to free mobility. See the analysis of various immigration rules by Jehiel and Scotchmer (2001).

It should be clear that free mobility is drastically restricted. Free mobility under agreement simply requires that no group $S_\ell \cup i$ or i weakly blocks. Therefore, arguing as above, one straightforwardly obtains the following:

Under smooth payoffs, a coalition structure that satisfies free entry satisfies free mobility under agreement as well.

Therefore, even if feasible sets are not increasing, a free-entry structure can indeed be considered stable provided that coalitions are able to screen potential newcomers and possibly to forbid them to join.[30] In a variety of situations however, a group is unable to exclude some individuals – at least without bearing a cost. For example, exclusion policies based on identity only or on some criteria may be forbidden. Also a group, especially a large one, is often poorly informed on the newcomers' characteristics. Section 5.4 investigates this situation.

5.3.6. Restrictions on Free Entry or on Preferences

We have seen that free-entry structures do not necessarily exist. We examine here which restrictions on free entry or on preferences help to restore existence.

Restrictions on Free Entry. If there are limits to free entry, stable coalition structures should be more likely to exist. The question is, To which extent must free entry be limited to guarantee stability? We investigate here[31] the situation in which some coalitions simply cannot form. Such restrictions naturally arise in some settings. Let us give two examples.

Marriage and Assignment Games. The society is partitioned into two groups – for instance, men and women, buyers and sellers, colleges and students. Let us consider the marriage problem (Gale and Shapley 1962). Only singletons and pairs consisting of one man and one woman can form. A marriage defines a set of couples, each individual having at most one spouse. The marriage is stable if (1) no new couple can form in which both the man and the woman prefer each other to their standing partner (no couple blocks) and (2) no person would prefer to stay single (no individual blocks). Gale and Shapley show that a stable marriage always exists.

Connected Coalitions in a Network. If communication among individuals is constrained by a network, quite naturally only the coalitions that are connected in the

---

[30] The possibility of forbidding entry can be reasonably assumed in a small population as, for example, in the analysis of partnerships of Farrell and Scotchmer (1988). See also Chapter 13 of this volume, which analyzes the formation of coalitions of countries (a "player" is a country). Once a coalition of countries is formed, each country within the coalition decides on its own contribution to a growth-enhancing public good. Owing to difference in endowments across countries, increasing returns to coalitions fail. Assuming the possibility for a coalition of countries to exclude a (poorer) country makes sense.

[31] Other types of restrictions to entry could be considered. For example, a new group can form only if it is a subset of an existing group (internal stability within a group) or if it is the union of two existing groups. We are not aware of any general result under such restrictions.

graph can form.[32] If the network is a simple path, individuals are completely ordered, and only intervals can form: a *consecutive* game is obtained as considered by Greenberg and Weber (1993). More generally, if the network is a tree, individuals are partially ordered, as in Demange (1994).

How much must free entry be restricted to guarantee stability regardless of the preferences? This leads to the following definition, as introduced by Kaneko and Wooders (1982).

Definition 5.10. *Given a set C of coalitions of N, a coalition structure is said to be C-stable if it is blocked by no coalition in C. The set C guarantees stability if any game admits a C-stable coalition structure.*

Clearly, the more coalitions that are allowed to block (i.e., the larger the set C), the stronger the stability concept. If all coalitions can form, we know that stable coalition structures may not exist. At the opposite, if only the whole society and the singletons are allowed to block, C-stability coincides with Pareto optimality and individual rationality: stability is guaranteed.

Consider the preceding examples. Stability is guaranteed in marriage games. In networks, stability is guaranteed if the network is a line or more generally is a tree but fails if the network contains a cycle. There are no other known examples that are associated to meaningful contexts.[33] One can say, however, that free entry must be drastically restricted to guarantee stability. To understand this, the following condition, based on triples of coalitions, is helpful. Let us define a *Condorcet triple* as three coalitions that intersect each other and whose overall intersection is empty:

$$S_i, i = 1, 2, 3, \quad \text{with } S_i \cap S_j \neq \emptyset \quad \text{and} \quad S_1 \cap S_2 \cap S_3 = \emptyset.$$

One can show that if a set C of coalitions guarantees stability, then it contains no Condorcet triple. The argument is by contradiction. Take a family C that contains a Condorcet triple. Consider the transferable utility game with characteristic function $V: V(N) = 1$, $V(S) = b$ if S is a strict subset of N that contains at least one S_i, $i = 0, 1, 2$, and $V(S) = 0$ otherwise. For b smaller than 1 the game is superadditive, but for b strictly smaller than $2/3$, any feasible payoff is blocked by one of the S_i. Note that stability fails in numerous games. Hedonic games could be defined as well.

The absence of Condorcet triples is a strong restriction (which is furthermore not sufficient). Therefore, the lesson that can be drawn from this analysis is that, without restrictions on preferences, the blocking power of coalitions, or equivalently their possibility to form, must be quite drastically restricted to guarantee stability. We now examine restrictions on preferences.

---

[32] Kalai, Postlewaite, and Roberts (1978) were the first to analyze stability under this restriction. In an exchange economy, they perform some comparative statics on the set of stable allocations by allowing the graph to vary. Because, in an exchange economy the core is always nonempty, their concern clearly differs from ours.

[33] There are mathematical characterizations. Thanks to standard results on balanced games, one easily shows that C guarantees stability if and only if any balanced family of sets in C contains a partition. Kaneko and Wooders (1982) derive a characterization in terms of the extreme solutions to a system of linear equations.

Restrictions on Preferences. Under some restrictions on preferences, only the blocking possibilities of a restricted set of coalitions matter. Therefore, the previous approach is very helpful to get some insight into the kind of existence results that can be obtained by restricting preferences.

For example, why does a sustainable configuration exist under a one-dimensional intermediate preferences family (Theorem 5.1)? Thanks to the one-dimensional assumption, individuals can be ordered according to their characteristics. Therefore, there is a coalition structure formed with "intervals" of individuals that no interval blocks. Increasing returns to coalitions and intermediate preferences then imply that this coalition structure is blocked by no coalition at all. The same argument can be used if the characteristic belongs to a tree. This yields the following result, which extends Theorem 5.1 (Demange 1994).

Let preference characteristics belong to a tree. Under intermediate preferences and increasing returns to coalitions, a coalition structure that is stable under free entry exists.

Now consider characteristics to be multidimensional – bidimensional for instance – and still assume intermediate preferences. By a similar argument as the one just presented, a coalition structure formed with convex sets that is not blocked by a convex set satisfies free entry. However, such a structure may not exist because the family of convex sets does not guarantee stability: in a two-dimensional space, it is easy to find a Condorcet triple formed with convex sets. Similarly, given a graph with a cycle, the family of connected sets does not guarantee stability. This explains why a stable structure does not exist for a large set of parameters in the example of destructive competition in Section 5.2.3.1. This leads us to our second point.

That there are very few sets C that guarantee stability suggests that free-entry coalition structures do not exist except under specific assumptions. To be more precise, let us take the feasible sets as the primitives and assume preferences to be unknown. If the class of preferences is not rich, a stable coalition structure may exist without any restriction on the set of admissible coalitions.[34] If the class of possible preferences is rich enough, however, surely there are some profiles for which no stable coalition structure exists. This may provide a rationale for organizations such as tree-hierarchy structures that restrict the set of blocking coalitions (Demange 2004).

5.4. Public Decision Rules and Mobility

Some of the central questions regarding public decisions can be discussed through the tools introduced in the previous section. Choosing public goods levels and their financing or deciding on a redistributive policy are subject to objections stemming from part of the population. Also, these decisions are affected by the ability of individuals to move to another jurisdiction or to another country.

---

[34] For an example in a hedonic setup, see the top cycle property defined by Banerjee, Konishi, and Sonmez (2001).

To discuss these issues we first introduce a very simple economy in which a public good is financed through a tax system. Basic properties such as superadditivity and increasing returns to coalitions are shown to depend crucially on the fiscal tools available to a government and on the decision process used. That fiscal tools affect the efficiency frontier is well known from tax theory. It is less well known that fiscal tools affect stability as well. In particular, if redistributive policies are implemented, increasing returns to coalitions may fail: an individual may have a negative impact on a group he or she joins. Then free mobility does not follow from free entry and must be explicitly taken into account. Alternative equilibrium approaches to address the interaction between free entry and free mobility are discussed.

5.4.1. Fiscal Tools, Decision Rules, and Increasing Returns

We consider an economy[35] with two private goods, a consumption good and labor, and a public good. Both consumption and public goods are produced from labor through constant-returns-to-scale technologies. Up to a normalization, a unit of labor produces, respectively, c units of consumption and 1 unit of public good. Preferences over private and public goods are separable and represented for a θ-agent by

$$u(x, l, y, \theta) = v(x, l, \theta) + w(y), \tag{5.6}$$

where x, l, y are, respectively, the amounts of the consumption good, labor, and public good, and standard assumptions are made on v.

From the efficiency point of view, the whole society should join, leaving access to the public good to each agent. If personalized prices are implementable without cost, the incremental value generated by an individual's joining a coalition increases as the coalition grows. As a result, owing to a "snowballing" or "bandwagon" effect, there are many stable outcomes,[36] among them the Lindahl equilibrium (see Champsaur 1975 and Demange 1987, respectively, with and without transferable utility). Most often, however, public goods are financed through taxes because personalized prices cannot be charged owing, for example, to a lack of information. Tax systems restrict the possibilities of distributing the potential gains derived from public goods within the population.

Tax System and Feasible Sets. We consider here tax systems that are composed of a nonnegative tax on the consumption good, denoted by t, and a uniform lump sum tax, possibly negative, denoted by r in terms of units of labor. The overall tax burden for an individual is the sum of the amount of taxes on consumption and the lump sum r. Accordingly, a system (t, r) with r negative is described as being *redistributive* because some individuals may be net receivers. To handle constraints such as the absence of redistribution, or r not too large, we assume that r must be chosen in $[\underline{r}, \overline{r}]$. Thus, according to the previous remark, redistribution is excluded if $\underline{r} \geq 0$.

---

[35] The analysis here is close to Guesnerie and Oddou's (1981).

[36] In technical terms, the game is not only superadditive but also convex, as defined first by Shapley (1971).

The feasibility sets associated to these tax systems are determined as follows. Let a group of citizens S decide to form a community. If the tax system (t, r) is chosen by S, a unique equilibrium is derived as follows. Because returns to scale are constant, the competitive production price for the private good is equal to its constant average cost c, and the consumption price is $c + t$. Thanks to separable preferences, the consumer's demand, $x(t, r, \theta)$, $l(t, r, \theta)$, maximizes

$$v(x, l, \theta) \text{ over } (x, l) \text{ such that } (c + t)x \le l - r.$$

Thus, the budget surplus for community S can be expressed as

$$\pi(y, t, r, S) = \sum_{i \in S} tx(t, r, \theta_i) + r|S| - y. \tag{5.7}$$

Budget balance, $\pi(y, t, r, S) = 0$ determines the public good level. Furthermore, the market for consumption good clears through an appropriate production scale, and by Walras law the labor market also clears. Thus, given (y, t, r) that satisfies budget balance for community S, a payoff vector to each member of S is derived. Therefore, if no decision process is further specified, a group of citizens S can choose any policy that is budget balanced:

$$A(S) = \{(y, t, r) \text{ that satisfies } t \ge 0, r \in [\underline{r}, \overline{r}], \pi(y, t, r, S) \ge 0\}. \tag{5.8}$$

The preceding feasible set is quite large. If further constraints on the tax system, the decision process within a community, or both are added, the feasible sets are subsets of $A(.)$. Therefore, each set of constraints gives rise to a different game. We investigate the properties of the induced game, superadditivity, and increasing returns starting with the case in which no decision process within a community is fixed and proceeding with the majority rule.

No Fixed Decision Rule. Without fixed rule, feasible sets $A(.)$ are given by equation (5.4).

Increasing Returns. Monotonicity properties depend on whether redistribution is possible. Consider whether feasible sets are increasing, that is, whether a policy (y, t, r) feasible for S remains feasible if newcomers join it. Clearly, if the budget π given by equation (5.7) increases with S, feasible sets are increasing. The amount of taxes collected from consumption can only increase with S (t is nonnegative). Therefore, without redistribution (i.e., if $\underline{r} \ge 0$), π is nondecreasing with S so that feasible sets are increasing. Instead, with a redistributive policy ($r < 0$), the budget may decrease as the population is enlarged. Then feasible sets and returns to coalitions may not be increasing. The argument should be clear: the arrival of individuals who receive a positive net payment through the tax system (individuals with low consumption in the private good) has a negative impact on the budget and hurts the insiders. A similar argument applies if a proportional income tax is raised: newcomers whose income is low enough to be net tax receiver imposes a negative externality on incumbents.

Superadditivity. In a situation in which personalized prices cannot be charged, efficiency gains are not freely distributed among individuals. As a consequence, the game is not necessarily superadditive, and the formation of several groups cannot be excluded even from a Pareto point of view. This is illustrated by the following example, which has nothing pathological.

Example. Preferences are given by $\theta v(x, l) + w(y)$. Consider only a lump sum tax r so that an individual faces the budget constraint $cx \le l - r$. Defining $U(r) = \max_x v(x, cx - r)$ the indirect utility over the consumption good, a θ-individual derives the utility level $\theta U(r) + w(y)$ from public good level y and tax r.

Individuals' characteristics take two values only: θ_ℓ, $\ell = 1, 2$. Denote by N_ℓ the group of individuals with characteristic θ_ℓ and by n_ℓ its cardinality. Assume that N_ℓ forms. Because N_ℓ contains identical individuals, it optimally chooses the level of tax, r_ℓ, that maximizes $\theta_\ell U(r) + w(n_\ell r)$. Now if the whole society N forms and chooses r, individuals in N_ℓ are better off if the inequality

$$\theta_\ell U(r) + w(nr) \ge \theta_\ell U(r_\ell) + w(n_\ell r_\ell)$$

holds. The set of r that satisfies the inequality above is an interval I_ℓ that contains r_ℓ. All individuals can be made better off by forming N if the intersection $I_1 \cap I_2$ is nonempty (then N is universally efficient). The intersection, however, may be empty, leading to a nonsuperadditive game. With equal groups for example, the game is not superadditive if the difference between the valuations θ_ℓ for the private good is large enough.

Majority Rule. We examine now the case in which the tax system within each community is chosen under majority rule. To ensure the existence of a majority winner, assume that the tax parameter on which individuals vote is one-dimensional – for instance, they vote on the poll level r only. Returns to coalitions may fail to be increasing. To see this, consider the previous example. Inside the homogeneous group N_ℓ, the majority winner is r_ℓ. Now, assume N_1 to be more numerous than N_2. Under simple majority, society N chooses the decision r_1' that maximizes $\theta_1 U(r) + w(nr)$. Even if there are decisions that could make everybody better off, the majority may not choose one of them: even if I_1 and I_2 intersect, r_1' does not necessarily belong to the intersection.

In conclusion, this section has shown that the redistribution performed by jurisdictions most often generates negative externalities among citizens. Increasing returns to coalitions fail because of the *anonymity* of the tax policy – anonymity that may be due to various factors such as poor information. If a coalition could screen the newcomers who exert a negative effect on insiders, the difficulty would not be so serious as we have seen in Section 5.3.5. In most countries, citizens are allowed to move freely from one community to another and information is poor. In such a context, the interaction between free mobility and free entry is not trivial. Indeed, similar difficulties arise in defining competition in insurance markets, where negative externality stems from adverse selection (Rothschild and Stiglitz 1976).

We present first a possible definition of blocking in a general framework and then discuss it in our simple public good economy.

5.4.2. Blocking under Negative Externality

Under negative externalities and free mobility, a group setting its policy has to take into account not only the welfare within the group but also the attractiveness the policy may have on outsiders. Also, a tentative blocking coalition must derive some information on the characteristics of its members in order to assess the feasibility of a secession. A natural point of view is to base this information on *self-selection* arguments. In this approach, the possible moves of the citizens are derived in assessing their incentives to do so and given the utility levels at the candidate equilibrium. This leads to the following definition of credible blocking.

Definition 5.11. *Coalition T credibly blocks via b the structure $(a_\ell, S_\ell)_{\ell=1,...,L}$ if the action b is feasible for T and if T is the whole set of individuals who strictly prefer b to the current policy of the community to which they belong:*

$$u_i(b) > u_i\left(a_{\ell(i)}\right) \text{ for any } i \text{ in } T$$
$$u_i(b) \le u_i\left(a_{\ell(i)}\right) \text{ for any } i \text{ not in } T. \tag{5.9}$$

Credible blocking entails two conditions: (1) as usual, each member of the blocking coalition has incentives to join and (2) no outsider wants to do so.

What kind of process enables a coalition to block? This question is important because we are interested in situations in which individuals cannot be screened. Consider the public good model. Let policy (y, t, r) be proposed. Assume that citizens (or at least a city manager) *rationally* expect the coalition T of individuals who are attracted by this proposal. Then coalition T credibly blocks if the policy is budget feasible for T, that is, if $\pi(y, t, T) \ge 0$, where π is defined by equation (5.7). Otherwise, if $\pi(y, t, T) < 0$, a tâtonnement process can be contemplated, for example, as follows: the level of public goods is adjusted down to y' so as to satisfy the budget constraint $\pi(y', t, T) = 0$, which leads to a new set T', and so on. If the process converges to a nonempty coalition, a credible coalition is obtained. Note that only the information on the distribution of characteristics is necessary, not the identity of individuals.

Similar ideas have been used in various contexts with asymmetric information: in a credit market with two types of individuals (Boyd and Prescott 1986), in an income taxation model à la Mirrlees with nonlinear income tax schedules (Berliant 1992), in a mechanism design setup (Demange and Guesnerie 2001), and finally within a local public good economy subject to congestion with homogeneous consumers (Conley and Konishi 2002). To our knowledge, neither the existence nor the properties of stable outcomes have been analyzed in a general framework. Actually, the analysis of blocking under asymmetric information is still in progress.[37] Finally, self-selection

---

[37] Wilson (1978) first tackles the problem by defining several concepts according to the communication system used by a coalition if it forms. The incentives to abide by the communication system are however not considered: individuals ex ante commit to a given communication system. Since this

arguments are also implicit in the analysis of redistribution by Epple and Romer (1991) that we discuss now.

5.4.3. Free Mobility with a Fixed Number of Jurisdictions

As seen in Section 5.4.1, redistribution within jurisdictions typically generates negative externalities. Epple and Romer precisely address the impact that free mobility may have on communities' decisions. To simplify, we present here their approach in the public good economy of the previous section. Distinctive features from the analysis of competition across groups carried out in Section 5.3 are that

(1) the number of communities is fixed – for example, a community is associated with a given geographical zone with fixed boundaries;

(2) stability is assessed from the point of view of insiders: a new policy may destabilize a community only if the current inhabitants agree to it – possibly taking into account the population changes triggered by the new policy.

To simplify, let us restrict to two communities. A structure is given by the set of inhabitants in each community together with a budget-balanced policy: $(a_1, S_1), (a_2, S_2)$, where $a_\ell = (y_\ell, t_\ell, r_\ell)$ satisfies $\pi(y_\ell, t_\ell, r_\ell, S_\ell) = 0$, $\ell = 1, 2$. To make the model more realistic, we allow individuals to be concerned with some intrinsic, exogenous characteristics of a community: u_i is a function of both the decision a taken by a community and the community "identity" l. Free mobility says, as usual, that no citizen wants to move to the other community and takes both policies as given:

$$\text{for any } i, u_i\left(a_{\ell(i)}, \ell(i)\right) \geq u_i(a_k, k), k = 1, 2.$$

Citizens in a community vote on the tax parameters (t, r) and the level of the public good is determined by budget balance over the population within the community. Decisions are taken under q-majority, where q is between one-half (majority) and one (unanimity).

To form a (voting) equilibrium, a structure must satisfy two conditions: (1) free mobility, and (2) in each community no alternative policy destabilizes the current policy according to the voting rule. The second condition means that no policy gets a proportion larger than q of the votes within the community against the current policy. The difficulty is to predict how citizens vote. Indeed, different equilibrium outcomes may arise according to the level of voters' farsightedness. When a voter in a given community compares different policies, he or she may or may not take into account the impact that each policy has on the composition of the population living in the community. Let us start with "myopic" voters.

A voter is *myopic* if he or she assumes that the composition of the population is unaffected by policy decisions and derives the feasible policies accordingly: living in a community with population S and contemplating another tax decision (t, r), he

pioneering work, another line of research studies the ex ante coalitional stability of such mechanisms, which are implemented at the interim stage (see the special issue of *Economic Theory* 2001).

or she expects the level y of public good to be given by budget balance applied to population S. This gives the following definition.

Definition 5.12. *A two-communities structure* $(a_1, S_1), (a_2, S_2)$ *forms an equilibrium with myopic voters if it satisfies free mobility and*

(no destabilizing policy) for each community $\ell = 1, 2$, *there is no* $b = (y, t, r)$ *with* $\pi(y, t, r, S_\ell) \geq 0$ *that is preferred to* a_ℓ *by a proportion of the population in* S_ℓ *larger than* q.

Under unanimity, a destabilizing policy is simply a policy that Pareto-dominates the current policy of a community. Without unanimity, destabilizing is easier. Therefore, at an equilibrium, surely each jurisdiction chooses a Pareto-efficient decision for itself. Accordingly, both intragroup efficiency and free mobility must be met at equilibrium (and are even sufficient under unanimity).

In assessing stability, the various policies that are considered as destabilizing do not account for free mobility: if an alternative policy b feasible for S_ℓ were indeed implemented, some outsiders might immigrate to community ℓ, and some citizens might leave it (the latter case can happen if $q < 1$ because then some citizens in ℓ may be worse off under b than under a_ℓ and so might prefer to move to the other community). These moves altogether affect the feasibility of b, which has to be adjusted. Voters, even slightly farsighted or "sophisticated", should be aware of the interaction between a policy and the incentives of the citizens to move.

A voter is *sophisticated* if he or she takes into account population moves: this person forms some expectations on how the citizens of both communities react to a policy change. Actually, it is not that easy to define such expectations. In what follows, individuals base their expectations on self-selection arguments, as introduced in the previous section. Because the intrinsic characteristics of a community matter, credible blocking has to be adjusted as follows.

Given a structure $(a_1, S_1), (a_2, S_2)$, coalition T *credibly blocks* via $b = (y, t, r)$ community ℓ if $\pi(y, t, r, T) \geq 0$ (feasibility), and T contains all individuals who are better off to live in community ℓ under policy b rather than under their current situation:

$$u_i(b, \ell) > u_i\big(a_{\ell(i)}, \ell(i)\big) \text{ for any } i \text{ in } T \quad \text{and}$$
$$u_i(b, \ell) \leq u_i\big(a_{\ell(i)}, \ell(i)\big) \text{ for any } i \text{ not in } T.$$

Because individuals care about the intrinsic characteristics of a community, a coalition T may credibly block one community but not the other one (the utility levels on the left-hand side depend on ℓ). Without intrinsic characteristics, we fall back on Definition 5.11 of credible blocking.

Definition 5.13. *A two-communities structure* $(a_1, S_1), (a_2, S_2)$ *forms an equilibrium with sophisticated voters if it satisfies free mobility and*

(no destabilizing credible blocking) for each community $\ell = 1, 2$, *there is no* (b, T) *that credibly blocks community* ℓ, *and such that* b *is preferred to* a_ℓ *by a proportion larger than* q *of the population of* S_ℓ.

A free-mobility structure that is not credibly blocked at all is clearly an equilibrium. But credible blocking is allowed at equilibrium. If (b, T) credibly blocks ℓ, all the citizens of community ℓ who prefer b to the current policy a_ℓ belong to T (by definition of credible blocking). Thus, (b, T) is destabilizing only if $S_\ell \cap T$ contains more than the proportion q of the population of ℓ. Under unanimity, this means that each current inhabitant of ℓ is better off.

The no-destabilizing condition can be interpreted as follows. Let (t, r) be an alternative to the current decision proposed to community ℓ. Current citizens forecast a level of public expenditures y together with a set T that is exactly formed by the citizens who would live in ℓ if (y, t, r) were feasible and implemented. The alternative is destabilizing if it defeats the current policy in ℓ under q-majority when the current citizens S_ℓ vote according to these expectations. An equilibrium is obtained if there is no alternative for which this occurs.

How does each equilibrium concept relate to each other and with stability under free entry? Comparisons are clearly much easier when the unanimity rule is used, and so let us restrict to $q = 1$. The relationships are clear under increasing returns to coalitions. First, an equilibrium with sophisticated voters is surely an equilibrium with myopic voters: if a new policy destabilizes the current policy with myopic voters, it makes every inhabitant better off when applied to the current population; if the new policy attracts citizens of the other community, under increasing returns to coalitions, sophisticated voters would a fortiori destabilize the current policy (note that the argument is not valid under simple q majority because sophisticated voters take into account that some inhabitants may leave the community). Second, a structure that satisfies free entry is surely an equilibrium with sophisticated voters: under free entry, an entire new group may be formed without the agreement of the inhabitants who are not members of this new group. These simple results suggest that stability is the good concept when there are increasing returns to coalitions. However, the assumption of increasing returns does not hold in the problems with negative externalities.

In a model with redistribution, the adverse selection phenomena come up naturally. They are also present in more subtle ways through price effects in other models as well. In a quite similar model, Epple, Romer, and Sieg (2001) consider a fixed number of communities differing a priori only in the (exogenous) housing service offer function. A posteriori communities also differ in the chosen level of tax on housing service, land, the level of public good, and the equilibrium housing price. Interestingly, Epple et al. provide an empirical analysis using data from the Boston metropolitan area and conclude that voters are indeed quite sophisticated. It would be interesting to perform similar analyses on different policy issues or in different countries.

5.5. Conclusion

This chapter has shown that the standard cooperative game theory is useful for analyzing the formation of groups. In particular, it has displayed conditions under which competitive pressures exercised by individuals and groups lead to an efficient and stable organization. On the theoretical side, a major failure of the approach is its current inability to handle situations under negative externalities. Another open problem is the definition of an equilibrium concept that covers situations in which heterogeneity among individuals is richer, as arises if individuals differ along several dimensions. Finally, it would be of interest to test the theory in the situations in which the conditions under which stability can be reached are likely to be met.

BIBLIOGRAPHY

[1] Alesina, Alberto and Enrico Spolaore (1997), "On the Number and Size of Nations," *Quarterly Journal of Economics* 112, 1027–1056.

[2] Aumann, Robert and Jacques Dreze (1974), "Cooperative Games with Coalition Structures," *International Journal of Game Theory* 3, 217–237.

[3] Banerjee, Santanu, Hideo Konishi, and Tayfun Sonmez (2001), "Core in a Simple Coalition Formation Game," *Social Choice and Welfare* 18, 135–153.

[4] Baumol, William J., John C. Panzer, and Robert D. Willig (1982), *Stable Markets and the Theory of Industry Structure*, New York: Harcourt Brace Jovanovich.

[5] Berliant, Marcus (1992), "On Income Taxation and the Core," *Journal of Economic Theory* 56, 121–141.

[6] Bewley, Truman F., (1981), "A Critique of Tiebout's Theory of Local Public Expenditures," *Econometrica* 49, 713–740.

[7] Bogomolnaia, Anna and Matthew O. Jackson (2002), "The Stability of Hedonic Coalition Structures,"*Games and Economic Behaviour* 38, 201–230.

[8] Boyd, John H. and Edward C. Prescott (1986), "Financial Intermediary Coalitions," *Journal of Economic Theory* 38, 221–232.

[9] Buchanan, James M. (1965), "An Economic Theory of Clubs," *Economica* 33, 1–14.

[10] Champsaur, Paul (1975), "How to Share the Cost of a Public Good?" *International Journal of Game Theory* 4, 113–129.

[11] Conley, John P. and Hideo Konishi (2002), "Migration-proof Tiebout Equilibrium: Existence and Asymptotic Efficiency," *Journal of Public Economics* 86, 243–262.

[12] Currarini, Sergio (2003), "On the Stability of Hierarchies in Games with Externalities," mimeo, Università di Venezia.

[13] Demange, Gabrielle (1987), "Nonmanipulable Cores," *Econometrica* 55, 1057–1074.

[14] Demange, Gabrielle (1994), "Intermediate Preferences and Stable Coalition Structures," *Journal of Mathematical Economics* 23, 45–58.

[15] Demange, Gabrielle (2004), "On Group Stability in Hierarchies and Networks," *Journal of Political Economy*; vol 112, no. 4, 754–778.

[16] Demange, Gabrielle and Roger Guesnerie (1997), "Nonemptiness of the Core: Low Dimensional Decisions Spaces and One-Dimensional Preferences," *Research in Economics* 51, 7–17.

[17] Demange, Gabrielle and Roger Guesnerie (2001), "On Coalitional Stability of Anonymous Interim Mechanisms," *Economic Theory* 18, 367–389.

[18] Demange, Gabrielle and Dominique Henriet (1991), "Sustainable Oligopolies," *Journal of Economic Theory* 54, 417–428.

[19] Economic Theory (2001), *Symposium Differential Information Economics* 18, 2.

[20] Epple, Dennis and Thomas Romer (1991), "Mobility and Redistribution," *Journal of Political Economy* 99, 828–858.

[21] Epple, Dennis, David Romer and Holger Sieg (2001), "Interjurisdictorial Sorting and Majority Rule: An Empirical Analysis," *Econometrica* 69, 1437–1466.

[22] Farrell, Joseph and Suzanne Scotchmer (1988), "Partnerships," *The Quarterly Journal of Economics* 103, 279–297.

[23] Gabszewicz, Jean J. and Jean-François Thisse (1986), "Spatial Competition and the Location of Firms," in *Location Theory*, Gabszewicz, Thisse, Fujita, and Schweizer (eds.). Chur; Harwood Academic Publishers.

[24] Gabszewicz, Jean J. and Jean-François Thisse (2002), *Microeconomic Theories of Imperfect Competition*, Old Problems and New Perspectives, Elgar Reference collection. Northampton, MA:

[25] Gale David, and Lloyd S. Shapley (1962), "College Admissions and Stability of Marriage," *The American Mathematical Monthly* 60, 9–15.

[26] Grandmont, Jean-Michel (1978), "Intermediate Preferences and the Majority Rule," *Econometrica* 46, 317–330.

[27] Greenberg, Joseph and B. Shitovitz (1988), "Consistent Vong Rules for Competitive Local Public Good Economies," *Journal of Economic Theory* 46, 223–236.

[28] Greenberg, Joseph and Shlomo Weber (1986), "Strong Tiebout Equilibrium under Restricted Preferences Domain," *Journal of Economic Theory* 38, 101–117.

[29] Greenberg, Joseph and Shlomo Weber (1993), "Stable Coalition Structures with Unidimensional Set of Alternatives," *Journal of Economic Theory* 60, 62–82.

[30] Greenberg, J. and S. Weber (1994) "Stable Coalition Structures in Consecutive Games," in *Frontiers in Game Theory*, Binmore, K., A. Kirman, and P. Tani (eds.), Cambridge, MA: MIT Press.

[31] Guesnerie, Roger and Claude Oddou (1981), "Second Best Taxation as a Game," *Journal of Economic Theory*, 25, 1, 67–91.

[32] Guesnerie, Roger and Claude Oddou (1987), "Increasing Returns to Size and Their Limits," *Scandinavian Journal of Economics* 90, 259–273.

[33] Haeringer, Guillaume (2000), "Stable Coalition Structures with Fixed Decision Schemes," UFAE and IAE Working Papers 471.00.

[34] Hotelling, Harold (1929), "Stability in Competition," *Economic Journal* 39, 4–57.

[35] Jehiel, Philippe and Suzanne Scotchmer (2001), "Constitutional Rules of Exclusion in Jurisdiction Formation," *Review of Economic Studies* 68, 393–413.

[36] Kalai, Ehud, Andrew Postlewaite, and John Roberts (1978), "Barriers to Trade and Disadvantageous Middlemen: Nonmonotonicity of the Core," *Journal of Economic Theory* 19, 200–210.

[37] Kaneko, Mamoru and Myrna Wooders (1982), "Cores of Partitioning Games," *Mathematical Social Sciences* 3, 313–327.

[38] Kemeny, John G. and J. Laurie Snell (1962), *Mathematical Models in the Social Sciences*. New York: Ginn.

[39] Rose-Ackerman Susan (1979): "Market Models of Local Governments: Exit, Voting and the Land Market," *Journal of Urban Economics* 6, 319–337.

[40] Rothschild, Michael and Joseph Stiglitz (1976), "Equilibrium in Competitive Insurance Markets: An Essay on the Economics of Imperfect Information," *Quarterly Journal of Economics* 90, 629–649.

[41] Shaked, Avner and John Sutton (1983), "Natural Oligopolies," *Econometrica* 51, 1469–1483.

[42] Shapley, Lloyd S. (1967), "On Balanced Sets and Cores," *Naval Research Logistics Quarterly* 14, 453–460.

[43] Shapley, Llyod, S. (1971), "Cores of Convex Games," *International Journal of Game Theory* 11–26.

[44] Sharkey, William W. (1982), *The Theory of Natural Monopoly*, Cambridge University Press.

[45] Tiebout, Charles (1956), "A Pure Theory of Local Expenditures," *Journal of Political Economy* 64, 416–424.

[46] Westhoff, F. (1977), "Existence of Equilibria in Economies with a Local Public Good," *Journal of Economic Theory* 17, 84–112.

[47] Wilson, Robert (1978), "Information, Efficiency, and the Core of an Economy," *Econometrica* 52, 1365–1368.

[48] Yi, Sang-Seung (1997), "Stable Coalition Structures with Externalities," *Games and Economic Behavior* 20, 201–237.

6

Games and Economies with Near Exhaustion of Gains to Scale

Alexander Kovalenkov and Myrna Wooders

6.1. Games with Many Players as Models of Large Economies

In this chapter we model economies as coalitional games, provide some new results, and review results showing that under apparently mild conditions games with many players share properties of markets. The examples include economies with pure or local public goods, economies with large or small clubs, coalition production economies, and economies with ever-increasing returns to firm size. The framework presented, of parameterized collections of games, includes cooperative games as discussed in Chapters 5 and 8 of this volume. For the case of quasi-linear utilities, the framework also incorporates games derived from the club and local public good economies treated in Chapter 7 of this volume.

Roughly, the key assumptions we require on economies and their derived games are that

1. The economies are *essentially superadditive*, that is, a group of players can freely break into smaller groups.
2. Gains to forming increasingly larger coalitions become small as coalitions become large.

The second condition simply rules out unboundedly large average payoffs as population size increases. We stress that the conditions permit both situations in which optimality requires that the total player set be partitioned into relatively small groups as well as some situations with a fixed, finite number of firms, clubs, or jurisdictions. We review results showing that, under our two conditions, economies and the games they generate have nonempty approximate cores and that the games are approximated by market games, that is, games generated by private goods economies in which all players have concave, quasi linear monotonic increasing objective functions (utility functions or production functions).

For accessibility, we restrict our attention to economies with quasi-linear utilities and games with side payments, but note, however, that our most general results,

We are grateful to the University of Warwick for generous research support of our collaboration.

published elsewhere, apply to economies and games without side payments.[1] Several examples are provided to clarify the intuition. We highlight examples with large optimal groups and illustrate how they fit into our assumptions. A simple example with large optimal groups is a coalition production economy in which firms face a fixed cost plus a constant marginal cost. Another simple example is a situation in which individuals have preferences over the size of some public facility, between zero and one for instance, and each individual using the facility must pay the average cost of the facility he or she uses.

In this chapter, we relate markets to parameterized collections of games. Games in a parameterized collection are described by certain parameters: (a) the number of approximate types of players and the goodness of the approximation and (b) the size of nearly effective groups of players and their distance from exact effectiveness. Exact bounds are obtained, as a function of the parameters describing a collection of games, on the difference between games in the collection and market games. We also discuss the "pregame" framework used in several previous papers and the equivalence of games with many players and market games for pregames (Wooders 1994a).[2]

The result that games with many players are market games has significant implications for economics and the sorts of models considered in much of Part Two of this volume. First, note that the free-entry condition of cooperative game theory is simply the no-improvement condition of the core – in a cooperative free-entry equilibrium, no group of players, using only the resources under the control of its members, can coordinate activities and allocate resources to make everyone in the group better off. Free mobility, in the context of the research in Part Two of this volume, is a nonexclusion condition; given the mechanism by which costs and benefits of group formation are distributed among the members of a group and the rules governing movement into existing groups, in a free-mobility equilibrium no individual can benefit by changing his or her group membership.[3] Mobility is free only in the sense that the rules apply to everyone; no individual can be discriminated against on the basis of his or her name, for example. The properties of a free-mobility equilibrium depend crucially on the mechanisms that govern the conditions under which an individual can move. As an illustration of one possible rule, suppose a group of individuals decides on a collective activity such as the size of some public project and then other individuals are able to move into the group provided that they pay the resulting per capita cost for the given public project; although costs to those members of the original group may change, the size of the project may not (see, for example, Konishi, Le Breton, and Weber 1998). Or it may be that when an individual moves into a group providing some public project, essentially a new group

---

[1] See Kovalenkov and Wooders (2001a, 2001b, 2003a) for treatment of NTU (nontransferable utility) games and economies.

[2] A pregame is formally defined in Section 6.4. For now, we remark that a pregame consists of a set of player types and a function assigning a payoff to any possible group of players described by the numbers of players of each type in the group.

[3] An exposition of possible rules governing free mobility appears in Chapter 8 of this volume.

is formed, including the individual joining the group; in this situation, whether or not the size of the public project remains unchanged, the payments made by group members may change. In other cases, free mobility may mean simply that players are free to respond to nondiscriminatory prices; workers, for example, can choose between the best employment opportunities for which they are qualified, and in a free-mobility equilibrium no individual worker prefers another position to his or her current employment.

The equivalence of games and markets relates to both free entry and free mobility. Nonemptiness of the core means that a free-entry equilibrium exists. Now suppose that the rules governing the mobility of individuals between groups are given by competitive prices for participants in groups (e.g., clubs, firms, jurisdictions). The equivalence of games and markets means that we can represent the game (or the economy that generates the game) as a private goods economy or as a production economy in which the commodities are player types or types of labor and all individuals or firms have concave objective functions. Moreover, for the "standard" representation of the game as a market, it holds that the core of the game is equivalent to the set of outcomes of price-taking equilibrium.

Shapley and Shubik (1969, 1975) demonstrate that any totally balanced game (a game with the property that all subgames have nonempty cores) is equivalent to a game generated by a market and that the core of the game is equivalent to the set of outcomes of price taking. This result, however, is not interpretable as a core-equilibrium equivalence result in the sense of Debreu and Scarf (1963) or Aumann (1964) because, as Shapley and Shubik show in their 1975 paper, for any compact convex subset of the game's core there is a market representing the game that has this subset as the set of price-taking equilibrium outcomes. Moreover, strong assumptions are required on economic models to ensure that the games derived from the economies are totally balanced.

The situation changes dramatically when there are many players, that is, when the games are large. For games derived from pregames, where the worth of a coalition depends on the number of players of each type in the coalition, under our two seemingly mild conditions given above, large games have nonempty approximate cores and the approximation can be allowed to become "close" for sufficiently large games. Moreover, the games are approximately market games and limiting equivalence of the core and the set of price-taking equilibrium outcomes holds. In addition, if we restrict the number of commodities in the market to equal to the number of types of players, then the market representing the game is completely determined. This means that, if one takes the mechanism governing movement of players into groups as that given by the competitive price-taking equilibrium, the free-mobility equilibrium outcomes are efficient and equivalent to the outcomes of the free-entry equilibrium (the core).[4]

---

[4]   See Wooders (1994a) and references therein for the equivalence of games and markets.

We first review basic definitions for games with side payments. In the next section, we introduce the framework of parameterized collections of games for this case. For purposes of comparison and to strengthen the reader's intuition, we then review the framework of cooperative pregames. Next, some of the results for parameterized collections of games are presented. We then turn to market games and results demonstrating that large games satisfying our two conditions are approximated by market games. We also determine bounds on the distance of a game from a market game in terms of the parameters describing the game. Although this is not a comprehensive survey, in a several examples we relate our research to much other literature, including research on coalition production economies (for example, Böhm 1974), economies with a fixed and finite number of jurisdictions (for example, Westhoff 1977 and Epple, Romer, and Sieg 2001), exchange economies (for example, Shapley and Shubik 1966), and economies with clubs and endogenous choice of crowding types (for example, Conley and Wooders 2001). We defer a discussion of further motivation for our approach to a concluding section.

Finally, because of space considerations we do not discuss in any detail the foundational papers in game theory upon which this research builds. We have in mind Shubik (1959), which shows, for an example with two types of players, that cores of large market games (which have the property that all subgames have nonempty cores) converge to equal-treatment cores;[5] Shapley and Shubik (1966), which shows that under apparently mild assumptions on utility functions approximate cores of large exchange economies with transferable utility are nonempty; Bondareva (1962) and Shapley (1967), which introduce the concept of "balancedness" and show that a game with side payments is balanced if and only if it has a nonempty core; and Shapley and Shubik (1969), which shows that games derived from convex exchange economies with quasi-linear utilities are equivalent to market games. These papers, along with Aumann (1964), Aumann and Shapley (1974), Debreu and Scarf (1963), and Tiebout (1956) are, in our view, seminal to the line of research discussed in this chapter.

6.2. Games with Side Payments

A *game with side payments* (also called a *TU game*) is a pair (N, v), where $N = \{1, \dots, n\}$ is a finite set of players and v is a worth function from subsets of N to the nonnegative real numbers with the property that $v(\emptyset) = 0$. Subsets of N will be called groups, clubs, or coalitions. A *group* is the most general term and is to be interpreted simply as a subset of players without any suggestion of joint activity. A *club* is to be understood as a group of players that engages in some collective activity. A *coalition* is a group of players assumed to act together. The term "coalition" is intended to suggest an alliance.

A game (N, v) is *superadditive* if $v(S) \geq \sum_k v(S^k)$ for all groups $S \subset N$ and for all partitions S^k of S. In games and economies in which the realization of maximum

---

[5] The equal treatment core consists of those payoffs in the core that treat identical players identically.

total payoff may require that a group of players subdivide into smaller coalitions, superadditivity does not necessarily hold. Instead, we assume that games are *essentially superadditive*, that is, a possibility open to a group S is to divide into subgroups and achieve the total payoff realizable by the subgroups. Thus, we define the *superadditive cover* (N, v^s) of the game (N, v), where

$$v^s(S) \overset{\text{def}}{=} \max \sum_k v(S^k)$$

and the maximum is taken over all partitions $\{S^k\}$ of S.[6] In interpretation we might think of each S^k as a club and S as a group or coalition. Definitions of solution concepts below will take this feature into account.

Given a nonnegative real number $\delta \geq 0$, two players i and j are δ-*substitutes* if for all groups $S \subset N$ with $i, j \notin S$, it holds that

$$|v(S \cup \{i\}) - v(S \cup \{j\})| \leq \delta.$$

For any group S, let $\mathbb{R}^S$ denote the $|S|$-dimensional Euclidean space with coordinates indexed by elements of S and let $|S|$ denote the number of players in the group S.

For $x \in \mathbb{R}^N$, which is called a *payoff vector*, x_S will denote its restriction to $\mathbb{R}^S$. Given a game (N, v), a payoff vector $x \in \mathbb{R}^N$, and a group $S \subset N$, we define

$$x(S) \overset{\text{def}}{=} \sum_{i \in S} x_i.$$

The assumption of "per capita boundedness," simply bounding the supremum of per capita payoffs over all games considered, has played a major role in the study of games with many players.[7] We introduce the assumption here, for it will be required in various contexts in the following: Let $\{(N, v)\}$ be a collection of games. Suppose there is a constant K such that, for all games in the collection,

$$\frac{v(N)}{|N|} \leq K.$$

Then the collection satisfies *per capita boundedness* with bound K. Note that if a collection of games $\{(N, v)\}$ satisfies per capita boundedness, then so does the collection $\{(N, v^s)\}$ and conversely.

Let (N, v) be a game and let $x \in \mathbb{R}^N$. Consistent with our assumption of essential superadditivity, a payoff vector x is *feasible* if

$$x(N) \leq v^s(N).$$

---

[6] The superadditive cover appears in Chapters 5 and 8 of this volume and is also implicit in Chapters 7 and 13. In the theory of cooperative games with many players, the superadditive cover appears in Wooders (1979,1983) and in many other papers.

[7] See, for example, Wooders (1983) for early results showing nonemptiness of approximate cores of games with many players requiring essentially only per capita boundedness and a fixed distribution of players of each of a finite number of types. Kaneko and Wooders (1986) uses a weak form of per capita boundedness for games with a continuum of players; the conditions are required to hold only near the population proportions given by the measure on the set of players. Note that the results of Wooders (alone and with her collaborators in several papers) do not depend on any "balancedness" assumptions but only on the condition that there are sufficiently many players, in contrast to Weber (1979, 1981) for example.

Given $\varepsilon \geq 0$, the payoff vector x is in the ε-*core* of the game (N, v) if x is feasible and

$$v(S) - \varepsilon |S| \leq x(S) \text{ for all coalitions } S \subset N.$$

When $\varepsilon = 0$, the 0-core is called simply the *core*. For games with side payments the concept of the core is attributed to D.B. Gilles (1953) and unpublished research of Lloyd Shapley. The ε-core was introduced for a game with side payments derived from an exchange economy in Shapley and Shubik (1966).

The notion of the ε-core allows transfers between groups of players. Consider, for example, a game in which any two players can earn \$1.00 and there are eleven players. Then the ε-core is nonempty for $\varepsilon \geq \frac{1}{22}$. In effect, five two-person groups can form, and any such group can give $\frac{5}{11}$ to each of its members and make a transfer of $2\varepsilon \geq \frac{1}{11}$ to the "leftover" player in a one-person group. This leftover player receives a total transfer $10\varepsilon \geq \frac{5}{11}$, and thus no two-player coalition (or any other coalition) can improve the payoffs to its members by more than $\frac{1}{22}$ for each of its members.

In some situations that may arise in noncooperative game theory, for example, it is useful to have another notion of an approximate core in which a relatively small subset of agents – "leftovers" – are ignored.

Let (N, v) be a game and let $x \in \mathbb{R}^N$. A payoff vector x belongs to the ε-*remainder core* if x is feasible and if, for some group $S \subset N$,

$$\frac{|N| - |S|}{|N|} \leq \varepsilon \text{ and}$$

x_S belongs to the core of the subgame (S, v).

The concept of the ε-remainder core is based on the idea that all requirements of the core should at least be satisfied for almost all players with the remainder of players representing a small fraction of "unemployed" or "underemployed" players.[8]

Another core notion, the ε_1-remainder ε_2-core, combines the approximate natures of both the ε-core and the ε-remainder core.[9]

Let (N, v) be a game and let $x \in \mathbb{R}^N$. A payoff vector x belongs to the ε_1-remainder ε_2-core if x is feasible and if, for some group $S \subset N$,

$$\frac{|N| - |S|}{|N|} \leq \varepsilon_1 \text{ and}$$

x_S belongs to the ε_2-core of the subgame (S, v).

Notice that 0-remainder ε_2-core is equivalent to the ε_2-core and that the ε_1-remainder 0-core is equivalent to the ε_1-remainder core.

---

[8] The ε-remainder core is suggested in Shubik (1971) for an example involving bridge games and formally introduced in Woodars (1981). The ε-remainder core subsequently appeared in Shubik and Wooders (1983a), Kaneko and Wooders (1982), and other papers. This approximate core notion is frequently used as a stepping stone to other notions of approximate cores. There are game-theoretic situations, however, in which the notion of the ε-remainder core may naturally arise – for example, the demand games of Selten (1981) or multisided matching games with bounds on the numbers of players in an effective group.

[9] This notion was introduced in Kovalenkov and Wooders (2003a). But the notion of the ε_1-remainder ε_2-core was previously used for $\varepsilon_1 = \varepsilon_2 = \varepsilon$ and named the weak ε-core in Shubik and Wooders (1983a,b) and other papers.

6.3. Parameterized Collections of Games

In this section, we describe the Kovalenkov–Wooders[10] notion of parameterized collections of games restricted to the case of games with side payments. Informally, a game (N, v) is a δ, T–type game if the player set N can be partitioned into T subsets where all players within each subset are approximate (δ) substitutes for each other. The game has β-effective B-bounded groups if within β per capita of all gains to collective activities can be realized by some partition of the player set into groups containing no more than B members. If there are many players, then such a game has the properties that there are many near substitutes for most players and almost all increasing returns to group size are exhausted.

Example 6.1. A simple illustration of the idea of a δ-substitute partition and β-effective B-bounded groups follows. *Let (N, v) be a game. Suppose that players can be ranked in the $[0, 1]$ interval and that the total payoff to any two players is the sum of their ranks. Suppose also that the payoff $v(S)$ to any other group S is zero. Then, for any $\beta \geq 0$ and any $B \geq 2$, the game has β-effective B-bounded groups. Given $\delta \geq 0$, if the distance between players i and j is less than δ, then i and j are δ-substitutes. Thus, players may be divided in T classes of δ-substitutes for $T \geq 1/\delta$. Typically, the division is not unique.*

Formally, given an integer T and $\delta \geq 0$, a partition $\{N^t\}_{t=1}^T$ of N into subsets is a δ-*substitute partition* if all players in each subset are δ-substitutes for each other. The set N^t is called a *type* or an approximate type.

Let B be a given integer. A game (N, v) has *strictly effective B-bounded groups*[11] if for every group $S \subset N$ there is a partition $\{S^k\}$ of S into subgroups with $|S^k| \leq B$ for each k and

$$v^s(S) = \sum_k v(S^k).$$

A multisided matching game is another example of a game with strictly effective B-bounded groups. An example of such a game is one with two sets of players – for instance a set of men and a set of women – and a payoff function v that assigns positive payoffs only to pairs consisting of one man and one women. In general, a multisided matching game may have T types of players and only certain clubs consisting of no more than B players may yield positive payoffs. Coalition production economies for which admissible firm size, either by technological or legal considerations, is bounded by B are an example.

It turns out that large classes of games can be approximated by games with strictly effective B-bounded groups. This motivates the following definition.

Let B be a given integer and let β be a nonnegative real number. A game (N, v) has β-*effective B-bounded groups* if for every group $S \subset N$ there is a partition $\{S^k\}$

---

[10] See Wooders (1994b) and Kovalenkov and Wooders (2001a,b; 2003a,b). Kovalenkov and Wooders (2003c) provides a review focusing on the special case of games with side payments.

[11] See Wooders (1979, p. 17; 1983, 1992a,b) for this concept in games with and without side payments. In Wooders (1983) the condition is called "mimimum efficient scale."

of S into subgroups with $|S^k| \leq B$ for each k and

$$v^s(S) \leq \sum_k v(S^k) + \beta |S| .$$

Given nonnegative real numbers δ and β and positive integers T and B, a *parameterized collection of games with side payments,* denoted by $\Gamma((\delta, T), (\beta, B))$, is a collection of games with the properties that for each game (N, v) in the collection

1. there is a δ-substitute partition of N into no more than T subsets $\{N[t] : t = 1, \ldots, T', T' \leq T\}$, and
2. the game has β-effective B-bounded groups.

Let us first note that a parameterized collection of games $\Gamma((\delta, T), (\beta, B))$ does not require that all gains to collective activities be realized by groups bounded in size. Consider the following example.

Example 6.2. Nonexhaustion of gains to scale by finite coalitions. *Consider a collection of games $\{(N^k, v_k)\}$ in which all players are substitutes for each other, $|N^k| = k$, and for any $S \subset N^k$*

$$v_k(S) = |S| - 1.$$

It is clear that there are forever-increasing returns to population size. Also, given any $\beta > 0$, the collection of games $\{(N^k, v_k)\}$ is contained in the collection $\Gamma((0, 1), (\beta, \lceil 1/\beta \rceil))$, where $\lceil 1/\beta \rceil$ denotes the smallest integer greater than or equal to $1/\beta$.

Although more and stronger results can be obtained with strictly effective B-bounded groups, some results do not depend on this. Roughly, strictly effective B-bounded groups enable the equivalence of the core and price-taking equilibrium outcomes in finite-sized economies, but β-effective B-bounded groups suffice for approximation results. In the following we present some examples with more economic interpretations.

6.4. Pregames

The concept of parameterized collections of games grew out of the concept of a pregame. Informally, a pregame consists of a set of player types or attributes and a (single) payoff function specifying the payoff to any conceivable group of players described by the numbers of each player type in the group. In the context of a pregame, *small group effectiveness* (SGE), the property that almost all gains to collective activities can be realized by groups of players bounded in absolute size, plays a crucial role. As we will demonstrate by examples, SGE is the mildest assumption permitting the results and in particular the result that games with many players derived from a pregame are approximately market games. Economies that fit into the framework of this section include private goods exchange economies with indivisibilities, nonconvexities, and nonmonotonicities; economies with clubs in which individuals may belong to multiple clubs; economies with local public goods; and even some economies with pure public goods and with ever-increasing returns to scale. The pregame framework is especially well suited to limiting results; in fact, one could simply take the player set as a nonatomic continuum.[12] The advantages of the framework of parameterized collections of games are discussed at the end of the section.

Although most of the results described have been obtained with a compact metric space of player types, we confine our attention to the central case of pregames with a finite number T of types. A *pregame* is simply a pair (T, Ψ), where Ψ is a superadditive function from $\mathbb{Z}_+^T$, the T-fold Cartesian product of the nonnegative integers, to the real numbers. A vector $n \in \mathbb{Z}_+^T$ is called a *profile*. That Ψ is a *superadditive function* means that for any two vectors $n, n' \in \mathbb{Z}_+^T$ it holds that

$$\Psi(n) + \Psi(n') \le \Psi(n + n').$$

In interpretation, given $n = (n_1, \ldots, n_T) \in \mathbb{Z}_+^T$, the value $\Psi(n)$ is the payoff achievable by any group of players consisting of n_t players of type t, $t = 1, \ldots, T$. Let $\|n\|$ denote the number of players in a group described by n, that is, $\|n\| = \sum n_t$. Note that for ease in exposition we have simply assumed that Ψ itself is superadditive, but only essential superadditivity is required for our results.

When we interpret a vector $m \in \mathbb{Z}_+^T$ as a description of a total player set, then m and the function Ψ determine a game as just defined.[13] Specifically, given $m \in \mathbb{Z}_+^T$, define

$$N \overset{\text{def}}{=} \{(t, q); \ t = 1, \ldots, T \text{ and } q = 1, \ldots, m_t\}.$$

For each group $S \subset N$, define

$$v(S) = \Psi(s),$$

where $s \in \mathbb{Z}_+^T$ is called the *profile of* S and is defined by its coordinates

$$s_t \overset{\text{def}}{=} |\{(t, q); \ q = 1, \ldots, m_t\} \cap S|.$$

It is apparent that when there are many players of each of a finite number of types, pregames satisfying the mild condition of *per capita boundedness* (PCB, which is boundedness of the supremum of average payoff over all populations n)[14] can be approximated by games satisfying *strict SGE*.[15] This leads to the formulation of SGE.[16]

---

[12] See Kaneko and Wooders (1996), for example.

[13] Many examples of pregames appear in the literature before the introduction of the concept in Wooders (1979). For example, a statement that any two players can earn a dollar and all other coalitions are ineffective describes the pregame $\Psi(n) = 1$ if $n = 2$ and $\Psi(n) = 0$ otherwise. See Wooders (1991; 1992a,b; 1994a,b) for more complete discussions of pregames satisfying small group effectiveness.

[14] See for example, Wooders (1983) and Shubik and Wooders (1982; 1983a,b).

[15] The notion of strictly effective small groups is an extension of the notion of exhaustion of gains to scale or "minimum efficient scale" from Wooders (1979). See also Wooders (1983) for an NTU version.

[16] See Wooders (1992a,b; 1994a).

A pregame (T, Ψ) satisfies SGE if, for each $\varepsilon > 0$, there is an integer $\eta(\varepsilon)$ such that for every profile $n \in \mathbb{Z}_+^T$ there is a partition $\{n^k\}$ of n satisfying

$$\|n^k\| \leq \eta(\varepsilon) \text{ for each subprofile } n^k \text{ and}$$

$$\Psi^s(n) - \Sigma_k \Psi(n^k) \leq \varepsilon \|n\|,$$

where

$$\Psi^s(n) \stackrel{\text{def}}{=} \max \Sigma_k \Psi(m^k)$$

and the maximum is taken over all partitions of n into subprofiles (collections of profiles satisfying $\Sigma_k m^k = n$). SGE dictates that, given $\varepsilon > 0$, there is a group size $\eta(\varepsilon)$ such that within ε per capita of the gains to group formation can be realized by the collective activities of groups containing no more than $\eta(\varepsilon)$ players.

The advantage of SGE over the prior combination of conditions of per capita boundedness and of many players of each type is that SGE allows arbitrarily small percentages of players of each type. With "thickness" requiring that there be many close substitutes for each player in any game, SGE and PCB are equivalent.

Proposition 6.1. *(Woaders 1994a, Theorem 4): With "thickness," SGE = PCB.*

(1) Let (T, Ψ) be a pregame satisfying SGE. Then the pregame satisfies PCB.

(2) Let (T, Ψ) be a pregame satisfying PCB. Then, given any positive real number ρ, construct a new pregame (T, Ψ_ρ) for which the domain of Ψ_ρ is restricted to profiles f where, for each $t = 1, \ldots, T$, either $\frac{f_t}{\|f\|} > \rho$ or $f_t = 0$. Then (T, Ψ_ρ) satisfies SGE on its domain.

We note that the preceding equivalence does not in general hold for parameterized collections of games.

Example 6.3. Nonequivalence of SGE and PCB for parameterized collections. *Consider a sequence of inessential games*[17] *$\{(N^k, v_k)\}$, where, in the kth game, a group S can realize the total payoff $|S|k$. Clearly, even one-player groups are strictly effective, but the sequence of games does not satisfy PCB.*

One can wonder how big the gap is between SGE and assumptions ensuring that a game can be approximated by one with a continuum of players. A new definition is needed to illustrate that in fact SGE is implicit in continuum models such as that of Aumann (1964) and many subsequent papers. The condition of *small-group negligibility* (SGN), to follow, is that small groups of players cannot have significant effects on economic outcomes. Note that a model with an atomless continuum of players has the property that a small group of players (a set of measure zero) can be ignored. For economies with many players (but a finite number) and quasi-linear

---

[17] An *inessential game* has the property that there are no strict gains to forming coalitions containing more than one player.

utilities to be well approximated by a model with an atomless continuum of players it is necessary that small groups of players not have large impacts. This is illustrated in the following example.

Example 6.4. SGE resolves the problem of "scarce types." *Consider a sequence of games* $\{(N^k, v_k)\}$ *with two types of players. Suppose that the payoff to any group S of players with n_1 players of type 1 and n_2 players of type 2 is given by*

$$v_k(S) = \begin{cases} n_1 + n_2 & \text{if } n_1 > 0 \\ 0 & \text{otherwise.} \end{cases}$$

A limiting continuum representation of such a game cannot treat situations with measure zero of players of type 1. If each game in the sequence $\{(N^k, v_k)\}$ *has a positive proportion of players of type 1 but this proportion becomes negligible – type 1 becomes "scarce" – then the continuum does not provide a good approximation to large finite games in the sequence. Examples of this type are easy to develop.*

Given a pregame (T, Ψ) and a profile $f \in \mathbb{Z}_+^T$, let $\sigma(f)$ denote the *support of* f, that is, the set $\{t : f_t \neq 0\}$. A pregame (T, Ψ) satisfies SGN introduced in Wooders (1994c), if, for any sequence of profiles $\{f^\nu\}$ such that

$$\|f^\nu\| \to \infty \text{ as } \nu \to \infty,$$

$$\sigma(f^\nu) = \sigma(f^{\nu'}) \text{ for all } \nu \text{ and } \nu', \text{ and}$$

$$\lim_{\nu \to \infty} \frac{\Psi(f^\nu)}{\|f^\nu\|} \text{ exists,}$$

and for any sequence of profiles $\{\ell^\nu\}$ with

$$\lim_{\nu \to \infty} \frac{\|\ell^\nu\|}{\|f^\nu\|} = 0,$$

it holds that

$$\lim_{\nu \to \infty} \frac{\Psi(f^\nu + \ell^\nu)}{\|f^\nu + \ell^\nu\|} \text{ exists, and}$$

$$\lim_{\nu \to \infty} \frac{\Psi(f^\nu + \ell^\nu)}{\|f^\nu + \ell^\nu\|} = \lim_{\nu \to \infty} \frac{\Psi(f^\nu)}{\|f^\nu\|}.$$

The property of SGN appears quite mild. It simply ensures that in "thick" games – ones with many players of a few types, a small group of possibly distinct player types cannot significantly affect per capita payoffs of members of the large player set. When it is postulated that a small group of participants cannot affect aggregate outcomes it is also of necessity postulated that all gains to collective activities can be realized by small groups.

Proposition 6.2. *(Wooders 2004a): With PCB, SGE = SGN. Let (T, Ψ) be a pregame satisfying PCB. Then (T, Ψ) satisfies SGE if and only if it satisfies SGN.*

This equivalence is not as paradoxical as it may at first seem. Consider, for example, a marriage game with many males and many females of either a finite number of types or with attributes in some compact metric space. All gains to collective activities are realizable by two-player coalitions consisting of a male and a female and singleton sets (consisting of single people). If any small group of players were to withdraw from the game, the maximal per capita payoff to the remaining players would be "nearly" unchanged – small groups are negligible relative to economic aggregates. However, in a marriage game, clearly small groups are effective!

A pregame may be naturally suited to the study of limiting games with a continuum of players, but this concept is not completely satisfactory for analysis of finite economies. First, as Proposition 6.1 and the following example illustrate, the pregame framework itself has hidden consequences – in general, SGE does not imply PCB nor the converse. The aspect of a pregame that the payoff to a group is independent of the total player set in which it is contained rules out widespread externalities and has implications of economic substance. Moreover, it appears more difficult to gain intuition into "boundary cases" in which some player types become negligible percentages of the population.

The pregame framework may also hide what makes the results work: that there are many close substitutes for most players and that groups bounded in size can nearly exhaust gains to collective activities. In addition, because the pregame framework specifies conditions on payoffs for all groups, no matter how large, in general it is difficult, if not impossible to estimate the pregame function Ψ. In contrast, within the framework of parameterized collections, there are only four parameters to be estimated: δ, T, β, and B. This point is stressed in the Kovalenkov–Wooders papers. The notion of β-effective B-bounded groups makes explicit how close coalitions bounded in size by B are to being able to realize all gains to collective activities for a given game.

6.5. Nonemptiness of Approximate Cores of Games in Parameterized Collections

It is well known that games with many players derived from pregames have nonempty approximate cores; the first such results were obtained in Woivders (1979, 1983) for games with and without side payments, respectively. In this section we consider nonemptiness of approximate cores of games in parameterized collections, where we can place an exact lower bound on ε, in terms of the parameters describing the games, for the games in the collection to have nonempty ε-cores. The first result is obtained for the ε-remainder core of a game with T exact types of players and with strictly effective B-bounded groups. This result is new but follows easily from the proof of Lemma 1 in Kovalenkov and Wooders (2001b). Notice that the bound applies uniformly to all games in the collection. This bound will be shown to be exact for some games; see Examples 6.6 and 6.7.

Proposition 6.3. *Nonemptiness of the ε-remainder core. Let $(N, v) \in \Gamma((0, T)$, $(0, B))$ and let ε be a positive real number. Then, if*

$$\varepsilon \geq \frac{T(B-1)}{|N|},$$

the ε-remainder core of (N, v) is nonempty.

The preceding result may suggest that whether a population consists of the "right" numbers of players of each type is in some sense crucial to whether there exists stable outcomes. One would want to have a result that allows for approximate player types and not necessarily strictly effective groups. The following new result is exactly that, and it follows easily from the previous proposition.

Proposition 6.4. *Nonemptiness of the ε_1-remainder ε_2-core. Let $(N, v) \in \Gamma((\delta, T)$, $(\beta, B))$, let ε_1 be a positive real number and let ε_2 be a nonnegative real number. Then, if*

$$\varepsilon_1 \geq \frac{T(B-1)}{|N|} \quad \text{and} \quad \varepsilon_2 \geq \delta + \beta,$$

the ε_1-remainder ε_2-core of (N, v) is nonempty.

One possible criticism of the preceding results may be that a subset of agents is ignored.[18] It is not difficult to imagine that there is some small percentage of "unemployed" or "underemployed" players who create some friction and some instability but that their effects are minor. For example, suppose the population consists of a million and one identical individuals, only two-person clubs are effective, and each period an underemployed person can only negotiate with one other person; then, most of the time, almost all individuals can be in two-person clubs. Ongoing research on the noncooperative foundations of economies with clubs is making this sort of intuition clear (cf. Arnold and Wooders 2002).

Another approach to addressing the possible instability of an economy is to allow transfers from individuals who happen to be in more favorable clubs to those less favorably situated. To obtain such a result for games in a parameterized collection, per capita boundedness is indispensable.

Proposition 6.5. *(Kovalenkov and Wooders 2001a): Nonemptiness of the ε-core. Let $(N, v) \in \Gamma((\delta, T), (\beta, B))$, where (N, v) has a per capita bound of C. Let ε be a positive real number. Then, if*

$$\varepsilon \geq \frac{TC(B-1)}{|N|} + \delta + \beta$$

the ε-core of (N, v) is nonempty.

The following simple example illustrates how Propositions 6.3–6.5 can be applied.

---

[18] In fact, this has a precedent in the properties of approximate price-taking equilibrium in exchange economies.

Example 6.5. Applications of our nonemptiness results. *Let us consider a game* (N, v) *with two types of players. Assume that any player alone can realize only 0 units or less of payoff, that is,* $v(\{i\}) = 0$ *for all* $i \in N$. *Also assume that any coalition of two players of types* i *and* j *can get up to* γ_{ij} *units of payoff to divide. Let* γ_{11}, $\gamma_{12} = \gamma_{21}$ *and* γ_{22} *be some numbers from the interval* $[0, 1]$. *An arbitrary coalition can gain only what it can obtain in partitions in which no member of the partition contains more than two players; the game is essentially superadditive. We leave it to the reader to check that* $(N, v) \in \Gamma((0, 2), (0, 2))$ *and has a per capita bound of* $1/2$. *Thus, it follows from Proposition 6.3 that for* $\varepsilon \geq \frac{2}{|N|}$ *the* ε-*remainder core of* (N, v) *is nonempty, from Proposition 6.4 that for* $\varepsilon_1 \geq \frac{2}{|N|}$ *and* $\varepsilon_2 \geq 0$ *the* ε_1-*remainder* ε_2-*core of* (N, v) *is nonempty, and from Proposition 6.5 that for* $\varepsilon \geq \frac{1}{|N|}$ *the* ε-*core of* (N, v) *is nonempty. Notice that these results hold uniformly for all possible numbers* γ_{11}, $\gamma_{12} = \gamma_{21}$, *and* γ_{22}.

In some cases the bounds given in Propositions 6.3–6.5 are exact. The following two examples illustrate this first for inessential and then for some essential games.

Example 6.6. The bounds are exact for inessential games. *Let* (N, v) *be a game in which all coalitions are inessential (that is, only singleton coalitions matter). Such a game has a nonempty core. Thus, for every* $\varepsilon \geq 0$, *the* ε-*remainder core, the* ε-*remainder* ε-*core, and the* ε-*core of* (N, v) *are nonempty and the lower bound on epsilon is zero. To apply the propositions, notice that* $(N, v) \in \Gamma((0, |N|), (0, 1))$ *and has some per capita bound. The lower bounds given in Propositions 6.3–6.5 are all zeros because* $\delta = \beta = 0$ *and* $(B - 1) = 0$. *Even in this extreme case, the bounds work well.*

Example 6.7. The bounds are exact for some essential games. *Consider games in which, given some positive real number* K, *within each game all players are identical, only two-player coalitions are effective, and any two-player coalition can earn a payoff of less than or equal to* $2K$. *Obviously all these games belong to the class* $\Gamma((0, 1), (0, 2))$ *and have a per capita bound of* K. *In this case, the bounds from Propositions 6.3–6.5 become* $\frac{T(B-1)}{|N|} = \frac{1}{|N|}$, $\delta + \beta = 0$, *and* $\frac{TC(B-1)}{|N|} + \delta + \beta = \frac{K}{|N|}$. *The core is empty if the number of players is odd. We immediately see that the lower bound on the proportion of the remainders is* $\frac{1}{|N|}$, *as Propositions 6.3 and 6.4 have predicted. The bound for Proposition 6.5 requires more details. Let* $|N| = 2m + 1$ *for some positive integer* m. *We can determine the least lower bound on* ε *so that the* ε-*core is nonempty for any game* (N, v) *in the collection with* $|N| = 2m + 1$. *In particular, suppose we assign each of the first* $2m$ *players the payoff* $K - \varepsilon$ *and the remaining player the payoff* $2m\varepsilon$. *Suppose* ε^* *solves* $K - \varepsilon^* = 2m\varepsilon^*$. *Then the* ε-*core is nonempty for any game in the collection for any* $\varepsilon \geq \varepsilon^*$ *but may be empty otherwise. (Take, for example,* $K = 1$ *and* $m = 1$. *Then* $\varepsilon^* = \frac{1}{3}$ *and the* ε-*core is empty for any* $\varepsilon < \frac{1}{3}$.) *Solving for* ε^*, *we obtain*

$$\varepsilon^* = \frac{K}{(2m + 1)} = \frac{K}{|N|}.$$

This bound coincides with the bound given by the Proposition 6.5. Thus, the bounds from Propositions 6.3–6.5 are the best possible bounds for this collection.

In the next and later sections we present more economical examples.

6.6. Examples of Coalition Production Economies with Small or Large Optimal Firms

For brevity, the following example, illustrating the application of our results to a familiar situation, is somewhat informal. Although the example is worded in terms of firms and workers, as in Crawford and Knoer (1981), for example, it could easily be modified to treat the hospital and intern matching problem as in Roth (1984) or any such assignment problem. The example also illustrates the application of our results to situations in which there is a compact metric space of player types, essentially a special case of the parameterized collection of games framework, and an extension of the finite-type pregame framework above.

Example 6.8a. Coalition production with small optimal groups. *Suppose there are two sorts of players, firms and workers. The set of possible types of workers is given by the points in the interval $[0, 1]$, and the set of possible types of firms is given by the points in the interval $[1, 2]$. To derive a game from this information, let N be any finite player set and let ξ be an attribute function, that is, a function from N into $[0, 2]$. In interpretation, if $\xi(i) \in [0, 1]$, then i is a worker, and if $\xi(i) \in [1, 2]$, then i is a firm. Firms can profitably hire up to three workers, and the payoff to a firm i and a set of workers $W(i) \subset N$ containing no more than three members is given by $v(\{i\} \bigcup W(i)) = \xi(i) + \sum_{j \in W(i)} \xi(j)$. Workers and firms can earn positive payoff only by cooperating, and thus $v(\{i\}) = 0$ for all $i \in N$. For any group $S \subset N$, define $v(S)$ as the maximum payoff the group S could realize by splitting into groups containing either workers only or one firm and no more than three workers. This completes the specification of the game.*

We leave it to the reader to verify that for any positive integer m every game derived from the pregame is a member of the collection $\Gamma((1/m, 2m), (0, 4))$ and has a per capita bound of 2.

Proposition 6.3 does not apply to this collection.

Proposition 6.4 implies that for $\varepsilon_1 \geq \frac{6m}{|N|} + \frac{1}{m}$ and $\varepsilon_2 > 1/m$, the game (N, v) has a nonempty ε_1-remainder ε_2-core. Thus, by taking first m and then $|N|$ as very large numbers both ε_1 and ε_2 can be made arbitrarily small.

Proposition 6.5 implies that, given $1/m < \varepsilon$, if $\varepsilon \geq \frac{12m}{|N|} + \frac{1}{m}$, then the game (N, v) has a nonempty ε-core. One can easily see that for any $\varepsilon > 0$ the ε-core of (N, v) is nonempty for a large enough $|N|$.

We can revise the preceding example so that firm sizes are unbounded and it is optimal for each firm to be as large as possible but yet the conditions required in Proposition 6.4 are satisfied.

Example 6.8b. Coalition production with large optimal groups. *Take as given the same information as in Example 6.8a except we now think of $\xi(i)$ as representing the fixed cost of the firm i and consider only games in which, for some given $\rho > 0$,* *the number of firms is at least a positive proportion ρ of the total number of play-ers. The payoff to a firm i and a nonempty set of workers $W(i) \subset N$, is given by $v(\{i\} \cup W(i)) = \sum_{j \in W(i)} \xi(j) - \xi(i)$. It can be verified that given $\beta > 0$, every game derived from this information has a per capita bound of 1 and is a member of $\Gamma((\frac{1}{m}, 2m), (\beta, B^*))$, where B^* denotes the smallest integer greater than or equal to $\max(2/\beta, 1/\rho)$. Thus Propositions 6.4 and 6.5 again can be applied to get a bound on $|N|$ for the nonemptiness of the ε_1-remainder ε_2-core or the ε-core for an arbitrarily small $\varepsilon_1, \varepsilon_2$, and ε. Let us rule out the case in which an optimal outcome would leave all workers unemployed. Then an optimal outcome would assign all workers to a firm i' (if there are any firms in the player set) satisfying $\xi(i') \leq \xi(i)$ for all firms i; an optimal group consists of the entire player set.*

Although we will not do so here, it is obvious that one could modify the models described in Chapter 7 of this volume to allow large clubs. Indeed, this is done in a general setting in Allouch and Wooders (2004) and in situations with multiple memberships in Chapter 8 of this volume.

We note that early works on coalition production economies include Böhm (1974), Sondermann (1974), and Hildenbrand (1974). Böehm assumes constant returns to population size, thereby ruling out the possibility of ever-increasing returns. Several other examples of coalition production economies allowing increasing returns are contained in Shubik and Wooders (1983b).

6.7. Equal Treatment of Similar Individuals

An important result for the competitiveness of large economies with limited gains to coalition formation is that cores and approximate cores treat all or most similar players nearly equally. Indeed, such results have been known for economies with private goods since Debreu and Scarf (1963).[19] It is easy to develop examples to demonstrate that not all players of the same type are necessarily treated approximately equally by an ε-core payoff. For example, consider an inessential game (N, v) in which each coalition S has value of $|S|$. Thus, all players are identical. For any $\varepsilon > 0$, the payoff $x = (1 + (|N| - 1)\varepsilon, 1 - \varepsilon, \ldots, 1 - \varepsilon)$ is in the ε-core. For large $|N|$, the first player will be treated much better than others.

The following result for pregames shows that most players of the same type are of necessity treated approximately equally in the ε-cores.

Proposition 6.6. *(Wooders 1992b): Equal treatment propoerty of the ε-core. Let (T, Ψ) be a pregame satisfying small group effectiveness. Given any real numbers $\delta > 0$ and $\lambda > 0$ there is a real number $\varepsilon^* > 0$ and an integer $\rho(\delta, \lambda, \varepsilon^*)$ such that for each $\varepsilon \in [0, \varepsilon^*]$ and for every game n with $\|n_t\| \geq \rho(\delta, \lambda, \epsilon^*)$, if x is in the*

---

[19] For TU (and NTU) games with a finite set of player types and in which all gains to coalition formation are exhausted by coalitions bounded in size, all payoff vectors in the core have the equal treatment property (Wooders 1983, Theorem 3). For TU games, approximate cores of games with many players treat most identical players nearly equally; see Wooders (1992b) and references therein. In the context of economies with general preferences, see especially Hildenbrand and Kirman (1973), who show that, in large economies, unequal-treatment allocations in the core disappear.

ε-core of the derived game with player set N, then

$$|\{(t,q) : |x_{(t,q)} - z_t| > \delta\}| < \lambda\|n\|,$$

where $z_t = \frac{1}{n_t}\sum_{q=1}^{n_t} x_{(t,q)}$, which is the average payoff received by players of type t.

Note that from the equivalence, with thickness of the player set, of small group effectiveness and PCB, Proposition 6.6 holds when we replace SGE by PCB. An extension of the preceding result to pregames with a compact metric space of player attributes appears in Wooders (2004b).

For parameterized collections of games, our proofs of nonemptiness of approximate cores typically demonstrate existence of a point that treats players of the same approximate type equally, but this, of course, does not imply any equal treatment result for all payoffs in approximate cores. In Kovalenkov and Wooders (2001a), however, we introduce the concept of limited side payments and show that for games in parameterized collections satisfying limited side payments all payoffs in approximate cores treat similar players nearly equally. Limited side payments rule out large transfers between groups of players.

For example, consider a $2n$-player matching or marriage game with n identical males and n identical females. Suppose that the payoff to being unmatched is 0 and the payoff to any male–female pair is 1. It is well understood that for such a game the core has the equal treatment property. Moreover, for any payoff vector in the $ε$-core, the percentage of players of any gender whose payoff differs significantly from the average for their gender becomes small as n grows large – most players of the same type are assigned nearly the same payoffs. This follows from the observation that, because every matched pair must receive at least $1 - 2ε$, the payoff that can be transferred to players receiving more than the average for their genders is bounded. For any $ε > 0$, however, payoff vectors in the $ε$-core may be far from equal treatment. If side payments are unlimited (as in a TU game), there are $ε$-core payoff vectors that assign one player $2nε$ more than any other player of the same gender. Now suppose that utility is transferable only within marriages but not between marriages. We might think of a matched pair of players as indulging in some activity that yields pleasure only to them. Alternatively, we may suppose that for some reason – political infeasibility, for example – transfers are not made between coalitions or that there is simply no reason for such transfers to be made. With this restriction, the behavior of $ε$-core payoff vectors changes dramatically. Now any payoff vector x in the $ε$-core for our example must have the property that for any two players i and j of the same gender, $|x_i - x_j| \le 2ε$. Note that this depends on some transferability of utility within marriages. If we rule out any side payments even within marriages so that, for example, each member of a marriage could realize at most $\frac{1}{2}$, then we again lose the equal treatment property of the core and the result that $ε$-core payoff vectors treat similar players similarly.

Thus, to obtain a result that all players of the same type are treated approximately equally by all the payoff vectors in the $ε$-core of a game, we must require that there be some degree of side payments within nearly effective small groups but must rule out unlimited side payments. Such a class of games is addressed in detail in Kovalenkov and Wooders (2001a). In this chapter we concentrate on the properties of games with side payments.

We note that another sort of limiting equal treatment result is presented in Engl and Scotchmer (1996) for games with side payments and economies with quasi-linear utilities. There, the authors show that for small epsilon, ε-core payoffs to sufficiently large *groups* of players can be approximated by equal treatment payoffs. Engl and Scotchmer is more general in allowing divisibility of players but requires and relies on differentiability of the limiting payoff function.

6.8. Games and Markets

Recall that a market is defined as an exchange economy in which all agents have quasi-linear, continuous, and concave utility functions.[20] Shapley and Shubik (1969) introduce the notion of a direct market derived from a totally balanced game (one with the property that the game and all its subgames have nonempty cores). Shubik and Wooders (1982) note that Wooders' nonemptiness of approximate cores results imply that games with many players and a fixed distribution of player types are approximately market games. Wooders (1994a) characterizes the equivalence of games with many players satisfying small group effectiveness (or PCB and "thickness" of the total player set) and market games. Here, we characterize parameterized collections of games as market games.

In the Shapley and Shubik direct market, each player is associated with a commodity and all agents in the economy have the same utility function. Here, we take the player types of the game as the commodity or attribute types and assign all participants in the market the same utility function, which is derived from the worth function of the game.[21] We first review the notion of a market as defined in Shapley and Shubik (1969, 1975) and then the notion of the direct market. The concept of a direct market is modified, however, to take account of the feature that there may be agents who are perfect substitutes for each other.

6.8.1. Markets

Let the set of participants in the economy be

$$N = \{(t, q) : t = 1, \ldots, T, \text{and } q = 1, \ldots, n_t\}.$$

Let $(y, \xi) \in \mathbb{R}_+^T \times \mathbb{R}$ denote a commodity bundle. Assume that all participants have the same concave utility function given by $\widehat{u}(y, \xi) = u(y) + \xi$, where $y \in \mathbb{R}_+^T$ and

---

[20] This is fairly standard terminology in the literature of game-theoretic general equilibrium c.f. Shapley and Shubik (1969, 1975).

[21] This dates back to the earliest papers on large games as markets, Wooders (1992b, 1994a), including a 1988 CORE DP version of 1994a, and Winter and Wooders (1990). See also Shubik and Wooders (1982).

　　For our purposes in this paper it suffices to restrict attention to premarkets in which all participants in the economy have the same utility function. More complete treatments are in Wooders (1992b, 1994a) and Shapley and Shubik (1969, 1975). These papers show equivalence of market games and large games with small effective groups.

$\xi \in \mathbb{R}$. The endowment of the (t, q)th participant of the first T commodities is $a^{tq} \in \mathbb{R}_+^T$. For simplicity and without loss of generality, we can assume that no participant is endowed with any nonzero amount of the $(T + 1)$th good, the "money" or medium of exchange. With the price of the $(T + 1)$th commodity ξ set equal to 1, a *competitive outcome* is a price vector π in $\mathbb{R}^T$ listing prices for the first T commodities and an allocation $\{(y^{tq}, \xi^{tq}) \in \mathbb{R}_+^T \times \mathbb{R} : (t, q) \in N\}$ for which

$$u(y^{tq}) - \pi \cdot (y^{tq} - a^{tq}) \geq u(\widehat{y}) - \pi \cdot (\widehat{y} - a^{tq}) \text{ for all } \widehat{y} \in \mathbb{R}_+^T, (t, q) \in N,$$

$$\sum_{(t,q)\in N} y^{tq} = \sum_{(t,q)} a^{tq}, \text{ and}$$

$$\sum_{(t,q)\in N} \xi^{tq} = 0.$$

Given a competitive outcome with allocation $\{(y^{tq}, \xi^{tq}) \in \mathbb{R}_+^T \times \mathbb{R} : (t, q) \in N\}$ and price vector π, the *competitive payoff vector* is given by

$$(u(y^{tq}) - \pi \cdot (y^{tq} - a^{tq}) : (t, q) \in N).$$

In the following we will assume that for each t, all participants of type t, $\{(t, q) : q = 1, \ldots, n_t\}$, have the same endowment, that is, $a^{tq} = a^{tq'}$ for all q, q'. In this case, a competitive payoff has the equal treatment property; that is, $u(y^{tq}) - \pi \cdot (y^{tq} - a^{tq}) = u(y^{tq'}) - \pi \cdot (y^{tq'} - a^{tq'})$ for each t and all q, q'. Thus, in this case, a competitive payoff vector can be represented by a vector in $\mathbb{R}^T$ with one component for each player type.

6.8.2. Direct Markets

The direct market generated by a game simply endows each participant in the economy with one unit of one commodity, him- or herself. Our construction differs in that we take the types of players as the types of commodities.

Let (N, v), where $N = \{(t, q) : t = 1, \ldots, T \text{ and } q = 1, \ldots, n_t\}$, be a game with T types of players. To construct the Shapley–Shubik direct market generated by the game, but in which the player types are the commodities, suppose that each agent of type t is endowed with one unit of the tth commodity and thus has endowment $\mathbf{1}_t = (0, \ldots, 0, 1, 0, \ldots, 0) \in \mathbb{R}_+^T$, where the "1" is in the tth position. (There is no need to make the idealized money, the $(T + 1)$th commodity of the preceding subsection, explicit.) The total endowment of the economy is then given by $\sum n_t \mathbf{1}_t = (n_1, \ldots, n_T) = n$. Given $S \subset N$, let *profile*(S) denote the vector in $\mathbb{Z}_+^T$ defined by its components

$$profile(S)_t \overset{\text{def}}{=} |S \cap \{(t, q) : q = 1, \ldots, n_t\}|.$$

A profile of a set S simply lists the numbers of players of each type in S.

For any vector $y \in \mathbb{R}_+^T$, define[22]

$$u(y) \overset{\text{def}}{=} \max \sum_{S \subset N} \gamma_S v(S),$$

---

[22] The reader might notice that the definition of u is similar to the definition of the worth function of the balanced cover of a game in which the "numbers" of players of each type are given by y.

the maximum running over all $\{\gamma_S \geq 0 : S \subset N\}$ satisfying

$$\sum_{S \subset N} \gamma_S \, profile(S) = y.$$

If we mimic the proof of Shapley and Shubik (1969), but for the types case, it can be verified that the function u is concave and one-homogeneous.[23] Taking the utility function u as the utility function of each agent $i \in N$, we have generated a market, called the *direct market*, from the game (N, v). Let $[u; (N, v)]$ denote the direct market generated by the game (N, v) and let (N, v^u) denote the game derived, using the standard procedure, from the direct market, where

$$v^u(S) \overset{\text{def}}{=} u(profile(S)) \quad \text{for } S \subset N.$$

Remark. As shown by Shapley and Shubik (1969) (for the case in which each agent is his or her own unique type), the game (N, v^u) generated by the direct market is the totally balanced cover of (N, v).[24]

Let $\widehat{\Pi}(N, v^u) \subset \mathbb{R}^T$ denote the equal treatment core[25] of the game (N, v^u). Note that

$$\widehat{\Pi}(N, v^u) = \{\pi \in \mathbb{R}_+^T : \pi \cdot n = u(n) \text{ and } \pi \cdot s \geq u(s) \text{ for all } s \in \mathbb{Z}_+^T, s \leq n\}.$$

The following proposition extends a result due to Shapley and Shubik (1975). The only difference is that Shapley and Shubik do not have player types.

Proposition 6.7. *Core-equilibrium equivalence. For the direct market $[u; (N, v)]$ the set of competitive price vectors for $[u; (N, v)]$ coincides with the equal treatment core $\widehat{\Pi}(N, v^u)$.*

This proposition states that the set of competitive price vectors for the direct market coincides with the equal treatment core of the game obtained from this market. In general, many different markets can be constructed that generate the same game, but the core-equilibrium equivalence does not hold for some of these markets (see Shapley and Shubik 1975, Theorem 2). The direct market representing a game is just one of these markets that has an advantage of simplicity and for which the core-equilibrium equivalence holds.

6.8.3. Approximation of Games by Markets

We first briefly review the main result of Wooders (1994a) on the equivalence of games and markets. Let (T, Ψ) be a pregame satisfying SGE. For each vector x in $\mathbb{R}_+^T$, define

$$U(x) \overset{\text{def}}{=} \|x\| \lim_{v \to \infty} \frac{\Psi(f^v)}{\|f^v\|},$$

---

[23] Note also that u is continuous and is independent of whether the game is superadditive.

[24] The *totally balanced cover* of (N, v) is a game (N, v^b), where for all $S \subset N$: $v^b(S) \geq v(S)$ and as small as possible consistent with the nonemptiness of the core of (S, v^b).

[25] As noted previously, the equal treatment core of a game has a long history dating back to Shubik (1959). It was introduced in the context of pregames in Wooders (1979) and appears also in Wooders (1983) and Shubik and Wooders (1983a).

where the sequence $\{f^\nu\}$ satisfies

$$\lim_{\nu \to \infty} \|f^\nu\| = \infty \text{ and}$$

$$\lim_{\nu \to \infty} \frac{f^\nu}{\|f^\nu\|} = \frac{x}{\|x\|}.$$

In Wooders (1994a), it is shown that with SGE for any $x \in \mathbb{R}_+^T$ the preceding limit exists and $U(\cdot)$ is well defined. Moreover, as first noted by Aumann (1987),[26] the function U is concave. Briefly, the main result is as follows:

Proposition 6.8. *(Wooders 1994a). Large games are market games. Let (T, Ψ) be a pregame satisfying SGE and let U be as defined immediately above. Then, given $\varepsilon > 0$ there is an integer $\eta(\varepsilon)$ such that if f is a profile with $\|f\| > \eta(\varepsilon)$, then*

$$\frac{U(f)}{\|f\|} - \frac{\Psi(f)}{\|f\|} < \varepsilon.$$

The preceding proposition implies that we can approximate a large game by a market game in which the utility or payoff function of all participants in the economy is given by the function U and each participant owns one unit of one commodity, of his or her "type." It also holds that the core payoffs of the market game given by the subgradients of the function U, provide an approximation to ε-cores of games derived from the pregame. Given a population profile n, the subgradients of the function U, evaluated at n, are core payoffs and also are prices for player types in the market generated by the game. Note also that because a market (as defined in Shapley and Shubik 1969 and in this chapter) has a nonempty core, the equivalence of markets and games confirms Wooders' (1979, 1983) and subsequent results showing that games with many players have nonempty approximate cores.[27]

Turning to the framework of parameterized games, we will treat one case – a game with many players and exact player types say $(N, v) \in \Gamma((0, T), (\beta, B))$. Given (N, v), let us take the smallest ε^* such that the game (N, v) has a nonempty ε^*-core. By Proposition 6.5, $\frac{TC(B-1)}{|N|} + \beta \geq \varepsilon^*$.

Then let us construct a game (N, w) in the following way: $w(N) = v(N)$ and $w(S) = \max(0, v(S) - \varepsilon |S|)$. Obviously, the game (N, w) will have a nonempty core. By a convexity argument the core will include an equal treatment payoff. Hence, the equal treatment core of (N, w) is nonempty.

Therefore, if we construct a corresponding direct market $[u; (N, w)]$, then a game derived from this market (N, v^u) will be a totally balanced cover of the game (N, w). Moreover, by Proposition 6.7, the set of competitive price vectors for $[u; (N, v)]$ coincides with $\widehat{\Pi}(N, v^u)$, which belongs to the ε-core of the original game (N, v). Moreover, by construction $u(profile(N)) = v^u(N) = w(N) = v(N)$ and $u(profile(S)) = v^u(S) \geq w(S) = v(S) - \varepsilon^*|S|$. Thus the following approximation result is obtained.

---

[26] Although under a stronger condition, bounding gains to group formation.
[27] We note that, in a recent contribution, Flam, Owen, and Saboya (2002) show that, for an economy, SGE and differentiability of utility or payoff functions imply nonemptiness of strong ε-cores.

Proposition 6.9. *Approximation of games by markets. Let* $(N, v) \in \Gamma((0, T),$ $(\beta, B))$. *Assume that* (N, v) *has a per capita bound of* C. *Let*

$$\varepsilon = \frac{TC(B-1)}{|N|} + \beta.$$

Then there is a market with T *types of commodities and player set* N *and in which each individual owns one unit of one commodity and has the same continuous, concave utility function* u *such that*

(i) $\frac{u(profile(N))}{|N|} = \frac{v(N)}{|N|}$,

(ii) $\frac{u(profile(S))}{|S|} \geq \frac{v(S)}{|S|} - \varepsilon$ *for all* $S \subset N$ *and*

(iii) the competitive outcomes of the market are in the ε-*core of the game.*

Notice that the games from the parameterized collection $\Gamma((\delta, T), (\beta, B))$ with $\delta > 0$ can easily be approximated by games from $\Gamma((0, T), (\beta, B))$ and thus also by markets described in Proposition 6.9. The authors are planning to investigate further the representation of games in parameterized collections as markets in a separate paper.

6.9. Examples of Local Public Goods Economies

6.9.1. An Example of an Economy with Few Jurisdictions

The example of this section illustrates application of our results to an economy with local public goods and a fixed number of jurisdictions. The example relates to the material in Chapter 5 of this volume on the trade-offs between increasing returns and preference diversity and also to several other models including, for example, those of Westhoff (1977); Vohra (1987); Epple, Romer, and Sieg (2001); and Fernandez and Rogerson (1996).

Example 6.9. A local public goods economy with few jurisdictions. *Suppose that there are* K *jurisdictions; let* $\mathcal{J} = \{J_1, \ldots, J_K\}$ *denote a set of jurisdictions. Each jurisdiction* $J_1, \ldots, J_K$ *can produce a public good* y *at a cost of* 1 *per unit. We take jurisdictions in* $\mathcal{J}$ *to be profit maximizing and let the payoff function of jurisdiction* J_k, *producing* $y_k \in \mathbb{R}_+$ *units of the public good, be given by* $\tau_k - y_k$, *where* τ_k, *determined endogenously, is the total contribution of private good to public goods provision in jurisdiction* J_k. *Note that because jurisdiction* J_k *can choose to produce* 0 *units of the public good, the individual rationality of* J_k *would imply that* $\tau_k \geq y_k$.

Let $N = \{1, \ldots, n\}$ denote a set of consumers. Let

$$u_i(y_i, \zeta_i) \stackrel{\text{def}}{=} h_i(y_i) + \zeta_i$$

be the utility function of the agent i, where $\zeta_i \in \mathbb{R}$ denotes the amount of private good that i consumes and $y_i \in \mathbb{R}_+$ denotes the amount of public good produced in the jurisdiction of which i is a member. Let us assume that all functions h_i are concave and differentiable and that $\lim_{y \to \infty} \frac{dh_i}{dy}(y) = 0$. Note that the individual rationality of consumer i would imply that i provides private goods only to one jurisdiction, where i is a member. Let ω_i denote the endowment of private good of consumer i.

In interpretation, there are K jurisdictions that may produce the public good at different levels. We will allow the possibility that some consumers do not belong to any of the jurisdictions J_k. Implicitly, there is an outside option – the possibility of free movement to some place where no public goods are provided.

The preceding information determines an economy and also a derived game with side payments. The total player set is $\mathcal{J} \cup N$, the jurisdictions, and the consumers. A *feasible state of the economy* is a partition $\mathcal{P}$ of consumers into jurisdictions and singleton sets, an amount $y_k \in \mathbb{R}_+$ of public good for each jurisdiction J_k, $k = 1, \ldots, K$, an amount of private good $\zeta_i \in \mathbb{R}$ for each player i, and an amount of revenue $\tau_k \in \mathbb{R}_+$ for each jurisdiction J_k satisfying

$$\sum_k \sum_{i \in J_k} \zeta_i + \sum_{J_k} \tau_k = \sum_k \sum_{i \in J_k} \omega_i$$

(the amount of private good used in consumption plus that used in production of public good equals the total initial endowment). It is assumed that those consumers in singleton sets – that is, not in any of the jurisdictions in $\mathcal{J}$ – simply consume their endowments.

With any feasible state of the economy we can associate a payoff vector

$$u = (\tau_1 - y_1, \ldots, \tau_K - y_K, u_1(y_1, \zeta_1), \ldots, u_n(y_n, \zeta_n)),$$

where $\tau_k - y_k$ is the payoff to jurisdiction J_k, $k = 1, \ldots, K$, and $u_i(y_i, \zeta_i)$ is the payoff to consumer i, $i = 1, \ldots, n$. Also, for any subset of consumers and jurisdictions, we can define the maximum total payoff achievable by the group. Thus, a game in characteristic form is determined.

Note that all jurisdictions $J_1, \ldots, J_K$ are perfect substitutes for each other. If we suppose that all endowments of private good are contained in some compact interval $[0, \overline{\omega}]$ and the functions $h_i(\cdot)$ are all in some compact set H, then given any $\delta > 0$ we can determine an integer T so that players can be partitioned into T classes of δ-substitutes. Moreover, a bound C on per capita utility can be determined, and given any $\beta > 0$ we can determine an integer B so that the game has β-effective B-bounded groups. Thus, from Proposition 6.5, if the number of consumers n is "large," then the ε-core is nonempty for small ε. Moreover, an explicit bound can be computed on how large n should be.

One of the major research issues for economies with local public goods is whether consumers will segregate into jurisdictions consisting of similar individuals; see for example, Chapters 5, 7, 8, and 13 and references therein of this volume. The model of this example can also be modified to address this question. Let us suppose that all consumers have the same valuation function h for the public good so $h_i = h$ for all consumers $i = 1, \ldots, n$ and that h is concave. Suppose also that $\omega_i \leq \omega_{i'}$ if $i \leq i'$. Then, this example is still encompassed by the framework of parameterized collections of games and satisfies conditions ensuring that the derived game is consecutive.

Some of the models noted above, such as that of Epple, Romer, and Sieg (2001) have majority voting rather than profit-maximizing entrepreneurs. With majority voting within jurisdictions on the level of public goods to be provided, it is more complicated to adopt the quasi-linear framework of this chapter. The NTU framework of Kovalenkov–Wooders, however, may be more easily applied, but treatment of this issue is beyond the scope of this chapter.

An issue of particular interest in this line of research is whether similar individuals sort into similar jurisdictions. We note that results showing approximate cores treat similar individuals similarly are relevant. To address the issue of sorting, we note here that, under the assumptions of essential superadditivity and SGE, the nearly equal treatment of most agents who are similar implies that jurisdictions largely consist of similar individuals. Note also that equal treatment does not apply to jurisdictions.

6.9.2. An Example of an Economy with Free Entry

This example is taken from Shubik and Wooders (1983a) and included here especially to demonstrate that, with congestion, convexity of preferences and production sets is not sufficient to guarantee nonemptiness of the core of the economy. The example also demonstrates how our nonemptiness results apply.

Example 6.10. An economy with a local public good and free entry. *The economy has one private good x and one local public good y. A jurisdiction (or club) is a subset of players who jointly produce the public good for their exclusive consumption. There are T types of consumers, and all consumers of the same type have the same endowments and utility functions. Let N denote the set of agents, $N = \{(t, q) : t = 1, \ldots, T$ and $q = 1, \ldots, n_t\}$, and let $n = (n_1, \ldots, n_T)$ denote the profile of N. Let ω^t denote the endowment of a consumer of type t of the private good, and let $\omega = (\omega^1, \ldots, \omega^T)$.*

Let the utility function of any consumer of type t in a jurisdiction with profile s be

$$u^t = u^{tq}(s, x, y) = xy + c^t(s),$$

where $c^t(\cdot)$ is a function from $\mathbb{Z}_+^T$ to $\mathbb{R}$. Let us define $c(\cdot) = (c^1(\cdot), \ldots, c^T(\cdot))$.

A jurisdiction with profile s has access to the production function

$$x + b(s)z = 0,$$

where x is output of the local public good, z is the input (signed negatively) of private good required to produce x, and $b(\cdot)$ is a function from $\mathbb{Z}_+^T$ to $\mathbb{R}_+$.

Using standard techniques, we can construct a coalitional game (N, v) from this information in which, for any group $S \subset N$, $v(S)$ denotes the maximal total utility achievable by the group if it forms a jurisdiction and produces the public good exclusively for the use of the jurisdiction members. Also, for any profile $s \in \mathbb{Z}_+^T$, define $\Psi(s)$ as the maximal total utility achievable by a group with profile s. It can be verified that

$$\Psi(s) = \frac{b(s)}{4}(s \cdot \omega)^2 + s \cdot c(s).$$

As in the preceding, we also define the superadditive covers v^s and Ψ^s.

For various natural specifications of the functions $b(\cdot)$ and $c(\cdot)$, the core might be empty, but our results on the nonemptiness of approximate cores do apply. To illustrate this point, let us consider a simple case in which all agents are identical, $b(s) = 1$ for all $s \in \mathbb{Z}_+$, and $c(s) = -s^2$. Let the endowment of each agent in the economy be $\omega = 8$. Thus, a per capita payoff in a group with s agents is

$$\frac{\Psi(s)}{|s|} = 16s - s^2.$$

This expression is maximized for $s = 8$. Thus, if the number n of agents in the economy is greater than eight, the core of the economy is nonempty if and only if the agents can be partitioned into jurisdictions each containing eight members. Increasing the size of a jurisdiction beyond eight has negative congestion effects.

Notice that the problem of the emptiness of the core is not due to indivisibility of agents and not resolved by convexity. If we will allow agents to be part-time members of jurisdictions, then the only change will be that we now can consider noninteger group sizes s in the expression of the per capita payoff in a group: $16s - s^2$. But this expression is still maximized only for $s = 8$. Hence, again for $n > 8$, the core is nonempty if and only if n is an integer multiple of 8.

Note that the utility function $u(s; x, y) = xy - s^2$ as a function from $\mathbb{R}_+^3$ to $\mathbb{R}$ is concave. Thus, preferences as well as the production sets are convex. This indicates that when there is a mix of external economies and diseconomies, standard methods of exploiting the convexifying effect of large numbers may not immediately apply.

The game however belongs to the class $\Gamma((0, 1), (0, 8))$ and has a per capita bound of 64. Thus, for any $\varepsilon > 0$, Proposition 6.3 implies that the ε-remainder core of the game is nonempty if $n \geq 7/\varepsilon$, and Proposition 6.5 implies that the ε-core of the game is nonempty if $n \geq 348/\varepsilon$.

6.10. Attribute Games and Exchange Economies

One common interpretation of a game with side payments is to regard the players in the game as commodities or inputs. We call this an *attribute game*, and the equal treatment core is called the *attribute core*.[28]

Now let us assign ownership of *bundles* of commodities to consumers (or other individual units, such as teams or divisions within a firm, as in the literature on subsidy-free pricing); then, another cooperative game is generated. In this game, essentially some players in the original attribute game are "syndicated" or glued together to become one player. Such a game is identical to a Shapley and Shubik (1969) exchange economy.

---

[28] Of course this simply gives a name to a familiar concept – the equal treatment core of a game.

Example 6.11. Application of the results to attribute games. *Consider a glove game in which each player is a RH glove or a LH glove and the payoff to a coalition consisting of n_1 RH glove players and n_2 LH glove players is $\Psi(n_1, n_2) := \min\{n_1, n_2\}$. Suppose that in total there are f_1 RH gloves and f_2 LH gloves. It is immediate that our results apply to this interpretation of a game. Note that this game is a member of the collection $\Gamma((0, 2), (0, 2))$.*

From the data given above, we can construct new games in which players may be endowed with bundles of gloves. By endowing players in this game with various numbers of RH and LH gloves, we create games with possibly several types of players. For specificity, suppose that

1. m_1 players of type 1 are endowed with two RH gloves each;
2. m_2 players of type 2 are endowed with a RH glove; and
3. m_3 players of type 3 are endowed with a LH glove.

Given that there are, in total f_1 RH gloves and f_2 LH gloves, for consistency it must hold that $2m_1 + m_2 = f_1$ and $m_3 = f_2$. Now it is not so immediate that our main results can be applied. However, from the data given, with the three possible endowments of gloves stated above, we can determine a number of types T and a bound B so that the game constructed, say (M, w) for instance, is a member of the collection $\Gamma((0, T), (0, B))$. It is immediate that we can choose $T = 3$. It is fairly obvious, and we leave it for the reader to verify, that $B = 3$ suffices; for this particular example, the largest coalitions that need to form to realize all gains to collective activities consist of one player of type 1 and two players of type 3. Thus, we have that $(M, w) \in \Gamma((0, 3), (0, 3))$, and our results apply to games in $\Gamma((0, 3), (0, 3))$.

We refer the reader to Wooders (1993) for further discussion of attribute games and to Kovalenkov and Wooders (2003b,d) for more recent relationships to the literature on economies and comparative statics in games with many players.

The attribute core was introduced in Wooders (1993) to demonstrate convergence of approximate cores of economies to competitive outcomes. The attribute core is, in fact, closely related to competitive prices for commodities. We note that an alternative approach appears in Engl and Scotchmer (1996). They also consider 'prices' for attributes and payoffs to individuals are determined by the value of the attributes that they own. In Engl and Scotchmer, however, coalitions consist of individuals who may own bundles of commodities. In contrast, the attribute core takes the commodities themselves as players. To illustrate, for the example above the games considered in Engl and Scotchmer (1996) would have $m_1 + m_2 + m_3$ players while the corresponding attribute game would have $2m_1 + m_2 + m_3$ players. As noted previously for games, Engl and Scotchmer obtain the the result that ε-core payoffs for sufficiently large coalitions of individuals are approximated by the values of the endowments of the coalition members.

6.11. Some Relationships to the Literature

6.11.1. The Tiebout Hypothesis and Near Exhaustion of Gains to Scale

A first suggestion in the spirit of this chapter was made by Tiebout (1956), who observed that if public goods are local rather than pure and it is optimal to have many jurisdictions providing such public goods, then the movement of consumers to their preferred jurisdictions will lead to a "market-type," near-optimal outcome and the free-rider problem of economies with pure public goods will not arise. This is the celebrated Tiebout hypothesis. This chapter argues that the Tiebout hypothesis is much more broadly applicable than the local public good environment suggested by Tiebout.[29]

Tiebout's ideas and discussion focus on the provision of differing levels of public goods in a large number of communities. Each community is assumed to tax its residents to cover the costs of public good provision within the community. The movement of consumers to communities in which their wants are best satisfied subject to their budget constraints and competition between communities for residents is conjectured to lead to a near-optimal, marketlike outcome. A basic structural feature of an economy with local public goods, implicit in Tiebout's discussion, is that, although large communities containing many participants are not ruled out, large communities are not essential for the realization of near-optimal outcomes. Another crucial feature of Tiebout's conception of an economy is that there is "sufficient" choice of communities to enable the consumer to choose the optimal community. The set of offerings of local public goods must be sufficiently large.

Although Tiebout's model is quite informally expressed – there are no precise definitions or conjectures – he does describe a "severe" comparison model that could easily be formalized. In his severe model (Tiebout 1956, 421), Tiebout supposes an infinite number of communities exist, each offering a different public goods package (implicitly, so that all possible levels of public goods are provided). There is no congestion or any increasing returns to scale within jurisdictions, and per capita costs of providing the public goods on offer within a community are constant and independent of the number of members in a community. In such a situation, the consumer-voter can move to the community in which his or her demands for public goods are exactly satisfied. Tiebout himself, as he makes clear, did not view this severe model as a good approximation to reality. For one thing, for the exact satisfaction of consumer demands, the number of (nonempty) communities may well need to be equal to the number of types of consumers, but the model was intended to illustrate how his informally described ideas may work.

Example 6.12. An Illustration of Tiebout's Severe Model. *Suppose all levels of public goods are possible. Thus, let us suppose that "community" $x \in \mathbb{R}_+$ offers quantity (or quality) x of the public good. Suppose that the costs of providing x to n consumers are $\$xn$ and that a consumer who chooses community x must pay the*

---

[29] Wooders (1999) provides a short but comprehensive survey on the Tiebout hypothesis.

cost (or tax) x. Each consumer $i \in N$ has a quasi-linear utility function

$$u^i(x, \xi) = f^i(x) + \xi.$$

Also, assume $f^i(x)$ is concave. Then, consumer i faces the problem

$$\text{maximize}_x \, f^i(x) + \xi - x.$$

Because $f^i(x) - x$ is concave, a maximum exists and, with free mobility,[30] *the utility-maximizing consumer may move to exactly a community that maximizes his or her preferences (subject to that consumer's budget constraint).*

Note that in this simple example the size of the population is of no real relevance. It could be finite or (with appropriate technical measure-theoretic conditions) a continuum (with or without atoms but would present no real problem either way). Also, the fundamental problem of sorting individuals into groups is trivial.

A key feature of Tiebout's severe model is the assumption of "no crowding effects." First, the average cost of providing a fixed level of the public good within each community is constant irrespective of population size. Also, individuals are indifferent to the characteristics of other individuals within the same community. If either of these features are relaxed, then even Tiebout's severe model can run into problems.

The results outlined in this chapter apply to private goods exchange economies, to economies with pure public goods, to economies with clubs in which individuals can belong to multiple clubs, to coalition production economies, and so on. Models of games with many players also allow congestion effects and positive externalities between members of the same group. Although Tiebout allows choice by positing a continuum of jurisdictions offering a continuum of public good levels, we allow choice by permitting free entry. Although Tiebout requires constant returns to population size within a jurisdiction, we require only that gains to population size be nearly exhausted – gains to forming increasingly larger coalitions become small as coalitions become large.

6.11.2. Buchanan Clubs

The Tiebout hypothesis and the literature on economies with many participants and small effective groups have become quite closely linked to club theory. A *club* consists of a group of individuals who collectively engage in some activity. Buchanan (1965) posited that clubs are of economic importance and discussed first-order conditions characterizing optimal club size and club good provision. Buchanan assumes the existence of an *optimal size* for a club – a preferred number of people in a swimming pool, for example, so that a swimmer is neither bored by doing solitary laps nor bothered by excessive numbers of other swimmers in the pool. More formally, an optimal club size maximizes the utility of a representative consumer under the assumption of equal sharing of costs. A natural application of

---

[30] Note that "free mobility" here is easily understood. A consumer can move to any community provided that he or she pays the per capita cost of the public good. Because this is independent of the numbers of residents of a community, no issue arises about what the consumer takes as given. In general, "free mobility" must be carefully defined.

this idea is to economies with local public goods. By common definitions of local public goods, they may become congested and there may be optimal, finite club (community, or jurisdiction) sizes. Unlike Tiebout, Buchanan did not appear to have in mind economies with many participants. But note that there is really not much difference between a Buchanan club and a Tiebout jurisdiction in Tiebout's informal model – at least at this point in the development of the literature. (Hence, we see authors using both the terms "club economy" and "Tiebout economy.")

As we have stressed in this chapter, our results do not require the existence of optimal club sizes – larger and larger clubs may yield larger and larger per capita payoffs. Moreover, although we have not treated the case in which individuals can belong to multiple clubs in this chapter, this is allowed by the assumptions of our model.[31]

6.11.3. Stable and Optimal Outcomes

Tiebout's informal model assumes a large number of jurisdictions and that consumers face a rich choice set. If the choice of jurisdictions is insufficient, then clearly consumers cannot reveal their preferences by their choice of community. Suppose, for example, all jurisdictions offer the same level of the public good; then, unless all consumers have the same "demands" for the public good, which happen to coincide with the level offered, "voting with one's feet" will not be effective because there is no good place to go. One way to deal with this problem is to allow individuals to form groups collectively to provide public goods for the group membership. This approach has been widely adopted, and the game-theoretic concept of the core has been applied in a variety of Tiebout-type models. The core consists of all those outcomes that are stable in the sense that they cannot be improved upon by any group of consumers or, equivalently, those outcomes with the property that no group of consumers can benefit by "opting out" or by seceding.[32] One can also consider the core to be a set of outcomes that arise as an equilibrium with free entry, and thus in equilibrium, no new group (or club) wishes to form and arrange its activities to the mutual benefit of the group members.

Remark. The distinction between a coalition, as typically used in cooperative game theory, and free entry as used in the more applied literature, is that "free entry" refers to the formation of firms, jurisdictions, clubs or other organizations, taking prices for private goods as given (or with the assumption that there is only one private good). In the chapters in this part, most of the discussion concerns economies with one private good or idealized money. Thus, we can equate free-entry equilibrium with the core; in more general contexts this is not possible.

There have been two distinct lines of research investigating stable group formation in Tiebout-type models in which groups form for the purpose of sharing a public good or the costs and benefits of a public project. The first approach is to

---

[31] See Shubik and Wooders (1982), Kovalenkov and Wooders (2003a,c), and Allouch and Wooders (2001).

[32] The reverse interpretation of "opting out" of a situation is to "enter." If a group of individuals decides to opt out of their club memberships to create a new club, then they (a) secede from the existing pattern of club memberships and (b) enter as a new club.

impose conditions on the model that permit nonemptiness of the core. One example is Wooders (1978), who assumes that for each type of consumer there is a range of "optimal" group sizes ensuring that in sufficiently large economies, consumers can be partitioned into optimal groups for their types and the core is nonempty. Other papers related to this approach impose assumptions on the structure of preferences of members of the economy so that, for some ordering of players, optimal groups consist of players who are consecutively ordered or in which the ordering has some treelike structure. This important line of research was initiated by Greenberg and Weber (1986); these, and related papers, are discussed in more detail in Chapters 5 and 8 of this volume. Note that at this point in the development of this line of research, players are not directly affected by the characteristics of other players – for example, their gender or whether they prefer ballroom dancing to hip hop.

Another approach underlying the research reported in this chapter is to consider situations in which there are many consumers, potentially many jurisdictions (effectively, free entry), and the possibility of congestion. Analyzing clubs via cooperative game theory appears to have been initiated by Pauly (1970). There, Pauly considers a model with essentially identical consumers and an optimal club size.[33] Pauly argues that unless the total player set can be partitioned into clubs of optimal sizes, the core will be empty. As a simple example, suppose all people are identical and that a two-person club maximizes the equal treatment payoff to its members. Let us go further and suppose that all other club sizes yield zero utility. If the population can be partitioned into two-player clubs, there are stable outcomes. If the total population is sufficiently large, then there is at most one "leftover" player and, with various notions of stability, approximately stable outcomes exist. Because Pauly assumes essentially identical consumers, the fundamental problem of optimal sorting of individuals into groups consisting of different types of consumers is not touched – only group size is relevant.

Cores and approximate cores for club economies with local public goods, heterogeneous consumers, and anonymous crowding – that is, consumers and producers are affected only by the numbers of consumers in a club (or jurisdiction) but not their characteristics – were investigated in Wooders (1978, 1980). As is demonstrated, except when different types of individuals have the same implicit "demands" for public goods and congestion, clubs in core states of the economy are homogeneous. This feature makes possible an extension of the intuition of Pauly to the heterogeneous types case.

Consumers, however, may care about the characteristics of other members of their club, that is, crowding may be differentiated (or nonanonymous). Then the difficulty of the possible emptiness of the core is more subtle. However, games with many players have nonempty approximate cores under seemingly mild assumptions.[34] The

[33] In Pauly (1970), the two types of agents may appear to differ but, as shown by one of the authors in her Ph.D. dissertation, the fact that both types of agents make identical marginal contributions to clubs implies that only the size and not the composition of clubs is relevant.

[34] See Wooders (1979, 1983) for first results and Wooders (1999) for another survey. This research is distinct from prior research on games with large numbers of players satisfying "balancedness"

approach of this chapter grew out of works on the study of cores and approximate cores of economies with local public goods and extensions of this research to games with many players. An increasing amount of literature continues to confirm that, when small groups of participants can realize almost all gains to collective activities, then economies with many participants resemble or are competitive markets analogous to large exchange economies with many participants. The most basic result is that, with many players, approximate cores are nonempty and treat most players who are similar nearly equally.

This chapter is based on recent research resulting from the authors' introducing a new approach simply describing a game (or economic situations underlying the game) by the size of the group required to realize almost all gains to collective activities. An appealing feature of the framework is that the model can actually be estimated and is sufficiently nonrestrictive to possibly apply to real-world situations. The advantage of our results over the prior Shapley and Shubik (1969) results showing that exchange economies with quasi-linear preferences have nonempty approximate cores is that they can be applied to any economy satisfying the conditions, including economies with clubs and with local public goods. Kovalenkov and Wooders (2003a) discuss the most recent results showing nonemptiness of approximate cores.

6.12. Conclusions

6.12.1. Free Entry and Free Mobility

Both the issues of free mobility and free entry appear several times in this volume. The research reviewed in this chapter and also in Chapter 7 of this volume relates to both these concepts.

The equivalence of games with many players and market games and also the limiting equivalence of the core and the set of competitive outcomes of the representing markets have implications for questions of free entry and free mobility in games and economies with many players. Think of the player types as types of commodities or as types of labor. Then, as shown for a fixed game by Shapley and Shubik (1969,1975), if the game has a nonempty core, the set of price-taking equilibria of the market generated by the game is equivalent to the core of the game. The price-taking equilibrium captures the idea that labor (or players) can migrate to those coalitions in which their earnings are highest. When games satisfy minimal conditions ensuring that small groups become negligible (small group negligibility), then approximate cores converge to price-taking equilibrium. The core is the outcome of free entry, whereas the price-taking equilibrium captures free mobility; their outcomes are equivalent.

The nonequivalence of free-mobility equilibrium and free entry in large economies arises owing to the mechanisms whereby the benefits and costs of coalition formation are allocated. (This is on the assumption that in economies with many

conditions (cf. Weber 1979, 1981) and games derived from exchange economies (cf. Aumann and Shapley 1974).

players, small groups of players or individual players are near negligible – small group negligibility.) If these mechanisms do not reflect the marginal costs and benefits caused by the migration of an individual to a nonequilibrium jurisdiction, then the equivalence of free-entry equilibrium and free-mobility equilibrium simply cannot hold. Let us suppose, for example, as in our discussion in the introduction, that in equilibrium individuals within a jurisdiction pay average costs and that anyone willing to pay the average costs in a jurisdiction can move into a jurisdiction. Then, except in special circumstances, even in large economies an equilibrium outcome may not exist and, if it does, will not be in the core. See also Conley and Wooders (1998) and Chapter 7 of this volume for further examples of equilibrium concepts in which the free-mobility aspect of equilibrium is inconsistent with the optimality of free entry.

In this chapter, free entry, as in the other chapters in this part, is captured by using the concept of the core and approximate cores. The free-entry condition and the no-improvement condition of the core are equivalent because there is no motivation for trade or other exchanges between coalitions (clubs, groups, or firms). Free mobility is interpreted as freedom to join any group if one is willing to pay the admission price (or taxes) required to belong to that group. When free mobility and free entry both hold, the core (or approximate cores) can be supported by price-taking equilibria. The equivalence of games with many players and of market games (in which the player types are the commodities) implies the equivalence of price-taking equilibrium and free-entry equilibrium.[35]

Because this chapter is already long, we have not included any discussion of comparative statics and monotonicity properties of games with many players. The most recent treatments of this topic can be found in Kovalenkov and Wooders (2003b,d).

We conclude with some discussion of our approach.

6.12.2. Motivation for Approximate Cores and Approximate Equilibrium

A major motivation for cores and approximate cores is that they are defined for cooperative games and thus can accommodate a variety of economic situations. It is clear that special assumptions are required on the economic models. This same point is made in Chapter 8 of this volume. In contrast, this chapter illustrates that only apparently very mild conditions covering diverse economic and game-theoretic models are required to ensure nonemptiness of approximate cores and existence of approximate equilibrium.

If we focus on competitive outcomes and the core, it is well understood that, except in highly idealized situations, cores of games may be empty and competitive equilibrium of economies may not exist. For example, within the context of an exchange economy, the conditions required for existence of equilibrium typically include convexity, which implies infinite divisibility of commodities, and also nonsatiation.[36]

---

[35] We refer the reader to Chapter 7 of this volume for further discussion of the equivalence of free-entry equilibria (the core) and price-taking equilibrium outcomes where prices are admission prices to jurisdictions offering packages of public goods, and to Chapters 5 and 8 of this volume for further discussion of free entry with other notions of free mobility.

[36] There are many exceptions – for example, Quinzii (1984).

Even these two conditions may well not be satisfied; goods are usually sold in pre-specified units, and there are some commodities that many individuals prefer not to consume. As was demonstrated in this chapter, in economies with congestion, even if preferences and production sets are convex, the core of the economy may be empty.[37] In the context of economies with coalition structures, such as economies with clubs, local public goods, or both, the added difficulties of endogenous group formation compound the problem; even if, given club memberships, all conditions for existence of equilibrium and nonemptiness of the core are satisfied in each club, the core may be empty. One possible approach to the problem of existence of equilibrium is to restrict attention to models in which equilibria exist – for example, economies with continuums of agents. But a model with a continuum of agents can only be an approximation to a finite economy. Another approach is to consider solution concepts for which existence is more robust – in particular, approximate equilibria and cores. It seems reasonable to suppose that frictions typically prevent an exact competitive equilibrium from being attained. Possibly, many readers of this volume may have, at one time, found that they were unable to purchase some item at the going price because suppliers were sold out. Moreover, most purchases might be made at prices that are only close to equilibrium prices; perhaps many of the readers of this volume have found that the same article does not necessarily sell for the same price in different shops. It also seems reasonable to suppose that typically there are costs of forming coalitions; anyone who has ever tried to form a group – even a group of colleagues to go to dinner – perhaps agrees. Observations such as these motivate the study of the existence of approximate equilibria and nonemptiness of approximate cores.

Besides assumptions on the structure of the economies or games considered, solution theory also requires behavioral assumptions: the competitive equilibrium mobility requires that individuals take prices as given (by some unknown source) and optimize, whereas the core is based on the idea that, if a group of individuals can be better off by forming a coalition and reallocating resources and activities within that coalition, then they will do so. These behavioral assumptions are problematic – those of the core perhaps no more so than those of the competitive equilibrium. An alternative to the behavioral assumption of the core that may be easier for economists to accept is that entrepreneurs form coalitions whenever an opportunity exists to profit from doing so; there is a long literature taking this approach or closely related approaches – for example, Pauly (1967), Shapley and Shubik (1969), and Bennett and Wooders (1979).[38] The literature on contestable markets (e.g., Baumol, Panzer, and Willig 1982) takes a similar approach; roughly, this literature suggests that the presence of entrepreneurs who are ever-ready to enter a market if there is an opportunity to profit ensures that prevailing prices are perfectly competitive. Thus, there is some motivation for both the core and the competitive equilibrium in the idea that, if prices or payoffs are not competitive, profit-maximizing firms will enter.

---

[37] An example making this point was taken from Shubik and Wooders (1983a).

[38] Pauly treats the case of essentially identical players and economies with quasi-transferable utilities. Wooders (1979) treats multiple types; these results are applied in Bennett and Wooders (1979) to problems of firm formation. See also Section 6.8 in this chapter.

From the viewpoint of the behavioral assumptions required, there are arguments in favor of both the core and the competitive equilibrium.

In a frictionless world perfectly and completely described by the payoffs attainable to any set of consumers (or to any club), approximate cores may not be applicable. In economies with local public goods, clubs, or both, however, at any point in time people are all located somewhere. Even the homeless must bed down someplace. We can imagine that there are costs associated with relocation, moving to another community, or more generally changing one's pattern of consumption. Then the same payoff set facing a club or community in place is distinct from a payoff set that would face the members of the club if they wished to form a new club. With costs of forming new clubs, nonemptiness of approximate cores in the absence of such costs implies nonemptiness of exact cores with club formation costs (cf. Allouch and Wooders 2001 and references therein for such an approach). Also, strategic games can have equilibria whose outcomes are in approximate cores. Results demonstrating this are in their infancy, but we anticipate that they will be demonstrated to hold broadly.

BIBLIOGRAPHY

[1] Allouch, A. and M. Wooders (2001), "Price Taking Equilibrium in Club Economies with Multiple Memberships and Unbounded Club Sizes," University of Warwick Department of Economics discussion paper No. 639 (revised).

[2] Arnold, T. and M. Wooders (2002), "Dynamic Club Formation," University of Warwick Department of Economics Working Paper No. 640.

[3] Aumann, R. J. (1964), Markets with a Continuum of Traders, *Econometrica* 32, 39–50.

[4] Aumann, R. J. (1987), "Game Theory," in *The New Palgrave: A Dictionary of Economics*, J. Eatwell, M. Milgate, and P. Newman (eds.), New York: The Macmillan Press.

[5] Aumann, R. J. and Shapley, L. S. (1974), *Values of Nonatomic Economies*, Princeton University Press.

[6] Baumol, W. J., J. C. Panzer, and R. D. Willig (1982), *Contestable Markets and the Theory of Industry Structure*, San Diego: Harcourt, Brace, Jovanovich.

[7] Bennett, E. and M. Wooders (1979), "Income Distribution and Firm Formation," *Journal of Comparative Economics* 3, 304–317.

[8] Böhm, V. (1974), "The Limit of the Core of an Economy with Production," *International Economic Review* 15, 143–148.

[9] Bondareva, O. (1962), "Theory of the Core in an *n*-Person Game," *Vestnik LGU* 13, 141–142 (in Russian).

[10] Buchanan, J. (1965), "An Economic Theory of Clubs," *Economica* 33, 1–14.

[11] Conley, J. and M. Wooders (1998), "Anonymous Lindahl Pricing in a Tiebout Economy with Crowding Types," *Canadian Journal of Economics* 31, 952–974.

[12] Conley, J. and M. Wooders (2001), "Tiebout Economies with Differential Genetic Types and Endogenously Chosen Crowding Characteristics," *Journal of Economic Theory* 98, 261–294.

[13] Crawford, V. and E. Knoer (1981), "Job Matchings with Heterogeneous Firms and Workers," *Econometrica* 49, 437–450.

[14] Debreu, G. and H. Scarf (1963), "A Limit Theorem on the Core of an Economy," *International Economic Review* 4, 235–246.

[15] Engl, G. & S. Scotchmer (1996), "The Core and Hedonic Core: Equivalence and Comparative Statics," *Journal of Mathematical Economics* 26, 209–248.

[16] Epple, D., T. Romer, and H. Sieg (2001), "Interjurisdictional Sorting and Majority Rule; An Empirical Analysis," *Econometrica* 69, 1437–1466.

[17] Fernandez, R., and R. Rogerson (1996), "Income Distribution, Communities, and the Quality of Public Education," *The Quarterly Journal of Economics*, 111(1), 135–164.

[18] Flam, S., G. Owen, and M. Saboya (2002), "Large Production Games and Approximate Core Solutions," Typescript (submitted).

[19] Gilles, D. B. (1953), "Some Theorems on *n*-Person Games," Ph.D. Dissertation, Department of Mathematics, Princeton University.

[20] Greenberg, J. and S. Weber (1986), "Strong Tiebout Equilibrium with Restricted Preference Domain," *Journal of Economic Theory* 38, 101–117.

[21] Hildenbrand, W. (1974), *Core and Equilibria of a Large Economy*, Princeton University Press.

[22] Hildenbrand, W., and A. P. Kirman (1973), "Size Removes Inequality," *Review of Economic Studies* 30, 305–314.

[23] Kaneko, M. and M. Wooders (1982), "Cores of Partitioning Games," *Mathematical Social Sciences* 3, 313–327.

[24] Kaneko, M. and M. Wooders (1986), "The Core of a Game with a Continuum of Players and Finite Coalitions: The Model and Some Results," *Mathematical Social Sciences* 12, 105–137.

[25] Kaneko, M. and M. Wooders (1996), "The Nonemptiness of the f-core of a Game without Side Payments," *International Journal of Game Theory* 25, 245–258.

[26] Konishi, H., M. Le Breton, and S. Weber (1998), "Equilibrium in a Finite Local Public Goods Economy," *Journal of Economic Theory* 79, 224–244.

[27] Kovalenkov, A. and M. Wooders (2001a), "Epsilon Cores of Games with Limited Side Payments; Nonemptiness and Equal Treatment," *Games and Economic Behavior* 36, 193–218.

[28] Kovalenkov, A. and M. Wooders (2001b), "An Exact Bound on Epsilon for Nonemptiness of Epsilon Cores of Games," *Mathematics of Operations Research* 26, 654–678.

[29] Kovalenkov, A. and M. Wooders (2003a), "Approximate Cores of Games and Economies with Clubs," *Journal of Economic Theory* 110, 81–120.

[30] Kovalenkov, A. and M. Wooders (2003b), "Laws of Scarcity for a Finite Game – Exact Bounds on Estimations," to appear in *Economic Theory.*

[31] Kovalenkov, A. and M. Wooders (2003c), "Advances in the Theory of Large Cooperative Games and Application to Club Theory: The Side Payments Case," in *The Endogenous Formation of Economic Coalitions,* Carlo Cararro ed., Cheltenham, UK/Northampton, MA: Edward Elgar, 9–34.

[32] Kovalenkov, A. and M. Wooders (2003d), "Comparative Statics and Laws of Scarcity for Games," to appear in a volume of essays in honor of Marcel K. Richter, D. McFadden, R. Matzkin and J. Moore (eds).

[33] Pauly, M. (1967), "Clubs, Commonality and the Core: An Integration of Game Theory and the Theory of Public Goods," *Economica* 34, 314–324.

[34] Pauly, M. (1970), "Cores and Clubs," *Public Choice* 9, 53–65.

[35] Roth, A. (1984), "The Evolution of the Labor Market for Medical Residents and Interns: A Case Study in Game Theory," *Journal of Political Economy* 92, 991–1016.

[36] Quinzii, M. (1984), "Core and Competitive Equilibria with Indivisibilities," *International Journal of Game Theory* 13, 41–60.

[37] Scarf, H. E. (1967), "The Core of an n-Person Game," *Econometrica* 35, 50–67.

[38] Selten, R. (1981), "A Non-cooperative Model of Characteristic Function Bargaining," in *Essays in Game Theory and Mathematical Economics in Honor of O.*

Morgenstern, V. Böhm and M. Nachtkamp (eds.), Mannheim, Vienna, Zürich: Bibliographical Institüt.

[39] Shapley, L. S. (1967), "On Balanced Sets and Cores," *Naval Research Logistics Quarterly* 14, 453–460.

[40] Shapley, L. S. and M. Shubik (1966), "Quasi-cores in a Monetary Economy with Nonconvex Preferences," *Econometrica* 34, 805–827.

[41] Shapley, L. S and M. Shubik (1969), "On Market Games," *Journal of Economic Theory* 1, 9–25.

[42] Shapley, L. S. and M. Shubik (1975), "Competitive Outcomes in the Cores of Market Games," *International Journal of Game Theory* 4, 229–237.

[43] Shubik, M. (1959), "Edgeworth Market Games," in *Contributions to the Theory of Games IV, Annals of Mathematical Studies 40,* F. R. Luce and A. W. Tucker (eds.), Princeton University Press.

[44] Shubik, M. (1971), "The 'Bridge Game' Economy: An Example of Indivisibilities," *Journal of Political Economy* 79, 909–912.

[45] Shubik, M. and M. Wooders (1982), "Near-Markets and Market-Games," Cowles Foundation Discussion Paper No. 657, published as "Clubs, Near-Markets and Market-Games," in *Topics in Mathematical Economics and Game Theory; Essays in Honor of Robert J. Aumann,* M. Wooders (ed.), Fields Institute Communication Volume, Providence: American Mathematical Society, 1999.

[46] Shubik, M. and M. Wooders (1983a), "Approximate Cores of Replica Games and Economies: Part I. Replica Games, Externalities, and Approximate Cores," *Mathematical Social Sciences* 6, 27–48.

[47] Shubik, M. and M. Wooders (1983b), "Approximate Cores of Replica Games and Economies: Part II, Set-up Costs and Firm Formation in Coalition Production Economies," *Mathematical Social Sciences* 6, 285–306.

[48] Sondermann, D. (1974), "Economies of Scale and Equilibria in Coalition Production Economies," *Journal of Economic Theory* 8, 259–271.

[49] Tiebout, C. (1956), "A Pure Theory of Local Expenditures," *Journal of Political Economy* 64 , 416–424.

[50] Vohra, R. (1987), "Local Public Goods as Indivisible Commodities," *Regional Science and Urban Economics* 17, 191–208.

[51] Weber, S. (1979), "On ϵ-cores of Balanced Games," *International Journal of Game Theory* 8, 241–250.

[52] Weber, S. (1981), "Some Results on the Weak Core of a Non-sidepayment Game with Infinitely Many Players," *Journal of Mathematical Economics* 8, 101–111.

[53] Westhoff, F. (1977), "Existence of Equilibrium in Economies with a Local Public Good," *Journal of Economic Theory* 14, 84–112.

[54] Winter, E. and M. Wooders (1990), "On Large Games with Bounded Coalition Sizes," University of Bonn, Sonderforschungsbereich 303 Discussion Paper A-317.

[55] Wooders, M. (1978), "Equilibria, the Core, and Jurisdiction Structures in Economies with a Local Public Good," *Journal of Economic Theory* 18, 328–348.

[56] Wooders, M. (1979), "A Characterization of Approximate Equilibria and Cores in a Class of Coalition Economies," Stony Brook Department of Economics Working Paper No. 184, 1977; revised 1979; on-line at http://www.myrnawooders.com/

[57] Wooders, M. (1981), "The Epsilon Core of a Large Game," Cowles Foundation Discussion Paper 612.

[58] Wooders, M. (1983), "The Epsilon Core of a Large Replica Game," *Journal of Mathematical Economics* 11, 277–300.

[59] Wooders, M. (1991), "The Efficaciousness of Small Groups and the Approximate Core Property in Games without Side Payments," University of Bonn Sonderforschungs-bereich 303, Discussion Paper No. B-17.

[60] Wooders, M. (1992a), "Inessentiality of Large Groups and the Approximate Core Property; An Equivalence Theorem," *Economic Theory* 2, 129–147.

[61] Wooders, M. (1992b), "Large Games and Economies with Effective Small Groups," Sonderforschingsbereich 303 University of Bonn Discussion Paper No. 215; revised September 1992, in *Game Theoretic Approaches to General Equilibrium Theory*, J.-F. Mertens and S. Sorin (eds.), Dordrecht- Boston- London: Kluwer Academic Publishers, 1994.

[62] Wooders, M. H (1993), "The Attribute Core, Core Convergence, and Small Group Effectiveness; The Effects of Property Rights Assignments on the Attribute Core," University of Toronto Working Paper No. 9304, to appear in a volume in honor of Martin Shubik (Pradeep Dubey and John Geanakoplos, eds.) Revised 2003.

[63] Wooders, M. (1994a), "Equivalence of Games and Markets," *Econometrica* 62, 1141–1160.

[64] Wooders, M. (1994b), "Approximating Games and Economies by Markets," University of Toronto Working Paper No. 9415.

[65] Wooders, M. (1994c), "On Aumann's Markets with a Continuum of Traders; The Continuum, Small Group Effectiveness, and Social Homogeneity," University of Toronto Discussion Paper 9401.

[66] Wooders, M. (1999), "Multijurisdictional Economies, the Tiebout Hypothesis, and Sorting," *Proceedings of the National Academy of Sciences* 96, 10585–10587, on-line at http://www.pnas.org/cgi/content/full/96/19/10585.

[67] Wooders, M. (2004a), "Small Group Negligibility and Small Group Effectiveness; Two Sides of the Same Coin," University of Warwick Department of Economics Working Paper (to appear).

[68] Wooders, M. (2004b) "Small Group Effectiveness and the Equal Treatment Property of the Core of a Game," University of Warwick Department of Economics Working Paper (to appear).

Coalitions and Clubs: Tiebout Equilibrium in Large Economies

John Conley and Stefani Smith

7.1. Introduction

A central problem in public economics is how to achieve optimal outcomes through price-based mechanisms in economies with public goods. One of the key papers in this area is Samuelson (1954), which provides a formalization of Lindahl's approach. Unfortunately, the implied system of personalized prices requires agents to reveal their preferences for public goods truthfully. As Samuelson notes, an agent may therefore have an incentive to misrepresent his true preferences. Thus, it is doubtful that market mechanisms based on the Lindahl prices defined by Samuelson would generally be able to provide public goods efficiently.

In response, Tiebout (1956) argued that many types of public goods are subject to crowding and congestion, resulting in the possibility of their provision by local jurisdictions rather than national governments. Jurisdictions offering consumers various bundles of public goods can condition residence in the jurisdiction (and therefore consumption of the public goods) on the payment of taxes. Thus, agents in effect are forced to reveal their willingness to pay for public goods through their locational choice. Tiebout asserted that, in "large" economies, when localities compete for residents and agents, in turn, "vote with their feet" to express demand for public goods, such goods will be efficiently provided.[1]

Tiebout (1956) stimulated a large theoretical investigation. Subsequent researchers have shown that, although efficient Tiebout sorting may not occur in completely general circumstances, adding economic restrictions that are natural in the study of clubs or local public goods provides support for Tiebout's hypothesis. For example, Wooders (1978) showed that when congestion is anonymous (only the number of agents sharing the public good matters) and all gains to coalition forming are realized in small coalitions, the core can be decentralized with anonymous prices. Although Wooders (1978) was an early result, many other works also provide support for the Tiebout hypothesis. These works will be surveyed throughout this chapter.

---

[1] See Chapter 6 of this volume for a discussion of Tiebout's intuition and his severe "comparison model."

Bewley (1981) is sometimes cited as an early attempt to formalize the Tiebout hypothesis but his conclusions were not promising. He argued that, in some cases, anonymous decentralization of efficient outcomes is not possible and, in other cases, anonymous prices may only decentralize inefficient outcomes. However, in Bewley (1981) the number of jurisdictions is fixed and public goods are not subject to congestion. And so, in important ways, Bewley (1981) does not present a Tiebout model of the type the literature has come to accept. This notwithstanding, Bewley makes a key point that any meaningful interpretation of Tiebout's hypothesis must embed the idea that decentralizing prices are anonymous in the sense that they do not depend on agents' unobservable characteristics.

The *local public goods* approach to the provision of congestible public goods centers on an agent's locational choice among competing jurisdictions that offer distinct public goods bundles. Broadly taken, local public goods models address the general equilibrium question of how best to sort the entire population of a large economy into nonoverlapping and exhaustive coalitions. Alternatively, the *club* approach to the provision of congestible public goods usually involves partial equilibrium models of private membership organizations such as country clubs or private schools. Club models generally address the profit-maximizing decisions of a club with price-taking members. Early models of tolls and congested roads by Pigou (1920) and Knight (1924) are considered club models. However, Buchanan (1965) was the first to develop a formal club model and is often credited with beginning the modern club literature. It should be noted that the language that we use to distinguish clubs from local public goods is not universal. Berglas, Helpman, and Pines (1982); Sandler and Tschirhart (1980); and Cornes and Sandler (1996) offer distinct taxonomies. For example, Cornes and Sandler refer to local public goods economies as club economies whose population is partitioned.

The club literature has developed in myriad directions since Buchanan published his seminal paper. Pauly (1967, 1970) explored the issue of optimal club size and the stability of club membership in situations with homogeneous populations. Tollison (1972), Ng and Tollison (1974), Berglas (1976), and DeSerpa (1977) present clubs in which crowding is differentiated.[2] Wooders (1978) considered a model with heterogeneous populations, anonymous crowding[3] and anonymous pricing – prices that do not depend on unobservable characteristics of agents. McGuire (1974) addresses whether club membership will be homogeneous when agents differ in tastes or endowments. Questions of core and equilibrium existence in club economies and equivalence of their outcomes arose in works such as Pauly (1967, 1970) and Wooders (1978). Issues of costs for excluding unwanted members of an exclusive club are presented by Davis and Whinston (1967); Millward (1970); Nichols, Smolensky, and Tideman (1971); Oakland (1972); and Kamien, Schwartz, and

---

[2] The early authors did not use the terminology "differentiated crowding," which is the current language used to describe congestion caused by agents' characteristics rather than club size only. Note also that sometimes the term *nonanonymous crowding* is used; this term may incorrectly suggest that individual agents are not anonymous – that names matter.

[3] Anonymous crowding means that individuals care only about the numbers of agents in the same jurisdictions and not about their characteristics.

Roberts (1973). Early explorations of uncertainty in club models include DeVany and Saving (1977) and Hillman and Swan (1979). Cornes and Sandler (1996) survey each of these expansive research areas and provide an introduction to more recent directions of investigation, such as multiproduct, variable usage, and intergenerational clubs.

Our purpose in this chapter is to draw attention to a recent approach to formalizing Tiebout's central insight into the local public goods tradition, the crowding-types model introduced in Conley and Wooders (1997a). The chapter is organized as follows. In Section 7.2 we introduce the agents who populate the local public goods economy presented and discuss the various forms of crowding that have been studied. Section 7.3 describes our local public goods economy. Optimality and decentralization results are given in Section 7.4. In Section 7.5, existence results are presented. Section 7.6 discusses noncooperative solution concepts, and Section 7.7 discusses other results and future research.

7.2. Agents and Crowding

We consider an economy with I agents, each of whom resides in exactly one jurisdiction and consumes one private good, $x \in \Re$, and M local public goods, $y \in \Re_+^M$.[4] The set of agents $\mathcal{I}$ is given by $\mathcal{I} \equiv \{1, \ldots, i, \ldots, I\}$, where $i \in \mathcal{I}$ is an individual. In this economy, agents will typically find it optimal to form many small jurisdictions to consume local public goods. Therefore, the coalitional structures we study are partitions. An arbitrary jurisdiction of agents is denoted $s \subset \mathcal{I}$, and $\mathcal{S}$ denotes the set of all possible jurisdictions. A list of jurisdictions $\{s^1, \ldots, s^P\} \equiv S$ is a *partition* if $\cup_p s^p = \mathcal{I}$ and $s^p \cap s^{\bar{p}} = \emptyset$ for all $s^p, s^{\bar{p}}$ such that $p \neq \bar{p}$.

An agent possesses one of T different types of tastes or preferences indexed by $t \in \{1, \ldots, T\} \equiv \mathcal{T}$. The mapping $\tau : \mathcal{I} \to \mathcal{T}$ assigns a taste type and a corresponding endowment ω_t to each agent in the economy. Thus, if agent i possesses taste type t, then $\tau(i) = t$. It will sometimes be useful to describe the population of a jurisdiction by the number of agents of each taste type in that jurisdiction. The total population of agents in the economy is given by $N = (N_1, \ldots, N_t, \ldots, N_T)$, where N_t is interpreted as the number of agents of type t in the economy. Similarly, a jurisdiction s has population $N^s = (N_1^s, \ldots, N_t^s, \ldots, N_T^s)$, where N_t^s is the number of agents of type t in jurisdiction s.

Agents are also distinguished by their crowding characteristics. The crowding type of an agent captures all aspects of the agent that generate external effects on other members of the same club or jurisdiction. These effects could be positive or negative, and we will assume that they are publicly observable. For example, one's gender, race, height, or intelligence may confer costs or benefits to one's coalition-mates.

---

[4] Until we consider models with linear price systems, the Euclidian structure of the public goods space is not used. Thus, it is trivial to alter the model to allow an abstract set of public projects. It is not as trivial to generalize the results to multiple private goods, although the results carry through to continuum economies in this case and hold approximately for finite economies.

Formally, each agent is classified as having one of C publicly observable crowding types indexed by $c \in \{1, \ldots, C\}\mathcal{C}$. The mapping $\kappa : \mathcal{I} \to \mathcal{C}$ associates a crowding type with each agent in the economy.[5] That is, $\kappa(i) = c$ indicates that agent i possesses crowding characteristic c. Let $\mathcal{K}$ be the set of all such mappings. Denote a profile of crowding characteristics by $n = (n_1, \ldots, n_c, \ldots, n_C) \in Z_+^C$, where Z is the set of integers and n_c is interpreted to be the number of agents of type c. For any assignment of agents to crowding types $\kappa \in \mathcal{K}$, the crowding profile of a jurisdiction $s \in \mathcal{S}$ is the mapping $K : \mathcal{K} \times \mathcal{S} \to Z_+^C$ given by

$$K(\kappa, s) \equiv (|s_1|, \ldots, |s_C|),$$

where $i \in s_c$ if and only if $i \in s$ and $\kappa(i) = c$ and $|\cdot|$ denotes the cardinality.

The commonly available public goods production technology is given by the cost function $f : \Re_+^M \times Z_+^C \to \Re$, where

$$f(y, n)$$

is the cost in terms of private goods of producing the public goods levels y for a jurisdiction with crowding profile given by n. Note that crowding effects are also permitted. For example, it may be cheaper to construct public buildings if agents are not vandals, and it may be easier to establish a good departmental research reputation if the department is populated by smart and hard-working types.

One focus of these coalitional economy models is to explore the form of crowding or congestion effects. Crowding can take many forms. Here we consider anonymous crowding, differentiated crowding, exogenous crowding types, endogenous crowding types where agents have equal abilities, and endogenous crowding types where agents have differentiated genetic endowments. In the remainder of this section, we describe these various forms of crowding.

7.2.1. Anonymous Crowding

When crowding is anonymous, each agent cares only about the number of individuals in his jurisdiction. For example, when patrons stand in line at the movie theater, only the length of the queue is directly relevant, not the theatergoers' heights, professions, or even their tastes in movies. Formally, anonymous crowding implies that there is only one exogenously given crowding type, $\kappa(i) = c$ for all $i \in \mathcal{I}$, and the crowding profile of a jurisdiction, $K(\kappa, s) = (|s_c|)$, is simply the number of agents in the jurisdiction. An agent i has a utility function

$$u_{\tau(i)} : \Re \times \Re_+^M \times Z_+ \to \Re$$

given by $u_t(x_i, y, |s|)$, where x_i is agent i's private good level, s is the jurisdiction in which i resides, and y is the public goods levels in jurisdiction s. Note that this specification of preferences ensures that agents are only affected by the number of people sharing the public good and not by their taste types. Anonymous crowding

---

[5] Note that, in the specifications that follow, this mapping will sometimes be exogenously given and will sometimes be endogenous.

may also have an effect on the cost of public goods production. In this case, the cost in terms of the private good of producing the public goods bundle y in jurisdiction s may be written $f^A(y, |s|)$. Models of local public goods in which crowding is anonymous include Wooders (1978, 1980), Berglas and Pines (1980), Boadway (1980), Scotchmer and Wooders (1987), and Barham and Wooders (1998). Barham and Wooders (1998) provide a survey of the many other contributions in which crowding is anonymous.

7.2.2. Differentiated Crowding

Often agents care about the types of their fellow residents in a jurisdiction and not just their number. For example, when one dines out, the numbers of smokers and nonsmokers affect the enjoyment of dinner, not just the total number of people in the restaurant. In this case, an agent's unobservable preferences, whether he enjoys smoking in restaurants, may be perfectly correlated with an observable crowding characteristic, that is, whether the agent actually smokes in the restaurant. Thus, if crowding is differentiated, an agent's crowding type is exogenously given and perfectly correlated with tastes. As a result, the crowding-type index, $c \in C$, and the taste-type index, $t \in T$, may be used interchangeably, and a jurisdiction's crowding profile is simply its population given by $K(\kappa, s) = (|s_1|, \ldots, |s_c|, \ldots, |s_C|) = (n_1, \ldots, n_T)$. An agent i has utility function $u_{\tau(i)} : \Re \times \Re_+^M \times Z_+^T \to \Re$ given by $u_t^D(x_i, y, (n_1, \ldots, n_T))$, where x_i is the level of private goods, s is the jurisdiction in which i resides, and y is the public goods level in jurisdiction s. If differentiated crowding is manifest in public goods production, then the cost in terms of the private good of producing the public goods bundle y in jurisdiction s can be written $f(x, y, (n_1, \ldots, n_T))$.

Early studies of differentiated crowding naturally arose in the context of labor complementarities and peer-group effects. Notable contributions along those lines include Berglas (1976), in which differentiated crowding was introduced, de Bartolome (1990), McGuire (1991), Schwab and Oates (1991), Benabou (1993), and Brueckner (1994). General equilibrium local public goods models in which crowding is differentiated are formalized in Wooders (1981,1988,1989), Scotchmer and Wooders (1986), and Allouch and Wooders (2004). Models of cooperative games with player types capturing economies with local public goods and differentiated crowding as special cases were introduced in Wooders (1983); see also Shubik and Wooders (1983a,b) and, for further references, the preceding chapter of this volume. Wooders (1999) provides a short survey linking these models of cooperative games to economies with local public goods and Tiebout sorting.

7.2.3. Exogenous Crowding Types

In an important way, differentiated crowding is an unsatisfactory generalization of the anonymous crowding model. In general, it would be somewhat surprising if agents' unobservable tastes were perfectly correlated with their observable crowding types. For example, at a dance club, an agent's gender is an observable crowding characteristic. For any individual, one gender crowds positively whereas the other is simply in the way. Both genders, however, have some members who prefer rock music to jazz and others who prefer jazz to rock. Tastes in this case are unobservable and unrelated to how agents crowd each other. To capture this formally, we allow utility and cost functions to depend on a jurisdiction's crowding profile but not on agents' tastes. We assume, as in differentiated crowding, that an agent's crowding type is exogenously assigned; that is, we assume that the mapping κ is fixed and known by all agents. An agent i has a utility function $u_{\tau(i)} : \Re \times \Re_+^M \times Z_+^C \to \Re$ given by $u_t(x_i, y, n)$, where x_i is the private goods level, y is the public goods levels, and n is the crowding profile in the jurisdiction in which i resides. Similarly, when only crowding characteristics matter, the cost in terms of private good of producing the public goods bundles y in jurisdiction s can be written $f(y, n)$. Conley and Wooders (1997a) introduce this crowding-types model, and other results are included in Conley and Wooders (1997b), Conley and Wooders (1998), and Conley and Smith (2003).

Cartwright and Wooders (2001) examine the theory of equalizing differences (see Rosen 1986, 1988) in the context of the crowding types model and show that increasing the number of workers of a specific crowding type may lead to an increase in their earnings even when small groups are strictly effective; note that this is in contrast to the situation in differentiated crowding models where increasing abundances of a type of player lead to a (weak) decrease in core payoffs to players of that type (see the preceding chapter for references and further discussion).

7.2.4. Endogenous Crowding Types, Equal Abilities

The exogenous crowding-types model is most appropriately applied to situations in which agents have no control over their crowding types. For example, agents have no control over race, height, national origin, and basic mental abilities and very little control over others such as gender, looks, charisma, and so on. An exogenous crowding-types approach may also be appropriate when an agent's crowding type results from a past irreversible decision such as learning a second language. However, many observable characteristics that affect the welfare of others are the result of choices made in response to clear market signals. For example, when a graduate student chooses a major field, the knowledge of demand for the various types of economists may play a role in the decision. Crowding characteristics such as profession, marital status and number of children, and level of participation in the community are chosen at least partly in response to expected costs and benefits.

To capture this, suppose that an agent may choose, subject to the constraints of educational costs, his own observable crowding characteristics. The cost to any agent of choosing to become any given crowding type is given by the mapping $\epsilon : C \to \Re$, which is called the educational cost function. For example, $\epsilon(c)$ gives the educational cost that an agent must incur to obtain crowding type c. Note that agents are "equally able" in that they all face the same educational cost of obtaining a particular skill. An agent i has a utility function $u_{\tau(i)} : \Re \times \Re_+^M \times C \times Z_+^C \to \Re$ given by $u_{\tau(i)}(x_i - \epsilon(c), y, c, n)$, where x_i is the gross private goods level, c is the chosen crowding characteristic, and y and n are the public goods level and crowding profile, respectively, in the jurisdiction in which i resides. Note that each agent pays the full cost of his education and that $x_i - \epsilon(c)$ is his private good consumption net of education costs. Note also that "c" is an argument in the utility function. This is to capture the idea that agents may have preferences over which crowding type they acquire. For example, I may wish to be a rock star or a poet but choose the dreary life of an economist because of the expected wages, and this, after all, is preferred to being an accountant. Of course, the crowding profile of a jurisdiction may also affect production. In this case, the cost in terms of the private good of producing the public goods bundles y in a jurisdiction with crowding profile n can be written $f(y, n)$. This model was introduced in Conley and Wooders (1996).

7.2.5. Endogenous Crowding and Differential Genetic Types

Often, an agent's genetic abilities affect the cost of acquiring a particular skill crowding type. For example, a 7-foot-tall person is likely to have a lower cost of becoming a professional basketball player than a 5-foot-tall person. An intelligent person may find it easy get a doctorate in physics but may have no facility for typing. Note also that we would not generally expect an agent's preferences to be related to his genetic endowments. For example, many professional athletes would rather be movie stars and many movie stars would rather be politicians.

Agents in this case are described by their preferences and genetic endowments. We assume these are uncorrelated and not publicly observable. Each agent may choose, subject to the constraints of educational costs, his own observable crowding characteristic. Only an agent's crowding type directly affects the welfare of others. An agent's educational cost of obtaining a particular crowding characteristic depends on his genetic endowment. Again, independent of this cost, individuals have preferences over which skill is acquired.

Formally, each agent $i \in \mathcal{I}$ is described by his preference type $\tau(i)$, and one of G different types of genetic endowments indexed by $g \in \{1, \ldots, G\} \equiv \mathcal{G}$. The mapping $\gamma : \mathcal{I} \to \mathcal{G}$ exogenously ascribes a genetic endowment to each agent in the economy. Each agent chooses to acquire one of the C publicly observable crowding characteristics. Agents with different genetic endowments may have different abilities and will therefore face different costs of acquiring a given crowding type. In this case, the educational cost function is given by $\epsilon_{\gamma(i)} : \mathcal{I} \to \Re$, where $\epsilon_{\gamma(i)}(c)$ gives the cost to agent i of obtaining crowding characteristic c. Note that this cost may be negative because some types of education may generate positive net income.

An agent i has a utility function $u_{\tau(i)} : \Re \times \Re_+^M \times C \times Z_+^C \to \Re$, given by

$$u_{\tau(i)}(x_i - \epsilon_{\gamma(i)}(c), y, c, n),$$

where x_i is the gross private good level, c is the chosen crowding characteristic, and y and n are the public goods levels and crowding profile of the jurisdiction in which

i resides. As noted, an agent pays the full cost of his education, and so $x_i - \epsilon_{\gamma(i)}(c)$ is the private good consumption level net of education costs. Crowding is treated in the standard way.

This most recent approach to modeling crowding characteristics is introduced by Conley and Wooders (2001). It is easy to see that each of the approaches just described can be obtained as special cases. For example, if each agent has the same genetic type and the same costlessly acquired crowding characteristic, the model becomes the anonymous crowding model of Wooders (1978, 1980). Suppose, instead, that agents all have the same genetic type, that the number of crowding types is the same as the number of taste types ($T = C$), that the cost of acquiring any crowding characteristic is zero, and that an agent with taste type t always prefers to be crowding type $c = t$ rather than any other $\bar{c} \neq t$. Then, in equilibrium, all agents sharing a taste type will choose the same crowding type; taste and crowding characteristics are perfectly correlated. The special case described leads to an outcome indistinguishable from that of the differentiated crowding model. To obtain the exogenous crowding-types model, suppose that the number of genetic types G is equal to the number of crowding types C. Furthermore, for genetic type g the cost of obtaining crowding type $c = g$ is zero and the cost of obtaining any other crowding type $\bar{c} \neq g$ is greater than the private goods endowment. Then, in equilibrium, the genetic and crowding characteristics are perfectly correlated – in effect, the crowding characteristic is exogenously identified with the genetic characteristic. Finally, to obtain the endogenous crowding-type model with equal abilities, suppose all agents possess the same genetic type and they are all indifferent over their choices of crowding characteristic. That these different crowding forms can be stated as special cases of the endogenous crowding with differential genetic abilities allows us to state definitions and results in terms of this most general case.

7.2.6. Extensions

Thus far, only crowding effects that relate to an agent's coalition membership have been considered. Clearly, this approach is too simple for some economic situations. The classic cases of toll roads and athletic clubs are other examples of situations in which an agent's utility can depend not only on the size of a facility, y, and the crowding profile of those with whom he shares, n, but also on the number of visits he makes to the club, v_i, as well as the total number of visits made by each crowding type $(V_1, \ldots, V_c, \ldots, V_C)$. For example, Arnott and Kraus (1998) conjoin the urban transportation and congestible facilities models with the club literature in a model with crowding and anonymous prices. We could also consider how production technology may be affected in a coalitional economy in which agents decide the distribution of their endowments across various coalitions. For example, the bright colleague who never shows up for seminars creates few positive externalities. On the other hand, the annoying colleague who always shows up at faculty meetings creates many negative external effects.

Alternatively, we could consider a model of local consumption externalities. It may be that external effects flow not from an exogenous or endogenous characteristic but through the actions of agents. For example, I do not care whether you enjoy smoking (a taste) or even whether you are a smoker (a crowding characteristic). What I do care about is how many cigarettes you smoke in my presence. Similarly, I care about whether you renovate your house because it affects my property values. To our knowledge, these effects have not been thoroughly explored in coalitional economies.

7.3. A Local Public Goods Economy

In this section we define a local public goods economy and the core and provide theorems for the equal treatment property of the core and for the 'equal implicit contributions' of core allocations.

A feasible state of the economy is a list

$$(X, Y, \kappa, S) \equiv ((x_1, \ldots, x_I), (y^1, \ldots, y^P), \kappa, (s^1, \ldots, s^P, \ldots, s^P)),$$

where X is an allocation of private good for each agent, Y gives the level of each public good for each jurisdiction, κ is an assignment of agents to crowding types, and $S = (s^1, \ldots, s^P)$ is a partition of the population such that

$$x_i - \epsilon_{\gamma(i)}(\kappa(i)) \geq 0, \quad \text{for all } i \in \mathcal{I},$$

and

$$\sum_{i \in \mathcal{I}} (\omega_{\tau(i)} - x_i) - \sum_p f(y^p, \mathcal{K}(\kappa, s^p)) \geq 0 \quad \text{for all} \quad p = 1, \ldots P.$$

We denote the set of feasible states as F. A pair $(\bar{x}, \bar{y})$ is a feasible allocation for a jurisdiction $\bar{s}$ under crowding assignment $\bar{\kappa}$ if

$$\bar{x}_i - \epsilon_{\gamma(i)}(\bar{\kappa}(i)) \geq 0, \quad \text{for all } i \in \mathcal{I},$$

and

$$\sum_{i \in \bar{s}} (\omega_{\tau(i)} - \bar{x}_i) - \sum_p f(\bar{y}, K(\bar{\kappa}, \bar{s})) \geq 0.$$

We denote the set of feasible allocations for a jurisdiction $\bar{s}$ under crowding assignment $\bar{\kappa}$ as $A(\bar{s}, \bar{\kappa})$.

A jurisdiction $\bar{s} \in S$ under crowding assignment $\bar{\kappa}$ producing $(\bar{x}, \bar{y}) \in A(\bar{s}, \bar{\kappa})$ *improves upon a feasible state* $(X, Y, \kappa, S) \in F$ if, for all $i \in \bar{s}$,

$$u_{\tau(i)}[\bar{x}_i - \epsilon_{\gamma(i)}(\bar{\kappa}(i)), \bar{y}, \bar{\kappa}(i), K(\bar{\kappa}, \bar{s})] \geq u_{\tau(i)}[x_i^p - \epsilon_{\gamma(i)}(\kappa(i)), y^p, \kappa(i), K(\kappa, s^p)],$$

where $i \in s^p \in S$ in the original feasible state, and, for some $j \in \bar{s}$,

$$u_{\tau(j)}[\bar{x}_j - \epsilon_{\gamma(j)}(\bar{\kappa}(j)), \bar{y}, \bar{\kappa}(j), K(\bar{\kappa}, \bar{s})]$$
$$> u_{\tau(j)}[x_j^{\hat{p}} - \epsilon_{\gamma(j)}(\kappa(j)), y^{\hat{p}}, \kappa(j), K(\kappa, s^{\hat{p}})],$$

where $j \in s^{\hat{p}} \in S$ in the original feasible state. A feasible state $(X, Y, \kappa, S) \in F$ is a *core state* if it cannot be improved upon by any allocation. The *core* of the economy is the set of all core states.

What drives an economy to display the "localness" of public goods provision suggested by Tiebout is that all gains from forming coalitions can be realized by groups that are small compared with the size of the population. Tiebout (1956) suggested that seven assumptions would guarantee that efficient allocations in a local public goods economy could be decentralized. His sixth assumption ("[f]or every pattern of community services . . . there is an optimal community size") informally defines a local public goods economy. There are several alternative formulations of the idea of an optimal group size, including exhaustion of blocking opportunities distinguished numbers, and minimum efficient scale. See Conley and Wooders (1997b) for a more detailed discussion of these alternatives. In this chapter, we use the idea of *strict small group effectiveness* to formalize Tiebout's sixth assumption. Strict small-group effectiveness (SSGE) is a variant of exhaustion of gains to scale or "minimum efficient scale" from Wooders (1983).[6] Formally, an economy satisfies SSGE if exists a positive integer $B \in Z_+$ such that

(1) for all core states (X, Y, κ, S) and for all $s^p \in S$ it holds that $|s^p| \leq B$;

(2) if a feasible state (X, Y, κ, S) can be improved upon, then there exists a coalition $\bar{s} \in S$ such that $|\bar{s}| \leq B$, and $\bar{s}$ can improve upon (X, Y, κ, S);

(3) for all $t \in T$ and $g \in C$, either $|\{i \in \mathcal{I} \mid \tau(i) = t$ and $\gamma(i) = g\}| > B$ or $\{i \in \mathcal{I} \mid \tau(i) = t$ and $\gamma(i) = g\} = \emptyset$.

The first condition states that core state jurisdictions are "small" or bounded in size. The second condition states that all possibilities for improving upon a state are realized in small coalitions. And the last condition guarantees that if any type of agent is actually represented in the economy, then there must be enough agents of that type to populate that largest potentially optimal jurisdiction. Note that in the one private good case, a jurisdiction improves upon a feasible state without trading private goods outside the jurisdiction because no gains from such trade are possible. One interpretation of this model is that there are multiple unspecified private goods whose prices are taken as given and the one specified private good is the economy's "money." If the economy included multiple private goods, gains from trading among jurisdictions would be possible.

An immediate consequence of strict small-group effectiveness is the equal treatment property of the core. This follows from Wooders (1983, Theorem 3) and is proven specifically for this economy in Conley and Wooders (2001). Theorem 7.1 states that any two agents with the same taste, crowding, and genetic type are treated equally in the core.

Theorem 7.1. *Let (X, Y, κ, S) be a core state of an economy satisfying SSGE. For any two individuals $i, \hat{i} \in I$ such that $\tau(i) = \tau(\hat{i})$ and $\gamma(i) = \gamma(\hat{i})$, if $i \in s^p$ and $\hat{i} \in s^{\hat{p}}$, then*

$$u_t(x_i - \epsilon_g(\kappa(i)), y^p, \kappa(i), K(\kappa, s^p)) = u_t(x_{\hat{i}} - \epsilon_g(\kappa(\hat{i})), y^{\hat{p}}, \kappa(\hat{i}), K(\kappa, s^{\hat{p}})).$$

---

[6] Another variant of strict small group effectiveness appears in the previous chapter of this volume. While strict small group effectiveness may appear quite restrictive, in situations with many agents, it can fruitfully approximate situations satisfying the apparently mild condition of per capita boundedness (Wooders 1994, theorem 4).

A second consequence of strict small-group effectiveness is that agents residing in two jurisdictions with the same crowding profile and public goods levels who each choose to become the same crowding type must make the same implicit contributions to their jurisdictions for public goods productions. This result, given in the following theorem from Conley and Wooders (2001), is crucial to the competitive properties of club economies; it enables the result that implicit decentralizing, first-best prices can be anonymous – they need not depend on agents' tastes. Note that this extends the equal treatment result of Wooders (1978, Theorem 5) from situations with anonymous crowding to the crowding types model. In contrast, for prior models with differentiated crowding it was only known that individuals with the same tastes and crowding types must be treated equally. This theorem is from Conley and Wooders (1997a).

Theorem 7.2. *Let (X, Y, κ, S) be a core state of an economy satisfying SSGE, and let $s^p, s^{\hat{p}} \in S$ be a pair of jurisdictions in S such that $y^p = y^{\hat{p}}$ and $K(\kappa, s^p) = K(\kappa, s^{\hat{p}})$. Then for any crowding type $c \in C$ and any pair of agents $i \in s^p$ and $\hat{i} \in s^{\hat{p}}$ such that $\kappa(i) = \kappa(\hat{i}) = c$, it holds that*

$$\omega_{\tau(i)} - x_i - \epsilon_{\gamma(i)}(c) = \omega_{\tau(\hat{i})} - x_{\hat{i}} - \epsilon_{\gamma(\hat{i})}(c).$$

7.4. Optimality and Decentralization

In this section we define the price-taking equilibrium concept from Conley and Wooders (2001) and present their core equivalence results. Let $\mathcal{N}^c$ denote the set of crowding profiles that include at least one agent of crowding type c:

$$\mathcal{N}^c \equiv \{n \in Z_+^C \mid K(\kappa, s) = n \text{ for some } s \in S \text{ and } \kappa(i) = c \text{ for some } i \in s\}.$$

An anonymous admission price system for an agent possessing type c is given by the mapping $\rho_c : \Re_+^M \times \mathcal{N}^c \to \Re$ where $\rho_c(y, n)$ is the price an agent with crowding type c would have to pay to join a jurisdiction producing public goods level y and having a crowding profile $n \in \mathcal{N}^c$. We call this system anonymous because prices depend only on observable characteristics (crowding types) and not on any private information (tastes or genetic endowments). A Tiebout admission price system ρ is a collection of such price systems – one for each crowding type.

A Tiebout equilibrium is a feasible state $(X, Y, \kappa, S) \in F$ and a Tiebout admission price system ρ such that

(1) for all $s^p \in S$, all individuals $i \in s^p$, any alternative crowding profile $\bar{n} \in Z_+^C$, all alternative crowding choices c satisfying $\bar{n} \in \mathcal{N}^c$, and all alternative public goods levels $\bar{y} \in \Re_+^M$,

$$u_{\tau(i)}[\omega_{\tau(i)} - \rho_{\kappa(i)}(y^p, K(\kappa, s^p)), y^p, \kappa(i), K(\kappa, s^p)]$$

$$\geq u_{\tau(i)}[\omega_{\tau(i)} - \rho_c(\bar{y}, \bar{n}), \bar{y}, c, \bar{n}];$$

(2) for all potential jurisdictional crowding profiles $\bar{n} = (\bar{n}_1, \ldots, \bar{n}_c \ldots, \bar{n}_C) \in Z_+^C$ and public goods levels $\bar{y} \in \Re_+^M$,

$$\sum_{\{c \in C \mid \bar{n}_c > 0\}} \bar{n}_c \rho_c(\bar{y}, \bar{n}) - f(\bar{y}, \bar{n}) \leq 0;$$

(3) and, for all $s^p \in S$,

$$\sum_{i \in s^p} \rho_{\kappa(i)}(y^p, K(\kappa, s^p)) - f(y^p, K(\kappa, s^p)) = 0.$$

Condition (1) states that all agents must maximize their utilities over jurisdiction type, public goods levels, and crowding assignments. Condition (2) states that, given the price system, no firm can make positive profits by entering the market and offering any other crowding profile with any other public goods levels. Condition (3) requires that equilibrium jurisdictions cover their costs exactly.

A Tiebout admission price equilibrium is, in most respects, a standard competitive equilibrium notion. Given prices, consumers are assumed to maximize utility and firms to maximize profits. Just as would be expected from a price-taking equilibrium for private goods, prices are anonymous in that the prices faced by consumers and firms do not depend on any unobservable traits. In this respect, the Tiebout admission prices are very different from the personalized prices of a Lindahl equilibrium concept. One undesirable feature of Tiebout admission prices, however, is that they require jurisdictions with each possible crowding profile and every possible public goods level to have a separate price. Generally, this requires an infinite number of prices. Thus far, attempts to reduce the dimensionality of the price space have come at the expense of generality: core equivalence results with alternative price mechanisms are typically only attainable for a smaller class of economies. Those results are presented at the end of this section. We now state core equivalence theorems for the Tiebout admission price equilibrium. Theorem 7.3 states that all Tiebout admission price equilibrium states are also core states. An immediate corollary of Theorem 7.3 is a first welfare theorem.

Theorem 7.3. *If the state* $(X, Y, \kappa, S) \in F$ *and the price system* ρ *constitute a Tiebout admission price equilibrium, then* (X, Y, κ, S) *is a core state.*

Theorem 7.4 states that every core state can be decentralized as a Tiebout admissions price equilibrium for some Tiebout admission price system. Theorems 7.3 and 7.4 combine to prove that the set of equilibrium states of the economy is equivalent to the core. Proofs of both results are provided in Conley and Wooders (2001).

Theorem 7.4. *If an economy satisfies SSGE and for all* $t \in T$, u_t *is continuous in* x, *then for each state* (X, Y, κ, S) *in the core, there exists a price system* ρ *such that* ρ *and* (X, Y, κ, S) *constitute a Tiebout equilibrium.*

As stated in Section 7.2.5, each of the various models of crowding are special cases of the differential genetic types and endogenous crowding-types model. As a result, the preceding core equivalence result shows that anonymous decentralization is possible in each of these submodels. Note, however, that "anonymous," when applied to the *differentiated* crowding model, loses its meaning. Although prices formally depend only on crowding types, in this special subcase crowding types and taste types are exogenous and perfectly correlated. Thus, prices in effect depend on taste and are not truly anonymous.

To address the issues of nonlinearity and infinite dimensionality of admission prices, alternative price structures have been explored. The most prominent alternative price structure is that of Lindahl prices. A Lindahl price system in the context of this local public goods model specifies two prices: a per unit price list for the public goods production levels and a participation price. A Lindahl price system is anonymous if those prices are independent of agents' tastes. For the case of anonymous crowding, Wooders (1978) showed the first core decentralization result for anonymous Lindahl prices.[7] (For this and all of the alternative price structures, all of the core equivalence results require some kind of small-group effectiveness assumption.) Notably, however, the Wooders (1978) result is restricted to an economy with constant-returns-to-scale production technology. Boadway (1980), Berglas and Pines (1980), Scotchmer and Wooders (1987), Barham and Wooders (1998), and many others confirm this result. In the case of differentiated crowding, nonanonymous Lindahl price equilibrium states and the core are equivalent, but anonymous Lindahl price equilibrium states are generally strictly contained in the core (see Conley and Wooders 1998; Scotchmer and Wooders 1986; Wooders 1981, 1989). In the crowding-types framework, the core is equivalent to the set of nonanonymous Lindahl price equilibria and is generally larger than the set of anonymous Lindahl price equilibria (see Conley and Wooders 1998). Thus, although Lindahl prices offer a more appealing price system because they are finite dimensional, the only anonymous core decentralization results seem to be attainable for the small class of economies in which production technology is linear. (For this and all of the alternative price structures, all of the core equivalence results require some kind of small-group effectiveness assumption.)

Another pricing system, finite cost shares, addresses the infinite dimensionality of admission prices but with slightly less structure than Lindahl prices. Finite cost shares specify two prices for each crowding type and for each jurisdiction: a list of shares of the cost of providing any levels of public goods, and a jurisdiction participation price. This slight restriction on the pricing structure allows an anonymous core decentralization result in the anonymous crowding framework without requiring linear technology. Conley and Smith (2003) show that if the cost of producing the public good is increasing (but not necessarily linear), the core and the set of anonymous finite cost-share equilibrium states are equivalent when crowding is anonymous. However, this result does not hold for more than one crowding type and the slight generalization comes at a price: a finite cost-share system requires that agents fully know the cost structure for public goods production.

7.5. Existence

One problem with the core and equilibrium approach to coalition economies is that, in general, the core may be empty. Pauly (1970) shows, and Wooders (1978)

---

[7] In Pauly (1970), agents are essentially identical and hence anonymous decentralization trivially holds.

confirms, that even large and very nice economies generally have empty cores. The problem arises because most local public goods economies are characterized by jurisdictional structures that are optimal in that they maximize per capita utility.[8] But, unless the population can be divided into optimal jurisdictions, the core will be empty. For examples of this phenomenon, see Conley and Wooders (1997b). It should also be noted that this is not simply an integer problem resulting from the indivisibility of agents. It is more closely related to the problem of nonexistence of price-taking equilibrium in an economy with free entry of firms and when firms have U-shaped average cost curves; it may not be possible for all firms to produce at minimum average cost.[9] Note that these average cost curves may depend on the total endowment of the economy just as optimal jurisdictions may depend on the numbers of agents of each type in the economy.

The nonexistence remains a significant theoretical issue. However, the theoretical issue may not be of very much real-world importance because, although the *exact* core may fail to exist, *approximate ε-cores* will in general exist for small ε and large economies. In the context of local public economies, the approximate core has a natural interpretation. Basically, we need only require potential blocking coalitions to pay a small cost of defecting. It can be shown that the core exists for arbitrarily small jurisdiction formation costs (for a sufficiently large population); this idea is employed in Wooders (1988, 1989) and Allouch and Wooders (2004). Various formulations of cores and approximate cores as well as corresponding existence results may be found in Wooders (1980), Kaneko and Wooders (1982), Shubik and Wooders (1983), and Wooders (1983). Alternatively, although the exact core may not exist in finite economies, several recent papers show that it will exist in continuum versions. For examples of the continuum approach, see Kaneko and Wooders (1986, 1996); Hammond, Kaneko, and Wooders (1989); Cole and Prescott (1997); Conley and Wooders (1997b); and Ellickson et al. (1999). For a discussion of nonemptiness of approximate cores and related results, see the preceding chapter.

7.6. Noncooperative Solutions

The preceding discussion of existence issues suggests that the core as a solution concept may be too strong. Under the core approach, coalitions have control over who is admitted to their membership. For example, firms, academic departments, and condominium cooperatives control admittance to their clubs. Furthermore, co-ordinated moves such as coalitional defections are often considered. Under standard Nash approachs, individual agents are freely mobile because coalitions must admit anyone who applies (and pays the necessary price); that is, our society institutionally enforces an individual's right to migrate freely between jurisdictions. However, Konishi, Le Breton, and Weber (1998) show that the Nash equilibrium approach

---

[8] More formally, optimal jurisdictions can be characterized as those that yield core payoffs to their memberships in a related game with a nonempty core (the "balanced cover" game). See, for example, Wooders (1983) for a discussion of balanced cover games.

[9] For production economies, this problem is treated in Novshek and Sonnenschein (1978), which introduces the concept of "minimum efficient scale," a noncooperative analogue of strict small-group effectiveness but for firms rather than clubs or jurisdictions.

is generally too weak. When it exists, the Nash equilibrium in a finite local public goods economy is often not efficient.[10] Showing the existence of equilibria in the Nash-based approaches often runs into the same problems we find with the core approach: the population size (and proportion of types) must be just right.[11]

Conley and Konishi (2002) offer a refinement of Nash equilibrium for local public goods economies called the *migration-proof Tiebout equilibrium*. In this approach, both coalitional and unilateral deviations are permitted, but all deviations must be credible in the sense that they are stable against new migration. That is, deviations are credible if none of the agents who were left behind would want to follow the deviators to the new coalition. Conley and Konishi show that the exact migration-proof Tiebout equilibrium exists and is unique in large finite economies. Furthermore, they find that these equilibria are asymptotically efficient. However, this has only been proven for a small class of economies (identical agents with single-peaked preferences), and how far this approach can be extended is unclear.

Another approach is to consider dynamic models in which agents are myopic and some agents may chose to move to a new jurisdiction each period. To illustrate, suppose that an optimal jurisdiction contains only two people but there is an odd number of individuals in the population and a three-person jurisdiction is preferred to a singleton jurisdiction. Arnold and Wooders (2002) define a k-remainder as an equilibrium in which only individuals in the same club can coordinate their actions and in which for each period only k individuals can benefit from moving. They demonstrate existence of such an equilibrium for k smaller than the optimal group size. Again, Arnold and Wooders deal with a special case, and it is unclear how far this approach can be extended.

We refer the reader to Chapters 6 and 9 of this volume for further treatment of noncooperative (and non-price-taking) equilibria.

7.7. Other Results and Future Research

An interesting question in these coalitional economies and an issue that has been important to the Tiebout literature is how agents sort themselves by tastes. If optimal jurisdictions are taste homogeneous, much can be concluded about efficient organization of our social and economic institutions. For example, the best way to educate college students would be in schools of like-minded students, such as the London School of Economics and the Juilliard School of the Arts. Wooders (1978) shows that when crowding is anonymous, optimal jurisdictions will be taste homogeneous. When crowding is differentiated and when crowding types are exogenous, optimal jurisdictions will generally be taste heterogeneous. See Wooders (1989), Wooders (1997), Conley and Wooders (1995), and Conley and Wooders (1997a) for these results. If crowding types are endogenous and agents have the same genetic abilities, Conley and Wooders (1996) show that optimal jurisdictions will be taste

[10] This approach was first pursued by Kalai, Postlewaite, and Roberts (1979) and Guesnerie and Oddou (1979, 1981) with additional work by Konishi, Le Breton, and Weber (1998). See Konishi (1996) and Nechyba (1997) for a survey of work in this area.
[11] See Pauly (1970) and Wooders (1978).

homogeneous. Finally, if crowding types are endogenous and agents have different genetic abilities, equilibrium jurisdictions will generally be taste integrated.

The literature discussed herein has focused primarily on single-membership jurisdictions. However, we could also consider a "club" approach in which agents are allowed to be members of multiple clubs that provide different public goods. Buchanan (1965) first introduced the idea of a club good, and the club approach to Tiebout's hypothesis constitutes a large part of the public economics literature. If agents are allowed to join multiple clubs, several interesting modeling questions arise: Should an agent's preferences depend directly on the intensity of his own and others' club usage? Or should agents be endowed with a finite amount of time that they may allocate across clubs? And to what extent will clubs specialize in a particular service rather than offering a spread of public goods? Although there are a few papers that consider multiple memberships in clubs (Shubik and Wooders 1982; Ellickson et al. 1999; and Allouch and Wooders 2001), the models posit some restrictions on admissible club structures but otherwise are closely related to those already treated in the literature and do not address any of the issues raised here.

Although these local public goods models are based on locational choice in the sense that each agent is choosing a jurisdiction in which to reside, land allocation has not been explicitly modeled. Of course, land allocation has been extensively explored in urban economics and regional science, but these studies do not generally treat the issues in the manner of game theoretic coalitions. There are likely to be many interesting spillovers between the two approaches.

Finally, to place this chapter in the context of others in this volume, we note that our model permits situations in which there is a tension between increasing returns to forming large clubs and heterogeneity of preferences over optimal facility sizes or levels of public goods, as in Chapters 5 and 8 of this volume. Our assumption of SSGE – that *all* gains to collective activities can be realized by groups bounded in size – is in contrast to the assumptions used by Demange, however, to obtain existence of equilibrium. Although relaxing SSGE to the conditions described in Chapter 6 of (this volume) can be done for several results, the existence of first best equilibrium with anonymous pricing in such environments is problematic. (Recall that Kovalenkov and Wooders in Chapter 6 of this volume treat only the core and approximate cores as well as limiting situations.) Our model, as the others in Part Two allows free entry. The equilibrium concepts also allow free mobility, but the prices an individual faces when considering relocation to another club or jurisdiction depend on his crowding type, the composition of the jurisdiction, and the level of the public project provided in that jurisdiction; prices or cost shares are competitive. The restrictions on the mechanisms by which the costs and benefits of group formation are distributed in Chapters 5 and 8 of this volume typically are inconsistent with the admission price systems treated in this chapter.

BIBLIOGRAPHY

[1] Allouch, A. and M. Wooders (2001), "Price Taking Equilibrium in Club Economies with Multiple Memberships and Unbounded Club Sizes," University of Warwick Department of Economics Discussion Paper. No. 639 (revised).

[2] Arnold, T. and M. Wooders (2002), "Dynamic Club Formation with Coordination," University of Warwick Department of Economics Discussion Paper.

[3] Arnott, R. and M. Kraus (1998), "When Are Anonymous Congestion Charges Consistent with Marginal Cost Pricing?" *Journal of Public Economics* 67, 45–64.

[4] Barham, V. and M. Wooders (1998), "First and Second Welfare Theorems for Economies with Collective Goods," in *Topics in Pubic Finance*, D. Pines, E. Sadka, and I. Zilcha (eds.), Cambridge University Press.

[5] Benabou, R. (1993), "Workings of a City: Location, Education, and Production," *Quarterly Journal of Economics* 105, 619–652.

[6] Berglas, E. (1976), "Distribution of Tastes and Skills and the Provision of Local Public Goods," *Journal of Public Economics* 6, 409–423.

[7] Berglas, E., E. Helpman, and D. Pines (1982), "The Economic Theory of Clubs: Some Clarifications," *Economics Letters* 10, 343–348.

[8] Berglas, E. and D. Pines (1980), "Clubs, as a Case of Competitive Industry with Goods as a Variable Quality," *Economics Letters* 5, 363–366.

[9] Berglas, E. and D. Pines (1981), "Clubs, Local Public Goods and Transportation Modes; A Synthesis," *Journal of Public Economics* 15, 141–162.

[10] Bewley, T. (1981), "A Critique of Tiebout Theory of Local Public Expenditure," *Econometrica* 49, 713–740.

[11] Boadway, R. (1980), "A Note on the Market Provision of Club Goods," *Journal of Public Economics* 13, 131–137.

[12] Brueckner, J. (1994), "Tastes, Skills and Local Public Goods," *Journal of Urban Economics* 35, 201–220.

[13] Buchanan, J. M. (1965), "An Economic Theory of Clubs," *Economica* 32, 1–14.

[14] Cartwright, E. and M. Wooders (2001), "On the Theory of Equalizing Differences; Increasing Abundances of Types of Workers May Increase Their Earnings," *Economics Bulletin*, Vol. 4, no. 4, 1–10.

[15] Cole, H. and E. Prescott (1997), "Valuation Equilibria with Clubs," *Journal of Economic Theory* 74, 19–39.

[16] Conley, J. and H. Konishi (2002), "Migration-Proof Tiebout Equilibrium: Existence and Asymptotic Efficiency," *Journal of Public Economics* 86, 243–262.

[17] Conley, J. and S. C. Smith (2003), "Finite Decentralization in a Tiebout Economy with Crowding Types," *Social Choice and Welfare* 20, 49–75.

[18] Conley, J. and M. Wooders (1995), "Hedonic Independence and Taste-Homogeneity of Optimal Jurisdictions in the Core of a Tiebout Economy with Crowding Types," University of Illinois Office of Research Working Paper, pp. 95–118 (to appear in *Annales d'Economie et de Statistique*).

[19] Conley, J. and M. Wooders (1996), "Taste-Homogeneity of Optimal Jurisdictions in a Tiebout Economy with Crowding Types and Endogenous Educational Investment Choices," *Recherche Economiche* 50, 367–387.

[20] Conley, J. and M. Wooders (1997a), "Equivalence of the Core and Competitive Equilibrium in a Tiebout Economy with Crowding Types," *Journal of Urban Economics* 41, 421–440.

[21] Conley, J. and M. Wooders (1997b), "Anonymous Pricing in Public Goods Economies," in *Topics in Pubic Finance*, D. Pines, E. Sadka, and I. Zilcha (eds.), Cambridge University Press.

[22] Conley, J. and M. Wooders (1998), "Anonymous Lindahl Pricing in a Tiebout Economy with Crowding Types," *Canadian Journal of Economics* 31, 952–974.

[23] Conley, J. and M. Wooders (2001), "Tiebout Economies with Differential Genetic Types and Endogenously Chosen Crowding Characteristics," *Journal of Economic Theory* 98, 261–294.

[24] Cornes, R. and T. Sandler (1996), *The Theory of Externalities, Public Goods and Club Goods*, Cambridge University Press, Second Edition.

[25] Davis, O. A. and A. B. Whinston (1967), "On the Distinction between Public and Private Goods," *American Economic Review* 57, 360–373.

[26] de Bartolome, C. (1990), "Equilibrium and Efficiency in a Community Model with Peer-Group Effects," *Journal of Political Economy* 98, 110–133.

[27] DeSerpa, A. C. (1977), "A Theory of Discriminatory Clubs," *Scottish Journal of Political Economy* 24, 33–41.

[28] DeVany, A. S. and T. R. Saving (1977), "Product Quality, Uncertainty, and Regulation: The Trucking Industry," *American Economic Review* 67, 583–594.

[29] Ellickson, B. (1979), "Local Public Goods and the Market of Neighborhoods," in *The Economics of Neighborhoods*, D. Segal (ed.), New York: Academic Press, 263–294.

[30] Ellickson, B. and B. Grodal, S. Scotchmer, and W. Zame (1999), "Clubs and the Market," *Econometrica* 67, 1185–1218.

[31] Guesnerie, R. and C. Oddou (1979), "On Economic Games Which Are Not Necessarily Superadditive," *Economic Letters* 3, 301–306.

[32] Guesnerie, R. and C. Oddou (1981), "Second Best Taxation as a Game," *Journal of Economic Theory* 25, 67–91.

[33] Hammond, M., M. Kaneko, and M. Wooders (1989), "Continuum Economies with Finite Coalitions: Core, Equilibria and Widespread Externalities," *Journal of Economic Theory* 49, 113–134.

[34] Hillman, A. L. and P. L. Swan (1979), "Club Participation under Uncertainty," *Economics Letters* 4, 307–312.

[35] Kalai, E., A. Postlewaite, and J. Roberts (1979), "A Group Incentive Compatible Mechanism Yielding Core Allocations," *Journal of Economic Theory* 20, 13–22.

[36] Kamien, M. I., N. L. Schwartz, and D. J. Roberts (1973), "Exclusion, Externalities, and Public Goods," *Journal of Public Economics* 2, 217–230.

[37] Kaneko, M. and M. Wooders (1982), "Cores of Partitioning Games," *Mathematical Social Sciences* 3, 313–327.

[38] Kaneko, M. and M. H. Wooders (1986), "The Core of a Game with a Continuum of Players and Finite Coalitions: The Model and Some Results," *Mathematical Social Sciences* 12, 105–137.

[39] Kaneko, M. and M. H. Wooders (1989), "The Core of a Continuum Economy with Widespread Externalities and Finite Coalitions: From Finite to Continuum Economics, *Journal of Economic Theory* 49, 135–168.

[40] Kaneko, M. and M. H. Wooders (1996), "The Nonemptiness of the f-core of a Game without Side Payments," *International Journal of Game Theory* 25, 245–258.

[41] Knight, F. H. (1924), "Some Fallacies in the Interpretation of Social Cost," *Quarterly Journal of Economics* 38, 582–606.

[42] Konishi, H. (1996), "Voting with Ballots and Feet: Existence of Equilibrium in a Local Public Good Economy," *Journal of Economic Theory* 68, 480–509.

[43] Konishi, H. (1997), "Free Mobility Equilibrium in a Local Public Goods Economy with Congestion," *Research in Economics* 51, 19–30.

[44] Konishi, H., M. Le Breton, and S. Weber (1998), "Equilibria in Finite Local Public Goods Economies," *Journal of Economic Theory* 79, 224–244.

[45] McGuire, M. (1974), "Group Size, Group Homogeneity, and the Aggregate Provision of a Pure Public Good under Cournot Behavior," *Public Choice* 18, 107–126.

[46] McGuire, M. (1991), "Group Composition, Collective Consumption, and Collaborative Production," *American Economic Review* 81, 1391–1407.

[47] Millward, R. (1970), "Exclusion Costs, External Economies, and Market Failure," *Oxford Economic Papers* 22, 24–38.

[48] Nechyba, T. (1997), "Existence of Equilibrium and Stratification in Local and Hierarchical Tiebout Economies with Property Taxes and Voting," *Economic Theory* 10, 277–304.

[49] Nichols, D., E. Smolensky, and T. N. Tideman (1971), "Discrimination by Waiting Time in Merit Goods," *American Economic Review* 61, 312–323.

[50] Ng, Y. K. and R. D. Tollison (1974), "A Note on Consumption Sharing and Non-Exclusion Rules," *Economica* 41, 446–450.

[51] Novshek, W. and H. Sonnenschein (1978), "Cournot and Walras Equilibrium," *Journal of Economic Theory* 19, 223–266.

[52] Oakland, W. H. (1972), "Congestion, Public Goods, and Welfare," *Journal of Public Economics* 1, 339–357.

[53] Pauly, M. (1967), "Clubs, Commonality, and the Core: An Integration of Game Theory and the Theory of Public Goods," *Economica* 34, 314–324.

[54] Pauly, M. (1972), "Cores and Clubs," *Public Choice* 9, 53–65.

[55] Pigou, A. C. (1920), *The Economics of Welfare*. London: Macmillan.

[56] Rosen, S. (1978), "Substitution and Division of Labour," *Economica* 45, 235–250.

[57] Rosen, S. (1986), "The Theory of Equalising Differences," Chap. 12 of the *Handbook of Labor Economics, Volume 1*, O. Ashenfelter and R. Layard (eds.), Elsevier Science Publishers.

[58] Samuelson, P. (1954), "The Pure Theory of Public Expenditures," *Review of Economics and Statistics* 36, 387–389.

[59] Sandler, T. and J. Tschirhart (1980), "The Economic Theory of Clubs: An Evaluative Survey," *Journal of Economic Literature* 18, 1481–1521.

[60] Schwab, R. and W. Oates (1991), "Community Composition and the Provision of Local Public Goods: A Normalize Analysis," *Journal of Public Economics* 44, 217–237.

[61] Scotchmer, S. and M. Wooders (1986), "Optimal and Equilibrium Groups," *Harvard Discussion Paper* 1251.

[62] Scotchmer, S. and M. Wooders (1987), "Competitive Equilibria and the Core in Economies with Anonymous Crowding," *Journal of Public Economics* 34, 159–174.

[63] Shubik, M. and M. Wooders (1982) "Near Markets and Market Games," Cowles Foundation Discussion Paper No. 657, in *Topics in Game Theory and Mathematical Economics; Essays in Honor of Robert S. Aumann*, M. Wooders (ed.) Fields Institute Communication Vol. 32, The American Mathematical Society (1999).

[64] Shubik, M. and M. Wooders (1983a), "Approximate Cores of Replica Games and Economies: Part I. Replica Games, Externalities, and Approximate Cores," *Mathematical Social Sciences* 6, 27–48.

[65] Shubik, M. and M. Wooders (1983b), "Approximate Cores of Replica Games and Economies: Part II. Set-up Costs and Firm Formation in Coalition Production Economies," *Mathematical Social Sciences* 6, 285–306.

[66] Tiebout, C. (1956), "A Pure Theory of Local Expenditures," *Journal of Political Economy* 64, 416–424.

[67] Tollison, R. D. (1972), "Consumption Sharing and Non-Exclusion Rules," *Economica* 39, 279–291.

[68] Westhoff, F. (1977), "Existence of Equilibria in Economies with a Local Public Good," *Journal of Economic Theory* 14, 84–112.

[69] Wooders, M. (1978), "Equilibria, the Core, and Jurisdiction Structures in Economies with a Local Public Good," *Journal of Economic Theory* 18, 328–348.

[70] Wooders, M. (1980), "The Tiebout Hypothesis: Near Optimality in Local Public Good Economies," *Econometrica* 48, 1467–1486.

[71] Wooders, M. (1981), "A Limit Theorem on the ϵ-Core of an Economy with Public Goods," National Tax Institute of Japan, Paper No. 20.

[72] Wooders, M. (1983), "The Epsilon-Core of a Large Replica Game," *Journal of Mathematical Economics* 11, 277–300.

[73] Wooders, M. (1988), "Stability of Jurisdiction Structures in Economies with a Local Public Good," *Mathematical Social Sciences* 15, 24–29.

[74] Wooders, M. (1989), "A Tiebout Theorem," *Mathematical Social Sciences* 18, 33–55.

[75] Wooders, M. (1992), "Inessentiality of Large Groups and the Approximate Core Property; An Equivalence Theorem," *Economic Theory* 2, 129–147.

[76] Wooders, M. (1994), " Equivalence of Games and Markets," *Econometrica* 62, 1141–1160.

[77] Wooders, M. (1997), "Equivalence of Lindahl Equilibrium with Participation Prices and the Core," *Economic Theory* 9, 115–127.

[78] Wooders, M. (1999) "Multijurisdictional Economies, the Tiebout Hypothesis, and Sorting" *Proceedings of the National Academy of Sciences* 96, 10585–10587, on line at http: //www.pnas.org/cgi/content/full/96/19/10585.

Secession-Proof Cost Allocations and Stable Group Structures in Models of Horizontal Differentiation

Michel Le Breton and Shlomo Weber

8.1. Introduction

In many social, political, and economic situations individuals form groups rather than operate on their own. For example, communities are formed to share the costs of producing local public goods among the residents, or workers join a labor union to attain a better working contract. In these situations individuals utilize the increasing returns to scale provided by large groups. On the other hand, given the heterogeneity of agents' characteristics and tastes, the decision-making process of a large group may lead to outcomes quite undesirable for some of its members. This observation supports the claim that benefits of size are not unlimited and, on some occasions, a decentralized organization is superior to a large social structure. Thus, instead of a grand coalition containing the entire population, we may observe the emergence of group structures consisting of groups smaller than the grand coalition. The reason for the existence of groups that contain more than one agent but less than the entire society lies in the conflict between increasing returns to scale on the one hand and heterogeneity of agents' preferences on the other.[1]

In this chapter we consider a society consisting of a finite or infinite number of individuals. who are allowed to create subsocieties that lead to a partition of the society into pairwise disjoint groups. Each group in the partition selects an alternative within a policy space available to this group. The notion of policy (or project) in this chapter is similar to that of *public project* introduced by Mas-Colell (1980). It can accommodate virtually any interpretation as long as the benefit derived by an agent from the selected project within the given group is not affected by the composition and size of the group.

The two basic elements of group formation described here, namely, the composition of formed groups and their policy choices do not provide, however, the complete description of the collective decision problem. What is missing here is a mechanism of sharing the policy costs among agents within the same group. Indeed, a government has to select an explicit scheme to tax its citizens in order to cover the

---

[1] See also Chapters 5, 6, and 7 of this volume.

cost of public policies, whereas a community must determine the tax burden of its residents for financing local public projects. Thus, when a partition of individuals has been formed, a set of appropriate policies has been chosen, the allocation of the cost among the agents should be determined. Suppose now that the partition of individuals into groups has been formed, where each group in the partition chooses a policy and decides on allocation of policy costs among its members. For an arbitrarily chosen cost allocation, however, there could be a single individual or a group of agents who would object to the proposed arrangement. We provide a detailed analysis of "secession" threats taking into account various stability notions.

It is important to point out a clear separation between "horizontally differentiated" and "vertically differentiated" projects. If the interpretation of the policy space is given by a choice of geographical location of public facilities (schools, hospitals, libraries, etc.), then the individuals display distinct preferences over the policy space and the location turns to be the parameter of horizontal differentiation. If, on the other hand, the agents exhibit identical preferences over quantity or quality attributes of public projects, we will have a model of "vertical differentiation."[2] In this chapter we focus mainly on models with horizontal differentiation in which individuals have different rankings over elements of policy space.[3]

When analyzing possible cost allocations, we have to take into account that in many cases a variety of institutional, legal, informational, and technological constraints may rule out some cost allocation schemes for certain groups of individuals. We therefore will distinguish between two cases:

(1) *Unrestricted set of cost allocations.* In this case there are no restrictions on the set of cost allocations, and thus every group that forms or contemplates its formation is allowed to use any cost-sharing scheme among its members. The only condition is that the aggregated individual contributions of the members of the group cover the cost of their chosen policies.

(2) *Restricted set of cost allocations.* Here some groups face institutional or social limitations on the sets of possible cost allocations they can use. We examine several specific cost-sharing schemes such as

Equal Share Allocations – All individuals within the same group, regardless of their characteristics and policy preferences, make equal contributions towards policy costs;

Rawlsian Allocations – The cost allocations are designed to equalize the after-contribution utilities and eliminate utility gaps among all members of the given group.

In this chapter we do not examine the issue of feasibility of public projects. The limitations on feasibility may incorporate constraints generated by institutions, rules,

---

[2] The general framework developed in this chapter allows for the examination of the existence and structure of Tiebout equilibria. Our approach is by no means exclusive. For example, economies with local public goods and economies with clubs have been analyzed within the Arrow–Debreu general equilibrium framework (see, e.g., Conley and Wooders 1997; Ellickson et al. (1999); Wooders 1978, 1980).

[3] See also Chapters 5, 6, and 7 in this volume that deal with horizontal and vertical differentiation.

or social norms. If the "projects" under consideration are allocations of goods, feasibility, as usual, means that, owing to resource constraints, some alternatives that are available for some groups could be out of reach for others. One case is that of increasing returns when larger groups have an access to larger sets of projects. For example, a merger of two groups may create a pool of resources that was not available in the pre-merger state. Obviously, there are situations when the opposite is true, as in the case when the chances to reach an acceptable solution for all members would diminish in large groups. All these situations are beyond the scope of our analysis here.[4]

It is quite natural to expect that the existence of stable structures is crucially dependent on the dimensionality of the policy space. In general, the severity of preferences' divergence increases when the number of policy dimensions grows, in which case the search for a stable group structure and an appropriate cost-share allocation becomes more challenging. We will focus here on unidimensional policy spaces that allow us to obtain a large set of interesting results and in the same time to indicate the difficulties that arise in the *multidimensions* setting.

8.2. The Model

We consider a framework with one private good that plays the role of numeraire. The society ϵ is defined by a sextuple (N, X, C, T, W, U), where N is a set of individuals, X is a set of projects, C is a cost correspondence that determines the cost (in terms of the numeraire) incurred by a coalition S when it selects a project $x \in X$, T is a cost-share correspondence that assigns the set of feasible cost-share allocations for every coalition S and every project $x \in X$, W is a profile of initial endowments (incomes) $\{w(i)\}_{i \in N}$ in terms of the numeraire, and $U = \{u_i\}_{i \in N}$ is a profile of individuals' utility functions that represent their preferences over pairs of public projects and a consumption of private good $u_i : X \times \Re_+ \to \Re_+$.

Note that we examine both "nonatomic" and finite sets of individuals. In the first case every individual is negligible and the set of individuals N is represented by the measure space $\{N, \mathcal{S}, \lambda\}$, where λ is an atomless measure and $\mathcal{S}$ is a set of nonnegligible, measurable subsets of N. A canonical example that will be used throughout this chapter is the case of the unit interval, where $N = [0, 1]$, $\mathcal{S}$ is the Borel σ-algebra of $[0, 1]$, and λ is the Lebesgue measure on $[0, 1]$. In the case of finite societies, which underline the importance of individual actions, we denote by n the number of individuals in N, and $\mathcal{S}$ will simply denote the collection of all nonempty subsets of N.

Every group of individuals that forms can choose an alternative from X. In most of our applications we consider a finite-policy space X. However, in some cases it is more appropriate to consider an infinite-policy space. We assume that X is a convex and compact subset of the unidimensional set $\Re$ and also require that all policies in X are feasible for all coalitions.[5]

---

[4] See Le Breton and Weber (2003b,c) for the comparison of two polar cases when the feasible sets are expanding and shrinking with the size of a group.

[5] We do not examine here a possibility that, owing to resource constraints, institutional rules, or social norms, some policies could be out of reach for some coalitions. See Wooders (1978), Kaneko and

The cost correspondence $C : X \times S \rightarrow \Re_+$ determines the cost incurred by coalition S when it selects the public project x. In our framework, the cost of every project assumes the separable form $C(S, x) = \tilde{C}(S) + c(x)$. On many occasions the function $\tilde{C}(S)$ is an increasing function of the mass of members of S, and thus the group-specific component of the public project cost increases with the size of the group served by this project. Because our focus is on distinct preferences over projects, we do not examine here the cost differentials across projects. We often assume that the project-specific component of the project cost, $c(x)$, is independent of x.

For every coalition $S \in S$ and a project $x \in X$, any cost allocation should guarantee that the aggregated contributions of members of S cover the cost of the project $C(S, x)$. The set of all cost allocations for S and x is denoted by $T^*(S, x)$. Owing to possible institutional, technological, or other types of constraints, the set of feasible cost-allocation $T(S, x)$ for a coalition S and a project x could be smaller than the set of balanced cost-share allocations $T^*(S, x)$. If the cost-allocation correspondence is single valued, then, for $i \in S$, the value $T(i, S, x)$ will denote the cost share of individual i within S used to finance the project x. Otherwise, for every cost allocation $t \in T(S, x)$ we denote by $t(i)$ the cost share of individual i.

Each individual $i \in N$ is endowed with a positive amount of the private good $w(i)$. The utility function $u_i : X \times \Re_+ \rightarrow \Re$ represents the preferences of individual i over all bundles (x, m_i), consisting of a public project x and a consumption of private good $m(i)$. We assume that, for any given project x, every function $u_i(x, \cdot)$ is increasing with respect to the amount of private good. In addition, in models with the infinite set of projects X, for a given amount of private good, the utility function of every individual is quasi-concave in policy choices.

8.3. Cooperative Framework

Let us now turn to the cooperative approach of the group formation process and associate a society with a cooperative game in characteristic function form. To avoid the introduction of the heavy machinery required for the treatment of societies with the infinite number of individuals, we provide the formal definition of the game for a case with a finite number of individuals.

Let the cost allocation correspondence T be given. We then associate $\mathcal{E}$ with a cooperative game in characteristic form v^T, where for each coalition $S \subset N$, the set of utility levels attainable for the members S is determined. That is, a utility vector $u = (u_1, \ldots, u_n)$ is attainable for S if there exists a public project $x \in X$ and a cost-share allocation $t \in T(S, x)$ such that every member of $i \in S$ achieves at least the utility level u_i. Formally,

$$v^T(S) = \{u = (u_1, \ldots, u_n) \in \Re^n : \exists x \in X \text{ and } t \in T(S, x) \text{ s. t. } u_i$$
$$\leq u_i(x, w(i) - t(i)) \, \forall i \in S\}.$$

Wooders (1982), Greenberg and Weber (1993), Demange (1994), and Le Breton and Weber (2003b,c) among those who have examined this possibility as well as Chapter 6 of this volume.

If the sets of cost-share allocations are unrestricted, the game v^{T*} will be simply denoted by v.

As we show next, the cooperative game v^T is not necessarily *superadditive*; that is, it is possible that there exist coalitions $S, S' \subset N$ for which the inclusion $v^T(S) \cap v^T(S \setminus S') \subset v^T(S)$ does not hold. This means that there could be two disjoint coalitions such that their union does not necessarily guarantee all the members of two groups the utility levels they could achieve separately. We then define the cooperative game $\widehat{v}^T$, which is the *superadditive cover* of the game v^T. Denote by $\mathcal{P}$ the set of all partitions or group structures[6] of N and consider a partition $P = \{S^k\}_{1 \le k \le K} \in \mathcal{P}$. This partition yields the set of feasible payoff vectors given by the following intersection:

$$v^T(P) = \cap_{1 \le k \le K} v^T(S^k).$$

Then $\widehat{v}^T$ is defined by

$$\widehat{v}^T(S) = \cup_{P_S \in \mathcal{P}(S)} \cap_{S' \in P_S} v^T(S')$$

for all $S \subseteq N$, where $\mathcal{P}(S)$ denotes the set of partitions of S.[7] The game $\widehat{v}^T$ describes the set of payoffs attainable for coalitions on the assumption they can be partitioned in any arbitrary way. It is easy to verify that the games v^T and $\widehat{v}^T$ coincide if and only if the latter is superadditive.

Before introducing the notion of a T-stable outcome, we should point out that a T-attainable outcome consists of three elements: partition of the set of individuals in pairwise disjoint groups, public projects in X, and feasible (given T) cost-sharing allocations chosen by each group in the formed partition. This is expressed formally in the following definition:

Definition 8.3.1. *The set of triples $z = \{(S^k, x^k, t^k)\}_{1 \le k \le K}$ is called a T-attainable outcome, where*

$\{S^k\}_{1 \le k \le K}$ is a partition of the set of individuals N into pairwise disjoint groups;

$(x^1, \ldots, x^K)$ is a set of public projects with $x^k \in X$ being chosen by S^k for all $k = 1, \ldots, K$;

$(t^1, \ldots, t^K)$ is a set of cost-sharing allocations with $t^k \in T(S^k, x^k)$ being chosen by S^k for all $k = 1, \ldots, K$.

A T-attainable outcome z is stable if it is immune to all coalitional deviations. In other words, the utility vector associated with z belongs to the core of the corresponding game.[8]

---

[6] Cooperative games with a coalition structure were introduced by Aumann and Drèze (1974).
[7] See also Chapter 5 of this volume.
[8] Recall that a payoff vector $u = (u_1, \ldots, u_n) \in \mathfrak{R}^n$ is in the *core* of the game v if $u \in v(N)$ and there is no coalition $S \subseteq N$ and $u' = (u'_1, \ldots, u'_n) \in v(S)$ such that $u'_i > u_i$ for all $i \in S$.

Because the game v^T is not, in general, superadditive, we allow multigroup configurations and, as is typically done in economies with public goods or clubs,[9] we consider the game $\widehat{v}^T$ instead of v^T:

Definition 8.3.2. *A T-attainable outcome* $z = \{(S^k, x^k, t^k)\}_{1 \leq k \leq K}$ *is T-stable if the utility vector* $u = (u_1, \ldots, u_n)$, *where* $u_i = u_i(x^{k(i)}, w(i) - t(i))$ *for every* $i \in S^{k(i)}$, *belongs to the core of* $\widehat{v}^T$. *A T*-stable outcome will simply be called* stable.

If the outcome z is T-stable, then, given the partition of the set N and the choice of public projects, the contribution scheme $(t_1, \ldots, t_n)$ *associated with z is immune to any threat of coalitional deviations and is called a T-secession-proof. A T*-secession-proof scheme is simply* secession proof.

In the next section we study the existence of stable outcomes and provide a partial characterization of secession-proof allocations. In light of the discussion of this section, we proceed by examining the core of the game $\widehat{v}^{T^*} = \widehat{v}$.

8.4. Unrestricted Cost-Allocation Correspondence

We consider[10] a society consisting of agents with preferences over the set X of possible locations of public projects, where the set X is given by the interval $[0, 1]$. Every agent $i \in N$ has an ideal point θ^i in X and the preferences are symmetric and single peaked. The distribution of ideal points is given by a cumulative distribution function F defined over the space X. It is important to stress that for our main existence result in this section we do not impose any restrictions on the distribution function and allow for infinite or finite societies. We denote by μ the measure on X induced by the distribution function F with the total mass $\mu(X)$ equal to 1.

Every (measurable) group of individuals S can choose any location $x \in X$. The costs associated with any project x for the community S are given by $C(S, x) = \alpha\mu(S) + c(x)$. The project cost consists of two components: the variable cost, $\alpha\mu(S)$, which depends on the number of individuals in S (project users), where α is a nonnegative constant, and a positive fixed cost of setting and maintaining the project $c(x)$. We assume that $c(\cdot)$ is a continuous and positive valued function on X. In this section we do not restrict the set of balanced cost-share allocations, and for every measurable subset S of N and every $x \in X$, the set of feasible cost-share allocations, $T^*(S, x)$, consists of all measurable functions t on the set S that satisfy $\int_S t(i) d\mu(t) = C(S, x)$.

If an individual i belongs to the group S that chooses project $x \in X$, he or she incurs a disutility or "transportation" cost, $d(i, x)$, which is determined by the distance between i and the location x of the project. We only require that the cost function $d(i, x) = d(|\theta(i) - x|)$ be continuous and (strictly) increasing in the distance $|\theta(i) - x|$, with $d(0) = 0$. The utility of member i of group S, which chooses

---

[9] See Guesnerie and Oddou (1979, 1981) and Wooders (1978).
[10] See Cremer, De Kerchove, and Thisse (1985); Alesina and Spolaore (1997); Le Breton and Weber (2003a); and Haimanko, Le Breton, and Weber (2003, 2004) among others.

project x and the cost-share allocation t, consists of two terms, the transportation cost $d(i, x)$ and his or her net income $w(i) - t(i)$. Assuming separability, we may simply ignore initial endowments, and, without loss of generality, the utility of individual i will be given by $u_i(x, m_i) = -d(i, x) - t(i)$.

Now for every coalition S let the set $v(S)$ be given by

$$v(S) = \{u = (u_1, \ldots, u_n) \in \Re^n : \exists x \in X \text{ and } t \in T^*(S, x) \text{ s. t. } u_i$$

$$\leq -d(i, x) - t(i) \; \forall i \in S\},$$

and define the game $\widehat{v}$ as in the previous section. Definition 8.3.2 implies that a stable outcome exists if and only if the game $\widehat{v}$ has a nonempty core. We have the following existence result:

Proposition 8.4.1. *(Haimanko, Le Breton and Weber 2004). Suppose that the set of public projects X is the interval $[0, 1]$ and that the preferences of each $i \in N$ are symmetric and single peaked. Assume also that the costs associated with any project x for the community S are given by $C(S, x) = \alpha \mu(S) + c(x)$, where $\alpha \geq 0$. Then a stable outcome exists for all finite and infinite societies.*

Given the symmetry and single-peakedness of the individuals' preferences, all individuals in N can be ordered with respect to their peaks. The question that may arise is: Can one restrict the analysis to *consecutive* groups only as in Greenberg and Weber (1986) and Demange (1994) (see also Section 8.5). Recall that a group is consecutive S if it contains no holes, and thus if S contains individuals with peaks θ and θ' it also contains all those who have peaks between θ and θ'. The Greenberg–Weber and Demange results rely on the following property: if an outcome is rejected by a nonconsecutive coalition, there is a consecutive coalition that rejects the same outcome. However, this property does not hold in the framework of Proposition 8.4.1. One can construct an example in which an outcome is blocked by nonconsecutive coalitions only. Thus, the techniques of Greenberg–Weber and Demange cannot be applied to prove this proposition.

Haimanko et al. (2004) also show that if the society is nonatomic and is described by a strictly positive and continuous density, then, given the constant project-specific costs c for any stable outcome and any interval $S \subseteq N$, the number of groups in S, denoted $K(c, S)$, satisfies the following asymptotic formula called *the square-root principle*:

$$\lim_{c \to 0} \sqrt{c} K(c, S) = \frac{\sqrt{d'_+(0)}}{2} \int_S \sqrt{f(t)} dt,$$

where $d'_+(0)$ is the (well-defined) right-hand-side derivative of the function d at 0. The *square-root principle* implies that if c is small, the asymptotic ratio of the number of groups in intervals S and T is given by $\frac{\int_S \sqrt{f(t)} dt}{\int_T \sqrt{f(t)} dt}$. Note this ratio is different from the population ratio $\frac{\int_S f(t) dt}{\int_T f(t) dt} = \frac{\lambda(S)}{\lambda(T)}$ unless λ is generated by the uniform distribution!

Proposition 8.4.1 guarantees the existence of stable partitions under appropriate choice of projects and cost-share allocations, but it does not provide a characterization of the policy choices and, especially, of cost-allocation, secession-proof schemes. However, the issue of redistribution of economic costs across various groups has important theoretical and practical implications in many contexts, including the study of country formation and redistributive policies that aim at preventing conflicts within countries with heterogeneous populations. There are several sources of population heterogeneity that may cause dissatisfaction of significant groups of the society with the one-size-fits-all choices made by the central or regional governments. They include the country's geographic structure; attitudes towards protection of minority rights; promotion and preservation of distinctive local culture and language; disagreement over spending policies; the country's cultural, ethnical, religious, and language fractionalization; economic regional disparity, and so on. With sufficient heterogeneity and diversity of the country's population, government's inability to satisfy all the preferences in the country is bound to breed dissatisfaction within certain groups and regions, thereby creating a potential for internal conflicts and threats of secession. Because the consequences of conflicts (political instability, inadequate economic performance, etc.) are usually undesirable from the countrywide perspective, many countries have explicit transfer schemes to assist their disadvantaged regions.[11] Inasmuch as the existence of redistribution schemes has been examined in our framework by Proposition 8.4.1, the natural question that remains is, What set of policy instruments is available to the government to mitigate secessionist sentiments?

Suppose now through the rest of the section that the project-specific part of the cost $c(x)$ is project independent – that is, the costs associated with any project x for the community S are given by $C(S, x) = \alpha\mu(S) + c$, where c is a positive constant. We also assume that the transportation costs are linear, namely, $d(i, x) = |\theta(i) - x|$ for all $i \in N$ and all $x \in X$.

Because a seceding region has to incur the substantial costs of laying foundations for the new country and running its administration, the breakaway tendencies are countered by the economies of scale generated by being a united political entity. When the secession costs are too high, the stable outcome allows no partitions of the grand coalition.

Proposition 8.4.2. *(Haimanko Le Breton and Weber 2003). Suppose that the set of public projects X is the interval $[0, 1]$. The preferences of each $i \in N$ are symmetric and single peaked, and the transportation costs $d(i, x)$ are linear in the distance between project x and $\theta(i)$. Assume also that the costs associated with any project x for the community S are given by $C(S, x) = \alpha\mu(S) + c$, where $\alpha \geq 0$. Then there exists a value $\bar{c}$ such that a society admits a stable outcome consisting of the triple $\{N, x, t\}$, where $x \in X$ and $t \in T^*(N, x)$ if and only if $c \geq \bar{c}$. For a given distribution of individuals' ideal points F, we denote $c^F = \bar{c}$.*

---

[11] The examples include Russia, China, France, Italy, Belgium, Germany, Canada, Australia, and many other countries. See Ter-Minassian (1997), Ahmad and Craig (1997), and Le Breton and Weber (2003a).

Consider now nonatomic societies represented by an atomless distribution over the interval $X = [0, 1]$. We impose two assumptions on the cumulative distribution functions to be used in our analysis. The first is quite standard:

SY – Symmetry: The density function f is symmetric with respect to $\frac{1}{2}$, the center of X, that is, $f(i) = f(1 - i)$ for all $i \in X$.

As an introduction to the second assumption, for $i \in X$, denote by $L_i = [0, i]$ and $R_i = [i, 1]$. Let $l(i)$ and $r(i)$ be the medians of the sets L_i and R_i, respectively.[12] Note that $r(i) = 1 - l(1 - i)$ for every $i \in X$.

Suppose that the functions l and r are differentiable, except possibly at a finite number of points. We assume the following:

GEM – Gradually Escalating Median: The derivative $l'(i)$ satisfies $l'(i) \leq 1$ on the interval $[0, 1]$. Obviously, the symmetry assumption would imply $r'(i) \leq 1$.

We denote by $\mathcal{F}$ the set of distribution functions satisfying the symmetry and GEM assumptions.

Assumption GEM implies that if we increase the length of the interval $L_i = [0, i]$ by a small positive number δ, then the median of the interval $L_{i+\delta} = [0, i + \delta]$ is shifted to the right by an increment smaller than δ.

The class of distribution functions satisfying GEM contains the family of *log-concave functions*. That class, in turn, includes "truncated" versions of the uniform, the normal, and the exponential distributions.[13] There are, in addition, distribution functions that are not log-concave but nevertheless satisfy the GEM assumption, such as some classes of bimodal distributions.[14]

For every distribution function F that belongs to the class $\mathcal{F}$, the threshold value c^F defined in Proposition 8.4.2 has been explicitly derived in Haimanko et al. (2003).

Proposition 8.4.3. *Suppose that all assumptions of Proposition 8.4.2 hold. Then for every $F \in \mathcal{F}$ we have*

$$c^F = \frac{1}{2} - 4 \int_{l(\frac{1}{2})}^{\frac{1}{2}} i f(i) \, di,$$

where f is the density function of the cumulative distribution F. If the distribution f is uniform on $[0, 1]$, then $c^F = \frac{1}{8}$.

We now turn to the characterization of stable outcomes and secession-proof cost allocation. Obviously, if the project cost c is greater than or equal to c^F, then the grand coalition N should form. The symmetry of the distributions makes it natural

---

[12] If f is positive everywhere, then the functions l and r are well defined. Otherwise, the median locations are not unique and constitute an interval. In this case, the median will be represented by the midpoint of this interval.

[13] See Caplin and Nalebuff (1991) and Weber (1992).

[14] See Le Breton and Weber (2003a).

to consider the location of the public project x at the geographical center of X, $\frac{1}{2}$. We have the following result:

Proposition 8.4.4. *(Le Breton and Weber 2003a): Suppose that all assumptions of Proposition 8.4.2 hold. For a given project-cost value c, define the following cost allocation:*

$$t^c(i) = \begin{cases} r(i) + \beta & \text{if } i \leq \frac{1}{2} \\ r(1-i) + \beta & \text{if } i \geq \frac{1}{2}, \end{cases}$$

where β is chosen to satisfy the budget constraint: $\beta = c - \int_0^1 t^c(i)f(i)di$.
   Let $F \in \mathcal{F}$ be given. If the project cost c satisfies $c \geq c^F$, the triple $\{N, \frac{1}{2}, t^c\}$ is a stable outcome and, therefore, the cost allocation t^c is secession-proof.

   Note that the function t^c is symmetric around the center $\frac{1}{2}$, is increasing on the interval $[0, \frac{1}{2}]$, and is decreasing on the interval $[0, \frac{1}{2}]$. This implies that the closer an individual is to the center, the larger his or her cost share is. Thus, individuals who are located close to the endpoints are subsidized by those located closer to the center. However, the GEM implies the total contribution (including the transportation cost) given by $|i - \frac{1}{2}| + t^c(i)$ is still higher for those close to the endpoints. Thus, this allocation satisfies the principle of *partial equalization*, which means that, although some equalization takes place, it is not full. It is interesting to note that in the case of the uniform distribution the equalization rate is 50%.
   It is important to stress that two important allocations often studied in the literature are not necessarily secession proof when $c \geq c^F$. Consider the uniform distribution F whose density $f(i)$ is equal to 1 for all i on interval $[0, 1]$. First, consider an equal-share allocation t^E under which all individuals contribute the same amount $t^E(i) = c$ toward the project costs. Secondly, examine the Rawlsian allocation t^R that guarantees the equal total contribution (including transportation cost) for all individuals. That is, $t^R(i) + |i - \frac{1}{2}|$ should be the same for all $i \in N$. It is easy to derive

$$t^R(i) = \begin{cases} i - \frac{1}{4} + c & \text{if } i \leq \frac{1}{2} \\ -i + \frac{3}{4} + c & \text{if } i \geq \frac{1}{2}. \end{cases}$$

The remark below follows.

Remark 8.4.5 (Le Breton and Weber 2003a): Suppose that all assumptions of Proposition 8.4.2 hold. Let the distribution of individuals' ideal points on the interval $[0, 1]$ be uniform. Then

(i) there exists $c^* > \frac{1}{8}$ such that for every c, $\frac{1}{8} \leq c < c^*$, the triple $\{N, \frac{1}{2}, t^E\}$ is not a stable outcome. That is, the equal cost-share allocation t^E is not, in general, secession-proof.

(ii) For every c, $\frac{1}{8} \leq c < \frac{1}{4}$, the triple $\{N, \frac{1}{2}, t^R\}$ is not a stable outcome. That is, the Rawlsian cost-share allocation t^E is not, in general, secession-proof.

In the case of the equal cost-share allocation t^E, the individuals in the center do not provide equalization transfers to those close to the endpoints. Thus, there would be coalitions of distant individuals who might reject the proposed cost share. Indeed, there are coalitions $[0, i]$ with $\frac{1}{3} < i < \frac{1}{2}$ that would be better off on their own. Note that the seceding coalition should be sufficiently large to mitigate the increasing returns effect generated by the grand coalition N.

In the case of the Rawlsian cost-share allocation t^R, the individuals close to the center carry the major burden of equalization transfers to those close to the endpoints. Thus, there are coalitions of individuals in the center who would rather create their own group than fully subsidize the rest of the society.

We now turn to the case in which some coalitions are prevented from using all balanced cost-share allocations to finance public projects.

8.5. Restricted Cost-Allocation Correspondence

In this section we examine an extreme case in which the cost-allocation correspondence T is single valued. That is, for every coalition S and a public project $x \in X$, the coalition S possesses only one scheme to share the cost of a project $x \in X$ among its members. In this case every individual $i \in S$ contributes an amount $T(i, S, x)$ towards the project cost. It allows us to introduce the indirect utility function $v_i(S, x) : S^i \times X \to \Re$ for every individual i, where S^i is the set of all coalitions that contain i. This function is defined as follows: $v_i(S, x) = u_i(x, w(i) - T(i, S, x))$.

We impose the following important assumption that will be satisfied through the rest of the chapter.

Assumption PE – Positive Externality: The inequality $v_i(S, x) < v_i(S', x)$ holds for every individual $i \in N$, every project $x \in X$, and every two different coalitions $S, S' \in S^i$ and $S \subset S'$.

This assumption implies that if one or several individuals join the existing coalition, they would have a positive effect on the utility of existing members of the group. In the case of separable utilities, the PE assumption simply means that the monetary burden of financing a given project would be reduced in a larger group. Note that the PE assumption holds when, in particular, the cost of public projects is constant and the society uses either the equal cost-share correspondence T^E or the tax proportional rule, where each individual contributes the same proportion of his or her initial endowment.

In the next subsection we examine the issue of T-stability for the environments satisfying PE.

8.5.1. T-stability

Because the utility functions of all individuals depend only on the project and the coalition the individual i belongs to, one can reduce Definition 8.3.2 of a T-stable outcome to a choice of a partition and corresponding public projects. The corresponding cost-share allocations would be uniquely determined by the single-valued cost-allocation correspondence. Our first results in this framework are obtained when either the set of public projects X consists of two elements, as in many models with network externalities (Arthur 1989; Farrell and Saloner 1985, 1988; Tirole 1988), or set N contains two individuals. In both cases the existence of a T-stable outcome is guaranteed by PE:

Proposition 8.5.1.1.

(Konishi, Le Breton, and Weber 1997a): Let $|X| = 2$. Then under PE, *society $\mathcal{E}$ admits a T-stable outcome.*

Proposition 8.5.1.2. *(Konishi, Le Breton, and Weber 1997b): Let $|N| = 2$. Then, under* PE, *society $\mathcal{E}$ admits a T-stable outcome.*

Propositions 8.5.1.1 and 8.5.1.2 cannot be extended to the case in which the set of alternatives and set of individuals each contain more than two elements. Before describing the example showing that this is indeed the case, let us introduce the following assumption:

Assumption AN – Anonymity: The equality $v_i(S, x) = v_i(S', x)$ holds for every individual $i \in N$, every project $x \in X$, and every two coalitions $S, S' \in S^i$ with $|S| = |S'|$. If the society satisfies AN, we will write, without abuse of notation, $v_i(|S|, x)$ instead of $v_i(S, x)$.

This assumption holds under the equal-share cost allocation. However, it would not, in general, be satisfied if the society adopted the tax proportional rule. In this case, every individual would be better off in the same size group with wealthier individuals rather than with poorer ones.

The following example (Konishi et al. 1997a) shows that a T-stable outcome would fail to exist even if the society satisfied PE and AN and the indirect utility of each individual were quasi-linear:

Example 8.5.1.3. *Consider the society $\mathcal{E}$ for which the set of individuals is given by $N = \{1, 2, 3, 4, 5, 6, 7\}$ and the set of projects is given by $X = \{a, b, c\}$. The indirect utility function $v_i(S, x) = |S| + \tilde{v}_i(x)$ is quasi-linear for each $i \in N$, and*

$$\tilde{v}_1(a) = 6.5, \ \tilde{v}_1(b) = 8, \ \tilde{v}_1(c) = 4.3, \ \tilde{v}_2(a) = 4.3, \ \tilde{v}_2(b) = 8.5, \ \tilde{v}_2(c) = 6,$$

$$\tilde{v}_3(a) = 6, \ \tilde{v}_3(b) = 6.3, \ \tilde{v}_3(c) = 6.5, \ \tilde{v}_4(a) = 8, \ \tilde{v} - 4(b) = 0, \ \tilde{v}_4(c) = 0,$$

$$\tilde{v}_5(a) = 8, \ \tilde{v}_5(b) = 0, \ \tilde{v}_5(c) = 0, \ \tilde{v}_6(a) = 0, \ \tilde{v}_6(b) = 0, \ \tilde{v}_6(c) = 8,$$

$$\tilde{v}_7(a) = 0, \ \tilde{v}_7(b) = 0, \ \tilde{v}_7(c) = 8.$$

Then, $\mathcal{E}$ does not admit a T-stable outcome.

The challenge here is to describe a class of societies satisfying PE that admit T-stable outcomes. Trivially, this class of societies contains all "perfectly homogeneous" societies, where for all $S \subseteq N$, all $i, j \in S$, and all $x, y \in X$ the inequality $v_i(S, x) \geq v_i(S, x)$ implies $v_j(S, x) \geq v_j(S, y)$. This extreme case of homogeneity fully exploits the advantages of increasing returns to size and may suggest that a T-stable outcome will exist if a degree of homogeneity within the society is large enough. There is no uncontroversial definition of a measure of homogeneity associated to a profile of preferences, and we present here a result suggesting that a unidimensional heterogeneity may indeed yield a T-stable outcome.

The result imposes a condition on the profile of individual preferences that has been called *consecutiveness* (Greenberg and Weber 1986, 1994) or *intermediate preferences* (Demange 1994). It requires the existence of an ordering of the individuals with respect to their preferences:

> **Consecutiveness – CONS:** Let $\mathcal{E}$ be a society satisfying AN. $\mathcal{E}$ is consecutive if there exists an ordering $\prec$ over N such that for all $i, j, k \in N$, all $x, x' \in X$, and all positive integers r, r', if $i \prec j \prec k$, $v_i(r, x) < v_i(r', x')$ and $v_k(r, x) < v_k(r', x')$, then $v_j(r, x) < v_j(r', x')$.

The interpretation of this condition is that if any two individuals prefer a group with r' members and policy x' rather than a group with r members and policy x, then every intermediate individual (according to the ordering $\prec$) must share this choice.

The following result heavily relies on the assumption of consecutiveness:

Proposition 8.5.1.4. *(Le Breton and Weber 2003c): Every society $\mathcal{E}$ satisfying PE, AN, and CONS, admits a T-stable outcome.*

Proposition 8.5.1.4 allows for various alternative versions. In particular, AN is not essential, but the definition of consecutiveness without AN is more cumbersome. Further, as demonstrated by Demange (1994), the assumption of a complete ordering $\prec$ is not essential as well. Demange proved a version of Proposition 8.5.1.4, in which, instead of CONS, she assumes the existence of a *tree*[15] τ on N such that for all $x, x' \in X$, the sets[16] $\{i \in N : v_i(x) < v_i(x')\}$ and $\{i \in N : v_i(x) \leq v_i(x')\}$ are connected with respect to τ.

8.5.2. Individual T-stability

The discussion in the previous section indicates that the notion of T-stability, which requires a T-attainable outcome to be immune to any group deviation, is quite demanding. It would naturally lead us to attempt to examine a less restrictive concept of stability. We then consider a notion of individual T-stability in which an outcome has to be immune against individual deviations only. The difference between two concepts of stability is reminiscent of the distinction between the notion of Nash equilibrium and of strong Nash equilibrium (Aumann 1959).

---

[15] A tree τ on N is a graph on N such that there is a unique path between any two distinct elements of N; a subset $S \subseteq N$ is connected with respect to τ if $i, j \in S \Rightarrow k \in S$ whenever k is on the path from i to j.

[16] In her model, $v_i(S, x)$ does not depend on S.

Let $\mathcal{E}$ be a finite society and consider a pair $\{(S^k, x^k)\}_{1 \leq k \leq K}$, where $\{S^k\}_{1 \leq k \leq K} \in \mathcal{P}$ is a group structure and x^k are projects in X. Recall that T is a single-valued cost-allocation correspondence that determines individual contributions, and thus the focus is on groups and project selection only. In introducing the concept of *individual T-stability*, we allow for *free mobility* when every individual is free to stay alone or to join one of the existing groups. The outcome would be T-stable if no individual i would prefer staying alone rather than accepting the project $x^{k(i)}$ in the group $S^{k(i)}$ or would benefit by joining another coalition S^j in P choosing the project x^j:

Definition 8.5.2.1. *A T-attainable outcome $\{P, x^k\}_{1 \leq k \leq K}$, where $P = \{S^k\}_{1 \leq k \leq K} \in \mathcal{P}$ is a group structure, is considered individually T-stable if the following two inequalities hold for every $i \in N$:*

$$(i) \quad v_i \left(S^{k(i)}, x^{k(i)} \right) \geq \max_{x \in X} v_i(\{i\}, x)$$

$$(ii) \quad v_i \left(S^{k(i)}, x^{k(i)} \right) \geq \max_{S^j \in P} v_i \left(S^j \bigcup \{i\}, x^j \right).$$

One can consider situations in which free mobility is restricted. For example, under *contractual stability*, which was introduced in Drèze and Greenberg (1980), individual moves from one group to another are subject to approval of members of the new group, the old group, or both. Also, the notion of individual T-stability is provided for finite societies. For infinite nonatomic societies, one can consider a modified notion capturing the robustness of a T-attainable outcome to deviations by coalitions of an arbitrarily small size (see Section 8.5.3).

It is easy to verify that, under PE, the notion of individual t-stability is weaker than T-stability. In fact, the following example (Konishi et al. 1997b) shows that there exists a society that satisfies AN and PE but does not admit even an individually stable T-outcome.

Example 8.5.2.2. *Consider the society $\mathcal{E}$ for which the sets of individuals N and projects X are given by $N = \{1, 2, 3\}$ and $X = \{a, b, c\}$, respectively. (By Propositions 8.5.1.1 and 8.5.1.2 these are the minimal sizes of N and X that may generate an absence of stability.) The society $\mathcal{E}$ satisfies AN and PE, and the individuals' utility functions of individuals satisfy the following inequalities:*

$$v_1(2, b) > v_1(2, a) > v_1(1, a) > v_1(1, b) > v_1(3, c);$$
$$v(2, c) > v_2(2, b) > v_2(1, b) > v_2(1, c) > v_2(3, a);$$
$$v_3(2, a) > v_3(2, c) > v_3(1, c) > v_3(1, a) > v_3(3, b).$$

Then $\mathcal{E}$ does not admit an individually T-stable outcome.

This rather simple example shows that one has to impose much more demanding conditions to guarantee the existence of individually T-stable outcomes in societies with more than two individuals and two projects. The following proposition (Konishi et al. 1997a) demonstrates that the more demanding condition is sufficient for the existence of an individually T-stable outcome. The proposition also shows that the result is tight in the sense that relaxing any of the assumptions would deny the existence result.

Proposition 8.5.2.3. *Let $\mathcal{E}$ be a society satisfying* PE *and* AN. *Moreover, the utility functions*[17] *of each $i \in N$ are quasi-linear: $v_i(S, x) = |S| + \tilde{v}_i(x)$. Then the society $\mathcal{E}$ admits an individually T-stable outcome.*

The proof of this proposition is quite instructive and proceeds by constructing a real-valued function on the set of n-tuples $(x^1, \ldots, x^n)$ of individuals' project choices. It turns out that every local maximum of this function (the existence of which is guaranteed by the finiteness of the domain) yields an individually T-stable outcome. This method of proof is similar to the one used by Rosenthal (1973), who introduced the class of "potential games" studied further by Monderer and Shapley (1996).

8.5.3. Equal Cost-Sharing Rule

We now examine finite societies with a single-valued cost-allocation correspondence T^{E}, where, in order to finance the cost of public projects, each coalition can use only the equal cost-sharing rule. We assume that for every project $x \in X$ the cost $C(S, x)$ is independent of group S and that the utility functions of all individuals are quasi-linear. Then the indirect utility of an individual i who is a member of group S, which chooses project x, is given by

$$v_i(S, x) = \tilde{v}_i(x) + w(i) - \frac{C(x)}{|S|}.$$

We assume that the initial endowment of every individual is sufficiently large to cover contributions to all projects and that no confusion will arise if we delete the term $w(i)$.

The existence of an individually T^{E}-stable outcome in this framework can be derived from Proposition 8.5.2.3. It is interesting to note, however, that individually T^{E}-stable outcomes can be inefficient. The following example (Konishi, Le Breton, and Weber 1998) shows that there is a society with multiple T^{E}-stable outcomes, some of which are Pareto inferior to others.

Example 8.5.3.1. *Consider a society $\mathcal{E}$ with two individuals, $N = \{1, 2\}$, and three public projects, $X = \{a, b, c\}$. Let the utilities of individuals be given by*

$$\tilde{v}_1(a) = 30, \quad \tilde{v}_1(b) = 0, \quad \tilde{v}_1(c) = 0, \quad \tilde{v}_2(a) = 0, \quad \tilde{v}_2(b) = 0, \quad \tilde{v}_2(c) = 25,$$

and the project costs are $C(a) = C(b) = C(c) = 20$.

This society has two individually T^{E}-stable outcomes, one in which individual 1 chooses project a and individual 2 chooses project b and the other in which both choose project c. The utility vectors associated with two outcomes are

---

[17] See Konishi and Fishburn (1996) for the assumptions needed for this utility representation.

$(10, -20)$ *and* $(15, 15)$, *respectively. Thus, the first outcome is Pareto inferior to the second.* $\square$

Example 8.5.3.1 illustrates a conventional inefficiency arising from a pure coordination problem. To evaluate the potential inefficiency scope of T-stable outcomes, consider the following much weaker efficiency requirement:

Definition 8.5.3.2. *A T^E-attainable outcome* $\{P, x^k\}_{1 \le k \le K}$, *where* $P = \{S^k\}_{1 \le k \le K}$ *is a partition of N and $x^k \in X$ are public projects chosen by S^k, is intragroup efficient if there is no $S^k \in P$ and $y \in X$ such that* $\tilde{v}_i(y) - \frac{C(y)}{|S^k|} \ge \tilde{v}_i(x) - \frac{C(x)}{|S^k|}$ *for all $i \in S^k$ with a strict inequality for, at least, one i.*

Intragroup efficiency rules out arrangements across groups and does not allow for their breakup. It simply requires that no group in P can find an alternative public project preferred to the chosen one by all members of the group. The following example (Konishi et al. 1998) demonstrates that intragroup efficient, individually T^E-stable outcomes may fail to exist. This obviously implies that T^E-stable outcomes may fail to exist as well.

Example 8.5.3.3. *Consider a society $\mathcal{E}$ with five individuals, $N = \{1, 2, 3, 4, 5\}$, and four public projects, $X = \{a, b, c, d\}$. Let utilities of individuals be given by*

$$\tilde{v}_1(a) = 10025, \quad \tilde{v}_1(b) = 10110, \quad \tilde{v}_1(c) = 0, \quad \tilde{v}_1(d) = 10061,$$

$$\tilde{v}_2(a) = 10026, \quad \tilde{v}_2(b) = 10089.8, \quad \tilde{v}_2(c) = 0, \quad \tilde{v}_2(d) = 10030,$$

$$\tilde{v}_3(a) = 10030, \quad \tilde{v}_3(b) = 10120, \quad \tilde{v}_3(c) = 9900, \quad \tilde{v}_3(d) = 9900,$$

$$\tilde{v}_4(a) = 10000, \quad \tilde{v}_4(b) = 10240, \quad \tilde{v}_4(c) = 10200, \quad \tilde{v}_4(d) = 9900,$$

$$\tilde{v}_5(a) = 9900, \quad \tilde{v}_5(b) = 9900, \quad \tilde{v}_5(c) = 10090, \quad \tilde{v}_5(d) = 10061,$$

and the project costs are $C(a) = 50$, $C(b) = 240$, $C(c) = 90$, and $C(d) = 60$.

This society has a unique, individually T^E-stable outcome in which individuals $1, 2, 3$ choose a whereas 4 and 5 choose c. However, this outcome is not intragroup efficient because individuals $1, 2, 3$ would be better off by jointly switching to project b.

We now consider the infinite nonatomic framework examined in Section 8.4. In doing so we will modify the notion of an individually T-stable outcome to take into account the deviation of arbitrarily small coalitions (see also Jehiel and Scotchmer 2001 and Le Breton and Weber 2003c):

Definition 8.5.3.4. *Let $\mathcal{E}$ be an atomic society and $z = \{(S^k, x^k)\}_{1 \le k \le K}$ be a T^E-attainable outcome. Let u be the utility vector associated with z, where for every $i \in N$:*

$$u_i = -|\theta(i) - x^{k(i)}| - \frac{C(S^{k(i)}, x^{k(i)})}{\mu(S^{k(i)})}.$$

The outcome z is considered locally *T*-stable *if there exists* $\delta > 0$ *such that there is no coalition S with* $\mu(S) \leq \delta$ *and* $x \in X$ *such that*

$$u_i(S, x) = -|\theta(i) - x| - \frac{C(S, x)}{\mu(S)} > u_i$$

for all $i \in S$.

By this definition, a T^E-attainable outcome is locally T^E-stable if there is no coalition of positive but arbitrary small measure for which it would be profitable to deviate. Such an outcome is less demanding than T^E-stability, for the test against coalitional deviations applies only to "small" coalitions. Obviously, the set of locally stable T^E-outcomes is smaller than the set of individually T^E-stable outcomes and is larger than the set of T^E-stable outcomes.

Alesina and Spolaore (1997) study the implication of local T^E-stability and consider a version of contractual stability in which a new group can be created or an existing group can be eliminated if the change is approved by majority vote in each of the groups affected by that decision. Under the assumption of the uniform distribution, they show that a group structure consisting of groups of equal size is stable in that sense if and only if the number of groups is the largest integer smaller than $\frac{1}{\sqrt{2c}}$. Alesina and Spolaore also demonstrate that if secession threats are limited to subgroups of the group structure, then a group structure consisting of groups of equal size is stable if and only if the number of groups is larger than $\frac{1}{(\sqrt{6}+2)\sqrt{c}}$.

We now turn to a finite variant of the model presented in Section 8.4, where $X \subseteq \Re$ and $v_i(x, m(i)) = -d(i, x) + m(i)$ for all $i \in N$. As we indicated while presenting the setting, x is interpreted as a location decision and $d(i, x)$ as the transportation cost incurred by i when he or she "consumes" a public project located at x. If the incomes of all individuals are the same, the existence of an individually T^E-stable outcome follows from Proposition 8.5.2.3. Let us now examine the existence of T^E-stable outcomes. The following result follows from Proposition 8.5.1.4:

Proposition 8.5.3.5. *Suppose that for every project* $x \in X$ *the project costs are the same for all groups of the same size, that is,* $C(S, x) = C(T, x)$ *if* $|S| = |T|$. *Assume that individuals' utility functions are quasi-linear and the distribution of individuals' locations is uniform on* X. *Also, let the transportation cost function be of the form* $d(i, x) = g(|\theta(i) - x|)$, *where* $d : \Re_+ \to \Re_+$ *is increasing and convex. Then, there exists a* T^E-*stable outcome.*

In this proposition, it is assumed that the transportation cost of any individual is an increasing function of his or her distance to the public project and that this function is the same for all individuals. In particular, the transportation cost function of any individual is symmetric with respect to that person's peak. It is easy to see that under the assumptions of this proposition, any T^E-stable outcome is *stratified* in the sense that each group is an interval according to the order $\prec$. The following example shows that, in general, this is not the case:

Example 8.5.3.6. *Consider a society consisting of four individuals,* $N = \{1, 2, 3, 4\}$, *with their locations* $\theta(1) < \theta(2) < \theta(3) < \theta(4)$ *given by* $\theta(2) = \theta(1) + \gamma$,

$\theta(3) = \theta(1) + 2\gamma, \theta(4) = \theta(1) + 3\gamma$, where γ is a positive parameter. The transportation costs are determined as follows:

$$d(1, x) = \begin{cases} \frac{x - \theta(1)}{\varepsilon} & \text{if } x > \theta(1) \\ \varepsilon(\theta(1) - x) & \text{if } x < \theta(1) \end{cases}$$

$$d(2, x) = \begin{cases} \varepsilon(x - \theta(2)) & \text{if } x > \theta(2) \\ \frac{\theta(2) - x}{\varepsilon} & \text{if } x < \theta(2) \end{cases}$$

$$d(3, x) = \begin{cases} \frac{x - \theta(3)}{\varepsilon} & \text{if } x > \theta(3) \\ \varepsilon(\theta(3) - x) & \text{if } x < \theta(3) \end{cases}$$

$$d(4, x) = \begin{cases} \varepsilon(x - \theta(4)) & \text{if } x > \theta(4) \\ \frac{\theta(4) - x}{\varepsilon} & \text{if } x < \theta(4) \end{cases},$$

where $0 < \varepsilon < \min[\frac{2\gamma}{3c}, \frac{c}{4\gamma}]$. Finally, the project costs $C(x) = c$ for all $x \in X$. Then for every T^E-stable outcome $\{P, x^1, \ldots, x^K\}$, the partition P consists of two pairs, $\{1, 3\}$ and $\{2, 4\}$.

First, we show that in a T^E-stable outcome the pairs of individuals 1, 2 and 3, 4 cannot be in the same group. Suppose, in negation, that 1 and 2 are in the same group S with a public project located in x. Then, either $d(1, x) \geq \frac{\gamma}{2\varepsilon}$ or $d(2, x) \geq \frac{\gamma}{2\varepsilon}$. Therefore, either $v_1(S, x) \leq -\frac{\gamma}{2\varepsilon} - \frac{c}{4}$ or $v_2(S, x) \leq -\frac{\gamma}{2\varepsilon} - \frac{c}{4}$. On the other hand, $v_1(\{1\}, \theta(1)) = -c$ and $v_2(\{2\}, \theta(2)) = -c$. Thus, if $\varepsilon < \frac{2d}{3c}$, then either $v_1(S, x) < v_1(\theta(1), \{1\})$ or $v_2(S, x) < v_2(\theta(2), \{2\})$, which contradicts our assumption that S is part of a T^E-stable outcome. A similar argument applies to the pairs $\{3, 4\}, \{1, 4\}, \{2, 3\}$.

In conclusion, it remains to show that 1 and 3 prefer to be together rather than staying alone. But $v_1(\{1, 3\}, \theta(1)) = -\frac{c}{2}$ and $v_3(\{1, 3\}, \theta(1)) = -2\varepsilon\gamma - \frac{c}{2}$. Thus, $v_1(\{1, 3\}, \theta(1)) > v_1(\{1\}, \theta(1))$ and $v_3(\{1, 3\}, \theta(1)) > v_3(\theta(3), \{3\})$ whenever $\varepsilon < \frac{c}{4\gamma}$.

BIBLIOGRAPHY

[1] Ahmad, E. and J. Craig (1997), "Intergovernmental Transfers," in *Fiscal Federalism in Theory and Practice*, T. Ter-Minassian (ed.), Washington DC: International Monetary Fund.

[2] Alesina, A. and E. Spolaore (1997), "On the Number and Size of Nations," *Quarterly Journal of Economics* 113, 1027–1056.

[3] Arthur, W. B. (1989), "Competing Technologies, Increasing Returns, and Lock-in by Historical Events," *Economic Journal* 99, 116–131.

[4] Aumann, R. J. (1959), "Acceptable Points in General Cooperative *n*-Person Games," in *Contributions to the Theory of Games*, Vol. IV, A. W. Tucker and R. D. Luce (eds.), Princeton University Press.

[5] Aumann, R. J. and J. Drèze (1974), "Cooperative Games with Coalition Structure," *International Journal of Game Theory* 3, 217–237.

[6] Caplin, A. and B. Nalebuff (1991), "Aggregation and Social Choice: A Mean Voter Theorem," *Econometrica* 59, 1–24.

[7] Conley, J. P. and M. H. Wooders (1997), "Anonymous Pricing in Tiebout Economies and Economies with Clubs," in *Topics in Public Finance*, D. Pines, E. Sadka, and Y. Zilcha (eds.), Cambridge, UK: Cambridge University Press.

[8] Cremer, H., A. M. De Kerchove, and J. Thisse (1985), "An Economic Theory of Public Facilities in Space," *Mathematical Social Sciences* 9, 249–262.

[9] Demange, G. (1994), "Intermediate Preferences and Stable Coalition Structures," *Journal of Mathematical Economics* 23, 45–58.

[10] Drèze, J. and J. Greenberg (1980), "Hedonic Coalitions: Optimality and Stability," *Econometrica* 48, 987–1003.

[11] Ellickson, B., B. Grodal, S. Scotchmer and W. R. Zame (1999), "Clubs and the Market," *Econometrica* 67, 1185–1217.

[12] Farrell, J. and G. Saloner (1985), "Standardization, Compatibility, and Innovation," *Rand Journal of Economics* 16, 70–83.

[13] Farrell, J. and G. Saloner (1988) "Coordination through Committees and Markets," *Rand Journal of Economics* 19, 235–252.

[14] Greenberg, J. and S. Weber (1986), "Strong Tiebout Equilibrium under Restricted Preferences Domain," *Journal of Economic Theory* 38, 101–117.

[15] Greenberg, J. and S. Weber (1993), "Stable Coalition Structures with a Unidimensional Set of Alternatives," *Journal of Economic Theory* 60, 62–82.

[16] Greenberg, J. and S. Weber (1994), "Stable Coalition Structures in Consecutive Games," in *Frontiers in Game Theory*, K. Binmore, A. Kirman, and P. Tani (eds.), Cambridge, MA: MIT Press.

[17] Guesnerie, R. and C. Oddou (1979), "On Economic Games Which Are Not Necessarily Super-additive," *Economic Letters* 3, 301–306.

[18] Guesnerie, R. and C. Oddou (1981), "Second Best Taxation as a Game," *Journal of Economic Theory* 25, 67–91.

[19] Haimanko, O., M. Le Breton, and S. Weber (2003), "Transfers in a Polarized Country: Bridging the Gap between Efficiency and Stability," *Journal of Public Economics*, forthcoming.

[20] Haimanko, O., M. Le Breton, and S. Weber (2004), "Voluntary Formation of Communities for the Provision of Public Projects," *Journal of Economic Theory* 115, 1–34.

[21] Jehiel, P. and S. Scotchmer (2001), "Constitutional Rules of Exclusion in Jurisdiction Formation," *Review of Economic Studies* 68, 393–413.

[22] Kaneko, M. and M. H. Wooders (1982), "Cores of Partitioning Games," *Mathematical Social Sciences* 3, 313–327.

[23] Konishi, H. and P. C. Fishburn (1996), "Quasi-linear Utility in a Discrete Choice Model," *Economic Letters* 51, 197–200.

[24] Konishi, H., M. Le Breton, and S. Weber (1997a), "Pure Strategy Nash Equilibria in a Group Formation Game with Positive Externalities," *Games and Economic Behavior* 21, 161–182.

[25] Konishi, H., M. Le Breton, and S. Weber (1997b), "Group Formation in Games without Spillovers: A Noncooperative Game-Theoretical Approach," in *New Directions in the Economic Theory of the Environment*, C. Carraro and D. Siniscalco (eds.), Cambridge, UK: Cambridge University Press.

[26] Konishi, H., M. Le Breton, and S. Weber (1998), "Equilibrium in a Finite Local Public Goods Economy," *Journal of Economic Theory* 79, 224–244.

[27] Le Breton, M. and S. Weber (2003a), "The Art of Making Everybody Happy: How to Prevent a Secession," *IMF Stuff Papers*, 50, 403–435.

[28] Le Breton, M. and S. Weber (2003b), "Stable Partitions in a Model with Group-Dependent Feasible Sets," University of Copenhagen Discussion paper 417.

[29] Le Breton, M. and S. Weber (2003c), "Group Formation in Strategic Environments without Widespread Externalities," mimeo. Southern Methodist University and University of Toulouse.

[30] Mas-Colell, A. (1980), "Efficiency and Decentralization in the Pure Theory of Public Goods," *Quarterly Journal of Economics* 94, 625–641.

[31] Monderer, D. and L. S. Shapley (1996), "Potential Games," *Games and Economic Behavior* 14, 124–143.

[32] Rosenthal, R. W. (1973), "A Class of Games Possessing a Pure-Strategy Nash Equilibrium," *International Journal of Game Theory* 2, 65–67.

[33] Ter-Minassian, T. (ed.) (1997), *Fiscal Federalism in Theory and Practice*, Washington, DC: International Monetary Fund.

[34] Tirole, J. (1988), *Industrial Organization,* Cambridge, MA: MIT Press.

[35] Weber, S. (1992), "On Hierarchical Spatial Competition," *Review of Economic Studies* 59, 407–425.

[36] Wooders, M. H. (1978), "Equilibria, the Core and Jurisdiction Structures in Economies with a Local Public Good," *Journal of Economic Theory* 18, 328–348.

[37] Wooders, M. H. (1980), "The Tiebout Hypothesis: Near Optimality in Local Public Goods Economies," *Econometrica* 48, 1467–1486.

PART THREE

Groups, Clubs, and Alliances in Political and Economic Environments

9

Political Parties and Coalition Formation

Amrita Dhillon

9.1. Introduction

Political parties have long been treated in both the theoretical political science and economics literature as unitary actors. Take, for example, the Downsian model of political competition (Downs 1957), the multidimensional spatial models (e.g., Enelow and Hinich 1984), and even the more recent models of redistributive politics (e.g., Dixit and Londregan 1996, Lindbeck and Weibull 1987). In many of these models, important results about policy outcomes hinge on specific assumptions about party objectives.

This begs the question of what political parties actually are: What is the notion of party that theorists should be interested in? Are they agglomerations of the policy positions of individual candidates (Osborne and Tourky 2002) or are they informative brand names aimed at voters (Snyder and Ting 2002)? Are they mechanisms to economise on the costs of standing for elections (Riviere 1999; Osborne and Tourky 2002) or simply credible commitment mechanisms (Levy 2004; Morelli 2004)?

One may go further and ask if we should really be looking at "parties" as coalitions of individuals or at coalitions of "parties" or groups of individuals – whether preelection or postelection – because, in many electoral systems, it is such coalitions that affect actual policy outcomes.

If we care about choice in politics, we should worry about the number of parties that a country has, their size, and the platforms they take. Presumably, systems dominated by one party – as in many African dictatorships – are less desirable than a multiparty system in which parties have divergent platforms. On the other hand, if party positions converge, then outcomes may not be different between these two systems. Indeed, if these are important criteria for a well-functioning democracy, we should also be interested in why different electoral systems generate different party structures. Duverger (1954) conjectured that majoritarian systems like those of the United Kingdom and United States would cause fewer parties to emerge than proportional representation systems used in some European countries (Duverger's

I thank Martin Osborne, Massimo Morelli, and Matt Jackson for helpful comments.

hypothesis). As one of the most important informal "laws" in political science, Duverger's (1963) law states that plurality rule systems have a tendency towards a two-party system. Recent research on political parties analyses exactly these types of questions.

This chapter attempts to survey some of the theoretical work being done in this area. My aim is to present the most recent work that has not been covered elsewhere and thus to provide a flavour of the types of factors that economists and political scientists consider to be salient in party formation. Hence, this chapter is not meant to be an exhaustive survey but rather focuses on a few papers in detail.

The format followed is to categorise the models into those that consider parties to be coalitions of individual candidates who are motivated to form parties by electoral considerations (preelectoral coalition formation) and those that focus on parties in the legislature – that is, coalitions of groups of individual candidates interested in forming a government (postelectoral coalition formation).

The chapter is organised as follows: Section 9.2 is concerned with preelectoral coalitions and Section 9.3 with postelection coalitions. My conclusions are presented in Section 9.4.

9.2. Preelectoral Coalitions

To understand the role of a party, we first need to understand what happens *without* parties: a world in which only independent candidates stand for election. Such a world has been modelled recently by two sets of authors: Besley and Coate (1997) and Osborne and Slivinski (1996). These authors were the first to endogenise the candidacy decision and the factors that influence an individual citizen's decision to enter as a candidate or not to do so, that is, the trade-off between the costs of candidacy and the benefits of getting the best policy for a particular candidate implemented. Candidates were assumed not to be able to commit credibly to anything but their own ideal policies. Thus, policy platforms were inflexible in direct contrast to the Downsian model.

But it seems clear that forming coalitions in this setup would have dividends! Candidates could share the costs of candidacy if they made a "party" of like-minded individuals, or they could improve their chances of electoral victory if they could join a coalition of individuals with different policy positions, thus ensuring commitment to a *set* of policies rather than just their own best policies. Parties could also act as mechanisms to coordinate voters' decisions. The first set of authors we survey considers exactly these variations on the citizen candidate model.

I will now focus on models of preelectoral coalition formation. The common ingredients of most models involve

(i) a policy space Q, which can be uni- or multidimensional Euclidean space;

(ii) a private good X; and

(iii) a set of citizens partitioned (according to policy preferences) into N homogenous groups. It is assumed that citizens care only about policy, each citizen has an ideal policy, and preferences are Euclidean (hence single peaked in unidimensional policy space). Thus, each group represents an ideal policy position.

(iv) Finally, some models have a cost of candidacy.

The models differ in the main motivations for parties to form, the predictions on the size and number of parties, and the models and the equilibrium concepts employed. Among the motivations for preelectoral coalitions to form, the first one we present is the cost-sharing motivation. Riviere (1999) and Osborne and Tourky (2002) are both models of parties as cost-sharing organisations. Although the models are considerably different in detail, both assume unidimensional policy space. Riviere (1999) assumes plurality rule, whereas Osborne and Tourky (2002) present a more general model applicable to both plurality rule and proportional representation.

In Riviere (1999), the policy space is restricted to three points on a line: $Q \subset \mathcal{R} = \{-1, 0, 1\}$. Thus, citizens are of three types ($N = 3$). The model is a modified version of the Besley–Coate (1997) citizen candidate model. The median voter is not known at the party formation stage; otherwise, only one party would ever form. There is a cost to entering as a candidate that is assumed to be not "too large," and thus entry is possible in the game.

As in Besley–Coate (1997), there are four stages: (i) the entry stage, (ii) revelation of the median voter, (iii) voting on the set of candidates, and (iv) policy implementation.

Voting may be strategic, but weakly dominated strategies are eliminated iteratively. This equilibrium is called a *refined voting equilibrium*.

Two scenarios are compared:

(1) Candidates are not allowed to share costs.
(2) Candidates can decide to form parties that are cost-sharing organisations.

In case (2), a preentry stage is added in which each citizen may simultaneously decide whether to become a party president or a member of a party (i.e., to nominate a president) or to stay independent.[1] Then the same four stages as in Case (1) are played out.

Coalition-proofness is demanded at the party formation stage in equilibrium. This ensures that parties will form, for coordination failures are easy in Nash equilibrium. If all citizens expect others not to become members, then parties are useless and no citizen will have an incentive to create one; moreover, each type can have at most one party.

The equilibrium concept is essentially subgame perfectness with the additional refinements on equilibria at the entry stage (and preentry stage in scenario (2)) – coalition-proofness – and at the voting stage – iterated elimination of weakly dominated strategies. In scenario (1) the equilibrium concept is *coalition-proof political equilibrium* (CPPE). It consists of a vector s of entry decisions ($s \in \{0, 1\}$) and a function α that describes voting behaviour such that (i) s is a coalition-proof Nash

---

[1] The role of party presidents and members is asymmetric: only citizens of the same type can be in a party, only presidents can decide to enter as candidates, costs are shared equally between all members, and citizens can be members of at most one party.

equilibrium (Bernheim, Peleg, and Whinston 1987) of the entry game given α and (ii) for all nonempty candidate sets C and any state of nature I, $\alpha^I(C)$ is a voting equilibrium.

In scenario (2) the equilibrium concept is analogously the subgame perfect equilibrium of the whole game, which is now called a *coalition-proof complete political equilibrium* (CPCPE).

The main results are that, without parties, the number of candidates who stand for election is decreasing in the cost of candidacy. When parties are allowed, (i) active parties are minimal winning coalitions: this conclusion is driven by the fact that members share the costs of candidacy, so each member must be "decisive" in the sense that without him the party would not form. (ii) Secondly the Duvergerian hypothesis that there is a tendency for only two parties to form in equilibrium holds. The paper has a full characterisation of the CPCPE.

Intuitively, this is a result of the fact that both extremist parties (all citizens are risk averse) may prefer not to run rather than not to have a centrist candidate. Centrists therefore have a higher power in a collusion with an extremist party. Thus, there are equilibria in which only a centrist party and an extremist run. Compared with case (1) (no cost sharing), more candidates stand for election in case (2), as expected.

Thus, parties in Riviere (1999) are viewed as coalitions of like-minded individuals who share the fixed costs of campaigning. However, a self-enforcing collusion between heterogenous parties can arise in equilibrium in the sense that entry decisions of different parties are coalition-proof.

Another set of authors that considers parties to be mainly cost-sharing organisations is Osborne and Tourky (2002). Unlike Riviere (1999), however, they are more interested in modelling situations in which a *group* of legislators makes policy decisions rather than a single party and candidates are not restricted to choosing their own ideal policy. Moreover, the rule chosen for translating policy announcements by legislators into policy is that the median of the announcements is chosen. Thus, parties in the Osborne–Tourky model are a group of legislators who vote for and support the same position. The reasons for forming parties are costly participation and the economies of scale that result from the formation of large parties.

The model consists of a set of players (finite) who decide whether or not to participate in decision making and, if so, which policy to champion. The policy space is unidimensional (it can be multidimensional as long as candidates can be ordered on a line according to their favourite positions), and the outcome is the median of the policies championed. The first assumption about payoffs is called *costly participation* and is defined as follows:

Costly Participation (C): If a participating player's switching to nonparticipation does not change the policy, then his or her payoff increases.

The second assumption is called *Economies of Party Size (E)* and is defined as follows:

Economies of Party Size (E): If a participant's switching to a larger party does not change the median championed policy, then his or her payoff increases.

We discuss an example of committee voting from the paper in the appendix. Example A.1 shows how the model works. The main result is that Example A.1 can be generalized, and two-party equilibria are characterized in the paper. Regarding equilibrium platforms, they show that the smaller the cost of participating, the closer will be the two parties' positions to each other.

The authors weaken the economies-of-scale axiom to allow different types of games: for example, two-stage games in which players can be candidates and voters and in a variety of games satisfying these conditions find the tendency towards a two-party system, thus verifying Duverger's law. Indeed, other outcome functions are explored in the paper that describe two-stage games satisfying similar axioms.

Notice that although Riviere (1999) has the entry decision subsequent to the party formation stage, Osborne and Tourky (2002) have a simultaneous entry and party formation decision. Moreover, Riviere has exogenously given platforms, whereas they are endogenous in Osborne and Tourky. Even then, some version of Duverger's law seems to emerge in the two papers. In Riviere (1999) the motivating factor is that the policy compromise achieved by having two parties (one extreme and one centrist) rather than two extremes is favoured by the two extremists, whereas in Osborne and Tourky (2002) the motivating factor is cost savings and the fact that the outcome does not change if the median does not. If participation were costless, it would be a weakly dominating strategy to announce the true favourite position; however, the two-party equilibrium is still a Nash equilibrium.[2]

Similar in spirit to the Osborne and Tourky (2002) model is one proposed by Gomberg, Marhuenda, and Ortuno-Ortin (2001). However, the motivation is different – indeed, Gomberg et al. assume that there are two parties to begin with. Their main contributions are a definition of political equilibrium and demonstration of its existence. They consider multidimensional policy spaces and introduce the notion of a party as a coalition of voter members who support a given policy that depends on their primary electorate's composition. The overall social outcome is a weighted average of the parties' positions, the weights being proportional to the share of votes received by each party. Equilibrium is a situation in which no coalition of voter members can obtain a preferred outcome by changing its voting. Existence of equilibrium is the main result.

In the appendix (Example A.2) I show that in a simple unidimensional setting the platforms chosen by the two parties in the Gomberg et al. solution are the same as the platforms chosen by the endogenous parties in the Osborne and Tourky solution. Of course the main points in Gomberg et al. are to generalize the solution to multidimensional spaces and prove existence.

---

[2] A related paper by Gerber and Ortuno-Ortin (1998) shows another two-party emergence result. Here, the policy space is unidimensional and voting takes place on this space. Voting basically means that each player proposes a policy. The policy adopted is a compromise between the proposals made. There is a continuum of voters, and each type has single-peaked preferences. The outcome function is assumed to be continuous and superadditive. The main result is that a unique, strong Nash equilibrium exists in the voting game that involves only two parties. The proposals are polarised, though the adopted policy is a compromise between these. The results do not generalize to the case of finite types because the continuity of the outcome function is necessary. Voting (participation) is costless.

Levy (2004) models party formation differently: the main rationale for parties to form, in her view, is their ability to solve the commitment problem of independent candidates. Parties are able to commit to a larger set of policies – in particular they are able to commit to any policy in the Pareto set of party members. The trade-off that an individual citizen faces in joining a party is between the gain in terms of the probability of winning against the costs of compromising on policy. Levy defines the notion of *effectiveness* of parties, namely, parties are effective if the outcome is different when they are allowed to form as against when they are not. Her main result is that parties are not effective in a unidimensional policy space.

Levy's (2004) model has N players; there is a representative agent in each group. A continuum of voters exists, and they are assumed to vote sincerely. The model has two phases of analysis: The platform game: Assume a partition π of voters into coalitions, a typical coalition being denoted S. Each coalition chooses a policy in its Pareto set to maximise its chances for election. Not choosing a policy is akin to choosing not to run. The winning policy is chosen by plurality rule. For each policy chosen in an equilibrium of the platform game, expected utility is given using a continuous and concave utility function for each member of each party. An equilibrium of the platform game is a set of platforms $\{\delta_S\}_{S \subset \pi} \equiv \delta(\pi)$ such that δ_S is a policy in the Pareto set of its members given δ_{-S}. Proposition 1 in Levy 2004 shows that an equilibrium of this game exists. Now for each possible coalition structure, choose an equilibrium of the corresponding platform game. Denote this pair as $(\pi, \delta(\pi))$. This yields an induced utility $U_i(\delta(\pi))$ for each player from this pair. An unstable partition is one that is not supported by any equilibrium of the platform game.

The stability concept is taken from Ray and Vohra (1997). From a given partition, the only deviations allowed are to break parties into smaller ones. Deviations can be unilateral or multilateral, but the deviators must be subcoalitions of the existing coalitions. Also, deviations take future deviations into account, both by members of their own coalitions and also members of other coalitions. Credible threats are deviations to finer partitions that are stable themselves. Thus, the definition is recursive. The technical details of the definition are presented in the appendix.

Let k^* denote the dimensionality of a Euclidean space V spanned by the N ideal policies in society.

Levy's main result (Levy 2004, Propositions 2 and 3) is that parties are not effective when $k^* = 1$. The only stable outcome is the median voters' ideal policy. When $k^* > 1$, parties are effective even if a Condorcet winner exists in the absence of parties. A sufficient condition for parties to be effective when the Condorcet winner is a unique equilibrium in π^0 and preferences are Euclidean is that $k^* = N - 1$.

Unlike Riviere (1999), Levy assumes that there is a representative candidate in each group given exogenously and that there is no cost sharing. But the dependence of the entry decision on the costs of campaigning and on risk aversion is similar in the two models.

In a companion paper, Levy (2002) verifies the robustness of the "party effectiveness" result under various stability concepts.

Morelli (2004) differs from the two authors above by looking at multidistrict elections and proportional representation. He is concerned, too, with whether "heterogeneous" parties form in equilibrium and whether parties are "effective," although these terms are interpreted differently from their use in Levy (2002). Parties are effective if they can be part of the government without considering their effect on the actual policy implemented. He is mainly concerned with the conditions under which the number of effective parties is larger under proportional representation than under plurality voting (Duverger's 1954 hypothesis). Parties are *active* if they run for election in at least one district.

As in Levy (2004), citizens are partitioned into N groups, each group composed of identical individuals (i.e., identical preferences). Preferences are single peaked and defined on a unidimensional policy space. There are three types of citizens (as in Riviere 1999); thus, $Q \subset \mathcal{R} = \{-1, t_C, 1\}$, where t_C denotes the ideal policy of the centrist voters, $t_C \leq 0$. There are also three districts with a measure $1/3$ of total citizens and each with its own distribution of voter preferences. Party leaders are given exogenously, and so are the set of potential candidates from each homogeneous party. Thus, with three districts, each district will have three potential candidates with a total of nine potential candidates given exogenously. The role of party leaders is to make coalitions of homogeneous parties, called the *heterogeneous* parties. The first stage entails party formation. In the second stage, each party decides whether to enter the election in each district. Then voting takes place. Voting can be sincere or "strategic" (because there is a continuum of voters, this needs to be defined). Two electoral systems are considered – plurality voting (PV) and proportional representation (PR). They differ in the way that vote shares in each district translate into seats in a legislature. There are three seats (one for each district). Under PV, a seat is allotted to a candidate if he or she wins (i.e., receives the maximum vote share) in a district. The party that receives a majority of seats will decide policy. If there is a tie, then the centrist party dictates the policy. Under PR, seats are allotted according to the Hare rule. Here we look first at the maximum vote share (summed across districts) for each party. This party (call it L) is awarded the first seat. Now we subtract $1/3$ from the total vote share for party L and compare this result with the original vote shares for the other two parties. The party that has the maximum vote share among these gets the second seat (call it C). Again, subtract $1/3$ from the total vote share for party C and compare this result with the remainder for part L, the remainder for party C, and the total votes for party R. The party that receives the maximum vote share among these gets the third seat. The party that has a majority of seats makes the policy decision it has chosen. If there is a tie, again C gets to make policy.[3]

Exogenously given candidates get a utility from winning the election as well. There is a cost to entry denoted by c. Thus, we may see candidates standing for election in a district even when they will not influence the policy given the voting equilibrium.

The strategic voting equilibrium needs to be described, for it is unusual. Strategic voting is thought of as voting recommendations made by each heterogeneous

---

[3] This is an important difference from the way that PR is usually modelled. Here policy is determined by the majority party in both plurality and proportional representation, and it is only the way in which winners are chosen that differs between the two.

party to its own group of voters across districts. Thus, a voting recommendation by a heterogeneous party composed of L and C would be a 3-tuple giving recommendations to its voters (L and C voters) in districts 1, 2, and 3. An equilibrium with strategic voting is a Nash equilibrium in recommendations – that is, given the voting recommendations of all other parties and on the assumption that all other voters follow the recommendations, a voter in party i should be weakly better off following the recommendation. Let π (as before) denote the partition into parties in equilibrium.

A voting equilibrium is *strong* if no *coalition* of parties $C \in 2^\pi$ can improve on the recommendations for voters in their coalition given the recommendations of all other parties.

An equilibrium of the whole game calls for subgame perfection.

In this model politicans may want to run for election even if they do not matter in the determination of policy. The main question analysed is whether parties are "effective," that is, Does the party have at least one candidate who wins in the whole country?

Each group has an incentive to have its own policy implemented. Suppose we focus on sincere voting and PV. If two districts have the same median voter, then that group can always win two seats in PV; thus, no heterogeneous parties form and at most two parties are effective generically. An interesting case arises when the median is different in all three districts. In this case, if all three parties stand and win one seat, then the centrist policy is the default option. Thus, in the bargaining stage of the game, both extreme parties offer the centrist voter his or her most preferred policy. This means that policy does not change in equilibrium whether heterogeneous parties form or not. Indeed, the equilibrium policy is always the centrist parties' most preferred position, and this is shown to be true as well for strategic voting (Proposition 1, Morelli 2004). Thus, parties are *not* "effective" in the sense that policy cannot change as the result of party formation. Levy (2002) showed this (Propositions 2 and 3, Levy 2004) for a single district with unidimensional policy space.

The main result is a full description of the configurations of voter preferences in the three districts under which PV has three active and effective parties (Corollary 2, Morelli 2004) and the configurations under which PR has at most two active and effective parties (Corollary 3, Morelli 2004). This allows us to come up with the conditions needed for Duverger's hypothesis to hold.

I compare the three models just discussed and their main results with the help of a simple example taken from Levy (2004) and presented in the appendix.

All the models considered so far assume complete information on all sides at the voting stage. Snyder and Ting (2002), in contrast, present a completely different view of parties. They view parties as "brand names" that inform voters credibly about the policy positions their members will take. In contrast to Levy (2004) and Morelli (2004), who assume that candidates cannot credibly commit to any policy except their own most preferred point and therefore need parties to be able to offer other platforms, Snyder and Ting (2002) assume that candidates cannot commit to any platform at all and need parties to credibly their true policy preference signal. Parties act as screening devices á la Spence (1974). The main issue is to explain how the precise meanings associated with different parties (e.g., Republicans are fiscally conservative, Democrats are liberal, etc.) arise as equilibrium phenomena. The model is based on two assumptions:

(i) Party membership carries costs. This assumption applies to the previously discussed models – that is, joining a party means compromise. These costs are higher the farther away the ideal policy of a candidate is from the party position.

(ii) Voters know little about preferences of candidates but much more about parties. This second assumption is in stark contrast to the citizen candidate models (Osborne and Slivinski 1996; Besley and Coate 1997) and all the models considered before. Thus, parties must be given exogenously in the model, as is indeed the case.

There are three types of players in the model: parties, candidates, and voters. There is a continuum of voters divided into a continuum of constituencies. Each constituency elects its own (single) representative by plurality rule from among the candidates who stand. The winning candidates take office and implement policy. The policy space is unidimensional, and again $Q = [-1, 1]$. Two situations are considered: one party only and two parties called L and R. Each party must choose its platform to maximise the share of offices won by its candidates. Candidates are driven by the rewards of office and, if elected, policy. Candidates' ideal points are random draws from a uniform distribution on $[-1, 1]$. However, candidates cannot credibly communicate to voters except through their affiliation choice, which is common knowledge. These choices are denoted by a: candidates may run unaffiliated ($a = 0$, independents) or join a party ($a = L, R$). The game consists of parties choosing platforms x_L and x_R. Then nature randomly draws an infinite sequence of candidates i.i.d from $[-1, 1]$. Candidates are offered affiliation with party L first, and the individual candidate must decide whether to affiliate or not. Party R offers affiliation to the second candidate, and so on. The remaining candidates may choose not to run or to run unaffiliated. Only one candidate is chosen to affiliate in each district. Then voting takes place, and the winner is chosen by plurality rule. The median across districts is the point 0.

By choosing its platform, a party implicitly selects its mean and variance because it can anticipate the set of candidates who join it. These are the crucial determinants of electoral success. Voters like less uncertainty and platforms close to their own ideal points.

When only one party is allowed, candidates may still choose to affiliate to reduce the uncertainty that voters have about their policy preferences. But the specifics of the model are such that in this case the party can locate at 0 and win all districts. By locating at 0, the party will have the same mean as an unaffiliated candidate but will have a lower variance because extremist candidates will not join the party – it is not worthwhile for them. The party thus screens out candidates who are too far in the policy space. Thus, equilibrium calls for consistency between the platform chosen and the ideal points of the candidates who join it.

When there are two parties, the equilibrium can be of two types: convergent or divergent as determined by the value of the costs and benefits of winning for a candidate. When the relative benefits of holding office are low, then the equilibrium is convergent: it involves both parties locating at the point 0, which ensures that they each will win half the districts. Unaffiliated candidates are sure to be defeated in every district. When the relative benefits of holding office are large, however, candidates may get divergent equilibria that involve parties locating at a distance (the same distance) away from the mean and on opposite sides of 0. This location ensures that

(i) unaffiliated candidates lose all districts again because, when the median is on the left side of the mean, the left party wins and vice versa; and

(ii) each party wins half the districts. The reason that 0 is no longer an equilibrium when the benefits of holding office are large is that more candidates will affiliate with the result that variance at 0 is very high. If one party locates at 0 (e.g., the R party), the other party (the L party) can do better by moving left of 0 to reduce its variance and attract more voters – without losing out to unaffiliated candidates.

In this model, parties are therefore viewed as entities that will choose platforms to attract certain types of candidates in order to maximise the chances of winning overall given the policy chosen by the other party. The factors that influence party membership are

(i) the policy chosen by the other party;

(ii) the benefits for candidates to affiliate with a party (payoff from winning, costs of standing, and the costs of policy compromise); and

(iii) the degree to which uncertainty is decreased (and electoral success enhanced) by having a particular set of candidates relative to unaffiliated candidates.

9.3. Postelection Coalitions

The common thread linking all the authors mentioned so far is the importance of the party formation process in the voting behaviour that follows. However, some authors suppress the role of voters and assume the legislative composition as given. The seminal work of Riker (1962) was the first to study this kind of coalition behaviour. His predictions still form the basis for recent research on this topic: he focused on a narrow interpretation of the objectives of political parties, namely, that they are interested in the spoils of office. Thus, the game is a zero-sum game, and this led to his insight called "the size principle." This is the notion that coalitions must be minimal winning coalitions so as to maximise the gains from forming them. Traditionally, the study of coalitions among political scientists has focused on postelection coalitions between parties.[4] In the interest of brevity and to avoid

---

[4] The literature has a long tradition in public choice. The themes that dominate have been the move from unidimensional to multidimensional policy space and the resulting potential for chaos if decisions are made by plurality vote (e.g., McKelvey 1976). Several cooperative game-theoretic solutions were

redundancy I will focus on work that is more recent and refer the interested reader to the reviews mentioned in footnote 4.

Jackson and Moselle (2002) model the benefits of party formation in the context of a legislative bargaining game. They use the legislative bargaining game of Baron and Ferejohn (1989) and extend it to the case in which bargaining between legislators takes place on two dimensions – a private goods dimension and a public goods dimension (whereas in the original legislative game bargaining was only over the distribution of a fixed amount of a private good). As in Levy (2002) and Riviere (1999), the outcome of the game is compared when parties can form and when they cannot. The main issue in the context of this chapter is to examine whether the equilibrium outcomes of the legislative game are different with and without parties, which is the question we saw in Levy (2002): Are parties *effective*? In terms of the extension of the simple legislative game to two dimensions, the equilibria show that the two dimensions interact in interesting ways even though legislators' preferences are separable on the two dimensions. In short, the motivation to form "parties" or coalitions may be to increase the power of a legislators' ideology or to garner extra benefits for their own constituencies in the budgetary process (the distributive dimension).

I will describe the model and then focus on one of the examples in the paper that illustrates the intuition for the main results.

The legislative game has n players (legislators), $n \geq 3$, is an odd number. A *decision* is a vector $(y, x_1, x_2, \ldots, x_n)$ consisting of an ideological decision y and a *distributive* decision about the division of a fixed pie of size X. The set of feasible public decisions is $[0, Y]$ and $Y \in [0, 1]$. The set of feasible distributive decisions consists of those that have $x_i \geq 0$ for all i and $\sum_i x_i = X$. Preferences of legislator i are assumed to be separable in x_i and y. They are single peaked in y and strictly increasing in x_i for every y. We can order legislators in increasing order by their ideal points for the public good: $i \leq j$ iff $y_i \leq y_j$. They have a uniform discount rate $0 < \delta \leq 1$, and the utility for i of reaching an agreement $(y, x_1, x_2, \ldots, x_n)$ at time t is $\delta^t u_i(y, x_i)$. The *legislative game* consists of sessions $t = 1, 2, \ldots$. At the beginnning of each session a legislator is chosen randomly, with probability p_i for legislator i, to make a proposal and the probabilties are the same in each session. Then legislators are called upon to vote yes or no on the proposal in a fixed order. The proposer can choose to propose on one dimension or both. The authors show that there is no loss of generality in restricting the rules of the game to be such that both dimensions are proposed simultaneously. A default utility is specified in case the

proposed to address this indeterminancy in the outcome of the legislative voting game. Thus, for example, the Core may be empty in multidimensional spaces. Some reviews of the extensive work on spatial theories of legislatures are Austen-Smith (1983), Calvert (1986), and Shepsle (1986). The approach taken to solve this theoretical problem was to consider detailed versions of the legislative process (i.e., to introduce institutions as a way to add more structure in the problem and to make meaningful predictions). Shepsle (1979), for example, proposed a *structure-induced equilibrium* by adding a role for committees that specialise in making decisions on particular issues. In contrast to the much later model of Jackson and Moselle (2002) (discussed in detail in this section), Shepsle argues that the operation of the committee system will not allow issues to be linked, and it is not possible to make trades on policy issues.

game never ends. All actions are observable, and the game is a perfect information game.

Equilibrium is a subgame perfect equilibrium of the game in stationary strategies (i.e., strategies that do not depend on history of past play). Because a legislator needs a majority to pass a proposal, there are exactly $M = \frac{n-1!}{[(n-1)/2]!}$ sets of other legislators such that he or she can get a majority. A *simple equilibrium* is a stationary equilibrium in which a legislator can randomize over a maximum of M proposals and each such proposal can be identified with a distinct coalition C of $(n-1)/2$ other legislators who vote yes on the proposal.

Because I am more interested in the pregame coalitions that form, I will not describe these results in detail but instead focus, as before, on examples taken from the paper. The main conclusions emerging from the legislative game are described in Section 6:

(i) Simple equilibria always exist.

(ii) In such equilibria, both dimensions are considered together and a decision will be approved in the first session.

(iii) Each legislator has a positive probability of being excluded from some decision that has a chance of being approved.

(iv) Generically there are at least two different ideological decisions that have a chance of being approved.

To understand the model better I present an example taken from Jackson and Moselle (2002) in the appendix (Example A.4). A party is modelled as a binding agreement between the members to act as a single unit in the legislative game. The benefits to the legislators are measured relative to the payoffs in the legislative game. The set of utility levels possible for legislators in a coalition $\{i, j\}$ is described by the set of decisions that the coalition can make in the legislative game. The disagreement point is given by the expected utility of the legislator in the legislative game without parties.

Let $u_i^{NB}(\{i, j\})$ denote the utility that i gets from party $\{i, j\}$ using the Nash bargaining solution to split the gains from party formation. The following definition applies to the three-player game discussed by Jackson and Moselle.

Definition: A party $\{i, j\}$ is stable if $u_i^{NB}(\{i, j\}) \geq u_i^{NB}(\{i, k\})$ and $u_j^{NB}(\{i, j\}) \geq u_j^{NB}(\{j, k\})$.

In our example, therefore, the stable parties are $\{1, 2\}$ and $\{2, 3\}$. Several examples in the paper show that with different parameter values very different stable parties can emerge. Some interesting comparative statics are derived.

Thus, Jackson and Moselle (2002) conclude that parties are effective in the sense that legislative outcomes are significantly altered when parties can form but that the changes depend on parameters like preference intensities.

Jackson and Moselle (2002) focus on the differences in outcomes when parties can form as opposed to when they cannot when there are two dimensions in the legislative game. They do not have predictions of the types of parties that form apart from some examples. Can we say anything about the types of coalitions that form? When legislators care about power as well as policy outcomes, this question is addressed in the unidimensional case by Bandyopadhyaya and Oak (2003). They consider a model of legislative coalition formation under a proportional representation (PR) system.

Although the role of voters was suppressed in the literature reviewed above, the models of Austen-Smith and Banks (1988) and Baron (1993) combine voting in elections with coalition formation at the legislative stage. Both focus on proportional representation. Austen-Smith (1986) focuses on multidistrict plurality rule elections but does not model the legislative game explicitly. In addition to deriving predictions about the equilibrium coalitions that emerge, these authors also derive the electoral platforms chosen by the parties endogenously. In this sense, these models are more general than the models of postelection coalitions I reviewed in Section 9.2.

The idea in Austen-Smith and Banks (1988) is that voters will anticipate the coalitions that form at the legislative stage and vote strategically to achieve their best policy. Although three parties compete on a unidimensional policy space, there is a distributional dimension as well to the legislative game in that parties can also bargain over the spoils of office. Parties are interested in minimising the difference between their electoral platforms and the policy ultimately implemented along with the spoils of office.

The timing is as follows: first the three parties announce electoral platforms; then an election takes place and vote shares are determined. Finally, policy is decided by bargaining between the different parties. The weights in the bargaining game are determined by the share of votes of each party: this happens endogenously through the legislative game in which the party with the highest vote share gets to propose a policy and distribution of the private good first. If the proposal is accepted by a majority, it is implemented; otherwise, the party with the next highest vote share gets to make a proposal, and so on. The subgame-perfect equilibrium of this is the solution to the legislative game for given vote shares. Finally, policy is implemented. A party needs at least s votes to get into the legislature, where $s \in [3, \frac{1}{3}n]$ is odd and n denotes the number of voters. Vote shares of the parties determine their weights in the implemented policy. If a party has an absolute majority in votes, then it can implement its own announced policy and corner all the private benefits. Assume that each party gets at least s votes.

Coalition formation in the legislative stage entails each party's making a proposal consisting of a coalition, a policy, and a distribution of private benefits. The members of the coalition can accept or reject the proposal. This proposal is passed if a majority of the coalition members decide to accept it. Otherwise, in the next legislative session the party with the second highest vote share attempts to make a winning coalition, and so on. If no government has formed after the third party makes its attempt, then a caretaker government is formed that makes its decision equitably. Equilibrium in this game is a subgame-perfect equilibrium of the whole game. The legislative game thus differs in the detailed description from that of Jackson and Moselle (2002) – in particular because proposals are made simultaneously in the latter model. However, the inefficiency of the legislative bargaining process is also a feature of the Austen-Smith–Banks model. This inefficiency is driven by the risk aversion of party members and the uncertainty in the equilibrium outcome. The legislative game is solved using a noncooperative bargaining approach – an idea employed subsequently by Jackson and Moselle (2002). An important insight from the coalition formation or legislative stage is that coalitions that form are minimal winning coalitions (almost by definition) but not necessarily of minimum size (i.e., size is not decided arbitrarily but is determined by proportional representation). Also, winning coalitions are not necessarily connected; that is, there may be equilibria in which the two extreme parties form a coalition – it is the parties with the highest and lowest weights that form a coalition. This is because the party that proposes would prefer to do so when it has to compromise less. The electoral equilibrium is fully characterised. Unlike plurality rule, the legislative influence of a party is not monotonic in vote shares. The expected policy in equilibrium is the median voters' position, although realised policy may be different. Finally, not all voters vote sincerely in equilibrium.

Some conclusions are similar to, and anticipate the results of, Jackson and Moselle (2002): legislators with extreme preferences may end up forming a coalition (unconnected coalitions), the median voter is an anchor for the different policy positions in equilibrium, and the inefficiency of the outcomes. Baron (1993) has a very similar model to that of Austen-Smith and Banks (1988) except that parties aim to maximise the aggregate welfare of their supporters and voting is sincere. The main result is that, unlike plurality voting systems, a convergence of policy positions may not occur.

9.4. Conclusions

What are the main insights that emerge from this survey of party formation? The first important insight is that, although most models of politics are unidimensional, this is not an innocuous assumption. Indeed, the question of whether it is important to study parties as an analytical construct may depend crucially on this assumption. Both Levy (2004) and Jackson and Moselle (2002) show, in different settings, that parties are effective when the issue space is multidimensional but not necessarily when the issue space is unidimensional.

What are the motivations to forming parties? As aptly summarised by Strom (1990), the literature has focused on three main motivations: office seeking, policy seeking, and vote seeking. Most of the models have similar motivating factors: economies of party size (Osborne and Tourky 2002), cost sharing (Riviere 1999), and improved ability to commit to and obtain good policy positions (Levy 2004; Morelli 2004; Jackson and Moselle 2002; Austen-Smith and Banks 1988). The costs of forming parties are the costs of compromise in many of the models.

Several of the papers surveyed confirm the minimal winning coalition idea of Riker (1962) – in particular when there is a distributive dimension to party formation (e.g., Riviere 1999; Austen-Smith and Banks 1988; Bandyopadhyay and Oak 2003). However, many instances are shown of parties not being connected (e.g., Jackson and Moselle 2002; Austen-Smith and Banks 1988).

Many of the papers focus on showing the conditions under which Duverger's (1954) law holds. Thus, for example, Riviere (1999) shows the conditions under which two parties emerge endogenously in single-district plurality rule elections, whereas Morelli (2004) shows the configurations of voter preferences under which Duverger's (1954) hypothesis (that there are typically more parties under proportional representation than under plurality rule) is true.

What determines the number of parties? Among the authors for whom this is an endogeneous variable; Levy (2004) seems to suggest that it is the original partition of groups of citizens with identical preferences (although this is not a prediction of the model): Her Example 2 shows that when there are three groups, there will be two parties in equilibrium. In Morelli (2004), it is the electoral institution and the original preference distribution that predict the number of parties that form, whereas in Austen-Smith and Banks (1988) and Jackson and Moselle (2002) it is the legislative bargaining game and the gains from trade and ultimately the preference intensities of legislators that determine the number of legislative coalitions that will form. On the other hand some papers simply show the conditions under which a two-party result emerges (e.g, Morelli 2004; Osborne and Tourky 2002). Of course, although Osborne and Tourky (2002) have sufficient conditions that guarantee Duvergerian outcomes for every distribution of preferences and for every electoral system, Morelli (2004) shows that preferences and electoral systems determine everything.

In terms of predictions about which policy will ultimately be implemented, the asymmetric importance of the median is a common theme in both unidimensional and multidimensional models. Finally, equilibrium concepts in most of the papers surveyed here are noncooperative, and most called for subgame perfection. An exception is Levy (2002), which explicitly uses some cooperative game theoretic equilibrium concepts as well. Jackson and Moselle (2002) use a combination approach – they employ the Nash bargaining solution as well as noncooperative bargaining in their model.

I conclude by observing that an important question is, Given the importance of the median in most models, do parties exaggerate the role of the majority? In practice, parties coexist with other coalitions – like interest groups or coalitions of voters – and thus outcomes are far from those predicted in this survey. Indeed, coalitions may form between parties and their "clients" in ways that are detrimental to the majority. Apart from Morelli (2004), most authors do not focus on the welfare aspects of party formation, and this remains an open (albeit normative) question in this newly emerging literature.

APPENDIX

Example A.1. (Osborne and Tourky 2002). *Each member of a committee of n individuals has to choose whether to champion a policy (assumed to be in an interval X) and, if so, which one. The payoff function depends on the actual policy chosen, which is the median of the announced positions. If a person participates, he or she* incurs a cost $c_i(k(x))$, where k is the number of people announcing the same policy $x \in X$. The cost is positive and decreasing in k. Each player has the strategy set $X \bigcup \theta$, where θ stands for no participation. This payoff function (see Example 2.1 in Osborne and Tourky 2002), satisfies the two axioms C and E discussed in Section 9.2. So what equilibria might we expect? What drives the two-party equilibrium result?

Thus, for example, let us consider why it is an equilibrium for an even number of participants to agglomerate at exactly two positions. Suppose the number of players is six and the policy space is $X = [0, 1]$. Preferences are single peaked and given by $u_i(x) = -(x - x_i)^2$, where x_i represents the ideal point of player i. They can be ordered on the policy space from 0 to 1 on the basis of their ideal point. Because the number of participants is even, the median is halfway between the two middle positions. For simplicity, assume that we have two people at 0, one at 1/4, two at 3/4, and one person at 1. Then, the mean of the two medians is 1/2. Assume that the function $c(k)$ (cost as a function of the number of members of the party) is given by C/k. The outcome function takes the announced positions and maps them to the unique median if the number of announcements is odd and takes the mean of the two median positions if the number of announcements is even.

Then, if $C \leq \frac{9}{16}$, there is a two-party equilibrium with the left party's position x given by 1/4 and the right party's position y given by 3/4. To see this, notice that members of the left party whose favourite point is to the left of 1/4 do better by participating than by not (gain $= -[(1/2) - 0]^2 + [(3/4) - 0]^2 = \frac{5}{16}$), whereas the cost per capita is $C/3 = \frac{3}{16}$. The members of the left party at 1/4 just break even and are indifferent between participating and not. By symmetry, this is true for the right party as well. Hence, this is an equilibrium, and so is any other pair (x', y') that gives the same medians and satisfies $x' < 1/4$ and $y' > 3/4$. This is because, if $x' > 1/4$, $y' < 3/4$ (to maintain the same medians), we have that the gain for members located at 1/4 is strictly less than $\frac{3}{16}$, and thus all such members will choose not to participate.

No player can profitably deviate from such a two-party location (x, y). If any member leaves, he or she will change the outcome to the other party's position, and we determined that this member prefers to participate given the other player's positions. Members do not want to move farther to the left given this configuration because they do not change the outcome but have higher costs.

There can also be two-party equilibria in this example with each party composed of two members each if costs are given by $C = \frac{75}{576}$. For example, let $x = 1/3$ and $y = 3/4$ so that the mean is $\frac{13}{24}$. At this level of cost, the candidates with favourite position at 3/4 will be indifferent between announcing 3/4 and not participating. So let us assume that one of them participates and the other does not. Candidates at the position 1/4 do not participate because the costs are too high relative to their gain. Candidates at 0 will participate in the left party, and the candidate at 1 will participate in the right party.

The intuition for the result is the following: the trade-off between joining a party and choosing to be an independent is the savings in costs versus the costs of compromise. However, if a legislator's favourite position is to the left of the median, then *joining a party that is also left of the median in a way that does not change the median position is a strategy that makes the individual no worse off in terms of policy outcome but makes him strictly better off in terms of cost savings. Thus, left-leaning legislators are better off joining a left-leaning party, and, similarly, right-leaning legislators are better off joining a right-leaning party.*

Example A.2. (Osborne and Tourky 2002, Gomberg et al. 2001). *Let us analyse a simpler version of the Gomberg et al. model with a unidimensional policy space and a finite set of agents. We may take the same example (Example A.1). In this model, however, the number of parties is fixed at two. Let us assume that the actual policy implemented will be the weighted mean of the two party positions with weights given by the share of votes. I want to show that $x = 1/4$, $y = 3/4$, with members of the left party being given by all the citizens who have ideal points to the left of $1/4$ and members of the right party given by all citizens who have ideal points to the right of $3/4$, is an equilibrium. Once these platforms are announced, no coalition of agents can do better by switching to voting for the other party, for this will shift the implemented policy away from their preferred point. This is an equilibrium in the sense of Gomberg et al. Of course, the main point is to generalise to the multidimensional case and prove existence. The idea in Osborne and Tourky (2002), on the other hand, is to show how a two-party equilibrium arises in a unidimensional space (or a multidimensional one that can be ordered by best points).*

Levy (2004), Definition of Stable Partition

Denote the finest partition structure, the single-member coalition partition, by π^0 and, because no deviations are possible for this, $(\pi^0, \delta(\pi^0))$ is defined as stable for all $\delta(\pi^0))$.

Let $R(\pi)$ denote the set of coalition structures that are refinements of π. A coalition $\tilde{\pi}$ is *induced* from π if $\tilde{\pi}$ is formed by breaking a coalition π into two. Suppose that, for some π, all stable coalitions with their respective equilibria are defined for all $\pi' \in R(\pi)$.

Definition. $(\pi^1, \delta(\pi^1))$ *is sequentially blocked by* $(\pi', \delta(\pi'))$ *if* $\exists$ *a sequence* $\{(\pi^1, \delta(\pi^1)), (\pi^2, \delta(\pi^2)), \ldots, (\pi^m, \delta(\pi^m))\}$, *such that:*

1. $(\pi^1, \delta(\pi^1)) = (\pi, \delta(\pi))$, $(\pi^m, \delta(\pi^m)) = (\pi', \delta(\pi'))$, *and for every* $j = 2, \ldots, m$ *there is a deviator* S^j *that induces* π^j *from* π^{j-1};
2. $(\pi', \delta(\pi'))$ *is stable;*
3. $(\pi^j, \delta(\pi^j))$ *is not stable for any* $\delta(\pi^j)$ *and* $1 < j < m$;
4. $U_i(\delta(\pi')) > U_i(\delta(\pi^{j-1}))$ *for all* $j = 2, \ldots, m$ *and* $i \in S$.

Then $(\pi, \delta(\pi))$ is stable if there is no $(\pi', \delta(\pi'))$ for $\pi' \in R(\pi)$ that sequentially blocks $(\pi, \delta(\pi))$.

Example A.3. Comparison of Riviere (1999), Levy (2004), and Morelli (2004). *There are three districts, each of which has $N = 3$. We can assume that each group is composed of n_i citizens. The citizens in each group i have the preferences*

$u_i(x) = -(i_x - x)^2$, where i_x denotes the ideal point of voter $i \in \{a, b, c\}$. Let $a_x = 0, b_x = 1, c_x = 2$. The policy space is restricted to be the interval $[0, 2]$. No group has an absolute majority in District 1 (thus the median is b), whereas a and b have absolute majorities in Districts 2 and 3, respectively. We consider plurality rule and sincere voting. There is a cost to candidacy c. Riviere and Levy (2004) focus on single-district solutions. Thus, in District 1, Levy predicts that no (heterogeneous) parties form; if all three types run, the equilibrium will have b winning the election. If a, b form a party against c, they can offer anything in $(0, 1]$ and win, whereas if b, c form a party against a, then they can offer anything in $[1, 2)$ and win. What about ac against b? This coalition can win only if it offers the median position 1; otherwise, b can enter and win on this platform. To see which coalitions are stable, consider that the trivial one is stable by definition and the only other coalitions that are stable will have the policy platform offered being equal to 1; otherwise, b can deviate by itself and do better. The grand coalition is stable if the platform is 1 again; hence, there are multiple stable partitions, but the policy outcome is the same. This is Levy's main result: for policy outcomes to be different from the benchmark case of no parties, we need more than one dimension in the policy space. Riviere (1999) focuses on how many members there would be within the homogenous groups. Morelli (2004) and Levy (2004) treat this as exogenously given, and the cost-sharing motivation for forming parties is not considered. Riviere (1999) requires some uncertainty over the median voter – without this only the median candidate would ever enter. So let us focus on District 1 and assume that there are n citizens in each group (i.e., whose preferences are common knowledge to begin with). In stage 1, citizens in the three groups announce their membership; they can choose to announce themselves as president or members of a party or stay independent (parties are restricted to be homogeneous).[5] Let N' denote the total number of citizens in the district. The ideology of the other $N' - 3n$ citizens is uncertain and determines the state of the world. The probability that the median voter is type a, b, or c is $3/10, 4/10,$ or $3/10$, respectively. Once citizens make their announcements, parties are formed, and in the second stage candidates announce whether they will run or not. Candidates can be independents or party presidents only. The median type is then realised, and voting takes place. Finally, policies are implemented by the winner. The expected gain from standing for election for a candidate depends on the other candidates who stand for election (because this determines the probability of winning) as well as the cost and the number of members willing to share the cost. Would candidates from a, b, c stand independently? The answer depends on costs of candidacy – candidates trade off the cost against the policy gain of winning. If costs are small enough, we can have all three candidates standing. Now let us consider the costs to be high enough so that no independent candidate will consider standing. When parties are allowed to form, the fact that equilibria at the party formation stage are coalition-proof means that coalitions will be minimal winning coalitions, that is, only as many members will join the party as are needed to make the party president of party i stand for

---

[5] This is like the membership game of Levy (2002).

election given the rest of the candidates.[6] *The size of the minimal coalition for a party of type i is determined by the gain to a member of i from a candidate of type i running for election given the rest of the candidate set. Denote by $M_i(C)$ the size of the minimal winning coalition for party i given the candidate set C – that is, on the assumption that all candidates $C/\{i\}$ stand for election. Consider a typical member of party a. His or her preferences over the set of candidates running for election are the following: $(a) \succ_a (a, b) \succ_a (a, b, c) \succ_a (b, c) \succ_a (c)$. A candidate of type c has symmetric preferences to these, but a candidate of type b is slightly different: $(b) \succ_b (a, b) \succ_b (a, b, c) \succ_b (a, c) \succ_b (a)$. He or she is indifferent between (a, b) and (b, c) and between (a) and (c).*

For the following calculations I assume that the ideal policy of a is -1, that of b is 0, and that of c is 1 in order to have the same numbers as Riviere (1999) has. Also, I assume, as in Riviere's paper, that default utility when no one stands is -4. These preferences imply that $M_a(a) \leq M_a(a, b) \leq M_a(a, c) \leq M_a(a, b, c)$. Indeed, we can explicitly calculate these: given that the cost of candidacy is $\delta > 4$, M_a is the number that equates the per capita cost of candidacy in the party to the expected gain from standing for election inasmuch as no other candidate is standing: in this case $\frac{\delta}{M_a(a)} = 4$ because the gain from standing is 4. Thus, $M_a(a) = \frac{\delta}{4}$. Similarly, $\frac{\delta}{M_a(a,b)} = \frac{3}{10}$, and so $M_a(a, b) = \frac{10\delta}{3}$; in the same way, $M_a(a, c) = \frac{\delta}{2}$, and $M_a(a, b, c) = \frac{10\delta}{3}$. The numbers for party C are symmetric. For party b we have $M_b(b) = \frac{\delta}{4}, M_b(b, c) = M_b(a, b) = \frac{10\delta}{7}$, and $M_b(a, b, c) = \frac{10\delta}{4}$.

Consider what happens when all three parties have candidates. Can this be an equilibrium (CPCPE)? No, because all three parties can do better by deviating collectively to a situation in which the centrist party b wins. To illustrate the caculation, consider party a. If all three run, this party gets $\frac{3}{10}(-4) + \frac{4}{10}(-1)$, whereas if only b runs, a gets -1.

Can it be an equilibrium for a centrist party b to be the only one running? This situation is less straightforward and more interesting because parties are using their size strategically to support this equilibrium. The answer is yes; it is clear that no coalition involving the b party can succeed because these citizens are getting their best possible policy. However, there is a prisoner's dilemma between the a types and the c types: in the absence of party size as a strategic variable, it is a dominant strategy for them to enter given that the candidate set is (b). This prisoner's dilemma exists in the absence of any commitment mechanism. But note that in this model, the size of the party is a credible commitment device.[7] Given that the size of the b party is such that it can support a candidate set (b) but nothing bigger, this means that the extremist parties (for instance a) expect to reach the situation (a, c) or (a) if they enter the race. The size of party c is such that it can support (a, c); thus, both extremist parties expect to reach (a, c) if they enter, which is worse for them than b standing alone.

---

[6] This makes the president indifferent between standing and not standing. Note that the entry decision is taken only after the size of parties is determined, thus it can be made contingent on the size.

[7] The entry decision takes place after the party formation stage.

It can also be an equilibrium for one extremist party to stand against the centrist party. Consider the situation in which a, b stand for election. Why does party c not deviate and stand as well (because it prefers the outcome (a, b, c))? Again, the reason is that the centrist party can use its size strategically to convince the c party that if it were to enter, the outcome would be (a, c) rather than (a, b, c), and the c party prefers the situation (a, b) to the situation (a, c) by risk aversion. The main result is this: the set of rational expectations that supports the two-party equilibrium is much bigger than the set that supports the one- (centrist) party equilibrium in the sense that the latter requires more restrictions on the size of parties.

Let us consider what happens when a party is interested in maximising the number of districts it can win. How many parties can form in such a case, and what platforms do they offer (Morelli 2004)? Party a has an absolute majority in District 2 and c in District 3. If no heterogeneous parties form, in the voting subgame we will have each group winning one seat only and the policy implemented is the median of the three, that is, 1. If instead we have a, b together versus c, then a, b will win the first two and c the third district, and vice versa if we have c, b versus a. In each of these cases the policy implemented must still be 1; otherwise, in the bargaining subgame the other extreme party will offer 1 to b and this will be accepted. Competition in bargaining leads to the median policy (for the country) being offered in every equilibrium. There is no (strict) incentive for heterogenous parties to form. Thus, all three groups are effective in the sense of Morelli but not effective in the sense of Levy.

What happens with PR? With a distribution of preferences such that the median is different in every district, suppose we have the following additional restrictions: party a has a (sincere) share of votes that is the maximum across the three districts but is strictly less than 1/2 the total votes. It also has a sincere share of votes that would allow it to get another seat under the Hare quota if all three parties were to run in every district. Thus, if all three parties ran, the policy would be 0. The other extreme party, c, will, however, decide not to run in this situation if the net gains from running are less than the policy gain of letting the b party win. Consequently, there will be at most two effective parties under PR in this scenario, whereas there were three parties under PV. This situation is the opposite of what is predicted by Duverger's hypothesis. To see situations in which the hypothesis does hold, consider the preferences in which no party has a majority in any district, but across districts, using the Hare quota gives each party one seat if they all run. In this case, all parties are effective under PR. Under PV, however, it would pay for a hetrogeneous party to form so that it can win two seats and implement 0. Thus, there would be only two effective parties in equilibrium under PV.

Example A.4. (Jackson and Moselle 2002, Example 1). *There are three legislators. $Y = X = 1$, $\delta = 1$. Each legislator has an equal chance of being recognised (called upon to make a proposal). Their peaks are $\hat{y}_1 = 0$, $\hat{y}_2 = 1/2$, $\hat{y}_3 = 1$. Thus, the median is $1/2$. The preferences of legislators are given by the quasi-linear utility functions $u_i = -b_i |y - \hat{y}_i| + x_i$. Possible minimal winning coalitions for any one legislator consist of one other legislator. Legislators have well-defined ex* ante expected utilities for a given strategy profile, and, in view of the stationarity, these are also the continuation utilities denoted by v_i if the current proposal is not accepted. A proposal from i to j denoted y_{ij}, x_{ij} is a proposal that includes legislators i and j, that is, promises them a utility at least as high as the continuation utilities and excludes legislator k ($k \neq, i, j$) if his or her utility from that proposal is strictly less than that legislator's continuation utility. Let $b_1 = 1, b_2 = 3$, and $b_3 = 6$. Thus, the marginal rate of substitution of public for private goods is given by b_i for each legislator i. To find the equilibrium, we need to determine the probabilities a_{ij} that legislator i will make a proposal to j as well as the proposal vectors y_{ij}, x_{ij}. The ex ante utility of each legislator (e.g., legislator 1) is given by $v_i = 1/3[a_{12}(u_1(y_{12}, x_{12})) + a_{13}(u_1(y_{13}, x_{13}))] + 1/3[a_{21}(u_1(y_{21}, x_{21})) + a_{23}(u_1(y_{23}, x_{23}))] + 1/3[a_{31}(u_1(y_{31}, x_{31})) + a_{32}(u_1(y_{32}, x_{32}))]$. (Note that $\sum_i(a_{ij}) = 1$.)

In a simple stationary equilibrium, the utilities from the proposals that are accepted must equal the continuation utilities, that is, proposals made by a legislator in equilibrium must give him or her a utility at least as high as that legislator's continuation utility, and proposals that exclude a legislator must give a utility strictly less than his or her continuation utility. The solution to this is $a_{12} = a_{23} = a_{31} = 1$. The corresponding decisions are $y_{12} = \frac{1}{2} - \frac{1}{6}$, $x_{12} = (1, 0, 0)$,; $y_{23} = \frac{1}{2} + \frac{1}{6}$, $x_{23} = (0, 1, 0)$,; and $y_{31} = 1, x_{31} = (1, 0, 0)$. Let us check the conditions for equilibrium. In the solution we must have $u_1(y_{12}, x_{12}) \geq u_1(y_{31}, x_{31}) = v_1 > u_1(y_{23}, x_{23})$. Note that $u_1(y_{12}, x_{12}) = \frac{5}{6}, u_1(y_{31}, x_{31}) = 0$, and $u_1(y_{23}, x_{23}) = -\frac{5}{6}$. In addition, $v_1 = \frac{1}{3}(\frac{5}{6}) + \frac{1}{3}(0) + \frac{1}{3}(-\frac{5}{6})$, thus confirming the condition above. The same reasoning obtains for legislators 2 and 3.[8] Thus equilibrium utility values of the legislators are $v_1 = 0, v_2 = -\frac{1}{2}$, and $v_3 = -2$. Note that this is not an efficient allocation; for example, the decision $y = \frac{3}{4}, x = (\frac{1}{2}, \frac{1}{2}, 0)$ would give strictly higher utilities to each of the three players of $u_1 = \frac{1}{4}, u_2 = -\frac{1}{4}$, and $u_3 = -\frac{3}{4}$. This is because (1) legislators are risk averse and (2) the fact that, for sufficiently high discount factors, there is always a positive probability that a legislator will be excluded from some proposal (see Proposition 4). Thus, legislators can gain from binding agreements that guarantee a certain utility.

A party is modelled as a binding agreement between the members to act as a single unit in the legislative game. The benefits to the legislators are measured relative to the payoffs in the legislative game. The set of utility levels possible for legislators in a coalition $\{i, j\}$ is described by the set of decisions that the coalition can make in the legislative game. The highest utility that legislator 2 can make if, for example, a coalition forms between 2 and 3, is given by equilibrium utility for 2 when 2 proposes to 3. Because in equilibrium this is accepted by 3 in the legislative game, it must give 3 at least his or her disagreement payoff. Thus, this is the best that 2 can do, whereas 3 gets at least his or her disagreement utility. In cases in which there is no equilibrium proposal from a legislator to the other person in his or her coalition, a direct computation must be done. Therefore, in the same example, because in equilibrium 3 does not make a proposal to 2, we must compute his or

---

[8] This solution is generalised in the paper to different parameter values for the b_i's.

her highest utility directly: if 2 is kept at his or her disagreement utility, $v_2 = -\frac{1}{2}$, the best that 3 can do is the decision $y = 1$, $x = (0, 1, 0)$, and this gives the utility $u_3 = 0$. Thus, we obtain a linear utility possibility frontier by varying y between $\frac{2}{3}$ and 1. The disagreement utilities are given by the continuation utilities in the legislative game: $v_2, v_3 = -\frac{1}{2}, -2$. The Nash bargaining solution is applied to this problem and gives the utilities associated with the two players forming a party. For further details of finding the utility possibility frontier when both y and x change in the optimal decisions, see Jackson and Moselle (2002). Finally, calculating utilities in this way, we find that legislator 1 prefers the party $\{1, 2\}$ to the party $\{1, 3\}$, 2 is indifferent between parties $\{1, 2\}$ and $\{2, 3\}$, and 3 is indifferent between the parties $\{1, 3\}$ and $\{2, 3\}$.

BIBLIOGRAPHY

[1] Aldrich, John H. (1995), *Why Parties? The Origin and Transformation of Political Parties in America*, Chicago: University of Chicago Press.

[2] Austen-Smith, D. (1983), "The Spatial Theory of Electoral Competition: Instability, Institutions and Information," *Environment and Planning* C 1, 439–459.

[3] Austen-Smith, D. (1986), "Legislative Coalitions and Electoral Equilibrium," *Public Choice* 50, 185–210.

[4] Austen-Smith, D. and J. Banks (1988), "Elections, Coalitions and Legislative Outcomes," *American Political Science Review* 82, 405–422.

[5] Axelrod, R. (1970), *The Conflict of Interest*, Chicago: Marham.

[6] Bandyopadhyay, S. and M. P. Oak (2003), "Party Formation and Coalitional Bargaining in a Model of Proportional Representation," mimeo.

[7] Baron, D. (1989), "A Non-Cooperative Theory of Legislative Coalitions," *American Journal of Political Science* 33, 1048–1084.

[8] Baron, D. P. and J. A. Ferejohn (1989), "Bargaining in Legislatures," *American Political Science Review* 83, 1181–1206.

[9] Baron, David P. (1993), "Government Formation and Endogenous Parties," *American Political Science Review* 87, 1, 34–47.

[10] Bernheim, D., B. Peleg and M. Whinston (1987), "Coalition Proof Nash Equilibria I. Concepts," *Journal of Economic Theory* 42, 1–12.

[11] Besley, T. and S. Coate (1997), "An Economic Model of Representative Democracy," *Quarterly Journal of Economics* 112, 1, 85–106.

[12] Calvert, R. (1986), *Models of Imperfect Information in Politics*, London: Harwood Academic.

[13] Dixit, A. and J. Londregan (1996), "The Determinants of Success of Special Interests in Redistributive Politics," *Journal of Politics* 58, 1132–1155.

[14] Downs, A. (1957), *An Economic Theory of Democracy*, New York: Harper and Row.

[15] Duverger, M. (1954), *Political Parties*, New York: Wiley and Sons.

[16] Duverger, M. (1963), *Political Parties: Their Organisation and Activity in the Modern State*, B. North and R. North (tr.), New York: Wiley, Science Ed.

[17] Enelow, J. M. and M. J. Hinich (1984), *The Spatial Theory of Voting: An Introduction*, Cambridge, UK: Cambridge University Press.

[18] Gerber, A. and I. Ortuno-Ortin (1998), "Political Compromise and Endogenous Formation of Coalitions," *Social Choice and Welfare* 15, 445–454.

[19] Gomberg, A. M., F. Marhuenda and I. Ortuno-Ortin (2001), "Equilibrium in a Model of Endogenous Political Party Formation," forthcoming in *Economic Theory*.

[20] Jackson, M. O. and B. Moselle (2002), "Coalition and Party Formation in a Legislative Voting Game," *Journal of Economic Theory* 103, 1, 49–87.

[21] Krehbiel, K. (1993), "Where's the Party?," *British Journal of Political Science* 23, 235–266.

[22] Levy, G. (2002), "Endogenous Parties: Cooperative and Non-cooperative Analysis," mimeo, London School of Economics.

[23] Levy, G. (2004), "A Model of Political Parties," *Journal of Economic Theory* 115, 250–277.

[24] Lindbeck, A. and J. Weibull (1987), "Balanced Budget Redistribution as the outcome of Political Competition," *Public Choice* 52, 273–297.

[25] McKelvey, R. (1976), "Intransitivities in Multi-dimensional Voting Models and Some Implications for Agenda Control," *Journal of Economic Theory* 12, 471–482.

[26] Morelli, M. (2004), "Party Formation and Policy Outcomes under Different Electoral Systems," *Review of Economic Studies* Vol. 71, Issue 3.

[27] Osborne, M. J. and A. Slivinski (1996), "A Model of Political Competition with Citizen-Candidates," *Quarterly Journal of Economics* 111, 65–96.

[28] Osborne, M. J. and R. Tourky (2002), "Party Formation in Collective Decision Making," mimeo, University of Toronto.

[29] Ray, D. and R. Vohra (1997), "Equilibrium Binding Agreements," *Journal of Economic Theory* 73, 30–78.

[30] Riker, W. H. (1962), *The Theory of Political Coalitions*, New Haven: Yale University Press.

[31] Riviere, A. (1999), "Citizen Candidacy, Party Formation and Duverger's Law," mimeo, Royal Holloway, University of London.

[32] Roemer, J. (2001), *Political Competition: Theory and Applications*, Harvard University Press.

[33] Schofield, N. J. (1993), "Party Competition in a Spatial Model of Coalition Formation," in *Political Economy: Institutions, Competition and Representation*, W. A. Barnett, M. J. Hinich, and N. J. Schofield (eds.), Cambridge, UK: Cambridge University Press, pp. 135–174.

[34] Shepsle, K. (1979), "Institutional Arrangements and Equilibrium in Multi-dimensional Voting Models," *American Journal of Political Science*, 23, 27–60.

[35] Shepsle, K. (1986), "The Positive Theory of Legislative Coalitions: An Enrichment of Social Choice and Spatial Models," *Public Choice* 50, 135–78.

[36] Snyder, J. and M. Ting (2002), "An Informational Rationale for Political Parties," *American Journal of Political Science* 46, 1, 90–110.

[37] Spence, A. M. (1974), "Market Signalling," Cambridge, MA: Harvard University Press.

[38] Strom, K. (1990), "A Behavioural Theory of Competitive Political Parties," *American Journal of Political Science* 34, 565–598.

10

Power in the Design of Constitutional Rules

Mika Widgrén

10.1. Introduction

Influence is a crucial element in any decision-making institution. The role of the decision-making rules or, more generally, institution design, is to affect power relations in institutions where decisions are made.

Quantitative analysis of decision-making rules can be divided into two parts: one based on cooperative games and the other on noncooperative games. Recently, there has been a lively debate between two schools of thought on the appropriate tools and approaches for assessing and designing different constitutional decision-making rules.

Scholars of cooperative game theory apply different power indices to assess the effects of different decision-making rules on actors' influence in decision making. The considered agents have no particular preferences and form winning coalitions that then implement unspecified policies. Individual chances of being part of and influencing a winning coalition are then measured by a *power index*. The actual distribution of power can be evaluated by defining some desirable distribution of actors' power.[1]

The second approach uses noncooperative game theory to analyze the impact of explicit decision procedures and given preferences over a well-defined policy space.[2] In this approach, conclusions are based on equilibrium analysis. This requires more detailed information regarding the players' preferences. As such, the noncooperative approach is not suitable for the design of constitutional rules, but by considering several realizations of actors' preference configurations, one is able to draw conclusions on the performance of the constitutional rules. This unified approach can also be seen as a bridge between the two distinct approaches, as will be demonstrated later in Section 10.2.3.[3]

---

[1] See, for example, Laruelle and Widgrén (1998), Baldwin et al. (2000, 2001), Felsenthal and Machover (2001), and Leech (2002) for recent applications of traditional power indices. Felsenthal and Machover (1998) and Nurmi (1998) contain a more general discussion regarding index-based analyses of power.

[2] See, for example, Steunenberg (1994), Tsebelis (1994, 1996), Crombez (1996, 1997), and Moser (1996, 1997).

[3] See Steunenberg, Schmidtchen, and Koboldt (1999) and Napel and Widgrén (2004).

This chapter surveys different ways to assess power relations in decision-making institutions using the distinction between cooperative and noncooperative game theories as the starting point. The emphasis of the analysis is on a priori evaluation of power and hence the constitutional analysis of decision-making rules. The main issues considered in this part of the chapter are the design of decision-making rules, how different ways of assessing decision making can influence rule design, and the kinds of questions the different approaches are able to answer.

Section 10.3 illustrates the use of measures in the design of the European Union's (EU's) decision-making rules, which is a topical issue in the context of EU enlargement and the ongoing constitutional debate. Experiences of European integration, especially the Nice reforms in 2000, also demonstrate that the design of decision-making procedures and voting rules is among the most difficult parts of constitutional arrangements. Because institutional arrangements and decision making in the EU are based more on ad hoc solutions than clear constitutional principles, unnecessary additional costs cannot be avoided. Moreover, because the entry of new member states requires the unanimous agreement of incumbent countries, threats of vetoing a candidate country's entry can be used to gain influence in negotiations on required reforms in institutional rules. To reduce the bias of decision-making institutions to seek short-run gains, the task of the constitution is to design the institutional structure and decision-making rules using principles that are acceptably transparent and as neutral to changes in membership as possible.

We begin the chapter by presenting classical power measure tools. Then we proceed to what is termed the *unified approach*. It is based on equilibrium analysis of the legislative phase using the constitutional rules of playing that stage. Because in this case the main emphasis is on how well the rules work, the unified approach takes several legislative games and hence several players' preference configurations into account. These approaches are applied to EU decision making, and the results are compared.

10.2. Measuring Power

In this section, we survey and illustrate the concepts that are often used in the design of constitutional rules.

10.2.1. Traditional Intrainstitutional Approach

A frequent subject of decision power studies in cooperative games is a weighted-coalitional-form voting game v characterized by a set of players, $N = \{1, \ldots, n\}$, a voting weight for each player, $w_i \geq 0$ ($i \in N$), and a minimal quota of weights needed for a passage of a proposal, $q > 0$. Subsets of players, $S \subseteq N$, are called *coalitions*, and if a coalition S meets the quota (i.e., $\sum_{i \in S} w_i \geq q$), it is a winning coalition. Formation of a winning coalition is assumed to be desirable to its members because, for example, they can jointly pass policy proposals that are in their interest. More generally, a winning coalition need not be determined by voting weights.[4] One can conveniently describe an abstract decision body v by taking v to be a mapping from the set of all possible coalitions, $\wp(N)$, to $\{0, 1\}$, where $v(S) = 1$ (0) indicates that S is winning (losing). The difference $v(S) - v(S - \{i\}) := \Delta_i v(S)$ is known as player i's marginal contribution to coalition S. Players' marginal contributions to coalitions, and hence outcomes, form the basis for power measurement in cooperative games.

To answer the question of individual effect generally for all coalitions in $\mathcal{P}(N)$, we need to specify, for example, a probability model for the voting process. An agent's behavior is specified as a probability distribution P for players' acceptance rates denoting the probabilities of a yes vote by individual players. A particular player's a priori power is then taken to be his or her probability of casting a decisive vote to pass a proposal that would not have passed had he or she voted no instead of yes.

Because we are dealing with the distribution of power in one voting body, the power index approach is straightforward. Using the class of winning coalitions as the basis for analysis counts how often players are in a swing position given the chosen probability model. Let x_i be the probability that player i favors a proposal and x an n-vector of these probabilities called *the acceptability vector* (see Straffin 1988 for details). If we randomize the issue of voting, the acceptability vector gives the probabilities that player i belongs to an arbitrary coalition S, that is, the probabilities that he or she will support the passage of a randomly chosen proposal. On the assumption that players vote yes or no independently of each other, we can write, for any fixed $S \subset N$, the probability $P\{\mathcal{S} = S\} = \prod_{i \in S} x_i \prod_{i \notin S}(1 - x_i)$. If we take the sum of these probabilities multiplied by values of the characteristic function over all possible coalitions, we will have the mathematical expectation for the value of function v. This expectation is often called the *multilinear extension* $f(x_1, \ldots, x_n)$ of v (Owen 1972). Write

$$f(x_1, \ldots, x_n) = \sum_{S \subset N} \left[\prod_{i \in S} x_i \prod_{i \notin S}(1 - x_i) \right] v(S).$$

It can be shown that the ith partial derivative of $f(x_1, \ldots, x_n)$ is the expected value of player i's marginal contribution to the coalition S, where the summation is taken over the class $\mathcal{V}_i$ of *vulnerable winning coalitions* with respect to player i in voting games. Thus, each $\mathcal{M}_i$ contains the coalitions in which i is a swing player, and we get

$$E[\Delta_i v(S)] = \frac{\partial f(x_1, \ldots, x_n)}{\partial x_i} = \sum_{S \in \mathcal{M}_i} \prod_{i \in S - \{i\}} x_i \prod_{j \in N - S} (1 - x_j), \quad (10.2.1)$$

which can be interpreted as the expectation of an agent's power. For calculation purposes, we need to define the x_i probabilities explicitly. To disregard players' preferences fully we adopt the *independence assumption* whereby probabilities x_i are independently, uniformly distributed on $[0, 1]$. This assumption is closest to pure constitutional analysis of voting rules. An alternative is to assume that voters are

---

[4] The simple dual-majority rule proposed by the EU Commission during the intergovernmental conference in 2000 serves as an example.

homogeneous, that is, their acceptance rates to a proposal are positively correlated. This yields $x_i = t$, and t is uniformly distributed on $[0, 1]$.[5] If we now calculate the expectation of individual effect assuming independence,

$$\frac{\partial f(x_1, \ldots, x_n)}{\partial x_i} = \sum_{S \in \mathcal{M}_i} \left(\frac{1}{2}\right)^{n-1} = \beta_i, \tag{10.2.2}$$

which is the Penrose–Banzhaf measure (PBM). The PBM can be interpreted as player $i's$ probability of having a *swing* in a vulnerable coalition, that is, in a coalition that can be turned from winning into losing by at least one of its members. To assess relative power, one can normalize the PBM, which is then referred to as the (normalized) Banzhaf index (NBI). It can be written as follows:

$$\frac{\sum_{S \in \mathcal{M}_i} \left(\frac{1}{2}\right)^{n-1}}{\sum_{j=1}^{n} \sum_{S \in \mathcal{M}_j} \left(\frac{1}{2}\right)^{n-1}} = \beta_i'. \tag{10.2.3}$$

Note that swings are defined using players' positions in coalitions but that the NBI gives a player's share of all swings as defined by equation (10.2.3). This implies that the probability model illustrating the PBM is destroyed by normalization.[6]

Assuming homogeneity, we obtain the *Shapley–Shubik index* (SSI) as follows:

$$\frac{\partial f(x_1, \ldots, x_n)}{\partial x_i} = \sum_{S \in \mathcal{M}_i} \frac{(n-s)! \cdot (s-1)!}{n!} = \Phi_i. \tag{10.2.4}$$

In the classical voting power literature of institutional design, either the PBM or NBI is more often applied than the SSI. A frequent explanation for this choice is based on the *behind-the-veil-of-ignorance* argument. The PBM and the NBI consider all possible coalitions of actors equally likely; that is, all coalitions have equal weight in power calculations. This ignores, among other things, actors' preferences, which can be considered a clear benefit in the design of voting rules. The SSI does not assume any particular preferences either, but it gives equal weights to different coalition sizes from 1 to n if n gives the number of actors and, moreover, all coalitions that are of equal size, for instance $m \leq n$, have equal weights. One can argue that this requires more specific information than the assumptions behind the PBM or the NBI. The assumption that all coalitions have the same probability of occurrence, like the PBM and the NBI do, can also be expressed as an abstract voting model in which all actors have 50-percent probability of voting yes and 50-percent probability of voting no. The number of yes votes is then binomially distributed with $p = \frac{1}{2}$. This in turn gives more weight to the middle-sized coalitions.

---

[5] For a more detailed discussion, see Straffin (1977, 1988) or Owen (1972, 1995).

[6] Probabilistic interpretation of the NBI is somewhat problematic. We need to assume that players are indifferent between voting yes and no but furthermore that a vulnerable coalition is formed, each swing within each vulnerable coalition has the same weight, and the actual swing players obtain the whole fixed value of a vulnerable coalition (for details see Widgrén 2001).

10.2.2. Interinstitutional Power in the Cooperative Approach

Interinstitutional aspects play a significant role in the design of constitutional decision-making rules and procedures. For instance, the EU treaties explicitly define the actors involved in decision making and the procedures, or sequence of moves, for making decisions. This also means that procedural aspects are important because the sequence in which the main institutions act in decision making is defined as a part of the voting rules.

In cooperative games, the traditional way to approach interinstitutional relations is to model the procedures as composite games.

Definition 10.5. *Let $M_1, \ldots M_n$ be n disjoint nonempty sets of players and let $g_1, \ldots g_n$ be simple games in $(0, 1)$ normalization with player sets $M_1, \ldots M_n$, respectively. Let v be a nonnegative game over the set $N = \{1, 2, \ldots n\}$. Then the v-composition of n disjoint subgames $g_1, \ldots g_n$, denoted $u = v[g_1, \ldots g_n]$ is a game with player set $M = \bigcup_{j=1}^{n} M_j$ and characteristic function $u(S) = v\left(\left\{j \mid g_j(S \cap M_j) = 1\right\}\right)$ for $S \subset M$.*

The composition of games can be interpreted as a division into committees or institutions involved in a decision-making procedure. As a model for EU procedures, the composite game approach reduces the decision-making process into one simultaneous move game, M_j. The multilinear extension of the composite game v can now be expressed as

$$h(x) = f(g_1(x^1), \ldots g(x^n)),$$

and the general power measure for a composite games is

$$\frac{\partial h(x_1, \ldots, x_n)}{\partial x_i} = \frac{\partial f(g_1, \ldots, g_n)}{\partial g_j} \frac{\partial g_j(x_1, \ldots, x_n)}{\partial x_i},$$

where we can apply the same vector of acceptance rates $(x_1, \ldots, x_n)$ as presented in Section 10.2.1.

10.2.3. Unified Approaches

As mentioned in Section 10.1, the noncooperative approach serves as an alternative for investigating decision-making institutions. In the literature, criticism of the co-operative approach is twofold. First, despite some attempts,[7] the indices cannot take strategic interinstitutional or procedural aspects of EU decision making into account and, second, they do not explicitly consider players' preferences but rather attempt to model voting behavior more directly, using acceptance probabilities for instance.[8] The latter drawback is not, however, necessarily severe in the design of constitutional rules. It can also be seen as a reason to support the abstract cooperative approach, but the first drawback has to be taken more seriously even in constitutional analysis.

---

[7] See, for example, Kirman and Widgrén (1995) and Laruelle and Widgrén (2001).
[8] See, however Widgrén (1995), Hosli (2002), or Kirman and Widgrén (1995).

When more than one decision-making institution is involved or when one is investigating the interaction between several institutions, the classical power index approach is problematic because it assumes that players are voting or moving simultaneously, which is rarely the case in decision-making procedures. Consider a simple agenda-setting game in which we have an institution that makes a legislative proposal to a decision-making body that either accepts or rejects the proposal. The simultaneous coalition-based approach can only use the fact that all winning coalitions must contain the acceptance of the agenda-setting institution plus a required majority in the decision-making institution. This approach, however, completely disregards the fact that the agenda setter moves first – decision making is procedural not simultaneous. Suppose, for simplicity, that the agenda setter is a single player and the passage of a proposal requires unanimous acceptance in the decision-making body. Then the power index approach suggests that each player in the latter is as powerful as the former, but it is not trivially true because the agenda setter moves first.

Partly as a reply to this critique (see, e.g., Tsebelis and Garrett 1997, 1999a, 2001) a recent literature, which attempts to combine the desirable elements of the cooperative and noncooperative approaches has developed. Steunenberg et al. (1999) have proposed a framework that explicitly describes agents' choices in a political procedure and (their beliefs about) agents' preferences. Steunenberg et al. consider a spatial voting model with n players and an m-dimensional outcome space. Let $N = \{1, \ldots, n\}$ be the set of players and $X \subseteq \mathbb{R}^m$ be the outcome or policy space; Γ denotes the procedure or game form describing the decision-making process, and $q \in X$ describes the status quo before the start of decision making. Players are assumed to have Euclidean preferences with $\lambda_i \in X$ ($i \in N$) as player i's ideal point. A particular combination of all players' ideal points and the status quo point define a *state of the world* ξ. On the assumption that the equilibrium exists and is unique, let $x^*(\xi)$ denote the equilibrium outcome of the game based on Γ and ξ. Steunenberg et al. are aware of Barry's (1980) distinction between power and luck and explicitly strive to isolate "the ability of a player to make a difference in the outcome" (p. 362). They note that "[h]aving a preference that lies close to the equilibrium outcome of a particular game does not necessarily mean that this player is also powerful" (p. 345). Therefore, they suggest considering not one particular state of the world ξ but many.

In particular, one can consider each λ_i and the status quo q to be realizations of random variables $\tilde{\lambda}_i$ and $\tilde{q}$, respectively. If P denotes the joint distribution of random vector $\tilde{\xi} := (\tilde{q}, \tilde{\lambda}_1, \ldots, \tilde{\lambda}_n)$ and $\|\cdot\|$ the Euclidean norm, then

$$\Delta_i^\Gamma := \int \left\| \tilde{\lambda}_i - x^*(\tilde{\xi}) \right\| dP \tag{10.2.5}$$

gives the expected distance between the equilibrium outcome for decision procedure Γ and player i's ideal outcome. The strategic power index of Steunenberg et al. (1999) is based on the expected distance between the equilibrium outcome and its ideal point. In order to obtain not only a ranking of players but a cardinal measure of their power, Steunenberg et al. proceed by considering a dummy player d whose preferences vary over the same range as the preferences of actual players but who does not have any decision-making rights. This leads to their definition of the *strategic power index (StPI)* as

$$\Psi_i^\Gamma := \frac{\Delta_d^\Gamma - \Delta_i^\Gamma}{\Delta_d^\Gamma}.$$

However, equation (10.2.5) turns out to define Δ_i^Γ, as player i's *expected success*. Just as actual distance measures success (a function of luck and power), so does average distance measure average success. Unless one regards average success as the defining characteristic of power (which neither Steunenberg et al. nor many others do), taking expectations will only by coincidence achieve what Steunenberg et al. aim at, namely, to "level out the effect of 'luck' or a particular preference configuration on the outcome of a game" (p. 362). This point is discussed in considerable detail in Napel and Widgrén (2004). There, various examples illustrate that the StPI is a good measure of expected success but in general fails to capture power.

Under special conditions, which eliminate all strategic aspects from the StPI, there exists a link between the StPI and the PBM discovered by Felsenthal and Machover (2001a) (see also Widgrén and Napel 2002).

The criticism of classical power indices just discussed does not mean, however, that the core of the traditional power index approach, namely a player's marginal contribution to the outcome, is useless. For this reason, Widgrén and Napel (2002) propose to extend the preceding analysis from the simple coalition framework of a priori power measurement and the very basic voting game to a more general framework. First, take a player's marginal contribution as the best available indicator of his or her potential or ability (i.e., *a posteriori power*) to make a difference. Second, if it is of normative interest or a necessity for lack of precise data, calculate a priori power as expected a posteriori power. Expectation can be with respect to several different aspects of a posteriori power, such as actions, preferences, or procedures.

In this approach, impact is relative to a what-if scenario or what Widgrén and Napel (2002) call the shadow outcome. The shadow outcome is the group's decision that would have resulted if the player whose power is under consideration had chosen differently than he or she a posteriori did (e. g., if this player had stayed out of coalition S when he or she a posteriori belongs to it). In simple games, the difference between shadow outcome and actual outcome is either 0 or 1. A richer decision framework allows for more finely graded a posteriori power.

To illustrate this more in detail, let $\Lambda = (\lambda_1, \ldots, \lambda_n)$ be the collection of n players' ideal policy positions in R^m as above. An $m \times n$ matrix, having the λ_i-vectors as columns, represents players' ideal points. In a policy space $X \subseteq R^m$, the opportunities even for only marginal changes of preference are manifold. A given ideal point λ_i can be shifted locally to $\lambda_i + h$, where h is an arbitrary vector in R^m with small norm. Which tremble directions it is reasonable to consider will depend on the application. Multiples of the vector $(1, 1, \ldots, 1) \in R^m$ seem reasonable if the m-policy dimensions are independent of each other.

In any case, if the vector h that describes the direction of preference trembles has norm $\|h\|$ and thus $\alpha = (\alpha_1, \ldots, \alpha_m) = \frac{h}{\|h\|}$ is its normalized version, one can define

$$D_i(\Lambda) := \lim_{t \to 0} \frac{x^*(\lambda_i + t\alpha, \lambda_{-i}) - x^*(\lambda_i, \lambda_{-i})}{t} = \frac{\partial_\alpha x^*(\lambda_i, \lambda_{-i})}{\partial \lambda_i} \quad (10.2.6)$$

as a reasonable measure of player i's ex post power provided that the limit above exists. This is simply the directional derivative of the equilibrium outcome in the direction h or α. Other measures for the multidimensional case can be based on the gradient of $x^*(\lambda_i, \lambda_{-i})$ (holding λ_{-i} constant). Using the ex post power above we can define a corresponding ex ante measure as

$$\xi_i = \int D_i(\Lambda) dP.$$

Using a suitable probability distribution of players' ideal policy positions, let us refer to this index as the *strategic measure of power* (SMP).

10.3. Applying Power Indices to the EU

10.3.1. Classical Power Indices and Institution Design

As mentioned in Section 10.2.1 classical power indices fit best in a priori analysis of intrainstitutional power. Within the context of the EU, this means the Council of Ministers, where national interests are represented. An important question then is, Does the distribution of power treat citizens in all member states equally? To our knowledge, all existing studies on this issue use the NBI as their power measure.

The one-person, one-vote (OPOV) principle is a cornerstone in designing democratic institutions and the fair allocation of power in a federation or in two-tiered decision making in general.[9] In large states, citizens have less power in choosing their national government than citizens in small states. This requires that the large states be compensated in the Council voting weights. The right compensation to ensure the OPOV principle is the well-known square-root rule due to Penrose (1946). Applied to the EU Council, the fair power of countries should be determined by their square-root shares of population. Hence, the fair power of country i can be expressed as

$$\beta^* = \frac{\sqrt{m_i}}{\sum_{j=1}^{n} \sqrt{m_j}}, \quad (10.3.1)$$

where m_i denotes the population of country i and β^* the fair (Banzhaf) index of power.

Laruelle and Widgrén (1998) pose the question of whether the distribution of power in the EU is fair. They conclude first that the answer depends on the definition of the EU, and in their analysis they consider all possible alternatives between an

---

[9] For earlier analysis on the EU, see Laruelle and Widgrén (1998), Widgrén (2001), and Leech (2002).

association of states and a federal state. The former is defined by requiring that each member state have the same power, whereas the latter requires that all citizens, regardless of their nationality, be equally powerful, which leads to the square-root rule. The alternative definitions of the EU can be expressed as convex combinations of the two extremes. In their analysis, Laruelle and Widgrén conclude that the existing distribution of power in the Council of Ministers does not systematically favor or disfavor any country with the exception of The Netherlands, which is less powerful than it should be regardless of the EU's definition. Using the existing distribution of power in the Council of Ministers, Laruelle and Widgrén estimate the regression

$$\beta = 0.78 \frac{\sqrt{m_i}}{\sum_{j=1}^{n} \sqrt{m_j}} + 0.22 \left(\frac{1}{15} \right), \tag{10.3.2}$$

which gives the revealed definition of the EU based on the distribution of power in the Council of Ministers. The Treaty of Nice changed the distribution of power in the Council of Ministers. Using the new distribution in the EU-15, we obtain

$$\beta = 0.97 \frac{\sqrt{m_i}}{\sum_{j=1}^{n} \sqrt{m_j}} + 0.03 \left(\frac{1}{15} \right), \tag{10.3.3}$$

which is quite close to the OPOV principle. The enlargement to EU-27 changes the result because the coefficient of the square-root share (i.e., OPOV principle), decreases to 0.92 (see Baldwin et al. 2001).

During the intergovernmental conference in 2000, the Swedish delegation proposed that the re-weighting of votes in the Treaty of Nice should approximately follow the square-root rule. The proposal was to give each member state the number of votes determined by its square-rooted population in millions multiplied by two and rounded to the closest integer. Although power is not equal to the voting weight, this proposal quite naturally leads to a power distribution that is very close to the square-root rule. Moreover, if votes are determined by square-roots of populations, the system is, indeed, very transparent.

There is, however, one undesirable property in weighting based on square roots of populations, namely, it requires very high majority threshold to avoid the possibility that a minority of member states could pass proposals. The square-root shares of populations of the ten biggest EU member states sum up to 63 percent in the EU-27. The same property holds for the decided voting weights as well. One way to exclude undesirable winning coalitions is to introduce an additional requirement that explicitly does this. It is noteworthy that such a safety net has an impact on power distribution.

The Treaty of Nice introduced a twofold safety net requiring that a qualified majority should, in addition to sufficient vote threshold, contain an absolute majority of member states and represent at least 62 percent of EU population.

In the intergovernmental conference 2000 (IGC-2000), the Commission proposed and advocated the so-called simple dual (SD) majority voting rule in the Council. The SD rule reflects the Union of nations and union of citizens principle because,

Table 10.1: *The regression coefficient of the square-root rule and the sum of squared differences between fair and actual power in the EU-15 and EU-27*

Rule	Coefficient of the square-root rule		Sum of squared differences, $\cdot 10^{-3}$	
	EU-15	EU-27	EU-15	EU-27
D50	0.931	0.911	2.166	2.037
D62	1.051	1.071	3.588	2.690
D74	1.113	1.165	5.805	6.234
SD50	0.868	0.836	6.100	4.668
SD62	0.991	0.982	0.100	0.057
SD74	0.978	0.986	0.252	0.051
Nice	0.971	0.919	0.749	5.494

when it is applied, a legislative proposal needs the acceptance of a majority of member states and a majority of EU citizens to pass. Member-state governments do not have voting weights, but the rule itself determines proposal passage and the distribution of power among member states. Transparency makes SD majority voting rule desirable.

The Commission proposal was designed for the Council. More generally, SD rule is typical for federal states. For instance, in the United States, the majority-of-states part of the definition is reflected by the decision-making rules in the Senate and the majority-of-citizens part in the House of Representatives. If both chambers are equally powerful, as in the United States, and the assessment is only interested in national distribution of power, the analysis gives the same conclusions in one- and two-chamber decision making.

Table 10.1 summarizes differences between normalized Banzhaf indices when two alternative dual majorities are used in the Council of EU-15 and EU-27. The table gives the regression coefficients of the square-root rule in a simple regression. In the table, D50 refers to simple dual majority (i.e., absolute majority of states and citizens), D62 to absolute majority of states and a 62-percent majority of citizens,[10] and D74 to an absolute majority of states and a 74-percent majority of citizens. The alternatives SD50, SD62, and SD74 refer to similar dual majorities in which an absolute majority of member states and a 50-, 62-, and 74-percent majority of member states' square-rooted population are needed to pass legislation. Let us refer to these rules as *square-root dual majorities*.

Interestingly, Table 10.1 suggests that a 62-percent majority of the square-rooted population together with an absolute majority of member states implement the square-root rule almost exactly. In the EU-27, a higher square-rooted population threshold seems to work slightly better. In dual majorities of member states and their population, a lower than 62-percent population quota seems to mimic the

[10] The choice of 62 percent was inspired by the Nice reform, which defines the voting rules in the Council as a mixture of voting weights and D62 rule.

square-root rule better. As an overall conclusion, a simple dual majority proposed by the Commission in IGC-2000 performs slightly worse than the voting weights agreed upon in Nice if the emphasis is on the coefficient. The Nice weights also imply a smaller sum of squared differences, according to the square-root rule, between fair and actual allocation of power in the EU-15 but not in the EU-27. In fact, there is a substantial increase in this respect when Nice weights are used in the EU-27, indicating that, despite the better average performance, the differences at the level of individual member states show worse performance.

In summary, the results in Table 10.1 suggest that weighted voting turns out to be unstable in fulfilling the square-root rule at the one-actor level. This is mainly because determination of voting weights is based not on the characteristics, such as population, of one country but many. Member states are divided into clusters of countries, and the division lines are partially arbitrary. Dual majority rules can be interpreted as weighted voting games with a safety net guaranteeing the support of an absolute majority of member states for the passage of a proposal. Contrary to the Nice rules, dual majorities have theoretical foundations. Dual majority rule applies the definition of the EU as the union of citizens and the union of states, whereas square-rooted dual majority applies fairness criterion for two-tiered decision making more directly.

Should we ever rely on the SSI in the design of constitutional rules? The standard answer is no. The PBM assumes that all coalitions have the same probability of occurrence. This supports its use as the index, for indeed, the PBM takes "behind the veil of ignorance" literally.[11] If the voting rules are understood as triples of voting weights, vote thresholds, and procedures, not all the information available in the procedure will necessarily be used. In the unified approaches considered next, the basis of ex ante assessment is ex post equilibrium analysis, which makes the setup more game theoretic and may support use of the SSI as an appropriate power measure. More specifically, on the assumption of spatial preferences, the SMP allocates power according to the SSI at the intrainstitutional level. This gives theoretical support for using it.

10.4. Power in EU Procedures

10.4.1. The Main Procedures of the EU

In composite games, it is implicitly assumed that the actors move simultaneously.[12] This gathers dark clouds upon their applicability to EU procedures. Intuitively these measures are likely to overestimate the power of late movers and underestimate the power of the first mover such as the agenda setter. In this section, we investigate

---

[11] See, for example, Laruelle and Valenciano (2002) for a probabilistic voting model of the PBM, which leads to a similar conclusion. Felsenthal and Machover (1998) give the probabilistic interpretation to the PBM using repeated Bernoulli experiments for which each repetition is like a yea or nay vote.

[12] See, however, Laruelle and Widgrén (2001), who model the EU procedures as sequences of composite games.

Table 10.2: *Interinstitutional Penrose–Banzhaf power measures in the EU-15 and EU-27*

	Codecision procedure				Consultation procedure	
	CD1	CD1E	CD2	CD2E	CN	CNE
Commission	0.039	0.014	0.000	0.000	0.078	0.028
Council	0.253	0.152	0.506	0.303	0.506	0.303
Parliament	0.039	0.014	0.078	0.028	0.000	0.000

interinstitutional power in the EU and the difference between the results based on the composite game and unified approaches.

The EU has three main decision-making bodies (i.e., the Commission, the Council, and the European Parliament [EP]) and two main decision-making procedures (i.e., consultation and codecision). In the consultation procedure, the Commission proposes and the Council decides. A unanimous Council can amend a Commission proposal. The Commission can also decide not to propose, and then the legislative status quo 0 prevails. The Commission thus exerts agenda-setting and gate-keeping powers, and the Council wields decision-making power. These cannot be separated appropriately in standard cooperative analysis, but our equilibrium-based analysis gives a better picture of different powers. In our models, the Commission is assumed to be a unitary actor – that is, national views are assumed not to play a role.[13] The Council is considered to be a voting body (currently 15 members) and, after eastern enlargement has fully taken place, will comprise 27 member states. The EP is modeled following the standard tradition as a unitary actor as well.

A cooperative, coalition-based model can approach the consultation procedure simply by defining the win-sets of a game. In the consultation procedure they are

- the Commission plus a qualified majority in the Council (refer to column CN in Tables 10.2 and 10.3);
- unanimity in the Council (refer to column CNE in Tables 10.2 and 10.3).

The codecision procedure is more complicated. The main difference from the consultation procedure is that codecision gives significant powers to the EP. A Commission proposal goes to the EP for its first reading and can either be accepted or amended. In each case, the proposal – the original or amended – goes to the Council, where it can be accepted or further amended. The former action leads to outcome x_1, and the latter to a proposal x_2 that can be then accepted, amended, or rejected by the EP. This stage of the procedure also gives the EP some agenda-setting powers. A proposal x_3 is then studied by the Commission. It can reject or accept this proposal but may not amend it further. The next mover is the Council, which can accept x_3 by qualified majority in the case of Commission acceptance and unanimously in the case of Commission rejection. Note that, in fact, the Commission view does not bind

---

[13] For analyses where this has not been assumed, see Bindseil and Hantke (1997) and Baldwin et al. (2000, 2001).

Table 10.3: *Interinstitutional Shapley–Shubik power indices in the EU-15 and EU-27*

	Codecision procedure				Consultation procedure	
	CD1	CD1E	CD2	CD2E	CN	CNE
Commission	0.254	0.253	0.000	0.000	0.248	0.268
Council	0.492	0.494	0.690	0.696	0.752	0.732
Parliament	0.254	0.253	0.310	0.304	0.000	0.000

the Council at all because by overruling it, the Council can start conciliation with the EP. The Conciliation Committee is chaired by the Vice President of the EP and a representative of the member state that is holding presidency in the Council. Before the Committee meets, the member state holding the presidency has, however, a leading role. This suggests that one alternative way to model decision making in the Conciliation Committee is a simple agenda-setting approach in which the member state holding the presidency in the Council makes a take-it-or-leave-it proposal that has to be accepted by an absolute majority in the EP and qualified majority in the Council. Let us refer to this model as the *presidency model*.[14]

In the composite game approach to the codecision procedure, we obtain two potential win-sets as follows:

- The Commission, a qualified majority in the Council, and an absolute majority in the EP (refer to column CD1 in Tables 10.2 and 10.3)
- A qualified majority in the Council and an absolute majority in the EP (refer to column CD2 in Tables 10.2 and 10.3).

Again, it is worth noting, however, that the Commission has the right to initiate or decide not to initiate. This gate-keeping role of the Commission means that the true distribution of power lies in both procedures between the two cases – with and without amendments – and depends on preferences.

10.4.2. The Composite Game Approach

Table 10.2 gives the interinstitutional power in the EU-15 using the pre-Nice voting weights and the PBM. Column heads CD1 and CD2 refer to the codecision procedure and CD1E and CD2E to their respective counterparts after the enlargement. In CD1 and CD1E, it is assumed that the Commission exerts power as a member of a winning coalition, and in CD2 and CD2E it is assumed that the Commission exerts only gate-keeping power. Abbreviations CN and CNE denote the consultation procedure before and after enlargement, respectively. Table 10.3 gives the respective SSIs.

---

[14] The presidency model is not the only way to approach the codecision procedure. We use it here for the sake of comparing the analysis of Steunenberg and Dimitrova (1999) that applies StPI with codecision modeled using the presidency model. For alternative approaches, see Napel and Widgrén (2003), where codecision is modeled as Rubinstein's alternative offers bargaining game.

The numerical data in Tables 10.2 and 10.3 show that the interinstitutional balance of power is practically not affected by eastern enlargement. This conclusion is very robust regardless of the enlargement and hence the number of new member states added. The most notable effect is a 2-percent decline of the Council's power in consultation procedure. This is due to expanding membership as unanimous Council can amend the Commission proposal and unanimity is harder to achieve in the EU-27 than in EU-15.

According to the classical power indices, the Council is the most powerful actor in both procedures. This contradicts the standard conclusion of spatial voting games that the Commission is the most powerful actor (e.g., Steunenberg et al. 1999) due to its first-mover advantage.

The results are also different when different classical power indices are used for measurement. The SSI suggests that interinstitutional power remains practically unchanged after the enlargement, whereas the PBM suggests that the enlargement has a significant impact on actors' power and also on the intrainstitutional distribution of power. In absolute terms, all actors lose, and the change in relative power affects the Commission or the EP more than the Council. In summary, the cooperative analysis suggests that expanding membership may decrease all actors' power mainly because the probability of passing a random proposal declines. In the EU-27, it is more likely that the status quo will prevail than it is in the EU-15. This does not hold, however, to the same extent if actors' acceptance rates for proposals are positively correlated, which is the case in the SSI. Let us next consider interinstitutional power in a strategic environment and then compare the results with those just presented.

10.4.3. Strategic Power in the EU

10.4.3.1. Consultation Procedure

Let us restrict the policy space to a unit interval for which the reference point is normalized to zero, and let us denote the ideal policies in the Council by $\mu = (\mu_1, \ldots, \mu_n)$. The ideal policies of median voters in the EP and the Commission are denoted by π and γ, respectively. For the sake of comparability with classical power indices, let us assume that the policy space is unit interval $[0, 1]$. Because here the interest is in interinstitutional power and not the distribution of power in the Council, we simply assume that each Council member has one vote.[15] The majority rule is $m \leq n$.

There are two alternative ways to approach the consultation procedure: the standard model and the presidency model. In the former, the Commission's draft proposal is challenged by a unanimous Council. If all Council members are either to the right or to the left of the Commission's ideal policy position, then either the left-most or the right-most Council member is crucial for the outcome. Another modeling

---

[15] This is the usual assumption made in the spatial voting game. To our knowledge there are no studies in which strategic power is analyzed in the weighted spatial voting game.

strategy in the literature (see Steunenberg and Dimitrova 1999) gives a role to the member state holding the presidency in the Council. It is assumed that the state holding the presidency is able to make a proposal that makes either the left-most or right-most Council member indifferent when faced with a choice between the Commission's ideal policy and a proposal made by the presidency. But knowing that, the best that the Commission can do is to propose the ideal policy outcome from the viewpoint of the left-most or right-most Council member. That proposal cannot be beaten by any unanimous compromise. Let μ^L and μ^R denote the left-most and right-most members of the Council. More formally, we get the following subgame-perfect Nash equilibrium proposal in the consultation procedure χ^* with spatial preferences

$$\Omega^*(\gamma, \mu^*, \mu^L, \mu^R) = \chi^*(\gamma, \mu^*) = \begin{cases} \mu^L & \text{if } \mu^L \geq \gamma \\ \gamma & \text{if } \mu^* \geq \frac{1}{2}\gamma \wedge \mu^R > \gamma \\ \mu^R & \text{if } \mu^* \geq \frac{1}{2}\gamma \wedge \mu^R \leq \gamma \\ \min(\mu^R, 2\mu^*) & \text{if } \mu^* \in (0, \frac{1}{2}\gamma), \end{cases}$$

where Ω^* refers to the equilibrium outcome, μ^* refers to the ideal policy position of the pivotal player accepted by voters $(n), \ldots, (n - m + 1)$ and by any $(n - m), \ldots, (l)$, $n - m \geq l \geq 1$, for whom $(\mu_i - \chi^*)^2 \leq \mu_i^2$ holds. Hence, $\Omega^*(\gamma, \mu) = \chi^*(\gamma, \mu^*)$.[16] This states more formally that, first, only the spatial swing player $(n - m + 1)$ *may have* an influence on the outcome and, second, he or she actually *has* an influence only for particular preference constellations.

For the Commission γ we obtain the a posteriori (strategic) power

$$D_\gamma(\gamma, \mu^*) = \frac{\partial \Omega^*(\gamma, \mu^*)}{\partial \gamma} = \begin{cases} 1; & \text{if } \frac{1}{2}\gamma < \mu^* < 1 \\ 0; & \text{if } \mu^* < \frac{1}{2}\gamma, \end{cases}$$

and for a member state in the Council i

$$D_i(\gamma, \mu^*) = \frac{\partial \Omega^*(\gamma, \mu^*)}{\partial \mu_i} = \begin{cases} 2; & \text{if } \mu^* < \frac{1}{2}\gamma \wedge \mu^* < \frac{1}{2}\mu^R \wedge \mu_i = \mu^* \\ 1 & \text{if } (\mu^L \geq \gamma \wedge \mu_i = \mu^L) \\ & \quad \vee (\mu^* \geq \frac{1}{2}\gamma \wedge \mu^R \leq \gamma \wedge \mu_i = \mu^R) \\ 0; & \text{otherwise.} \frac{1}{2}\gamma < \mu^* < 1. \end{cases}$$

For ex ante considerations, suppose that the ideal policy positions are uniformly distributed on $[0, 1]$. We get

$$\xi_k = \int D_k(\gamma, \mu^*) dP,$$

where $k \in \{\gamma, \mu^*\}$.

---

[16] Note that the ideal point $\lambda_{(n-m+1)}$ of the pivotal player is unique. In qualified majority voting there are two potential pivotal players, but agenda setting makes the equilibrium unique.

10.4.3.2. Codecision Procedure

Here we assume that the government of a member state that is holding the presidency exerts agenda-setting power in the Conciliation Committee. This assumption may, however, overestimate the role of the Council because the meetings of the committee are cochaired by a vice president of the EP and a minister of the member state holding the presidency. Suppose first that the presidency exerts agenda-setting power in the Conciliation Committee. In the post-Amsterdam version of the codecision procedure, the Commission does not have a role in the Conciliation Committee. In the Conciliation Committee we get the following subgame-perfect Nash equilibrium:

$$\Omega_{CC}^*(\gamma, \mu'\mu^P, \pi) = \chi^*(\gamma, \mu'\mu^P, \pi)$$

$$= \begin{cases} \mu^P & \text{if } \min\{\mu', \pi\} \geq \frac{1}{2}\mu^P \\ 2\min\{\mu', \pi\} & \text{if } \min\{\mu', \pi\} \in [0, \frac{1}{2}\mu^P) \\ 0 & \text{if } \gamma < \min\{\frac{1}{2}\mu^P\mu', \pi\}, \end{cases}$$

where μ^P refers to the ideal point of the member state holding the presidency and μ' refers to the ideal point of a *semipivotal* player of a subgame in the Council without the government holding the presidency. Note that the Commission exerts only gate-keeping power in this procedure. This holds in terms of a posteriori power because

$$D_\gamma(\gamma, \mu'\mu^P, \pi) = \frac{\partial \Omega_{CC}^*(\gamma, \mu'\mu^P, \pi)}{\partial \gamma} = 0 \quad \text{if } \min\{\mu', \mu^P, \pi\} \neq 0,$$

and in terms of a priori power because $P\{\min\{\mu', \frac{1}{2}\mu^P, \pi\} = 0\}$ has zero measure. The EP wields influence if $\pi < \mu'$ and $\pi < \frac{1}{2}\mu^P$. The Council members have two channels to exert power: when holding the presidency, as a semipivotal player, or both.

We denote a posteriori power for the EP by

$$D_\pi(\gamma, \mu'\mu^P, \pi) = \frac{\partial \Omega_{CC}^*(\gamma, \mu'\mu^P, \pi)}{\partial \pi}$$

$$= \begin{cases} 2; & \text{if } \pi < \mu' \wedge \pi < \frac{1}{2}\mu^P \\ 0; & \text{if otherwise,} \end{cases}$$

and for the government that is holding presidency by

$$D_{\mu^P}(\gamma, \mu'\mu^P, \pi) = \frac{\Omega_{CC}^*(\gamma, \mu'\mu^P, \pi)}{\partial \mu^P}$$

$$= \begin{cases} 1; & \text{if } \frac{1}{2}\mu^P < \mu' \wedge \frac{1}{2}\mu^P < \pi \\ 0; & \text{if otherwise;} \end{cases}$$

Table 10.4: *The effects of the Nice reforms and enlargement on strategic interinstitutional power in consultation procedure*

	Current EU		Enlarged EU		Difference	
	CM	EC	CM(E)	EC(E)	DCM	DEC
Q = 71 percent	0.813	0.531	0.744	0.592	−0.069	0.061
Q = 74 percent	0.922	0.477	0.831	0.549	−0.092	0.072
Difference	0.109	−0.054	0.086	−0.043	0.017	0.018

finally, for the semipivotal position in the Council, we write

$$D_{\mu'}(\gamma, \mu'\mu^{P}, \pi) = \frac{\Omega^{*}_{CC}(\gamma, \mu'\mu^{P}, \pi)}{\partial \mu'}$$

$$= \begin{cases} 2; & \text{if } \frac{1}{2}\mu^{P} > \mu' \wedge \pi < \pi \\ 0; & \text{if otherwise.} \end{cases}$$

On the assumption of uniformly distributed ideal points, this gives us the following a priori power for the actors:

$$\xi_{k} = \int D_{k}(\gamma, \mu'\mu^{P}, \pi) dP,$$

where $k \in \{\pi, \mu, \mu^{*}\}$.

10.4.3.3. Assessment

Let us next evaluate the procedures using the SMP and StPI presented in Section 10.2.3. Tables 10.4 and 10.5 give the strategic power indices and the effects of the Nice reforms on the majority threshold before and after the enlargement and the effects of enlargement under pre-Nice and post-Nice quota.[17] The total effect can be computed either by taking the effect of enlargement under the old threshold and then the threshold effect or by taking the effect of the change in threshold and then the effect of the enlargement under the new threshold. The total effects are shown on the two right-most columns of the third row. As before, EP refers to the European Parliament, CM to the Council, and EC to the Commission. In both tables, columns 2 and 3 give the preenlargement data, columns 4 and 5 list the postenlargement data, and columns 6 and 7 give the differences.

Tables 10.4 and 10.5 demonstrate that the Council gains in both procedures. The Commission gains in the consultation procedure, and the EP loses in the codecision procedure. In both cases the total effects are very small. Note that the Commission is powerless in the codecision procedure – it only exerts gate-keeping power. The

---

[17] Here we disregard the effects of the changes in the intra-Council distribution of power. According to the earlier results, the power distribution within the Council does not have a significant effect on interinstitutional distribution of power at the aggregate level.

Table 10.5: *The effects of the Nice reforms and enlargement on strategic interinstitutional power in codecision procedure*

	Current EU		Enlarged EU		Difference	
	EP	CM	EP(E)	CM(E)	DEP	DCM
Q = 71 percent	0.178	0.658	0.173	0.668	−0.005	0.010
Q = 74 percent	0.162	0.731	0.162	0.727	0.000	−0.004
Difference	−0.016	0.073	−0.011	0.059	−0.016	0.069

equilibrium outcome does not depend on the Commission's preferences unless it refuses to initiate action and the legislative status quo prevails.[18]

The results in Tables 10.4 and 10.5 share the common property that the inter-institutional power in the EU seems to be very stable as far as the membership is concerned. This especially holds in the codecision procedure in which the effects are in third decimals when the membership expands from 15 to 27. In the consultation procedure, the magnitude of these effects is somewhat greater. Comparison of the impact of considerable enlargement with a small change in quota from 71 to 74 percent puts these effects into perspective. In the codecision procedure, the impact of increasing the quota from 71 to 74 percent has a much greater effect than the expansion of membership from 15 to 27, and in the consultation procedure the effects are roughly of the same magnitude.

Let us next compare three different approaches to measure interinstitutional power, namely, the composite game approach and two variants of strategic power measures. In the former, we concentrate on the SSI. Because, to our knowledge, there are no studies using the StPI of Steunenberg et al. (1999) in evaluating the post-Nice rules, we concentrate on EU-15 and the majority thresholds that are currently in use.

Tables 10.6 and 10.7 give the respective results in consultation and codecision procedures. The first observation in both cases is that the composite game SSI and the SMP give qualitatively rather similar results and that the StPI differs from these significantly. In fact, in both procedures the StPI ranks the actors differently from the composite game SSI and the SMP. In the consultation procedure, these results suggest that the Commission is more powerful than the Council and, in the codecision procedure, that the EP exerts more power than the Council. These differences illustrate the fundamental difference between the StPI, which uses the average distances between outcomes and actors' policy positions as the source of power, whereas the two other indices rely on marginal contributions.

A major difference between the composite game SSI and the SMP is that the former considers the procedures as simultaneous decisions whereas the latter models the procedures as procedural noncooperative games. This raises the question of the first-mover advantage. In the consultation procedure, the Commission is the

---

[18] This makes the procedure inefficient because not all gains from trade are realized if the Commission uses its gate-keeping power (see Widgrén 2003 for details).

Table 10.6: *Interinstitutional power measures in consultation procedure in the EU-15*

	Composite game SSI		SMP		StPI	
	QMV	Unanimity	QMV	Unanimity	QMV	Unanimity
Commission	0.248	0.063	0.531	0.000	0.350	0.100
Council	0.752	0.937	0.813	1.875	0.110	0.070

Sources: Columns 1–4: own calculations; columns 5–6: Steunenberg et al. (1999).

first mover in making a proposal, but a unanimous Council can amend the proposal, which keeps the first-mover advantage almost completely in the hands of the Commission. In the codecision procedure, the situation is different. Like the equilibrium analysis in Section 10.4.3 suggested above, the Commission's role is considerably diminished. This occurs because the EP and the Council apply the same quota for acceptance of the Commission proposals and for amendments that do not require the Commission's support. In the analysis we have moreover assumed that the member state that is holding the Council presidency has an initiator's role in the Conciliation Committee.

Tables 10.6 and 10.7 show that, in the consultation procedure, indeed, the SMP gives a higher power score to the Commission than the composite game SSI (CGSSI). In the case of the Commission, the theoretical maximum power is 1 in both cases. The CGSSI is based on the Commission's presence in a winning coalition and can therefore be seen as a measure of the Commission's gate-keeping power. The difference between the SMP and CGSSI illustrates, on the other hand, the Commission's agenda-setting power. Note that unanimity rule diminishes gate-keeping power. It is more likely that the Commission is (on average) worse off than when the legislative status quo prevails if it compares a compromise made by a qualified majority (QMV) of the Council instead of unanimous Council with the legislative status quo. This makes the need for using gate-keeping power (on average) less urgent under unanimity rule than in qualified majority voting (QMV).

For the Council, the theoretical maximum value of the CGSSI is 1, and the maximum of the SMP index is 2.[19] Relative to these maxima, the Council exerts less power according to the SMP than to the CGSSI. This conclusion is intuitively plausible because of the Commission's gains owing to its agenda-setting power in the NWI. The Council's absolute power figures remain almost identical, however.

The StPI gives different results. It gives a higher power score to the Commission than to the Council, and both actors' power decreases when QMV is replaced by unanimity rule. The theoretical maxima are 1 for both actors. This value is obtained because power stems from a small distance between the ideal policy positions and outcomes. Unanimity rule tends to shift the equilibrium outcome towards the extreme positions, whereas, under QMV, outcomes are closer to the center of the policy space.

---

[19] This can be seen from the equilibrium analysis in Section 10.4.3.

Table 10.7: *Interinstitutional power measures in the codecision procedure in the EU-15*

	Composite game SSI		SMP		StPI	
	QMV	Unanimity	QMV	Unanimity	QMV	Unanimity
Commission	0.000	0.000	0.000	0.000	0.000	n.a.
Council	0.690	0.938	0.658	1.668	0.089	n.a.
Parliament	0.310	0.062	0.178	0.033	0.140	n.a.

Sources: Columns 1–4: own calculations; column 5: Steunenberg and Dimitrova (1999).

In the codecision procedure, the CGSSI and the SMP suggest that the Council is more powerful than the EP, whereas the StPI suggests the opposite. The latter gives, however, more power to the member state holding the presidency in the Council than to the EP. The Council's power in the StPI column of the Table refers to an average Council member on the assumption that each member state has a $\frac{1}{15}$ likelihood of holding the presidency. The separate figures, according to the StPI, are 0.50 for the member state holding the presidency and 0.06 for other Council members. Also, this property differs from the SMP and the CGSSI, which suggests that the member state holding the presidency exerts less power than the rest of the Council, the respective figures being 0.260 and 0.398.

10.5. Concluding Remarks

This chapter has surveyed different methods of evaluating actors' power in voting games. Our emphasis was on ex ante assessment of power. The standard tools for this are the classical power indices of cooperative games. Power indices have been criticized because they disregard actors' preferences, all strategic aspects, and interinstitutional relationships. If power indices are used in the design of constitutional rules, the first source of criticism does not hit the target. The fact that power indices abstract preferences can be seen as a desirable property when the objective is to design institutions. The two other sources of criticism should, however, be taken more seriously. They are both closely related to the fact that legislation and decision making in institutions like the EU are procedural whereas power indices are static concepts.

In power index literature, there have been some attempts to capture the inter-institutional aspects using the composite game approach. Because it is as static as standard coalitional-form voting games and hence power indices, the composite game approach does not explain the strategic and interinstitutional aspects satisfactorily.

In the recent literature of power indices, there have been several attempts to reply to criticism toward power indices or (abstract) of the a priori approach in general. The first wave of this literature (see, e.g., Widgrén 1995; Kirman and Widgrén 1995) concentrated on making different assumptions concerning actors' preferences. In power index models, these assumptions are often made on players' rates of acceptance towards a proposal or on probabilities of supporting a proposal. This line of research rather investigates and models different voting situations and, therefore, does not fit into the design of constitutional rules.

Another and more recent approach stems from the noncooperative models of voting and decision-making procedures. This unified approach is based on equilibrium analysis of the decision-making procedure. The rules of the game are understood more widely than in cooperative games because the explicit procedure is included. Ex ante analysis is then carried out by randomizing actors' preferences. In this line of research there are two variants: the one in which power is defined as the expected distance between the outcome and an actor's ideal policy position and, the one in which the original definition of power as a marginal contribution in coalitional form games is restored. The former approach is limited to spatial voting whereas the latter is not.

In this chapter, we used EU decision making as an example to demonstrate how different approaches work. We argued that the classical cooperative approach is still valid in dealing with intrainstitutional distribution of power, such as the EU Council of Ministers. Here, the usual approach relies on the Banzhaf index of power, but this chapter demonstrates that the use of the Shapley–Shubik index may be justified as well. In interinstitutional relations, the unified approach is more appropriate. Here the composite game approach seems, however, to give a consistent picture with the unified approach based on marginal contribution. Nevertheless, this picture is only partial.

BIBLIOGRAPHY

[1] Baldwin, R., E. Bergl, F. Giavazzi, and M. Widgrén (2000), "The EU Reforms for Tomorrow's Europe," CEPR Discussion Paper 2623.

[2] Baldwin, R., E. Bergl, F. Giavazzi, and M. Widgrén (2001), "Nice Try: Should the Treaty of Nice Be Ratified?" Monitoring European Integration 11. London: Centre for Economic Policy Research.

[3] Bindseil, U. and Hantke, C. (1997), "The Power Distribution in Decision-Making among EU Member States," *European Journal of Political Economy* 13, 171–185.

[4] Crombez, C. (1996), "Legislative Procedures in the European Community," *British Journal of Political Science* 26, 199–228.

[5] Crombez, C. (1997), "The Co-Decision Procedure in the European Union," *Legislative Studies Quarterly* 22, 97–119.

[6] Felsenthal, D. and M. Machover (1998), *The Measurement of Voting Power: Theory and Practice, Problems and Paradoxes*. Cheltenham: Edward Elgar.

[7] Felsenthal, D. and M. Machover (2001a), "Myths and Meanings of Voting Power," *Journal of Theoretical Politics* 13, 81–87.

[8] Felsenthal, D. and M. Machover (2001b), "The Treaty of Nice and Qualified Majority Voting," *Social Choice and Welfare* 18, 431–464.

[9] Garrett, G. and G. Tsebelis (1999a), "Why Resist the Temptation to Apply Power Indices to the EU?" *Journal of Theoretical Politics* 11, 291–308.

[10] Garrett, G. and G. Tsebelis (1999b), "More Reasons to Resist the Temptation to Apply Power Indices to the EU," *Journal of Theoretical Politics* 11, 331–338.

[11] Garrett, G. and G. Tsebelis (2001), "Even More Reasons to Resist the Temptation to Apply Power Indices to the EU," *Journal of Theoretical Politics* 13, 99–105.

[12] Holler, M. and M. Widgrén (1999), "Why Power Indices for Assessing EU Decision-Making?" *Journal of Theoretical Politics* 11, 321–330.

[13] Hosli, M. (1993), "Admission of European Free Trade Association States to the European Community: Effects on Voting Power in the European Community's Council of Ministers," *International Organization* 47, 629–643.

[14] Hosli, M. (2002), "Preferences and Power in the European Union," *Homo Oeconomicus* XIX(3), 311–327.

[15] Kirman, A. and M. Widgrén (1995), "European Economic Decision-Making Policy: Progress or Paralysis?" *Economic Policy* 21, 421–460.

[16] Laruelle, A. and M. Widgrén (1998), "Is the Allocation of Power among EU States Fair?" *Public Choice* 94, 317–339.

[17] Laruelle, A. and M. Widgrén (2001), "Voting Power in a Sequence of Cooperative Games," in *Voting Power and Coalition Formation*, Manfred Holler and Guillermo Owen (eds.), Dordrecht and Boston: Kluwer Academic Publishers.

[18] Laruelle, A. and F. Valenciano (2002), "Assessment of Voting Situations: The Probabilistic Foundations," Discussion Paper No. 26/2002, Departamento de Economia Aplicada IV, Basque Country University, Bilbao, Spain.

[19] Leech, D. (2002), "Designing the Voting System for the Council of Ministers of the European Union." Forthcoming in *Public Choice*.

[20] Moser, P. (1996), "The European Parliament as a Conditional Agenda Setter: What Are the Conditions? A Critique of Garrett and Tsebelis (1994)," *American Political Science Review* 90, 834–838.

[21] Moser, P. (1997), "A Theory of the Conditional Influence of the European Parliament in the Cooperation Procedure," *Public Choice* 91, 333–350.

[22] Napel, S. and M. Widgrén (2001), "Inferior Players in Simple Games," *International Journal of Game Theory* 30, 209–220.

[23] Napel, S. and M. Widgrén (2004), "Strategic Power Revisited," CESifo Working Paper No. 736, Munich.

[24] Nurmi, H. (1998), *Rational Behavior and the Design of Institutions*. Cheltenham: Edward Elgar.

[25] Owen, G. (1972), "Multilinear Extensions of Games," *Management Science* 18, 64–79.

[26] Owen, G. (1995), *Game Theory*. San Diego: Academic Press.

[27] Penrose, L. (1946), "The Elementary Statistics of Majority Voting," *Journal of the Royal Statistical Society* 109, 53–57.

[28] Shapley, L. (1953), "A Value for *n*-Person Cooperative Games," in Harold Kuhn and Al Tucker (eds.), *Contributions to the Theory of Games*, Princeton University Press. *Annals of Mathematical Studies* 28, 307–317.

[29] Shapley, L and M. Shubik (1954), "A Method of Evaluating the Distribution of Power in a Committee System," *American Political Science Review* 48, 787–792.

[30] Steunenberg, B. (1994), "Decision-Making under Different Institutional Arrangements: Legislation by the European Community," *Journal of Theoretical and Institutional Economics* 150, 642–669.

[31] Steunenberg, B. and Dimitrova (1999), "Interests, Legitimacy and Constitutional Choice: The Extension of the Codecision Procedure in Amsterdam," University of Twente, mimeo.

[32] Steunenberg, B., D. Schmidtchen, and C. Koboldt (1999), "Strategic Power in the European Union: Evaluating the Distribution of Power in Policy Games," *Journal of Theoretical Politics* 11, 339–366.

[33] Straffin, P. D. (1977), "Homogeneity, Independence and Power Indices," *Public Choice* 30, 107–118.

[34] Straffin, P. D. (1978), "Probability Models for Power Indices," in *Game Theory and Political Science*, Peter C. Ordeshook (ed.), New York University Press.

[35] Straffin, P. D. (1988), "The Shapley–Shubik and Banzhaf Power Indices as Probabilities," in *The Shapley Value: Essays in Honor of Lloyd Shapley*, Alvin E. Roth (ed.), Cambridge, UK: Cambridge University Press.

[36] Straffin, P. D., M. D. Davis, and S. J. Brams (1982), "Power and Satisfaction in an Ideologically Divided Body," in *Voting and Voting Power*, Manfred J. Holler (ed.), Würzburg: Physica-Verlag.

[37] Tsebelis, G. (1994), "The European Parliament as a Conditional Agenda Setter," *American Political Science Review* 88, 128–142.

[38] Tsebelis, G. (1996), "More on the European Parliament as a Conditional Agenda Setter: Response to Moser." *American Political Science Review* 90, 839–844.

[39] Tsebelis, G. and G. Garrett (1997), "Why Power Indices Cannot Explain Decision-Making in the European Union," in *Constitutional Law and Economics of the European Union*, Dieter Schmidtchen and Robert Cooter (eds.), Cheltenham: Edward Elgar.

[40] Widgrén, M. (1994), "Voting Power in the EU and the Consequences of Two Different Enlargements," *European Economic Review* 38, 1153–1170.

[41] Widgrén, M. (1995), "Probabilistic Voting Power in the EU Council: The Cases of Trade Policy and Social Regulation," *Scandinavian Journal of Economics* 97, 345–356.

[42] Widgrén, M. (2001), "On Probabilistic Relationship between Public Good Index and Normalized Banzhaf Index," in *Coalition Formation and Power Indices*, Holler, M. and Owen, G. (eds.), Kluwer.

[43] Widgrén, M. and S. Napel (2002), "The Power of a Spatially Inferior Player," *Homo Oeconomicus* 19, 327–343.

11

Group and Network Formation in Industrial Organization: A Survey

Francis Bloch

11.1. Introduction

Recent years have witnessed a surge of interest in the formation of groups and networks in industrial organization. Most of this interest stems from the emergence of new forms of cooperation and competition between firms. The development of strategic alliances, the acceleration in the creation of joint ventures and joint production, and research facilities have given rise to a new strategic environment in which firms cooperate in some domains and compete in others. At the same time, new noncooperative approaches have been introduced in game theory to analyze the endogenous formation of coalitions and networks, providing simple tools that can be applied to study the formation of alliances and networks of firms. These approaches typically model the formation of groups as a two-stage process in which firms initially join in groups or alliances and compete in the market in the second phase.

The objective of this chapter is to provide a selective survey of recent applications of models of group and network formation to industrial organization. Given the abundance of work on the formation of groups of firms (e.g., cartels in oligopolies and bidding rings in auctions), we drastically had to limit the topics covered in the survey. We focus on models that explain the size and structure of groups and networks. Important issues, such as the enforceability of group agreements, the design of mechanisms for cost revelation, or the empirical literature on groups and networks of firms, will not be reviewed in this chapter.

More specifically, this chapter considers three aspects of group and network formation: (i) the formation of collusive agreements, (ii) the formation of cost-reducing alliances, and (iii) the formation of trade networks. For each of these topics, we discuss a small number of basic models and give a brief account of the extensions studied in the literature. Although the material covered in the survey is limited, the reference list is rather exhaustive, and we direct the reader to these references for a deeper understanding of specific issues. We also note that most of the literature focuses on the case of symmetric players. The determination of endogenous groups

I am grateful to Sanjeev Goyal and especially Gabrielle Demange for critical comments in the preparation of this chapter.

and networks in the general case is a formidable task, and very little research has been done in this area.

Collusive agreements cover cartels choosing quotas (as in many commodity markets), price-fixing agreements, and bidding rings as well as market sharing or exclusive territories agreements. The striking feature of collusive agreements, which has already been pointed out by Stigler (1950), is that the formation of a cartel is a public good and induces positive externalities on firms outside the cartel. Hence, firms have an incentive to free ride on the cartels formed by other firms, and collusive agreements are highly unstable. Most of the models discussed in this survey aim at enriching the basic model to explain the formation of stable cartels and collusive agreements on the market.

Cost-reducing alliances have recently been the focus of attention by many industrial economists and policy makers. These alliances may pursue different objectives such as the development of new products and processes, the definition of common standards, or the joint use of facilities. As opposed to collusive agreements, cost-reducing alliances typically induce negative externalities on other firms in the industry. Hence, the analysis of the formation of these alliances usually leads to very different conclusions than the study of the stability of cartels.

Trade networks correspond to a market setting that has recently attracted the attention of many economists in industrial organization and development economics. By contrast to traditional centralized markets, trade networks are based on bilateral agreements between buyers and sellers, which exclusively deal with one another. The architecture of these networks has been the object of descriptive studies, but theoretical models of trade networks remain scarce.

The rest of the chapter is organized as follows. In Section 11.2, we present the basic models of group and network stability. Section 11.3 discusses the formation of cartels and collusive networks. In Section 11.4 we address the formation of alliances and networks of collaboration among firms, and Section 11.5 is devoted to the study of trade networks.

11.2. Group and Network Stability

In this section, we present the basic tools for the analysis of group and network formation in industrial organization. Traditional analyses from cooperative game theory cannot be directly applied to the formation of groups of firms because the values of groups depend on the groups formed by other players. In other words, the basic representation of coalitional gains must be a game in *partition function form* (which depends on the entire coalition structure) rather than one in *coalitional form* (which only depends on the coalition). The presence of spillovers among groups also implies that, whenever players form groups, they must anticipate the reaction of other players to the formation of the group. This is a very important distinctive feature of the formation of groups of firms, and it plays a fundamental role in the modeling of group and network formation in industrial organization.

The earliest formal games of coalition formation were introduced by Selten (1973) and d'Aspremont et al. (1983). These games correspond to *open membership games* in which players cannot exclude other players from the group. Later models, inspired by Hart and Kurz (1983), allowed for exclusion in the process of coalition formation. Two different models have been studied, the γ and δ models, which differ in the specification of the reaction of coalition members to a defection. Bloch (1996) and Ray and Vohra (1999) proposed a game of coalition formation in extensive form based on Rubinstein's (1982) alternating offers procedure. Finally, the main concept of network stability applied to industrial organization is Jackson and Wolinsky's (1996) concept of pairwise stability.

11.2.1. Open Membership Games

In an open membership game, all players simultaneously announce yes or no, and the group is formed by all players announcing yes. A stable cartel is then defined as the Nash equilibrium outcome of the game. Clearly, for a cartel K to be stable, two conditions need to be satisfied:

- No member wants to leave the cartel (condition of *internal stability*).
- No outsider wants to join the cartel (condition of *external stability*).

Notice that this game always admits a trivial equilibrium in which all players announce no. The focus of the analysis is on nontrivial equilibria for which a cartel of size $k \geq 1$ emerges on the market.[1]

11.2.2. Exclusive Membership Games

In an exclusive membership game, all players simultaneously announce a coalition S that they want to form. In the γ model, the coalition is formed only if all coalition members unanimously announce the same coalition. In the δ model, partial coalitions are formed by all players who announce the same coalition, but unanimity is not required. Hence, if $S = \{i, j, k\}$ and players i and j announce S, but not player k, the coalition is not formed and all players remain singletons in the γ model whereas the partial coalition $\{i, j\}$ is formed in the δ model. Because this game typically admits several Nash equilibria reflecting coordination failures among players, Hart and Kurz (1983) propose to refine the set of equilibria by considering strong Nash equilibria, which are immune to coalitional deviations. Yi (1997) has studied another refinement, the coalition-proof Nash equilibrium, which only allows for coalitional deviations that are immune to further deviations.

11.2.3. Sequential Bargaining Games

Bloch (1996) and Ray and Vohra (1999) propose a sequential procedure in which players are forward looking and take into account the consequences of their choices for the behavior of the other players. More specifically, this procedure is based on an extension of Rubinstein's (1982) alternating offers game. (See also Selten 1981 for an early paper on a bargaining model of group formation.) At each period t,

---

[1] We adopt the following convention: For any group S, s denotes the size of the group.

one firm is chosen to make a proposal (a coalition to which it belongs), and all the prospective members of the coalition respond in turn to the proposal. If the proposal is accepted by all, the coalition is formed and another firm is designated to make a proposal at $t + 1$; if some of the firms reject the proposal, the coalition is not formed, and the first firm to reject the offer makes a counteroffer at period $t + 1$. The identity of the different proposers and the order of response are given by an exogenous rule of order. There is no discounting in the game, but all players receive a zero payoff in case of an infinite play. Because the game is a sequential game of complete information and infinite horizon, we use *stationary perfect equilibrium* as a solution concept.

When firms are ex ante identical, it can be shown that the coalition structures generated by stationary perfect equilibria can also be obtained by analyzing the following simple finite game. The first firm announces an integer k_1, corresponding to the size of the coalition it wants to see formed, firm $k_1 + 1$ announces an integer k_2, and so on until the total number n of firms is exhausted. An equilibrium of the finite game determines a sequence of integers adding up to n, which completely characterizes the coalition structure because all firms are ex ante identical.

11.3. Cartels and Collusive Networks

In this section, we discuss the formation of collusive groups – cartels, bidding rings, and collusive networks in which firms form reciprocal agreements not to enter each other's market. For each of these collusive groups, we present a basic economics model highlighting the economic forces leading to the formation of the group. In the case of cartels, which have been extensively studied, we also propose a brief guide to the literature.

11.3.1. Cartels and Horizontal Mergers

11.3.1.1. The Basic Model

To illustrate the basic problem of cartel stability, consider a Cournot market with n firms and a linear inverse demand:

$$P = 1 - Q.$$

All firms have an identical constant marginal cost, normalized at 0, and thus each firm's profit is given by

$$\pi = \frac{1}{(n + 1)^2}.$$

Suppose that k firms form a cartel or merge on the market. Because marginal costs are constant, the cartel (or merged firm) has no cost advantage over the other firms. Inasmuch as there are now $n - k + 1$ firms on the market, each firm obtains

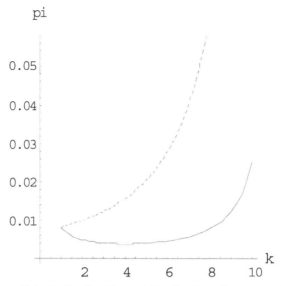

Figure 11.1: Profits of insiders, outsiders in a linear Cournot cartel.

a profit

$$\pi^I(k) = \frac{1}{(n - k + 2)^2},$$

but members of the cartel share the total profits, and so cartel members receive a payoff

$$\pi^K(k) = \frac{1}{k(n - k + 2)^2}.$$

Figure 11.1 graphs the profit of a cartel member (solid line) and an external firm (dashed line) on a market of ten firms for values of k ranging from 1 to 10.

Figure 11.1 shows that the profit of an outsider is always higher than the profit of an insider. Furthermore, as first observed by Salant, Switzer, and Reynolds (1983), there is a minimal size of the merger for which the merger becomes profitable. This minimal size $\underline{k}$ is computed as the first integer following the solution to the equation

$$\frac{1}{(n + 1)^2} = \frac{1}{k(n - k + 2)^2}$$

and is around 80 percent of the total number of firms in the industry.

Because external firms receive a higher profit than cartel members, the formation of a cartel can be interpreted as the provision of a public good. Cartel members reduce their production to increase price, but this price increase benefits external firms more than cartel members. This is the source of cartel instability, which was first pointed out by Stigler (1950): every firm would like to see a cartel formed, but none of the firms wants to be part of the cartel!

The stability of a cartel can be tested using various models of group formation. Three facts have to be noted:

- No cartel of size lower than $\underline{k}$ can be formed. Any insider has an incentive to leave the cartel, for the lowest profit it would realize after leaving the cartel (when n firms are present on the market) is always greater than the profit it earns in the cartel. Hence, *at most one cartel can form on the market.*
- If a cartel of size $k \geq \underline{k}$ forms, no outsider has an incentive to join the cartel because the maximal profit it would make by joining the cartel (in the case of complete monopolization) is lower than the profit it would make as an outsider:[2]

$$\pi^I(k) - \frac{1}{(n-k+2)^2} > \frac{1}{4n} = \pi^K(n) \forall k \geq \underline{k}.$$

Hence, the only relevant condition to check is whether *insiders have an incentive to leave the cartel.*

- An insider in a cartel of size k always realizes a lower profit than an outsider when a cartel of size $k - 1$ is formed, that is,

$$\pi^I(k-1) = \frac{1}{(n-k+3)^2} > \frac{1}{k(n-k+2)^2} = \pi^K(k).$$

Hence, *no cartel is stable if, after the departure of a member, all insiders stay together.*

This last remark shows that the stability of a cartel depends crucially on the anticipations that players form on the behavior of cartel members after a firm leaves the cartel. In the γ model, a coalition is dissolved after the departure of a member, and hence any cartel of size greater than $\underline{k}$ is stable. In the δ model, the coalition stays together after a defection, and no coalition is stable because the profit an outsider obtains when a cartel of size $k - 1$ is formed exceeds the profit of a member of a cartel of size k.

In the sequential bargaining game, Bloch (1996) shows that the only stationary, perfect equilibrium results in the first $(n - \underline{k})$ firms forming singletons and the last $\underline{k}$ firms grouping in a cartel. Clearly, when $\underline{k}$ firms are left in the game and previous players have formed singletons, the optimal strategy of the remaining players is to form a cartel. No cartel of smaller size is viable; thus, the only choice is between remaining as singletons and forming a cartel, and by definition, forming a cartel is a better option if $k = \underline{k}$. Anticipating this behavior, the first $(n - \underline{k})$ players have an incentive to leave as singletons and free ride on the formation of the cartel by subsequent firms.

11.3.1.2. Extensions

Although we presented the model in the linear Cournot case, the analysis can be extended to symmetric Cournot models with arbitrary cost and demand functions.

---

[2] This inequality can be verified by the following computation. For all $k \geq \underline{k}$, $4nk > (n+1)^2$ because, at $k^* = (n+1)^2/4n$, $\pi^K(k^*) < \pi^I(1)$. Now, if $k/(n+1)^2 > 1/4n$, for all $k \geq \underline{k}$, $1/(n-k+2)^2 > k/(n+1)^2 > 1/4n$.

Yi (1997) studies in detail the properties of cost and demand functions needed to conduct the analysis of stable cartels. Farrell and Shapiro (1990) discuss general Cournot models.

The main conclusion of the basic model is that cartel instability will prevent the formation of any cartel on the market. Thus, in order to explain the observed formation of cartels in some industries, the model needs to be enriched in such a way that cartel members enjoy an advantage over outsiders. This can be done in several ways. Perry and Porter (1985) and Farrell and Shapiro (1990) consider situations in which horizontal mergers (or the formation of cartels) create synergies in such a way that the production cost of cartel members is lower than the cost of outsiders. In that case, a stable cartel size emerges. In an interesting recent analysis, Nocke (1999) studies the formation of cartels when firms face capacity constraints. Because cartels have access to more capacity, they enjoy an advantage when the individual firms' capacity constraints are binding. Hence, in particular, large cartels are easier to sustain when capacity is reduced or demand expands. Espinosa and Macho-Stadler (2003) incorporate moral hazard in the Cournot model by assuming that every firm is a team of independent players. The moral hazard problem becomes more important as the size of the cartel increases, and hence at first glance, it appears that cartels have a cost disadvantage with respect to outsiders. However, interestingly, the moral hazard problem also affects intermediate coalitions, and large cartels may be easier to sustain because the defection of players results in an intermediate cartel, which cannot be sustained. In fact, Espinosa and Macho-Stadler (2003) solve numerically for the solution of the sequential bargaining game and show that the introduction of moral hazard might help to stabilize large cartels.

Using a different approach, d'Aspremont et al. (1983), Donsimoni (1985), and Donsimoni Economides, and Polemarchakis (1986) study the formation of cartels that act as a dominant firm facing a competitive fringe. In that case again, the cartel enjoys a larger profit than outsiders, and a stable cartel size exists. Currarini and Marini (2002) make a similar point in a model in which cartel members act as Stackelberg leaders and thus benefit from a first-mover advantage.

Deneckere and Davidson (1985) study the formation of cartels in a differentiated products market in which firms choose prices. The incentives to form cartels are stronger in the Bertrand model than in the Cournot model. In particular, an insider's profit is always increasing in the size of the cartel. Deneckere and Davidson (1985) show that stable cartels are easier to sustain under Bertrand competition and that complete market monopolization is a stable outcome for some parameter values.

When firms are heterogeneous, the analysis of stable cartels is much more complex, and has only been done in very restricted settings. Donsimoni (1985) studies heterogeneous cartels in a dominant firm model in which firms have different linearly increasing marginal cost. Brown and Chiang (2003) discuss cartel formation at length in a three-player Cournot oligopoly with different constant marginal costs. Fauli-Oller (2000) studies mergers among four firms when two firms have a lower marginal cost than the two others.

Kamien and Zang (1990, 1991) propose a different original approach to the study of horizontal mergers. In their acquisition game, players simultaneously announce a bidding price for all the other players and an asking price for their participation in a coalition. Player i can "buy" player j if $i's$ bidding price for player j exceeds $j's$ asking price. Because many different acquisitions can occur given a vector of bid and ask prices, one needs to define a tie-breaking rule to select the coalitions formed. Kamien and Zang (1990) propose several rules to resolve the ties (e.g., no sale if two players can acquire another, global exogenous priority rule, etc.). In the acquisition game, no merger will occur at equilibrium. To understand this fact, note that when forming a cartel of size k, a firm must compensate all the other firms for its participation in the cartel. Because an outsider obtains a payoff $\pi^I(k-1)$ if it does not join the cartel, its asking price will be set at this amount. But absent of meger synergies, $k\pi^K(k) < (k-1)\pi^I(k-1)$, and thus no firm will ever propose to form a cartel in equilibrium. (This line of reasoning is reminiscent of the free-riding problem associated with takeovers in the corporate finance literature.)

Recent contributions to the literature on cartel stability have also emphasized new models of coalition formation. Thoron (1998) proposes a model in which cartel members can choose whether to stay or break apart. Diamantoudi (2001) proposes a solution concept based on a cooperative solution concept (the stable set) with forward-looking players. Macho-Stadler, Perez-Castrillo, and Porteiro (2002) consider a model in which mergers occur through bilateral agreements, show that complete market monopolization is eventually reached and characterize the sequence of mergers leading to monopoly.

11.3.2. Bidding Rings

Bidding rings are groups of buyers who submit their bids cooperatively in auctions. Graham and Marshall (1987) and Mailath and Zemsky (1991) have analyzed bidding rings in second-price private value auctions. Suppose that all valuations are distributed independently according to the common distribution F with density f.

In a second-price auction, the optimal bidding strategy is to submit a bid equal to the valuation, and the expected benefit of a buyer is given by

$$U = \int_0^\infty \int_0^z (z-y)(N-1)F(y)^{N-2}f(y)f(z)dydz,$$

where $(N-1)F(y)^{N-2}f(y)$ is the density of the distribution of the highest bid among $(N-1)$ bidders.

If a bidding ring of size k forms, the density of the distribution of the highest bid among the ring members is $kF(z)^{k-1}f(z)$, whereas the density of distribution of the highest bid among the independent bidders is given by $(N-k)F(y)^{N-k-1}f(y)$. Hence, the expected benefit of a bidding ring member is

$$U^R = \frac{1}{k}\int_0^\infty \int_0^z (z-y)(N-k)F(y)^{N-k-1}f(y)kF(z)^{k-1}f(z)dydz,$$

and the expected benefit of an independent bidder is $U^I = U$.

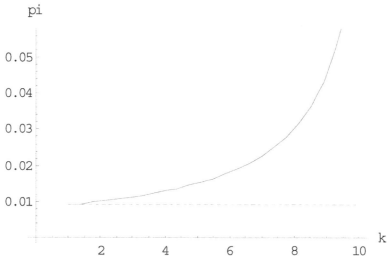

Figure 11.2: Expected utility of bidders in a uniform second-price auction.

In the special case in which the distribution is uniform over $[0, 1]$, expected benefits are equal to $U^I = \frac{1}{N(N+1)}$, $U^R = \frac{1}{(N-K+1)(N+1)}$.

Figure 11.2 graphs the expected utility of a ring member and of an independent bidder in the uniform case as a function of k for $N = 10$.

It appears that the expected benefit of an independent bidder is independent of k and always lower than the expected benefit of a ring member. Furthermore, the utility is increasing in the size of the ring. We conclude that firms always have an incentive to join the bidding ring and that the stable ring size is the grand coalition $k = n$.

Mailath and Zemsky (1991) consider a game with heterogeneous bidders and prove a stronger result. In a second-price auction, the total utility of a bidding ring is independent of the structure of rings formed by other bidders, and hence the situation can be represented as a game in coalitional form. It can be shown that this game is convex and therefore has a nonempty core. In any of the core allocations, a single bidding ring encompassing all the bidders is formed.

The situation is much more complex in first-price private value auctions. If a ring of size k forms, the auction between the bidding ring and independent bidders is asymmetric, for the bidding ring draws its highest value from a distribution with density $k F(z)^{k-1} f(z)$ whereas independent bidders draw their valuations from a distribution with density $f(y)$. Even when the distribution F is assumed to be uniform, there is no explicit analytical formula for the equilibrium strategies. Marshall et al. (1994) provide numerical computations of the optimal strategies and the expected utilities of ring members and independent firms in the uniform case.

McAfee and McMillan (1992) compute equilibrium strategies when valuations follow a discrete distribution with two values $v = 0$, $v = 1$ and $p = \Pr\{v = 1\}$. The expected benefits of a ring member and an independent bidder are given by

$$U^R = \frac{1}{K}(1 - p)^{N-K}(1 - (1 - p)^K), U^I = p(1 - p)^{N-K}.$$

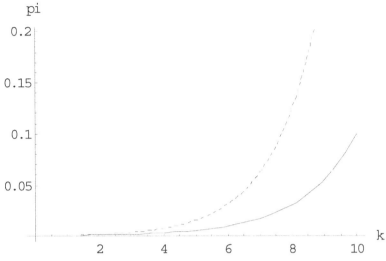

Figure 11.3: Expected utility of bidders in a discrete first-price auction.

Figure 11.3 graphs the expected benefit of a ring member and an independent bidder as a function of k for $N = 10$ and $p = 1/2$.

As opposed to second-price auctions (but in line with cartels in oligopolies), the utility of a ring member is always lower than the utility of an independent bidder. Notice, however, that the inequality

$$\pi^I(k-1) > \pi^K(k)$$

does not necessarily hold and that ring members do not necessarily have an incentive to defect from the cartel. In fact, McAfee and McMillan, using the open membership game, show that a unique cartel size k^* exists for which the cartel is both internally and externally stable. This is the unique value k satisfying

$$\frac{1 - (1-p)^k}{k} \geq p(1-p) \geq \frac{1 - (1-p)^{k+1}}{k+1}.$$

It can be shown that k^* is always larger than 3, increases in p, and converges to infinity when p goes to 1.

11.3.3. Collusive Networks

Collusive networks emerge when firms form reciprocal market-sharing agreements by which they refrain from entering each other's market. This geographical division of markets has been analyzed by Belleflamme and Bloch (2004) using recent models of strategic network formation.[3] Suppose that firms are initially present on different markets. By forming a link ij, the firms i and j commit to stay out of each other's market. For any graph g on the set N of firms, we can compute $n_i(g)$, the number

---

[3] See also Chapter 1 of this volume.

of firms present on market i. On the supposition that all firms are identical, we let $\pi(n_i(g))$ denote the profit made by each firm on market i. For any firm i, the total profit it makes is the sum of profits on each market where it is present, that is,

$$\Pi^i(g) = \pi(n_i(g)) + \sum_{j,ij\notin g} \pi(n_j(g)).$$

The equilibrium concept used here is pairwise stability. A network g is pairwise stable if no player has an incentive to sever a link unilaterally, and no pair of firms has an incentive to form a link. Formally, letting $g - g_{ij}$ (respectively $g + g_{ij}$) denote the network obtained from g by deleting (adding) the link between firms i and j, a network g is *(pairwise) stable* if and only if (i) $\forall i$, j s.t. $g_{ij} = 1$, $\Pi^i(g) \geq \Pi^i(g - g_{ij})$ and $\Pi^j(g) \geq \Pi^j(g - g_{ij})$; and (ii) $\forall i$, j s.t. $g_{ij} = 0$, if $\Pi^i(g + g_{ij}) > \Pi^i(g)$, then $\Pi^j(g + g_{ij}) < \Pi^j(g)$.

Belleflamme and Bloch (2004) characterize pairwise stable collusive networks when profit functions are decreasing and log-convex in the number of active firms on the market. They show that

(i) every stable network involves complete components – all firms are linked to each other in a component;

(ii) components in a stable network must be of different sizes; and

(iii) there exists a minimal threshold on alliance size, m^*, which is the minimal number such that $\pi(N - m + 1)/\pi(N - m + 2) \geq 2$.

The formulation of collusive networks is general enough to encompass oligopoly and auction models. In a linear Cournot oligopoly with inverse demand $P = 1 - Q$, it is easy to see that $m^* = N$. Hence, the only stable collusive networks are the complete and empty networks. In an auction with uniform distribution of values, one computes the ex ante profit of a bidder as $\pi(n) = 1/[n(n + 1)]$. Hence, $m^* = N - 1$, and there are three stable, collusive networks: the empty network, the complete network, and a network with a complete component of size $N - 1$ and an isolated bidder.

11.4. Alliances and Networks of Collaboration

Firms form alliances for a variety of reasons: to lobby for pieces of legislation, to agree on common standards, to develop new products and processes, to launch joint marketing campaigns, to produce common inputs, to jointly use some facilities, and so on. Although there is a large variety of strategic alliances, their objective is always to reduce the cost of production or increase market demand for alliance members. Hence, to model the role of alliances on a market, we suppose that firms can benefit from synergies that lead to a reduction in the constant marginal cost of production (or equivalently to an increase in the scale parameter of demand). We distinguish between two types of agreements: multilateral agreements, in which synergies depend on the size of the alliance formed, and bilateral agreements, in which synergies accrue to pairs of firms forming a collaborative link.

11.4.1. Alliances

11.4.1.1. The Basic Model

Cost-reducing alliances have been extensively studied in the context of cooperative research joint ventures (see Katz 1986; d'Aspremont and Jacquemin 1988; Kamien, Muller, and Zang 1992; Suzumura 1992; and Kamien and Zang 1993). In this theoretical literature, the structure of alliances is fixed. Either the alliance covers all the firms in the industry (as in Kamien et al. 1992 and Suzumura 1992), or the industry can be partitioned into symmetric alliances (Kamien and Zang 1993).

Bloch (1995) proposes a model to derive the structure of cost-reducing alliances in oligopolies endogenously. Consider a linear oligopoly with inverse demand $P = 1 - Q$. Let a_k denote the size of alliance A_k. We suppose that the constant marginal cost of production of a firm is linearly decreasing in the size of the alliance it belongs to. Formally, if firm i belongs to association $A_{k(i)}$, its marginal cost of production is given by

$$c_i = \lambda - \mu a_{k(i)}$$

The equilibrium profit of a firm belonging to an association of size a_i is given by

$$\pi_i = \left[\frac{1-\lambda}{n+1} + \mu a_{k(i)} - \frac{\mu \sum_k a_k^2}{(n+1)} \right]^2.$$

Two important features of alliance formation can be deduced from the profit expression given above.

- First, the formation of an alliance induces negative externalities on outsiders. Members of an alliance enjoy a lower marginal cost and are thus more aggressive on the market, reducing the profits of their competitors.
- Second, members of a larger alliance have higher profits than outsiders because they benefit from a cost advantage with respect to their competitors. Hence, if membership in an association is open, all firms will belong to the association.

If, on the other hand, membership is exclusive and firms can prevent other firms from entering the group, the association will not cover the entire industry. In fact, when a firm joins an association, cost benefits are asymmetric. The new member immediately benefits from all the synergies created within the group, whereas standing group members only receive the additional benefit of the new member. Hence, after the association has reached a given size, it has no incentive to accept new members. A careful look at the profit function shows that π_i is increasing in a_i until $n/2$ and then decreases.

However, the formation of an association of size $n/2$ is not the optimal strategy because it results in the formation of two symmetric associations. To increase the cost difference with its rivals, an association has an incentive to accept more than $n/2$ members. Anticipating that the remaining players will form an association of size $(n - a)$, the first association should optimally decide to admit up to $a^* = \frac{3n+1}{4}$ members. In the sequential game of coalition formation studied by Bloch (1996) and Ray and Vohra (1999), the unique equilibrium association structure thus results in the formation of two associations of unequal size, one with $\frac{3n+1}{4}$ members, the other with $\frac{n-1}{4}$.

11.4.1.2. Extensions

Bloch (1995) discusses the extension of the model to Cournot and Bertrand competition with differentiated products. As the level of product differentiation increases, competition on the market is less fierce and the dominant association becomes larger. Interestingly, the sizes of associations are identical under Cournot and Bertrand competition. Yi (1998) and Yi and Shin (2000) generalize the model by studying arbitrary demand and cost functions. They isolate conditions on demand and cost functions for which the grand coalition emerges in an open membership game. Belleflamme (2000) extends the model to asymmetric firms and shows that when firms and cost reductions are asymmetric, the grand coalition may not form in the open membership game. Morasch (2000) considers a related model in which firms in a strategic alliance propose contracts about cost and profit sharing in a production joint venture. In this environment, he numerically computes the endogenous association structures for small values of n.

11.4.2. Networks of Collaboration

As an alternative to multilateral alliances, we now analyze the formation of bilateral links among firms. Goyal and Joshi (2003) propose a model of networks of collaboration among firms. Consider a linear Cournot oligopoly with inverse demand $P = 1 - Q$ and suppose that firms can decrease their marginal production cost by collaborating with other firms on a bilateral basis. We suppose that the constant marginal cost of production is linearly decreasing in the number of agreements signed by each firm. For any graph g, we let $d_i(g)$ denote the degree of vertex i, namely, the number of agreements signed by firm i. We then have

$$c_i = \lambda - \mu d_i(g),$$

and the equilibrium profits are given by

$$\prod_i = \left[\frac{1}{n+1} + \mu d_i(g) - \frac{\mu \sum d_j(g)}{(n+1)} \right]^2.$$

Although the formulation is similar to the study of multilateral alliances, the analysis is very different. When two firms sign an agreement, they both enjoy a symmetric reduction in production cost. In fact, one can easily compute the marginal effect of an additional agreement on firm $i's$ equilibrium quantity as

$$\Delta q_i = \frac{n\mu}{n+1} > 0.$$

Because equilibrium profits are monotonically increasing in quantities, we observe that all bilateral agreements raise the firm's profit and thus that the only pairwise stable network is the complete graph.

When firms face a large fixed cost F of link formation, the complete network ceases to be stable. Instead, Goyal and Joshi (2003) show that stable networks have a "dominant group" architecture with one complete component and singleton firms.

Goyal and Moraga-Gonzales (2001) extend the analysis by supposing that firms endogenously choose their research effort and cost synergies depend on the research effort of the two collaborating firms. Clearly, research effort will be decreasing in the number of links formed by any firm; hence the addition of new links may actually result in a decrease in cost reduction on the market. In a linear Cournot model with homogeneous firms, Goyal and Moraga-Gonzales (2001) show that cost reduction is maximized when every firm is linked to exactly $n/2$ competitors. However, because the marginal benefit of an additional link remains positive for both firms for any number of links, the complete network is pairwise stable. Hence, in a model with endogenous choice of effort, firms may engage in excessive collaborative activities.

11.4.3. Cartels versus Alliances

We have clearly distinguished between two types of cooperation among firms: collusion on the market and collaboration in production. The two models exhibit striking differences. In models of collusion, the formation of groups induces positive externalities on outsiders (and the main difficulty for firms is to solve the free-rider problem), whereas in models of collaboration, the formation of groups induces negative externalities on outsiders (and the main difficulty for firms is to exclude other firms from the alliance). The two models also have very different implications for competitive policy. Antitrust authorities should encourage the formation of alliances but discourage the formation of cartels.

We should stress, however, that in practice, most cooperative agreements among firms are neither purely collusive nor purely collaborative and fall in a grey area consisting of some elements of collusion and cooperation in production. This is of course the challenge faced by antitrust authorities, and this explains why the rule of reason should be adopted in investigating mergers and cooperative agreements. The models we discussed can guide antitrust policy by describing the size and structure of collaborative agreements that would emerge on the market in the absence of regulation.

11.5. Trade Networks

The two models we discuss in this section analyze trading on fixed network structures. The importance of social networks in economics has long been recognized. Labor economists have emphasized the role of social networks in job search; industrial economists have analyzed the role of networks in the diffusion of products and innovations. The originality of the two models we present here is that they study how networks determine the number of agents exchanging commodities with one another. Hence, market power is endogenously determined by the structure of the network. Unfortunately, the complexity of the models makes it impossible to determine the architecture of trade networks endogenously. More work is needed to understand how agents form exchange networks.

11.5.1. Bargaining on Networks

Corominas-Bosch (2004) proposes a model in which buyers and sellers bargain over a network. Bargaining takes place according to a variation of the Rubinstein alternating-offer protocol. At even periods, sellers post prices and buyers respond to the offer; at odd periods, buyers make the offer and sellers respond. For trade to occur, two conditions must be met: (i) the buyer and seller must be connected through the network, and (ii) the buyer has to accept the seller's offer. If multiple trades are possible given the buyers and sellers' strategies, an exogenous priority rule determines the effective trades. After a buyer and a seller trade, they leave the game, and the remaining agents continue to bargain, thus preserving the network structure.[4]

Let n and m denote the number of sellers and buyers and δ the common discount factor of all agents. The competitive solution assigns all surplus to the short side of the market, and thus buyers get 1 and sellers 0 if $n > m$ and sellers get 1 and buyers 0 if $m > n$. When the numbers of buyers and sellers are equal, $m = n$, let z denote the outcome of a two-player bargaining game $z = 1/(1 + \delta)$ for the proposer and $1 - z$ for the respondent.

For $n = m = 2$, there are two connected networks: one in which s_1 is linked to both buyers, b_1 to both sellers, s_2 to b_1, and b_2 to s_1 (graph G_1) and the complete network (graph G_2). In the first graph, it might appear that a seller connected to both buyers is in an advantageous position, for he or she can play the two buyers against one another. However, this will not be the case: seller s_1 will never trade with b_1 because s_2 will always have an incentive to undercut. In essence, in graph G_1, traders will act as if there were two separate pairs, (s_1, b_2), (s_2, b_1), and the outcome will be that of a two player bargaining game, $z = 1/(1 + \delta)$. Similarly, in the complete graph G_2, the outcome will be the competitive outcome $z = 1/(1 + \delta)$.

The two-player example underscores that the important feature of the bipartite graph is the decomposition into subsets of buyers and sellers who trade with one another. For general values of n and m, Corominas-Bosch (2004) introduces the following description of a graph (which is known in the graph-theoretic literature on matching as the Edmonds–Gallai decomposition of bipartite graphs.)

Consider a subset V of buyers (respectively sellers) in a graph. This set V is considered nondeficient if in any subset V' of V, every buyer in V' is connected to at least V' sellers in the graph. Define then a graph G as a seller's graph G^S if $n > m$ and the set of sellers is nondeficient. Similarly, a buyer's graph is a graph G^B with $m > n$ and for which the set of buyers is nondeficient. Finally, if $m = n$,

---

[4] For details of the model, see Chapter 1 of this volume.

the graph G^E denotes a graph where one can find n matchings of pairs of agents. Corominas-Bosch (2004) shows that any graph G can be described as the union of subgraphs of types G^S, G^B, and G^E.

Using this description, we can answer the following two questions: (i) Which network structures support the competitive solution as one perfect equilibrium outcome and (ii) which network structures support the competitive solution as the unique subgame perfect equilibrium outcome?

The answer to the first question is that a graph G supports the competitive solution if and only if it is decomposed into subgraphs that are all of the same type. (Hence, if $n > m$, all subgraphs are sellers' graphs; if $m > n$, all subgraphs are buyers' graphs; and if $m = n$, all subgraphs have a perfect matching.) The proof of this result is constructive. If a graph satisfies this property, then the competitive solution can indeed be implemented on the graph because players are "connected enough" through the network. Conversely, it can be shown that if a graph does not satisfy this property, the competitive solution cannot be supported in equilibrium. (A decomposition of the graph into graphs of different types would imply that, at the competitive solution, some sellers get one and others zero; it can be checked that this is not an equilibrium.)

The answer to the second question is less clear. In the complete graph, the competitive solution is indeed the only perfect equilibrium of the bargaining game. Other graphs have the same property: for example, when in the Edmonds–Gallai decomposition all subgraphs are complete, the same result holds. However, these conditions are sufficient but not necessary.

11.5.2. Auctions on Networks

In a series of papers, Kranton and Minehart (2000a,b) and (2001) analyze the formation of buyer–seller networks. Kranton and Minehart (2001) propose a model in which buyers have random valuations for the good sold by the (identical) sellers and participate in an ascending auction to acquire the good. The number of sellers is assumed to be smaller than the number of buyers, $n < m$. The structure of the network determines the number of auctions that a particular buyer can participate in: a buyer can only acquire the object from a seller with whom he or she is linked.

Kranton and Minehart (2001) first characterized the equilibrium of the English auction. As prices increase, bidders drop from the competition until a subset of sellers and buyers remains for which demand equals supply. This is the price at which markets clear, and goods are then allocated in an efficient way among the buyers with the highest valuations. Notice in particular that, because bidders' prices do not depend on their valuation but on the second highest valuation, each buyer's dominant strategy is to bid up to his or her valuation, and efficiency obtains as in a classical Vickrey auction.

Kranton and Minehart (2001) then study the incentives to form links. They suppose that buyers establish links to sellers at a fixed cost c per link formed. The main result of their analysis is that *socially efficient networks always arise as an equilibrium outcome of the game of link formation.* This surprising result can be interpreted as follows. The marginal benefit of forming an additional link for a buyer is the difference between his or her expected payoff if this buyer is linked with $l - 1$ or l sellers. Because buyers compete for the good and the auction rules guarantee that the allocation of objects will be efficient, this marginal benefit is identical to the social marginal benefit of adding a new link; hence, the buyers' incentives to form links are aligned with social incentives. (Notice that in this argument it is of paramount importance that buyers [and not sellers] initiate the formation of links.)

The characterization of efficient network architectures is a difficult exercise. If $c = 0$, the complete network is obviously efficient. As c increases, the efficient network becomes less connected. Kranton and Minehart (2001) define "least-link allocatively complete" (LAC) networks as networks with the smallest number of links guaranteeing that the outcome will be efficient – buyers with the highest valuation always obtain the good from a seller. In an LAC network, each buyer is linked to one seller and each seller to exactly $m - n + 1$ buyers. For small but positive values of c, Kranton and Minehart (2001) show that LAC networks are indeed the socially efficient networks.

Kranton and Minehart (2000b) propose a variation of the model to study vertical relationships. Buyers are downstream suppliers who can either invest a to produce an input specific to the firm or acquire the input from sellers (upstream firms) and support a cost c per link formed. Uncertainty in demand results in random valuations of the buyers for the input, and the model is thus an extension of the theory of buyer–seller networks. The focus of the study is on the conditions under which network structures dominate (using ex ante welfare comparisons) a vertically integrated structure. Kranton and Minehart demonstrate that a set of parameters (a, c) for which the network structure is efficient always exists. Furthermore, because the network structure enables firms to benefit from economies of sharing flexible outputs, network structures become more efficient when the dispersion of buyer's valuations increases. The analysis can be extended to study the strategic choice of firms (firms initially choose whether to form links or produce the input internally) and the effects of vertical mergers.

Finally, Kranton and Minehart (2000a) propose a model of buyer–seller networks for which the exact trading process is left unspecified. For any network structure, any competitive price equating demand and supply can be realized. For any network, the set of competitive prices can be computed taking into account the outside opportunities of all the traders. These outside options are computed by tracing out "opportunity paths" for the traders in the network.

BIBLIOGRAPHY

[1] Belleflamme, P. (2000), "Coalition Structures with Open Membership and Asymmetric Firms," *Games and Economic Behavior* 30, 1–21.
[2] Belleflamme, P. and F. Bloch (2004), "Market Sharing Agreements and Collusive Networks," *International Economic Review*, forthcoming.

[3] Bloch, F. (1995), "Endogenous Structures of Association in Oligopolies," *Rand Journal of Economics* 26, 537–556.

[4] Bloch, F. (1996), "Sequential Formation of Coalitions in Games with Fixed Payoff Division," *Games and Economic Behavior* 14, 537–556.

[5] Bloch, F. (2004), "Bargaining in a Network of Buyers and Sellers," *Journal of Economic Theory* 115, 35–77.

[6] Brown, M. and S. H. Chiang (2003), *Coalitions in Oligopolies*. North Holland: Elsevier.

[7] Corominas-Bosch, M. (2004), "Bargaining in a network of buyers and sellers", *Journal of Economic Theory*, 115, 37–77.

[8] Currarini, S. and M. Marini (2002), "Sequential Play and Cartel Stability in Oligopoly," mimeo, University of Urbino, http://pesonal.lse.ac.uk/marinim/cartelstability 5.pdf

[9] d'Aspremont, C. and A. Jacquemin (1988), "Cooperative and Noncooperative R&D in a Duopoly with Spillovers," *American Economic Review* 78, 1133–1137.

[10] d'Aspremont, C., A. Jacquemin, J. J. Gabszewicz, and J. Weymark (1983), "On the Stability of Collusive Price Leadership," *Canadian Journal of Economics* 16, 17–25.

[11] Deneckere, R. and C. Davidson (1985), "Incentives to Form Coalitions with Bertrand Competition," *RAND Journal of Economics* 16, 473–486.

[12] Diamantoudi, E. (2001), "Stable Cartels Revisited," mimeo, University of Aarhus.

[13] Donsimoni, M. P. (1985), "Stable Heterogeneous Cartels," *International Journal of Industrial Organization* 3, 451–467.

[14] Donsimoni, M. P., N. Economides, and H. Polemarchakis (1986), "Stable Cartels," *International Economic Review* 27, 317–327.

[15] Espinosa, M. P. and I. Macho-Stadler (2003), "Endogenous Formation of Competing Partnerships with Moral Hazard," *Games and Economic Behavior* 44, 183–194.

[16] Farrell, J. and C. Shapiro (1990), "Horizontal Mergers: An Equilibrium Analysis," *American Economic Review* 80, 107–126.

[17] Fauli-Oller, R. (2000), "Takeover Waves," *Journal of Economics Management and Strategy* 9, 189–210.

[18] Goyal, S. and S. Joshi (2003), "Networks of Collaboration in Oligopoly," *Games and Economic Behavior* 43, 57–85.

[19] Goyal, S. and J. L. Moraga-Gonzales (2001), "R&D Networks," *RAND Journal of Economics* 32, 686–707.

[20] Graham, R. and G. Marshall (1987), "Collusive Bidder Behavior at Single Object Second Price and English Auctions," *Journal of Political Economy* 86, 1217–1239.

[21] Hart, S. and M. Kurz (1983), "Endogenous Formation of Coalitions," *Econometrica* 51, 1047–1064.

[22] Jackson, M. and A. Wolinsky (1996), "A Strategic Model of Social and Economic Networks," *Journal of Economic Theory* 71, 44–74.

[23] Kamien, M., E. Muller, and I. Zang (1992), "Research Joint Ventures and R & D Cartels," *American Economic Review* 82, 1293–1306.

[24] Kamien, M. and I. Zang (1990), "The Limits of Monopolization through Acquisition," *Quarterly Journal of Economics* 105, 465–499.

[25] Kamien, M. and I. Zang (1991), "Competitively Cost Advantageous Mergers and Monopolization," *Games and Economic Behavior* 3, 323–338.

[26] Kamien, M. and I. Zang (1993), "Competing Research Joint Ventures," *Journal of Economics and Management Strategy* 2, 23–40.

[27] Katz, M. (1986), "An Analysis of Cooperative Research and Development," *RAND Journal of Economics* 17, 527–543.

[28] Kranton, R. and D. Minehart (2000a), "Competition for Goods in Buyer-Seller Networks," *Review of Economic Design* 5, 301–332.

[29] Kranton, R. and D. Minehart (2000b), "Networks versus Vertical Integration," *RAND Journal of Economics* 31, 570–601.

[30] Kranton, R. and D. Minehart (2001), "Buyer-Seller Networks," *American Economic Review* 91, 485–508.

[31] Macho-Stadler, I., D. Perez-Castrillo, and N. Porteiro (2002), "Sequential Formation of Coalitions through Bilateral Agreements," mimeo, Universitat Autonoma de Barcelona.

[32] Mailath, G. and P. Zemsky (1991), "Collusion in Second Price Auctions with Heterogeneous Bidders," *Games and Economic Behavior* 3, 467–486.

[33] Marshall, G., M. Meurer, J. F. Richard, and W. Stronquist (1994), "Numerical Analysis of Asymmetric First Price Auctions," *Games and Economic Behavior* 7, 193–220.

[34] McAfee, P. and J. McMillan (1992), "Bidding Rings," *American Economic Review* 82, 579–599.

[35] Morasch, K. (2000), "Strategic Alliances as Stackelberg Leaders," *International Journal of Industrial Organization* 18, 257–282.

[36] Nocke, V. (1999), "Cartel Stability under Capacity Constraints: The Traditional View Restored," mimeo, University of Pennsylvania.

[37] Perry, M. and R. Porter (1985), "Oligopoly and the Incentives for Horizontal Merger," *American Economic Review* 75, 219–227.

[38] Ray, D. and R. Vohra (1999), "A Theory of Endogenous Coalition Structures," *Games and Economic Behavior* 26, 286–336.

[39] Rubinstein, A. (1982), "Perfect Equilibrium in a Bargaining Model," *Econometrica* 50, 97–109.

[40] Salant, S., S. Switzer, and J. Reynolds (1983), "Losses from Horizontal Mergers: The Effects of an Exogenous Change in Industry Structure on Cournot-Nash Equilibrium," *Quarterly Journal of Economics* 98, 185–199.

[41] Selten, R. (1973), "A Simple Model of Imperfect Competition When 4 Are Few and 6 Are Many," *International Journal of Game Theory* 2, 141–201.

[42] Selten, R. (1981), "A Noncooperative Model of Coalitional Bargaining," in *Essays in Game Theory and Mathematical Economics in Honor of Oskar Morgenstern*, V. Bohm and H. Nachtkamp (eds.), Mannheim: Bibliographisches Institut Mannheim, 131–151.

[43] Stigler, J. G. (1950), "Monopoly and Oligopoly by Merger," *American Economic Review* 40, 23–34.

[44] Suzumura, K. (1992), "Cooperative and Noncooperative R&D in an Oligopoly with Spillovers," *American Economic Review* 82, 1307–1320.

[45] Thoron, S. (1998), "Formation of a Coalition-Proof Stable Cartel," *Canadian Journal of Economics* 31, 63–76.

[46] Yi, S. S. (1997), "Stable Coalition Structures with Externalities," *Games and Economic Behavior* 20, 201–237.

[47] Yi, S. S. (1998), "Endogenous Formation of Joint Ventures with Efficiency Gains," *RAND Journal of Economics* 29, 610–631.

[48] Yi, S. S. and H. Shin (2000), "Endogenous Formation of Research Coalitions with Spillovers," *International Journal of Industrial Organization* 18, 229–256.

Institution Design for Managing Global Commons:
Lessons from Coalition Theory

Carlo Carraro

12.1. Introduction

In many cases, environmental quality is a public good. When the dimension of the environmental problem is global, as in the case of global commons (climate change, ozone layer, biodiversity, etc.), there is no supranational authority that can enforce provision of the optimal amount of environmental quality. In this case, sovereign countries must decide whether or not to improve environmental quality – namely, to provide the environmental global public good – on a voluntary basis. In practice, countries negotiate on an international agreement that defines emission targets for each signatory and often the way to achieve these targets as well.

Early contributions (cf. Hardin and Baden 1977) characterized the interaction among countries as a prisoners' dilemma inevitably leading to the so-called tragedy of the global common property goods. However, in the real world, at the same time, many international environmental agreements on the commons were signed, often involving subgroups of negotiating countries and sometimes transfers and links with other policies (trade, technological cooperation, etc.).

How can we explain that some countries sometimes decide to sign an international environmental agreement even when they could enjoy the same environmental benefits by letting other countries abate? In other words, when the environment is a global public good, a country that does not abate achieves – without paying any costs – the same environmental benefits as signatories that decide to abate. Can it then be concluded that there is no incentive for countries to sign an international agreement – that is, that the outcome of the negotiation process will be a situation without any environmental cooperation?

The recent literature on international environmental agreements provides a negative answer to this last question.[1] Several different papers have shown that

The author is grateful to Carmen Marchiori, Francesca Moriconi, and Sonia Oreffice for their valuable assistance and to the participants at the International Conference on Game Practice and the Environment, Alessandria, 12–13 April, 2002, for helpful comments. The usual disclaimer applies.

[1] The literature is now quite large. Let us just mention the works by Hoel (1991), Carraro and Siniscalco (1992, 1993), Barrett (1994), Heal (1994), and Chander and Tulkens (1995, 1997). Most papers are

cooperation can emerge even when the environment is a public good and each country decides independently, voluntarily, and without any forms of commitment or repeated interaction.[2]

To analyze the emergence of environmental cooperation, environmental economists have used a new game-theoretic approach in which cooperation (i.e., the formation of coalitions) is the outcome of a noncooperative game.[3] The noncooperative approach to coalition formation can be loosely described as follows (see Bloch 1997 or Yi 2003 for a detailed presentation). The decision of whether to join the coalition is a "metadecision" that precedes the cooperative strategy characterising the behaviour of coalition members once the coalition is formed. This metadecision is taken noncooperatively. Thus, the outcome of the metagame in which agents decide whether to join a coalition – and which coalition – is identified via a noncooperative equilibrium concept. In addition, the partition function approach can be applied, and interactions between coalitions are taken into account.

The literature on environmental negotiations has emphasised the importance of modelling the decision process through which countries decide to join an environmental coalition as a noncooperative game. The goal is to determine the so-called self-enforcing agreements, that is, agreements that are not based on countries' commitment to cooperate. Building on the history of environmental negotiations, in which a single treaty is usually under negotiation, the theory of coalition formation in environmental economics has focused on the emergence of a single coalition at the equilibrium. Therefore, the game that captures a country's decision process is usually assumed to be a two-stage game: in the first stage, a country noncooperatively decides whether to sign the treaty (join the coalition); in the second stage, a country sets its emission level (or, more generally, its environmental policy) by maximising its welfare function given the decisions taken in the first stage and the adopted burden-sharing rule.[4]

The aforementioned theoretical literature has produced some important conclusions (see Barrett 1997b; Carraro and Siniscalco 1998; Tulkens 1998; Carraro 2000; Carraro and Marchiori 2003; and Finus and Rundshagen 2003 for a few surveys):

- Even in the case in which there are positive spillovers (e.g., in the case of a public good provision) and even without any commitment to cooperation, countries may form a coalition, that is, may decide to sign a treaty in order to cooperate to achieve a common target (cf. Barrett 1994).

collected in Carraro (2002). Surveys of this literature are provided by Tulkens (1998), Barrett (1997a), Carraro (1997b, 2000), and Carraro and Galeotti (2003).

[2] Of course, to obtain this result, more than two players must be involved in the environmental negotiation and some conditions on countries' reaction functions must be met.

[3] It must be acknowledged that the first results on the noncooperative formation of coalitions in the presence of positive spillovers can be found in the oligopoly literature on stable cartels. See D'Aspremont and Gabszewicz (1986); Donsimoni, Economides, and Polemarchakis (1986); and Chapter 11 of this volume.

[4] Repeated interactions are usually ruled out for two reasons: first, because the threat mechanisms upon which the equilibrium is based are unrealistic in environmental situations, and second, because the grand coalition is one of the equilibria of the repeated game (given the usual conditions on the discount rate) and this is in contrast to a reality in which partial coalitions characterise the observed outcome of negotiations on the protection of global commons.

- This coalition is usually formed by a subgroup of the n negotiating countries (cf. Carraro and Siniscalco 1992; Barrett 1994, 1997a, 1997b).
- The sometimes small initial coalition can be expanded by means of transfers or through "issue linkage," but only under some restrictive conditions – in particular when countries are symmetric (cf. Carraro and Siniscalco 1993, 1995; Botteon and Carraro 1997a, 1997b).
- The outcome of the two-stage game just described crucially depends on the membership rules (open membership, exclusive membership, coalition unanimity) adopted by the n negotiating countries (cf. Carraro and Marchiori 2003; Finus and Rundshagen 2003).

This latter result highlights the importance of properly designing the institutions that govern the management of global commons. There is indeed a strict dependence of the outcome of negotiations over global commons on the institutions and rules adopted by the negotiating countries. Some examples of these institutions and rules are

(i) the way in which new signatories are accepted (e.g., in the EU, new member countries are accepted only with the unanimous consensus of all existing members);

(ii) the time sequence through which decisions are taken (e.g., whether signatories should decide to adhere to the treaty simultaneously or do so sequentially); and

(iii) the minimum participation level necessary for the treaty to come into force (e.g., in the Kyoto Protocol, at least 55 countries accounting for at least 55 percent of total emissions must sign the treaty in order for it to enter into force), and so on.

In actual environmental negotiations, these rules are very important and often carefully designed. For example, in the negotiations on climate change or the ozone layer, a sequential and open access to the coalition has been adopted. In more than one hundred environmental agreements there is a minimum participation clause for the coalition to form (i.e., for the treaty to come into force). In almost all environmental agreements, sanctions are designed by linking environmental cooperation to other economic issues. In particular, minimum participation and issue linkage are among the most important features of environmental treaties.

However, there has been little theoretical research on the consequences of these rules and, above all, on how these rules can be optimally designed. This chapter will next survey some of the main results recently achieved by environmental economists on institution design for managing global commons. Following Schotter (1981), we use the words *institutions* and *rules* interchangeably. Therefore, the next section will summarize some results on the relationship between institution design and the structure of the equilibrium coalition (the number and identity of the signatory countries). Then, we will analyze how decisions about institutions and rules are taken and whether there are the incentives to adopt the institutions that maximize the number of participants in the cooperative management of global commons.

Section 12.3 will analyse the role of a minimum participation rule in international environmental treaties, the incentives to adopt this rule, and how it can be optimally designed. Section 12.4 will do the same for issue linkage, which is another frequently adopted feature of international agreements on global commons. When defining the negotiation agenda, countries may decide to negotiate on one issue only (e.g., the cooperative management of a global common) or on several issues at the same time. In particular, negotiations over an environmental problem could be linked to negotiations on a different policy issue. When do countries have an incentive to link two different policy issues? Under what conditions? Section 12.4 will provide an answer to these questions by highlighting the trade-off between issue linkage and the benefits of separate negotiations. Section 12.5 addresses the issue of regional versus global environmental treaties. It is indeed argued that the incentives to sign regional environmental treaties, as in the case of trade blocs, are stronger than the incentives to sign a single global agreement. Again, Section 12.5 will explore this issue and provide conditions for regional agreements to emerge at the equilibrium. A concluding section summarises the results presented in this chapter.

12.2. Accession Rules and Equilibrium Environmental Coalitions

Assume negotiations take place among n countries, $n > 3$, each indexed by $i = 1, \ldots, n$. As noted in the previous section, countries play a two-stage game. In the first stage – *the coalition game* – they decide noncooperatively whether to sign the agreement (i.e., to join the coalition). In the second stage, they play the noncooperative emission game in which the countries that signed the agreement play as a single player and divide the resulting payoff according to a given burden-sharing rule (any of the rules derived from cooperative game theory).[5] Let us assume that in both stages countries decide simultaneously.[6]

If the second-stage emission game has a unique Nash equilibrium for any coalition structure, a partition function can be constructed (cf. Bloch 1996; Yi 1997). If countries are symmetric and inside each coalition countries act cooperatively to maximise the coalitional surplus – whereas coalitions (and singletons) compete with one another in a noncooperative way[7] – then the per member partition payoff function (partition function hereafter) can be denoted by $p(k; \pi)$, which represents the payoff of a player belonging to the *size-k* coalition in the coalition structure $\pi = \{c_1, c_2, \ldots, c_m\}$, where $\sum_{i=1}^{n} c_i = n$. As a consequence, the payoff received by the players depends on coalition sizes and not on the identities of the coalition members. If, in addition, countries negotiate on a single agreement, the partition function can be denoted by $p(k; \pi)$, where $\pi = \{c, 1_{(n-c)}\}$.

---

[5] This approach must be contrasted with the traditional cooperative game approach (e.g., Chander and Tulkens 1995, 1997) and with a repeated game approach (Barrett 1994, 1997b). Moreover, note that the regulatory approach often proposed in public economics is not appropriate given the lack of a supranational authority.

[6] By contrast, Barrett (1994) assumes that the group of signatories is Stackelberg leader with respect to nonsignatories in the second-stage emission game. In Bloch (1996) it is assumed that players play sequentially in the first-stage coalition game.

[7] This assumption is equivalent to the one adopted to define the core equilibrium in Chander and Tulkens (1995, 1997). It is also at the basis of the PANE equilibrium of Eyckmans and Tulkens (2001).

In the case of negotiations on global commons, the benefit arising from an increased emission abatement or from a lower exploitation of the common increases with the number of cooperating countries. The reason is that congestion effects are missing and all countries receive the same additional benefits when a new country signs the treaty and cooperates on emission control or the management of the global common (cf. Barrett 2002). Therefore, the partition function increases monotonically with respect to the coalition size (the number of signatories in the symmetric case).

Given the preceding assumptions, which are commonly adopted in most of the literature on international environmental agreements, it is possible to show that a nontrivial equilibrium coalition $c^* \geq 2$ generally exists even though the grand coalition $c = n$ is unlikely to form at the equilibrium.[8]

In other words, the "tragedy of commons" is not necessarily the outcome of the negotiations on a global common. However, the treaty is unlikely to be signed by all the negotiating countries. The existence and size of the equilibrium coalition depend, among other things, on the intensity of the strategic interactions among countries (i.e., on the slope of their reaction functions). When reaction functions are negatively sloped (e.g., in the presence of some forms of economic or environmental "leakage"), environmental negotiations may fail and no treaty will be signed (Carraro and Siniscalco 1993). The absence of leakage effects can be used to explain the success of the Montreal negotiations on the ozone layer. A country's decision to reduce its own production of chlorinated fluorocarbons (CFCs) could not lead to an increased production of CFCs in another country.[9]

Accession rules are also very important to determine the size of the equilibrium coalition. Three different accession rules (also called membership rules) are often considered (see also Chapter 11 of this volume): the open membership rule, the exclusive membership rule, and the coalition unanimity rule. In the *open membership game* (D'Aspremont et al. 1983; Carraro and Siniscalco 1993; Yi and Shin 1994), each player is free to join and to leave the coalition without the consensus of the other coalition members. The negotiation process is represented by the announcement of a message, "join" or "not join" for example, by each player. In this game, all the players who announce the same message form a coalition. This membership rule thus implies that a coalition accepts any new player who wants to join it. By contrast, in the *exclusive membership game*[10] (Yi and Shin 1994)[11] or game Δ[12] (Hart and

---

[8] Several papers have shown these results. See, for example, Carraro and Siniscalco (1993) in the case of simultaneous moves and Barrett (1994) in the case of sequential moves. A survey of the applications of coalition theory in environmental economics can be found in Finus and Rundshagen (2003).

[9] Of course, this is not the only reason. Another major explanation is the low cost of moving from the old CFC-intensive technology to the new CFC-saving technology.

[10] The exclusive membership game is "a game in which the existing members in the coalition are allowed to deny membership to outsider players" (Yi and Shin 1994).

[11] The open membership game is "a game in which membership in a coalition is open to all players who are willing to abide by the rules of the coalition" (Yi and Shin 1994).

[12] The game Δ is "a game in which the choice of a strategy by a player means the largest set of players he is willing to be associated with in the same coalition. Each set of all the players who chose the same C then forms a coalition (which may, in general, differ from C)," where C indicates a subset of players (Hart and Kurz 1983).

Kurz 1983), each player can join a coalition only with the consensus of the existing members, but he or she is free to leave the coalition. In this negotiation process, each player's message consists of a list of players with whom he or she wants to form a coalition. Then, players who announce the same list form a coalition, which is not necessarily formed by all players in the list. Finally, in the *coalition unanimity game*[13] (Chander and Tulkens 1995; Yi and Shin 1994; Bloch 1997) or game Γ[14] (Hart and Kurz 1983), no coalition can form without the unanimous consensus of its members. This implies that players are not free either to join the coalition or to leave it. In this negotiation process, players' messages consist of a list of players, as in the previous negotiation process. However, if a coalition is formed, it is necessarily composed of all players in the list, and, as soon as a player defects, the coalition breaks up into singletons.

Finus and Rundshagen (2003) analyse how the size of the equilibrium coalition depends on the accession rule. They find that coalition unanimity sustains full cooperation (i.e., if this rule is adopted, the environmental treaty is likely to be signed by all the negotiating countries). In addition, they find that "exclusive membership leads to more concentrated coalition structures [than open membership] and is therefore preferable from an ecological perspective." This result is counterintuitive because one would expect that, in global pollution control, countries that have decided to reduce emissions want other countries to join them and that unanimous agreement among coalition members, as applies in exclusive membership games, should make it more difficult to fight global pollution than in open membership games. However, it turns out that just the opposite is true, which suggests that the frequently observed and perceived obstacle in international politics, namely agreement by consent, may in fact be an advantage.

Carraro and Marchiori (2003) also analyse the relationship between different membership rules and the size of the equilibrium coalition. They also show that coalition unanimity can sustain the grand coalition at the equilibrium. However, they provide examples in which exclusive membership (which is meaningful only when the payoff is hump-shaped) may reduce the size of the equilibrium coalition with respect to the one that would emerge under open membership. This result is different from the one by Finus and Rundshagen (2003) previously described. The reason is the adoption of more general payoff functions. Carraro and Marchiori (2003) also show that, under open membership, a coalition emerges at the equilibrium only if leakage is small and discuss how the coalition size is related to the marginal returns from cooperation.

A result of the relationship between membership rules and coalition size that is often emphasised (cf. Tulkens 1998) is that coalition unanimity induces all negotiating countries to join the coalition. This is why, in some papers on international environmental negotiations, coalition unanimity is assumed (see Chander and Tulkens

---

[13] The coalition unanimity game is a game in which "a coalition forms if and only if all potential members agree to join it" (Yi and Shin 1994).

[14] The game Γ is a game in which "each player chooses the coalition to which he wants to belong. A coalition forms if and only if all its members have in fact chosen it; the rest of the players become singletons" (Hart and Kurz 1983).

1995, 1997). However, it is important to understand whether countries would actually adopt coalition unanimity when they are free to choose the membership rule.
This would suggest studying a three-stage game in which in the first stage negotiating countries decide the membership rule, in the second stage they decide whether
to sign the treaty, and in the third stage they set their environmental policy.

A possible way to endogenise coalition unanimity is based on the equivalence
between coalition unanimity and a minimum participation rule stating that a treaty
comes into force only if all negotiating countries sign it. This equivalence will be
used in the next section, where the game through which a decision on a minimum
participation rule is taken will be analysed.

12.3. Endogenous Minimum Participation Rules in International Environmental Agreements

Many international environmental treaties contain the clause that the treaty will
only come into force if a minimum number of signatories or a minimum degree
of effectiveness is achieved. For example, in the case of the Kyoto Protocol, the
clause is twofold: the Protocol comes into force only if at least 55 countries sign it
and the signatories represent at least 55 percent of total emissions. More generally,
according to Rutz (2001), only 2 out of the 122 multilateral environmental agreements provided by the Center for International Earth Science Information Network
do not contain any minimum participation rule. In 81 cases, the participation rule
asks for a minimum number of signatories. In 22 cases, unanimity is required for
the treaty to come into force – namely, all negotiating countries must sign and ratify the agreement for it to be effective. In the remaining 17 cases, the minimum
participation rule is coupled to other requirements (i.e., for these agreements it is
not sufficient that a certain number of countries ratify the treaty, but these countries
have to satisfy additional criteria). For example, the Montreal Protocol on the ozone
layer asks for 11 instruments of ratification representing at least two-thirds of 1986
estimated global consumption of the controlled substances.[15]

Despite the importance of the minimum participation rule (and of the unanimity
rule as a particular case), very few theoretical studies have analysed this issue. Black,
Levi, and de Meza (1992) show that the introduction of a minimum participation
constraint increases the number of signatories of an international environmental
agreement. However, they do not prove that countries actually have an incentive
to introduce a minimum participation constraint among the rules of a given treaty.
Similarly, Rutz (2001) shows, in a very specific case, that a minimum participation
rule, if it exists, can result in an increase in the number of signatories. However,
the rule is imposed exogenously and is therefore not an equilibrium outcome of the
game. In addition, in Black et al. (1992) the minimum participation constraint is
designed to solve a profitability problem (cooperation becomes profitable only if a
minimum number of countries sign the agreement), whereas we would like to focus

---

[15] This section is based on the results contained in Carraro, Marchiori, and Oreffice (2001).

on the solution of a stability problem (cooperation is undermined by the presence of free-riders).

Therefore, it is important to address the following questions: Why do countries agree to have a minimum participation constraint among the clauses characterising an international treaty? Is a minimum participation rule a way to offset free-riding incentives? Why do countries that know they have an incentive to free ride consent to "tie their hands" through the introduction of a minimum participation constraint? What is the endogenous equilibrium level of the minimum participation constraint?

This section answers the preceding questions by analysing a three-stage noncooperative coalition game. In the first stage, countries set the minimum participation rule (minimum coalition size), which is necessary for the treaty to come into force. In the second stage, countries decide whether to sign the treaty. In the third stage, the equilibrium values of their decision or policy variables are set. At the equilibrium, both the minimum participation constraint and the number of signatories (the coalition size) are determined.

Notice that the first stage of our game is somewhat like a constitutional stage in which the rules of the game are set. Therefore, decisions are taken under unanimity and, in addition, are assumed to be irreversible (i.e., once a minimum participation rule is set, it cannot be modified in the subsequent stages of the game). This assumption is useful to forestall the possibility that, in the second stage, countries will ask to renegotiate the minimum participation constraint set in the first stage.

The second stage of the game is again a binary choice game (joining the coalition or behaving as a lone free-rider) whose outcome is a single coalition structure $\{\pi = c, 1_{(n-c)}\}$. Given the presence of positive spillovers, the partition function of any player outside the coalition *(nonmember function)* increases in c for all values of c in $[1, n]$. Formally, $p(1; \pi)$, where $\{\pi = c, 1_{(n-c)}\}$, is an increasing function of c. Let us denote by $Q(c)$ the relative nonmember partition function $p(1; \pi) - p(1; \pi^s)$, where $\pi^s = \{1_{(n)}\}$. Similarly, the relative per-member payoff function $P(c)$ is equal to $p(c; \pi) - p(1; \pi^s)$.

Let the minimum participation rule be denoted by α, where α is the share of the n negotiating countries that must sign the treaty for it to come into force. The value of α can vary between 0 and 1. If $\alpha = 0$, no restriction is introduced and a treaty comes into force whatever the number of its signatories. This is the so-called open membership rule previously described. If $\alpha = 1$, a treaty comes into force only if all countries decide to sign it. In this case, we have what is termed the *coalition unanimity* rule or full participation constraint. If $\alpha = 0.55$ and countries are symmetric, we will have the 55-percent rule introduced in the Kyoto Protocol. Therefore, by endogenising α, we can determine whether it is optimal for countries to opt for the open membership rule, the coalition unanimity rule, or any other minimum participation rule defined by $\alpha \in [0, 1]$.

Let us start the analysis by considering the case in which no minimum participation rule is introduced. In this case, $\alpha = 0$ (open membership rule) and the equilibrium of the coalition stage is completely characterised by the two properties given below, which were first derived in cartel literature (D'Aspremont et al. 1983; see also

Chapter 11 of this volume for a survey) and then often used also in environmental literature (Carraro and Siniscalco 1993; Barrett 1994, and many others). A coalition c is the equilibrium of the coalition stage of the game if it is profitable and stable:

Profitable: $P(c) \geq P(1) = 0$ c in $[2, n]$,
where $P(1) = p(1; \pi^s)$ is the relative payoff associated to the singleton structure $\pi^s = \{1_n\}$.

Stable: $P(c) \geq Q(c - 1)$, $c \in [2, n]$ and $Q(c) > P(c + 1)$, c in $[2, n - 1]$.

Let c^* be the size of the equilibrium coalition when $\alpha = 0$ (open membership). Let us denote this coalition by $c^*(\alpha = 0)$. Then, under the assumptions of this chapter:

Proposition 12.1. *The equilibrium of the coalition game for any value of [0,1] is the coalition structure:*

$$\pi^*(\alpha) = \{c^*(\alpha = 0), 1_{(n-c^*)}\} \text{ for any minimum participation rule such that}$$
$$0 \leq \alpha \leq \alpha^*. \tag{12.1a}$$

$$\pi(\alpha) = \{\alpha n, 1_{\{n-\alpha n\}}\} \text{ for any minimum participation rule such that}$$
$$\alpha^* < \alpha \leq 1. \tag{12.1b}$$

Proof. If $\alpha^* \leq \alpha = c^*(\alpha = 0)/n$, the equilibrium coalition is not modified by the presence of a minimum participation constraint α. Indeed, if in the first stage players set a minimum participation rule $\alpha \leq c^*(\alpha = 0)/n$, the number of signatories necessary for the treaty to come into force is smaller than or equal to the number of countries that would sign the treaty anyway. Hence, the equilibrium coalition remains $c^*(\alpha = 0)$. If in the first stage players agree on a minimum participation rule $\alpha > \alpha^* = c^*(\alpha = 0)/n$, then in the second stage they have the choice either to form a coalition of size $c = \alpha n$ or not to form any coalitions at all. Indeed, all coalitions larger than c are unstable because all coalitions larger than $c^*(\alpha = 0)$ are unstable and $c > c^*(\alpha = 0)$. Moreover, no coalition smaller than $c = \alpha n$ can form by definition of minimum participation. Given that $Q(c - 1) > P(c) > P(1) = 0$ (by monotonicity), players prefer to form the coalition $c = \alpha n$. Q.E.D. ∎

Proposition 12.1 identifies the relationship between the minimum participation rule decided in the first stage of the game and the equilibrium of the coalition stage. This relationship between the value of α and the equilibrium of the coalition stage jointly with the incentive structure that supports the equilibrium coalition $c^*(\alpha = 0)$ are crucial to determine the equilibrium value of α in the minimum participation stage.

Let us now determine the equilibrium of the minimum participation stage of the game, that is, let us identify which minimum participation rule is chosen in the first stage of the game. When countries deal with the choice of the membership rule, they consider two aspects:

1. **if** it is convenient to introduce a minimum participation constraint rather than to negotiate under the open membership regime;
2. **which** minimum participation constraint is optimal.

As noted at the beginning of this section, the decision in the first stage of the game is taken independently and simultaneously by all players. Because no player can be forced to accept a minimum participation rule he or she does not agree upon, decisions in the first stage must be taken with the unanimous consensus of all players. To achieve a unanimous consensus on a given rule in the first stage, all players must prefer the equilibrium supported by that rule to the one that would emerge without a minimum participation rule. This is the case if, whatever the choice of a player in the second stage, a player's payoff when the minimum participation constraint is introduced is larger than the payoff he or she would receive in the absence of any minimum participation constraint.

Proposition 12.2. *In the first stage of the game, all players agree to introduce a minimum participation constraint $\alpha = c/n$ if*

$$P(c) \geq Q[c * (\alpha = 0)]. \tag{12.2}$$

Proof. For all players to agree on a minimum participation constraint, we must have

$P(c) \geq P(c^*)$, that is, all players who cooperate in $\{c, 1_{(n-c)}\}$ and in $\{c^*, 1_{(n-c^*)}\}$ are better off in $\{c, 1_{(n-c)}\}$;

$Q(c) \geq P(c^*)$, that is, all players who are free-riders in $\{c, 1_{(n-c)}\}$ but cooperators in $\{c^*, 1_{(n-c^*)}\}$ are better off in $\{c, 1_{(n-c)}\}$;

$P(c) \geq Q(c^*)$, that is, all players who cooperate in $\{c, 1_{(n-c)}\}$ but free ride in $\{c^*, 1_{(n-c^*)}\}$ are better off in $\{c, 1_{(n-c)}\}$;

$Q(c) \geq Q(c^*)$, that is, all players who free ride both in $\{c, 1_{(n-c)}\}$ and in $\{c^*, 1_{(n-c^*)}\}$ are better off in $\{c, 1_{(n-c)}\}$.

If these four conditions are satisfied, all players find it convenient to agree on the minimum participation constraint α that sustains $\{c, 1_{(n-c)}\}$. Notice that $c > c^*$(otherwise, the coalition structure is $\{c^*, 1_{(n-c^*)}\}$ by Proposition 12.1. Hence, $P(c) \geq P(c^*)$ by monotonicity. Moreover, $Q(c)$ is also monotonically increasing, which implies $Q(c) \geq Q(c^*)$ when $c > c^*$. These two results, the definition of c^* and $c > c^*$, imply $Q(c) > Q(c-1) > P(c) > P(c^*)$. As a consequence, inequality (12.2), that is, $P(c) \geq Q(c^*)$, is a necessary and sufficient condition for all players to agree on the selection of a minimum participation rule such that the equilibrium coalition structure becomes $\{c, 1_{(n-c)}\}$. Q.E.D. ∎

The geometric representation of condition (12.2) when met for $c \geq c^* + 2$ is provided in Figure 12.1.

Is this condition feasible? The answer is certainly yes. Given the monotonicity of the functions $P(c)$ and $Q(c)$, it is possible – if n is sufficiently large – to find a coalition c large enough to satisfy $P(c) \geq Q(c^*)$. In particular, assume that n is

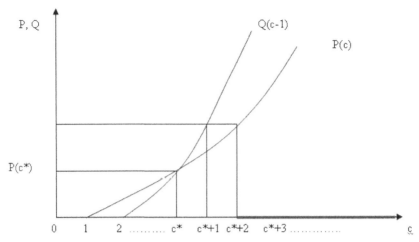

Figure 12.1: Geometric representation of condition (12.2) when met for $c \geq c^* + 2$.

such that there is a c' that satisfies $P(c') = Q[c^*(\alpha = 0)]$. The monotonicity of $P(c)$ implies that inequality (12.2) is met for all $c \in [c', n]$.

However, inequality (12.2) is only a necessary condition to identify the minimum participation constraint chosen by the n countries. The inequality (12.2) defines the set of minimum participation rules that would be voted upon with the unanimous consensus of all countries. Which rule is actually going to be adopted?

To answer this question, we must write the optimisation problem that each country solves when deciding the optimal minimum participation rule. Given symmetry, in the first stage of the game, a country does not know whether in the coalition stage it will be a cooperator or a free-rider. Therefore, it solves

$$\max_{c} EP(c) = \frac{c}{n} P(c) + \frac{n-c}{n} Q(c),$$
$$\text{s.t. } P(c') = Q[c^*(\alpha = 0)] \qquad 1 \leq c \leq n, \qquad (12.3)$$

where $EP(c)$ is a country's expected payoff in the first stage of the game and $\frac{c}{n}$ is the probability of being a cooperator in the second stage (given that the rule $\alpha = \frac{c}{n}$ is chosen in the first stage), whereas $\frac{n-c}{n}$ is the probability of being a free-rider in the second stage of the game.

The equilibrium minimum participation rule $\alpha^\circ = c^\circ / n$ is then the solution of the optimisation problem (12.3), where c° is the maximand of $EP(c)$ subject to inequality (12.2). Note that (12.3) identifies the trade-off that countries face. On the one hand, a high value of c, namely of α, increases the payoff of both cooperators and free-riders. On the other hand, a high value of α reduces the probability of being a free-rider in the second stage, thus reducing the probability of reaping the highest payoff.

Under what conditions is $EP(c)$ increasing with c for all values of c satisfying inequality (12.2)? This question is relevant because it identifies the case in which $c^\circ = n$ or $\alpha^\circ = 1$, that is, in which the minimum participation rule requires the ratification by all countries and therefore coalition unanimity. By differentiating $cP(c) + (n - c)Q(c)$ with respect to c, we obtain

$$P(c) - Q(c) + cP'(c) + (n - c)Q'(c), \tag{12.4}$$

where $P'(c)$ and $Q'(c)$ are the first derivatives of $P(c)$ and $Q(c)$, respectively. Let c^+ be the solution of $P(c^+) = Q(c^*)$. Then, inequality (5) is positive for all $c[c^+, n]$ if

$$\frac{\varepsilon_Q(n - c)}{n} + \frac{(1 + \varepsilon_p)P(c)}{Q(c)} \geq 1, \tag{12.5}$$

where ε_Q and ε_p are the positive elasticities of the functions $Q(c)$ and $P(c)$, respectively. Note that both terms on the left-hand side are positive. However, $(n - c)/n < 1$ because $c > c^*$ and $P(c)/Q(c) < 1$ for $c > c^*$ by definition of stability. Both $(n - c)$ and $P(c)/Q(c)$ decrease with c when P and Q are monotonic and $c^* \geq 2$. Therefore, unless the elasticities strongly increase with c, inequality (12.5) is less likely to be met for high values of c. The strongest condition to be met for $EP(c)$ to be increasing for all $c \geq c^+$, including $c = n$, is

$$\frac{(1 + \varepsilon_p)P(c)}{Q(c)} \geq 1, \tag{12.6}$$

which coincides with inequality (12.5) for $c = n$. This condition is satisfied only if ε_p is sufficiently large (i.e., the profitability function increases sufficiently rapidly with c). The intuition is that high and increasing values of $P(c)$ when c is close to n or equal to n offset the loss induced by the impossibility of free riding in the second stage.[16]

If inequality (12.6) is not met, there may exist values of c for which (12.6) is negative. In this case, the optimal rule $\alpha^\circ = c^\circ/n$ is smaller than 1. A minimum participation constraint $\alpha^\circ < 1$ implies that, at the equilibrium, some countries free ride on the cooperative behaviour of the other ones. However, given the constraint $P(c)Q[c^*(\alpha = 0)]$, the minimum participation rule, even when chosen endogenously and strategically, achieves the goal of inducing an equilibrium coalition larger than or equal to the one that would form without minimum participation constraint.[17]

The intuition behind this result is as follows. Even if players perfectly anticipate the consequences of their decision, in the first stage they have an incentive to reduce their freedom to free ride in order to achieve a larger payoff. However, this does not necessarily lead to the grand coalition (full cooperation) because all players also have an incentive to minimise this limitation to their freedom in order to increase the likelihood of being free-riders. The balance of these two incentives leads to the

---

[16] Assume $P(c)$ to be concave. Its elasticity becomes smaller and smaller as c moves towards n. At the same time, by definition of stability, the difference between $Q(c)$ and $P(c)$ increases with c. Therefore, $\frac{P(c)}{Q(c)} < 1$ also becomes smaller and smaller. As a consequence, $\frac{(1+\varepsilon_p)P(c)}{Q(c)}$ may become smaller than 1 and (12.6) may not be met. By contrast, if ε_p is large because, for example, $P(c)$ is convex, the ratio $\frac{P(c)}{Q(c)}$ is closer to one and (12.6) is more likely to be satisfied for $c = n$.

[17] The proof is easy. For all $c > c*$, $Q(c) > P(c - 1)$ by definition of stability. Therefore, $Q(c + 1) > P(c) \geq Q[c^*(= 0)]$, which implies $c + 1 > c^*$ because $Q(c)$ is monotonic. This implies $c \geq c^*$.

formation of a coalition that is larger than or equal to the one that would form when $\alpha = 0$ (no minimum participation constraint) but could be smaller than the grand coalition. The grand coalition is achieved only when the elasticity of $P(c)$ for c close to n is sufficiently large (i.e., the inequality (12.6) is met). In this latter case, coalition unanimity is the equilibrium rule and therefore all countries find it optimal to sign the environmental treaty.

These results could be used in the design of actual policy agreements. Two factors of information are crucial. First, the minimum participation constraint is effective only if the profitability condition is met for all countries. Otherwise, it may be counterproductive. Therefore, in real agreements, a minimum participation constraint could be associated with a transfer mechanism that makes the agreement profitable to all countries. Secondly, the slope of the coalition's payoff function is also crucial. If benefits from cooperation do not increase with the number of cooperators, or increase too slowly, then it is not optimal to adopt coalition unanimity, namely, a minimum participation constraint such that all countries must sign and ratify the treaty for it to come into force.

12.4. Endogenous Issue Linkage in International Negotiations

Another idea often proposed to reduce the incentives to free ride on global commons is issue linkage. The basic idea behind issue linkage is to design an agreement in which countries do not negotiate only on one issue (e.g., the environmental issue) but are forced to negotiate on two issues (e.g., the environmental one and another interrelated [economic] issue). For example, Barrett (1997c) proposes to link environmental negotiations to negotiations on trade liberalisation; Carraro and Siniscalco (1995, 1997) and Katsoulacos (1997) propose to link environmental negotiations to negotiations on R&D cooperation; and Mohr (1995) and Mohr and Thomas (1998) propose to link climate negotiations to negotiations on international debt cooperation.[18]

The idea of issue linkage was originally formulated by Folmer, van Mouche, and Ragland (1993) and Cesar and De Zeeuw (1996) to solve the problem of asymmetries among countries. The intuition is that some countries gain by cooperating on a given issue, whereas other countries gain by cooperating on a second one. By linking the two issues, the agreement in which the countries decide to cooperate on both issues may become profitable to all of them.

The idea of issue linkage can also be used to offset the free-riding incentives that characterise many environmental (or other public good) agreements. Suppose there is no profitability concern (either because countries are symmetric or because a transfer scheme is implemented to make the agreement profitable to all countries). Then, the equilibrium number of signatories of the linked agreement may be larger than the equilibrium number of signatories of the agreement affected by strong incentives to free ride (Carraro and Siniscalco 1995). Of course, this depends on the relative economic weights of the two agreements and on their nature. In particular,

---

[18] This section is based on the results contained in Carraro and Marchiori (2004).

to be successful, an agreement concerning a public good should be linked to an agreement concerning a quasi-club good.

Let us consider an example. Suppose the environmental negotiation is linked to the negotiation on R&D cooperation,[19] which involves an excludable positive externality (club good) and increases the joint coalition welfare. In this way, the incentive to free ride on the benefit of a cleaner environment (which is a public good fully appropriable by all countries) may be offset by the incentive to appropriate the benefit stemming from the positive R&D externality (which is a club good fully appropriable only by the signatories). The latter incentive can stabilise the joint agreement, thus also increasing its profitability because countries can reap both the R&D cooperation and the environmental benefit (this second benefit would be lost without the linkage).[20]

This idea is exploited in Carraro and Siniscalco (1995, 1997), Katsoulacos (1997), and Botteon and Carraro (1997b). Carraro and Siniscalco (1995, 1997) show that issue linkage may be a powerful tool to increase the number of signatories of an environmental agreement. For example, if developed countries on the one hand increase their financial and technological cooperation with developing countries and on the other hand make this cooperation conditional on the achievement of given environmental targets, then several countries are likely to be induced to join the environmental coalition (i.e., to sign a treaty in which they commit themselves to adequate reductions in their emission growth). Katsoulacos (1997), who accounts for information asymmetries, provides additional support to the conclusion that issue linkage can be very effective in guaranteeing the stability of an environmental agreement. By contrast, Botteon and Carraro (1998), in which asymmetric players are also considered, show that issue linkage may be counterproductive because of potential conflicts among asymmetric players on the "optimal" number of members of the R&D club.

All the aforementioned papers assume that issue linkage has been chosen by, or imposed upon, the negotiating countries.[21] Given this assumption, these papers analyse the effectiveness of issue linkage in increasing the equilibrium number of signatories of the joint agreement (with respect to the environmental agreement). However, the decision of linking two economic issues should also be considered as a strategic choice that players make. A game therefore describes the incentives to link two issues. This game could also be characterised by free riding. Hence, even if issue linkage increases the number of signatories – and therefore the amount of public good provided (e.g., emission abatement) – it may not be an equilibrium outcome. The crucial question is therefore the following: Do players have an incentive to link the negotiations on two different issues instead of negotiating on the two issues separately? Namely, is the choice of issue linkage an equilibrium of the game in which players decide noncooperatively whether or not to link the negotiations on two different economic issues?

To answer these questions, let us consider a game in which, in the first stage, players decide whether to link two issues on which they are trying to reach an

---

[19] See Carraro and Siniscalco (1997) for a full presentation of the model.

[20] An interesting exception is the paper by Tol, Lise, and van der Zwaan (1999).

[21] An interesting exception is the paper by Tol et al. (1999).

agreement or to negotiate on two separate agreements. If they decide not to link the two issues, in the second stage, they can decide whether to sign either one or both separate agreements. If they decide in favour of issue linkage, in the second stage, they decide whether to sign the linked agreement. Finally, in the third stage, they set the value of their policy variables (e.g., emission targets).

Let us assume again that the choice of the rule must be taken under unanimity voting. The choice of issue linkage precedes the beginning of actual negotiations and therefore should be taken with the consensus of all countries involved in the negotiations. Let c_u^* denote the equilibrium number of players who sign the linked agreement (i.e., when issue linkage is chosen in the first stage of the game). Then $P_u(c_u^*)$ is their equilibrium payoff. The remaining $n - c_u^*$ players are the free-riders of the linked agreement. Their equilibrium payoff is $Q_u(c_u^*)$.

If linkage is not adopted, we have two agreements. Let "a" identify the agreement whose benefits are not excludable (e.g., the environmental agreement), whereas "t" identifies the agreement with (partly) excludable benefits (e.g., the agreement on technological cooperation). Then, let c_a^* be the equilibrium number of players who sign the public good agreement, or "a-agreement," whereas c_t^* is the equilibrium number of signatories of the quasi-club good agreement, or "t-agreement." $P_a(c_a^*)$ is the equilibrium payoff of the former, whereas $P_t(c_t^*)$ is the equilibrium payoff of the latter. Finally, free-riders of the "a-agreement" obtain a payoff equal to $Q_a(c_a^*)$, whereas free-riders of the "t-agreement" obtain $Q_t(c_t^*)$.

For simplicity, let us assume that $P_u(c) = P_a(c) + P_t(c), \forall c$ and $Q_u(c) = Q_a(c) + Q_t(c), \forall c$. Hence, the payoff that can be obtained from linking the two agreements is equal to the sum of the payoffs of the two individual agreements, both for cooperators in the joint agreement and for its free-riders.

As just noted, c_u^* denotes the size of the equilibrium coalition when issue linkage is adopted. Given the preceding assumptions and the definition of profitable and stable coalition previously given, c_u^* is an equilibrium if

$$P_a(c_u^*) + P_t(c_u^*) \geq P_a(0) + P_t(0) \tag{12.7a}$$

$$P_a(c_u^*) + P_t(c_u^*) \geq Q_a(c_u^* - 1) + Q_t(c_u^* - 1) \tag{12.7b}$$

$$P_a(c_u^* + 1) + P_t(c_u^* + 1) < Q_a(c_u^*) + Q_t(c_u^*). \tag{12.7c}$$

From inequality (12.7a) it is clear that, if the two separate agreements are profitable, then the linked agreement is also profitable. However, a linked agreement may be profitable to all players even when the two separate agreements are profitable only to a fraction of the n players of the game (two different fractions for the two agreements). This is why, as just explained, issue linkage has been proposed to solve the profitability problem (cf. Cesar and De Zeeuw 1996).

Let us define the structure and the payoffs of the linkage game. If players decide to link the two issues and negotiate on a joint agreement, the equilibrium payoffs are

$$P_u(c_u^*) = P_a(c_u^*) + P_t(c_u^*) \text{ for a signatory of linked agreement;} \tag{12.8a}$$

$$P_u(c_u^*) = P_a(c_u^*) + P_t(c_u^*) \text{ for a free-rider.} \tag{12.8b}$$

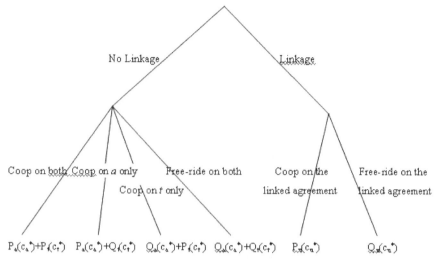

Figure 12.2: The structure of the game with endogenous issue linkage.

If, instead, players prefer not to link the two issues, they decide whether to participate in two different agreements. In this case, they obtain the following at the equilibrium:

$$P_a(c_a^*) + P_t(c_t^*) \text{ if they decide to cooperate on both issues;} \qquad (12.9a)$$

$$P_a(c_a^*) + Q_t(c_t^*) \quad \begin{aligned} &\text{if they cooperate in the ``a-agreement''} \\ &\text{(the public good agreement), but they free ride} \\ &\text{on the ``t-agreement'' (the club good agreement);} \end{aligned} \qquad (12.9b)$$

$$Q_a(c_a^*) + P_t(c_t^*) \quad \begin{aligned} &\text{if they cooperate in the ``t-agreement''} \\ &\text{but free ride on the other issue;} \end{aligned} \qquad (12.9c)$$

$$Q_a(c_a^*) + Q_t(c_t^*) \text{ if they free ride on both issues.} \qquad (12.9d)$$

Hence, without linkage, there are four "types" of countries, where the identity of countries is irrelevant because of symmetry. The structure of the linkage game and its payoffs are summarised in Figure 12.2.

Recall that decisions in the first stage of the game – the "constitutional" stage in which countries decide whether or not to adopt "issue linkage" – are taken with the unanimous consensus of all countries. As a consequence, all players, whatever their role, must be better off with "issue linkage" than without "issue linkage." Given monotonicity, this is the case if $P_u(c_u^*) \geq Q_a(c_a^*) + Q_t(c_t^*)$ (see Figure 12.2). This condition can also be written as

$$P_a(c_u^*) - Q_a(c_a^*) > Q_t(c_t^*) - P_t(c_u^*). \qquad (12.10)$$

How can condition (12.10) be interpreted? The right-hand side, $Q_t(c_t^*) - P_t(c_u^*)$, is the loss from reducing the coalition on the "t-agreement" from c_t^* to c_u^* (Carraro and Marchiori 2004 show that $c_t^* > c_u^*$). Notice that $Q_t(c_t^*) - P_t(c_u^*) > 0$, because it is equal to $[Q_t(c_t^*) - P_t(c_t^*)] + [P_t(c_t^*) - P_t(c_u^*)]$, where $[Q_t(c_t^*) - P_t(c_t^*)] > 0$ and $[P_t(c_t^*) - P_t(c_u^*)] > 0$, if $c_t^* > c_u^*$ and if $P_t(c_t)$ is monotonic.

The left-hand side, $P_a(c_u^*) - Q_a(c_a^*)$, is the environmental benefit that a free-rider on the "*a*-agreement" achieves when joining the expanded coalition. It can also be written as $[P_a(c_u^*) - P_a(c_a^*)] - [Q_a(c_a^*) - P_a(c_a^*)]$, where $[P_a(c_u^*) - P_a(c_a^*)]$ is the increased gain a cooperator on the "*a*-agreement" achieves from expanding the coalition, whereas $[Q_a(c_a^*) - P_a(c_a^*)]$ is a free-rider's relative gain when a coalition c_a^* forms.

The positivity of $Q_t(c_t^*) - P_t(c_u^*)$ implies that (12.10) holds if $P_a(c_u^*) - Q_a(c_a^*)$ is also positive, that is, if the increased gain that a cooperator on the "*a*-agreement" achieves from expanding the coalition is larger than a free-rider's relative gain when a coalition c_a^* forms.

This is only a necessary condition. The sufficient condition says that a free-rider on the public good agreement who enters the coalition on the linked agreement must not only increase his or her payoff, but this positive change must be larger than the loss a player might suffer because the club good coalition becomes smaller.

As a consequence, when proposing or advocating issue linkage, policy makers must be careful in assessing two crucial elements. The first crucial element is the relative change of the coalition sizes $c_u^* - c_a^*$ and $c_t^* - c_u^*$. The larger $c_u^* - c_a^*$ and the smaller $c_t^* - c_u^*$, the larger the likelihood that condition (12.10) will be satisfied. The second crucial element is the relative change of the players' payoffs. The larger the increased benefits induced by a larger cooperation on the public good issue, the larger the likelihood that issue linkage will be adopted. Similarly, the smaller the loss from a reduced cooperation on the "*t*-agreement," the larger the likelihood that issue linkage will be adopted.

Notice that these conditions neglect the likely increase of transaction costs when negotiating on two linked issues. However, introducing transaction costs would be trivial. They would simply be added to the right-hand side of condition (12.10). Finally, Carraro and Marchiori (2004) show that all equilibrium conditions become less restrictive in the presence of majority voting and when the degree of excludability of technological benefits is high.

12.5. Regional versus Global Environmental Treaties

Another idea sometimes proposed to reduce the free-riding incentives that undermine the possibility of achieving a global agreement on global commons is to give negotiating countries the freedom to sign different agreements at a regional level, which is similar to the approach adopted for trade agreements (cf. Carraro 1998; Stewart and Wiener 2003). It is argued that a regional cooperative management of global commons could more easily be achieved than a global management of global commons. This may raise a trade-off between the potential greater efficiency of a global agreement, which is however unlikely to be signed, and the possibly greater incentives to sign several regional agreements.

In real environmental negotiations on global commons, the focus has always been on a single agreement. However, the situation is gradually changing, mainly because of the difficulty in achieving a global agreement on climate change. As stressed by

Eric Haites, former head of the IPCC Technical Support Unit, in a recent personal e-mail,

In substance, even though not in form, the Kyoto Protocol on climate change reflects agreements among several different coalitions. It incorporates special provisions for several different groups of countries. The Non-Annex B countries have no commitments and can benefit from emission reduction investments through the Clean Development Mechanism (CDM). The most vulnerable Non-Annex B countries can also receive financial assistance for adaptation from the levy imposed on the CDM (and possibly on the other mechanisms). The economies in transition have generally less ambitious commitments and have the flexibility to choose their base year. The European Union has the ability under Article 4 to redistribute the emissions reduction burden. Australia got a special provision on land use emissions in Article 3.7.

Similarly, Egenhofer and Legge (2001) write that "it is increasingly becoming clear, that the Kyoto Protocol is less a global agreement than a set of differing regional approaches."

Therefore, the situation that is emerging in the context of environmental agreements is similar to the one that has already developed in the case of trade agreements. Since the early 1990s, the number of regional free-trade agreements has risen to over 200. Already before the failure of Cancun, according to the OECD, the percentage of world trade accounted for by regional trade arrangements is expected to grow from 43 percent now to 55 percent in 2005, if all envisaged regional free-trade agreements are realised.

As a consequence, it would be important to explore, from a theoretical viewpoint, whether countries, once free to choose different coalitions, actually decide to sign one or several environmental treaties. Let us therefore consider the case in which countries are allowed to form as many coalitions as they prefer. This is equivalent to assuming that any coalition can be free ridden by nonsingleton coalitions.

If multiple coalitions can form, then the outcome of the game is a coalition structure $\pi = \{c_1, \ldots, c_m\}$. However, the determination of the equilibrium coalition structure is not as easy as in the previous sections for several reasons. First, in a coalition game with externalities, the worth of any coalition depends on the behaviour of the complement set. In a single coalition game, free-riders can behave solely as singletons and thus the worth of the lone coalition is easily computable and the stability of a coalition structure coincides with the stability of the lone coalition. By contrast, in a multiple coalition game the complement-set behaviour can be defined in several different ways. As a consequence, a coalition does not have a unique worth, and any notion of stability cannot simply be referred to a coalition but must take into account the whole coalition structure to which such a coalition belongs. Second, the feasible coalition structures increase significantly when the number of players increases.

For these reasons, we restrict ourselves to one illustrative case in which decisions are taken simultaneously with open membership.[22] Therefore, the equilibrium

---

[22] We are not going to discuss the exclusive membership rule because it is relevant only when the payoff function is hump-shaped – a case that does not add much to the understanding of the formation of multiple coalitions. We are not going to discuss the coalition unanimity rule because it leads trivially to the grand coalition if the profitability condition is satisfied. For the same reason, we do not discuss the case of circular sequential moves.

structure will be identified by a stability condition (see below) which corresponds, as in previous sections, to the Nash equilibrium of the coalition game. We do not consider other solution concepts, such as those proposed by Bloch (1996), Ray and Vohra (1997, 1999), Chew (1994), and Mariotti (1997), that make use of either some forms of commitment or some forms of forward-looking behaviour.

Let us start by extending the definitions provided for the single coalition case to the case in which multiple coalitions can form.

Positive Spillovers. In any coalition structure, if coalitions merge to form a larger coalition, other coalitions not affected by the change are better off. Formally, consider two coalition structures π and π' and a coalition c_i such that $c_i \in \pi$, $c_i' \in \pi$, c_j, $c_k \in \pi'$, and $c_j \cup c_k \in \pi$. Then, $p(c_i; \pi) > p(c_i; \pi')$ for all players belonging to c_i.

Hence, the partition function is such that the payoff of a player belonging to a given coalition c_i is larger the larger the size and the lower the number of coalitions formed by players not belonging to c_i. This has an important implication. When players who do not join c_i decide to behave as singletons, they give rise to the worst possible complement structure for the coalition c_i (i.e., the minimax one). The single coalition game thus constitutes a benchmark for the multiple coalition one. For any fixed coalition size, the single coalition structure defines the minimum worth such a coalition can obtain.

Free Riding. In any coalition structure, small coalitions have higher per-member payoffs than big coalitions. Formally, for any coalition structure and any two coalitions c_i and c_k in π, $p(c_i; \pi) < p(c_k; \pi)$ if and only if $c_i > c_k$.

As in previous sections, let us assume monotonicity (an increase of cooperators increases the payoff of all players).

Profitability. A coalition structure π is profitable if any coalition c_i in π is profitable. A coalition $c_i \in \pi$ is profitable if any cooperating player belonging to c_i gets a payoff larger than the one he or she would get in the singleton structure. Formally, $p(c_i; \pi) \geq p(1; \pi^S)$ for all players in the coalition c_i and all coalitions in π.

Let us recall that the payoff of a player belonging to c_i increases with the size of the other coalitions in π, which provide positive spillovers. Geometrically, this implies that the payoff function in the multiple coalition case is shifted upward by the presence of more than one nontrivial coalition. Hence, the following conclusions are straightforward:

- If a coalition is profitable in the single coalition game, it is profitable in the multiple coalition game as well.
- If c^m denotes the minimal coalition size above which a coalition becomes profitable in a single coalition game, then this minimal size becomes equal or smaller in a multiple coalition game with more than one nontrivial coalition.

Let us also characterise the equilibrium of the game by extending the notion of Nash stability previously provided to the case of multiple coalitions. The internal and external stability conditions of Section 12.3 are again necessary conditions because it is still possible for any cooperating player to deviate to form a singleton and for a singleton to join a coalition. However, these two conditions are no longer sufficient to characterise the equilibrium coalition structure. With multiple coalitions, players choose both whether to join a coalition (as in the single coalition game) and which coalition to join. This is why a further stability condition on the entire coalition structure has to be added. We call this latter condition "intracoalition stability." Therefore:

Stability. A multiple coalition structure π is stable if each coalition $c_i \in \pi$ is internally stable, externally stable, and intracoalition stable. It is *internally stable* if no cooperating player would be better off by leaving the coalition to form a singleton. Formally, $p(c_i; \pi) \geq p(1; \pi')$ for all players in the coalition c_i and all coalitions in π, where $\pi' = \pi \setminus \{c_i\} \cup \{c_i - 1, 1\}$. It is *externally stable* if no singleton would be better off by joining any coalition belonging to the coalition structure π. Formally, $p(1; \pi) \geq p(c_i; \pi')$ for all players who do not belong to c_i or to any other nontrivial coalition in π, where $\pi' = \pi \setminus \{c_i, 1\} \cup \{c_i + 1\}$. It is *intracoalition stable* if no player belonging to c_i would be better off by leaving c_i to join any other coalition $c_j \in \pi$. Formally, $p(c_i; \pi) \geq p(c_j + 1; \pi')$ for all players in the coalition c_i and all coalitions in π, where $\pi' = \pi \setminus \{c_i, 1\} \cup \{c_i + 1\}$.

Suppose there is one coalition. Then a second coalition forms. Players in the first coalition receive a benefit (more abatement), but a benefit is also received by those players who do not join any coalition and keep enjoying a cleaner environment without cooperating on emission abatement. Will players in the first coalition continue to cooperate or will they free ride? There is a case in which the answer is easy. If there is no leakage (i.e., a country's best-reply functions are orthogonal), then cooperators in the first coalition and free-riders receive the same benefit from the second coalition abatement. Moreover, this benefit is additive, that is, it is possible to write the payoff of each player in the game as the payoff resulting from his or her choice of joining (or not joining) a coalition c_i plus the benefit (positive externality) produced by the other coalitions in π. In the sequel, we will focus on the no-leakage case (orthogonal free-riding), which helps to clarify the mechanism of multiple coalition formation.

Let us normalise to zero the noncooperative payoff $p(1, \pi^S)$. In the absence of leakage, it is then possible to write a player's payoff function as $p(c_i; \pi) = P(c_i) + \sum_{j \neq i} Q(c_j)$, where the index j denotes all coalitions belonging to the coalition structure π other than c_i. In words, a player in c_i achieves his or her cooperative payoff plus the payoff from free riding on the other coalitions that may form. In the case in which only two coalitions c_i and c_k form, the payoff would be $p(c_i; \pi) = P(c_i) + Q(c_k)$. From the definition of free riding, $p(c_i; \pi) \leq p(c_k; \pi)$ if and only if $c_i \geq c_k$. Hence, $P(c_i) + Q(c_k) \leq P(c_k) + Q(c_i)$, that is,

$$P(c_i) - P(c_k) \leq Q(c_i) - Q(c_k). \tag{12.11}$$

This is equivalent to saying that a player who moves to a larger coalition increases his or her payoff (by monotonicity) but the incremental benefit is lower than the incremental gain this player would achieve by free riding on the larger coalition.

Moreover, the case of orthogonal free-riding enables us to determine the stability function for a given coalition c_i belonging to π. If a player leaves a coalition c_i to be a singleton, he or she compares $p(c_i; \pi)$ and $p(1; \pi')$, $\pi = \pi \setminus c_i \cup (1, c_i - 1)$, where

$$p(c_i; \pi) - p(1; \pi') = \left[P(c_i) + \sum_{j \neq i} Q(c_j) \right] - \left[Q(c_i - 1) + \sum_{j \neq i} Q(c_j) \right]$$

$$= P(c_i) - Q(c_i - 1) \equiv L(c_i).$$

If $L(c_i)$ is nonnegative, no player would like to leave the coalition to be a singleton. In addition, if $L(c_i + 1)$ is nonpositive, no singleton would like to join the coalition c_i. If a player leaves a coalition c_i to join a different coalition c_k, he or she compares $p(c_i; \pi)$ and $p(c_k + 1; \pi'')$, $\pi'' = \pi \setminus c_i, c_k \cup (c_i - 1, c_k + 1)$, where

$$p(c_i; \pi) - p(c_k + 1; \pi'') = \left[P(c_i) + \sum_{j \neq i} Q(c_j) \right]$$

$$- \left[P(c_k + 1) + Q(c_i - 1) + \sum_{j \neq i, j \neq k} Q(c_j) \right]$$

$$= P(c_i) - P(c_k + 1) + Q(c_k) - Q(c_i - 1)$$

$$= L(c_i) - L(c_k + 1). \tag{12.12}$$

First, notice that $L(c_i) \geq 0$ is no longer a sufficient condition for the absence of free riding. Indeed, $p(c_i; \pi) - p(c_k + 1; \pi'')$ can be negative even when $L(c_i)$ is positive. Second, by definition of free riding, a rational player decides to leave c_i to join c_k only if $c_k < c_i$, which implies $c_k + 1 < c_i$. Hence, $p(c_i; \pi) - p(c_k + 1; \pi'') = L(c_i) - L(c_k + 1) \leq 0$ because the function $L(.)$ is decreasing when free riding is orthogonal. Hence, intracoalition stability is achieved only when $L(c_i) = L(c_k + 1)$, which implies $c_i = c_k + 1$. Therefore, at equilibrium, coalition sizes can differ by at most one player.

We can therefore conclude that a profitable and stable coalition structure must satisfy the following restrictions:

- it contains only coalitions whose size is smaller than or equal to c* (internal stability);
- it cannot simultaneously contain a singleton and a coalition smaller than c* (external stability);
- coalition sizes differ by at most one player (intracoalition stability), that is, at most two types of coalitions emerge at equilibrium.

These remarks lead to the following proposition (assumptions are not repeated for brevity):

Proposition 12.3. *The stable coalition structures of a simultaneous multiple coalition game with Nash conjectures and open membership are*

- $\pi^S = \{1_n\}$ *that is, the singleton structure, when* $c^m > c^*$
- $\pi^* = \{c^x_{(q)}(c^x - 1)_{(p)}\}$ *when* $c^m \leq c^*$

with $c^x \leq c^*$, *where p and q are two integers such that* $c^x q + (c^x - 1)p = n$.

Proof. See Carraro and Moriconi (1998). ■

For example, with four players, two size-2 coalitions form (unless $c^* = 4$, in which case there is only the grand coalition). If $c^* = 3$, a size-3 coalition could form. However, $P(c^*)$ – the payoff of a player in a size-3 coalition – is not larger than $P(c^* - 1) + Q(c^* - 1)$, the payoff of a player in a size-2 coalition when a second size-2 coalition forms. Indeed, $P(c^*) - Q(c^* - 1) \leq P(c^* - 1)$; that is, $L(c^*) \leq P(c^* - 1)$ because $L(c^*) \approx 0$ by definition of a stable coalition and $P(c^* - 1) > 0$ by profitability. If $c^* = 2$, the conclusion that two size-2 coalitions form follows immediately.

With five players, if $c^* = 5$, then the grand coalition forms. If $c^* = 4$, a size-3 and a size-2 coalition form. Indeed, if the argument just presented is used, $P(c^*) \leq P(c^* - 2) + Q(c^* - 1)$, where the left-hand side denotes the payoff a player achieves by leaving c^* and forming a size-2 coalition. This is larger than $Q(c^* - 1)$, the payoff a player achieves by leaving c^* and behaving as a singleton. If $c^* = 3$, again a size-3 and a size-2 coalition form. Indeed, $P(c^*) + Q(c^* - 1)$ – the payoff a player achieves when he or she belongs to a size-3 coalition and another size-2 coalition forms – is not lower than $Q(c^* - 1) + Q(c^* - 1)$, the payoff he or she would achieve by free riding on two size-2 coalitions (of course, it does not make sense to leave a size-3 coalition to join a size-2 coalition that then is formed by three players).

With six players, if $c^* = 6$, the grand coalition forms. If $c^* = 5$, $\{4, 2\}$ is preferred to $\{5, 1\}$ because $P(c^*) \leq P(c^* - 3) + Q(c^* - 1)$, that is, it is more profitable to form a small coalition and free ride on the larger one. However, the equilibrium is not $\{4, 2\}$. Indeed, by (12.12), a player in the size-4 coalition prefers to leave and join the size-2 coalition. We have that $P(c^* - 1) + Q(c^* - 3)$ – the payoff a player achieves in the size-4 coalition – cannot be larger than $P(c^* - 2) + Q(c^* - 2)$, the payoff he or she achieves by moving to the size-2 coalition. Indeed, $P(c^* - 1) + Q(c^* - 3) \leq P(c^* - 2) + Q(c^* - 2)$, that is, $P(c^* - 1) - P(c^* - 2) \leq Q(c^* - 2) - Q(c^* - 3)$. Moreover, there is no incentive to free ride on two size-3 and size-2 coalitions, that is, the structure $\{3, 2, 1\}$ is not an equilibrium because $P(c^* - 2) + Q(c^* - 2) \geq Q(c^* - 3) + Q(c^* - 2)$ by definition of c^*. Hence, the structure $\{3, 3\}$ is an equilibrium of the coalition game. However, this is not the only equilibrium because the structure $\{2, 2, 2\}$ can be shown to be an equilibrium as well. If $c^* = 4$, again $\{4, 2\}$ is not an equilibrium because $P(c^*) \leq P(c^* - 2) + Q(c^* - 1) \leq P(c^* - 1) + Q(c^* - 1)$. Hence, $\{3, 3\}$ is again an equilibrium of the coalition game. It can be shown that $\{2, 2, 2\}$ is also an equilibrium. Finally, if $2 \leq c^* \leq 3$, the application of Proposition 12.3 is straightforward. Two equilibrium structures exist (i.e., either three size-2 coalitions or two size-3 coalitions can emerge at the equilibrium).

When the number of players is larger than six, a similar analysis confirms the conclusions of Proposition 12.3. For example, if $n = 7$ and $c^* = 4$, then the NE coalition structures can be $\{4, 3\}$ and $\{3, 2, 2\}$. If $n = 8$, and $c^* = 7$, the NE coalition structures are $\{4, 4\}$, $\{3, 3, 2\}$, $\{2, 2, 2, 2\}$. This multiplicity of equilibria can be reduced by moving to a sequential order of moves or by using the coalition-proof Nash equilibrium concept.

The intuition behind Proposition 12.3 could be phrased as follows. A player prefers to free ride cooperatively rather than as a singleton if the coalition he or she joins is not larger than c^*. In this case, the player gets the double benefit of free riding on the other coalition's abatement and of cooperating with a small number of players. By definition of c^*, this second benefit is larger than the gain from free riding as a singleton.

The theoretical conclusion is therefore consistent with the observed dynamics of environmental and trade negotiations. An increasing number of regional agreements have been signed to enhance trade cooperation. Similarly, the difficulty of achieving an agreement on climate change control has stimulated the emergence of regional climate blocs and of subgroups of countries that, for economic or political reasons, have common environmental interests (e.g., the EU bubble, the Umbrella group, or the AOSIS). The results of this section suggest that this is the right direction to foster environmental cooperation and to manage global commons better in the absence of a supranational authority that can enforce an environmental regulation. In a recent paper, Buchner and Carraro (2003) apply the theoretical framework developed in this section to assess which coalition structure is most likely to emerge out of future negotiations on climate change control. By using a simple empirical integrated assessment model based on a Ramsey-type growth model, they analyse the incentives for the different world countries to sign either a single climate agreement or several regional agreements. Their main conclusion can be phrased as follows. A global agreement is the preferred output only for China and developing countries. The other negotiating countries, except the United States, prefer fragmented coalition structures in which climate blocs form. The United States, which presently does not participate in the Kyoto Protocol, is more likely to adopt unilateral policies than to join a coalition to control greenhouse gas emissions. Therefore, for the United States, the incentives to free ride seem to prevail. However, it is unlikely that, at least in the medium run, the United States will keep rejecting any form of cooperation on climate change control. If the United States decides to cooperate, the climate regime that provides the highest incentives to the cooperating countries is the one in which China and the United States cooperate bilaterally and the current Annex B countries remain within the Kyoto framework. Therefore, a two-bloc climate regime would emerge: on the one hand, a coalition formed by the United States and China, and on the other hand a coalition formed by the European Union, Japan, Russia and the other remaining Annex B countries.

Note that these conclusions are consistent with the theoretical results proposed in this section notwithstanding the presence in the empirical model of relevant economic asymmetries across the negotiating countries.[23]

---

[23] A similar analysis is also in Bosello et al. (2003), where the effect of different burden-sharing rules on the coalition size is analysed.

12.6. Conclusions

The main results presented in this chapter can be summarised as follows. In Section 12.2, we provided a brief overview of the effects of different institution designs on the possibility of achieving an effective cooperative management of global commons. Using a noncooperative, game-theoretic approach, we suggested that institutions matter and that different rules modify the incentives to sign a cooperative agreement to control polluting emissions or the use of natural resources. In particular, there exist rules (e.g., coalition unanimity) that can support a large participation in an international agreement to manage global commons.

The next issue that we addressed was therefore whether there are incentives to adopt these rules, that is, under what conditions countries are likely to adopt rules that offset their free-riding incentives. This chapter has analysed some of these possible rules and the related incentives to adopt them. In particular, as far as coalition unanimity is concerned, we showed that all countries find it profitable to reduce their freedom by introducing a minimum participation level that limits free riding, thus inducing countries to form a larger equilibrium coalition. In many cases, the minimum participation constraint is such as to require that all countries sign the agreement for it to come into force. Therefore, in these case, coalition unanimity is endogenously chosen by the negotiating countries even in the presence of strong free-riding incentives.

We also analysed the incentives to link negotiations on global commons to other economic negotiations. Our results highlighted under what conditions it is profitable for all countries to agree on the linkage of two different negotiations in a way that increases the number of signatories of the agreement on global commons.

Finally, we discussed the incentives to sign an environmental agreement when countries are free to choose whether to participate in a single global agreement or in several regional agreements. The answer is that incentives lead countries to form several agreements (coalitions). Therefore, unless there is evidence that several regional agreements are largely less environmentally effective than a single, often partial agreement, policy makers should design the rules of negotiations on global commons in a way that allows the formation of several environmental blocs.

BIBLIOGRAPHY

[1] Barrett, S. (1994), "Self-Enforcing International Environmental Agreements," *Oxford Economic Papers* 46, 878–894.

[2] Barrett, S. (1997a), "Heterogeneous International Environmental Agreements," in C. Carraro (ed.), *International Environmental Agreements: Strategic Policy Issues*, Cheltenham: E. Elgar.

[3] Barrett, S. (1997b), "Towards a Theory of International Cooperation" in C. Carraro and D. Siniscalco (eds.), *New Directions in the Economic Theory of the Environment*, Cambridge, UK: Cambridge University Press.

[4] Barrett, S. (1997c), "The Strategy of Trade Sanctions in International Environmental Agreements," *Resources and Energy Economics* 19(4), 345–361.

[5] Barrett, S. (2002), *Environment and Statecraft*, Oxford University Press.

[6] Black, J., M. D. Levi, and D. de Meza (1992), "Creating a Good Atmosphere. Minimum Participation for Tackling the Greenhouse Effect," *Economica* 60, 281–293.

[7] Bloch, F. (1995), "Endogenous Structures of Association in Oligopoly," *RAND Journal of Economics* 26, 537–556.

[8] Bloch, F. (1996), "Sequential Formation of Coalitions in Games with Fixed Payoff Division," *Games and Economic Behavior* 14, 537–556.

[9] Bloch, F. (1997), "Noncooperative Models of Coalition Formation in Games with Spillovers," in C. Carraro and D. Siniscalco (eds.), *New Directions in the Economic Theory of the Environment*, Cambridge, UK: Cambridge University Press.

[10] Bosello, F., B. Buchner, and C. Carraro (2003), "Equity, Development and Climate Change Control," *Journal of the European Economic Association* 2–3, 601–611.

[11] Botteon, M. and C. Carraro (1997a), "Burden-Sharing and Coalition Stability in Environmental Negotiations with Asymmetric Countries," in C. Carraro (ed.), *International Environmental Agreements: Strategic Policy Issues*, Cheltenham: E. Elgar.

[12] Botteon, M. and C. Carraro (1997b), "Strategies for Environmental Negotiations: Issue Linkage with Heterogeneous Countries," in H. Folmer and N. Hanley (eds.), *Game Theory and the Global Environment*, Cheltenham: E. Elgar.

[13] Buchner, B. and Carraro, C. (2003), "Emissions Trading Regimes and Incentives to Participation in International Present Climate Agreements," FEEM Working Paper 104.03, Milan.

[14] Carraro, C. (1997a) (ed.), *International Environmental Agreements: Strategic Policy Issues*, Cheltenham: E. Elgar.

[15] Carraro, C. (1997b), "Environmental Conflict, Bargaining and Cooperation" in J. van den Bergh (ed.), *Handbook of Natural Resources and the Environment*, Cheltenham: E. Elgar.

[16] Carraro C. (1998), "Beyond Kyoto: A Game-Theoretic Perspective," paper presented at the: "OECD Experts Workshop on Climate Change and Economic Modeling: Background Analysis for the Kyoto Protocol," Paris, September 17–18, 1998.

[17] Carraro, C. (2000), "Roads towards International Environmental Agreements," in H. Siebert (ed.), *The Economics of International Environmental Problems*, Tübingen: Mohr Siebeck.

[18] Carraro, C. (2002) (ed.), *Governing the Global Environment*, Cheltenham: E. Elgar.

[19] Carraro, C. and M. Galeotti (2003), "The Future Evolution of the Kyoto Protocol. Costs, Benefits, Incentives to Ratification and New International Regimes," in C. Carraro and C. Egenhofer (eds.), *Firms, Governments and Climate Policy: Incentive-Based Policies for Long-Term Climate Change*, Cheltenham: Edward Elgar.

[20] Carraro, C. and C. Marchiori (2003), "Stable Coalitions," in C. Carraro (ed.), *The Endogenous Formation of Economic Coalitions*, Cheltenham: Edward Elgar.

[21] Carraro, C. and C. Marchiori (2004), "Endogenous Strategic Issue Linkage in International Negotiations," in C. Carraro and V. Fragnelli (eds.), *Game Practice and the Environment*, Cheltenham: Edward Elgar.

[22] Carraro, C., C. Marchiori, and S. Oreffice (2001), "Endogenous Minimum Participation in International Environmental Treaties," Working paper presented at first EAERE-FEEM-VIU Summer School on Environmental Economics, Venice, 1–7 July, 2001 and at the Harvard Kennedy School of Government, Boston, 8 October 2003.

[23] Carraro, C. and F. Moriconi (1998), "Endogenous Formation of Environmental Coalitions," presented at the Coalition Theory Network Workshop on "Coalition Formation: Applications to Economic Issues," Venice, 8 October 1998.

[24] Carraro, C., F. Moriconi, and S. Oreffice (1999), "Rules and Equilibrium Endogenous Coalitions," presented at the 4th CTN Workshop on "Coalition Formation," Aix en Provence, 8–10 January 1999 and at the EAERE Annual Conference, Oslo, 24–26 June 1999.

[25] Carraro, C. and D. Siniscalco (1992), "The International Protection of the Environment: Voluntary Agreements among Sovereign Countries," in P. Dasgupta and K.G. Maler (eds.), *The Economics of Transnational Commons*, Oxford: Clarendon Press.

[26] Carraro, C. and D. Siniscalco (1993), "Strategies for the International Protection of the Environment," *Journal of Public Economics* 52, 309–328.

[27] Carraro, C. and D. Siniscalco (1995), "Policy Coordination for Sustainability: Commitments, Transfers, and Linked Negotiations," in I. Goldin and A. Winters (eds.), *The Economics of Sustainable Development*, Cambridge, UK: Cambridge University Press.

[28] Carraro, C. and D. Siniscalco (1997), "R&D Cooperation and the Stability of International Environmental Agreements," in C. Carraro (ed.), *International Environmental Agreements: Strategic Policy Issues*, Cheltenham: E. Elgar.

[29] Carraro, C. and D. Siniscalco (1998), "International Environmental Agreements. Incentives and Political Economy," *European Economic Review* 42, 561–572.

[30] Cesar, H. and A. De Zeeuw (1996), "Issue Linkage in Global Environmental Problems," in A. Xepapadeas (ed.), *Economic Policy for the Environment and Natural Resources*, Cheltenham: E. Elgar.

[31] Chander, P. and H. Tulkens (1995), "A Core-Theoretical Solution for the Design of Cooperative Agreements on Trans-Frontier Pollution," *International Tax and Public Finance* 2, 279–294.

[32] Chander, P. and H. Tulkens (1997), "The Core of an Economy with Multilateral Environmental Externalities," *International Journal of Game Theory* 26, 379–401.

[33] Chew, M. S. (1994), "Farsighted Coalitional Stability," *Journal of Economic Theory* 54, 299–325.

[34] D'Aspremont, C. A. and J. J. Gabszewicz (1986), "On the Stability of Collusion," in G. F. Matthewson and J. E. Stiglitz, eds., *New Developments in the Analysis of Market Structure*, MacMillan Press, New York, 243–264.

[35] D'Aspremont, C. A., A. Jacquemin, J. J. Gabszewicz, and J. Weymark (1983), "On the Stability of Collusive Price Leadership," *Canadian Journal of Economics* 16, 17–25.

[36] Donsimoni, M. P., N. S. Economides and H. M. Polemarchakis (1986), "Stable Cartels," *International Economic Review* 27, 317–327.

[37] Egenhofer, C. and T. Legge (2001), "After Marrakech: The Regionalisation of the Kyoto Protocol," CEPS Commentary, Brussels.

[38] Eyckmans, J. and H. Tulkens, (2001), "Simulating Coalitionally Stable Burden Sharing Agreements for the Climate Change Problem," *Resource and Energy Economics*, forthcoming.

[39] Finus, M. (2002), "Stability and Design of International Environmental Agreements: The Case of Global and Transboundary Pollution," in H. Folmer and T. Tietenberg (eds.), *International Yearbook of Environmental and Resource Economics, 2002/3*, Cheltenham: Edward Elgar.

[40] Finus, M. and B. Rundshagen (2003), "Endogenous Coalition Formation in Global Pollution Control: A Partition Function Approach," in C. Carraro (ed.), *The Endogenous Formation of Economic Coalitions*, Cheltenham: Edward Elgar.

[41] Folmer, H., P. van Mouche, and S. Ragland (1993), "Interconnected Games and International Environmental Problems," *Environmental Resource Economics* 3, 313–335.

[42] Hardin, G. and J. Baden (1977), *Managing the Commons*, New York: Freeman and Co.

[43] Hart, S. and M. Kurz (1983), "Endogenous Formation of Coalitions," *Econometrica* 51, 1047–1064.

[44] Heal, G. (1994), "The Formation of Environmental Coalitions," in C. Carraro (ed.), *Trade, Innovation, Environment*, Dordrecht: Kluwer Academic Publisher.

[45] Hoel, M. (1991), "Global Environmental Problems: The Effects of Unilateral Actions Taken by One Country," *Journal of Environmental Economics and Management* 20, 1, 55–70.

[46] Hoel, M. (1992), "International Environmental Conventions: The Case of Uniform Reductions of Emissions," *Environmental and Resource Economics* 2, 141–159.

[47] Hoel, M. (1994), "Efficient Climate Policy in the Presence of Free-Riders," *Journal of Environmental Economics and Management* 27, 259–274.

[48] Katsoulacos, Y. (1997), "R&D Spillovers, R&D Cooperation, Innovation and International Environmental Agreements," in C. Carraro (ed.), *International Environmental Agreements: Strategic Policy Issues*, Cheltenham: E. Elgar.

[49] Mariotti, M. (1997), "A Model of Agreements in Strategic Form Games," *Journal of Economic Theory* 73, 128–139.

[50] Mohr, E. (1995), "International Environmental Permits Trade and Debt: The Consequences of Country Sovereignty and Cross Default Policies," *Review of International Economics* 1, 1–19.

[51] Mohr, E. and J. P. Thomas (1998), "Pooling Sovereign Risks: The Case of Environmental Treaties and International Debt," *Journal of Development Economics* 55, 173–190.

[52] Nordhaus, W. (1999), "Global Public Goods," IDEI Annual Lecture, Toulouse, 14 June 1999.

[53] OECD (1993), *The Cost of Cutting Carbon Emissions: Results from Global Models*, Paris.

[54] Ray, D. and R. Vohra (1997), "Equilibrium Binding Agreements," *Journal of Economic Theory* 73, 30–78.

[55] Ray, D. and R. Vohra (1999), "A Theory of Endogenous Coalition Structure," *Games and Economic Behavior* 26, 286–336.

[56] Rutz, S. (2001), "Minimum Participation Rules and the Effectiveness of Multilateral Environmental Agreements," Working Paper 01/22, Centre for Economic Research, SFIT, Zürich.

[57] Schotter, A. (1981), *The Economic Theory of Social Institutions*, Cambridge University Press.

[58] Stewart, R. and J. Wiener (2003), *Reconstructing Climate Policy*, Washington, DC: American Enterprise Institute Press.

[59] Tol, R., W. Lise, and B. van der Zwaan (1999), "Technology Diffusion and the Stability of Climate Coalitions," FEEM Working Paper 20.2000, Milan.

[60] Tulkens, H. (1998), "Cooperation versus Free-Riding in International Environmental Affairs: Two Approaches," in H. Folmer and N. Hanley (eds.), *Game Theory and the Global Environment*, Cheltenham: E. Elgar. Also in C. Carraro (ed.), *Governing the Global Environment*, Cheltenham: E. Elgar.

[61] Yi, S. (1997), "Stable Coalition Structures with Externalities," *Games and Economic Behavior* 20, 201–223.

[62] Yi, S. (2003), "Endogenous Formation of Economic Coalitions: A Survey on the Partition Function Approach," in C. Carraro (ed.), *The Endogenous Formation of Economic Coalitions*, Cheltenham: Edward Elgar.

[63] Yi, S. and H. Shin (1994), "Endogenous Formation of Coalition in Oligopoly: I. Theory," mimeo, Dartmouth College.

[64] Yi, S. and H. Shin (2000), "Endogenous Formation of Research Coalitions with Spillovers," *International Journal of Industrial Organization* 18, 2, 229–256.

13

Inequality and Growth Clubs

Fernando Jaramillo, Hubert Kempf, and Fabien Moizeau

13.1. Introduction

As the various chapters of this book make clear, coalition theory is extremely useful for microeconomic issues. But what about macroeconomics?

If we adhere to the methodological program of modern macroeconomics to ground its research on explicit and firm microeconomic foundations, the answer is obviously yes. Actually, there are more precise reasons to think that coalitions matter for macroeconomic issues than the rather general and vague desire to build a bridge between microeconomics and macroeconomics:

1. Institutions exist at the macroeconomic level that shape and organize the functioning of an economy. The clearest example of this is the modern central bank, which indirectly provides liquidities to the economy and plays a prudential role in the banking sector. But these institutions in turn are formed and not created by some deus ex machina. The creation of the European Monetary Union amounts to the formation of a coalition of countries willing to share monetary sovereignty, and the debates on the economic viability of the eurozone are de facto on the viability of this coalition.
2. Public goods generating externalities on a wide scale, like education and public infrastructure, exist. But these goods depend on collective financing by a set of agents, be it a nation, a region or a neighborhood. More generally, externalities matter for macroeconomics, and they depend on the clusterings of agents and firms.
3. There is such a diversity between agents that the representative agent hypothesis appears as a gross device that more and more macroeconomists tend to abandon. Recent macroeconomic models incorporate heterogeneity between agents and clusters within an economy.

We are very grateful to the editors, Alain Desdoigts, Matthew Jackson, and participants at the *2003 Coalition Theory Network* workshop in Marseille and seminar in CERGE-EI (Prague) for helpful remarks on earlier versions of this paper.

It is likely that a circular sequence exists between the clustering of agents and the macroeconomic dynamics: the fragmentation of the economy into groups (sectors, trade unions, countries, unions, etc.) affects the macroeconomy, but in turn the macroeconomic outcomes shape the grouping of agents over time. There is therefore a compelling incentive to provide an understanding on how groups form for the macroeconomic research agenda. This is fully consistent with the desire to found the macroeconomic inquiry on an explicit analysis of optimizing behaviors. Coalition theory – that is, the study of the forming of groups – is a crucial set of techniques to be added to the toolbox of macroeconomists and used to investigate macroeconomic issues. This chapter aims at offering an illustration of this by looking at growth theory with the help of some concepts developed by coalition theory. In particular, we would like to show that the formation of groups matters for understanding the growth process because these groups both exploit and generate externalities. In so doing, stylized facts about growth could be given adequate microeconomic foundations.

In a recent survey on growth, Easterly and Levine (2001) document five stylized facts:

1. Productive factor accumulation does not suffice to explain income and growth differences across nations, and there is "something else" besides quantitative accumulation that is critical for understanding these differences.
2. These differences matter over the long run, and nations do not exhibit long-run per capita output convergence.
3. Growth is not regular, and the growth dynamics are highly dissimilar and fluctuate across countries. In contrast, capital accumulation is much more persistent than overall growth.
4. Growth is related to the spatial concentration of factors with capital flowing to the richest areas.
5. National public policies matter for long-run growth rates.

A similar inquiry led Prescott (1998) to stress that the total factor productivity[1] (corresponding to Easterly and Levine's "something else") is all-important for understanding growth. But total factor productivities (TFPs) differ across countries and cannot be linked to the stock of technical knowledge. Prescott concluded that a theory of TFP was needed that could explain why countries, and more generally communities, are characterized by different growth paths.

The second stylized fact is central for us because it bears on the following questions. If communities (nations, regions, localities) are characterized by such differences in their growth trajectories over time, can these differences be linked to the structural characteristics of communities? Is there something related to a given community that explains its idiosyncratic growth process and makes it resistant to convergence? Then, if the shapes and characteristics of communities happen to

---

[1] Also known as the "Solow residual."

have such important long-term properties, how are these communities formed and sustained?

The fourth stylized fact listed by Easterly and Levine suggests a first response to this last question: there is factor mobility, and this modifies the shape of communities over time. This is the answer provided by the new economic geography when applied to growth matters (see Baldwin and Martin 2003). But this answer is partial. First, the mobility of factors itself is shaped by collective decisions of communities. This is obvious from the fifth stylized fact. Second, labor migration and capital mobility take time and communities tend to coexist for a long time before one is absorbed by another, if ever. In other words, mobility presumes long-lasting communities and we are still in need of a theoretical explanation of their formation and existence that takes into account their consequence and more generally their interaction with growth.

This chapter supports the claim that coalition theory provides us with tools that can be used to answer these questions and illuminate the crucial facts characterizing growing economies. If individual decisions linked to factor accumulation do not suffice to understand growth and growth divergences, if we are in need of a theory of total factor productivity that implicitly has a collective dimension, then coalition theory may help us to understand how clusters of agents form to collectively exploit and shape collective sources of growth that surface in the yet-residual TFP.

This chapter is organized as follows. The next two sections put to the fore the connection between *stratification* and growth. We define stratification as follows. A society is *stratified* if it is grouped into clusters of agents such that each cluster groups agents "similar" in terms of some crucial attributes. For example, a society may be spatially stratified insofar as it is formed of *neighborhoods* such as clusters of "neighbor agents," or agents "similarly" located.[2] On the theoretical side, many authors assume some forms of stratification for growth analysis, but they rarely explain endogenously the formation of groups in relation to growth. On the empirical side, many studies support the view that growth is uneven and linked to stratification. The second section explores the relationship between growth and stratification from an empirical point of view, and the third section develops some theoretical arguments on this relationship.

Then, in the fourth section we relate the formation of coalitions to the growth process, using a dynamic model with capital accumulation and an endogenous growth engine linked to total factor productivity. This source of growth, the "something else" stressed by Easterly, Levine, and Prescott, depends on collective financing by agents. However, the "frontiers" and the number of financing communities are not exogenously set but endogenously determined. It is assumed that agents freely form these communities aimed at financing a productive public good. This results in a partition of society. The different coalitions composing the partition are justified because of the specific externalities accruing to the members of each coalition: The productive public good only benefits the financing community and, as such, is a

---

[2] Wooders (1978) relates the demands for public good and stratification of society in the case of one private good – one public good dilemma and anonymous crowding.

"club good."[3] Hence, the endogenously formed communities can be considered as "growth clubs." We use some coalition theory concepts to generate these clubs and then study the consequences for the ensuing growth process in the entire society. The partition of the society into growth clubs leads to the evidence of stratification as we defined it previously. In other words, stratification results from explicit microfoundations by means of coalition formation. In the fifth section, we address the possibility that stratification may change over time. Then we show that the growth process interacts over time with the formation of communities and generates a dynamic sequence of endogenous clubs, the frontiers of which vary over time. The last section is the conclusion.

13.2. Stratification and Growth: Evidence

In this section, we motivate our study of coalition building in a growing environment by a brief survey of the empirical relationship between stratification and growth.

13.2.1. Growth and Inequality between Nations

13.2.1.1. Growth and Convergence

There is yet no consensus among economists about the determinants of long-term growth. Over the recent past, the main controversy about economic growth has been between the advocates of the standard exogenous growth theory and economists favoring endogenous growth models. Empirically, this controversy is centered over the issue of convergence between poor and rich countries. A first interpretation of the neoclassical model is that it favors the absolute convergence hypothesis: if all countries are assumed to have similar structural characteristics (labor force growth, saving rate, etc.), per capita outputs in any country converge to the same level, and the long-run growth rate is exogenous and identical for all countries. Moreover, in the short run the growth rate for any given country depends on the difference between its present per capita output and the long-term steady-state per capita output. This is because the rate of return on capital is higher in less developed countries and therefore the incentives to save and accumulate capital are higher.

Two theoretical models have been used to explore this exogenous growth theory. First, Solow (1956) uses the equality between saving and investment and assumes an exogenous saving rate and a production function with decreasing marginal returns on capital. Then, a Ramsey–Cass–Koopmans model in which saving is endogenously determined has been developed and widely used (see Barro and Sala-i-Martin 1995). In this model, a representative agent with an intertemporal utility function is introduced. The results obtained with both models are similar.

On the whole, empirical evidence does not confirm the hypothesis of absolute convergence. Using country data, we do not observe that poor countries grow at a higher rate than rich countries (Pritchett 2000). Rather, it seems that a noticeable

---

[3] See chapters in part 2 of this volume for an analysis of clubs and clubs goods.

divergence between poor and rich countries occurs over the long run. According to Pritchett (2000), it is reasonable to think that in no region of the world in 1870 was the per capita output below the subsistence income level. Using several criteria, Pritchett considers that this subsistence level was around 250 $US (expressed in 1985 purchasing power). When the present per capita output for poor countries is compared with this level, it appears that the maximum growth rate for poor countries is much below the growth rate for rich countries with comparable data over the same period. Following Pritchett's computations, the ratio of per capita outputs for the richest and the poorest countries was equal to 8.7 in 1870 and 45.2 in 1990.[4]

Easterly and Levine (2001) use Maddison's (1995) data and show that per capita outputs diverged over the two last centuries. Bourguignon and Morrisson (2002) confirm this finding and show that individual income inequality increased over these two centuries in the world economy. They decompose this inequality between a part explained by intracountry differences and one explained by inequality between countries. In 1820, the first part is almost the sole component of inequality. But it steadily decreases over time, and thus in 1922 the second part represents the dominant component.

The absence of absolute convergence across countries does not necessarily contradict the exogenous neoclassical theory. If structural characteristics are assumed to differ across countries, the steady-state per capita output level differs for each country and depends on the equilibrium propensity to save, the population growth rate, and external public policies. This is the "conditional convergence" hypothesis. The steady-state growth rate is still exogenous and identical for all countries, but for each country the short-run rate now depends on its initial per capita output level and its own steady-state output level. Hence, in a cross-sectional analysis, the growth rate for a given country depends on its initial output level and on the determinants of the steady-state equilibrium.

Empirical studies such as those of Mankiw, Romer, and Weil (1992, later MRW) and Barro and Sala-i-Martin (1995) confirm this hypothesis when both physical and human capital are taken into account. The dynamics of output growth during the transition toward the steady state is mainly due to the decreasing marginal returns of capital, whereas the steady state growth is exogenous and identical for all countries. On the basis of a Cobb–Douglas production function, for reasonable values of the depreciation rate, the population growth rate, the output elasticity with respect to physical capital only, and the technological change component, the convergence rate[5] should be around 5 percent per year, which implies that countries should reduce the half of the distance between initial output and steady-state output in 14 years. In other words, the speed of the convergence process is rather high. However, the estimated coefficients obtained from regressions by MRW are not completely satisfactory, for

---

[4] See also Bairoch (1993).

[5] The speed of convergence is given by

$$\frac{d \ln y_t}{dt} = \lambda(\ln y_\infty - \ln y_t),$$

where λ is the convergence rate, y_t the per capita income at date t, and y_∞ the per capita income at the steady state.

they imply a rather high capital coefficient (and a speed of convergence equal to 0.6 percent).

To improve these estimates, MRW extend the Solow model and introduce a production function with constant returns to scale and physical capital, human capital, and efficient labor. Therefore, in the theoretical model, the steady-state output depends on the investment rates in physical capital and human capital and on the population growth rate. With output elasticities with respect to physical and human capital equal to 1/3 and plausible values for the other parameters, the convergence rate is around 2 percent per year, and the economy moves halfway to the steady-state in about 35 years. A wealth of studies has subsequently been produced with refinements in estimation techniques and the inclusion of additional explanatory variables. The broad conclusion that emerges from this literature is that a negative and robust relationship exists between output growth and an initial output level that tends to validate the modified exogenous growth model.

13.2.1.2. Growth and Convergence Clubs

However, if the estimates of convergence are robust to the inclusion of additional explanatory variables, this is not so with respect to variations in the set of countries used. Temple (1995) computed estimations of conditional convergence for different country data samples with different wealth levels. He observed that output elasticity with respect to capital and the convergence rate vary strongly across data sets. For example, when the data sets include countries with average wealth levels, the coefficients of the initial output level happen to be insignificant. However, a convergence pattern appears among poor countries, and the same is true for rich countries. In other words, convergence clubs exist. Inside a "club," countries converge, but there is no convergence between two countries belonging to two different "clubs."

Durlauf and Johnson (1995) used the method of regression trees to address the same issue. This method allows the subsets of countries to be identified, the behavior of which can be explained by the same statistical model. Regression trees split the set of countries into three groups: low income, average income, and high income. The low and average income country groups can then be split according to the level of education (high or low). Durlauf and Johnson observe that the coefficient for initial output is significant only for the low-income, low-education subgroup and for the average-income, high-education subgroup.

Using a similar methodology, Berthélémy and Varoudakis (1996) define four categories of countries associated with different combinations of initial output levels and financial sector development. The coefficients of the initial output levels are negative and significant in the regressions run for each group.

These results lead to the notion of "convergence clubs": The heterogeneity in the estimated parameters for countries characterized by different levels of development indicates that the dynamics of income distribution across countries do not depend solely on some aggregate characteristics of an overall growth process but are marked by the presence of subsets of countries. Conditional convergence happens within each subset but not between subsets.

To explore further this idea, Quah (1997) uses a different estimating method based on transition probability matrices. He then shows that income distribution across countries exhibits "twin peaks," which develop over time. These results confirm the existence of convergence clubs: in the long run, the world economy would tend towards a bimodal distribution. More precisely, Quah splits the set of countries into groups with respect to their initial output and computes the probability for a given country belonging to the *i*th group to join the *j*th group within a 15-year period. To avoid an arbitrary grouping of countries, Quah reasons within a continuous framework. The graph of the estimated stochastic kernel shows that most probabilities are concentrated around the principal diagonal. However, two peaks are observed that correspond to the existence of two attracting poles or, in other words, two convergence clubs.

Later findings corroborate this result. Bourguignon and Morrisson (2002) show that the world income distribution tends to be polarized. With the passing of time, the density functions of country per capita income exhibit two increasingly defined peaks. On a related matter, Mayer-Foulkes (2001) finds evidence of convergence clubs in the dynamics of the life expectancy distribution across countries.

According to Desdoigts (1999), convergence clubs can be explained by "a) structural characteristics that determine the steady state of an economy within a neoclassical framework (time preferences, labor force growth, economic policy, etc.), b) the initial conditions that govern a history-dependent growth model in the evolving world income distribution." Desdoigts (1999) p. 306 uses the so-called Exploratory Projection Pursuit (EPP) method to distinguish between these two alternative explanations. First, he identifies institutional (Organisation for Economic Co-operation and Development (OECD) versus non-OECD), cultural (Protestant and Catholic), and geographical (continents) clubs of economies that form endogenously on the basis of their economic structure. Then, corroborating explanation b), he finds that variables involved in the emerging structure correspond to the starting conditions of the growth process (e.g., initial stock of human capital).

In other words, econometric evidence, the computations of transition matrices, and the evolution of income distribution across countries show that a tendency exists toward divergence between poor and rich countries with respect to per capita income and that attracting poles are forming in both groups. The evolution of the world income distribution depends to a large degree on the growth processes characterizing countries, but poor countries do not succeed in converging toward the income levels obtained by the most developed countries.

13.2.2. Intranational Evidence

At more disaggregated levels, it is also possible to observe the uneven distribution of wealth. If we look within Europe, regional income disparities exist and exhibit a core-periphery pattern. Rich regions tend to be located in Europe's geographical center, whereas poorer ones are located on its periphery (i.e., the eastern and northern parts of Europe and the Mediterranean regions). Furthermore, most empirical works reject any convergence process across European regions over time for per capita output.[6] Boldrin and Canova (2001) find that there is no convergence in per capita output levels across European regions and rather suggest a convergence in long-run growth rates, although relative differences in per capita output levels persist between regions. However, finding no evidence that rich and poor regions are clustered in two separate clubs, Boldrin and Canova claim that stratification[7] is not driving the growth process. In contrast to this view, Canova (1998) and Quah (1996a, 1996b) conclude that clusters exist in European regions, each one having its own asymptotically stable per capita income level.

In the United States, the same stratification phenomenon takes place. Using a 3141-county database, Easterly and Levine (2001) sort counties by gross domestic product (GDP) per square mile and find that "50 percent of GDP is produced in counties that account for only 2 percent of the land, while the least dense counties that account for 50 percent of the land produce only 2 percent of GDP" (p. 200).

Cities are also places in which stratification based on income arises. In addition to the observed concentration of poverty in American inner cities or European suburbs, which is a visible manifestation of income stratification, many empirical works find that the spatial distribution of city residents displays income homogeneity of neighborhoods. For instance, studying patterns of residential segregation in the United States, Jargowsky (1996) shows that segregation by income increased for blacks, whites, and Hispanics in all U.S. metropolitan areas from 1970 to 1990. Epple and Sieg (1999) corroborate Jargowsky's findings on urban stratification from an examination of the Boston metropolitan area. A more anecdotal but striking evidence of American's urban stratification is the East–West dichotomy of the Washington metropolitan area between poor and rich zip codes (Easterly and Levine 2001). Studies on French data draw the same conclusions on the spatial concentration of income (Tabard 1993).

However, the empirical literature on the effect of metropolitan stratification on growth aggregate performance is very sparse. A well-known study that has stressed the effect of metropolitan stratification on growth is Rusk (1993). Focusing on four-teen American metropolitan areas, Rusk shows that there is a negative correlation between income segregation, measured by the ratio of central city to suburban mean incomes, and metropolitan per capita income growth (see Bénabou 1996b for a more complete exposition of Rusk's study). Although Rusk's findings are not based on econometric methods, they suggest that metropolitan stratification and growth performance are linked processes, thus motivating theoretical research on this issue.

13.3. Stratification and Growth: Theoretical Approaches

The conclusion we have just reached is that the growth process is empirically related to some stratification features – most evidently with respect to income distribution.

---

[6] Two types of convergence are usually sought: the β-convergence (or the conditional convergence hypothesis) and the σ-convergence, which corresponds to a convergence in the variability of output. Boldrin and Canova (2001) present a useful discussion of the empirical literature as well as original results on the matter.

[7] Boldrin and Canova use the term *polarization*.

This is true whether we consider international, regional, or urbanization data. This is in accordance with the view stressed by Easterly and Levine that "something else," besides capital accumulation matters for the growth process. In other words, this stratification phenomenon would both emphasize and explain the role of externalities in the growth process. But it is yet unclear whether the stratification processes, in particular based on income inequality, is the source or the consequence of the growth process heterogeneity. To have a proper explanation of this relationship, we have to resort to theory.

Indeed, several studies have attempted to explain the absence of per capita output convergence by the presence of multiple clusters of agents. In this section, we first review theoretical works that have prompted research on persistent inequality issues and emphasize nonconvexities and imperfect capital markets as key mechanisms to explain nonconvergence. We then focus on recent theoretical developments based on two different strands of literature stressing the role of local externalities on the growth process: the "new economic geography" literature and the "human capital neighborhood effects" literature. The first one analyzes the role of local productive externalities on clustering of industries and economic growth, and the second one is situated at a more disaggregated level and considers that neighbors' attributes and actions have an impact on the individual's economic success.

13.3.1. Nonconvexities and Incomplete Capital Markets

Two types of explanations have been initially put forward to account for a nondegenerate cross-sectional income distribution and hence for a nonconvergence process between countries. Both explanations emphasize the crucial role of initial inequality characteristics on the patterns of cross-country income-distribution dynamics.

The first argument that has been invoked by economists to account for multiple steady states and "poverty trap" phenomena[8] relies on the existence of some specific nonconvexities in technologies (see for instance Azariadis and Drazen 1990 and Durlauf 1993). These papers develop theoretical models that stress the path dependence of income trajectories and the crucial influence of initial conditions on capital accumulation rates. For instance, in Azariadis and Drazen, nonconvexities in the technology function arise because of the existence of a threshold level of capital above which (respectively, below which), the aggregate production function is characterized by high (respectively, low) technological spillovers. It turns out that such nonconvexities allow for multiple history-dependent steady-states. On the one hand, those economies with a high level of initial endowment above the threshold value benefit from high spillovers and experience high rates of capital accumulation. In the long run, these economies reach a "high" steady state with high levels of capital. On the other hand, for economies initially below the threshold value, low technological spillovers are activated and make those economies become stuck into

---

[8] Poverty trap phenomena refer to situations in which poorer countries are unable to catch up with the rest of the world economy. As we will see later, the notion can also be used within a country to distinguish between poverty-ridden neighborhoods, ghettos, or classes, and the rest of society.

a poverty trap with low capital endowments. Thus, nonconvexities allow for a non-convergence process that leads to a stratified world economy with distinct clusters of countries.

Related papers explore alternative specifications of the production process. Kremer (1993) develops the consequences of a multistage production process. The final output then depends on each task at each stage to be properly executed. He proves that firms will match workers of similar skills together. This setting implies "small differences in wages and output, so wage and skill differential between countries with different skill levels are enormous. .... In particular this is consistent with the tendency of rich countries to specialize in complicated products" (p. 573).

Murphy, Shleifer, and Vishny (1989a,b) explore the consequence of the size of national markets industrialization when world trade is costly. In this setting, they show that two conditions are necessary for industrialization: first, a leading sector must grow and provide the source of autonomous demand for industrial goods; second, income thus generated must be broadly distributed so as to generate demand for a broad range of industrial goods. These conditions explain why some countries might fail to industrialize whereas others succeed.

Besides the "nonconvexities" explanation, other theoretical works consider the imperfection of the credit market and explore its consequences for capital accumulation (see among others, Galor and Zeira 1993, Aghion and Bolton 1997, and Piketty 1997). In particular, Galor and Zeira represent the imperfection of the credit market by means of the spread between the lending and the borrowing interest rates. They then prove that a stratified economy emerges at the steady-state equilibrium. As determined by the initial distribution of income, two classes of agents form. The poorest are unable to obtain loans and are liquidity constrained; the richest do get access to credit. On the whole, capital accumulation and the growth rate reflect this stratification caused by financial motives. Other papers have exploited the theory of incomplete insurance and moral hazard to study the steady-state income distribution and growth. Introducing credit rationing in a standard capital accumulation model, Piketty (1997) exploits the fact that, inside a country, a fraction of families has no access to credit. If some economy-wide externality is assumed, this means that countries with a more unequal wealth distribution will grow less. Piketty shows that a self-reinforcing phenomenon takes place, leading to multiple steady-state wealth distributions that depend on initial interest rates. Aghion and Bolton (1997), on the other hand, use the presence of imperfect capital markets to support the "trickle-down" theory and give conditions under which a unique, steady-state output growth rate exists despite persistent income inequality.

The nature of credit market imperfections (i.e., the transaction and information costs borne by financial contracts) reflects deeper structural features, among which legal aspects rank high. Hence, differences in legal systems should matter and affect the interlinked financial development and economic growth. La Porta et al. (1998) exploit this view: they claim that the degree of legal protection of shareholders and the level of law enforcement regarding financial contracts matter for shaping the structure of a financial system. They then distinguish four families of legal systems: English common law, French civil law, Scandinavian civil law, and German civil law.

Writing before the Enron scandal and its sequel, La Porta et al. claim that the English common law system is the most efficiency-supporting system, whereas the French civil law system is the worst. Generally, legal characteristics are a good predictor of economic performance. In contrast, Chakraborty and Ray (2001) develop a model in which financial structure arises endogenously, and they show that two countries may have quite different financial systems and still enjoy similar growth rates over time. But on methodological grounds, it remains true that financial structural differences a priori lead to different growth dynamics.

On the empirical side of the problem, several studies are worth mentioning. Beck, Levine, and Loayza (1999) focus on the influence of finance on the sources of growth. Using panel data techniques, they examine the relationship between financial development and private saving rates as well as physical capital accumulation and total factor productivity (TFP) growth. They find that financial intermediaries exert a large positive impact on TFP growth and that the long-run links between financial intermediaries and both capital growth and private savings are tenuous. In other words, Schumpeter (1912) is vindicated. Finance influences the growth process and in particular affects the "something else" factor.

However, we would like to go one step farther again and speculate whether finance plays a role in the stratification of the growth process and may contribute to the existence of multiple convergence clubs. In a well-quoted article, King and Levine (1993), using cross-country data over the period 1960–1989, present evidence suggesting that the initial level of financial development is a good predictor of subsequent rates of economic growth, capital accumulation, and technology improvements. This result may be compatible both with a convergence view on growth, leading ultimately to financial integration, or with a view stressing stratification and no integration. The study by Berthélemy and Varoudakis (1996) is more one-sided because it empirically supports the view that financially determined stratification exists between countries with respect to their long-term development: some countries suffer from insufficient access to developed financial markets, which severely inhibits the ability to grow. A "poverty trap" phenomenon then takes place. Benhabib and Spiegel (2000) have undertaken a project similar to the one by Beck et al. (1999). They too confirm the link between finance and investment and total productivity growth; in addition they notice country-fixed effects. This may indicate that the financial development indicators are proxying for other country-specific characteristics or that financial systems play a different role in different countries. Spiegel (2001), pursuing this research, claims, for example, that the Asia Pacific Economic Cooperation countries appear to be more sensitive to financial development than the rest of the sample.

Up to now, most empirical studies have stressed that the discrepancy in development may be due to imperfections in financial systems and markets: different countries face different financial situations because the markets are segmented and different agents have different access to them. However, there is a widespread feeling, if not yet proper understanding of the phenomenon, that there is growing integration of financial markets. Does this mean that the finance-based stratification phenomena are likely to disappear? A first answer to this question is by Guiso, Sapienza, and

Zingales (2002). The originality of their study is that they look at the effect of local financial development within a single country, Italy, which is financially integrated: Are there financial neighborhood effects that matter for national growth of Italian regions even though each of them has the same access to an integrated financial market? The answer provided by Guiso et al. is yes: there are strong effects of local financial development on the growth process of regions. In particular, in the most financially developed regions, per capita GDP grows 1 percent per annum more than in the least financially developed one. They conclude that financial factors will still play a segmenting role in growth when the economy becomes financially more integrated.

In brief, this short survey of significant studies on finance and growth lends support to the view that financial channels lead to a heterogeneous and uneven growth process.

13.3.2. Geography and Growth

A straightforward type of stratification is spatial. A society using a given territory is divided into local communities. These spatial clusterings may persist and interact with growth processes. One of the main lines of division between communities may be in terms of wealth and income. A famous distinction in economic geography is between the core and the periphery of a country; the core being the region where all firms belonging to the modern sector locate, whereas the periphery is specialized in the traditional sector. The same distinction can be transposed at the international level. Indeed, a core and a periphery seem to exist in Europe, and this distinction is used to justify an ambitious regional policy in the European Union aimed at redistributing resources across regions. A widespread view, shared both by economists and laymen, is that, in the core, wealth accumulates more rapidly because it can attract more resources, including people, from the periphery, which then grows less rapidly. Indeed, data tend to confirm this view as we have seen from the section on the empirics of growth: countries grow at different paces over the long period. We did not insist yet on the spatial dimension of the divide. Tellingly, it is standard to oppose the "North" and the "South."

In spatial economics and in growth economics, externalities are at work. Increasing returns to scale and spillover effects exist and shape the geography of human activities. This is also true for growth. This explains why Fujita and Thisse (2002, 389) consider that "agglomeration is the territorial counterpart of growth."

Can we go further? Can we link both processes and say that they do not just coexist but are intimately interrelated because the same phenomena of increasing returns and spillovers have a spatial and an accumulation impact simultaneously? Lucas (1988) in a seminal paper on endogenous growth theory did not hesitate to view cities as engines of growth. In a circular way, agglomeration fosters growth and growth fosters agglomeration. Local externalities generate agglomeration and agglomeration generates productive externalities. Then growth affects the distribution of income and wealth, changes incentives and relative capacities, and therefore affects the decision of where to locate.

The link between growth and location has recently been addressed in a few theoretical papers. Three main claims come out of this literature despite the inconsistent results obtained with different models:

1. The growth of the global economy depends on the spatial organization of the innovation sector across regions.
2. Growth and agglomeration are interrelated.
3. This joint process tends to foster a widening of income distribution. The limit case of catastrophic agglomeration, as in the new geography model of Krugman (1991), may occur: the core draws all productive resources and the periphery is deserted.

The spatial externalities at work are restricted to a given area and are not global, affecting any agent in the economy wherever he or she is located. There are two types as follows:

1. Location-productive externalities come from the proximity of firms that produce similar goods: owing to these externalities, the individual firm's marginal cost is a function of the number of firms being present in the neighborhood.
2. Urbanization externalities are more of a pecuniary type. They come from the enlargement of market for a firm's products when a clustering of agents forms.

In their survey on the topic, Baldwin and Martin (2003) develop two sequences of circular causality. In a demand-driven one, the enlargement of the market in the "North" leads to higher profitability for firms located there and hence a higher capital accumulation and more profit and income in the North as well as feedbacks into the enlargement of northern markets. In a technology-driven sequence, local technological spillovers tend to foster local accumulation; this, in turn, activates the local innovation sector because of trade costs and generates more local technological spillovers. In either case, trade costs and factor mobility, in particular capital mobility, play a crucial role. In some cases, when capital mobility is absent, this can lead to catastrophic agglomeration in which the periphery vanishes as an economic region.

In two models developed in their chapter on agglomeration and growth, Fujita and Thisse (2002) combine the two types of externalities with labor mobility – in particular for the skilled workers employed in the R&D sector. They conclude that "an R&D sector appears to be a strong centripetal force at the multiregional level, thus amplifying the circular causation that lies at the heart of the core-periphery model" (p. 391).

Several papers use coalition theory tools to address the endogenous formation of neighborhoods (see the recent papers by Henkel, Stahl, and Walz 2000 and Konishi 2000). But these papers do not make the link with growth. Quah's (2002) work is a pioneering paper in this respect. It develops a model of economic growth in which location matters and simultaneously studies growth dynamics, location choices, and the evolution of inequality. The driving force is technology, which generates productive spatial spillovers. The result may be agglomeration phenomena. The spatial clustering of activities evolves over time, and this goes along with inequality dynamics even though there are no a priori physical differences between loci. Interestingly, these dynamics converge toward a steady-state egalitarian growth.

Empirical studies devoted to the relationship between agglomeration and growth are still rare. Looking at spatial externality effects, Glaeser et al. (1992) study U.S. cities between 1956 and 1987 and show that urbanization economies are prevalent. However, Henderson, Kuncoro, and Turner (1995) show evidence of the existence of localization externalities over the period between 1970 and 1987. In a recent study on French regions over the period between 1984–1993, Combes (2000) concludes that the impact of spatial organization differs for industries and services, pointing to the need for disaggregated data.

On the issue of the spatial clustering of R&D activities and the ensuing technological spillovers, the existing studies (a recent reference is Ciccone and Hall 1996) state that technology spillovers are neither global nor local. Regions are not equally affected by them, but there is some dispersion across regions. Knowledge and innovations spread over space, but this diffusion decreases with distance, which still gives some advantages to the district from which the technology spillovers originate (Keller 2002).

13.3.3. Education and Stratification

In the last decade the literature on inequality and poverty within countries based on the "neighborhood effects" explanation has dramatically rise in (see, among others, the survey of Durlauf 2000a). This strand of literature considers that residential neighborhoods have a crucial impact on individual educational attainment. Neighborhood effects may have different sources such as local taxation or human capital local externalities like peer effects or social network effects. Neighbors' characteristics, which determine the amount of local resources, appear to be crucial for any individual educational and economic success. For instance, if education is a normal good and is locally funded, the identity of neighbors matters, and obviously, any individual seeks the company of the richest. Persistent inequality and poverty arise because of the uneven distribution of individuals over the city, which leads to different local resources between neighborhoods.

More specifically, seminal articles by Bénabou (1993; 1996a,b) and Durlauf (1996) develop theoretical frameworks of human capital accumulation with neighborhood effects that explore cross-sectional inequality dynamics. They are then able to account for persistent disparity and poverty-trap phenomena characterized by poor agents residing in deprived communities and being unable to catch up with the rich-populated communities.

It is worth noticing that the key feature of groups considered in most of the literature is their spatial dimension. The process of neighborhood formation is based on the location choice of individuals. Individuals make their decision facing a basic trade-off between the payment of an entry cost, which can be the land rent or the local tax rate when local resources are raised by local fundings, and the benefits from the neighborhood effects. The most common type of equilibrium studied is the free-mobility equilibrium in which no one has an incentive to move.

To address the inequality dynamics and the growth issues, most papers in the literature develop theoretical frameworks sharing the same common feature of the human capital technology. Human capital accumulation can be formalized as follows:

$$h^i_{j,t+1} = h\left(h^i_{j,t}, h_{j,t}, h_t\right). \tag{13.3.1}$$

The human capital at date $t + 1$ of agent i who resides in neighborhood j at date t depends on the combination between three factors: (i) the individual level of human capital $h^i_{j,t}$, (ii) an aggregate of human capital wealth of inhabitants of neighborhood j denoted $h_{j,t}$, and (iii) an aggregate of human capital wealth of the whole society denoted by h_t. The first factor, which depends on Nature or inheritance, drives inequality dynamics. The second input is the crucial one. It captures neighborhood effects. The third component, h_t, corresponds to economy-wide knowledge spillovers.

To highlight the basic mechanism at work in this setup, let us be more specific and consider the following Cobb–Douglas technology:

$$h^i_{j,t+1} = \left(h^i_t\right)^{1-\nu-\beta} \left(h_{j,t}\right)^{\beta} \left(h_t\right)^{\nu} \tag{13.3.2}$$

with β, ν, and $1 - \nu - \beta \in [0, 1]$.

Basically, the resulting human capital dynamics depend on the interplay between convergence and divergence forces. On the one hand, owing to diminishing marginal returns to scale, both the individual component and the social externality input favor income convergence. On the other hand, the impact of neighborhood effects on the inequality dynamics may vary as influenced by the degree of social stratification. More precisely, if individuals perfectly sort themselves into groups according to income, then rich neighborhoods benefit from better local externalities than poorer communities and the neighborhood factor turns out to favor income divergence. In this case, the resulting dynamics are not easy to predict and depend on the interplay between these opposing forces. On the contrary, when individuals organize themselves into various communities such that local resources are the same across these areas, then neighborhood effects have a neutral impact on the inequality dynamics.[9] Thus, the three components of the human capital technology unambiguously lead to convergence.

A key result of the "human capital neighborhood effects" literature is that cross-sectional inequality dynamics may exhibit different history-dependent steady states. In one steady state, the society may end up unequal and stratified. Poor individuals are trapped into deprived communities, whereas rich agents merge together and benefit from substantial educational resources. In another steady state, the society may be integrated and equal in the long run. Local resources do not differ across communities, and thus per capita ouputs may converge. What is crucial is that the long-term behavior of the economy depends on the initial human capital distribution,

---

[9] An individual having a negligible relative weight has then no incentive to move from one community to another because these communities are identical. No agglomeration process is at work.

which determines the initial stratification. If an uneven initial distribution is assumed, the endogenous formation of neighborhoods will lead to a high degree of stratification, generating heterogeneity in the availability of local resources between neighborhoods. This favors inequality in the subsequent periods and the probability that the society will end up unequal and segregated is high. On the contrary, when initial human capital distribution is not too dispersed, individuals' location does not lead to a marked disparity in local resources between communities. In this case, the likelihood that the stationary human capital distribution will be ergodic is high.

Which social structure is the best engine for economic growth? Does a stratified and unequal society lower growth or is an integrated and equal society better for capital accumulation? One important contribution of Bénabou's works is to provide a clear discussion of the impact of the social structure on the long-term rate of growth. Let us consider the general function of equation (13.3.1). In particular, Bénabou stresses the crucial role of the curvature of both functions, $h_{j,t}$ and h_t. The basic idea is the following. When these functions are convex, stratification enhances growth. In such a case, owing to increasing marginal returns to scale, the marginal increase in individual human capital induced by a marginal rise in the concentration of the rich population within the same neighborhood supersedes the marginal decrease of individual human capital due to a marginal rise of the poverty rate in another area. It turns out that, in a stratified society, rich neighborhoods are characterized by a high rate of capital accumulation, which counterbalances the low level of growth within deprived communities. On the contrary, when these functions are concave, the integrated and equal society is better for growth. In this case, owing to decreasing marginal returns to scale, gains from a high concentration of rich individuals in some neighborhoods do not cover losses generated by a high rate of poverty in other communities.

Along the transitional path, cross-sectional income inequality dynamics can be very complex. Potentially, as long as income distribution evolves, a change in social stratification is possible. Multiple trajectories can then arise, making it difficult to identify conditions on initial distribution and elasticities β, v, $1 - v - \beta$ in equation (13.3.2) such that the society will be either stratified or integrated in the long run.

A vast empirical literature exists that supports the evidence of the influence of group membership on individual outcomes. (See Durlauf 2000a for an excellent survey of this literature covering ethnographic studies, statistical analyses, and quasi-experiments.)

A first piece of evidence on the significant role of peers in educational achievement can be found in the sociological literature on education and urban poverty. The Coleman Report (*Equality of Educational Opportunity*, 1966) galvanized the research community by stressing a strong and positive relation between a student's educational achievement and educational background as well as the aspirations of his or her classmates. Building on theories of "collective socialization" in which neighborhood role models and monitoring are key ingredients in a child's development, the influential study of Wilson (1987) on American ghettos shows how the lack of inhabitants experiencing economic success may harm aspirations and motivations of young people who grow up in these deprived communities and in turn may affect their educational attainment and professional success. Corroborating Wilson's view on the adverse effects of social isolation, Crane (1991) argues that concentration of social pathologies, like teenage pregnancy or dropping out of school, within poor neighborhoods may increase by "contagion" effects the likelihood for young inhabitants to get involved in such activities. Focusing on the fiscal channel of group effects, Kozol (1991) documents how the disparity in communities' resources due to local public finance can lead to persistent inequality.

Many empirical studies focus on the significant impact of group membership on individual outcomes. An early empirical work is the one of Henderson et al. (1978) that concludes, using Canadian data, that there is a marked correlation between average ability of classmates and educational outcome. Using the 1989 NBER survey of youths living in low-income, inner-city Boston neighborhoods, Case and Katz (1991) find that neighborhood characteristics exert a strong and significant effect on an individual's socioeconomic outcome. In particular, they show that young people living in a neighborhood with a high fraction of youths involved in crime or using illegal drugs have higher chances of exhibiting analogous behavior than youths with similar family backgrounds and personal characteristics residing in neighborhoods with a smaller proportion of young people engaged in such activities. For instance, Case and Katz estimate that a 10-percent increase in the number of young drug users in the neighborhood raises the chances for companions to fall in this category by 3.83 percent. Borjas (1995) is another well-known example of empirical work indicating the influence of neighborhood effects. Using American data sets, he shows that ethnic capital, as a good proxy for the socioeconomic background of the residential neighborhood of individuals, is a key determinant of intergenerational mobility.[10]

Thus, empirical studies supporting the evidence of group influences on an individual's outcome, highlight the prominent role played by local externalities on individual, and in turn, on aggregate human capital accumulation. These results also suggest the key impact of the organization of a society into distinct coalitions on its growth performance.

---

[10] However, there is considerable controversy concerning the measurement of the effect of group membership on individual outcomes. Ginther, Haveman, and Wolfe (2000) is an important contribution to the empirical literature that questions conclusions of many empirical works on the strong and significant effect of the neighborhood. Starting from the observation that estimates of neighborhood effects on children, outcomes vary widely among studies in their magnitude and existence, they ask whether this disparity is due to differences in the specification of family characteristics and hence to omitted variable bias. Using the Panel Study of Income Dynamics, they show that richer individual controls systematically reduce the magnitude of estimated neighboorhood influences, thus drawing the conclusion that findings of strong neighborhood effects are an artifact of the choice of the family background control variables. In fact, Ginther et al.'s findings illustrate the difficulties econometric analyses face in identifying social interactions. Durlauf (2000a, 2000b, 2002) are clear expositions of the econometric literature's difficulties, whereas Manski (1993) and Brock and Durlauf (2001a, 2001b) develop statistical frameworks that deal with these problems. Beyond the issue of identification of neighborhood effects, there is the problem of self-selection in the case of endogenous group membership. (See, among others, Evans, Oates, and Schwab (1992); Aaronson (1998); and Sacerdote (2001) for suggestions of empirical approaches dealing with this problem.)

13.4. Inequality, Stratification, and Growth

When we look at the growth process or at the sources of growth, the evidence of stratification is thus overwhelming. Growth is an uneven process that affects communities in different ways. In particular, the access to the various sources of growth seems to be affected by the differentiation of society into groups.

But does growth generate stratification or is the clustering process at the root of the uneven and unequal characteristics of growth? This is the question that comes immediately to mind given this evidence. In this section, we present an analysis of the growth process that suggests there is an intimate relationship between the formation of separate coalitions within a society and its growth process. The use of coalition theory allows us to offer a fully microeconomic explanation of "growth clubs" (i.e., of groups of agents that experience separated growth trajectories over time) and thus gives a theoretical explanation of the evidence of stratification and its impact on growth.

13.4.1. A Model of Growth Clubs

We consider a "society" $N = \{1, \ldots, n\}$ of individuals with infinite lives. This society is constituted at time $t = 0$. Each person enters society with an initial, strictly positive individual endowment a_i, where a_i is a scalar, because there is one good, and $\mathbf{a} = \{a_1, \ldots, a_n\}$ denotes the initial endowment distribution. The good may alternatively be saved, privately consumed, or used to finance a public good employed in the production process. Agents are ordered so that $a_1 > a_2 > \cdots > a_n$. The aggregate level of endowment is given by $\mathcal{A} = \sum_{i \in N} a_i$. This society is unequal insofar as initial endowments differ.

A club S is any nonempty subset of N. A club provides a productive "club good" formed from voluntary individual contributions made by its members. As based on Buchanan (1965), this good is nonrival and exclusive: it is beneficial to the members of the club only. Here, we assume that this club good positively affects the productive capacity of the club and therefore the intertemporal flows of income for its members. Hence, because a club influences growth, we refer to it as a "growth club." Given the benefits accruing to members of a club, agents may willingly form clubs.

The number and boundaries of clubs are not given ex ante but will be endogenously determined according to a three-stage process:

1. The partition stage. The very first decisions by agents are to form clubs. The characteristics of these decisions are that each individual voluntarily joins a club in which he or she is unanimously accepted. In other words, a club is formed when no individual or group of individuals wants to defect but joining a club is subject to approval.[11]
2. The contribution stage. Once a club is formed, each individual decides on his or her voluntary contribution to the productive club good. This decision is

---

[11] There is free entry but not free mobility. For developments on this distinction, see Chapter 5 of this volume.

taken noncooperatively, each member in a club taking as given the contributions made by all other members. The club good is supplied at the beginning of time once and forever. There is no obsolescence because it keeps its productive capacities forever.

3. The accumulation stage. Then, using his or her endowment net the contribution to the club good, each agent decides to save. This decision is made at time 0 and then is renewed at each period. Given that there is no ambiguity, it is as if each individual decides at 0 on her saving plan over the entire infinite future.[12]

The first two stages of this partition process are similar to the process in a static environment used by Barham et al. (1997) and Jaramillo, Kempf, and Moizeau (2003, later JKM). The first stage corresponds to a cooperative game without side payments, the second one corresponds to a noncooperative game on contribution, and the third one to a noncooperative game on savings. This amounts to saying that there is no commitment technology allowing an agent, before entering a club, to commit to the amount of good he or she will contribute and/or such that members of a club can punish another member who does not fulfill a promise to contribute or to save. In this section, we concentrate on the last two stages of the process. In the following section, we study the endogenous formation of growth clubs as coalitions.

Importantly, given the founding property of the club good and its everlasting consequences, it is convenient to stipulate that a club be formed at the beginning of history and forever.[13] No one has any possibility to reopen the case of the limits of clubs. Many growth clubs may form in the first stage. We refer to one of them as the *jth* club and denote it by S_j. The "once and forever" assumption amounts to saying that the club good, once it is supplied in quantity G_j in club S_j, will contribute to the productive process over the infinite growth path. Admittedly extreme, this assumption is not without empirical content. Many club goods are formed at the foundation of the club and last "forever": think about the location of the capital; the setting of public institutions; the definition of the legal apparatus, including property rights; the writing of a constitution; the discovery of a technological process, and so on.

The growth process is of the simple AK variety of endogenous growth models.[14] There is a unique accumulating resource, capital, characterized by constant returns to scale. The autonomous component A depends positively on the size of the productive club good G_j and negatively on the number of members in S_j, which we denote by n_j. This last assumption reflects the presence of congestion costs, which explain why an individual may not be willing to belong to a club that is too large or may not even be accepted. An additional member has the positive effect of an increase in the financing of the club good but the negative effect of increasing congestion. Intuitively, this

---

[12] As we will explain in the sequel, the first stage of this process is of a cooperative nature, whereas the second stage is of a noncooperative one. This contrasts with the construction used in Chapter 12 of this volume. Clearly, there is no unique way to model the endogenous formation of coalitions and the ensuing decisions. The precise choice depends on the nature of the problem at hand.

[13] This assumption will be relaxed in the next section.

[14] For an exposition of this variety of endogenous growth clubs, see Barro and Sala-i-Martin (1995).

trade-off shapes the sizes of clubs. Formally, for club S_j, the production function is as follows:

$$Y_j(t) = A(G_j, n_j)K_j(t) \tag{13.4.1}$$

with

$$K_j(t) = \sum_{i \in S_j} k_i(t), \tag{13.4.2}$$

where $k_i(t)$ denotes the level of productive capital accumulated at t by individual i. There is no depreciation of capital. We assume the following properties for function $A(G_j, n_j)$: $A_1 > 0$, $A_{11} < 0$, $A_2 < 0$. Moreover, we assume that a larger size does not make the marginal contribution of the public good to production be more productive ($A_{12} \leq 0$).[15] For simplicity, we assume that

$$G_j = \sum_{i \in S_j} g_i. \tag{13.4.3}$$

Once a club is formed, a growth process starts because its members will save and accumulate capital over time. This process will reflect the membership of the club – in particular the affluence of members – and its size. It is important to note that, once it is formed, each club is a productive autarky. There is economic interdependence within a club over time but not between clubs inasmuch as there is no economic relationship between existing clubs.[16] But because clubs are autarkies, there is no equilibrating process for capital returns, and different clubs entail (a priori) different capital returns. We denote by $r_j(t)$ the rate of return of capital at time t for club S_j, and we can write

$$r_j(t) = A(G_j, n_j).$$

Finally, individuals are identical and differ only in their initial endowments. We assume the following utility function for an individual i:

$$U_i = \int_0^{+\infty} e^{-\rho t} \ln c_i(t)dt, \tag{13.4.4}$$

where ρ denotes the discount factor and $c_i(t)$ the consumption of individual i at date t. Capital is remunerated at its marginal productivity. For any i belonging to S_j, $c_{i,t}^E$ and g_i^E are solutions of

$$\max_{g_i, c_{i,t}} \int_0^{+\infty} e^{-\rho t} \ln c_i(t)dt$$

---

[15] This differentiates our setting from the ones studied in Chapter 5 of this volume, which concentrates on the consequences of increasing returns on coalition formation.

[16] In other words, there are no spillovers between coalitions. To introduce such spillovers would be immensely interesting but beyond the scope of this chapter. For an introduction to such games, we refer to Bloch (1997) and Qin (1996).

subject to

$$\begin{cases} \dot{k}_i = r_j(t)k_i(t) - c_i(t) \\ a_i - g_i = k_i(0) \\ \lim_{t \to +\infty} e^{-\int_0^{+\infty} r_j(z)dz} k_i(t) \geq 0 \end{cases}.$$

The consumption path then satisfies the following Euler equation:

$$\frac{\dot{c}_i}{c_i} = r_j(t) - \rho = A(G_j, n_j) - \rho \qquad \forall i \in S_j. \tag{13.4.5}$$

As usual in AK models of endogenous growth, the capital accumulation rates and the growth rate are constant over time and equal to

$$\frac{\dot{k}_i}{k_i} = r_j(t) - \rho = A(G_j, n_j) - \rho \qquad \forall i \in S_j \tag{13.4.6}$$

$$\eta_j \equiv \frac{\dot{Y}_j}{Y_j} = A(G_j, n_j) - \rho. \tag{13.4.7}$$

This last equation makes clear that each club is characterized by a specific growth rate that is likely to differ from rates for other clubs. Moreover, the growth rate depends on the decisions regarding the membership and the contributions to the clubs. In this respect, despite the lack of spillovers between clubs, it is clear that the various growth processes are interdependent insofar as the formation of clubs is a global process. This will allow us to focus on the impact of inequality on club formation and its consequences for the growth process.

From (13.4.5), we deduce

$$c_i(t) = c_i(0)e^{(A(G_j, n_j) - \rho)t} \qquad \forall i \in S_j, \tag{13.4.8}$$

which gives the discounted value of the intertemporal level of utility denoted by

$$U_t = \frac{1}{\rho} \ln c_i(0) + \frac{1}{\rho^2} \left[A(G_j, n_j) - \rho \right] \qquad \forall i \in S_j. \tag{13.4.9}$$

In the contribution stage, once his or her club has been formed, an agent i belonging to S_j, has to decide over g_i. From the budget constraint and the value of $r_j(t)$, we know that

$$c_i(0) = \rho k_i(0) = \rho(a_i - g_i). \tag{13.4.10}$$

Agent i therefore solves

$$\max_{g_i} U_i = \frac{1}{\rho} \ln \rho(a_i - g_i) + \frac{1}{\rho^2} \left[A(G_j, n_j) - \rho \right].$$

The solution of this noncooperative stage is characterized by

$$g_i = a_i - \frac{\rho}{A_1(G_j, n_j)}. \tag{13.4.11}$$

The richer an individual in a club is, the more he or she contributes to the club good. However, the richer the other members are, the less an individual contributes. This expresses a free-riding behavior in the club owing to the noncooperative nature of this stage of the game. Finally, the larger a club is, the less an individual contributes (when $A_{12} \leq 0$) because the efficiency of a marginal contribution to the club good declines with membership and congestion.

It immediately follows that the club good at the noncooperative equilibrium of this stage equals[17]

$$G_j^* = \sum_{i \in S_j} a_i - \frac{n_j \rho}{A_1(G_j^*, n_j)}, \tag{13.4.12}$$

which is equivalent to

$$G_j^* = \Gamma \left(\sum_{i \in S_j} a_i, n_j \right) \tag{13.4.13}$$

with

$$\Gamma_1 > 0 \quad \text{and} \quad \Gamma_2 < 0. \tag{13.4.14}$$

For a given size, the richer (in aggregate) the club, the larger the club good: this reflects the increased financing ability of members, despite the negative free-riding effect. For a given financing ability (i.e., aggregate endowment), the larger a club, the smaller the club good. This reflects the aggregate effect of size (congestion) on the marginal provision of the club good ($A_{12} \leq 0$).

Note that because individual consumptions are equal and growing at the same rate over time, this economy is characterized by extreme intraclub convergence. All members of a club share the same intertemporal sequence of consumption and hence the same utilities.

It is easy to compute the present value of utility of agent i belonging to club S_j, which we denote $V_i(S_j)$:

$$V_i(S_j) = \frac{1}{\rho} \ln \rho^2 - \frac{1}{\rho} \ln A_1(G_j^*, n_j) + \frac{1}{\rho^2}[A(G_j^*, n_j) - \rho], \qquad \forall i \in S_j. \tag{13.4.15}$$

where S_j is associated with an amount of club good G_j^* and its cardinal n_j.

This formula makes clear some interesting properties of a growth club.

1. First, $V_i(S_j)$ does not depend on the individual endowment of i. All members of the growth club S_j benefit from the same intertemporal utility level denoted by $V(S_j)$. This is due to a characteristic well known in the case of the voluntary provision of public good first noticed by Bergstrom et al. (1986, 1992): When all members of a club have identical preferences, their individual arbitrage leads them to appreciate the same basket of goods and they give all their

---

[17] Bergstrom, Blume, and Varian (1986, 1992) show that Nash equilibrium exists and is unique when the club good is normal.

endowment in excess of a fixed amount left for private consumption. Here, we obtain this property in the case of growth clubs. Because of equation (13.4.11) and initial individual budget constraint, what is left for private purposes for i is his or her individual amount of capital $k_i(0)$, and it is independent of the individual initial endowment of i:

$$k_i(0) = \frac{\rho}{A_1(G_j, n_j)} \qquad \forall i \in S_j. \qquad (13.4.16)$$

This implies an equal amount of private consumption over time for all members of S_j:

$$c_i(t) = c_{i'}(t) \qquad \forall i, i' \in S_j. \qquad (13.4.17)$$

2. For a given size, the present utility value for members of a club is increasing in the aggregate endowment of the club $\sum a_i$. Altogether, despite the free-riding effect, a richer club generates a higher utility level because members contribute more to the club good.

3. On the other hand, the direct effect of the size n_j of club S_j on the present value of utility is ambiguous for a given aggregate endowment. The congestion effect negatively affects this utility level; however, the increase in the size decreases the free-riding effect on individual contributions because the average level of wealth within the group decreases when size increases. The net effect is ambiguous.

13.4.2. The Core and Growth Clubs

We now turn to the first stage of the process, when clubs are formed "forever." The resulting stratification of society into clubs is called a partition:

Definition 13.1. *A partition in J clubs of N is denoted by $S = \{S_1, \ldots, S_J\}$, $S_j \subset N$ and is such that $\cup_{j=1}^{J} S_j = N$ and $S_j \cap S_{j'} = \emptyset$.*

We define the pattern of growth associated with a given partition as follows.

Definition 13.2. *The pattern of growth associated with a given partition S is the set of growth rates characterizing the various clubs of this partition η_j, for $j = 1, \ldots, J$.*

Obviously, two different partitions are likely to induce different patterns of growth because the decisions for the financing of the club good and therefore for capital accumulation by a given individual depend on the size and the membership of the club to which this individual belongs. An agent with a given endowment opts for a different level of voluntary contribution according to the membership of the club to which he or she belongs because of the noncooperative nature of financing individual decisions. By generalization, given the noncooperative nature of the individual decisions, the entire pattern of growth depends on the partition of society associated with a given endowment distribution.

Here, we consider that the partition of the society in growth clubs belongs to the core given the cooperative nature of the formation of these clubs. Specifically, we consider the following definition of an equilibrium:

Definition 13.3. $[(c_{i,t}^E, g_i^E)_{i \in N, t \in [0,\infty[}, \mathcal{S}^E = (S_1^E; \ldots ; S_j^E)]$ *is an equilibrium if it satisfies*

i) *The equilibrium partition $\mathcal{S}^E$ belongs to the core, that is, is such that*

$$\nexists \mathcal{L} \subset N \text{ such that } \forall i \in \mathcal{L}, \ V_i(\mathcal{L}) > V_i(S_j^E), \quad (13.4.18)$$

where $V_i(S_j^E)$ denotes the utility for agent i being a member of S_j^E.

ii) *$c_{i,t}^E$ and g_i^E satisfy equations (13.4.8) and (13.4.11), for any i belonging to any $_j^E$.*

An equilibrium partition is such that there is no desirable defection to another possible coalition from anyone or group of agents or from any club in the equilibrium partition. The following proposition states that such a partition exists and details its important characteristics:[18]

Proposition 13.1. *For a given inequality schedule, there exists an equilibrium partition $S^E = \{S_1^E, \ldots, S_j^E, \ldots.\}$ that satisfies the following properties:*

i) *it is unique.*

ii) *it is stratified: if i and $\widetilde{i}$ belong to S_j^E, $i > \widetilde{i}$, then for all i^* such that, $i > i^* > \widetilde{i}$, $i^* \in S_j^E$. Thus, clubs can be indexed by decreasing endowments:*

$$\text{for any } j < j' \text{ and } i, i' \text{ such that } i \in S_j^E, i' \in S_{j'}^E, \quad \text{then } i < i'. \quad (13.4.19)$$

iii) *For any $i, i' \in S_j^E$, $V_i(S_j^E) = V_{i'}(S_j^E) \equiv V(S_j^E)$.*

iv) *Welfare ordering: Consider two clubs S_j^E and $S_{j'}^E$ such that $j < j'$; then, $V(S_j^E) > V(S_{j'}^E)$.*[19]

An immediate property of the equilibrium partition is that for any club of the equilibrium partition, any member contributes a strictly positive amount to the club good. This directly comes from the presence of congestion effects. Each new member of a club must represent a net gain for all other members. He or she inflicts some harm on them because of the increase in congestion. Therefore, this must be balanced by some advantage: this can only come from a positive contribution to the club good.

Basically, this proposition extends the properties of the equilibrium partition from the static case studied by JKM to the dynamic case with capital accumulation. These properties allow us to characterize the equilibrium partition by a sequence of pivotal agents. A pivotal agent is the poorest member of a given club.

Of course any individual would like to belong to the richest club S_1^E. But the richest individuals may not be willing to accept an agent who is too poor: given their own contributions, the poor agent contributes too little to cover the congestion costs he or she inflicts on the others. That is why the first club is formed of the richest individuals only up to the first pivotal agent. Then if this club is subtracted from

---

[18] The proofs of all propositions are left to the appendix.

[19] For consistency reason, we refer here to the stratification property. It is also known in the literature as the consecutiveness property. See Greenberg and Weber (1986).

society, the same reasoning explains why the second club is formed of the richest individual after the first pivotal agent, up to the second pivotal agent, and so on. The last club of the partition, formed of the poorer agents, is called a residual club. This property exemplifies the stratification of society into growth clubs. Given the voluntary provision to the club good assumption, we obtain that any member of a given club benefits from the same utility level as any other member of the same club.[20]

Stratification is uniquely determined by the initial endowment distribution. Inequality matters because it affects the relative contributing power of an individual, which is the fundamental factor of his or her unanimous acceptance in a club; therefore, inequality leads to the stratification of society into clubs. These clubs have an everlasting influence on the growth process inasmuch as each club allows its members to benefit from a productive club good. This club good happens to be one crucial engine of endogenous growth. Because there is no spillover between clubs, each club is then characterized by its own growth rate and no convergence force is at work that would lead to a unique steady-state growth rate for the whole economy. To summarize the whole process, inequality matters for growth divergence by means of endogenous stratification. We now turn to the study of the relationships between inequality and the pattern of growth.

13.4.3. Inequality, the Equilibrium Partition, and Growth

What then are the consequences of inequality for the pattern of growth via the equilibrium partition of society? Is inequality a cause of the nonconvergence of growth rates between clubs? Are there some relations between the characteristics of inequality and the pattern of growth of this society?

To answer these questions, we use an explicit form of the autonomous component to growth, $A\left(G_j, n_j\right)$. We assume that

$$A\left(G_j, n_j\right) = \ln\left(\frac{G_j}{e^{\alpha n_j}}\right). \tag{13.4.20}$$

This formulation satisfies the constraints imposed on the $A\left(\cdot\right)$ function in the previous section. It implies the following explicit values for the endogenous variables of interest:

$$G_j = \frac{\displaystyle\sum_{i \in S_j} a_i}{1 + n_j \rho} \tag{13.4.21}$$

$$\eta_j = \ln G_j - \alpha n_j - \rho = \ln\left(\sum_{i \in S_j} a_i\right) - \ln\left(1 + n_j \rho\right) - \alpha n_j - \rho \tag{13.4.22}$$

$$V\left(S_j^E\right) = C + \left(\frac{1}{\rho} + \frac{1}{\rho^2}\right)\ln\sum_{i \in S_j} a_i - \left[\left(\frac{1}{\rho} + \frac{1}{\rho^2}\right)\ln\left(1 + n_j \rho\right) + \frac{1}{\rho^2}\alpha n_j\right] \tag{13.4.23}$$

with $C = \frac{1}{\rho}\ln\rho^2 - \frac{1}{\rho}$.

---

[20] This property, related to the core and jurisdictons with local public goods, was first obtained by Wooders (1978). For production economies, it is also found in Bennett and Wooders (1979).

Because we will elaborate on these formulas, some comments are necessary. There are three effects on the growth rate of a given club. First, $\ln(\sum_{i \in S_j} a_i)$ expresses the positive impact of aggregate endowment on growth; given equal size, a richer club grows at a higher rate. Second, $\ln(1 + n_j \rho)$ expresses the aggregate effect of free-riding: for a given aggregate endowment, the larger a club is, the more free riding there will be, and this will depress the growth rate for this club. Finally, αn_j expresses the congestion effect and the direct depressing effect of size on the growth rate of a given club.

We shall reason from the formulas for answering the three preceding questions. We first pose two additional questions:

1. How do the characteristics of the inequality schedule affect the pattern of growth through the equilibrium partition?
2. Does an increase in inequality lead to a more segmented society and more divergence in club growth rates?

13.4.3.1. Inequality Characteristics and Growth

We begin by tackling the first question. What we want to answer is whether the stratification process we assume can lead to a "twin peaks" or a "many peaks" phenomenon in the distribution of per capita output over time, that is, generate a nonconvergence process of output levels or growth rate.

Of course, quite complex endowment distributions lead to complex partitions, and it would be difficult to trace down their consequences for the growth pattern. Here, we restrict our attention to endowment distributions characterized by some monotonicity properties. We are able to offer the following:

Proposition 13.2. *The equilibrium partition and the pattern of growth associated to it are related to the endowment distribution in the following way:*

i) *If and only if $a_{i-1}/a_i = a_i/a_{i+1}, \forall i \in N$, then $n_j^E = n_{j+1}^E$ and $\eta_j^E > \eta_{j+1}^E$, $\forall j \in \{1, \dots, J-1\}$.*

ii) *If and only if $a_{i-1}/a_i \geq a_i/a_{i+1}, \forall i \in N$, then $n_j^E \leq n_{j+1}^E$ and $\eta_j^E > \eta_{j+1}^E$, $\forall j \in \{1, \dots, J-1\}$.*

iii) *If and only if $a_{i-1}/a_i \leq a_i/a_{i+1}, \forall i \in N$, then $n_j^E \geq n_{j+1}^E$, $\forall j \in \{1, \dots, J-1\}$, but the rate of growth of the jth club η_j^E is an ambiguous function of j.*

This proposition conveys information both on the stratification of society and of its consequences on growth. The stratification of society is related to the relative sizes of clubs n_j^E. This part of the proposition is strictly identical to the characteristics of stratification obtained in the static case by JKM, and the explanations are therefore parallel. Basically, what matters in this dynamic environment is the relative importance of the endowment of the pivotal agent of a club and the aggregate endowment of the entire club, that is, on the whole distribution of the endowment ratios a_{i+1}/a_i between members of a club. In the case of constant ratios, this explains why they have a constant size. When these ratios are decreasing, the relative importance of endowment for an agent with the same ranking in a club tends to increase with the ranking of a club. In a poorer club, its kth agent is relatively richer than the kth agent in a richer club. That explains why the poorer club is larger. The reverse explanation is true when the endowment ratios increase.

The consequences on growth are substantial, and Proposition 13.2 relates the characteristics of the pattern of growth to the characteristics of the endowment distribution. When it is such that the endowment ratio a_i/a_{i+1} is never increasing (i.e. items i and ii), then the rates of growth of the richer clubs are bigger than those of the poorer club. When the endowment ratio increases with the ranking of agents, then there is an ambiguity in the sign of the variation of growth rates.

This can be explained as follows. Consider the case in which endowment ratios are equal and therefore clubs in the equilibrium partition have the same size. As we saw before (see (13.4.22)), the growth rate depends on three effects: the aggregate wealth of a club, a congestion effect, and a free-riding effect. The congestion effect and the free-riding effect are the same for two clubs in the equilibrium partition because both depend on the club size. Two clubs only differ because of the aggregate wealth effect; therefore, a richer club grows at a faster rate than a poorer club.

Then, consider the case in which the endowment ratios decline with the ranking of individuals. This means that the endowment ratio is larger between two rich successive agents than between two poorer successive agents. The relative capacity to contribute to the club good declines with the ranking of agents. As we have just noted, this implies that a richer club is smaller than a poorer club. Hence, the three effects on the growth rate work in the same direction. There is less congestion in a richer club than in a poorer club, because its size is smaller; there is less free-riding effect because it is also related to size, and each agent contributes more in a richer club because he or she is richer than agents in a poorer club. Altogether, the aggregate amount of productive club good is higher in a richer club than in a poorer one. Consequently, a club formed of richer agents experiences a higher growth rate than a club formed of poorer agents when the endowment distribution is such that endowment ratios decline with the ranking of agents.

However, this is not true when the endowment ratios increase with the ranking of individuals. This corresponds to the case in which the endowment leap is smaller between two rich individuals than between two poor ones. We have just seen that the size of a club tends to decrease with the ranking of this club: a club formed of richer agents is larger than a club formed of poorer agents. Hence, the three effects on the growth rate work in opposite directions: a richer club represents a higher aggregate financing capability than a poorer one, but because it is larger, there are more congestion and free riding, which have a depressing effect on the growth rate. Altogether, there is an ambiguity, and we cannot conclude that a richer club experiences a greater growth rate. It may be characterized by a lower growth rate than a poorer club because of the negative effects due to a greater size.

With respect to the issue of convergence, it is clear that in the case of decreasing or equal endowment ratios a poorer club is unable to catch up with a richer club.

No convergence, either in levels or even in growth rates, can be observed. The clubs will continuously drift apart. It is only in the case of increasing endowment ratios that a convergence in levels may be observed: there may be a date when two growth clubs will experience the same aggregate level of output because the poorest club benefits from a higher growth rate than the richest one. But we should realize that this convergence, if it exists, will not last because, after this period, the initially poorest club becomes richer than the initially richest club. Of course, this does not contradict the ranking in welfare established at the beginning of history with a positive discount factor.

The general implication we can draw from Proposition 13.2 is that the pattern of growth and the answer to the convergence debate rely on the characteristics of the initial endowment distribution.

13.4.3.2. Difference in Inequality and the Pattern of Growth

As we have seen in Section 13.2, a large body of evidence supports the view that stratification and growth are intimately related. However, it has been impossible to address this issue in a positive sense through analytical models of market economies in which agents do belong to political jurisdictions and share public goods and values but are autonomous and free to make their accumulation decisions. Here, we shed some light on this debate by addressing the following issue: How does an increase in inequality affect the pattern of growth associated with the equilibrium partition in our economy?

We know that the different impacts of different endowment distributions on the pattern of growth come through a different stratification of the society in clubs. To highlight this link, we need the following definition:

Definition 13.4. *A society $\widetilde{N}$ is weakly (strictly) more stratified than a society N if the number of nonresidual clubs in the equilibrium partition $\widetilde{S}^E$ associated with $\widetilde{N}$, $\widetilde{J} - 1$, is at least equal to (bigger than) the number of nonresidual clubs in the equilibrium partition S^E associated with N, $J - 1$, and the jth club in $\widetilde{S}^E$ is never larger than the jth club in S^E, for $j < J$.*

Consider two societies N and $\widetilde{N}$ having an equal number of agents having identical preferences, n. First, we make two assumptions about the endowment distributions **a** associated with N and $\widetilde{\mathbf{a}}$ associated with $\widetilde{N}$:

A1 both societies have an identical aggregate (average) endowment $\mathcal{A}$;
A2 **a** and $\widetilde{\mathbf{a}}$ are such that $\widetilde{a}_i / \widetilde{a}_{i+1} > a_i / a_{i+1}, \forall i \in \{1, \ldots, n\}$.

To make relevant comparisons, we assume an equal aggregate initial endowment because we want to single out the impact of an increase in inequality. The second assumption allows us to state that $\widetilde{\mathbf{a}}$ is more unequal than **a** because **a** Lorenz-dominates $\widetilde{\mathbf{a}}$.

Additional and more restrictive assumptions can be made about the ranking of successive endowment ratios. In particular, we use the two following ones:

A3 **a** and $\widetilde{\mathbf{a}}$ are such that $a_{i+1}/a_i = a_{z+1}/a_z, \forall i, z \in N$ and $\widetilde{a}_{i+1}/\widetilde{a}_i = \widetilde{a}_{z+1}/\widetilde{a}_z, \forall i, z \in \widetilde{N}$.

A4 **a** and $\widetilde{\mathbf{a}}$ are such that $a_{i-1}/a_i > a_i/a_{i+1}, \forall i \in N$ and $\widetilde{a}_{i-1}/\widetilde{a}_i > \widetilde{a}_i/\widetilde{a}_{i+1}, \forall i \in \widetilde{N}$.

It is likely but not necessary that an increase in inequality modifies the equilibrium partition of society, for we have seen that the stratification into growth clubs depends on the relative endowments of agents. Under the two first assumptions only, in the admittedly special case in which stratification is similar for the two endowment distributions **a** and $\widetilde{\mathbf{a}}$, we are able to offer the following:

Proposition 13.3. *Assume two endowment distributions* **a** *and* $\widetilde{\mathbf{a}}$ *satisfying A1 and A2 are such that stratification is not modified* ($S^E = \widetilde{S}^E$). *Then,*

i) *for any* S_j^E *such that all its members are characterized by an endowment higher than the median or mean endowment,* $\widetilde{\eta}_j > \eta_j$.

ii) *for any* S_j^E *such that all its members are characterized by an endowment lower than the median or mean endowment,* $\widetilde{\eta}_j < \eta_j$.

iii) $(\widetilde{\eta}_j - \widetilde{\eta}_{j+1}) > (\eta_j - \eta_{j+1}), \forall j \leq J - 1$.

Because stratification is assumed to be identical, we get the same number of clubs for both endowment distributions and the same pivotal agents. Note that higher endowment ratios lead to a higher (lower) ratio $\frac{a_i}{\bar{a}}$, where $\bar{a}$ denotes the constant mean endowment, for any individual who is richer (poorer) than the average individual. Then, any club j, the members of which are richer (poorer) than the society's average individual, is richer (poorer) in aggregate terms in $\widetilde{N}$ than in N. Therefore, the club grows more (less) rapidly in $\widetilde{N}$ than in N because the change in inequality schedule does not modify the congestion or the free-riding effect when we assume a constant stratification of society (and therefore no modification of size for clubs of the same ranking). This explains i) and ii).

Moreover iii) states that an increase in inequality, under the assumption that stratification remains constant, widens the difference in growth rates between two successive clubs. This means that the divergence in growth paths is increased in the more unequal society.

Now we relax the constraint that both societies are characterized by the same stratification in clubs. First, we would like to understand the impact of an increase in inequality on the stratification of society into growth clubs. We are able to offer the following:

Proposition 13.4. *Assume two societies* N *and* $\widetilde{N}$ *satisfying A1, A2, and A3 or A4. Then,* $\widetilde{N}$ *is weakly more stratified than* N.

This proposition extends in the dynamic case the result obtained in the static case by JKM. A more equal society (which is Lorenz-dominant) is weakly less stratified than a more unequal one: it has at most as many nonresidual clubs, and each of its nonresidual clubs is at least as large as the corresponding nonresidual club (with the same ranking index) in the more unequal society. Note that under A3, the first club $\widetilde{S}_1^E$ is at most equal in size to S_j^E because endowment ratios are larger in $\widetilde{N}$ than in N and that the size of clubs is constant in each partition because of Proposition 13.2. Hence, each club in $\widetilde{S}^E$ is at most as large as the corresponding club in S^E. Under A4, the size of clubs increases with the ranking of the club in each partition. Hence, inasmuch as the first club $\widetilde{S}_1^E$ is at most equal in size to S_j^E because endowment heterogeneity is greater in $\widetilde{N}$ than in N, and $\widetilde{n}_2^E$ is at most equal to $\widetilde{n}_1^E$, this implies that $\widetilde{n}_2^E$ is at most equal to n_2^E.

However, we cannot conclude that a more equal society is weakly less stratified then a more unequal one in the case in which the endowment ratios increase with i because then it may happen that the first club is larger than the second club in $\widetilde{N}$ and N.

Turning now to the impact of structural parameters (endowment distribution and congestion) on the growth patterns, we offer the following:

Proposition 13.5. *i) Assume two economies N and $\widetilde{N}$ satisfying A1, A2, and A3 or A4 and such that $\widetilde{N}$ is strictly more stratified than N. Then, the growth rate of $\widetilde{S}_j^E$ is higher than the growth rate of S_j^E for any club S_j^E such that all its members are characterized by an endowment higher than the median or mean endowment.*

ii) For a given endowment distribution, an increase in α leads to a weakly more stratified society but has ambiguous effects on growth rates.

This proposition may be explained by reasoning sequentially on clubs. Consider the impact on the first (the richest) club of an increase of inequality such that the endowment ratios are at most equal when the ranking of individuals increases. The higher endowment leap between two successive individuals tends to decrease the number of members in this first club. This generates less congestion. It also leads to less free riding. Finally, higher endowment ratios lead to more affluent members when clubs are formed with richer than average members, who are more able and more willing to pay for the club good. Therefore, the first club grows at a higher rate in the more unequal economy $\widetilde{N}$ than the first club of the partition associated with N. Looking at the second clubs in N and $\widetilde{N}$, and assuming that their members are richer than the average individual, we remark that the richest agent of $\widetilde{S}_2^E$ is richer than the agent in N with the same ranking because of assumptions A1 and A2, who is himself richer than the richest agent of S_2^E because of his or her lower ranking (since $\widetilde{n}_1^E$ is at most as large as than n_1^E). Because $\widetilde{n}_2^E$ is at most as large as n_2^E, this implies that in aggregate members of $\widetilde{S}_2^E$ are richer than members of S_2^E. Hence, all three effects make the growth rate associated with $\widetilde{S}_2^E$ higher than the growth rate associated with S_2^E. By repeating the reasoning on the following clubs, we obtain the same result as long as the club we consider is formed of individuals richer than the average individual. When this is not true, the aggregate endowment of a club of rank j in $\widetilde{N}$ may be lower than the aggregate endowment of the club of same rank j in N. This has a depressing effect on the growth rate that may overcome the effects of a smaller size.

An increase in the congestion parameter tends to decrease the size of clubs because each additional member has to overcome a higher marginal cost and be able to contribute more. However, this implies that the first club is at most as rich as before, and this depresses the aggregate ability to pay for the public good. Hence, the smaller size of the first club and its lower aggregate endowment have conflicting effects on the formation of the club good, which leads to an ambiguous effect on the growth rate of the first club. This reasoning generalizes to any successive club.

13.4.4. Discussion

This section addresses the theoretical underpinnings of the "twin peaks" phenomena. We focus on the impact of inequality over the pattern of growth and prove that the nonconvergence phenomena may ultimately be related to the underlying structural inequality between agents. This is concluded by means of an explicit analysis of the formation of growth clubs, that is, of clubs of agents that share a club good with continuing productive capacities over time. Using coalition theory, we prove that the partition of society into growth clubs depends on three effects: a contributing effect inasmuch as an individual's provision for the club good depends on his or her individual endowment, a congestion effect because the increase in club size is supposed to have negative productive consequences, and a free-riding effect common to clubs with voluntary contribution to the public good.

We are then able to relate the partition of society and consequently its pattern of growth to the initial endowment distribution over infinitely lived agents. We prove that clubs are not characterized by an identical growth rate and therefore do not converge to a unique steady-state growing path. Under special assumptions on the endowment distribution, a catching-up process may take place, for the poorer clubs may grow at a higher rate than richer clubs.

Our results depend on several restrictive assumptions. Their relaxation should allow us to further explore the links among inequality, economic and social stratification, and the characteristics of the pattern of growth and perhaps uncover new dimensions for empirical investigation. Many of the assumptions were made for simplicity and could be relaxed at the expense of clarity. Two of them are particularly important.

First, it is assumed that the provision of the club good is made at the beginning of history once and forever. Obviously, this does not cover the more plausible case in which the club good is provided period after period: think about R&D expenditures and public infrastructure that needs to be repaired and improved over time. But taking this fact into account raises the annoying point that the core partition may be reassessed every period. Clearly this raises difficult technical issues that could not be tackled in this chapter.

Second, it is assumed that once clubs are formed, there are no economic relationships between them. But this is another crude simplification. Trade between economies can be interpreted as an enduring relationship between clubs. In other words, we exploit externalities within clubs but not externalities (spillovers) between clubs. However, such externalities are likely to affect the growth pattern and the convergence properties of the growth dynamics. It should therefore be valuable to include interclub relationships.[21]

13.5. Club Formation Dynamics and Growth

Even if communities exist for long periods, their borders vary over time, and this is likely to be linked to growth: some economic groups get poorer and poorer and eventually disappear, some groups go ahead and develop, and others are able to catch up; therefore, the whole pattern of clustering varies over time during the growth process. The model in the previous section relies on a commitment assumption that there is no variation in the clusters of agents. But there are obvious dynamics in the frontiers of communities: witness the current process of European integration. Is it possible to overcome the limits of the previous model and capture the important phenomenon of cluster dynamics by means of coalition theory?

In this section, we answer this question affirmatively by developing a model tractable enough to allow us to characterize the pattern of intergenerational group formation and income dynamics. This model, based on Jaramillo and Moizeau (2002), is different in many ways from the model presented in the previous section, and we will briefly survey it.

We consider a society formed by $N = 3n$ agents characterized by different human capital endowments. There are three possible levels of initial endowment. This is the only source of heterogeneity. At time $t = 0$, endowments are characterized by the following inequalities: $0 < h_0^l < h_0^m < h_0^h$. Each initial endowment type is of size n. Each individual lives one period. An individual i living in neighborhood j who lives at time t has the following preferences:

$$U\left(c_{j,t}^i, h_{j,t+1}^i\right) = \ln c_{j,t}^i + \ln h_{j,t+1}^i, \tag{13.5.1}$$

where c_t^i denotes private consumption of individual i and $h_{j,t+1}^i$ is the human capital stock left to his or her offspring. This altruism component relies on a "joy of giving" motive for bequest. The inherited human capital forms individual i's income at t.

Individuals have no access to credit. They accumulate human capital according to the technology given by equation (13.3.2). We denote by $h_{j,t}$ the aggregate human capital in neighborhood j and by h_t the society's average human capital. The following function generates $h_{j,t}$:

$$h_{j,t} = \sum_{i \in S_{j,t}} g_t^i - n_{j,t}\omega.$$

The human capital in neighborhood j is raised by voluntary contributions of members denoted g_t^i. But a per capita linear congestion cost ω is assumed to hinder its formation.[22]

---

[21] On this point, see Beaudry, Cahuc, and Kempf (2000).

[22] For simplicity, we will consider that those costs are infinitesimal. However, the existence of congestion costs is required for the size of a community to be potentially smaller than total population (i.e., $3n$).

At each date t, two steps can be distinguished:

1. First, individuals decide on their neighborhood membership.
2. Second, in each neighborhood, individual members choose their voluntary provision to the financing of the neighborhood's human capital.

As in the previous section, we suppose that the formation process is accomplished cooperatively, whereas the second one is characterized by noncooperation. The equilibrium we are interested in is defined as follows:

Definition 13.5. $[(c_t^{iE}, g_t^{iE})_{i \in N}; S_t^E = (S_{1,t}^E, \ldots, S_{J,t}^E)]$ *is an equilibrium if, at each date t, it satisfies the following:*

i) *the equilibrium partition, S_t^E, is required to belong to the core of the coalition formation game;*
ii) *(c_t^{iE}, g_t^{iE}) is a Nash equilibrium that solves for any $i \in N$:*

$$\max_{g_t^i} U\left(c_t^i, h_{j,t+1}^i\right) = \ln c_t^i + \ln h_{j,t+1}^i$$

subject to

$$c_t^i + g_t^i \le h_t^i$$

$$h_{j,t+1}^i = \left(\sum_{z \in S_{j,t}} g_t^z\right)^\beta (h_t)^\nu \left(h_t^i\right)^{1-\nu-\beta}$$

$$g_t^i \ge 0, \text{ given } h_t^i, h_t.$$

To solve the model, we proceed backwards. The first-order condition to the second-stage optimization problem gives us the best reply function for individual i's contribution, when i belongs to neighborhood j:

$$g_t^i = \begin{cases} h_t^i - \dfrac{\sum\limits_{z \in S_{j,t}} g_t^z}{\beta} & \text{if } h_t^i > \dfrac{\sum\limits_{z \in S_{j,t}} g_t^z}{\beta} \\ 0 & \text{otherwise.} \end{cases}$$

Two properties about the individual's contributions are worth emphasizing. First, because the local public good is normal, it increases with respect to the human capital endowment. Second, there are strategic substitutabilities between members of $S_{j,t}$ because an individual contribution is decreasing with the aggregate provision of the neighborhood's human capital.

A Nash equilibrium exists at the second stage, and if we sum over the whole neighborhood population, the level of human capital $h_{j,t}$ equals

$$h_{j,t} = \frac{\sum\limits_{i \in S_{j,t}} h_t^i}{\beta + n_{j,t}}.$$

It turns out that human capital formed at t in neighborhood j increases with the sum of existing human capital endowments in the community, thus generating an incentive for any individual to be a member of the richest possible neighborhood.

The indirect utility for any individual i who belongs to $S_{j,t}$ easily obtains:

$$V_{i,t}(S_{j,t}) = (1 + \beta) \ln \left(\frac{\sum_{z \in S_{j,t}} h_t^z}{\beta + n_{j,t}} \right) - \ln \beta + (1 - \nu - \beta) \ln h_t^i + \nu \ln \overline{h}_t.$$

Moving to the coalition formation stage, we look for the equilibrium partition. Owing to the (infinitesimal) congestion effects, we can anticipate that, at equilibrium, no free-rider with zero provision will be accepted in a coalition because that individual's entry would only increase congestion costs. The various human capital ratios at time t are denoted by $\lambda_{h,m}^t = \frac{h_t^h}{h_t^m}$ and $\lambda_{m,l}^t = \frac{h_t^m}{h_t^l}$. We are able to show the following:

Proposition 13.6. *The equilibrium partition exists and is characterized as follows:*

i) $S_t^E = (\{h, m, l\})$ *if and only if* $\lambda_{h,m}^t < \frac{\beta+n}{n}$ *and* $(\frac{\beta+2n}{n})/(1 + \lambda_{h,m}^t) > \lambda_{m,l}^t$.

ii) $S_t^E = (\{h, m\}, \{l\})$ *if and only if* $\lambda_{h,m}^t < \frac{\beta+n}{n}$ *and* $(\frac{\beta+2n}{n})/(1 + \lambda_{h,m}^t) \leq \lambda_{m,l}^t$.

iii) $S_t^E = (\{h\}, \{m\}, \{l\})$ *if and only if* $\lambda_{h,m}^t \geq \frac{\beta+n}{n}$ *and* $\lambda_{m,l}^t \geq \frac{\beta+n}{n}$.

iv) $S_t^E = (\{h\}, \{m, l\})$ *if and only if* $\lambda_{h,m}^t \geq \frac{\beta+n}{n}$ *and* $\lambda_{m,l}^t < \frac{\beta+n}{n}$.[23]

Proposition 13.6 provides a characterization of the equilibrium partition for a particular pattern of human capital distribution. We can see that when there is at least one human capital ratio $\lambda_{h,m}^t$ or $\lambda_{m,l}^t$ that is too high, there is segregation in the sense that the core partition is not the grand coalition.

The basic intuition behind this result can be described as follows. Let us consider the case in which, in equilibrium, rich and middle-income categories merge together, leaving the poor agents to form their own community, $S_t^E = (\{h, m\}, \{l\})$. In this case, the human capital distribution is such that the rich and the middle-income types are close enough in the capital distribution, $\lambda_{h,m}^t < \frac{\beta+n}{n}$, and thus both categories find it worthwhile to form the coalition $\{h, m\}$ (they both contribute a positive amount to the financing of the local resources). However, poor agents lagging further behind in the capital distribution such that $(\frac{\beta+2n}{n})/(1 + \lambda_{h,m}^t) > \lambda_{m,l}^t$, are excluded from the richer group because they are not able to contribute a positive amount in coalition $\{h, m, l\}$. Moreover, as the result of linear congestion effects, coalitions in the equilibrium partition are such that if a particular agent of type i belongs to a neighborhood, it turns out that the entire income i type will be in that neighborhood.[24] As stressed in Section 13.4, the equilibrium partition is unique, stratified, and welfare ordered.

Stratification obtained at time t, linked from human capital distribution characterizing t, is crucial for the future of inequality dynamics and growth because it determines specific rates of human capital accumulation for each type of agent. We thus now turn to the study of the human capital distribution dynamics:

Proposition 13.7. *For any period t, inequality dynamics are given by the following equations as determined by the equilibrium partition prevailing at t:*

i) *When $S_t^E = (\{h, m, l\})$: $\lambda_{h,m}^{t+1} = (\lambda_{h,m}^t)^{1-\nu-\beta}$ and $\lambda_{m,l}^{t+1} = (\lambda_{m,l}^t)^{1-\nu-\beta}$.*

ii) *When $S_t^E = (\{h, m\}, \{l\})$: $\lambda_{h,m}^{t+1} = (\lambda_{h,m}^t)^{1-\nu-\beta}$ and $\lambda_{m,l}^{t+1} = (\frac{\beta+n}{\beta+2n})^\beta (1 + \lambda_{h,m}^t)^\beta (\lambda_{m,l}^t)^{1-\nu}$.*

iii) *When $S_t^E = (\{h\}, \{m\}, \{l\})$: $\lambda_{h,m}^{t+1} = (\lambda_{h,m}^t)^{1-\nu}$ and $\lambda_{m,l}^{t+1} = (\lambda_{m,l}^t)^{1-\nu}$.*

iv) *When $S_t^E = (\{h\}, \{m, l\})$: $\lambda_{h,m}^{t+1} = (\frac{\beta+2n}{\beta+n})^\beta (\frac{1}{1+(1/\lambda_{m,l}^t)})^\beta (\lambda_{h,m}^t)^{1-\nu}$ and $\lambda_{m,l}^{t+1} = (\lambda_{m,l}^t)^{1-\nu-\beta}$.*

This proposition stresses the role of stratification on inequality dynamics. Proposition 13.7 states that four partitions compatible with the core can be formed in this economy and that each one is characterized by a particular system of dynamic equations. At each period t, only one corresponds to the equilibrium partition. Importantly, in this setting nothing precludes the change of equilibrium partition over time. The accumulation of individual human capital at t may well explain why at $t + 1$ the next generation will choose to form another equilibrium partition different from the one that prevails at t. According to Proposition 13.7, note that, when the core partition at date t is $S_t^E = (\{h, m, l\})$, income dynamics are such that heterogeneity between the three income types vanishes, thus reinforcing incentives to form the grand coalition at date $t + 1$. However, there are other cases in which the core partition dynamics are more complex and difficult to predict. For instance, when $S_t^E = (\{h\}, \{m\}, \{l\})$, the resulting convergence in the human capital distribution increases incentives for income types to interact in common groups, leading to a new core partition.

The study of these dynamic systems allows us to show that two steady states may exist characterized as follows:

Proposition 13.8. *If and only if parameters β, ν, n are such that*

$$\beta/\nu \geq \Pi(\beta, n) = \ln\left(\frac{2n + \beta}{2n}\right) \Big/ \ln\left(\frac{2(n + \beta)}{2n + \beta}\right) > 1$$

there exist two steady states:

i) *The integrated equilibrium (IE) is characterized by a completely homogeneous population, that is, $\lambda_{h,m}^\infty = \lambda_{m,l}^\infty = 1$, which belongs to the same community, namely, $S_t^E = (\{h, m, l\})$. It is a globally stable steady state when $\lambda_{h,m}^t < \frac{\beta+n}{n}$ and $(\frac{\beta+2n}{n})/(1 + \lambda_{h,m}^t) > \lambda_{m,l}^t$.*

ii) *The stratified equilibrium (SE) is such that the high- and middle-income classes form an homogeneous community whereas the low-income class remains isolated, that is, $S_t^E = (\{h, m\}, \{l\})$. In this case, there is persistent inequality, namely, $\lambda_{h,m}^\infty = 1$ and $\lambda_{m,l}^\infty = (\frac{2n}{\beta+2n} * \frac{(\beta+n)}{n})^{\frac{\beta}{\nu}} > 1$. It is a locally stable steady state when $\lambda_{h,m}^t < \frac{\beta+n}{n}$ and $(\frac{\beta+2n}{n})/(1 + \lambda_{h,m}^t) \leq \lambda_{m,l}^t$. Otherwise, the integrated equilibrium is the unique steady state.*

> *Furthermore, the integrated equilibrium has a higher growth rate than the stratified one.*

In the integrated equilibrium, the whole population forms the grand coalition and benefits from the same local resources. Thus, as emphasized above, the three inputs of equation (13.3.2) together drive convergence of the human capital distribution. In the stratified equilibrium, both rich and middle-income classes have access to the same local resources and become identical, whereas poor agents remain excluded from this rich community and benefit from reduced local inputs. The stationary human capital distribution thus displays persistent inequality measured by a permanent income gap between these two coalitions equal to $(\frac{2(n+\beta)}{2n+\beta})^{\beta/\nu}$.

This proposition also highlights the crucial role of parameters ν and β. A stratified and unequal society may arise in the long run if and only if the effect of the local resources input, the intensity of which is given by the value of β, is high enough compared with the global externality impact measured by ν. In other words, the stratified equilibrium becomes possible when the local externality driving divergence supersedes the convergence force generated by the global externality.

With respect to the growth issue, it can be shown that stratification depresses growth. This directly refers to Bénabou's results on the impact of the social structure on the long-term rate of growth (reviewed in Section 13.3.3). More precisely, our framework is a particular case of Bénabou's theoretical settings (Bénabou 1996a,b), for we only consider a concave human capital technology implying that an integrated society is more favorable for growth because poor neighborhoods lose more from stratification than rich communities.

Let us now focus on transitional dynamics and consider an initial human capital distribution such that $\lambda_{h,m}^t \geq \frac{\beta+n}{n}$ and $\lambda_{m,l}^t \geq \frac{\beta+n}{n}$. In such a situation, inequalities are high and stratification is complete; that is, each human capital type forms its own group, $\mathcal{S}_0^E = (\{h\}, \{m\}, \{l\})$. Owing to decreasing marginal returns to scale and because each group is of size n, resulting dynamics are such that ratios $\lambda_{h,m}^t$ and $\lambda_{m,l}^t$ tend to reduce. Over a finite time, subsequent generations are closer in the human capital scale but then face the possibility of forming another partition of the society. Two possible scenarios arise: either the middle income class catching up with the rich is given the opportunity to form group $\{h, m\}$ (Scenario 1) or the middle and poor types are close enough that they decide to merge (Scenario 2). In fact, the trajectory of the economy depends on values reached by variables $\lambda_{h,m}^t$ and $\lambda_{m,l}^t$. If $\lambda_{m,l}^t$ becomes lower than the threshold value $\frac{\beta+n}{n}$ before $\lambda_{h,m}^t$, there is more homogeneity in the lower scale of the human capital ladder and, according to Proposition 13.6, inequalities are such that the equilibrium partition is $\mathcal{S}_t^E = (\{h\}, \{m, l\})$. The path dependency of income dynamics is illustrated by the fact that Scenario 2 (respectively Scenario 1) arises if and only if initial inequalities are such that $\lambda_{h,m}^0 > \lambda_{m,l}^0$ (respectively $\lambda_{h,m}^0 < \lambda_{m,l}^0$).

Suppose that income dynamics are such that $\mathcal{S}_t^E = (\{h\}, \{m, l\})$ occurs. In this case, the middle and poor types benefit from the same local linkages and thus become progressively more similar (i.e., $\lambda_{m,l}^t$ is reduced). Although rich agents in their own group produce higher local resources, a catching-up phenomenon occurs owing to decreasing marginal returns to scale and to a size effect ($\{m, l\}$ is of size $2n$ whereas $\{h\}$ is of size n). Consequently, at a given time t, the middle-income group experiences an upward-moving social mobility forming $\{h, m\}$, whereas the poor are downward moving and are left on their own, forming $\{l\}$. When this happens, rich and middle-income types then benefit from better local linkages and begin to move away from the poor. In this case, after a finite time, two transitions are possible. Either social polarization is enhanced and the economy converges to the stratified equilibrium, or, despite increasing $\lambda_{m,l}^t$, the low-income class is rich enough to be accepted eventually in the grand coalition $\{h, m, l\}$ and the dynamics of economy are modified. In this case, the economy evolves toward the integrated equilibrium. This transition is possible owing to the social externality effect and because heterogeneity within $\{h, m\}$ lowers its accumulation rate.

Human capital trajectories crucially depend on the parameter values. We are able to offer the following:

Proposition 13.9. *Let* $\Gamma(v, \beta, n)$ *be defined as follows:*

$$
\Gamma(v, \beta, n) = \ln\left(\frac{\frac{2n+\beta}{n}}{1 + \left(\frac{n+\beta}{n}\right)^{(1-v-\beta)}} \right)^{\frac{1}{v}} \bigg/ \ln\left(1 + \left(\frac{n}{\beta}\right)^{-1}\right) > \Pi(\beta, n).
$$

i) *When parameters* v, β, n *are such that* $\frac{\beta}{v} \geq \Gamma(v, \beta, n)$, *then if* $\lambda_{h,m}^0 < \frac{\beta+n}{n}$ *and* $(\frac{\beta+2n}{n})/(1 + \lambda_{h,m}^0) > \lambda_{m,l}^0$ *such that* $\mathcal{S}_0^E = (\{h, m, l\})$, *then the economy ends up integrated. Otherwise, the economy is stratified in the long run.*

ii) *When parameters* v, β, n *are such that* $\Gamma(v, \beta, n) > \frac{\beta}{v} \geq \Pi(\beta, n)$, *if for a given* $\lambda_{h,m}^0$, $\lambda_{l,m}^0 \geq \widetilde{\lambda}_{l,m}^0$, *then the economy evolves toward the stratified equilibrium.*

iii) *When parameters* v, β, n *are such that* $\Pi(\beta, n) > \frac{\beta}{v}$, *then the economy evolves toward the integrated equilibrium.*

It turns out that if the ratio $\frac{\beta}{v}$ is above the threshold value Γ, many economies are likely to end up unequal. In other words, Proposition 13.9 stresses that, if the divergence force generated by the local externality (measured by β) sufficiently exceeds the convergence force of the social externality (measured by v), then chances for an economy to end up integrated are small because this scenario only occurs in the unlikely case of an initial emergence of the grand coalition.

For lower values of $\frac{\beta}{v}$, predictions of the long-run behavior of the economy become more complicated. However, we can derive a sufficient condition for $\lambda_{l,m}^0$ that allows us to know whether a society will end up stratified. To this aim, we define the threshold value $\widetilde{\lambda}_{l,m}^0$ such that

$$
\widetilde{\lambda}_{l,m}^0 = \left(\frac{\beta + 2n}{2n} \right)^{\left[(1-v-\beta)^{t^*-\widehat{t}}(1-v)^{\widehat{t}} \right]^{-1}}
$$

with t^*, respectively $\widehat{t}$, with $t^* \geq \widehat{t} \geq 0$, the date at which $\mathcal{S}_t^E = (\{h, m\}, \{l\})$, respectively $\mathcal{S}_t^E = (\{h, m\}, \{l\})$, occurs for the first time.

If the initial distribution exhibits a wealth bias against the low-income type such that $\lambda_{l,m}^0 \geq \tilde{\lambda}_{l,m}^0$, then it turns out that the handicap of poor people is so serious that they never have the opportunity to catch up with richer income classes and become accepted in the community $\{h, m, l\}$.

In the last case, the global externality is sufficiently high compared with the local one such that whatever the initial distribution and the associated pattern of stratification, the economy will reach the integrated equilibrium.

In this section, a simple model of human capital accumulation with group effects has been developed to stress the feedback relationship between cross-sectional inequality and the social organization into distinct temporary coalitions. More precisely, we show that the pattern of income distribution leads at each period to a unique partition of a society that determines its growth performance and in turn the subsequent income distribution. There are therefore two interrelated dynamics: a social dynamics (the evolution of the partition over time) and an economic dynamics (the growth trajectories of the varying groups over time). These dynamics may then be characterized by multiple steady states. In particular, there may be a convergence to a steady-state stratified society or, alternatively, to a steady-state integrated society. The model allows us to predict the long-term behavior of an economy according to the magnitude of local and global externalities and initial inequality.

13.6. Conclusion

Our goal in this chapter was to prove that coalition theory is useful for addressing macroeconomic issues such as growth. Macroeconomics is slowly exploring issues that entail heterogeneity. Analyses being based on large aggregates are too crude. Disaggregation appears as a necessary preliminary to many studies. Thus, macroeconomists are in need of a theory to help them select the "right" level of aggregation. Is it local, regional, or national? Moreover, although recognizing the importance of externalities, macroeconomists are often at a loss when the task is to provide an understanding of the shape of these externalities. Why are some links between agents internalized and not others? Why do we witness partial but rarely global cooperation?

Coalition theory may be useful to answer both questions. Basically, some groups form in relation to a given macroeconomic issue. The "right" level of aggregation is therefore related to the shapes of groups. The formation of groups also has major impact on the type of externalities between agents. Some are internalized by means of group formation because agents want to cooperate in some manner within a chosen group; some are not internalized.

Growth is a domain in which these issues matter greatly: there is strong evidence that stratification is related to growth, both at the international and the intranational levels, and that group formation is important in shaping the numerous sources of growth, including the numerous factors hidden beneath the total factor productivity. This explains why we think that coalition theory should be a powerful tool for a better understanding of the growth processes.

Having documented stylized facts on the relationship between stratification and growth, we first offered a model linking the formation of coalitions and the ensuing characteristics of growth. We provided microeconomic foundations to the stratification of a society in growth clubs, using some coalition theory tools. Stratification was shown to depend on inequality, that is, on the characteristics of the initial individual endowment distribution. Then, we studied the growth processes over time of these clubs. In doing so, we addressed a major puzzling issue, namely, the nonconvergence over time of the entire economy to a unique steady state despite assumed similar technology and tastes. We proved that the formation of different growth clubs is likely to lead to different growth rates and thus to ever-increasing differences in output between clubs.

However, this first model is such that the partition of society into clubs is done once and forever. In other words, there are no actual dynamics in the shaping of groups over time. In the last section, we presented another model of growth with group formation in which such dynamics occur and we discussed the various trajectories that may develop given initial conditions. This illustrates the potential of using group formation tools to study growth. In particular, along with a given dynamic sequence of group formation, the growth process may exhibit irregularities such as "miracles" and "busts."

Of course, these models are limited by some strong assumptions made either on the process of group formation or on the type of growth externalities. We hope that, as they stand, they illustrate the potential of applying coalition theory tools to the study of growth and, more generally, to macroeconomic issues at large.

APPENDIX

13.A. – Proof of Proposition 13.1

13.A.1. Existence

Because voluntary individual contribution to the club good yields the same level of indirect utility for individuals belonging to the same club, our coalition formation game turns out to be identical to the one developed by Farrell and Scotchmer (1988) in the case of partnerships. Our proof thus follows their existence demonstration, which entails constructing an equilibrium partition.

First, let us consider the club S_1^E that maximizes the utility function $V(., \mathbf{a}, \alpha)$. Those agents belonging to S_1^E thus get the highest possible level of utility. Second, we can restrict our attention to the subset $N \backslash S_1^E$ and form a club S_2^E of agents remaining in this subset that maximizes $V(., \mathbf{a}, \alpha)$. We repeat the process until the set $\{S_1^E, \ldots, S_j^E, \ldots\}$ constitutes a partition of N. It then turns out that this partition $S^E = \{S_1^E, \ldots, S_j^E, \ldots\}$ belongs to the core of the coalition formation game. The reason is that no blocking coalition can contain any member of S_1^E because they obtain the highest possible level of utility. This argument is also true for those agents belonging to S_2^E, and so on.

13.A.2. Uniqueness

Suppose that there exist two equilibrium partitions $\mathcal{S}^E = \{S_1^E, \ldots, S_j^E, \ldots\}$ and $\mathcal{S}'^E = \{S_1'^E, \ldots, S_j'^E, \ldots\}$ with $S_1^E \subset S_1'^E$ and $V(S_1^E, \mathbf{a}, \alpha) = V(S_1'^E, \mathbf{a}, \alpha)$. We argue that this case is nongeneric. After small perturbations of initial individual endowments, there will no longer be two coalitions that would give the same maximal level of utility. Thus, if the club S_1^E that maximizes utility is unique, it must appear in any core partition, and so on. The core partition is then generically unique.

13.A.3. Stratification

Let us consider by contradiction that the equilibrium partition $\mathcal{S}^E = \{S_1^E, \ldots, S_j^E, \ldots\}$ is constituted by nonstratified clubs. Without loss of generality, we suppose that $S_1^E = \{1, \ldots, i, i+2, \ldots, n_1\}$ and $S_2^E = \{i+1, n_1+1, \ldots, n_1+n_2\}$ with $V(S_1^E, \mathbf{a}, \alpha) > V(S_2^E, \mathbf{a}, \alpha)$. If we form the new club $\pounds = (S_1^E \setminus \{n_1\}) \cup \{i+1\}$, because $a_{i+1} > a_{n_1}$, it is easy to show from the comparative statics on $V(S_j, \mathbf{a}, \alpha)$ that $\pounds$ is a blocking coalition. Because

$$\frac{\partial V(S_j, \mathbf{a}, \alpha)}{\partial \left(\sum\limits_{i \in S_j} a_i \right)} = -\frac{1}{\rho} \frac{\Gamma_1 A_{11}}{A_1(G_j^*, n_j)} + \frac{1}{\rho^2} \Gamma_1 A_1 > 0,$$

it implies

$$V(\pounds, \mathbf{a}, \alpha) > V\left(S_1^E, \mathbf{a}, \alpha\right) \forall i \in \pounds,$$

which contradicts the fact that $\mathcal{S}^E$ is an equilibrium partition.

13.A.4. Welfare Ordering

Let us consider by contradiction that the equilibrium partition $\mathcal{S}^E = \{S_1^E, \ldots, S_j^E, \ldots\}$ does not satisfy the welfare-ordering property. Without loss of generality, we suppose that the club S_1^E containing the richest members provides less utility than the club S_2^E, that is,

$$V\left(S_2^E, \mathbf{a}, \alpha\right) > V\left(S_1^E, \mathbf{a}, \alpha\right).$$

In this case, any agent $i \in S_1^E$ has an incentive to propose the following group $\pounds = (S_2^E \setminus \{z\}) \cup \{i\}$ with $z \in S_2^E$ that satisfies

$$V(\pounds, \mathbf{a}, \alpha) > V\left(S_2^E, \mathbf{a}, \alpha\right) > V\left(S_1^E, \mathbf{a}, \alpha\right),$$

which contradicts the fact that $\mathcal{S}^E$ belongs to the core.

13.B. – Proof of Proposition 13.2

We now denote the endowment ratio a_i/a_{i+1} by $\lambda_{i,i+1}$. First, let us provide a formal definition of a pivotal agent.

Definition 13.6. *For a given equilibrium partition* $S^E = \{S_1^E, \ldots, S_j^E, \ldots\}$, *a pivotal agent of a club* S_j^E *indexed by* p_j *is defined by the following inequalities:*

$$a_{p_j} \geq \sum_{z=p_{j-1}+1}^{p_j-1} a_z \left(e^{\frac{\alpha}{1+\rho}} \frac{1+n_j^E \rho}{1+(n_j^E-1)\rho} - 1 \right) \tag{13.A1}$$

and

$$a_{p_j+1} < \sum_{z=p_{j-1}+1}^{p_j} a_z \left(e^{\frac{\alpha}{1+\rho}} \frac{1+n_j^E \rho + \rho}{1+n_j^E \rho} - 1 \right). \tag{13.A2}$$

In other words, the pivotal agent is such that the marginal benefit of his or her entry into a club covers the subsequent marginal cost but the marginal benefit of the entry of the agent immediately after him or her (indexed $p_j + 1$) in the inequality schedule does not cover the subsequent marginal cost.

We rewrite (13.A1) and (13.A2) as follows:

$$1 \geq \left(e^{\frac{\alpha}{1+\rho}} \frac{1+n_j^E \rho}{1+(n_j^E-1)\rho} - 1 \right) \sum_{z=p_{j-1}+1}^{p_j-1} \left(\prod_{x=z}^{p_j-1} \lambda_{x,x+1} \right) \tag{13.A3}$$

and

$$1 < \left(e^{\frac{\alpha}{1+\rho}} \frac{1+n_j^E \rho + \rho}{1+n_j^E \rho} - 1 \right) \sum_{z=p_{j-1}+1}^{p_j} \left(\prod_{x=z}^{p_j} \lambda_{x,x+1} \right). \tag{13.A4}$$

Second, we focus on the link between the size of the nonresidual clubs and the endowment distribution **a**. Let us consider the inequality schedule such that $\lambda_{i,i+1} \geq \lambda_{i+1,i+2}$, $\forall i \in N$. We write $n(i)$ (resp. $n(i')$) to denote the optimal size of the club when i (resp. i', $i' < i$) is its richest member. Hence, according to inequalities (13.A2), $n(i)$ and $n(i')$ are the smallest integers such that the following inequalities are satisfied:

$$1 < \left(e^{\frac{\alpha}{1+\rho}} \frac{1+n(i)\rho + \rho}{1+n(i)\rho} - 1 \right) \sum_{z=i}^{i+n(i)-1} \left(\prod_{x=z}^{i+n(i)-1} \lambda_{x,x+1} \right)$$

and

$$1 < \left(e^{\frac{\alpha}{1+\rho}} \frac{1+n(i')\rho + \rho}{1+n(i')\rho} - 1 \right) \sum_{z=i'}^{i'+n(i')-1} \left(\prod_{x=z}^{i'+n(i')-1} \lambda_{x,x+1} \right).$$

Because $\lambda_{x,x+1} \geq \lambda_{x+1,x+2}$, $\forall x \in N$, it turns out that

$$\left(e^{\frac{\alpha}{1+\rho}} \frac{1+n(i)\rho + \rho}{1+n(i)\rho} - 1 \right) \sum_{z=i'}^{i'+n(i)-1} \left(\prod_{x=z}^{i'+n(i)-1} \lambda_{x,x+1} \right)$$

$$\geq \left(e^{\frac{\alpha}{1+\rho}} \frac{1+n(i)\rho + \rho}{1+n(i)\rho} - 1 \right) \sum_{z=i}^{i+n(i)-1} \left(\prod_{x=z}^{i+n(i)-1} \lambda_{x,x+1} \right),$$

which implies that $n(i') \leq n(i)$, $\forall i' < i$, i' and $i \in N$.

Now, we show that $n(i') \le n(i)$, $\forall i' < i$, i' and $i \in N$ implies that $\lambda_{x,x+1} \ge \lambda_{x+1,x+2}$, $\forall x \in N$. Given that $n(i') \le n(i)$, we can write

$$\left(e^{\frac{\alpha}{1+\rho}} \frac{1 + n(i')\rho + \rho}{1 + n(i')\rho} - 1\right) \sum_{z=i'}^{i'+n(i')-1} \left(\prod_{x=z}^{i'+n(i')-1} \lambda_{x,x+1}\right)$$

$$\ge \left(e^{\frac{\alpha}{1+\rho}} \frac{1 + n(i')\rho + \rho}{1 + n(i')\rho} - 1\right) \sum_{z=i}^{i+n(i')-1} \left(\prod_{x=z}^{i+n(i')-1} \lambda_{x,x+1}\right),$$

leading to the inequality

$$\sum_{z=i'}^{i'+n(i')-1} \left(\prod_{x=z}^{i'+n(i')-1} \lambda_{x,x+1}\right) \ge \sum_{z=i}^{i+n(i')-1} \left(\prod_{x=z}^{i+n(i')-1} \lambda_{x,x+1}\right),$$

which is true when $\lambda_{x,x+1} \ge \lambda_{x+1,x+2}$, $\forall x \in N$. Thus, we can conclude that for a given equilibrium partition, whatever $j \in \{1, \ldots, J-1\}$, $n_{j+1}^E \ge n_j^E$ if and only if $\lambda_{x,x+1} \ge \lambda_{x+1,x+2}$, $\forall x \in N$. The proof is similar for $\lambda_{x,x+1} = \lambda$ and $\lambda_{x,x+1} \le \lambda_{x+1,x+2}$, $\forall x \in N$.

Third, we now concentrate on the link between the pattern of growth and the inequality characteristics of a society. For a given equilibrium partition $S^E = \{S_1^E, \ldots, S_j^E, \ldots\}$, and according to (13.4.22), we have, whatever $j, j' \in \{1, \ldots, J-1\}$ and $j \ne j'$:

$$\eta_j - \eta_{j'} = \ln\left(\frac{\sum_{i \in S_j^E} a_i}{\sum_{i \in S_{j'}^E} a_i}\right) - \ln\left(\frac{1 + n_j^E \rho}{1 + n_{j'}^E \rho}\right) - \alpha\left(n_j^E - n_{j'}^E\right) \tag{13.A5}$$

and

$$V\left(S_j^E, \mathbf{a}, \alpha\right) - V\left(S_{j'}^E, \mathbf{a}, \alpha\right)$$

$$= \left(\frac{1}{\rho} + \frac{1}{\rho^2}\right)\left[\ln\left(\frac{\sum_{i \in S_j^E} a_i}{\sum_{i \in S_{j'}^E} a_i}\right) - \ln\left(\frac{1 + n_j^E \rho}{1 + n_{j'}^E \rho}\right)\right] - \frac{\alpha}{\rho^2}\left(n_j^E - n_{j'}^E\right).$$

Thus, when $n_{j+1}^E = n_j^E$ whatever $j \in \{1, \ldots, J-1\}$, we have

$$\eta_j - \eta_{j+1} = \ln\left(\frac{\sum_{i \in S_j^E} a_i}{\sum_{i \in S_{j+1}^E} a_i}\right),$$

which is positive whatever $j \in \{1, \ldots, J-1\}$ given the stratification property.

According to the welfare ordering property, if $j < j'$, we have

$$V\left(S_j^E, \mathbf{a}, \alpha\right) - V\left(S_{j'}^E, \mathbf{a}, \alpha\right) > 0$$

which is equivalent to

$$\ln\left(\frac{\sum\limits_{i\in S_j^E} a_i}{\sum\limits_{i\in S_{j'}^E} a_i}\right) > \ln\left(\frac{1+n_j^E \rho}{1+n_{j'}^E \rho}\right) + \frac{\alpha}{\rho+1}\left(n_j^E - n_{j'}^E\right).$$

Given equation (13.A5), it turns out that

$$\eta_j - \eta_{j'} > \frac{-\alpha\rho}{\rho+1}\left(n_j^E - n_{j'}^E\right).$$

As a consequence, when $n_{j+1}^E \geq n_j^E$ whatever $j \in \{1, \ldots, J-1\}$, we can easily conclude that $\eta_j - \eta_{j+1} > 0$ whatever $j \in \{1, \ldots, J-1\}$. However, in the case in which $n_j^E \geq n_{j+1}^E$ whatever $j \in \{1, \ldots, J-1\}$, the sign of $\eta_j - \eta_{j+1}$ is ambiguous.

13.C. – Proof of Proposition 13.3

Let us consider two economies N and $\widetilde{N}$ satisfying A1 and A2. We thus know that, whatever $i \in N$ with $a_i > \frac{A}{n}$ (respectively, $a_i < \frac{A}{n}$), we have $\widetilde{a}_i > a_i$ (respectively, $\widetilde{a}_i < a_i$). Let us now consider two equilibrium partitions $S^E = \{S_1^E, \ldots, S_j^E, \ldots\}$ and $\widetilde{S}^E = \{\widetilde{S}_1^E, \ldots, \widetilde{S}_j^E, \ldots\}$, respectively, associated with $\mathbf{a}$ and $\widetilde{\mathbf{a}}$ satisfying A1 and A2 and such that (i) for clubs S_j^E with $j = \{1, \ldots, \underline{j}\}$ we have $a_i > \frac{A}{n} \forall i \in S_j^E$, and (ii) for clubs S_j^E with $j = \{\overline{j}, \ldots, J-1\}$, $\overline{j} > \underline{j}$, we have $a_i < \frac{A}{n} \forall i \in S_j^E$.

Given equation (13.A5), the growth rate difference between clubs emerging with endowment distributions $\mathbf{a}$ and $\widetilde{\mathbf{a}}$ can be expressed as follows:

$$\eta_j - \widetilde{\eta}_j = \ln\left(\frac{\sum\limits_{i\in S_j^E} a_i}{\sum\limits_{i\in \widetilde{S}_j^E} \widetilde{a}_i}\right).$$

It is then straightforward to deduce that $\eta_j - \widetilde{\eta}_j > 0$ for any $j = \{1, \ldots, \underline{j}\}$ and $\eta_j - \widetilde{\eta}_j < 0$ for any $j = \{\overline{j}, \ldots, J-1\}$. This proves items i) and ii) of Proposition 13.3.

For endowment distributions $\mathbf{a}$ and $\widetilde{\mathbf{a}}$ satisfying A1, A2, and A3, the growth rate difference between two successive clubs equals

$$\eta_j - \eta_{j+1} = \begin{cases} \ln\left(\dfrac{\sum\limits_{i\in S_j^E} a_i}{\sum\limits_{i\in S_{j+1}^E} a_i}\right) & \text{with } \mathbf{a} \\[2em] \ln\left(\dfrac{\sum\limits_{i\in \widetilde{S}_j^E} \widetilde{a}_i}{\sum\limits_{i\in \widetilde{S}_{j+1}^E} \widetilde{a}_i}\right) & \text{with } \widetilde{\mathbf{a}} \end{cases}.$$

Knowing that $n_j = n_{j+1} = \widehat{n}$ for all $j \in \{1, \ldots, J-1\}$, we obtain

$$\eta_j - \eta_{j+1} = \begin{cases} \widehat{n}\ln\lambda & \text{with } \mathbf{a} \\ \widehat{n}\ln\widetilde{\lambda} & \text{with } \widetilde{\mathbf{a}} \end{cases}.$$

Hence, $\eta_j - \eta_{j+1}$ is higher with $\tilde{\mathbf{a}}$ than with $\mathbf{a}$, which completes the proof of Proposition 13.3.

13.D. – Proof of Proposition 13.4

If $n(i)$, respectively $\tilde{n}(i)$, is used to denote the size of the stratified club whose richest member is i and i's welfare is maximized with $\mathbf{a}$, respectively with $\tilde{\mathbf{a}}$, we have

$$\left(e^{\frac{\alpha}{1+\rho}} \frac{1 + n(i)\rho + \rho}{1 + n(i)\rho} - 1 \right) \sum_{z=i}^{i+n(i)-1} \left(\prod_{x-z}^{i+n(i)-1} \tilde{\lambda}_{x,x+1} \right)$$

$$> \left(e^{\frac{\alpha}{1+\rho}} \frac{1 + n(i)\rho + \rho}{1 + n(i)\rho} - 1 \right) \sum_{z=i}^{i+n(i)-1} \left(\prod_{x=z}^{i+n(i)-1} \lambda_{x,x+1} \right).$$

Hence, it is easy to deduce that $\tilde{n}(i) \leq n(i)$, $\forall i \in N$. This implies that the first pivotal agent with $\mathbf{a}$ has a lower index than with $\tilde{\mathbf{a}}$, that is, $\tilde{p}_1 < p_1$. Moreover, $\tilde{n}(\tilde{p}_1) \leq n(\tilde{p}_1)$. Under inequalities (13.A3), using Proposition 13.3, we know that $n(\tilde{p}_1) = (<) n(p_1)$. Combining these two inequalities, we find that the second club is smaller with $\tilde{\mathbf{a}}$ than with $\mathbf{a}$. Repeating this reasoning completes the proof of Proposition 13.4.

13.E. – Proof of Proposition 13.5

Let us consider two endowment distributions $\mathbf{a}$ and $\tilde{\mathbf{a}}$ satisfying assumptions A1, A2, and A3 or A4. We thus know that whatever i with $a_i > \frac{A}{n}$ (respectively $a_i < \frac{A}{n}$), we have $\tilde{a}_i > a_i$ (respectively $\tilde{a}_i < a_i$).

We consider two equilibrium partitions $\mathcal{S}^E = \{S_1^E, \ldots, S_j^E, \ldots\}$ and $\tilde{\mathcal{S}}^E = \{\tilde{S}_1^E, \ldots, \tilde{S}_j^E, \ldots\}$ respectively associated with the endowment distributions $\mathbf{a}$ and $\tilde{\mathbf{a}}$ such that (i) for clubs S_j^E with $j = \{1, \ldots, \underline{j}\}$ we have $a_i > \frac{A}{n}$ $\forall i \in S_j^E$, and (ii) for clubs S_j^E with $j = \{\overline{j}, \ldots, J - 1\}$, $\overline{j} > \underline{j}$, we have $a_i < \frac{A}{n}$ $\forall i \in S_j^E$.

We now concentrate on the clubs S_j^E and $\tilde{S}_j^E$ with $j = \{1, \ldots, \underline{j}\}$. We want to show that the following difference is positive:

$$V\left(\tilde{S}_j^E, \tilde{\mathbf{a}}, \alpha \right) - V\left(S_j^E, \mathbf{a}, \alpha \right)$$

$$= \left(\frac{1}{\rho} + \frac{1}{\rho^2} \right) \left[\ln \left(\frac{\sum_{i \in \tilde{S}_j^E} \tilde{a}_i}{\sum_{i \in S_j^E} a_i} \right) - \ln \left(\frac{1 + \tilde{n}_j^E \rho}{1 + n_j^E \rho} \right) \right] \frac{\alpha}{\rho^2} \left(\tilde{n}_j^E - n_j^E \right).$$

Given that $\tilde{S}_1^E$ belongs to the equilibrium partition, we can write

$$\not\exists \pounds \subset \tilde{N} \text{ such that } \forall i \in \pounds, \ V_i(\pounds, \tilde{\mathbf{a}}, \alpha) > V_i\left(\tilde{S}_j^E, \tilde{\mathbf{a}}, \alpha \right).$$

Therefore, we deduce that

$$\forall i \in S_j^E, \ V_i\left(\tilde{S}_j^E, \tilde{\mathbf{a}}, \alpha \right) > V_i\left(S_j^E, \tilde{\mathbf{a}}, \alpha \right),$$

and because

$$V_i\left(S_j^E, \widetilde{\mathbf{a}}, \alpha\right) - V_i\left(S_j^E, \mathbf{a}, \alpha\right) = \left(\frac{1}{\rho} + \frac{1}{\rho^2}\right) \ln \left(\frac{\sum\limits_{i \in S_j^E} \widetilde{a}_i}{\sum\limits_{i \in S_j^E} a_i}\right) > 0$$

we can then deduce that

$$V_i\left(\widetilde{S}_j^E, \widetilde{\mathbf{a}}, \alpha\right) > V_i\left(S_j^E, \mathbf{a}, \alpha\right),$$

which is equivalent to

$$\ln \left(\frac{\sum\limits_{i \in \widetilde{S}_j^E} \widetilde{a}_i}{\sum\limits_{i \in S_j^E} a_i}\right) > \ln \left(\frac{1 + \widetilde{n}_j^E \rho}{1 + n_j^E \rho}\right) + \frac{\alpha}{\rho + 1}\left(\widetilde{n}_j^E - n_j^E\right).$$

Given inequality (13.A5), it turns out that

$$\widetilde{\eta}_j - \eta_j > \frac{-\alpha\rho}{\rho + 1}\left(\widetilde{n}_j^E - n_j^E\right).$$

According to Proposition 13.5, we have $\widetilde{n}_j^E \le n_j^E$. We thus deduce that

$$\widetilde{\eta}_j - \eta_j > 0.$$

BIBLIOGRAPHY

[1] Aaronson, D. (1998), "Using Sibling Data to Eliminate the Impact of Neighborhoods on Children's Educational Outcomes," *Journal of Human Resources* 33, 915–946.

[2] Aghion, P. and P. Bolton (1997), "A Trickle-Down Theory of Growth and Development with Debt Overhang," *Review of Economic Studies* 64, 151–172.

[3] Azariadis, C. and A. Drazen (1990), "Threshold Externalities and Economic Development," *Quarterly Journal of Economics* 105, 501–526.

[4] Bairoch P. (1993), *Economics and World History: Myths and Paradoxes*, University of Chicago Press.

[5] Baldwin, R. and P. Martin (2003), "Agglomeration and Regional Growth," mimeo, forthcoming in V. Henderson and J.-F. Thisse (eds.), *Handbook of Urban and Regional Economics*, forthcoming, North-Holland.

[6] Barham, V., B. Boadway, M. Marchand, and P. Pestieau (1997), "Volunteer Work and Club Size: Nash Equilibrium and Optimality," *Journal of Public Economics* 65, 9–22.

[7] Barro, R. and X. Sala-i-Martin (1995), *Economic Growth*, New York: McGraw-Hill.

[8] Beaudry, P., P. Cahuc, and H. Kempf (2000), "Is It Harmful to Allow Partial Cooperation?" *Scandinavian Journal of Economics* 102, 1–21.

[9] Beck, T., R. Levine, and N. Loayza (1999), "Finance and the Source of Growth," *Journal of Financial Economics*, 58, 261–300.

[10] Bénabou, R. (1993), "Workings of a City: Location, Education, and Production," *Quarterly Journal of Economics* 108, 619–652.

[11] Bénabou, R. (1996a), "Heterogeneity, Stratification and Growth: Macroeconomic Implications of Community Structure and School Finance," *American Economic Review* 86, 584–609.

[12] Bénabou, R. (1996b), "Equity and Efficiency in Human Capital Investment: The Local Connection," *Review of Economic Studies* 63, 237–264.

[13] Benhabib, J. and M. J. Spiegel (2000), "The Role of Financial Development in Growth and Investment," *Journal of Economic Growth* 5, 341–360.

[14] Bennett, E. and M. Wooders (1979), "Income Distribution and Firm Formation," *Journal of Comparative Economics* 3, 304–317.

[15] Bergstrom, T., L. Blume, and H. Varian (1986), "On the Private Provision of Public Goods," *Journal of Public Economics* 29, 25–50.

[16] Bergstrom, T., L. Blume, and H. Varian (1992), "Uniqueness of Nash Equilibrium in Private Provision of Public Goods," *Journal of Public Economics* 49, 391–392.

[17] Berthélémy, J. C. and A. Varoudakis (1996), "Economic Growth, Convergence Clubs and the Role of Financial Development," *Oxford Economic Papers* 48, 300–328.

[18] Bloch, F. (1997), "Non-cooperative Models of Coalition Formation Games with Spillovers," in C. Carraro and D. Siniscalco (eds.), *New Directions in the Economic Theory of the Environment*, Cambridge University Press.

[19] Boldrin, M. and F. Canova (2001), "Inequality and Convergence: Reconsidering European Regional Policies," *Economic Policy* 32, 207–253.

[20] Borjas, G. J. (1995), "Ethnicity, Neighborhoods, and Human Capital Externalities," *American Economic Review* 85, 365–390.

[21] Bourguignon, F. and C. Morrisson (2002), "Inequality among World Citizens: 1820–1992," *American Economic Review* 92, 727–744.

[22] Brock, W. and S. Durlauf (2001a), "Interactions-Based Models," in J. Heckman and E. Learner (eds.), *Handbook of Econometrics,* Vol.5, Amsterdam: North-Holland.

[23] Brock, W. and S. Durlauf (2001b), "Discrete Choice with Social Interactions," *Review of Economic Studies* 68, 235–260.

[24] Buchanan, J. (1965), "An Economic Theory of Clubs," *Economica* 33, 1–14.

[25] Canova F. (1998), "Testing for Convergence Clubs: A Predictive Density Approach," mimeo, Universitat Pompeu Fabra.

[26] Case, C. A. and L. F. Katz (1991), "The Company You Keep: The Effects of Family and Neighborhoods on Disadvantaged Youth," NBER Working Paper 3705.

[27] Chakraborty, S. and T. Ray (2001), "Bank Finance vs Market Finance: A Growth Perspective," mimeo, University of Oregon.

[28] Ciccone, A. and R. E. Hall (1996), "Productivity and the Density of Economic Activity," *American Economic Review* 87, 54–70.

[29] Coleman, J., E. Campbell, C. Hobson, J. M. C Partland, A. Mood, F. Weinfeld, and R. York (1966), *Equality of Educational Opportunities*, Washington DC: U.S. Government Printing Office.

[30] Combes, P.-P. (2000), "Economic Structure and Local Growth: France, 1984–1993," *Journal of Urban Economics* 47, 329–355.

[31] Crane, J. (1991), "The Epidemic Theory of Ghettos and Neighborhood Effects on Dropping Out and Teenage Childbearing," *American Journal of Sociology* 96, 1226–1259.

[32] Desdoigts, A. (1999), "Patterns of Economic Development and the Formation of Clubs," *Journal of Economic Growth* 4, 305–330.

[33] Durlauf, S. N. (1993), "Nonergodic Economic Growth," *Review of Economic Studies* 60, 349–366.

[34] Durlauf, S. N. (1996), "A Theory of Persistent Income Inequality," *Journal of Economic Growth* 1, 75–93.

[35] Durlauf, S. N. (2000a), "The Membership Theory of Poverty: The Role of Group Affiliations in Determining Socioeconomic Outcomes," mimeo, University of Wisconsin.

[36] Durlauf, S. N. (2000b), "A Framework for the Study of Individual Behavior and Social Interactions," mimeo, University of Wisconsin.

[37] Durlauf, S. N. (2002), "Groups, Social Influences and Inequality: A Memberships Theory Perspective on Poverty Traps," mimeo, University of Wisconsin.

[38] Durlauf, S. N. and P. A. Johnson (1995), "Multiple Regimes and Cross-Country Growth Behavior," *Journal of Applied Econometrics* 10, 365–384.

[39] Easterly, W., and R. Levine (2001), "What Have We Learned from a Decade of Empirical Research on Growth? It's Not Factor Accumulation: Stylized Facts and Growth Models," *World Bank Economic Review* 15, 177–219.

[40] Epple, D. and H. Sieg (1999), "Estimating Equilibrium Models of Local Jurisdictions," *Journal of Political Economy* 107, 645–681.

[41] Evans, W., W. Oates, and R. Schwab (1992), "Measuring Peer Group Effects," *Journal of Political Economy* 100, 966–991.

[42] Farrell, J. and S. Scotchmer (1988), "Partnerships," *Quarterly Journal of Economics* 103, 279–297.

[43] Fujita, M. and J.-F. Thisse (2002), *Economics of Agglomeration*, Oxford University Press.

[44] Galor, O. and J. Zeira (1993), "Income Distribution and Macroeconomics," *Review of Economic Studies* 64, 151–172.

[45] Ginther, D., R. Haveman, and B. Wolfe (2000), "Neighborhood Attributes as Determinants of Children's Outcomes: How Robust Are the Relationships?" *Journal of Human Resources* 35, 603–642.

[46] Glaeser, E. L., H. Kallal, J. Scheinkman, and A. Shleifer (1992), "Growth in Cities," *Journal of Political Economy* 100, 1126–1152.

[47] Greenberg, J. and S. Weber (1986), "Strong Tiebout Equilibrium under Restricted Preferences Domain," *Journal of Economic Theory* 38, 101–117.

[48] Guiso, L., P. Sapienza, and L. Zingales (2002), "Does Local Financial Development Matter?," *NBER Working Paper* No. 8923.

[49] Henderson, J. V., A. Kuncoro, and M. Turner (1995), "Industrial Development in Cities," *Journal of Political Economy* 103, 1067–1090.

[50] Henderson, J. V., P. Vernon, P. Mieszkowski, and Y. Sauvageau (1978), "Peer Group Effects and Educational Production Functions," *Journal of Public Economics* 10, 97–106.

[51] Henkel J., K. Stahl, and U. Walz (2000), "Coalition Building in a Spatial Economy," *Journal of Urban Economics* 47, 136–163.

[52] Jaramillo, F., H. Kempf, and F. Moizeau (2003), "Inequality and Club Formation," *Journal of Public Economics* 87, 931–955.

[53] Jaramillo, F. and F. Moizeau (2002), "Inégalités, Mobilité Sociale et Croissance," *Annales d'Economie et de Statistique* 65, 85–116.

[54] Jargowsky, P. A. (1996), "Take the Money and Run: Economic Segregation in U.S. Metropolitan Areas," *American Sociological Review* 61, 984–998.

[55] Keller, W. (2002), "Geographic Localization of International Technology Diffusion," *American Economic Review* 92, 120–142.

[56] King, R. G. and R. Levine (1993), "Finance and Growth: Schumpeter Might be Right," *Quarterly Journal of Economics* 108, 717–737.

[57] Konishi, H. (2000), "Formation of Hub Cities: Transportation Cost Advantage and Population Agglomeration," *Journal of Urban Economics* 48, 1–28.

[58] Kozol, J. (1991), *Savage Inequalities: Children in America's School*, New York: Crown Publishers.

[59] Kremer, M. (1993), "The O-ring Theory of Economic Development," *Quarterly Journal of Economics* 108, 551–576.

[60] Krugman, P. (1991), "Increasing Returns and Economic Geography," *Journal of Po-litical Economy* 99, 483–499.

[61] La Porta, R., F. Lopez-de-Silanes, A. Schleifer, and R. Vishny (1998), "Law and Finance," *Journal of Political Economy* 106, 1113–1150.

[62] Levine, R. (1997) "Financial Development and Economic Growth: Views and Agenda," *Journal of Economic Literature* 35, 688–726.

[63] Lucas, R. E., Jr. (1988), "On the Mechanics of Economic Development," *Journal of Monetary Economics* 22, 3–42.

[64] Maddison, A. (1995), *Monitoring the World Economy: 1820–1992*, Paris: Development Centre of the Organisation for Economic Cooperation and Development.

[65] Mankiw, N. G., D. Romer, and P. Weil (1992), "Contributions to the Empirics of Economic Growth," *Quarterly Journal of Economics* 107, 407–437.

[66] Manski, C. (1993), "Identification of Social Endogenous Effects: The Reflection Problem," *Review of Economic Studies* 60, 531–542.

[67] Mayer-Foulkes, D. (2001), "Convergence Clubs in Cross-Country Life Expectancy Dynamics," Wider discussion paper, DP No. 2001/134.

[68] Murphy, K. M., A. Shleifer, and R. Vishny (1989a), "Industrialization and the Big Push," *Journal of Political Economy* 97, 1003–1026.

[69] Murphy, K. M., A. Shleifer, and R. Vishny (1989b), "Income Distribution, Market Size and Industrialisation," *Quarterly Journal of Economics* 104, 537–564.

[70] Piketty, T. (1997), "The Dynamics of Wealth Distribution and the Interest Rate with Credit Rationing," *Review of Economic Studies* 64, 173–189.

[71] Prescott, E. C. (1998), "Needed: A Theory of Total Factor Productivity," *International Economic Review* 39, 525–551.

[72] Pritchett, L. (2000), "Understanding Patterns of Economic Growth: Searching for Hills amongst Plateaus, Mountains, and Plains," *World Bank Economic Review* 14, 221–250.

[73] Qin, C.-Z. (1996), "Endogenous Formation of Cooperation Structure," *Journal of Economic Theory* 69, 218–226.

[74] Quah, D. (1996a), "Regional Convergence Clusters Across Europe," *European Economic Review* 40, 951–958.

[75] Quah, D. (1996b), "Twin Peaks: Growth and Convergence in Models of Distribution Dynamics," *Economic Journal* 106, 1045–1055.

[76] Quah, D. T. (1997), "Empirics for Growth and Distribution: Stratification, Polarization and Convergence Clubs," *Journal of Economic Growth* 2, 27–59.

[77] Quah, D. (2002), "Spatial Agglomeration Dynamics," Centre for Economic Policy Resarch DP No. 3208.

[78] Rusk, D. (1993), *Cities without Suburbs*, Baltimore: Johns Hopkins University Press.

[79] Sacerdote, B. (2001), "Peer Effects with Random Assignments: Results for Dartmouth Roommates," *Quarterly Journal of Economics* 116, 681–704.

[80] Schumpeter, J. A. (1912), *Theorie der Wirtschaftlichen Entwicklung*, Leipzig: Dunker and Humblot, (Trans. *A Theory of Economic Development*, Cambridge, MA: Harvard University Press, 1934).

[81] Solow, R. (1956), "A Contribution to the Theory of Economic Growth," *Quarterly Journal of Economics* 70, 65–94.

[82] Spiegel, M. J. (2001), "Financial Development and Growth: Are the APEC Nations Unique?," Pacific Basin Working Paper Series, Wp No. PB01–04.

[83] Tabard, N. (1993), "Des quartiers pauvres aux banlieues aisées: une représentation sociale du territoire," *Economie et Statistique* 270, 5–22.

[84] Temple, J. (1995), "Testing the Augmented Solow Model," Economics papers nuf:econwp:0018.

[85] Wilson, W. J. (1987), *The Truly Disadvantaged: The Inner City, the Urban Underclass and Public Policy*, University of Chicago Press.

[86] Wooders, M. (1978), "Equilibria, the Core and Jurisdiction Structures in Economies with a Local Public Good," *Journal of Economic Theory* 18, 328–348.

14

Informal Insurance, Enforcement Constraints, and Group Formation

Garance Genicot and Debraj Ray

14.1. Introduction

This chapter, largely based on Genicot and Ray (2003), discusses group formation in the context of informal insurance arrangements with enforcement constraints.

14.1.1. Risk-Sharing Agreements

Risk is a pervasive fact of life for most people – especially so in developing countries. A high and often extreme dependence on volatile labor markets or agricultural production, widespread poverty, and the lack of access to formal insurance and credit serve to create a particularly acute problem of consumption smoothing. It is not surprising, then, that formal insurance arrangements are supplanted by widespread informal arrangements. Such arrangements are not based on contracts that are upheld by a court of law but on the implicit promise of future benefits from continued participation and its attendant mirror image: the threat of isolation from the community as a whole in the event of noncompliance.

It hardly needs mentioning that there is considerable evidence of mutual insurance in village communities (Morduch 1991; Deaton 1992; Townsend 1994; Udry 1994; Jalan and Ravallion 1999; Ligon, Thomas, and Worrall 2002; Grimard 1997; Gertler and Gruber 2002; Foster and Rosenzweig 2001). What is more interesting is that the same studies reveal a large departure from the ideal of perfect insurance. It is only natural to invoke various incentive constraints to explain the shortfall. Asymmetry of information, moral hazard, and the lack of enforceability are all potential impediments to widespread risk sharing.

Of these three factors, it appears that the most important constraint arises from the inability to enforce risk-sharing agreements. Udry (1994), for instance, finds this constraint to be the most important in describing the structure of reciprocal agreements in rural northern Nigeria. In the absence of explicit, legally binding

We thank Fabien Moizeau for useful comments on an earlier draft.

contracts, these agreements must be designed to elicit voluntary participation. This constraint often seriously limits the extent of insurance informal risk-sharing agreements can provide.

Posner (1980, 1981) was the first to posit that voluntary risk sharing can emerge between self-interested individuals if future reciprocity is expected. Following his insight, there has been a growing body of literature, both theoretical and empirical, on *self-enforcing* risk-sharing agreements. Some important theoretical contributions are Kimball (1988), Coate and Ravallion (1993), Kocherlakota (1996), Kletzer and Wright (2000), and Ligon, Thomas, and Worrall (2002). All these studies define self-enforcing agreements as those that are proof from noncompliance by individual members of the group.[1] According to the theory, the individual defector is isolated from the community and thus must self-insure. With this insight in place, the common practice in the literature has been to define self-enforcing risk-sharing agreements as subgame perfect equilibria of a repeated game (in which self-insurance is always an option) and to characterize the Pareto frontier of such equilibria.

This kind of analysis has two important consequences. First, large groups always do better than smaller groups. Hence, efficient agreements have to be at the level of the "community."[2] This is why most empirical tests of insurance take the unit of analysis as exogenous and study the extent of insurance at the level of the village or even larger groups. Second, a higher need for insurance, stemming for instance from a higher degree of risk aversion, relaxes the enforcement constraint and must therefore increase the extent of risk sharing within a community.

14.1.2. Groups in Risk Sharing

Our starting point is the following natural observation: If a large group – for instance, the village community or a particular caste or kin group within the community – can foresee the benefits of risk sharing and reach an agreement, why are smaller groups unable to do the same? Indeed, one may go a step farther and entertain the possibility that subgroups may agree to defect *jointly* and subsequently share risk among themselves. It follows that, to be truly self-enforcing, an informal risk-sharing agreement should be robust to joint deviations by subgroups.

At the same time, such group deviations must be themselves credible. To be of any value, or to pose a credible threat to the group at large, a deviating coalition should also employ self-enforcing arrangements. These embedded constraints characterize the concepts of self-enforcing risk-sharing agreements and stable coalitions that we define in Genicot and Ray (2003). We study group formation in informal insurance within communities, recognizing that not just the extent of insurance within a given

---

[1] In the words of Telser (1980), "In a self-enforcing agreement each party decides *unilaterally* whether he is better off continuing or stopping his relation with the other parties (p. 27)."

[2] Of course, considerations of asymmetric information or some other cost of group formation may close off group size before the community limit is reached. See below for further discussion of this point.

group is endogenous but that this affects, and is affected by, the process of group formation itself.

This realization has two important implications that sharply contrast with the individual-deviation model. First, subgroups of individuals may destabilize insurance arrangements among the larger group, thereby limiting group size. Second, an increase in the need for insurance – stemming from a change either in the environment or in some behavioral parameter such as the degree of risk aversion – can actually decrease the extent of risk sharing among the population by reducing the maximal stable group size.

Indeed, the few papers that address the issue of risk sharing among subgroups actually find convincing evidence for the existence of subgroups. Lomnitz (1977) finds that reciprocity networks in Cerrada del Cóndor, a shantytown of about 200 dwellings in the southern sector of Mexico City, are composed of an average of 3.65 nuclear families. Fafchamps and Lund (2003) address a similar question in the context of the rural Philippines. Although gifts and loans circulate among networks of friends and relatives, risk is far from efficiently shared at the village level. Likewise, Murgai et al. (2002) investigate water transfers among households along a watercourse in Pakistan's Punjab and find that reciprocal exchanges are localized in units smaller than the entire watercourse community.

To be sure, there are other potential explanations for observed limits on group size. Geographical proximity (or lack thereof), the limited observability of actions or types, a varying ability to punish slackers, or positive covariance in the income distribution: all these factors can explain differences in the extent of insurance and the tendency for some clusters of individuals to make more transfers to each other than to others outside their cluster. However, except in extreme cases, all agents would be expected to transact with each other directly or indirectly – at least to some extent. Murgai et al. suggest that the explanation for the formation of these subgroups must lie in the existence of setup costs with the number of participants in the risk-sharing agreement: "If establishing and maintaining partnerships is indeed costless, there is no reason for a mutual insurance group not to be community-wide or world-wide. Real world limits to group size must therefore be the result of costs relating to the formation and maintenance of partnerships" (Murgai et al. 2002, p. 251). However, this chapter suggests that there may be more fundamental reasons for group splintering.

14.1.3. Chapter Outline

In Section 14.2, we illustrate the group formation question by means of the simplest possible model. In this setup, a group that forms *must* insure each other to the maximum extent possible (we call this the *equal-sharing norm*). Adherence to such a norm at the group level does not, of course, do away with the enforcement constraint. Splinter subgroups (conceivably individuals but often nondegenerate groups) may well break off from the larger group. Subsequently, they, too, must follow the equal-sharing group, and their stability will be tested in exactly the same way.

In Section 14.3, we extend the model to allow for the recognition (by a group) that it may be constantly under threat from potential deviants. Such recognition will generally entail a departure from equal sharing with more limited transfers. To be sure, in the interests of consistency, we must permit a similar self-exploration on the part of deviant subgroups. Thus, as we expand the possibilities for the group as a whole, we also expand the range of threats to its stability. Finally, in Section 14.4, we comment on a further widening of insurance schemes to include history-dependent quasi-credit.

The emphasis throughout this chapter is on specific examples rather than on full generality. Readers interested in the details of a more general analysis are invited to consult Genicot and Ray (2003).

14.2. Group Formation under Equal Sharing

A community of n identical agents engages in the production and consumption of a perishable good at each date. Each agent produces a random income that is high, h, with probability p and low, ℓ, with probability $1 - p$. Income realizations are independent and identical over people as well as dates. Each agent has the same utility function, which is increasing, smooth, and strictly concave in consumption. They discount future at a rate $\delta \in (0, 1)$.

Consider any grouping of individuals in this community and suppose that its members are pledged to mutually insure one another against consumption fluctuations. We assume that such insurance is to the maximum extent possible, that is, group output is shared equally among all the members. We refer to this practice as equal sharing. (It is obvious that this is the first-best symmetric scheme.)

Let $\tilde{v}(n)$ denote the expected utility from the equal-sharing scheme. When k individuals draw h, all group members consume $\frac{k}{n}h + \frac{n-k}{n}\ell$. This implies a per-period expected utility of

$$\tilde{v}(n) \equiv \sum_{k=0}^{n} p(k, n)u\left(\frac{k}{n}h + \frac{n - k}{n}\ell\right),\tag{14.2.1}$$

where $p(k, n)$ is just the probability of k highs out of n draws.[3]

Equal-sharing stability may be defined recursively as follows. By definition, singletons or individuals are equal-sharing stable, and the worth of a singleton group is just $\tilde{v}(1)$. Recursively, having assessed equal-sharing stability for all $m = 1, \ldots, n - 1$, we consider a coalition of size n to be equal-sharing stable if, for all $k = 1, \ldots, n - 1$,

$$(1 - \delta)\left[u(h) - u\left(\frac{k}{n}h + \frac{n - k}{n}\ell\right)\right] \leq \delta\left(\tilde{v}(n) - \tilde{v}(s)\right)\tag{14.2.2}$$

for every equal-sharing stable $s \leq k$. This constraint requires that the short-term deviation gain from not making the transfer, on the left-hand side, be smaller than the long-term gain from remaining in the risk-sharing agreement rather than deviating

---

[3] That is, $p(k, n) = \frac{n!}{k!(n-k)!}p^k(1 - p)^{n-k}$.

in a group of size s, on the right-hand side. If n is equal-sharing stable, then its worth is simply $\tilde{v}(n)$. Note that for a given equal-sharing stable size s, it actually suffices to check the constraint for $k = s$ because the left-hand side is decreasing in k.

Proposition 14.1. *Independently of the overall community size, there is a finite upper bound on the equal-sharing stable sizes.*

It is easy to see why Proposition 14.1 is true (see the formal proof in the appendix). If the assertion were false, there would be an infinity of stable sizes. But we do know that the marginal "diversification gain" from an increase in size ultimately tends to zero. Therefore, for a very small ϵ, we may pick a stable size n such that a coalition of size n is able to reap most of the benefits of sharing risk: a larger stable group improves the per capita utility of its members by no more than ϵ. Because the set of stable sizes is infinite, we can choose a stable coalition sufficiently larger than n such that the short-term gain of deviating from this coalition when n agents have a good shock is strictly larger than the relative long-term gain from being in this larger coalition rather than in a group of n.

Moreover, it is possible to show that for a large range of preferences, the set of equal-sharing stable sizes is a "connected" set of integers. To identify this range, consider the following condition:

[QC] For every k, $(1 - \delta)u(\frac{k}{n}h + \frac{n-k}{n}\ell) + \delta\tilde{v}(n)$ is quasi-concave in n for all $n \geq k$.

The condition [QC] is satisfied for several utility functions. It is true, for instance, for all utility functions exhibiting a relative risk aversion of at least 2 as well as for quadratic or cubic preferences. Now we may state the following proposition (see the appendix for proof):

Proposition 14.2. *For all utility functions satisfying [QC], if a group of size n is not equal-sharing stable then a group of size $n' > n$ is not equal-sharing stable either.*

For instance, with a utility function given by $u(x) = -\frac{1}{2}(B - x)^2$ for some $B > h$ it is possible to show that n is stable if and only if for every $1 \leq k \leq n - 1$,

$$\frac{C}{k} + \frac{k}{n} \geq \frac{2}{\theta} + 1, \tag{14.2.3}$$

where $C = \frac{\delta}{1-\delta}p(1 - p)$ and $\theta = \frac{h-\ell}{B-h}$ (this latter variable will later reappear as our proxy for the need for insurance).

From the inequality (14.2.3) it is easy to see that for the same k and n, a mean preserving spread in the income distribution (higher θ) and a higher patience δ relax the constraints. Hence, these increase (or at least leave unchanged) the set of equal-sharing stable sizes. Similarly, higher values of $p(1 - p)$ (p closer to 1/2) correspond to a higher variance and therefore, if anything, increase the set of stable sizes.

Condition (14.2.3) may also be used to obtain a tighter description of the maximal equal-sharing stable group. We illustrate this by neglecting integer constraints (which are easily accounted for). Observe that the left-hand side of condition (14.2.3) is minimized (in k) when $k = \sqrt{nC}$, this condition being applicable when $n > C$. Solving for the minimum value, we see that the maximal group size M is bounded above by the inequality

$$M \leq \max \left\{ C, \frac{4C}{\left(\frac{2}{\theta} + 1\right)^2} \right\}. \tag{14.2.4}$$

Notice that M is bounded *uniformly* in θ. With our later interpretation of θ as a measure of the need for insurance, this means that maximal stable size cannot rise indefinitely in need.

14.3. Stationary Transfers

To be sure, even when an equal-sharing agreement is not possible, individuals may be able to design a risk-sharing agreement by limiting transfers in states for which the enforcement constraint is binding. Kimball (1988) and Coate and Ravallion (1993) study the best stationary risk-sharing agreements. In this section, we emulate the approach of these authors to find the best constrained risk-sharing agreement. At the same time, we also bear in mind that groups as well as individuals may deviate. In short, we develop the theory of group enforcement constraints under the assumption that each coalition or group, once formed, attempts to implement some *symmetric and stationary* risk-sharing arrangement.

As in the previous section, group stability is defined recursively. Once again, individuals (or singleton coalitions) are stable. The lifetime utility of an individual in isolation (normalized by the discount factor to a per-period equivalent) is simply

$$v^*(1) \equiv pu(h) + (1 - p)u(\ell).$$

This is the *stable worth* of a "singleton group."

Recursively, having defined stability (and stable worths) for all $m = 1, \ldots, n - 1$, consider some coalition of size n. We first define a (symmetric and stationary) *transfer scheme*. This may be written as a vector $\mathbf{t} \equiv (t_1, \ldots, t_{n-1})$, where t_k is to be interpreted as the (nonnegative) transfer or payment by a person in the event that his or her income is h *and* k individuals draw h. We only consider nontrivial schemes in which $t_k > 0$ for some k.

With a transfer scheme in mind we can easily infer what a person receives if his or her income draw is ℓ and k individuals produce h. The total transfer is then kt_k, which is to be divided equally among the $n - k$ individuals who produce l. Thus, a transfer scheme $\mathbf{t}$ implies the following: if there are k high draws, then a person consumes $h - t_k$ if he or she produces h, and $\ell + \frac{kt_k}{n-k}$ if he or she produces ℓ. It follows that the expected utility from a transfer scheme $\mathbf{t}$ is given by

$$v(\mathbf{t}, n) \equiv p^n u(h) + (1 - p)^n u(\ell)$$
$$+ \sum_{k=1}^{n-1} p(k, n) \left[\frac{k}{n} u(h - t_k) + \frac{n - k}{n} u \left(\ell + \frac{kt_k}{n - k} \right) \right], \tag{14.3.1}$$

where $p(k, n)$ – as before – is the probability of k highs out of n draws. Define a (nontrivial) transfer scheme **t** to be *stable* if for all $k = 1, \ldots, n - 1$,

$$(1 - \delta)u(h - t_k) + \delta v(\mathbf{t}, n) \geq (1 - \delta)u(h) + \delta v^*(s) \qquad (14.3.2)$$

for every stable $s \leq k$.

The interpretation of stability is quite simple. We require that for all possible income realizations the stipulated transfers actually be carried out. If inequality (14.3.2) fails for some k and $s \leq k$, this means that there is a stable coalition of size s that would rather refuse to pay what they are required to pay (when k individuals draw high) and share risk with each other such that this transfer would actually not be made.

It is useful to compare our definition of self-enforcing insurance with the one used in the literature in which only the individual enforcement constraint must be respected. We call this *individual stability*, or *i-stability* for short. Fix a population of n individuals and let $\widehat{v}(n)$ denote the maximum value of expression (14.3.1) when inequality (14.3.2) is only invoked for $s = 1$. In other words, $\widehat{v}(n)$ is the solution to the following problem:

$$\max_{\mathbf{t}} v(\mathbf{t}, n) \qquad (14.3.3)$$

subject to

$$(1 - \delta)u(h - t_k) + \delta v(\mathbf{t}, n) \geq (1 - \delta)u(h) + \delta v^*(1) \qquad (14.3.4)$$

for all $k = 1, \ldots, n - 1$.

If there is some nontrivial transfer scheme that solves this problem, we say that a group of size n is i-stable.

In what follows, we will show that the concepts of stability and i-stability have very different implications for the extent of insurance we expect a community to achieve. For this purpose, it will be useful to measure the need for insurance as the ratio $\frac{u'(\ell) - u'(h)}{u'(h)}$, which we henceforth denote by θ. (The reader can check that this definition reduces precisely to the corresponding θ in the example of the previous section.) If everything else is held constant, a mean preserving spread between h and ℓ increases θ. Moreover, for the same income distribution, a utility function that exhibits a higher risk aversion throughout its domain will translate into a higher need for insurance. Hence, our measure incorporates both environmental uncertainty and attitudes towards risk, albeit in summary form.

We now proceed in further characterizing the sets of i-stable and stable sizes.

First, notice that if a group is not i-stable it cannot be stable because stability only adds constraints to the problem. Hence, the set of stable size is included in the set of i-stable sizes.

Next, note from inequality (14.3.4) that for the same transfer to be made today, and therefore the same short-term gain to be realized from deviating, being in a larger group means larger long-term benefits. This implies that if a group size is i-stable, any larger size must be stable too. In particular, in Genicot and Ray (2003) we show that a group size n is i-stable if and only if

$$\theta > \frac{1-\delta}{\delta p(1 - p^{n-1})}.$$ (14.3.5)

Clearly, the right-hand side of inequality (14.3.5) is decreasing in n and bounded below by $\underline{\theta} \equiv \frac{1-\delta}{\delta p}$. It follows that, if the need for insurance θ is no larger than $\underline{\theta}$, there is no i-stable or stable risk-sharing agreement and only autarky is possible. In contrast, if $\theta > \underline{\theta}$, not only is the set of i-stable sizes nonempty but it is infinite. The smallest i-stable group size is the smallest value of n such that inequality (14.3.5) holds and any larger size is i-stable too.

Now suppose that $\theta > \underline{\theta}$. What can we say about the set of stable sizes? Consider the smallest i-stable size. Because no smaller size is stable, no deviations other than individual deviations are credible. Hence, the same risk-sharing agreement is stable and this group size is also the smallest stable group size. With larger group sizes, however, this argument breaks down. Once groups of intermediate size are stable, they begin to pose credible threats to groups of larger size, and i-stability no longer implies stability.

This raises the question of whether there can be an infinite number of *stable* groups. Proposition 14.2 suggests the answer is no, but because we are no longer restricted to the equal-sharing norm the argument here is more subtle. In Genicot and Ray (2003) we show that, indeed, only a finite number of sizes can be stable and therefore that the set of stable sizes has a finite upper bound. To see why this must be true, assume as earlier that the assertion is false and therefore that there is an infinity of stable sizes. As before, we can then pick a stable size n such that a coalition of size n is able to reap most of the benefits of sharing risk: a larger stable group improves the per-capita utility of its members by only a small amount. The difference with equal-sharing stability is that now one can limit the transfer to satisfy the enforcement constraints. This means that in any larger stable coalition, the transfers made whenever at least n people have a good shock have to be close to 0. But, because the set of stable sizes is infinite, we can choose this stable coalition sufficiently large such that the probability of at least n people having a good shock is close to 1. This implies that the worth of such a coalition can be brought arbitrarily close to autarkic utility, but this contradicts the presumed stability of that coalition.

The preceding findings are summarized in the following proposition (proof omitted) and illustrated in Figure 14.1.

Proposition 14.3. *(Genicot and Ray 2003) For each level of need for insurance* $\theta > \frac{1-\delta}{\delta p}$, *there are thresholds* $\bar{n}(\theta)$ *and* $\underline{n}(\theta)$ *such that*

$$2 \le \underline{n}(\theta) \le n \le \bar{n}(\theta) < \infty$$ (14.3.6)

for every stable group size n. Moreover,

$$\underline{n}(\theta) \uparrow \infty \text{ as } \theta \downarrow \frac{1-\delta}{\delta p}.$$ (14.3.7)

In addition, from Proposition 14.3 follows a general "nonmonotonicity" result: a higher need for insurance can actually translate into lower group sizes. This can be

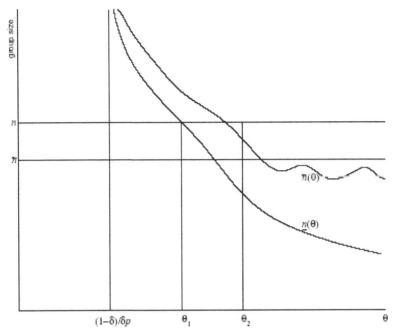

Figure 14.1: An illustration of Proposition 14.3.

seen directly from Figure 14.1. Pick a community size $\tilde{n}$ that lies above the "stable correspondence" at some point. Then, for any $n \geq \tilde{n}$, we can find two degrees of uncertainty θ_1 and θ_2, with $\theta_2 > \theta_1$, such that n is stable under θ_1 but not under θ_2. It is easy enough to pick θ_1 to be such that n is the smallest stable size that can be supported under θ_1 and pick θ_2 such that the largest stable size under θ_2 is strictly less than falls below n. This accounts for the nonmonotonicity.

The following example from Genicot and Ray (2003) illustrates well the main features of our concept of stability.

Example 14.1. *Consider a community of 10 individuals with a constant relative risk aversion utility function*

$$u(c) = \frac{1}{1 - \rho} c^{1-\rho},$$

where ρ is the Arrow–Pratt coefficient of relative risk aversion. Assume the following values for the specific parameters: $\delta = 0.83$, $\rho = 1.6$, $p = 0.4$, $\ell = 2$, and $h = 3$.

We evaluate – for each group size ranging from 1 to 10 – the return to informal insurance. One natural way to do this is to look at the gain over and above autarky compared with the corresponding per capita gain that the first-best provides in the community of all 10. If $\tilde{v}$ denotes this latter value and $\hat{v}(n)$ is the i-stable value for a group of size n, then the i-stable gain may be reported as

$$\frac{\hat{v}(n) - v(1)}{\tilde{v} - v(1)} \times 100$$

Table 14.1: *Stable gains are limited*

n	Stable?	i-Stable gain (%)	Stable gain (%)
1	✓	0	0
2	✓	10	10
3	✓	50	38
4	×	61	0
5	×	69	0
6	×	75	0
7	×	78	0
8	×	81	0
9	×	84	0
10	×	85	0

in percentage terms. Similarly, if $v^*(n)$ is the stable value for a group of size n, then the stable gain is described as

$$\frac{v^*(n) - v(1)}{\tilde{v} - v(1)} \times 100$$

again in percentage terms.

The results for this example are reported in Table 14.1.

It turns out that within this population of 10 and for the parameter values described, only individuals and groups of size 2 and 3 are stable. The question arise then, which groups do we expect to see, and, if there are groups of different sizes, which payoffs do we look at? Because we are looking at constrained efficient schemes among identical agents, a good contender is the partition of the population into stable groups that maximizes the expected utility of an agent under the assumption that his or her probability to be in any given group is proportional to the size of the group. In this example, the rule predicts that the population will break into three stable groups of three individuals each and one singleton group (which means a 90-percent chance of getting $v^*(3)$ and a 10-percent chance of obtaining $v(1)$). That is, an individual's stable payoff gain is 38 percent (see Table 14.1) with probability 9/10 and 0 otherwise. This implies a stable gain of only 34 percent, which is less than *half* the return (85 percent) were we not to account for coalition formation.

One might object that Example 14.1 is only described for a very special set of parameter values. So, to build Table 14.2 we took similar parameters but considered different values for the probability of a high income p and for the need for insurance θ. Table 14.2 reports the stable group sizes for the different values of p and θ.

Table 14.2: *Stable sizes*

p\θ	.75	1	2
.2	1	1	1,2
.4	1,3	1,2	1,2
.6	1,3	1,2,5	1,2
.8	1,3,5	1,3	1,2,7

To summarize the discussion so far, we see that

(1) The stability of smaller sizes may impede the stability of larger sizes.

(2) Much has been written on "social capital" in the past few years. In the insurance context, one could measure the return to such capital very much as we have done here. However, recognizing the possibility of coalition deviations dramatically reduces the estimated return on social capital.

(3) Computations for several parameter values reveal both robustness and sensitivity in the following senses. Changing the parameters even slightly causes some stable sizes to become unstable and vice versa, as Table 14.2 illustrates. Yet the results are surprisingly robust in the sense that potential coalitional deviations inevitably cause a large fraction of the potential benefits from insurance not to be reaped.

(4) Moreover, at $p = 0.4$, if the need for insurance θ increases from 0.75 to 1, the largest stable size decreases from 3 to 2. This suggests that even an *increase* in risk may destroy previously successful insurance arrangements as previously nonviable subgroups now become viable, destroying the viability of the larger community.

One can extend this analysis to heterogeneous agents. Heterogeneity is a natural feature of life and is likely to play an important role in group formation. Kinship, family, clan, and religious affiliation are important in this respect because they help in punishing and imposing strict norms on members (Platteau 1991; Fafchamps 1992). At the same time, characteristics that strengthen risk sharing between some individuals will tend to worsen the performance of risk-sharing agreements within a larger group or even destroy altogether the stability of these larger groups.

We illustrate this with a simple example. Consider two households each composed of two members. We assume that households have means of punishing their own members who would defect from a risk-sharing agreement but not individuals outside their households. Assume logarithmic utility and the following values for the parameters: $\ell = 1$, $h = 1.488$, $p = 0.5$, and $\delta = 0.9$. The appendix shows that, in this case, the ability of individuals to share risk perfectly within their household *prevents* them from sharing risk across households. Indeed, no stationary insurance agreement can be designed involving positive transfer between the two households. As a result, individuals enjoy a utility of $\tilde{v}(2)$ per period. However, in the absence of any enforcement power within households, these individuals would be able to all share risk with each other and enjoy $v^*(4)$. This, although still imperfect, would represent a 16-percent increase in the gain from insurance![4]

14.4. General Results: Asymmetric Treatment and History Dependence

The last section went a long way towards endogenizing both group formation and risk-sharing agreements. However, the latter were restricted to be symmetric and

---

[4]   The gain is evaluated as $\frac{v^*(4)-\tilde{v}(2)}{\tilde{v}(4)-v(1)} \times 100$.

stationary. In this section, we explain why risk-sharing agreements will generally make use of history dependence and of asymmetric strategies in subgames and discuss the robustness of our results.

The reader familiar with the recent literature on insurance knows that when the lack of enforcement limits risk sharing, the optimal i-stable risk-sharing agreement is nonstationary. The reason is simple. With stationary transfers, all agents face the same continuation utility regardless of their current shock. However, when perfect risk sharing is not possible, an agent suffering from a low shock today has a higher marginal utility than an agent with a high income. It follows that there exists a mutually beneficial modification in the agreement in which the low-income agent trades off some of his or her continuation utility in exchange for a slightly higher transfer today. The low-income agent promises to make some transfer (within the self-enforcing range) to the high-income agent in the event that both of them draw a high or a low shock next period. Thus, the efficient scheme tends to equalize the intertemporal rates of substitution between the agents. As Kocherlakota (1996) showed, all the history dependence of the optimal i-stable risk-sharing agreement is captured in the ratios of marginal utility of the agents. Given last period's ratio of marginal utilities, the continuation expected utilities of the agents follows a stationary distribution. Because the ratio of marginal utilities is one possible measure of the agents' relative needs, the structure of history-dependent schemes fits the empirical evidence well.

Numerous studies in the economic and anthropological literature provide evidence that informal risk-sharing agreements and informal credit arrangements are not clearly separated (see, for instance, Evans-Pritchard 1940; Platteau and Abraham 1987; Udry 1994). These studies report a large reliance on what is observationally equivalent to informal loans with an implicit repayment scheme contingent on the lender's needs and the borrower's ability to repay. Ligon et al. (2002), Foster and Rosenzweig (2001), and Fafchamps and Lund (2003) all find that the history-dependent scheme fits the data better than the benchmark of perfect risk pooling and the stationary limited commitment model.

Now, a particular source of history dependence and asymmetry stems specifically from our consideration of group formation. When group deviations are important, symmetry necessitates that we compensate *all* potential deviants in a subgroup in order to prevent a deviation. If that symmetry is broken, then not all deviants need to be so treated. A subset containing the minimal number that must be compensated in order to avoid the deviation will suffice. For instance, to prevent two individuals from deviating, the scheme may require a sufficiently low transfer from one of them so that he would not participate in a joint deviation while demanding from the other a higher transfer (but not too high in order to ensure that individual deviations are still not worthwhile). This will be the case even if both agents experienced the same history of shocks. Clearly, randomization will play an important role in this case to decide who gets to make the lower transfer. (Randomization would retain symmetry ex ante.) With these asymmetries, it is no longer necessary to compensate every member of every potential subgroup; it is only necessary to compensate some members of every potential subgroup.

In contrast, in a symmetric and stationary equilibrium, every member of a potentially deviant subgroup must be simultaneously compensated for staying with the ambient group. Such compensations become impossible because the marginal gains to group size vanish, whereas deviation gains are bounded away from zero, precipitating the boundedness result in the stationary case. In the general case, it is possible to switch carefully to asymmetric strategies following appropriate histories of good and bad draws.

To allow for history dependence, asymmetries, and randomization, insurance schemes need to be redefined. For a group of size n, let $\mathbf{y}$ be a vector of *realized incomes*; that is, y_i is either h or ℓ for each $i = 1, \ldots, n$. Let $\mathbf{c}$ be a nonnegative vector of consumptions. Say that $\mathbf{c}$ is *feasible* (under $\mathbf{y}$) if $\sum_i c_i = \sum_i y_i$. For any date s, an s-history – call it H_s – is a list of all past income realizations and (feasible) consumption vectors. (At $s = 0$, simply use any singleton to denote the 0-history.)

Define $\mathcal{M}(\mathbf{y})$ to be the set of all probability measures over consumption vectors $\mathbf{c}$ such that $\mathbf{c}$ is feasible for $\mathbf{y}$. An *insurance arrangement* is a list of functions $\sigma = \{\sigma_s\}_{s=0}^{\infty}$ such that for all $s \geq 0$, σ_s maps the product of s-histories and current income realizations $\mathbf{y}$ to lotteries in $\mathcal{M}(\mathbf{y})$. We will say that an insurance arrangement is *nontrivial* if it places positive probability on schemes that involve nonzero transfers for some states.

Note that an insurance arrangement generates a vector of expected payoffs following every s-history H_s; call this vector $\mathbf{v}(H_s, \sigma, n)$. (These are discounted, normalized expected payoffs for each individual in the group *before* the realization of current incomes and, of course, the consumption lottery.)

To define *stability*, we proceed recursively just as in the stationary case. Individuals (or singleton coalitions) are automatically branded stable. Indeed, there is only one stable payoff for an "individual coalition," which is just the no-insurance payoff at every date. That is, if we define

$$v^*(1) \equiv pu(h) + (1 - p)u(\ell), \qquad (14.4.1)$$

then the set of stable payoffs is just $V^*(1) \equiv \{v^*(1)\}$.

Now suppose that we have defined stable payoff sets $V^*(m)$ for all $m = 1, \ldots, n - 1$ (some of these may be empty). Pick a group of size n and a nontrivial insurance arrangement σ for this group. Say that σ is *stable* if the following two conditions are satisfied:

(PARTICIPATION.) For no s-history H_s is there a subgroup of individuals (of size $m < n$) and a stable payoff vector $\mathbf{v} \in V^*(m)$ such that $v_i(H_s, \sigma, n) < v_i$ for all $i = 1, \ldots, m$.

(ENFORCEMENT.) The following is a zero-probability event under σ: there is an s-history H_s, an income realization $\mathbf{y}$, and a prescribed consumption allocation $\mathbf{c}$ such that for some subgroup of individuals (of size $m < n$) and some stable payoff vector $\mathbf{v} \in V^*(m)$,

$$(1 - \delta)u(y_i) + \delta v_i > (1 - \delta)u(c_i) + \delta v_i(H_{s+1}, \sigma, n), \qquad (14.4.2)$$

where H_{s+1} is the $(s + 1)$-history obtained by concatenating H_s with $\mathbf{y}$ and $\mathbf{c}$.

If σ is stable, then say that $\mathbf{v}(h_0, \sigma, n)$ is a *stable payoff vector* for n. If no such vector exists, we say that n is *unstable* and set $V^*(n)$ to the empty set.

In Genicot and Ray (2003) we show that our main result extends to this fully general case. For every value of θ such that some stable group exists, the maximal stable group size is finite.

14.5. Some Final Remarks

We end with two remarks, one methodological and the other specific to the study of insurance arrangements.

The reader familiar with the recent literature on endogenous coalition formation (see, e.g., Bloch 1996; Chapter 11 of this volume; Ray and Vohra 1997, 1999, 2001) will see the close parallel to our approach. However, there is one important difference. In the literature on endogenous coalition formation, coalitions respond to a proposed ex ante arrangement. That is, coalitional constraints are evaluated at the level of the "participation constraints." In contrast, in this chapter, coalitions respond after learning the *realization* of income shocks at every date and after learning what their actions are to be. These ex post considerations are closer to "incentive constraints." In this sense, our approach also bears a connection to the coalition-proof Nash equilibrium (Bernheim, Peleg, and Whinston 1987).

Moreover, the existence of an *upper* bound on stable groups is in stark contrast to the existence of infinitely many stable sizes in the coalition formation literature (see, e.g., Bloch 1996 and Ray and Vohra 1997 for results on stable cartels in oligopoly, and Ray and Vohra 2001 for results on the efficient provision of public goods). This is peculiar to the insurance problem.

APPENDIX

Proof of Proposition 14.1

Suppose that Proposition 14.1 is false. Then there exists an infinite set $\mathcal{N}$ such that for all $n \in \mathcal{N}$, n is stable. Because $\tilde{v}(n)$ is increasing, if n and n' are both in $\mathcal{N}$ and $n < n'$, then $\tilde{v}(n) \leq \tilde{v}(n')$. Moreover, $\{\tilde{v}(n)\}_{n \in \mathcal{N}}$ is bounded. It follows that for any $\epsilon > 0$, there exists $n(\epsilon) \in \mathcal{N}$ such that for all $n \in \mathcal{N}$ with $n > n(\epsilon)$,

$$\tilde{v}(n) - \tilde{v}(n(\epsilon)) < \epsilon. \tag{14.A.1}$$

Moreover, it is easy enough to choose $n(\epsilon)$ satisfying both inequality (14.A.1) and the requirement that

$$\epsilon < \frac{1-\delta}{\delta}[u(h) - u(\ell)] - A \tag{14.A.2}$$

for some $A > 0$. Now consider some stable $n > n(\epsilon)$. It is obvious that as $n \to \infty$,

$$u(h) - u\left(\frac{n(\epsilon)}{n}h + \frac{n - n(\epsilon)}{n}\ell\right) \to u(h) - u(\ell). \tag{14.A.3}$$

It follows that as $n \to \infty$,

$$u(h) - u\left(\frac{n(\epsilon)}{n}h + \frac{n - n(\epsilon)}{n}\ell\right) > \tilde{v}(n) - \tilde{v}(n(\epsilon)),$$

which contradicts the stability of n. ∎

Proof of Proposition 14.2

For any k and any $n \geq k$, define

$$I(k, n) \equiv -(1 - \delta)\left[u(h) - u\left(\frac{k}{n}h + \frac{n - k}{n}\ell\right)\right] + \delta\left(\tilde{v}(n) - \tilde{v}(k)\right). \quad (14.A.4)$$

Invoking [QC], one can easily see that $I(k, n)$ must be quasi-concave in n. Because $I(k, k) = 0$, the quasi-concavity of $I(k, n)$ implies that if $I(k, n) < 0$ for any $n > k$, then the same must be true of any $n' > n$. ∎

Details of the Final Example in Section 14.3

Within a household, perfect risk sharing can be achieved. This implies that in the absence of any transfers across household pairs, a household's member income effectively takes on three values h, ℓ, and $m = \frac{h+\ell}{2}$ with probability $p_h = p^2$, $p_\ell = (1 - p)^2$, and $p_m = 2p(1 - p)$. Thus, a typical household enjoys utility

$$\tilde{v}(2) = p_h u(h) + p_m u(m) + p_\ell u(\ell). \quad (14.A.5)$$

A sufficient condition for households not to be able to make any transfer to each other is that

$$-(1 - \delta)u'(h) + \delta\left[-p_m p_h u'(h) + p_m p_h u'(m) - p_h p_\ell u'(h)\right.$$

$$\left. + p_h p_\ell - p_m p_\ell u'(h) + p_h p_\ell \frac{u'(h)}{u'(m)}\right] < 0. \quad (14.A.6)$$

Let $\ell = 1$, $h = 1.488$, $p = 0.5$, $\delta = 0.9$, $n = 4$ and assume a log utility. It can be checked that for these parameters inequality 14.A.6 is violated. Hence, households would enjoy an insurance gain of 66 percent ($\frac{\tilde{v}(2)-v(1)}{\tilde{v}(4)-v(1)} \times 100$). Moreover, in the absence of better enforcement power within households, our simulations reveal that they would enjoy an insurance gain ($\frac{v^*(4)-v(1)}{\tilde{v}(4)-v(1)} \times 100$) of 72 percent. Hence, this implies an additional gain of 16 percent.

BIBLIOGRAPHY

[1] Bernheim, D., B. Peleg, and M. Whinston (1987), "Coalition-proof Nash Equilibria. I. Concepts," *Journal of Economic Theory* 42, 1–12.

[2] Bloch, F. (1996), "Sequential Formation of Coalitions with Fixed Payoff Division," *Games and Economic Behavior* 14, 90–123.

[3] Coate, S. and M. Ravallion (1993), "Reciprocity without Commitment: Characterization and Performance of Informal Insurance Arrangements," *Journal of Development Economics* 40, 1–24.

[4] Deaton, A. (1992), *Understanding Consumption*. Oxford: Clarendon Press.

[5] Evans-Pritchard, E. (1940), *The Nuer: A Description of the Modes of Livelihood and Political Institutions of a Nilotic People*. Oxford: Clarendon Press.

[6] Fafchamps, M. (1992) "Solidarity Networks in Preindustrial Societies: Rational Peasants with a Moral Economy," *Economic Development and Cultural Change* 41, 147–174.

[7] Fafchamps, M. (1996), "Risk Sharing, Quasi-Credit, and the Enforcement of Informal Contracts," mimeo., Department of Economics, Stanford University.

[8] Fafchamps, M. and S. Lund (2003), "Risk Sharing Networks in Rural Philippines," *Journal of Development Economics* 71, 233–632.

[9] Foster, A. and M. Rosenzweig (2001), "Imperfect Commitment, Altruism, and the Family: Evidence from Transfer Behavior in Low-Income Rural Areas," *Review of Economics and Statistics* 83, 389–407.

[10] Genicot, G. and Ray, D. (2003), "Endogenous Group Formation in Risk-Sharing Arrangements," *Review of Economic Studies* 70, 87–113.

[11] Gertler, P. and J. Gruber (2002), "Insuring Consumption against Illness," *American Economic Review* 92, 51–70.

[12] Grimard, F. (1997), "Household Consumption Smoothing through Ethnic Ties: Evidence from Côte D'Ivoire," *Journal of Development Economics* 53, 391–422.

[13] Jalan, J. and M. Ravallion (1999), "Are the Poor Less Well Insured? Evidence on Vulnerability to Income Risk in Rural China," *Journal of Development Economics* 58, 61–81.

[14] Kimball, M. (1988), "Farmer Cooperatives as Behavior toward Risk," *American Economic Review* 78, 224–232.

[15] Kletzer, K. and B. Wright (2000), "Sovereign Debt as Intertemporal Barter," *American Economic Review* 90, 621–639.

[16] Kocherlakota, N. (1996), "Implications of Efficient Risk Sharing without Commitment," *Review of Economic Studies* 63, 595–609.

[17] Ligon, E., J. Thomas, and T. Worrall (2002), "Mutual Insurance and Limited Commitment: Theory and Evidence in Village Economies," *Review of Economic Studies* 69, 115–139.

[18] Lomnitz, A. L. (1977), *Networks and Marginality: Life in a Mexican Shantytown*. New York: Academic Press.

[19] Morduch, J. (1991) "Consumption Smoothing across Space: Tests for Village Level Response to Risk," Harvard University, mimeo.

[20] Murgai, R., P. Winters, E. Sadoulet, and A. de Janvry (2002), "Localized and Incomplete Mutual Insurance," *Journal of Development Economics* 67, 245–274.

[21] Platteau, J-Ph. (1991), "Traditional Systems of Social Security and Hunger Insurance: Past Achievements and Modern Challenges," in *Social Security in Developing Countries*, E. Ahmad, J. Dreze, J. Hills, and A. Sen (eds.). Oxford: Clarendon Press.

[22] Platteau, J-Ph. and A. Abraham (1987), "An Inquiry into Quasi-Credit Contracts: The Role of Reciprocal Credit and Interlinked Deals in Small-Scale Fishing Communities," *Journal of Development Studies* 23, 461–490.

[23] Posner, R. (1980), "A Theory of Primitive Society, with Special Reference to Law," *Journal of Law and Economics* 23, 1–53.

[24] Posner, R. (1981), *The Economics of Justice*. Harvard University Press.

[25] Ray, D. and R. Vohra (1997), "Equilibrium Binding Agreements," *Journal of Economic Theory* 73, 30–78.

[26] Ray, D. and R. Vohra (1999), "A Theory of Endogenous Coalition Structures," *Games and Economic Behavior* 26, 286–336.

[27] Ray, D. and R. Vohra (2001), "Coalitional Power and Public Goods," *Journal of Political Economy* 109, 1355–1384.

[28] Telser, L. (1980), "A Theory of Self-Enforcing Agreements," *Journal of Business* 53, 27–44.

[29] Thomas, J. and T. Worrall (2002), "Gift-Giving, Quasi-Credit and Reciprocity," *Rationality and Society*, 14(3), 307–351.

[30] Townsend, R. (1994), "Risk and Insurance in Village India," *Econometrica* 62, 539–591.

[31] Udry, C. (1994), "Risk and Insurance in a Rural Credit Market: An Empirical Investigation in Northern Nigeria," *Review of Economic Studies* 61, 495–526.

15

Spontaneous Market Emergence and Social Networks

Marcel Fafchamps

15.1. Introduction

In contrast to other chapters in this volume, the main purpose of this chapter is not to examine how networks are formed. Here, we take social networks as predetermined by nonmarket forces (such as ethnic, religious, and family affiliation) and investigate how market exchange is partly shaped by these social networks. Prior to market exchange, social networks exist but are devoid of economic content: little if any valuable information is available to be channeled through the network, and reputation mechanisms are not in place. As networked agents start trading with each other, however, they gain valuable experience about each other's type. As a result, parts of preexisting networks get activated as business networks and acquire economic value. It is this process we focus on.

The inspiration for this chapter comes from ten years of research on market institutions in Africa.[1] Microevidence from surveys of manufacturing firms and traders in various parts of the world shows that markets do not operate in the manner predicted by standard economic textbooks. Legal institutions are not important, and courts are seldom used to enforce commercial contracts – partly because the amounts involved are small and partly because debtors have no assets to foreclose upon (Fafchamps 1996; Bigsten et al.2000; Fafchamps and Minten 2001a; McMillan and Woodruff 1999a). Prevention is the dominant solution to the contract enforcement problem; this generates efficiency losses (e.g., [Fafchamps, Gunning, Isaksson, Oduro, Oostendorp, and Patillo,]). Ex post renegotiation is the main dispute resolution mechanism (Bigsten et al. 2000). If renegotiation fails, breach of contract occurs, and the relationship is severed. Similar findings are reported by, for example, McMillan and Woodruff (1999b), Johnson, McMillan, and Woodruff (2000);

This chapter draws extensively on "Spontaneous Market Emergence," Topics in Theoretical Economics, Berkeley Electronic Press at www.bepress.com, 2(1), Article 2, 2002. I benefitted from discussions with and comments from Avner Greif, Masa Aoki, Robert Cooter, Jonathan Conning, Lin Zhou, and seminar participants at Stanford University, Duke University, the University of Montreal, Namur University, and the American Law and Economics Association conference.

[1] This work is brought together in Fafchamps (2004).

Woodruff (1998); Johnson, McMillan, and Woodruff (2002) for various parts of the world.

In this chapter, we construct a model that mimics several of the features of the African markets I have studied empirically. These markets appear to operate as a two-tiered system with a core of sophisticated firms and traders and a fringe of small enterprises operating on a purely cash-and-carry basis. Core firms are in long-term relationships and deal with each other in a more trusting manner by placing orders and offering supplier credit and warranty (e.g., Fafchamps 1997). Fringe firms operate largely in an anonymous fashion and leave as little room as possible to breach of contract (e.g., Fafchamps and Minten 2001a). Core firms often are networked to each other in the sense that they interact outside business – in religious and family events as well as at sports events (e.g., Marris 1971; Himbara 1994; Fafchamps 2000). Firms with better networks receive more supplier credit and make more money (e.g., Fafchamps and Minten 2001b, 2002). These findings echo earlier work by other social scientists (e.g., Amselle 1977; Meillassoux 1971; Geertz, Geertz, and Rosen 1979).[2]

What is remarkable is that these features have been observed in many different economies irrespective of culture or legal history. Bernstein (1992) has described similar features among New York diamond traders and Midwestern grain traders. Her findings mirror the work of Granovetter (1995) on the U.S. job market. It is only in organized markets such as stock exchanges, commodity exchanges, or the U.S. real estate market that rules of operation differ. It therefore appears that, left to their own device, markets naturally develop along or into networks of relational contracting.

Building on these empirical regularities, this chapter shows how the simultaneous presence of core and fringe agents is essential to the spontaneous emergence of market exchange. This is because the two intereact to create a unique self-disciplining market structure. The main characteristic of this structure is that, as in Ghosh and Ray (1996), heterogeneity of agents and expense of search make the equilibrium entirely decentralizable. Unlike Kandori (1992), there is no need for coordinated punishment strategy; metapunishments are not required. Unlike in court-based exchange – where anonymous transactions are, in principle, feasible – personalized exchange is the rule and commercial relationships are long lasting. Excluding cheaters from future trade is not required for trade to arise. As markets emerge, so do networks of relational contracting in a way similar to the process described in Kali (1999).

Within this structure, preexisting social networks enable certain individuals or groups to prosper. This is because of the sharing of information among agents in the network. We also demonstrate that, when the screening of potential commercial partners is sufficiently costly, newcomers may find themselves excluded from trade.

---

[2] Historical descriptions of markets follow a similar vein. Historians have long noticed that business and trade are often in the hands of specific ethnic groups (e.g., Lombards and Genoese merchants in Western Europe, Jews in the Mediterranean, Armenians in the Middle East). See, for instance, Braudel (1986) and Greif (1993, 1994).

Business then becomes monopolized by a social network possibly sharing the same ethnic or religious affiliation.

This chapter formalizes some of the insights in Platteau (1994a,b), for example, and extends previous work by Greif (1993, 1994) and Milgrom, North, and Weingast (1991) on medieval merchants and by Shapiro and Stiglitz (1984) and Montgomery (1991) on labor markets. It complements previous work by Kranton (1996), who also considers the interaction between a reciprocal exchange market and a monetary market exchange but focuses on the minimization of search costs instead of commitment failure. Unlike these papers, which rely on static or steady-state models, we offer a thorough treatment of equilibrium dynamics and examine how relational contracting may foster the spontaneous emergence of markets. We also expand on these previous works by allowing for the circulation of information among agents.

15.2. A Model of Relational Contracting

Research by anthropologists, sociologists, historians, political scientists, and economists has brought to light the nearly universal reliance on interpersonal relations at early stages of market development (e.g., Hopkins 1973; Greif 1993; North 1990; Meillassoux 1971; Amselle 1977; Jones 1959; Bauer 1954; Sahlins 1972). Recent work has similarly noted the widespread existence of long-term relationships between manufacturers and their suppliers and clients in developed (e.g., Lorenz 1988; Aoki 1988; Dore 1987; Fukuyama 1995) and developing economies alike (Stone, Levy, and Paredes 1992). The prevalence of long-term personalized relationships is also the norm in employment contracts.

Detailed case studies conducted in several African countries suggest that the main reason why firms enter into long-term trading relationships with their suppliers and clients is to save on screening costs and minimize breaches of contract. Firms indeed realize that suppliers and clients differ in competence and honesty; consequently, finding reliable commercial partners is difficult and costly. The same justification is given by Granovetter (1995) to explain why employers and employees enter into long-term employment contracts. Empirical results further indicate that firms that are able to share information about clients and suppliers save on screening costs, identify reliable partners more easily, and can more readily switch among potential suppliers and clients (e.g., Fafchamps and Minten 1999; Gabre-Madhin 1997; Fafchamps and Minten 2002).

To further our understanding of these phenomena, we contruct a model that reproduces many of the stylized features of markets in developing countries. We begin with a model of relational contracting and examine how relational equilibria unfold over time. This model is largely inspired by earlier work of Fafchamps (2002b). The reader is referred to that article for proofs and modeling details. We focus here on the role of networks and interpersonal relationships in such a stylized economy. We first give a description of the economy, the action set of each player, and their payoffs.

15.2.1. The Economy

The stylized economy we consider is constructed around two organizing concepts: contract enforcement and hidden types. As my empirical research has shown (Fafchamps 2004), contract enforcement is a major concern of economic agents in poor countries because the threat of court action is not credible for most commercial transactions – either because transactions are too small, debtors are too poor, or courts are too ineffective. As has long been recognized, commitment problems can be solved through repeated interaction. This is the approach adopted here. For reasons that will become clear, we call the resulting type of exchange a *spontaneous market*.

Hidden types are another central feature of our model. Empirical work has indeed indicated that screening potential business partners is another major concern of economic agents. If contractual obligations are to be enforced by repeated interaction, agents must have a long enough horizon to be trusted. They must also be competent in the sense that their payoff from repeated interaction is positive. If either of these conditions is violated, the threat of discontinuing a commercial relationship has no bite. Survey results as well as numerous conversations with entrepreneurs in various countries have convinced me that economic agents are acutely aware of the importance of these two features and that they focus on them when screening potential business relations. By far the most popular – and relatively foolproof – screening method is to propose a small contract to newcomers that it is in their short-term interest to breach. Those who fulfill the contract demonstrate that they are competent – they delivered the goods or paid on time. They also show that they have some interest in establishing a long-term relationship. The testing period is typically set long enough to test the patience of the sophisticated crooks.

These features are captured in the model as follows. We consider an infinitely lived economy with a continuum of agents, indexed from 0 to 1 who trade over time and discount the future with a common discount factor $\hat{\delta}$. There are two types of agents: competent and incompetent. Their proportions G and $B = 1 - G$ in the economy are constant and known to all agents, but an agent's type is not directly observable. Competent agents require one unit of a homogeneous good per period. Incompetent agents can only earn a positive payoff by breaching contracts with competent agents. Agents' payoffs are private, nonverifiable information.

As based on Fafchamps (2002b), the economy combines random matching with relational contracting. It consists of an infinitely repeated sequence of trading rounds during which agents either trade, screen, or do nothing. External contract enforcement is assumed nonexistent. Each trading round is divided into three stages: the matching stage, the contracting stage, and the compliance stage. All agents are initially unmatched. At the beginning of the matching stage, agents decide either to continue trading together or to find a new partner, in which case they join the pool of unmatched agents. Trade is voluntary; if one agent decides to stop a relationship, his or her partner becomes unmatched. Unmatched agents are randomly paired; they observe each other's identity but not each other's type. The contracting stage begins with agents making one of three possible contracting offers: trade, screen, or do nothing. If players choose to do nothing, they collect an instantaneous payoff of

0 and move to the next trading round. If they choose to screen each other, they incur a screening cost c, obtain information about the other player's type, and move to the next round.[3] If both choose to trade, they move to the compliance stage.

To keep the economy dynamic, we introduce two types of shocks: death and quarrels. Death means the dispartition of an agent, who is then replaced by a new agent of the same type in the next period. In the context of this model, "death" encompasses any event that entails the dispartition of an economic agent such as bankruptcy, firm closure, and retirement. In any period agents disappear with probability $1 - \theta$ ($0 < \theta \le 1$).

Quarrels, in contrast, only lead an agent to sever a relationship. The reason for a quarrel can be irrational – for example, misunderstanding – or rational – e.g., unexpected change in economic conditions and trade patterns that requires a change in trading partner.[4] To keep things simple, we regard the occurence of quarrels as exogenous. Quarrels ensure that even good agents occasionally breach contracts: without assuming the occurence of quarrels, agents in our model would remain in a trade relationship until they die. Formally, we assume that in each period an agent has $1 - \hat{\tau}$ chance of wanting to sever the relationship he or she is in. To focus on contract enforcement, we assume that agents discover that they die or must sever the relationship *after* having incurred contractual obligations but *before* complying with them. This means that agents are able to complete the transaction but no longer make any profit from it.

From these assumptions, there are three states s in which a player can be at the end of the compliance stage: n, normal state; d, disappearing state; and b, breaking-up state. The probabilities of being in the normal, breaking-up, and disappearing states are $\hat{\tau}\theta$, $(1 - \hat{\tau})\theta$, and $1 - \theta$, respectively. Knowing the state they are in – but not the state in which their partner is – agents take one of two actions: comply or breach. An agent's action may only depend on its own type and current state as well as on the known history of play. If both agents are competent and in the normal state, their payoffs take the familiar prisoner's dilemma form:

	Comply	Breach	
Comply	$\hat{\alpha}, \hat{\alpha}$	$-1, 1$	(P)
Breach	$1, -1$	$0, 0$	

with $\hat{\alpha}$ representing agents' profit margin if both comply. If a competent agent is in either the disappearing or breaking-up state, his or her payoff from compliance is 0 instead of $\hat{\alpha}$. Incompetent agents derive a negative payoff from compliance; for them, cheating is the only way to get a positive payoff.

15.2.2. Trading Networks and Information Sharing

There are two types of networks in our economy: trading networks and information-sharing networks. Trading networks are nothing but the links between agents in

---

[3] Screening cost c is the solution to a screening subgame that we choose not to model in detail here (e.g. Datta 1996; Watson 1999).
[4] See Greif (1993) and Ghosh and Ray (1996, Section 4.2.1) for similar assumptions.

long-term commercial relationships. Consequently, trading networks are just another word for the pattern of trade in the economy. In this chapter, we assume away any form of inbreeding bias that may affect the creation of trading networks. I model and discuss such bias in detail in Fafchamps (2004). In Fafchamps (2002a), I provide evidence from three African countries that discrimination on the basis of ethnicity or gender does not affect trading networks.

Information-sharing networks serve to channel information, not goods. The weak and strong links discussed in Granovetter (1995) are examples of information-sharing networks. Such networks can potentially convey information about types and about behavior. As we will illustrate with our model, channeling these two types of information serves different functions and has different effects on contract enforcement. Sharing information about types makes it easier for good agents to be recognized as such when approaching a new potential trading partner. Sharing information about behavior makes it possible to orchestrate collective punishment for breach of contract. We examine in detail the effect both types of information sharing have on spontaneous markets.

Formally, informal information sharing is represented by the assumption that, with probability κ_i, an agent i obtains a costless and accurate report summarizing the past actions of the agent it has been matched with. Behind this assumption is the idea that agents form informal and partially connected information-sharing networks (e.g., Raub and Weesie 1990).[5] The origins of these networks of interpersonal relationships can be extremely varied, for example, consanguinity, marriage, vicinity, kinship, sport, religion, school, army. As their origin indicates, many interpersonal relationships arise from noncommercial activity and can be regarded as predetermined. For this reason, we assume throughout this chapter that κ_i is exogenous and time invariant. Information circulates in both directions, so that κ_i is also the proportion of agents who get a report on i.

The information channeled by networks depends on whether the agent has traded in the past or not. If an agent has never traded, his or her type is unknown, even to the person making the report. New agents are therefore called "untested." In contrast, agents who have traded at least once in the past have demonstrated that they are competent: their type has been revealed. They remain a good type even if they subsequently renege on a contract, which is something they might do if they quarrel. Information on past actions therefore conveys information both about type and behavior.

15.2.3. Relational Strategies

Having characterized the economy, we now examine the conditions under which relational contracting enables agents to trade. We proceed as in Fafchamps (2002b). We first define a set of relational strategies. On the basis of these strategies we

---

[5] Lang and Nakamura (1990) argue that agents may not find it in their immediate interest to share information with others for fear of losing reliable partners to them. In the model presented here, this issue does not arise since, by assumption, unmatched agents do not choose their partners but are matched at random.

compute expected payoffs conditional upon the state agents are in. Next, we derive the laws of motion of the economy, given these strategies, and we derive the properties of the long-term steady state. We then study the parameter configurations for which relational strategies are subgame perfect.

Define simple relational strategies as strategies in which two agents trade with each other until a breach of contract occurs, at which point they look for another partner. Within this broad class of strategies we first consider one specific set of strategies, which we denote SRS_a, and show that, for some parameter values, it constitutes a subgame perfect equilibrium and satisfies the bilateral rationality condition of Ghosh and Ray (1996). Strategies SRS_a are as follows.

- *Matching stage:* At time t, agents offer to continue trading with the agent with whom they were matched in the previous round unless, at $t - 1$, (1) screening has revealed that the agent is incompetent; (2) a breach of contract occurred; or (3) they discovered that they must break up the relationship. In all these cases, the agent seeks a new partner. New agents always seek a new partner.
- *Contractual stage:* Competent agents offer to trade if they have chosen to continue trading with the same partner. In the case of a new match, they offer to trade if the credit report shows that the agent has complied at least once in the past; otherwise they offer to screen.
- *Compliance stage:* Competent agents comply with their contractual obligations unless their payoff falls to 0 (i.e., they disappear or must break the relationship), in which case they breach the contract. Incompetent agents always breach. No stigma is attached to breach of contract because, with probability 1, all competent eventually breach. Stigma is revised in Section 15.3.

We now investigate the conditions under which these strategies form a sustainable, subgame-perfect equilibrium, which we denote RE_a. Expected payoffs of incompetent agents are constant and are ignored from now on. Expected long-term payoffs for competent agents are derived as follows. At the beginning of each period, competent agents are in one of three possible states: matched (M), tested and unmatched (K), or untested and unmatched (U). Matched agents are those who are in a long-term relationship. Tested agents are those that have been screened as competent, and untested agents are those who have never been screened. Let V_t^M, V_t^K, and V_t^U denote the expected continuation payoff of a matched, unmatched but tested, and untested agent at the beginning of period t, respectively. All payoffs to an agent i depend on his or her network contacts κ_i, although we omit this dependence from the notation to keep this readable. We obtain

$$V_t^M = \widehat{\alpha}\,\widehat{\tau}^2\theta^2 + (1 - \widehat{\tau}^2\theta)\theta\widehat{\delta}V_{t+1}^K + \widehat{\tau}^2\theta^2\widehat{\delta}V_{t+1}^M. \tag{15.2.1}$$

The first part is the agent's instantaneous payoff times the probability that both agents comply. The second term is the expected continuation payoff if either of the two agents breaks up the relationship and they must find a new partner. The third term is the continuation payoff if the relationship continues. Equation (15.2.1) incorporates the fact that disappearing agents have a continuation payoff of 0. To simplify the notation, let $\tau^2 \equiv \widehat{\tau}^2\theta$, $\delta \equiv \widehat{\delta}\theta$, and $\alpha \equiv \widehat{\alpha}\theta$. Equation (15.2.1) can then be rewritten more succinctly as

$$V_t^M = \alpha\tau^2 + (1 - \tau^2)\delta V_{t+1}^K + \tau^2 \delta V_{t+1}^M. \tag{15.2.2}$$

To derive the expected payoff of unmatched agents, let I_t be the proportion of tested agents at time t, a fraction K_t of which are unmatched at the beginning of the period. Next, let U_t stand for the fraction of untested, and thus unmatched, agents. By construction, the proportion of competent agents G is equal to $G = I_t + U_t$ at all t. Let μ_t be the proportion of untested agents among the unmatched, and let p_t be the proportion of incompetent agents among the untested. By definition, we have

$$\mu_t \equiv \frac{B + U_t}{B + U_t + K_t} \tag{15.2.3}$$

$$p_t \equiv \frac{B}{B + U_t}. \tag{15.2.4}$$

The expected payoff of a tested unmatched agent V_t^K can then be written as

$$\begin{aligned} V_t^K &= (1 - \mu_t)\kappa\left(\alpha\tau^2 + (1 - \tau^2)\delta V_{t+1}^K + \tau^2\delta V_{t+1}^M\right) \\ &\quad + \left((1 - \mu_t)(1 - \kappa) + \mu_t(1 - p_t)\right)\left((1 - \tau^2)\delta V_{t+1}^K + \tau^2\delta V_{t+1}^M\right) \\ &\quad + \mu_t p_t \delta V_{t+1}^K - (\mu_t + (1 - \mu_t)(1 - \kappa))c. \end{aligned} \tag{15.2.5}$$

The first term represents the expected payoff from being matched with a known tested agent and trading from the start. This option is not open to untested agents because they are undistinguishable from incompetent agents and therefore never trade at their first encounter. The second and third terms are the expected payoff from being matched with an unknown but competent agent, and with an incompetent agent, respectively. The last term is the screening cost. A similar equation can be derived for untested agents:

$$V_t^U = (1 - \mu_t p_t)\left((1 - \tau^2)\delta V_{t+1}^U + \tau^2\delta V_{t+1}^M\right) + \mu_t p_t \delta V_{t+1}^U - c. \tag{15.2.6}$$

If $\kappa = 0$, it is easy to verify that $V_t^K = V_t^U$ for all t.

Together, equations (15.2.2), (15.2.5), and (15.2.6) constitute a set of recursive equations that can be used to compute agents' payoffs provided we know μ_t and p_t. Because the number of agents is infinite, the laws of motion of K_t and U_t are given by

$$K_{t+1} = \theta(1 - \tau^2)I_t + \theta\tau^2\mu_t p_t K_t \tag{15.2.7}$$

$$U_{t+1} = (1 - \theta)G + \theta[1 - \tau^2(1 - \mu_t p_t)]U_t. \tag{15.2.8}$$

The economy's laws of motion do not depend on κ_i. This is because, unlike in Kranton (1996), social networks are not used to speed up the search for reliable commercial partners. The economy starts with all agents in the untested, unmatched category, that is, with $U_0 = G$, $I_0 = 0$, and $K_0 = 0$. The initial proportion μ_0 of untested agents in the population is equal to 1. Equations (15.2.7) and (15.2.8) constitute a self-contained system of difference equations describing the law of motion of μ_t

and p_t over time. Let p^* and μ^* denote the steady state of this system. Linearizing these equations around p^* and μ^*, we can verify that the system is locally stable and that it is approached monotonically from below. Numerical simulations further suggest that the system is globally stable and that K_t increases monotonically over time.[6]

It can be shown that steady-state payoffs V^M, V^K, and V^U are increasing in α, κ, δ, and τ and decreasing in c, μ^*, and p^* (Fafchamps 2002b). More interesting for our purpose is that for all t, payoffs V_t^M, V_t^K, and V_t^U increase with κ. This means that the returns to social network capital are unambiguously positive: agents with a high κ_i enjoy higher payoffs than those with low κ_i during all trading rounds.[7] They do so because they save on screening costs and can trade immediately. The sharing of information thus improves market efficiency even though reputation is used only to circulate information about types, not to stigmatize cheaters. This kind of reputation effect has been ignored in much of the theoretical literature because agent heterogeneity is typically not considered (e.g., Kandori 1992; Greif 1993; Milgrom et al. 1991; Raub and Weesie 1990; Ellison 1994).

An immediate policy implication is that the welfare of market participants can be raised by favoring the circulation of information about types. This can be accomplished in various ways, such as by creating a credit reference bureau, circulating information on potential workers, or fostering business associations and meetings. Identification of firms and agents, an essential ingredient of an information-sharing system, can itself be facilitated by setting up a business registration system. The circulation of inaccurate or ill-intended information can be punished as defamation or fraud.

Although information about types raises payoffs, it is not always unambiguously beneficial because, in certain cases, it can undermine commitment and thus market exchange. To show this formally, we now turn to equilibrium conditions.

15.2.4. Equilibrium Conditions

We now examine the conditions for which relational strategies RE_a form a self-enforcing, subgame-perfect equilibrium. Although many individual rationality conditions need to be satisfied, only three types of conditions deserve to be investigated in detail: continuation of relationship (CR) conditions that ensure that matched agents continue to trade with each other; breach deterrence (BD) conditions that ensure that contractual obligations are respected; and willingness to screen (WS) conditions that ensure that agents willingly screen each other.

---

[6] If $\theta = 1$ – competent agents are never renewed – the number of untested agents eventually tends to 0 and $p_* = 1$: in the long run, untested agents are all incompetent. If $\theta < 1$, the presence of newcomers among the unmatched ensures that p_* remains below 1: a certain proportion of unmatched agents remains competent even in the long run. It can also be verified that p^* and μ^* increase with θ. Moreover, the proportion of competent agents among the unmatched falls with time, and the product $\mu_t p_t \equiv \frac{B}{B+U_t+K_t}$ rises monotonically as initially untested agents progressively become known.

[7] Remember that i subscripts have been dropped from the notation to improve readability but are implicit in Propositions 15.1 and 15.2 and all that follows.

For CR conditions to be satisfied, agents' payoffs must be higher when matched than unmatched, that is,

$$V_t^M \geq V_t^K. \tag{CR}$$

This is always true because unmatched agents incur the cost of identifying a reliable agent whereas matched agents do not. Next, consider breach deterrence. In a relational equilibrium, opportunistic breach is deterred by the prospect of having to incur the cost and risk of screening new potential partners. For agents in the "normal" state, the breach deterrence condition is

$$\tau\left(\alpha + \delta V_{t+1}^M\right) + (1 - \tau)\left(-1 + \delta V_{t+1}^K\right) \geq \tau + \delta V_{t+1}^K,$$

which can be rewritten more simply as

$$V_{t+1}^M - V_{t+1}^K \geq \frac{1 - \alpha\tau}{\tau\delta}. \tag{BD}$$

This condition cannot be satisfied unless V_{t+1}^M is strictly larger than V_{t+1}^K. For agents who have discovered that they will disappear or that they must find a new partner, however, deterrence is ineffective. To deter willful breach by breaking up agents, it would have to be true that

$$\tau\left(1 + \delta V_{t+1}^K\right) + (1 - \tau)\delta V_{t+1}^K \leq \tau\delta V_{t+1}^K + (1 - \tau)\left(-1 + \delta V_{t+1}^K\right),$$

which boils down to $1 \leq 0$, which is an impossibility. A similar impossibility is found for disappearing agents because they have a zero continuation payoff. Breach by breaking up agents cannot be fully deterred for two reasons. First, the economy does not stigmatize cheaters and cannot, therefore, penalize breaking-up agents above and beyond the loss that they already suffer from having to end a commercial relationship. This is true even though agents share information about each other through an informal reputation mechanism. Second, the economy is large enough that the chance that agents would be paired with the same agent again in the future is vanishingly small. If the number of agents were finite and sufficiently small, agents would worry that cheating some agents might seriously reduce their chances of finding a new commercial partner, which is a process that could, by itself, support cooperation (e.g., Kandori 1992; Ellison 1994). This possibility is ignored here.

Let us now turn to willingness to screen conditions. First, it must be better for unmatched agents to screen unknown agents rather than withdraw from trade altogether, that is,

$$V_t^K \geq 0 \tag{WS1K}$$

$$V_t^U \geq 0 \tag{WS1U}$$

Second, untested agents must prefer to screen now instead of waiting for the next trading round:

$$V_t^U \geq \delta V_{t+1}^U. \tag{WS2U}$$

Finally, tested agents must prefer to screen now rather than wait until next period in the hope that they will be matched with a known agent and will not have to incur the screening cost:

$$((1 - \mu_t)(1 - \kappa) + \mu_t(1 - p_t))((1 - \tau^2)\delta V_{t+1}^K + \tau^2 \delta V_{t+1}^M) + \mu_t p_t \delta V_{t+1}^K$$
$$- (\mu_t + (1 - \mu_t)(1 - \kappa))c \geq (\mu_t + (1 - \mu_t)(1 - \kappa))\delta V_{t+1}^K,$$

which can be rewritten as

$$V_{t+1}^M - V_{t+1}^K \geq \frac{c(\mu_t + (1 - \mu_t)(1 - \kappa))}{\delta \tau^2(\mu_t(1 - p_t) + (1 - \mu_t)(1 - \kappa))}. \tag{WS2K}$$

If either of these conditions is violated, agents refuse to screen unknown agents. If the breach deterrence condition (BD) and the four willingness-to-screen conditions are satisfied, it can be verified that other individual rationality constraints are satisfied as well. Together, these conditions therefore define the set of model parameters for which the relational equilibrium RE_a is self-enforcing.

The properties of this equilibrium are discussed in Fafchamps (2002b). The one property that interests us here is that breach deterrence is harder for agents with a large κ_i. The reason is the absence of stigma: the large κ_i is, the easier it is for an agent to find a new trading partner. Because the cost of search is what deters breach of contract in this model, anything that makes search easier also reduces the incentive to comply with contractual obligations.

15.2.5. Pure Relational Equilibria

If information sharing dilutes incentives, can we conclude that a market exchange equilibrium is possible without any information sharing, that is, when $\kappa_i = 0$ for all i? The answer is yes. We call such an equilibrium a *pure relational equilibrium* because the only kind of network connections that arise are long-term relations between trading partners.

In pure relational equilibria, no information is circulated about agents' types. Consequently, agents must screen all unknown agents if they are to identify a suitable partner. Fafchamps (2002b) examines such equilibria in detail and concludes that pure relational equilibria are more likely to be sustainable when trading relationships are stable (high τ). Put differently, this implies that if pure relational equilibria were observed in practice, they would involve relatively long-lasting trading relationships. This is indeed what I have found in my empirical work (Fafchamps 2004): economic agents typically deal with the same suppliers for many years. Fafchamps (2002b) shows that, when gains from trade α are sufficiently high and screening costs c sufficiently low, market emergence is spontaneous: agents start trading in a decentralized manner without any exchange of information. Markets can nevertheless be vulnerable to shocks.

History abounds with examples of long-distance trading relationships that resemble pure relational strategies such as the spice and silk trade of the preindustrial world (Braudel 1986), long-distance cattle and kola trade in West Africa (Hopkins 1973), cattle trade in Kenya (Ensminger 1992), or gold trade along the Zambezi river (Shillington 1989). These ancient patterns of trade have in common high profitability (high α) and, if undisturbed, are extremely stable over time (high τ). Yet history suggests that they often are vulnerable to temporary trade disruptions in the sense that, once trading routes are disturbed by warfare or political turmoil these routes are difficult to reestablish.

It is still possible to find examples of similar trade patterns in contemporary Africa (e.g., Staatz 1979; Meillassoux 1971; Amselle 1977; Jones 1959). One of the reasons is that the semilegal nature of much cross-border African trade precludes recourse to courts. In addition, the small size of the transactions implies that suing is seldom an attractive option. The embryonic manufacturing sector of Ghana operates largely in the same manner (Fafchamps 1996). The reason appears to be that the Levantine businessmen who run much of the country's manufacturing sector are prohibited by law to run trading businesses. As a result, they find themselves sandwiched between suppliers and clients from other ethnic groups with whom socialization and thus the exchange of information is problematic. Trade in illegal drugs is another contemporary example of a pattern of exchange essentially based on relational contracting: the illegal nature of the trade prevents the use of courts to enforce contracts, and the fear of informants complicates the exchange of business information. Efforts by drug enforcement agencies to disrupt trade channels (e.g., by arresting dealers) in the hope of permanently stopping trade can be seen as an application of the idea that, in certain circumstances, markets can break down after a shock. These efforts, however, are bound to fail if gains from trade are sufficiently large so that market exchange spontaneously emerges again after a disruption.

15.2.6. Closed-Shop Equilibria

Things are somewhat different if networks $\kappa_i > 0$ and agents exchange information. To focus on an interesting special case, let us assume that competent agents are renewed slowly or are not renewed at all, that is, that $\theta = 1$. To keep the notation simple, we also assume that $\kappa_i = 1$ for all i. In this case, equilibrium conditions simplify to the following:

$$V_{t+1}^M - V_{t+1}^K \geq \frac{1 - \alpha\tau}{\tau\delta} \qquad \text{(BD')}$$

$$V_{t+1}^M - V_{t+1}^K \geq \frac{c}{\delta\tau^2(1 - p_t)} \qquad \text{(WS2K')}$$

plus (WS1K), (WS2U), and (WS1U).

Recall that p_t is the proportion of incompetent agents among the untested. It can be shown that when $c > 0$, however, condition (WS2K') is impossible to satisfy for values of p_t close enough to 1. In this case, the SRS_a strategies defined earlier are unsustainable in the long run. The reason is that tested agents cannot be convinced to incur screening cost $c > 0$ in order to sample untested agents when the latter are, in their great majority, incompetent. Tested agents prefer to limit their dealings to tested agents whom they can immediately trust. This means that as the economy evolves, there comes a time when tested agents refuse to deal with untested agents and prefer to wait until they are matched with a tested agent whose type is immediately available to them inasmuch as $\kappa_i = 1$ for all i. Because $p_t \to 1$ as $t \to \infty$ when $\theta = 1$, it follows that the RE_a as defined earlier is unsustainable in the long run. By extension, it is also unsustainable for θ or κ close enough to 1.

This does not imply that market exchange is impossible but only that market exchange must change from $p_t \to 1$. Early in the market emergence process, when p_t is small enough, waiting to be matched with another tested agent would take too long. Screening untested agents is likely to constitute a more profitable alternative even though it means incurring screening cost c. We therefore have the result that, when $\kappa = 1$, $\theta = 1$, and $c > 0$, the equilibrium involves changes of strategies over time. More specifically, there is a time $t^* \geq 0$ such that, for all $t < t^*$, SRS_a strategies presented earlier satisfy equilibrium conditions, but for all $t \geq t^*$, tested agents refuse to transact with untested agents. After t^*, absorption of agents into the group of tested agents is slower than before t^*. Moreover, there is also a time $t^{**} \geq t^*$ such that, for all $t \geq t^{**}$, untested agents refuse to screen each other. After t^{**}, untested agents are permanently excluded from trade. A formal proof of these results can be found in Fafchamps (2002b).

These findings imply that, if screening is costly, firms are long lasting, and information circulates freely among them, then trade is likely to take a "closed-shop" form: established firms deal only with other established firms and refuse even to consider unknown agents as potential partners. A similar result is derived by Taylor (2000) using different assumptions and a static setup. In our case, the reason is that in the long run there are too few competent agents among untested agents and it would be too costly to identify them. In such a world, agents with no payment history find it difficult if not impossible to be given a chance to prove themselves: the deck is stacked against newcomers. Possible real-life examples of such equilibria include, for instance, the difficulties that young inexperienced workers often encounter getting their first job and the problems that start-up companies face in qualifying for credit from banks and suppliers. Similar examples can be found in developing countries, where a closely knit business community has a hold on a particular economic activity (e.g., the Chinese in Indonesia, the Asians in Kenya, or the whites in Zimbabwe). Our model suggests that closed-shop equilibria are more likely in societies in which economic opportunities are unchanging over time (high τ) and firms are long lasting (high θ).

A corollary of the preceding is that setting up a mechanism to improve the circulation of business information among agents – such as a credit reference bureau – may result in excluding from the market those firms that have not yet established a name for themselves. This is true even though, in our model, new firms already are in an information-sharing network when they start business. The problem for newcomers comes precisely from the fact that their untested nature is revealed to other agents. When screening is costly and there are few competent agents among newcomers, then knowing that an agent is untested makes the other agent refuse to screen. The reason they refuse to screen is that they can wait.

Allowing established firms to better exchange information among themselves makes it easier for them to identify each other and thus to economize on screening costs by waiting to be matched with each other. Empirical work on Ghana, Kenya, and Zimbabwe manufacturing suggests that widespread circulation of information may indeed be detrimental to newcomers (Fafchamps 2004). The three countries differ greatly in the extent to which manufacturing firms exchange information. Ghanaian manufacturers share little information. In contrast, Kenyan manufacturers, who are predominantly of Asian origin, informally exchange information among themselves. In addition to informal information sharing, Zimbabwe also has a credit reference bureau. Of these three countries, it is also the one in which manufacturing appears the most closed to newcomers, especially blacks, whereas Kenya occupies an intermediate position and Ghana is the most open. This evidence is only suggestive, given that it is based on a small number of case studies in three countries, but it is consistent with the idea that information sharing may hurt newcomers. This issue deserves further investigation.

15.3. Stigmatization and Collective Punishment

So far we have shown that exchange can take place in the absence of formal institutions for the enforcement of contracts. Unlike much of the theoretical literature on informal contract enforcement, we have done so without resorting to any coordinated punishment or trigger strategy. Instead, we showed that the value that agents attach to commercial relationships can be sufficient to deter breach of contract whenever agents are heterogeneous. Better deterrence could, however, be achieved if breach of contract resulted in permanent exclusion from trade. Indeed, in the equilibria we have considered until now, a commercial relationship always ends with a breach of contract.

One possible solution to this problem is for agents to coordinate their actions to exclude cheaters. A sufficiently strong sense of community among agents and the existence of social sanctions could indeed be sufficient to enforce trigger strategies. This is the interpretation some economic historians and social scientists have given to the evidence of tightly knit trader communities. In my own empirical work, however, I have never come across examples of concerted punishment for breach of commercial contract (Fafchamps 2004). Never have survey and interview respondents said they refused to deal with a client or supplier because the person had cheated another firm. I also did not find any evidence of metapunishment: the idea that other economic agents could punish someone for dealing with a cheater never came up in interviews. Rather, economic agents reason their reluctance to deal with known cheaters in terms of inference about type: a cheater is seen as untrustworthy because of having a different payoff from a competent agent (lower profit $\widehat{\alpha}$ or lower discount rate δ). In particular, respondents often interpret cheating by an established agent as sign of impending exit, that is, as sign that they are leaving the business or going bankrupt.

In this section, we try to formalize these ideas by examining the conditions under which the threat of exclusion may be credible even without coordination between agents, that is, without metapunishment. The starting point of our argument is that agents who know they are leaving the business have no incentive to comply with their contractual obligations. Consequently, they are willing to take on contractual obligations they cannot fulfill and go bankrupt. We begin by showing that permanent exclusion of known cheaters serves as an additional deterrent to opportunistic breach. We then examine the conditions under which permanent exclusion is self-enforcing. We show that breach of contract may trigger permanent exclusion from trade if it is interpreted as a signal of impending bankruptcy. Self-enforcement then comes from what breachers reveal about themselves. Put differently, we identify conditions under which a trigger strategy satisfies the bilateral rationality condition of Ghosh and Ray (1996).

15.3.1. Exclusion from Trade

We investigate strategies in which agents who breach contracts are stigmatized and permanently excluded from trade. In this section, we abstract from the question of how the exclusion of cheaters is enforced; we revisit this issue later. We continue to assume that agents do not observe the other party's gains from trade, even ex post. Because agents cannot verify the conditions of a breach, all breaches must be equally punished. Let us define stigma-augmented relational strategies (*SARS*) as strategies in which only agents who are incompetent or going out of business cheat. Other agents never cheat, even after a quarrel. Cheaters are stigmatized: if they are matched with a competent agent who knows them, the agent refuses to trade with them. When matched with unknown agents, cheaters follow simple relational strategies. For the surplus, strategies are identical to simple relational strategies.

Because there is less cheating, it immediately follows that expected payoffs are higher and thus market exchange is more efficient. Conditions for $SARS_a$ to form a subgame-perfect equilibrium are unchanged except for a new breach deterrence condition along the equilibrium path:

$$\delta V_{t+1}^K \geq \theta + \delta V_{t+1}^C, \tag{BD''}$$

where V_{t+1}^C is the expected payoff to a one-time cheater. Manipulating equation (15.2.8) and combining it with payoff functions implied by the *SARS* yields that stigma-augmented relational strategies become more easily sustainable over time. The reason is simply that the gap between the expected payoff of a cheater V_t^C and that of an established noncheater V_t^K increases over time, thus making equation (15.2.8) easier to satisfy. The gap increases because the proportion of tested agents among the competent ones rises over time, making it difficult for cheaters to establish relationships with untested competent firms.

Another important finding is that *SARS* are more likely to be sustainable if κ_i is large for i. This follows because deterrence is more effective when the probability of punishment is higher. If we put the two results together, this means that, when information sharing is used to exclude cheaters, information-sharing networks facilitate market exchange while raising efficiency inasmuch as it makes exclusion possible. This stands in contrast with exchange of information about types, which raises payoffs but makes market exchange more difficulty to sustain as an equilibrium.

An immediate corollary of the preceding findings is that stigmatization is ineffective with totally unknown agents, that is, with agents whose $\kappa_i = 0$. Trade with such agents is only feasible via simple relational strategies. If agents differ with respect to their κ_i, stigmatization may be feasible only within a closely knit group. This opens the door to more complicated strategies whereby agents play stigma-augmented strategies with certain agents and relational strategies with others. For lack of space, we do not explore this possibility here, but it fits rather well the way Kenyan manufacturing firms interact: although Asian entrepreneurs share information with each other and refuse to deal with Asian cheaters, African entrepreneurs do not (Fafchamps 1997). A similar contrast among various business groups could be observed in Zimbabwe (e.g., Fafchamps, Pender, and Robinson 1995, Fafchamps 1997).

Another implication of the preceding observations is that changing one's identity must be sufficiently costly for a *SARS* to constitute a subgame-perfect equilibrium. A *SARS* cannot exist if agents who opportunistically breach a contract can subsequently hide among unknown agents. Stigmatization requires a precise way of identifying agents. In the absence of a formal identification system (e.g., business registration or an identity card system), stigmatization must remain confined to face-to-face interaction. This may explain why the threat of stigmatization is largely ineffective against so-called informal sector firms, which, as a rule, are not registered – and hence why transactions among informal sector firms remain quite unsophisticated. Interviews with entrepreneurs in Africa further suggest that running away to one's village – and resurfacing later with a different identity – is a widely used strategy to escape contractual obligations. Such strategy is typically not available to expatriate communities, which is a feature that may explain why stigmatization is easier among them and hence why breach is more easily deterred. This feature, by itself, could explain why expatriate communities dominate business in many agrarian societies of the Third World.

Finally, we note that a *SARS* shares essentially the same willingness to screen conditions as the simple relational equilibria discussed in Section 15.1. Consequently, previous findings also apply. For instance, if $c > 0$, $\kappa = 1$, and $\theta = 1$, established agents eventually refuse to trade with untested agents. Stigmatization does not preclude closed-shop equilibria.

15.3.2. Self-Enforcing Stigmatization

In much of the literature, the exclusion of cheaters from future trade is usually assumed to result from a trigger strategy whereby good agents coordinate around a punishment strategy. As pointed out earlier, in many years of empirical research on markets in Africa I have never come across evidence of such coordinated strategies. The reason is that, in the context of commercial transactions, it is costly to refuse trading with an agent who is known to be competent even if this agent has cheated in the past. The difficulty in coordinating around a joint exclusion punishment strategy may explain why I have also come across many stories in which agents fail to pay their commercial debt when they stop buying from a given supplier – what in this model we have called a "quarrel." Yet, many trading relationships end without breach of contract, contrary to what is predicted to occur in all relational equilibria we have examined so far. We now ask the question, Under what circumstances would the exclusion of cheaters be self-enforcing, that is, without requiring that agents who trade with cheaters be themselves punished?

We begin by noting that cheaters lucky enough to find someone willing to trade with them cannot be deterred from breaching the contract if a quarrel occurs: in their case BD″ cannot be satisfied because δV_t^C cannot be greater than $\theta + \delta V_t^C$. If a quarrel does not occur, however, breach deterrence is easier, that is, $V_t^N - V_t^C \geq V_t^M - V_t^K$. This is because a cheater has a harder time finding a new partner, making a commercial relationship more valuable to him or her than to a noncheater. Cheaters can therefore credibly promise that they will not cheat again while proposing to split gains from trade differently (e.g., by offering a bribe b such that the cheater gets a cooperation payoff of $\alpha - b$ and the stigmatization buster gets $\alpha + b$). Cheaters may, therefore, escape exclusion by credibly promising to amend their ways while anticipatively compensating the other agent for the fact that they will cheat when a quarrel occurs. The threat of permanent exclusion from trade is thus not credible, and a stigma-augmented relational strategy appears unsustainable without metapunishment.

There is, however, one possible mechanism by which stigmatization can be self-enforcing. So far, we have postulated that, with probability $1 - \theta$, competent agents leave business and are immediately replaced by new, untested competent agents. We now assume instead that these agents remain in the economy. This is equivalent to assuming that some good-type agents become bad but retain their identity and history of play. Let us call these agents *the walking dead*. Because the walking dead do not derive any gain from trade, they have no incentive to honor contracts. Like incompetent agents, they take advantage of every opportunity to cheat but, unlike them, they have been "tested" by the market and enjoy a long history of honored contracts. In a simple relational equilibrium, they could offer to trade with the tested agent they are matched with – and profit by cheating them. All they would have to do is pretend they cheated their previous commercial partner because of a quarrel, which is an event that affects all agents with probability $1 - \tau$.

In a simple relational equilibrium, therefore, the walking dead would find it in their interest to remain in the economy only to cheat others. Things are different with *SARS* because agents are instructed not to trade with known cheaters. The threat of exclusion deters cheating by all agents except those who have nothing to gain from any future trade. In equilibrium, therefore, all cheaters are either incompetent or walking dead, and no competent agent should deal with them. Refusing to deal with cheaters is then self-enforcing and the threat of exclusion credible. The conditions under which the economy would naturally switch from a pure relational equilibrium to an equilibrium with exclusion of cheaters are discussed in Fafchamps (2002b).

15.4. Networks and Markets

What does the analysis presented here have to say about the interface between networks and markets? In this section, we discuss briefly trading networks as well as information-sharing networks.

15.4.1. Trading Networks

In terms of trading networks, our model is not very instructive. The economy it generates can be represented by a very simple graph with diads, that is, simple one-to-one links between arbitrary pairs of identical agents. The symmetry of the pairing is one assumption that is relatively easy to do away with. Assuming, for instance, that matching takes place between buyers and sellers or between producers and consumers does not significantly alter our conclusions, as illustrated, for instance, in Fafchamps (2002a). One-sided commitment problems such as failed delivery or no payment can similarly be accommodated; the only change is that commitment issues then need to be solved for one side of the transaction only. Similarly, it is possible to generalize the model so that multiple types exist either only for buyers or only for sellers. In this case, some results change such as the emergence of closed-shop equilibria because incentives to screen depend on the existence of hidden types.

More complex trading patterns can of course be generated by assuming that agents specialize, for instance, in producers of raw material, processors, and consumers. Several layers of processing can also be imagined, resulting in multitiered trade patterns. Whatever the complexity of the resulting trading network, the same incentive problems must be solved. The model presented here can be used to depict the incentive issues surrounding screening and contract compliance at each stage of the tiered network (i.e., between producers of raw material and first processor, between first and second processor, etc.). At each stage, underlying parameters are likely to differ. Processors, for instance, have invested heavily in installed capacity and learning by doing; their horizon is thus likely to be long. In contrast, many traders and other intermediaries are transient, especially in poor countries. Consequently, one would expect margins α to be higher among traders than among processors because commitment is more problematic for the latter. Similar reasoning could be applied to other parameters of the model such as τ, θ, and c.

Here we have assumed pure random matching. A bias in matching could be introduced according to which certain types of agents are more likely to be matched with others perhaps because of social or geographical proximity. In Fafchamps (2002a), I examine how biased selection in the group of tested agents can endogenously result from statistical discrimination or information-sharing networks.

Heterogeneity in agents' size or gains from trade could also be introduced. In this case, pure random matching no longer constitutes a reasonable approximation because agents are likely to compete for more attractive commercial partners. Bidding for partners was first studied in the context of the marriage market but has since been extended to other markets (e.g., Becker 1981; Demange and Gale 1985; Shapley and Shubik 1972; Roth and Sotomayor 1990). Recent work in this area includes Bala and Goyal (2000) and Kranton and Minehart (2001), who provide examples of how the bidding process can influence the shape of the resulting trade network.

15.4.2. Information-Sharing Networks

In the model presented earlier, the variable κ_i represents in a succint fashion the information agents obtain through their contacts. The reader may wonder what form this transfer of information takes in practice. My experience from surveys and interviews is that the most common form in which information is conveyed between businesses is referral; this is also the form of information sharing Granovetter (1995) documents for the U.S. labor market. When a supplier is approached by a new client who asks for trade credit, he or she typically asks the client to provide a reference. If the client can provide a good referral from someone the supplier knows, then granting of trade credit is greatly facilitated. In practice, such a person is not always easy to find. In contrast, referrals from unknown sources are largely discounted if only because they can easily be falsified. Survey respondents indeed voice suspicion of the referrals even from known sources. This is because competition incites referees to distort the information – either by presenting a bad client as good (to hurt the supplier) or by presenting a good client as bad so that the referee keeps the client (Lang and Nakamura 1990). This explains why gossip is virtually ignored in the business world. This stands in contrast to assumptions often made in the theoretical literature. Survey respondents express extreme distrust vis-à-vis gossip. The main reason is that competitors have incentives to disinform by activating the rumor mill.

Parameter κ_i in our model represents the likelihood that client i would know someone who (1) can refer on i (i.e., knows enough about i's type and past actions) and (2) is known (and trusted) by the supplier. The second part is, by assumption, constant over time. But the first part depends on the history of client i. If i is a newcomer, no referral can be provided because i is not yet proven he or she is competent. From this we see that preexisting networks get activated by trade. If an agent has never been given a chance to prove himself or herself, having a very large network is useless. In fact, in some cases, a large network can hurt newcomers because, if established agents can easily identify each other, they have less incentive to screen untested agents. This is the closed-shop equilibrium we discussed earlier. In my empirical work, I have indeed encountered situations in which newcomers had strong networks but still were not given a chance.

If competent agents who have already been tested always provide references, someone's inability to provide references can be interpreted as evidence that either the agent is a newcomer or that he or she has cheated and therefore cannot provide a reference (at least not a flattering one). Extending the model to allow for this possibility is fairly straightforward. In my experience, the number of people who can provide a valid referral is in general very small, and thus the change in inference resulting from the absence of referral is small and can safely be ignored in most cases.

If we modify the model so that one side of the transaction is, for instance, a buyer whereas the other is a seller, we can also examine the value of different types of information. For instance, consider an economy with one type of buyer, one-sided commitment on the buyer side, and hidden supplier type. This corresponds to a situation in which the buyer does not know whether the supplier can deliver the kind of good needed (possibly because the supplier does not know whether his or her output is suitable or whether the buyer's requirements can be met). In this case, clients can save on screening costs by sharing information about suppliers. This information is immediately useful irrespective of the type of equilibrium (i.e., whether pure relational equilibrium or stigma augmented), and it always raises efficiency. Suppose in contrast that suppliers share information about buyers' actions. This information is useful only in a stigma-augmented equilibrium. If all buyers are of the same type, a stigma-augmented equilibrium would require coordinated action among suppliers (i.e., metapunishments). More complicated situations can be analyzed in the same fashion.

Membership in information-sharing networks can, on the basis of the circumstances, shape trading networks. One possibility is that matching remains unbiased, as assumed here, but established traders refuse to screen agents who do not belong to their information-sharing network. This possibility, which is apparent in our closed-shop equilibrium, is studied in further detail in Fafchamps (2002a). Matching itself could be biased because of social or geographical proximity. If agents search endogenously for a promising match, they are likely to use their information-sharing network to elicit information about trade opportunities (i.e., about competent agents currently unmatched). We have not studied this possibility here, but if agents find it easier to search among a subset of the population, a bias will arise. In fact, this possibility is so obvious that any bias in trading patterns is usually assumed to result from differential search. Our contribution here and in other work is to show that other phenomena – closed-shop equilibrium or statistical discrimination – can generate similar patterns.

Finally, in the analysis presented here, we have taken information-sharing networks as predetermined. This is of course a simplification. In practice, agents often engage in purposeful network building. Given the symmetry of our model, endogenizing the formation of information-sharing networks would result in identical values of κ_i for all without adding much substance to our findings. If, however, agents differed in the ease with which they could establish contacts, one would expect them to have different values of κ_i. What makes network establishment costs different among agents could be various things, such as their natural propensity for social interaction, their family background, or their personal history – all predetermined factors. In the end, the implication would be the same: agents would differ in their κ_i – with the same consequence on the type of sustainable market equilibrium. In my empirical work on returns to social network capital (e.g., Fafchamps and Minten 2002; Fafchamps and Minten 2001b), I have typically used agents' family background, personal history, and personal traits to instrument κ_i.

15.5. Conclusion

Approaching market exchange from the angle of commitment failure, we have examined the conditions under which markets can sustain themselves without external enforcement or coordinated metapunishment. We have shown that, when economic agents are differentiated, a fully decentralized market equilibrium can discipline itself provided gains from trade are large enough. Incompetent agents are screened away through a trial period, which also serves as sanction for breach of contract, as in Shapiro and Stiglitz (1984) and Ghosh and Ray (1996).

We discussed two types of networks, trading networks and information-sharing networks, and investigated the role that information sharing plays in spontaneous markets. We saw that, when agents are heterogenous, two types of information must be distinguished: information about revealed types and information about cheating. In the presence of screening costs, sharing information about types may lead agents to refuse screening unknown agents, thereby resulting in a closed-shop equilibrium in which newcomers are excluded from trade. We showed that such an outcome is more likely if agents are long lived and opportunities to trade are stationary – as is often the case for agricultural and other primary products. We interpreted this result as throwing light on the well-documented existence of closely knit business communities or networks the world over. Contrary to what one might expect, wider circulation of information about types (e.g., via a credit bureau) does not eliminate the problem; it only makes it worse. This might account for the virtual exclusion of black firms from the business mainstream in Zimbabwe despite the existence of an active credit reference agency (Fafchamps 1997).

We also investigated the conditions under which an economy might exclude cheaters from future trade. Strategies that condition on cheating behavior are not as easily enforceable as previously assumed in the literature (Kandori 1992). For exclusion of cheaters to be self-enforcing and decentralizable without metapunishment, breach of contract must be interpreted as a sign of impending bankruptcy.

Taken together, our results demonstrate that market exchange can exist with minimal intervention by the state but that it is unlikely to be fully efficient – at least initially. This is broadly consistent with observed characteristics of markets in Africa. Other features of the model, such as widespread reliance on relational contracting and the sharing of information about types along business networks, are also consistent with field observations. The model presented here thus provides a realistic framework for studying emerging markets.

This chapter contributes to our understanding of commercial networks in several respects. First, by distinguishing between trading networks and information sharing networks, our analysis brings to light their respective roles and suggests promising avenues for endogenizing the formation of either type of network. Second, the model presented here shows that exclusion of cheaters can be sustained without any coordinated action on the part of economic agents. This model prediction, which is in agreement with the absence of evidence for metapunishment and coordinated exclusion of cheaters in my empirical work, hinges on the existence of multiple types: provided that cheating is interpreted as a change in type, exclusion from trade becomes self-enforcing.

This is important because it provides an empirically backed theoretical justification for studying commercial networks not as groups or clubs but as decentralized, interactive structures. Economic agents may seek to build network relations with other not to promote or facilitate collective exclusion of cheaters, which is intrinsically hard to enforce, but simply to achieve agent-specific gains in terms of access to information. The decentralized action of many agents seeking to access information through networks can then lead, under certain conditions that have been made clear in this chapter, to information dissemination that helps enforce contracts and deter cheating. On the basis of my own experience studying market institutions in Africa since 1992, this approach to commercial networks offers the advantage of being more realistic. It is also in line with economists' emphasis on the decentralized virtues of the market.

BIBLIOGRAPHY

[1] Amselle, J.-L. (1977), *Les Negotiants de la Savanne*, Paris: Editions Anthropos.
[2] Aoki, M. (1988), *Information, Incentives and Bargaining in the Japanese Economy*. New York: Cambridge University Press.
[3] Bala, V. and Goyal, S. (2000), "A Non-Cooperative Model of Network Formation," *Econometrica* 68(5):1181–1229.
[4] Bauer, P. T. (1954), *West African Trade: A Study of Competition, Oligopoly and Monopoly in a Changing Economy*. Cambridge University Press.
[5] Becker, G. S. (1981), *A Treatise on the Family*, Cambridge, MA: Harvard University Press.
[6] Bernstein, L. (1992), "Opting Out of the Legal System: Extralegal Contractual Relations in the Diamond Industry," *Journal of Legal Studies* XXL: 115–157.
[7] Bernstein, L. (1996), "Merchant Law in a Merchant Court: Rethinking the Code's Search for Immanent Business Norms," *University of Pennsylvania Law Review* 144(5):1765–1821.
[8] Bigsten, A., P. Collier, S. Dercon, M. Fafchamps, B. Gauthier, J. W. Gunning, A. Isaksson, A. Oduro, R. Oostendorp, C. Patillo, M. Soderbom, F. Teal, and A. Zeufack (2000), "Contract Flexibility and Dispute Resolution in African Manufacturing," *Journal of Development Studies* 36(4):1–37.
[9] Braudel, F. (1986), *Civilization and Capitalism*, New York: Harper and Row.
[10] Datta, S. (1996), "Building Trust, London School of Economics," STICERD Discussion paper series TE/96/305, London.
[11] Demange, G. and D. Gale (1985), "The Strategy Structure of Two-Sided Matching Markets," *Econometrica* 53(4):873–888.
[12] Dore, R. (1987), *Taking Japan Seriously: A Confucian Perspective on Leading Economic Issues*. Stanford University Press.
[13] Ellison, G. (1994), "Cooperation in the Prisoner's Dilemma with Anonymous Random Matching," *Review of Economic Studies* 61:567–588.
[14] Ensminger, J. (1992), *Making a Market: The Institutional Transformation of an African Society*. New York: Cambridge University Press.
[15] Fafchamps, M. (1996), "The Enforcement of Commercial Contracts in Ghana," *World Development* 24(3):427–448.
[16] Fafchamps, M. (1997), "Trade Credit in Zimbabwean Manufacturing," *World Development* 25(3):795–815.
[17] Fafchamps, M. (2000), "Ethnicity and Credit in African Manufacturing," *Journal of Development Economics* 61(l):205–235.
[18] Fafchamps, M. (2002a), "Ethnicity and Networks in African Trade," mimeo.
[19] Fafchamps, M. (2002b), "Spontaneous Market Emergence. Topics in Theoretical Economics," 2(1), Article 2, Berkeley Electronic Press at www.bepress.com.
[20] Fafchamps, M. (2004), *Market Institutions in Sub-Saharan Africa*. Cambridge, MA: MIT Press.
[21] Fafchamps, M., T. Biggs, J. Conning, and P. Srivastava (1994), "Enterprise Finance in Kenya, Regional Program on Enterprise Development, Africa Region," Washington, DC: The World Bank.

[22] Fafchamps, M., J. W. Gunning, and R. Oostendorp (2000), "Inventory and Risk in African Manufacturing," *Economic Journal* 110(466):861–893.

[23] Fafchamps, M. and B. Minten (1999), "Relationships and Traders in Madagascar," *Journal of Development Studies* 35(6):1–35.

[24] Fafchamps, M. and B. Minten (2001a), "Property Rights in a Flea Market Economy," *Economic Development and Cultural Change* 49(2):229–268.

[25] Fafchamps, M. and B. Minten (2001b), "Social Capital and Agricultural Trade," *American Journal of Agricultural Economics* 83(3):680–685.

[26] Fafchamps, M. and B. Minten (2002), "Returns to Social Network Capital Among Traders," *Oxford Economic Papers* 54:173–206.

[27] Fafchamps, M., J. Pender, and E. Robinson (1995), "Enterprise Finance in Zimbabwe, Regional Program for Enterprise Development, Africa Division," Washington, DC: The World Bank.

[28] Fukuyama, F. (1995), *Trust: The Social Virtues and the Creation of Prosperity*. New York: The Free Press Paperbacks.

[29] Gabre-Madhin, E. (1997), "Grain Markets in Ethiopia," mimeo.

[30] Geertz, C., H. Geertz, and L. Rosen (1979), Meaning and Order in Moroccan Society. Cambridge: Cambridge University Press.

[31] Ghosh, P. and D. Ray (1996), "Cooperation in Community Interaction without Information Flows," *Review of Economic Studies* 63:491–519.

[32] Granovetter, M. S. (1995), *Getting a Job: A Study of Contacts and Carreers*. University of Chicago Press, 2nd edition.

[33] Greif, A. (1993), "Contract Enforceability and Economic Institutions in Early Trade: The Maghribi Traders' Coalition," *American Economic Review* 83(3): 525–548.

[34] Greif, A. (1994), "Cultural Beliefs and the Organization of Society: A Historical and Theoretical Reflection on Collectivist and Individualist Societies," *Journal of Political Economics* 102(5):912–950.

[35] Himbara, D. (1994), "The Failed Africanization of Commerce and Industry in Kenya," *World Development* 22(3):469–482.

[36] Hopkins, A. G. (1973), *An Economic History of West Africa*. London: Longman Group Ltd.

[37] Johnson, S., J. McMillan, and C. Woodruff (2000), "Entrepreneurs and the Ordering of Institutional Reform: Poland, Slovakia, Romania, Russia and Ukraine Compared," *Economics of Transition* 8(1): 1–36.

[38] Johnson, S., J. McMillan, and C. Woodruff (2001), "Property Rights and Finance," mimeo.

[39] Johnson, S., J. McMillan, and C. Woodruff (2002), "Courts and Relational Contracts," *Journal of Law, Economics, and Organization* 18(1):221–277.

[40] Jones, W. O. (1959), *Manioc in Africa*, Stanford University Press.

[41] Kali, R. (1999), "Endogenous Business Networks," *Journal of Law and Economic Organization* 15(3):615–636.

[42] Kandori, M. (1992), "Social Norms and Community Enforcement," *Review of Economic Studies* 59:63–80.

[43] Kranton, R. E. (1996), "Reciprocal Exchange: A Self-Sustaining System," *American Economic Review* 86(4):830–851.

[44] Kranton, R. and D. Minehart (2001), "A Theory of Buyer-Seller Networks," *American Economic Review* 91(3):485–508.

[45] Lang, W. W. and L. I. Nakamura (1990), "The Dynamics of Credit Markets in a Model with Learning," *Journal of Monetary Economics* 26:305–318.

[46] Lorenz, E. H. (1988), "Neither Friends nor Strangers: Informal Networks of Sub-contracting in French Industry," in D. Gambetta (ed.), *Trust: Making and Breaking Cooperative Relations*, New York: Basil Blackwell.

[47] Marris, P. (1971), "African Businessmen in a Dual Economy," *Journal of Industrial Economics* 19:231–245.

[48] McMillan, J. and C. Woodruff (1999a), "Dispute Prevention without Courts in Vietnam," *Journal of Law, Economics, and Organization* 15(3):637–658.

[49] McMillan, J. and Woodruff, C. (1999b), "Interfirm Relationships and Informal Credit in Vietnam," *Quarterly Journal of Economics* 114(4):1285–1320.

[50] Meillassoux, C. (1971). *The Development of Indigenous Trade and Markets in West Africa*, Oxford University Press.

[51] Milgrom, P. R., D. C. North, and B. Weingast (1991), "The Role of Institutions in the Revival of Trade: The Law Merchant, Private Judges, and the Champagne Fairs," *Economics and Politics* 2(19):1–23.

[52] Montgomery, J. D. (1991), "Social Networks and Labor-Market Outcomes: Toward an Economic Analysis," *American Economic Review* 81(5):1408–1418.

[53] North, D. C. (1990), *Institutions, Institutional Change, and Economic Performance*, Cambridge, UK: Cambridge University Press.

[54] Platteau, J.-P. (1994a), "Behind the Market Stage Where Real Societies Exist: Part I – The Role of Public and Private Order Institutions," *Journal of Development Studies*, 30(3):533–577.

[55] Platteau, J.-P. (1994b), "Behind the Market Stage Where Real Societies Exist: Part II – The Role of Moral Norms," *Journal of Development Studies* 30(4):753–815.

[56] Raub, W. and J. Weesie (1990), "Reputation and Efficiency in Social Interactions: An Example of Network Effects," *American Journal of Sociology* 96(3):626–654.

[57] Roth, A. and M. Sotomayor (1990), *Two-Sided Matching*, Cambridge University Press, Cambridge.

[58] Sahlins, M. (1972), *Stone Age Economics*. Chicago: Aldine-Atherton, Inc.

[59] Shapiro, C. and J. E. Stiglitz (1984), "Equilibrium Unemployment as a Worker Discipline Device," *American Economic Review* 74(3):433–444.

[60] Shapley, L. and M. Shubik (1972), "The Assignment Game I: The Core," *International Journal of Game Theory* 1(1):111–130.

[61] Shillington, K. (1989), *History of Africa*, New York: St. Martin's Press.

[62] Staatz, J. M. (1979), "The Economics of Cattle and Meat Marketing in the Ivory Coast," University of Michigan. Livestock Production and Marketing in the Entente States of West Africa.

[63] Stone, A., B. Levy, and R. Paredes (1992)," Public Institutions and Private Transactions: The Legal and Regulatory Environment for Business Transactions in Brazil and Chile," Technical Report, The World Bank, Washington, DC, Policy Research Working Paper No. 891.

[64] Taylor, C. R. (2000), "The Old-Boy Network and the Young-Gun Effect," *International Economic Review* 41(4):871–891.

[65] Watson, J. (1999), "Starting Small and Renegotiation," *Journal of Economic Theory* 85(1):52–90.

[66] Woodruff, C. (1998), "Contract Enforcement and Trade Liberalization in Mexico's Footwear Industry," *World Development* 26(6):979–991.

Index

Printed in the United States
By Bookmasters